MW01243255

Dear Students:

There is a saying that "knowledge is power." But for that to be true, knowledge must be based on an objective, independent thought process that tests new information against evidence, assumptions, bias, and other points of view. In other words, in order for you to gain new "knowledge," you must "think through" the related issues and ideas, understand them, satisfy yourself that they are reasonable, and make them a part of your personal knowledge base. Furthermore, you must be willing to re-evaluate that knowledge, and perhaps change it, as new issues and ideas arise.

In business, the saying is true—knowledge *is* power. Those who have it hold a competitive advantage over those who don't. Those who understand business information, and know how to interpret and use it, make the best business decisions.

A company's accounting reports, generated by its integrated accounting system, are a major source of business information. But when reading these reports, you must evaluate the information they contain by looking for supporting evidence, assumptions, and bias, and by considering other points of view. Furthermore, you must know how to *interpret* the information contained in these reports. To do this, you must understand how a company's integrated accounting system develops these reports, and what concepts, principles, and assumptions underlie the accounting information contained in these reports. With this in mind, we designed the two volumes of this book to address all of these issues.

After you graduate, you may work for a company and use its accounting information to make decisions as an "internal user." Or, you may consider investing in a company, or have some other reason to use its accounting information to make decisions as an "external user." Your ability to use the material in this book later to help you make effective business decisions (regardless of your career choice) depends on your making it a part of your own knowledge base. This means that you should "think through" the issues and ideas as you read about them, making sure that you understand them before you read further. This will require some effort on your part. As you read the book, read it critically. Test it in your mind. Does it make sense to you?

To help you learn this material and think about what you are learning, we have placed questions throughout the book, labeled with a "stop light," that we think are worth your time and effort to answer. Each time you encounter one of these questions, stop, think through the question, and answer it honestly. Base your answer on what you have learned in your life experiences, on your knowledge of accounting, business, and the world, and on your own common sense. By pausing in your reading and answering these questions, you will have time to process what you are reading and an opportunity to build new knowledge into your already-existing knowledge base.

Besides answering these questions as you read the book, think about what questions you have, or what else you would like to know about the subject at hand. Pursuing the answers to these questions, in class or otherwise, will help you add to your knowledge base and the quality of your later decisions.

We hope you find this book interesting and fun to read!! We also hope you find it useful in increasing your knowledge of accounting, your appreciation of the power of using accounting information for making business decisions, and your ability to use accounting information for your own business decisions.

Billie M. Cunningham Loren A. Nikolai John D. Bazley

UPDATED SECOND EDI-

# ACCOUNTING

## INFORMATION FOR BUSINESS DECISIONS

UPDATED 2E, VOLUME 1

BILLE M. CUNNINGHAM
*University of Missouri – Columbia*

LOREN A. NIKOLAI
*University of Missouri – Columbia*

JOHN D. BAZLEY
*University of Denver*

THOMSON

Australia · Canada · Mexico · Singapore · Spain · United Kingdom · United States

THOMSON

Accounting: Information for Business Decisions, Updated 2e Volume I

Billie M. Cunningham, Loren A. Nikolai, and John D. Bazley

**Executive Editors:**
Michele Baird, Maureen Staudt & Michael Stranz

**Project Development Manager:**
Linda deStefano

**Sr. Marketing Coordinators:**
Lindsay Annett and Sara Mercurio

**Production/Manufacturing Manager:**
Donna M. Brown

**Production Editorial Manager:**
Dan Plofchan

**Pre-Media Services Supervisor:**
Becki Walker

**Rights and Permissions Specialists:**
Kalina Hintz and Bahman Naraghi

**Cover Image**
Getty Images*



Printed in the United States of America
1 2 3 4 5 6 7 8 08 07 06

For more information, please contact Thomson Custom Solutions, 5191 Natorp Boulevard, Mason, OH 45040. Or you can visit our Internet site at www.thomsoncustom.com



The Adaptable Courseware Program consists of products and additions to existing Thomson products that are produced from camera-ready copy. Peer review, class testing, and accuracy are primarily the responsibility of the author(s).

Accounting: Information for Business Decisions / Updated 2e Volume I / Billie M. Cunningham, Loren A. Nikolai and John D. Bazley

ISBN-13: 9780759395428
ISBN: 0-759-39542-X

International Divisions List

**Asia (Including India):**
Thomson Learning
(a division of Thomson Asia Pte Ltd)
5 Shenton Way #01-01
UIC Building
Singapore 068808
Tel: (65) 6410-1200
Fax: (65) 6410-1208

**Australia/New Zealand:**
Thomson Learning Australia
102 Dodds Street
Southbank, Victoria 3006
Australia

**Latin America:**
Thomson Learning
Seneca 53
Colonia Polano
11560 Mexico, D.F., Mexico
Tel (525) 281-2906
Fax (525) 281-2656

**Canada:**
Thomson Nelson
1120 Birchmount Road
Toronto, Ontario
Canada M1K 5G4
Tel (416) 752-9100
Fax (416) 752-8102

**UK/Europe/Middle East/Africa:**
Thomson Learning
High Holborn House
50-51 Bedford Row
London, WC1R 4LS
United Kingdom
Tel 44 (020) 7067-2500
Fax 44 (020) 7067-2600

**Spain (Includes Portugal):**
Thomson Paraninfo
Calle Magallanes 25
28015 Madrid
España
Tel 34 (0)91 446-3350
Fax 34 (0)91 445-6218

# Brief Contents

## Volume 1

## Volume 2

# CONTENTS

## VOLUME 1

## PART 3 OPERATING, REPORTING, AND EVALUATING IN AN ENTREPRENEURIAL ENVIRONMENT 123

### CHAPTER 5 THE ACCOUNTING SYSTEM: CONCEPTS AND APPLICATIONS 124



### CHAPTER 6 THE INCOME STATEMENT: ITS CONTENTS AND USE 166

## VOLUME 2

## CHAPTER 18 MODERN DEVELOPMENTS IN MANAGING OPERATIONS 606



## CHAPTER 19 REPORTING INVENTORY 647



# MANAGING, REPORTING, AND EVALUATING NONCURRENT ASSETS IN A CORPORATE ENVIRONMENT 687

## CHAPTER 20 CAPITAL EXPENDITURE DECISIONS 688

# PREFACE

**CAUTION:**

*This textbook, the first of two volumes, has a number of themes that revolve around candy, and this preface is no exception. While this book has a lot of the great accounting ingredients you are used to (and all that you will need), it also "breaks the mold" as it incorporates a number of phrases and terms well known to candy lovers (and we believe that includes accountants) Our intent is that you will get a number of cravings while reading this preface, not the least of which is the desire to devour this book and to share its great taste with your colleagues and your students.*

## Two Great Courses that Make One Great Text . . .

You may recall hearing different food or beverage products promoting how natural and good they are for you by using the phrases "No artificial colors. No artificial sweeteners." Well, we would like to paraphrase those slightly to convey a similar message that is the initial premise as to why the two volumes of this text for the elementary accounting sequence is natural and good for you: "No artificial separation!"

In the real world, today's students will face an accounting environment where management accounting and financial accounting issues are integrated every day. The traditional—and artificial—separation of these topics in textbooks, however, tends to lead students to a perception that the two areas are unrelated. We also believe that traditional and highly technical "preparer-oriented" accounting textbooks (1) isolate accounting from general business decisions, (2) lose students' interest, and (3) reinforce a common misconception that accounting is best left only to accountants. Therefore, such a separation misses the big picture of an integrated accounting system that provides economic information to all users—which is what the overwhelming majority of your students in introductory accounting will be. Together, both volumes of this textbook thoroughly integrate management accounting and financial accounting topics in a way that is more reflective of the world students will face outside of the classroom.

## Sometimes You Feel Like a Debit, Sometimes You Don't . . .

A major focus of this textbook is on *using* management accounting and financial accounting information in various business settings. Therefore, we wrote this book at a "nontechnical" level for *all* business and nonbusiness students—not just those intending to be accounting majors. But, because two of us are heavily involved in teaching intermediate accounting and write an intermediate accounting textbook, we are also aware of the needs of your accounting majors. So we also discuss *accumulating* and *reporting* accounting information. We take a nonprocedural approach by explaining transactions in terms of the accounting equation (and entries into "account columns") and *the effect of these transactions on the financial statements* rather than in terms of debits and credits. But, we realize there is a need in many situations to teach procedures. To that end, we have provided a full chapter-length appendix (Appendix A) on recording, storing, and reporting accounting information. This appendix covers the accounting cycle, from journal entries (using debits and credits) through the post-closing trial balance. We designed it so that you may use it anywhere you see fit in the process of teaching from this book. We assure you that our accounting majors who have used this elementary accounting text are well-prepared to enter our intermediate accounting classes.

## Ingredients and Nutritional Information (Key Features of this Text)

### *An Introduction to Business Approach*

Chapters 1 and 10 take an "introduction to business" approach to orient students to the business environment—that is, the operations of a company, the different functions of business, managers' responsibilities, and the types of information, management reports, and financial statements the company's integrated accounting system provides for use in internal and external decision making. These chapters provide students with a basic understanding of business so they

can more effectively envision the context in which accounting information is collected and used, and the types of decisions users make in this context. This approach allows students to see the "big picture" more clearly.

### *Creative and Critical Thinking*

Chapter 2 is unique for accounting textbooks, and we integrate that uniqueness into the rest of the book. It introduces students to creative and critical thinking and demonstrates how they are used in decision making and problem solving. Both volumes of this book emphasize the type of analytical thinking that successful accountants and other business people use in a world that is constantly changing and becoming more complex. We believe that as you use analytical thinking in your decision process regarding this textbook, you will not only decide to adopt this two-volume book, but will also be able to use it in a way that will foster your students' growth.

In keeping with Chapter 2, the remaining chapters introduce students to various aspects of accounting and are designed to help them develop their thinking skills. "STOP" questions throughout the textbook (identified by a "stop light") ask students to take a break from reading, and to think about an issue and/or consider the outcome of a situation. We also ask them *why* they think what they think. The end-of-chapter (EOC) materials include both structured and unstructured questions and problems that emphasize the use of creative and critical thinking skills by the students. Therefore, some of the questions and problems do not have a "correct" answer. The focus is on the approach or process that students use to solve them. With the increasing complexity of business activities, we think our inclusion of creative and critical thinking materials will better prepare students to understand the substantive issues involved in new or unusual business practices.

### *The Simpler Things*

Earlier, we mentioned a "nontechnical" approach. Although we explain identifying, measuring, recording, and reporting of economic information, we discuss these activities at a basic level (increases and decreases in account balances) and do not include a discussion of debit and credit rules and journal entries in the main body of the text. We do emphasize the double-entry accounting system through the use of the accounting equation (Assets = Liabilities + Owners' Equity) and its linkage to the income equation (Income = Revenues − Expenses). We use account columns to record transactions, but we explain the increases or decreases in relation to the accounting equation, rather than as debits and credits. At the same time, we also emphasize the effects of the transactions on a company's financial statements and the impact they have on analysis of the company (e.g., its risk, liquidity, financial flexibility, operating capability). We chose this approach to better help students gain an understanding of the logic of the accounting system and its interrelationships, the effects of transactions on a company's financial statements, and the use of accounting information in decision making without getting them "bogged down" in the mechanics of the system. For those wanting to incorporate the mechanics of the system, as we mentioned earlier, we do provide a thorough coverage of debits, credits, and journal entries in Appendix A.

### *Because You've Kept Us Apart for Too Long...*

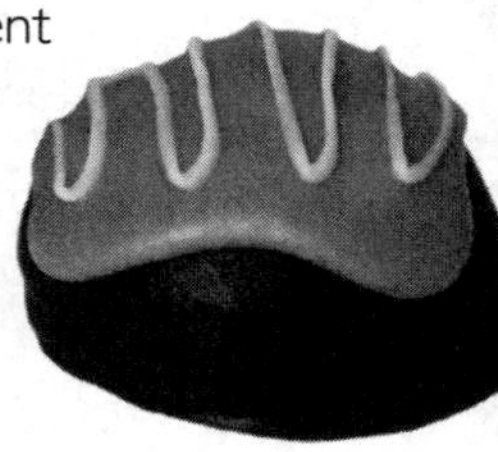

We also mentioned earlier that together, both volumes of this book integrate management accounting and financial accounting topics in a way that is more reflective of the world students will face outside of the classroom. In blending our discussion of management accounting and financial accounting, we address several management accounting topics prior to discussing specific financial accounting topics. In large part, a company must plan its activities before it communicates its plans to external users, and it must operate and evaluate its operations (internal decision making) before it communicates the results of its operations to external users. Therefore, in keeping with the "introduction to business" theme and the logical sequencing of business activities, we discuss accounting for planning first, and then for operating and evaluating (controlling)—discussing management accounting and financial accounting where they logically fit into this framework.

For instance, Chapter 3 covers cost-profit-volume (CVP) analysis for planning purposes. After students have an understanding of cost and revenue relationships, we introduce them to budgeting in Chapter 4. The discussion of the master budget includes projected financial statements, which links the coverage back to the financial statements we mentioned in Chapter 1. Chapter 5 then introduces accounting for the operations of a company. Chapters 6 through 8 describe a company's major financial statements and discuss how external users would use these statements to analyze the company.

Besides integrating management accounting and financial accounting topics, both volumes of this book also integrate business issues and values and international issues, where appropriate. This approach reinforces the idea that societal and global issues are not topics that can and should be dealt with separately from the other issues, but rather are an integral and significant part of business in today's world.

### *Plain—and with Peanuts (Building Block Approach)*

This textbook also uses a building-block approach. It begins with starting and operating a small retail candy store—a sole proprietorship—and then progresses through the operations of a more complex company in the form of a candy manufacturer—a corporation. This allows students to learn basic concepts first, and then later to broaden and reinforce those concepts in a more complex setting. Several of the same topics reemerge, but each time they are refined or enhanced by a different company structure, a different type of business, or a different user perspective. For example, because of its location at the beginning of the semester, the Chapter 3 discussion of CVP analysis is simple. We cover it again in greater depth in Chapter 11, after students have a better understanding of costs in a manufacturing setting. Each time we revisit an issue, we discuss the uses of accounting information for both internal and external decision making, as appropriate.

Likewise, we use a building-block approach to arranging the end-of-chapter materials according to levels of learning. To indicate these levels, we have divided the homework into sections on *Testing Your Knowledge, Applying Your Knowledge,* and *Making Evaluations.* These categories are arranged so that the answers to questions require students to use increasingly higher-order thinking skills as they move from one

category of question to the next. The *Testing Your Knowledge* section includes questions that test students' knowledge of specifics—terminology, specific facts, concepts and principles, classifications, and so forth. The *Applying Your Knowledge* section includes questions, problems, and situations that test students' abilities to translate, interpret, extrapolate, and apply their knowledge. The *Making Evaluations* section includes questions, problems, and cases that not only test students' abilities to apply their knowledge but also their abilities to analyze elements, relationships, and principles, to synthesize a variety of information, and to make judgments based on evidence and accounting criteria.

## New and Improved Flavor

In this updated second edition, as a result of our own use of the book and of feedback from other users, we have made both volumes of the book even better. These are the major changes and new features of the updated text.

1. We now illustrate transactions by showing their effect on specific accounts under the accounting equation. This is similar to recording in a computer system and much easier for students to understand. Marginal boxes next to these illustrations detail the effects of the transactions on the components of the affected financial statements.

| FINANCIAL STATEMENT EFFECTS |
|---|
| Decreases *net* property, plant, and equipment, and total assets on ***balance sheet***. Increases expenses, which decreases net income on ***income statement*** (and therefore decreases stockholders' equity on ***balance sheet***). |

2. We included more topics in Chapter 18 in the second volume that are oriented to internal users of accounting information, such as the balanced scorecard and economic value added.

3. We added a section on E-business in Chapter 10 and expanded the discussion of enterprise resource planning (ERP) systems. In later chapters, for many topics we refer to how a company's ERP system can be used to gather information for business decisions about these topics.

4. Additionally, in Chapter 10 we expanded the section on annual reports to include a discussion of (a) management's reporting on the effectiveness of a corporation's internal control and (b) the related extension of the audit to include an examination of the corporation's internal control over financial reporting.

5. We added more homework related to service companies. This reflects the growing service sector in our economy.

6. We expanded the appendix on the Profession of Accountancy by adding a discussion of current developments in the profession as well as the AICPA core competencies. We also moved the

appendix from the back of the book to Chapter 1, where it is closer to the introduction of the business environment.

7. We moved some topics to chapter appendices to keep them available to those who wish to teach them, but also to allow the chapters to be more focused. These topics include the indirect method cash flow statement (as an appendix to Chapter 8), as well as the periodic inventory system under FIFO, average cost, and LIFO (as an appendix to Chapter 19).

8. We updated the discussion of intangibles in Chapter 21, pension plans in Chapter 22, and stock options and the results of discontinued operations in Chapter 24 to reflect changes in GAAP.
9. We have revised the Summary Surfing section to update the Internet homework.
10. We have revised many "real" company examples in the text, and have also updated all of the "real" company problems in the homework.

We believe these changes enhance the "flavor" of the book and make its topics even more relevant and understandable to our students.

## Real-World/World-Wide/Total World:

Life is not a "textbook case." That's why we not only integrate management accounting and financial accounting topics, but also include information about real-world companies as examples for many of these topics. And, we include analyses of the financial information of some of these companies in the text and in the homework materials of many chapters. In conjunction with our Web site, the "Summary Surfing" section of each chapter gives students the opportunity to connect to some of these companies via the Internet for further evaluation.

Because each company's Web site may provide a unique path to its financial information, and each organization's Web site will be unique from each other organization's Web site, we provide helpful "surfing" instructions in the following two sections. You may want to direct your students' attention to these sections.

## Suggestions for Navigating (Surfing!) a Company's Web site:

Generally, you can access a company's home page by typing in the name of the company in place of "companyname" in the following generic Web address: http://www."companyname".com. If that fails, you can use a search engine, like Yahoo or Google, to locate the company's home page. After you have accessed a company's home page, you can locate its financial statements, annual reports, and other financial information by finding a link on the home page to "About Us," "Company," "Company Information," "Investors," "Investor Relations," "Investor information", or some combination of these terms.

After clicking on this link, you will be sent to the company's financial information. Many times, you can click on the company's annual report for a specific year to find all of the company's financial statements, notes to its financial statements, and related information. Sometimes, however, the company will show a "condensed" annual report which contains only "summary" financial statements. In this case, if you want complete financial information about the company for a specific year, you will need to find the company's SEC 10-K report for that year. Normally, the company's Web site will reference its10-K report by providing a link to "SEC Filings." To find the financial statements, after clicking on the link, go to Part 2, Item 8 of the 10-K report.

## Suggestions for Navigating (Surfing!) an Organization's Web site:

Generally, you can access an organization's (e.g., AICPA) home page by typing in the name of the organization in place of "organizationname" in the following generic Web address: http://www."organizationname".org. If that fails, you can use a search engine, like Yahoo or Google, to locate the organization's home page. After you have accessed an organization's home page, you will have to search the heading or body of that page, the drop-down menus, or "hot links" for an "entry" into the section of the Web site that is likely to contain the information for which you are looking. You may find that you have to go down several "paths" before you find the proper section. Unfortunately, because organizations' Web sites tend to be less standardized than those of corporations, you may find yourself using the "trial and error" method of finding information on those Web sites.

## Serving Suggestions (How to Use this Text)

*". . . a well thought out and very well-planned text. The explanations are easy to read and follow. I could teach myself from this book."*
*– Rebe Herling, Student*

Since we (and others) have used this book in our classes, we thought you might appreciate hearing what we have learned from this experience:

1. **Faculty Preferences:** For years, Hershey's made the Kiss only in plain chocolate. Although they had put almonds in a chocolate bar, they couldn't perfect doing so with a Kiss. Nonetheless, they kept trying, and as you know, succeeded several years ago. It has been a great success since then. You, too, can succeed in integrating the financial and managerial accounting areas for the best taste. For financial accounting faculty, the textbook is so well written (see student quote above) that the management accounting material is not difficult to teach. For management accounting faculty, the book leads with management accounting material and contains fewer financial procedures than traditional ones do, so it is not difficult to teach either. Although change doesn't occur without some effort, we have tried to make this change as easy as possible for both of you by providing a great support package that will help you step into the classroom with minimum effort.

2. **The Transfer Issue:** The two volumes of this book do not form an Oreo cookie. They are not designed so that you can split up the parts and eat them separately. Given that most transfer students will check out the receiving school's policies first, we suggest that receiving schools using our book advise transfer students that they should take their entire accounting sequence at one school or the other, but not half and half. To sending schools using our book, we suggest you give your students similar advice. For your course sequence, we suggest that you devote sufficient time to coverage of Appendix A (the accounting cycle, including debits and credits) so that your students who transfer to another school have an adequate foundation in accounting procedures.

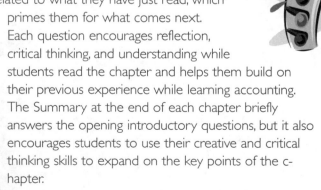

3. **Pedagogy:** We designed the pedagogical features of this book with the purpose of guiding the readers through it in a way that will help them learn the material in the book. Opening introductory questions for each chapter highlight the major topics and pique students' interest, as well as guide their reading. In support of these questions, as we mentioned earlier, "STOP" questions throughout each chapter ask students to pause and answer a question related to what they have just read, which primes them for what comes next. Each question encourages reflection, critical thinking, and understanding while students read the chapter and helps them build on their previous experience while learning accounting. The Summary at the end of each chapter briefly answers the opening introductory questions, but it also encourages students to use their creative and critical thinking skills to expand on the key points of the c-hapter.

Each time we use the accounting equation and account columns in the text to show the effect of a transaction on a company's accounts, we accompany that illustration with a description of the effect of the transaction on the company's financial statements. A marginal box next to the equation details this effect on the components of each of the financial statements affected by the transaction.

We include the financial section of Colgate-Palmolive's annual report in Appendix B (in the second volume of the book). We have homework assignments at the ends of many chapters that ask students questions about the financial information in this annual report.

4. **How to Use the End-of-Chapter Materials:** This book is constructed in a "building block" approach, and so is the homework. We suggest you assign it in the same manner: ask students to test their knowledge first, then apply their knowledge, and finally, after building a strong base of understanding, make evaluations. Each chapter has a Dr. Decisive problem that asks students to apply their new knowledge in a situation closer to one they might be currently experiencing, making accounting a little more personal and relevant for them. In a "Dear Abby" format, students are asked to answer a "problem" mailed in by a reader. We have found it to be a fun way for students to work on teams, where the team constructs an answer to the question or evaluates another team's answer to the question.

**DR. DECISIVE**

5. **Snickers®:** . . . by chuckling at the joke, the accounting concept it illustrated was planted firmly in my mind." – Lisa Mitchell, Student. The cartoons and photographs in the book are not just for levity. They provide visual enhancements of ideas, as well as humor, and help students apply their knowledge by interpreting cartoons and photos.

6. **Smooth or Crunchy?** Alternative Course: We wrote this book for the elementary accounting sequence, but the very nature of its design has led to its successful use in MBA and Executive MBA/Small Business Programs.

## Taste Tested (or "Show-Me")

We know there is always a concern about new editions, but you might have noted that two of us teach in Missouri—the "show-me" state. Having a need to "show ourselves" that the book works, we class-tested it at the University of Missouri-Columbia for eight semesters prior to the first edition. We continue to use both volumes in our elementary course sequence. We used student and instructor feedback (from our institutions and others) to make this two-volume book even better. Here is what we found, and it has been confirmed by other class testers:

- Students liked reading this book.
- The writing style is "user friendly" so that the topics are very understandable.
- The end-of-chapter homework ties in well with the topical coverage in the chapters.
- The Solutions Manual is very clean.
- Instructors found the book to be clear and easy to teach from.

Furthermore, to assure ourselves that the homework and solutions were error-free, we wrote and checked all the homework items and solutions ourselves. In addition, all the solutions were accuracy-checked by graduate students and teaching assistants.

## User Feedback

We would love to list all the positive quotes here that we've received from students and instructors who have used the book, but our editors say that would add significantly to the page count and thus to the cost of the book (which our marketing manager advises would result in negative comments from the students). So, we've listed one of each. This should help prove our point as well as illustrate that we have listened to the input of others in all stages of the development of this text.

> *"[Early in the first semester] I've had three students already tell me that they are really enjoying reading the text!! Wanted to let you know that I've been teaching accounting for 11 years and this is the first time I've ever heard any students make that comment. You should be very proud."*
>
> *– Instructor, Winthrop University*

> *"I enjoyed studying out of the book because it was written in a manner that is clear and easy to understand. The fact that the examples (Sweet Temptations, Unlimited Decadence) were used throughout the text was very helpful."*
>
> *– Nathan Troup, Student*

# Kudos!

THIS BOOK IS A WORK IN PROCESS, AND WE WILL APPRECIATE YOUR FEEDBACK AND SUGGESTIONS FOR IMPROVEMENT AS IT EVOLVES INTO THE THIRD EDITION. BUT IT WOULDN'T HAVE PROGRESSED THIS FAR WITHOUT THE HELP, CREATIVE IDEAS, ENCOURAGEMENT, AND HARD WORK OF NUMEROUS INDIVIDUALS, INCLUDING THE FOLLOWING:

## *Reviewers*

**Elizabeth Ammann,** Lindenwood University
**Janice Benson,** University of Wyoming
**Kathy Brockway,** Kansas State University at Salina
**Steven Campbell,** University of Idaho
**David Collins,** Bellarmine University
**Lola Dudley,** Eastern Illinois University
**Jean Hartman,** University of St. Thomas
**Jerry Kreuze,** Western Michigan University
**Leonard Long,** Bay State College
**Tracy Manly,** University of Tulsa
**Ken Mark,** Kansas City Community College
**Melanie Middlemist,** Colorado State University
**Gary Olsen,** Carroll College
**Keith Patterson,** Brigham Young University, Idaho
**Franklin Plewa,** Idaho State University
**James Pofahl,** University of Wisconsin, Oshkosh
**Alexander Sannella,** Rutgers Business School
**Cinday Seipel,** New Mexico State University
**Fred Smith,** Kansas State University
**John Waters, II,** University of Wyoming

## *Teaching Assistants/Class Testers at the University of Missouri-Columbia*

Jaime Bierk
Marcia Bunten
Cassi Costner
Rachel Davis
Carrie Duff
Gwen Ernst
John Faries
Katrinka Goldberg
Stacy Gower
Dave Gusky
Mark Gutwein
Mike Hart
Melissa Kahmann
Tim Koski
Lee Kraft
Shannon Lee
Jennifer Liesmann
Aaron Meinert
Holly Monks
Shannon Mudd
Lynn Nelson
Margaret Ofodile
Susan Parker
Cindy Patterson
Matt Peters
Katrina Pon
Mike Richey
Andrea Romi
Robbie Schoonmaker
Jennifer Seeser
Ken Smith
Dessie Stafford
Tom Stauder
Diane Sturek
Aaron Thorne
Robyn Vogt
Kelly Ward
Michael Weiss
Lisa Wright

## *Others who made invaluable contributions along the way:*

**Robin Roberts,** University of Central Florida, and **James Stallman,** University of Missouri-Columbia, for significant contributions to earlier versions of several chapters in this book.
**Tom Schmidt** for his insightful (and inciteful) comments on Chapter 2.
**Scott Summers,** Brigham Young University, and **Vairam Arunachalam,** University of Missouri-Columbia for their advice on certain database or computer issues.
**Jennifer Seeser** and **Diane Sturek** for the solutions they developed to the end-of-chapter homework.
**Cassi Costner, Herman Eckherle, Kelly Gallagher, Jason Janisse, Heather McWilliams,** and **Emily Reinkemeyer** for their accuracy checks of these solutions.
**Nathan (N8) Troup** for his assistance in the development of certain aspects of the text and ancillaries.
**Dana Cunningham** for her Chapter 8 photograph.
**Bob Hammerschmidt** for his Chapter 8 quote.
**Anita Blanchar** for her meticulous typing of various ancillaries.
**Karen Staggs** for typing parts of the manuscript.

The thousands of students who endured the class testing of previous editions, especially those students who noticed and reported errors, inconsistencies, and typos in previous versions.

## *Those who made conscientious efforts toward the production of this book:*

**Maureen Staudt, Jan Holloway, Laureen Palmisano Ranz** our Sr. Developmental Editor, **Dan Plofchan** our Production Editorial Manager **Nate Anderson, Beth Wolf** our project coordinator, and our compositor, **Integra**.

And thank you to all of the Thomson and Thomson Custom Solutions sales people for their observations, suggestions, and colossal past and future efforts to make this book known to those who dare to change.

*Billie M. Cunningham*
*Loren A. Nikolai*
*John D. Bazley*

# About The Authors

### *Billie M. Cunningham*

Billie Cunningham is an Adjunct Associate Professor in the School of Accountancy at the University of Missouri-Columbia (MU). She has a wide variety of teaching experience, having taught graduate and/or undergraduate courses at private universities, public universities, and community colleges. She has received several awards for outstanding teaching, including the MU College of Business *2005-2006 Raymond F. and Mary A. O'Brien Excellence in Teaching Award,* an MU Student-Athlete Advisory Council *2004 Most Inspiring Professor Award, Teacher of the Year, 2000* from the Association of Accounting Students, *Faculty Member of the Year, 2000* from the MU College of Business Student Council, an *Outstanding Faculty Award, 1998* from the Greek Councils of the University of Missouri-Columbia, and the *1995 Exemplary Accounting Educator Award* from the Missouri Association of Accounting Educators. Professor Cunningham has taught at Texas Christian University, University of Dallas, Collin County Community College, and the University of North Texas. She received her B.B.A., M.B.A., and Ph.D. from the University of North Texas. Professor Cunningham has conducted numerous workshops around the country on the use of writing exercises in accounting classes and on incorporating creative and critical thinking strategies into the accounting classroom. She was a coauthor of three previous books: *Accounting: Principles and Applications,* Fifth Edition (1986); *Financial Accounting: Principles and Applications,* Fifth Edition (1986); and *Accounting: Basic Principles,* Fifth Edition (1986); and a contributing author on *Cost Accounting: Principles and Applications,* Fourth Edition (1984) (all with McGraw-Hill Publishing Company).

Professor Cunningham has published articles in professional journals, including *Journal of Accounting Education, Issues in Accounting Education, Accounting Education: A Journal of Theory, Practice and Research, The CPA Journal, Research in Accounting Regulation, Management Accounting, Essays in Economic and Business History, The Community/Junior College Quarterly of Research and Practice Special Edition on College Teaching and Learning,* and *The Community/Junior College Quarterly of Research and Practice.* She received the *Outstanding Article Award* from the Two-Year College Section of the American Accounting Association. In addition, she serves on the Editorial Review Board of *Issues in Accounting Education* and has served as an ad hoc reviewer for *Advances in Accounting Education, Journal of Accounting Education,* and *Accounting Education: An International Journal.* Professor Cunningham is the faculty advisor for the Association of Accounting Students at MU. She is a member of the American Accounting Association (AAA) and wasChair of the Two-Year College Section and Chair of the Teaching and Curriculum Section. She served on the AAA Accounting Education Advisory Committee and as Vice-President and member of the Executive Committee of the AAA. Professor Cunningham has chaired or served on numerous Federation of Schools of Accountancy committees. She chaired the AICPA Core Competency Framework Best Practices Task Force and served on the AICPA Pre-certificationEducation Executive Committee. In fits of joy, Professor Cunningham sings in her car, dances in her living room, and is an aerobics enthusiast and avid golfer (and we use that term loosely).

### *Loren A. Nikolai*

Loren Nikolai is the Ernst & Young Professor and the Director of the Masters Programs in the School of Accountancy at the University of Missouri-Columbia (MU) where he has taught for over 30 years. He received his B.A. and M.B.A. from St. Cloud State University and his Ph.D. from the University of Minnesota. Professor Nikolai has taught at the University of Wisconsin at Platteville and at the University of North Carolina at Chapel Hill. Professor Nikolai has received an MU Student-Athlete Advisory Council *2004 Most Inspiring Professor Award,* the University of Missouri system-wide *1999 Presidential Award for Outstanding Teaching,* the MU College of Business and Public Administration *1999 Teacher of the Year Award,* the MU Alumni Association *1996 Faculty Award,* the MU College of Business and Public Administration *1994 Accounting Professor of the Year Award,* the Missouri Society of CPAs *1993 Outstanding Accounting Educator of the Year Award,* the MU *1992 Kemper Fellowship for Teaching Excellence,* the St. Cloud State University *1990 Distinguished Alumni Award,* and the Federation of Schools of Accountancy *1989 Faculty Award of Merit,* and was the co-recipient of the *1997 Holstein Creativity Award.* He holds a CPA certificate in the state of Missouri and previously worked for the 3M Company. Professor Nikolai is the lead author of *Intermediate Accounting,* Tenth Edition (2007, South-Western Publishing Company). He was the lead author of two previous textbooks, *Principles of Accounting,* Third Edition (1990) and *Financial Accounting,* Third Edition (1990, PWS-Kent Publishing), and was the coauthor of *Financial Accounting: Concepts and Uses,* Third Edition (1995, South-Western Publishing).

Professor Nikolai has published numerous articles in *The Accounting Review, Journal of Accounting Research, The Accounting Educator's Journal, Journal of Accounting Education, The CPA Journal, Management Accounting, Policy Analysis, Academy of Management Journal, Journal of Business Research,* and other professional journals. He was also lead author of a monograph published by the National Association of Accountants. Professor Nikolai has served as an ad hoc reviewer for *The Accounting Review* and *Issues in Accounting Education.* He has made numerous presentations around the country on curricular and pedagogical issues in accounting education. Professor Nikolai was the Faculty Vice-President of the Beta Alpha Psi chapter at MU for 18 years. He is a member of the American Accounting Association, the American Institute of Certified Public Accountants (AICPA), and the Missouri Society of CPAs (MSCPA). He has served on the AICPA's Accounting and Auditing Practice Analysis Task Force Panel and the Accounting Careers Subcommittee; he has also served on the MSCPA's Relations with Educators, Accounting Careers, and Accounting and Auditing Committees. Professor Nikolai has chaired or served on numerous Federation of Schools of Accountancy (FSA) and American Accounting Association (AAA) committees, was AAA Director of Education for 1985–1987, and was President of the FSA for 1994. Professor Nikolai is married and has two adult children and three grandsons. His family has one cat, and he is an avid basketball player, golfer, and weight lifter.

### *John D. Bazley*

John D. Bazley, Ph.D., CPA, is the John J. Gilbert Professor of Accountancy in the School of Accountancy of the Daniels College of Business at the University of Denver where he has received *the University 1990 Distinguished Teaching Award, the Vernon Loomis Award for Excellence in Advising, the Alumni Award for Faculty Excellence, the Jerome Kesselman Endowment Award for Excellence in Research,* and the *1995 Cecil Puckett Award of the Daniels College of Business.* Professor Bazley earned a B.A. from the University of Bristol in England and an M.S. and Ph.D. from the University of Minnesota. He has taught at the University of North Carolina at Chapel Hill and holds a CPA certificate in Colorado. He has taught national professional development classes for a major CPA firm and was a consultant for another CPA firm. Professor Bazley is co-author of Intermediate Accounting, Tenth Edition (2007, South-Western Publishing). He was also a co-author of *Principles of Accounting and Financial Accounting* (PWS-Kent Publishing Company).

Professor Bazley has published articles in professional journals including *The Accounting Review, Management Accounting, Accounting Horizons, Practical Accountant, Academy of Management Journal, The Journal of Managerial Issues,* and *The International Journal of Accounting,* and was a member of the Editorial Boards of *Issues in Accounting Education* and the *Journal of Managerial Issues.* He was also a co-author of a monograph on environmental accounting published by the National Association of Accountants. He has served as an expert witness for the Securities and Exchange Commission. He has served on numerous committees of The Federation of Schools of Accountancy (including Chair of the Student Lyceum Committee), the American Accounting Association, and the Colorado Society of CPAs (including the Continuing Professional Education Board).

# PART 1

# OVERVIEW: BUSINESS, ACCOUNTING, AND THE ROLE OF CREATIVE AND CRITICAL THINKING

CHAPTER 1
**INTRODUCTION TO BUSINESS AND ACCOUNTING**

CHAPTER 2
**CREATIVE AND CRITICAL THINKING, PROBLEM SOLVING, AND THEIR ROLES IN BUSINESS AND ACCOUNTING**

This section consists of two chapters which introduce you to business and accounting, and discuss the role of creative and critical thinking in business decisions. After reading these chapters, you will be able to:

- *understand the role of accounting information in business*
- *describe the planning, operating, and evaluating activities of managing a company*
- *know the difference between management accounting and finanacial accounting*
- *identify internal and external accounting reports*
- *explain the meaning of creative and critical thinking*
- *apply creative and critical thinking in business decisions*

CHAPTER
1

# Introduction to Business and Accounting

"Business is a game, the greatest game in the world if you know how to play it."

—Thomas J. Watson Sr.

1. Why is it necessary to have an understanding of business before trying to learn about accounting?
2. What is the role of accounting information within the business environment?
3. What is private enterprise, and what forms does it take?
4. What types of regulations do companies face?
5. What activities contribute to the operations of a company?
6. Are there any guidelines for reporting to company managers?
7. Are there any guidelines in the United States for reporting to people outside of a company?
8. What role does ethics play in the business environment?

What are you planning to do when you graduate from college—maybe become an accountant or a veterinarian, work your way up to marketing manager for a multinational company, manage the local food bank, or open a sporting goods store? Regardless of your career choice, you will be making business decisions, both in your personal life and at work. We have oriented this book to students like you who are interested in business and the role of accounting in business. You will see that accounting information, used properly, is a powerful tool for making good business decisions. People inside a business use accounting information to help determine and manage costs, set selling prices, and control the operations of the business. People outside the business use accounting information to help make investment and credit decisions about the business. Just what kinds of businesses use accounting? All of them! So let's take a little time to look at what *business* means.

1 Why is it necessary to have an understanding of business before trying to learn about accounting?

Business affects almost every aspect of our lives. Think for a moment about your normal daily activities. How many businesses do you usually encounter? How many did you directly encounter today? Say you started the day with a quick trip to the local convenience store for milk and eggs. While you were out, you noticed that your car was low on fuel, so you stopped at the corner gas station. On the way to class, you dropped some clothes off at the cleaners. After your first class, you skipped lunch so that you could go to the bookstore and buy the calculator you need; after buying a candy bar for sustenance, you headed to your next class. In just half a day, you already interacted with four businesses: the convenience store, the gas station, the cleaners, and the bookstore.

*Actually, you encountered a fifth business, your school. Why would you describe your school as a business?*

Although you were directly involved with four businesses, you were probably *affected* by hundreds of them. For example, two different businesses manufactured the calculator and the candy bar you purchased at the bookstore. Suppose that Unlimited Decadence Corporation manufactured the candy bar that you purchased. As we illustrate in Exhibit 1-1, Unlimited Decadence purchased the candy bar ingredients from many other businesses *(suppliers)*. Each supplier provided Unlimited Decadence with particular ingredients. Shipping businesses *(carriers)* moved the ingredients from the suppliers' warehouses to Unlimited Decadence's factory. Then, after the candy bars were manufactured, a different carrier moved them from Unlimited Decadence to the bookstore. Making and shipping the calculator would follow the same process. You can see that many businesses are involved with manufacturing, shipping, and selling just two products. Now think about all the other products that you used during the morning and all the businesses that were involved with the manufacture and delivery of each product. Before leaving your house, apartment, or dorm this morning, you could easily have been affected by hundreds of businesses.

Products and services affect almost every minute of our lives, and businesses provide these products and services to us. As you will soon see, accounting plays a vital role in both businesses and the business environment by keeping track of a business's economic resources and economic activities, and then by reporting the business's financial position and the results of its activities to people who are interested in how well it is doing. (This is similar to the way statistics are gathered and reported for baseball players and other athletes.)

2 What is the role of accounting information within the business environment?

Accounting focuses on the resources and activities of individual businesses. We will introduce you to accounting by first looking at private enterprise and the environment in which businesses operate. Our discussion will include the types and forms of business, as well as some of the regulatory issues associated with forming and operating a business. Then we will discuss the activities of managers within a business. Next we will introduce the role of accounting information within a business and in the business environment. Finally, we will discuss the importance of ethics in business and accounting.

**EXHIBIT 1-1** **BUSINESSES INVOLVED WITH THE MANUFACTURE AND SALE OF CANDY BARS**

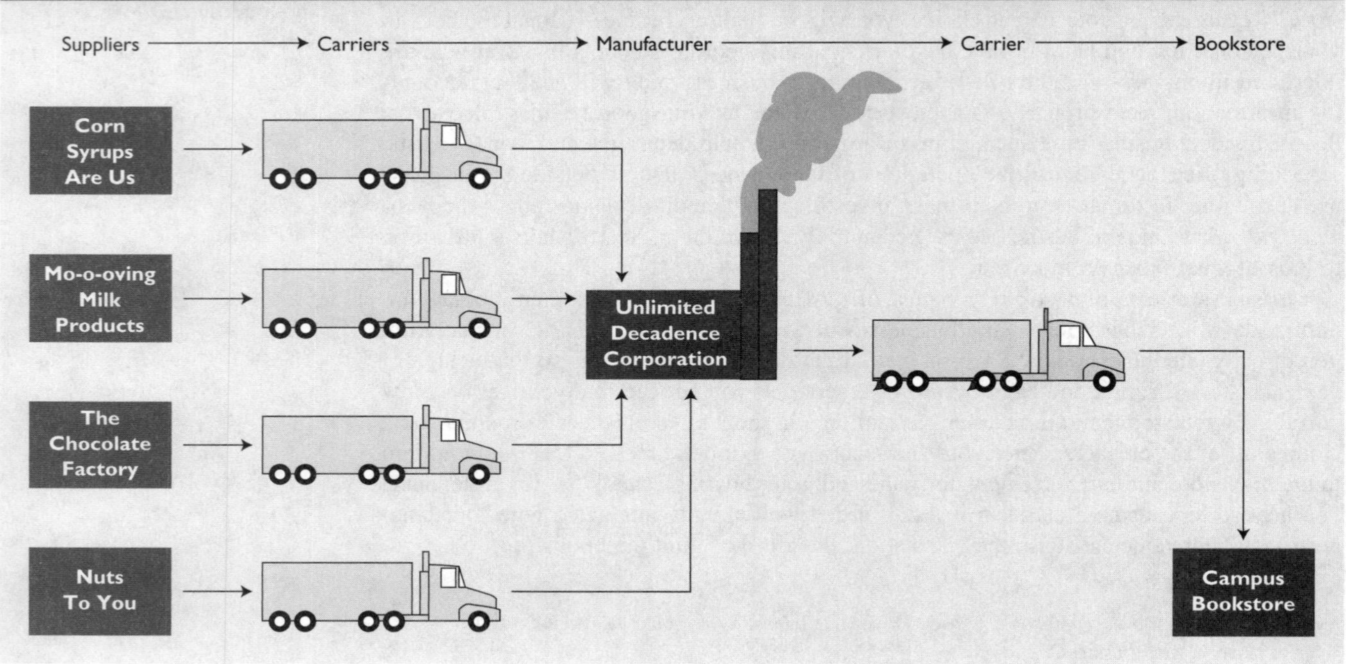


## PRIVATE ENTERPRISE AND CAPITALISM

3 What is private enterprise, and what forms does it take?

Businesses in the United States and most other countries operate in an economic system based on *private enterprise.* In this system, individuals (people like us, rather than public institutions like the government) own *companies* (businesses) that produce and sell services and/or goods for a profit. These companies generally fall into three categories: service companies, merchandising companies, and manufacturing companies.

### Service Companies

**Service companies** perform services or activities that benefit individuals or business customers. The dry cleaning establishment where you dropped off your clothes this morning provides the service of cleaning and pressing your clothes for you. Companies like **A Great Cut**, **Midas Muffler Shops**, **Merry Maids**, and **UPS**, and professional practices such as accounting, law, architecture, and medicine, are all service companies. Other companies in the private enterprise system produce or provide goods, or tangible, physical products. These companies can be either *merchandising companies* or *manufacturing companies.*

### Merchandising Companies

**Merchandising companies** purchase goods (sometimes referred to as *merchandise* or *products*) for resale to their customers. Some merchandising companies, such as plumbing supply stores, electrical suppliers, or beverage distributors, are *wholesalers.* Wholesalers primarily sell their goods to retailers or other commercial users, like plumbers or electricians. Some merchandising companies, such as the bookstore where you bought your calculator and candy bar or the convenience store where you bought your milk and eggs, are *retailers.* Retailers sell their goods directly to the final customer or consumer. **JCPenney**, **Toys 'R' Us**, **amazon.com**, and **Circuit City** are retailers. Other examples of retailers include shoe stores and grocery stores.

## Manufacturing Companies

**Manufacturing companies** make their products and then sell these products to their customers. Therefore, a basic difference between merchandising companies and manufacturing companies involves the products that they sell. Merchandising companies *buy* products that are physically ready for sale and then sell these products to their customers, whereas manufacturing companies *make* their products first and then sell the products to their customers. For example, the bookstore is a merchandising company that sells the candy bars it purchased from Unlimited Decadence, a manufacturing company. Unlimited Decadence, though, purchases (from suppliers) the chocolate, corn syrup, dairy products, and other ingredients to make the candy bars, which it then sells to the Campus Bookstore and other retail stores. **General Motors**, **Black & Decker**, and **Dana Corporation** are examples of manufacturing companies. Exhibit 1-2 shows the relationship between manufacturing companies and merchandising companies and how they relate to their customers.

The line of distinction between service, merchandising, and manufacturing companies is sometimes blurry because a business can be more than one type of company. For example, Dell Computer Corporation manufactures personal computers, sells the computers it manufactures directly to business customers, government agencies, educational institutions, and individuals, and services those computers (through installation, technology transition, and management).

*Do you think a supplier to a manufacturing company is a merchandising company or a manufacturing company? Why?*

Whether a company is a service, merchandising, or manufacturing company (or all three), for it to succeed in a private enterprise system, it must be able to obtain cash to begin to operate and then to grow. As we will discuss in the next sections, companies have several sources of cash.

**EXHIBIT 1-2 RELATIONSHIP OF MANUFACTURING AND MERCHANDISING COMPANIES**

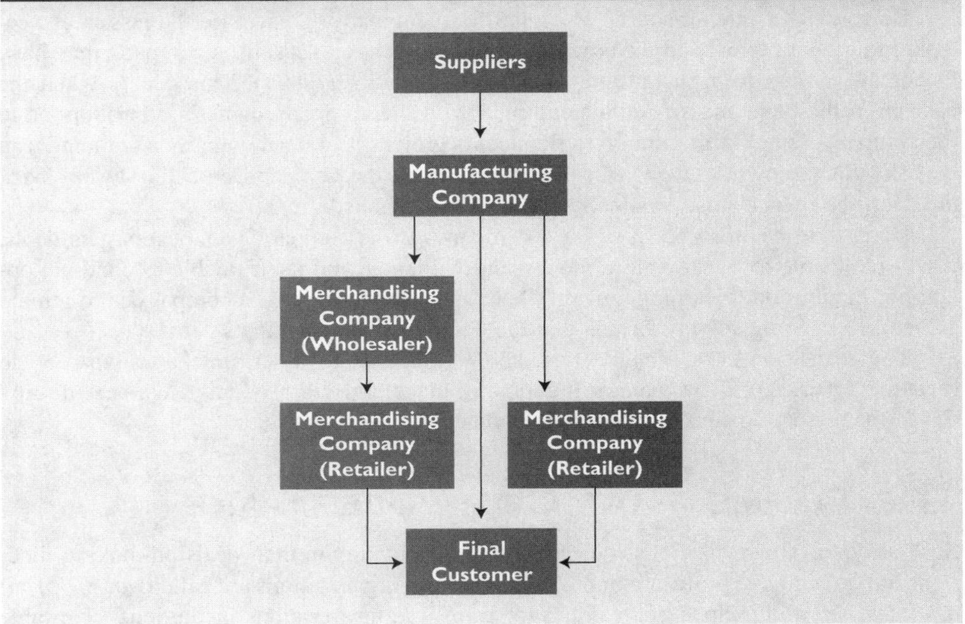

## Entrepreneurship and Sources of Capital

Owning a company involves a level of risk, along with a continuing need for **capital**. Although *capital* has several meanings, we use the term here to mean the funds a company needs to operate or to expand operations. In the next two sections we will discuss the risk involved with owning a company and possible sources of capital.

### Entrepreneurship

Companies in a private enterprise system produce and sell services and goods for a profit. So, profit is the primary objective of a company. Profit rewards the company's owner or owners for having a business idea and for following through with that idea by investing time, talent, and money in the company. The company's owner hires employees, purchases land and a building (or signs a lease for space in a building), and purchases (or leases) any tools, equipment, machinery, and furniture necessary to produce or sell services or goods, *expecting, but not knowing for sure, that customers will buy what the company provides.* An individual who is willing to risk this uncertainty in exchange for the reward of earning a profit (and the personal reward of seeing the company succeed) is called an **entrepreneur**. Entrepreneurship, then, is a combination of three factors: the company owner's idea, the willingness of the company's owner to take a risk, and the abilities of the company's owner and employees to use capital to produce and sell goods or services. But where does the company get its capital?

### Sources of Capital

One source of capital for a company is the entrepreneur's (or company owner's) investment in the company. An entrepreneur invests money "up front" so that the company can get started. The company uses the money to acquire the resources it needs to function. Then, as the company operates, the resources, or capital, of the company increase or decrease through the profits and losses of the company.

When an entrepreneur invests money in a company, he or she hopes to eventually get back the money he or she contributed to the company (a return *of* the contribution). Furthermore, the entrepreneur hopes to periodically receive additional money above the amount he or she originally contributed to the company (a return *on* the contribution). The entrepreneur would like the return *on* the contribution to be higher than the return that could have been earned with that same money on a different investment (such as an interest-bearing checking or savings account).

Borrowing is another source of capital for a company. To acquire the resources necessary to grow or to expand the types of products or services it sells, a company may have to borrow money from institutions like banks (called *creditors*). This occurs when the cash from the company's profits, combined with the company owner's contributions to the company, is not large enough to finance its growth. But borrowing by a company can be risky for the owner or owners. In some cases, if the company is unable to pay back the debt, the owner must personally assume that responsibility.

Borrowing can also be risky for a company. If the company cannot repay its debts, it will be unable to borrow more money and will soon find itself unable to continue operating. In addition to earning a profit, then, another objective of a company is to remain solvent. Remaining **solvent** means that the company can pay off its debts.

The terms *service, merchandising,* and *manufacturing* describe what companies do (perform services, purchase and sell goods, or make and sell products). We next discuss the forms that companies take, or how companies are organized.

# The Forms that Companies Take

Several types of organizations use accounting information in their decision-making functions but do not have profit-making as a goal. These organizations are called *not-for-profit organizations* and include many educational institutions, religious institutions, charitable

**EXHIBIT 1-3 TYPES OF BUSINESS ORGANIZATIONS (COMPANIES)**

| Sole Proprietorships | Partnerships | Corporations |
|---|---|---|
| • Single owner-manager<br>• Small companies<br>• Most common type of business organization | • Two or more owners (partners)<br>• Partnership agreement | • Stockholders have separate identity from company<br>• Capital stock<br>• Greatest volume of business |

organizations, municipalities, governments, and some hospitals. Since making a profit is not a goal of these organizations, some aspects of accounting for these organizations' activities are unique and beyond the scope of this book.

In this book we emphasize *business* organizations. These business organizations, or *companies,* are a significant aspect of the U.S. and world economies. As Exhibit 1-3 shows, a company may be organized as one of the following general types of business organizations: (1) sole proprietorship, (2) partnership, or (3) corporation.

## Sole Proprietorships

A **sole proprietorship** is a company owned by one individual who is the sole investor of capital into the company. Usually the sole owner also acts as the manager of the company. Small retail stores and service firms often follow this form of organization. The sole proprietorship is the most common type of company because it is the easiest to organize and simplest to operate. In 2003, about 72 percent of all companies were sole proprietorships.[a]

## Partnerships

A **partnership** is a company owned by two or more individuals (sometimes hundreds of individuals) who each invest capital, time, and/or talent into the company and share in the profits and losses of the company. These individuals are called *partners*, and their responsibilities, obligations, and benefits are usually described in a contract called a **partnership agreement**. Accounting firms and law firms are examples of partnerships. In 2003, just over 8 percent of all companies were partnerships.[b]

*If you and a friend decide to become business partners, do you think you need a formal partnership agreement? Why or why not?*

## Corporations

A **corporation** is a company organized as a separate legal entity, or body (separate from its owners), according to the laws of a particular state. In fact, the word *corporation* comes from the Latin word for body *(corpus).* In 2003, nearly 20 percent of all companies were corporations.[c]

By being incorporated, a company can enter into contracts, own property, and issue stock. A company issues shares of *capital stock* to owners, called *stockholders,* as evidence of the owners' investment of capital into the corporation. These shares are transferable from stockholder to stockholder, and each share represents part-ownership of the corporation.

A corporation may be owned by one stockholder or by many stockholders (these stockholders are called *investors*). In fact, many large corporations have thousands of stockholders. For example, in their 2005 annual reports, **The Gap** and **Intel Corporation** indicated that their stockholders owned 1,078,925,000 and 5,919,000,000 shares of stock, respectively!

The organization and legal structure of a corporation are more complex than that of a sole proprietorship or a partnership. Although sole proprietorships are the most common type of company, corporations conduct the greatest volume of business in the United States. In 2003, sole proprietorships made almost 5 percent, partnerships close to 12 percent, and corporations nearly 84 percent of all business sales in the United States.[d]

Since most of what we discuss in this text applies to all types of companies, we will use the general term *company* to apply to any company, regardless of structure. If the topic relates only to a specific type of company, we will identify the type of company.

## THE REGULATORY ENVIRONMENT OF BUSINESS

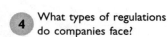

4 What types of regulations do companies face?

Companies affect each of us every day, but they also affect each other, the economy, and the environment. Just as individuals must abide by the laws and regulations of the cities, states, and countries in which they live and work, all companies, regardless of type, size, or complexity, must deal with regulatory issues.

Think again about that candy bar you had as a snack today. When Unlimited Decadence Corporation was formed, the company had to do more than build a factory, purchase equipment and ingredients, hire employees, find retail outlets to sell the candy bar, and begin operations. It also had to deal with the regulatory issues involved with opening and operating even the smallest of companies. Furthermore, its managers must continue to address regulatory issues as long as they continue to operate the company.

*Suppose a company is about to open a factory down the street from your house. What concerns do you have? What regulations might help reduce your concerns?*

Many different laws and authorities regulate the business environment, covering issues such as consumer protection, environmental protection, employee safety, hiring practices, and taxes. Companies must comply with different sets of regulations depending on where their factories and offices are located. We discuss these sets of regulations next.

### Local Regulations

City regulations involve matters such as zoning (parts of the city in which companies may operate), certificates of occupancy, and for some companies, occupational licenses and pollution control. Counties are concerned with issues such as the following: health permits for companies that handle, process, package, and warehouse food; registration of the unique name of each company; and control of pollution to air, land, or water.

### State Regulations

States also regulate the activities of companies located within their borders. Most states require corporations to pay some form of state tax, usually an income tax (a tax on profit), a franchise tax (a fee for the privilege of conducting corporate business in the state), or both. New companies (regardless of form) in most states must apply for sales tax numbers and permits. Each state has unemployment taxes that companies operating within that state must pay.

Practicing professionals, such as doctors, lawyers, and accountants, must get a license for each state in which they practice. Finally, states regulate companies that conduct certain types of business. For example, in Texas, companies that sell, transport, or store alcoholic beverages must obtain licenses from, and pay fees to, the state of Texas. Massachusetts regulations ban selling fireworks, whereas New Hampshire allows the sale of fireworks.

## Federal Regulations

The federal government has a variety of laws and agencies that regulate companies and the business environment. These laws and agencies relate to specific aspects and activities of companies, regardless of the city or state in which the companies are located.

### Internal Revenue Service

All companies have some dealings with the Internal Revenue Service (IRS). Each company must withhold taxes from its employees' pay and send these taxes to the IRS. Furthermore, the IRS taxes the profits of the companies themselves. The type of company determines who actually pays the taxes on profits, though. Corporations must pay their own income taxes to the IRS because, from a legal standpoint, they are viewed as being separate from their owners. Sole proprietorships and partnerships, however, do not pay taxes on their profits. Rather, owners of these types of companies include their share of the company profits along with their other taxable income on their personal income tax returns. This is because the tax law does not distinguish the owners of sole proprietorships and partnerships from the companies themselves.

### Laws and Other Government Agencies

A variety of laws and government departments and agencies (in addition to the IRS) regulate companies. Federal departments and agencies oversee the administration of laws governing areas such as competition (the Federal Trade Commission and the Department of Justice), fair labor practices (the Department of Labor), safety (the Occupational Safety and Health Administration), employee and customer accessibility (the Department of Justice), workplace discrimination (the Equal Employment Opportunity Commission), control of pollution to air, land, or water (the Environmental Protection Agency), and the like.

## International Regulations

When a company conducts business internationally, it also must abide by the laws and regulations of the other countries in which it operates. These laws and regulations address such issues as foreign licensing, export and import documentation requirements, tax laws, multinational production and marketing regulations, domestic ownership of company property, and expatriation of cash (how much of the company's cash can leave the country). Of course, these laws and regulations differ from country to country, so a company operating in several countries must abide by many laws and regulations. Exhibit 1-4 lists some of the more common regulatory issues facing companies operating in different jurisdictions.

*Suppose that as a manager of a manufacturing company, you have the opportunity to have many parts of your product manufactured in another country where the labor is much cheaper and the environmental regulations are less stringent. What are the pros and cons of taking advantage of this opportunity?*

**EXHIBIT 1-4 COMMON REGULATORY ISSUES COMPANIES FACE**

| City and County Issues | State Issues | Federal Issues | International Issues |
|---|---|---|---|
| zoning | state tax | federal taxes | foreign licensing |
| certificate of occupancy | sales tax | competition | exports and imports |
| occupational license | unemployment taxes | labor standards | taxes |
| environmental regulations | professional licenses | working conditions | multinational production and marketing |
| health permit | industry-specific regulations | workplace discrimination | property ownership |
| company name and registration | | | cash restrictions |

# INTEGRATED ACCOUNTING SYSTEM

A company is responsible to many diverse groups of people, both inside and outside the company. For example, its managers and employees depend on the company for their livelihood. Customers expect a dependable product or service at a reasonable cost. The community expects the company to be a good citizen. Owners want returns on their investments, and creditors expect to be paid back. Governmental agencies expect companies to abide by their rules.

People in all of these groups use accounting information about the company to help them assess a company's ability to carry out its responsibilities, and to help them make decisions involving the company. This information comes from the company's integrated accounting system. An **integrated accounting system** is a means by which accounting information about a company's activities is identified, measured, recorded, and summarized so that it can be communicated in an accounting report. A company's integrated accounting system provides much of the information used by the many diverse groups of people outside the company (these are sometimes called **external users**), as well as by the managers and employees within the company (these are sometimes called **internal users**). Two branches of accounting, management accounting and financial accounting, use the information in the integrated accounting system to produce reports for different groups of people. Management accounting provides vital information about a company to internal users; financial accounting gives information about a company to external users.

## Management Accounting Information

Management accounting information helps managers plan, operate, and evaluate a company's activities. Managers must operate the company in a changing environment. They need information to help them compete in a world market in which technology and methods of production are constantly changing. Moreover, in a world exploding with new information, managers must manage that information in a way that will let them use it more efficiently and effectively. Accounting is one of the critical tools of information management.

Since management accounting helps managers inside the company, it is free from the restrictions of regulatory bodies interested in how companies report to external users. Therefore, managers can request "tailor made" information in whatever form is useful for their decision making, such as in dollars, units, hours worked, products manufactured, numbers of defective units, or service agreements signed. The integrated accounting system provides information about segments of the company, products, tasks, plants, or individual activities, depending on what information is important for the decisions managers are making.

## Financial Accounting Information

Financial accounting information is organized for the use of interested people outside of the company. External users analyze the company's financial reports as one source of useful financial information about the company. For these users to be able to interpret the reports, companies reporting to outsiders follow specific guidelines, or rules, known as *generally accepted accounting principles,* (almost a one-size-fits-all approach to reporting). Since a company's financial reports are not tailored to specific user decisions, external users have to use care to find the information in these reports that is relevant to their decisions.

Financial accounting information developed by the integrated accounting system is expressed in dollars in the United States and in different currencies (such as yen, euros, and pesos) in other countries. This information emphasizes the whole company and sometimes important segments of the company.

Both internal and external users need accounting information to make decisions about a company. Since external users want to see the reported results of management activities, we discuss these activities next. Then we will discuss how accounting information supports both management activities and external decision making.

# MANAGEMENT ACTIVITIES

**5** What activities contribute to the operations of a company?

Managers play a vital role in a company's success—by setting goals, making decisions, committing the resources of the company to achieving these goals, and then by achieving these goals. To help ensure the achievement of these goals and the success of the company, managers use accounting information as they perform the activities of planning the operations of the company, operating the company, and evaluating the operations of the company for future planning and operating decisions. Exhibit 1-5 shows these activities.

## Planning

Management begins with planning. A clear plan lays out the organization of, and gives direction to, the operating and evaluating activities. **Planning** establishes the company's goals and the means of achieving these goals. Managers use the planning process to identify what resources and employees the company needs in order to achieve its goals. They also use the planning process to set standards, or "benchmarks," against which they later can measure the company's progress toward its goals. Periodically measuring the company's progress against standards or benchmarks helps managers identify whether the company needs to make corrections to keep itself on course. Because the business environment changes so rapidly, plans must be ongoing and flexible enough to deal with change before it occurs or as it is happening.

Managers of companies operating in more than one country have more to consider in their planning process than do those operating only in the United States. Managers of multinational companies must also consider such factors as multiple languages, economic systems, political systems, monetary systems, markets, and legal systems. In such companies, managers must also plan and encourage the communication between and among branches in several countries.

## Operating

**Operating** refers to the set of activities that the company engages in to conduct its business according to its plan. For Unlimited Decadence, these are the activities that ensure that candy bars get made and sold. They involve gathering the resources and employees necessary to achieve the goals of the company, establishing organizational relationships among departments and employees, and working toward achieving the goals of the company.

**EXHIBIT 1-5 MANAGEMENT ACTIVITIES**

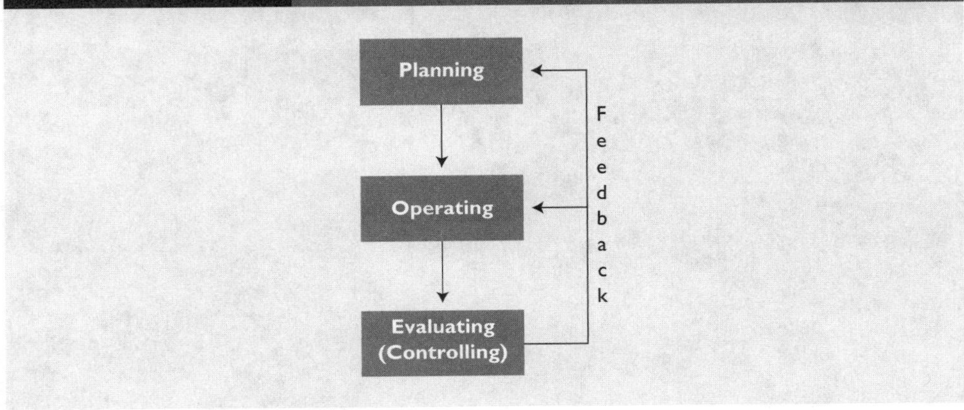

In operating the company, managers and work teams must make day-to-day decisions about how best to achieve these goals. For example, accounting information gives them valuable data about a product's performance. With this information, they can decide which products to continue to sell and when to add new products or drop old ones. If the company is a manufacturing company, managers and work teams can decide what products to produce and whether there is a better way to produce them. With accounting information, managers can also make decisions about how to set product selling prices, whether to advertise and how much to spend on advertising, and whether to buy new equipment or expand facilities. These decisions are ongoing and depend on managers' evaluations of the progress being made toward the company's goals and on changes in the company's plans and goals.

## Evaluating

**Evaluating** is the management activity that measures actual operations and progress against standards or benchmarks. It provides feedback for managers to use to correct deviations from those standards or benchmarks, and to plan for the company's future operations. Evaluating is a continuous process that attempts to prevent problems or to detect and correct problems as quickly as possible.

As you might guess, the more countries in which a company operates, the more interesting the evaluating activity becomes. Because of cultural and other differences, evaluation methods and feedback used in some countries may have little meaning in other countries. For example, it would be difficult to convince employees of the importance of high quality if these employees are used to standing in long lines for whatever quality and quantity of merchandise is available in their country. Managers must pay particular attention to the cultural effects of evaluation methods and feedback in order to achieve effective control.

*Even coaches of professional sports teams perform the activities of planning, operating, and evaluating. If a team's goal is to win the Super Bowl, how would the head coach implement each of these activities?*

Planning, operating, and evaluating all require information about the company. The company's accounting system provides much of the quantitative information managers use.

© RYAN MCVAY/GETTY IMAGES

Do you think these people are engaged in planning activities, operating activities, or evaluating activities? Why?

# Accounting Support for Management Activities

**Management accounting** involves identifying, measuring, recording, summarizing, and then communicating economic information about a company to *internal* users for management decision-making. Internal users include individual employees, work groups or teams, departmental supervisors, divisional and regional managers, and "top management." Management accountants, then, provide information to internal users for planning the operations of the company, for operating the company, and for evaluating the operations of the company. With the help of the management accountant, managers use this information to help them make decisions about the company.

The reports that result from management accounting can help managers *plan* the activities and resources needed to achieve the goals of the company. These reports may provide revenue (amounts charged to customers) estimates and cost estimates of planned activities and resources, and an analysis of these cost estimates. By describing how alternative actions might affect the company's profit and solvency, these estimates and analyses help managers plan.

In *operating* a company, managers use accounting information to make day-to-day decisions about what activities will best achieve the goals of the company. Management accounting helps managers make these decisions by providing timely economic information about how each activity might affect profit and solvency.

Accounting information also plays a vital role in helping managers *evaluate* the operations of the company. Managers use the revenue and cost estimates generated during the planning and decision-making process as a benchmark, and then compare the company's actual revenues and costs against that benchmark to evaluate how well the company is carrying out its plans.

Since managers are making decisions about their own company, and since each company is different, the information the management accountant provides must be "custom fitted" to the information needs of the company. This involves selecting the appropriate information to report, presenting that information in an understandable format (interpreting the information when necessary), and providing the information when it is needed for the decisions being made.

Management accounting responsibilities and activities thus vary widely from company to company. Furthermore, these responsibilities and activities continue to evolve as management accountants respond to the need for new information—a need caused by the changing business environment.

In response to this changing business environment, the Institute of Management Accountants (IMA) publishes guidelines for management accountants called Statements on Management Accounting (SMAs).

## Statements on Management Accounting

6 Are there any guidelines for reporting to company managers?

SMAs serve as guidelines for management accountants to use in fulfilling their responsibilities. The SMAs are nonbinding (they are not rules that must be followed), but because they are developed by professional accountants, as well as leaders in industry and colleges and universities, management accountants turn to SMAs for help when faced with new situations.

## Framework for Management Accounting

The responsibility for identifying issues to be addressed by SMAs lies with an IMA committee called the Management Accounting Committee. One of the first activities this committee undertook was to develop a framework for the work it was assigned to do. The "Framework for Management Accounting" developed by this committee defines the scope of the SMAs, including a statement of the objectives of management accounting and a description of the activities and responsibilities of management accountants.[e]

Company-specific responsibilities and unique elements of a company's internal reports may change, but the underlying goals of management accounting remain the same for all companies:

- To inform people inside and outside the company about past or future events or circumstances that affect the company
- To interpret information from inside and outside the company and to communicate the implications of this information to various segments of the company
- To establish planning and control systems that ensure that company employees use the company's resources in accordance with company policy
- To develop information systems (manual or computer systems) that contain, process, and manage accounting data
- To implement the use of modern equipment and techniques to aid in identifying, gathering, analyzing, communicating, and protecting information
- To ensure that the accounting system provides accurate and reliable information
- To develop and maintain an effective and efficient management accounting organization

In order to see how a company's accounting information helps managers in their planning, operating, and evaluating activities, briefly consider three key management accounting reports prepared with these goals in mind.

## Basic Management Accounting Reports

Budgets, cost analyses, and manufacturing cost reports are examples of management tools the accounting system provides. Exhibit 1-6 illustrates the relationships between management activities and these reports.

*Suppose you are the manager of your company's sales force. What type of information would you want to help you do your job?*

### Budgets

**Budgeting** is the process of quantifying managers' plans and showing the impact of these plans on the company's operating activities and financial position. Managers present this information in a report called a *budget* (or *forecast*). Once the planned activities have occurred, managers can evaluate the results of the operating activities against the budget to make sure that the actual operations of the various parts of the company achieved the established plans. For example, Unlimited Decadence might develop a budget showing how many boxes of candy bars it plans to sell during the first three months of 2008. Later, after actual 2008 sales have been made, managers will compare the results of these sales with the budget to determine if their forecasts were "on target" and, if not, to find out why differences occurred. We will discuss budgets further in Chapters 4 and 12.

### Cost Analyses

**Cost analysis**, or **cost accounting**, is the process of determining and evaluating the costs of specific products or activities within a company. Managers use cost analyses when making decisions about these products or activities. For example, Unlimited Decadence might use a cost analysis to decide whether to stop or to continue making the Divinely

**EXHIBIT 1-6 ACTIVITIES OF MANAGERS AND RELATED ACCOUNTING REPORTS**

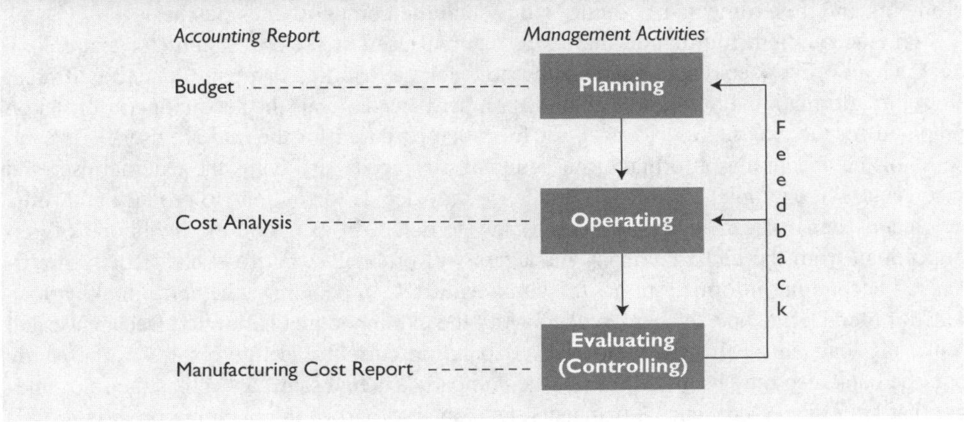


Decadent candy bar. The cost analysis report might show that the candy bar is not profitable because it earns less than it costs to make. If this is the case, the fact that this candy bar does not make a profit will be one factor in the managers' decision. The company's managers also will have to resolve the ethical issue of whether to lay off the employees who produced the candy bar. (Can you think of an alternative to a layoff?)

*Suppose you are a manager of a company that makes a food product thought to create major health problems after long-term use. What facts would you consider in trying to decide whether the company should drop the product or continue producing it?*

We will discuss cost analysis reports again in Chapter 15.

### Manufacturing Cost Reports

As we mentioned above, managers must monitor and evaluate a company's operations to determine if its plans are being achieved. Accounting information can highlight specific "variances" from plans, indicating where corrections to operations can be made if necessary.

For example, a manufacturing cost report might show that total actual costs for a given month were greater than total budgeted costs. However, it might also show that some actual costs were greater than budgeted costs while others were less than budgeted costs. The more detailed information will be useful for managers as they analyze why these differences occurred, and then make adjustments to the company's operations to help the company achieve its plans. We will discuss manufacturing cost reports again in Chapter 17.

## ACCOUNTING SUPPORT FOR EXTERNAL DECISION MAKING

*Say you have been offered a job at Unlimited Decadence. What economic information concerning Unlimited Decadence would you want to know about to help you decide whether to accept the job offer?*

Management accounting gives people inside a company vital business information about the company and its performance, but the company also must provide business information about its performance to people outside the company. **Financial accounting** involves identifying, measuring, recording, summarizing, and then communicating economic information about a company to *external* users for use in their various decisions. External users are people and groups outside the company who need accounting information to decide whether or not to engage in some activity with the company. These users include individual investors, stockbrokers and financial analysts who offer investment assistance, consultants, bankers, suppliers, labor unions, customers, and local, state, and federal governments and governments of countries in which the company does business.

The accounting information that helps external users make a decision (for example, a bank's loan officer deciding whether or not to extend a loan to a company) may be different from the information a manager within the company needs. Thus the accounting information prepared for the external user may differ from that prepared for the internal user. However, some of the accounting information the internal user needs also helps the external user and vice versa. For example, Unlimited Decadence may decide to continue to produce and sell a new candy bar if it can borrow enough money to do so. In weighing the likelihood of getting a loan from the bank, company managers will probably want to evaluate the same financial accounting information that the bank evaluates. In deciding whether to make a loan to Unlimited Decadence, the bank will consider the likelihood that Unlimited Decadence will repay the loan. Since this likelihood may depend on current and future sales of the candy bar, the bank also may want to evaluate the company's actual sales, as well as the sales budget that Unlimited Decadence's managers developed as part of the planning process.

Many external users evaluate the accounting information of more than one company, and need comparable information from each company. For example, a bank looks at accounting information from all of its customers who apply for loans, and must use comparable information in order to decide to which customers it will make loans. This need for comparability creates a need for guidelines or rules for companies to follow when preparing accounting information for external users. Over the years, because of the activities of several professional accounting organizations, a set of broad guidelines for financial accounting has evolved in the United States. These guidelines are referred to as *generally accepted accounting principles*.

## Generally Accepted Accounting Principles

7 Are there any guidelines in the United States for reporting to people outside of a company?

**Generally accepted accounting principles**, or **GAAP**, are the currently accepted principles, procedures, and practices that companies use for financial accounting and reporting in the United States. These principles, or "rules," must be followed in the external reports of companies that sell capital stock to the public in the United States and by many other companies as well. GAAP covers such issues as how to account for inventory, buildings, income taxes, and capital stock; how to measure the results of a company's operations; and how to account for the operations of companies in specialized industries, such as the banking industry, the entertainment industry, and the insurance industry. Without these agreed-upon principles, external users of accounting information would not be able to understand the meaning of this information. (Imagine if we all tried to communicate with each other without any agreed-upon rules of spelling and grammar!)

Several organizations contribute to GAAP through their publications (called "pronouncements" or "standards"). The three most important organizations that develop GAAP in the United States are the Financial Accounting Standards Board (FASB), the Securities and Exchange Commission (SEC), and the American Institute of Certified Public Accountants (AICPA). The FASB is a seven-member full-time board of professional accountants and businesspeople; it issues *Statements of Financial Accounting Standards,* which establish new standards or amend previously-established standards. The SEC is a branch of the U.S. government; it issues *Financial Reporting Releases* containing financial accounting guidelines. The AICPA is the professional organization of all certified public accountants (CPAs); it issues *Statements of Position* that also create accounting standards.[1]

[1]Each of these organizations issues other documents that influence and establish GAAP, but they are too numerous to mention here.

Accounting is less standardized worldwide than in the United States because of cultural, legal, economic, and other differences among countries. However, several organizations have made progress in developing worldwide accounting standards. Most notably, the International Accounting Standards Board (IASB) has issued over 40 standards covering issues such as accounting for inventories, property and equipment, and the results of a company's operations. Although compliance with these standards is voluntary, most of the accountancy organizations around the world that are represented on this board have agreed to eventually require the *International Accounting Standards* as part of their countries' generally accepted accounting standards.

Many GAAP pronouncements are complex and very technical in nature. In this book, we will introduce only the basic aspects of the generally accepted accounting principles that apply to the issues we discuss. It is important to recognize, however, that these principles do change; they are modified as business practices and decisions change and as better accounting techniques are developed.

## Basic Financial Statements

Companies operate to achieve various goals. They may be interested in providing a healthy work environment for their employees, in reaching a high level of pollution control, or in making contributions to civic and social organizations and activities. However, to meet these goals, a company must first achieve its two primary objectives: *earning a satisfactory profit* and *remaining solvent*. If a company fails to meet either of these objectives, it will not be able to achieve its various goals and will not be able to survive in the long run.

**Profit** (commonly referred to as *net income*) is the difference between the cash and credit sales of a company *(revenues)* and its total costs *(expenses)*. **Solvency** is a company's long-term ability to pay its debts as they come due. As you will see, both internal and external users analyze the *financial statements* of a company to determine how well the company is achieving its two primary objectives.

**Financial statements** are accounting reports used to summarize and communicate financial information about a company. A company's integrated accounting system produces three major financial statements: the income statement, the balance sheet, and the cash flow statement. It also produces a supporting financial statement: the statement of changes in owner's equity. Each of these statements summarizes specific information that has been identified, measured, and recorded during the accounting process.

### Income Statement

A company's **income statement** summarizes the results of its operating activities for *a specific time period* and shows the company's profit for that period. It shows a company's revenues, expenses, and net income (or net loss) for that time period, usually one year. Exhibit 1-7 shows what kind of information appears in a company's income statement. **Revenues** are the prices charged to a company's customers for the goods or services the company provided to them. **Expenses** are the costs of providing the goods or services. These amounts include the costs of the products the company has sold (either the cost of making these products or the cost of purchasing these products), the costs of conducting business (called *operating expenses*), and the costs of income taxes, if any. The **net income** is the excess of revenues over expenses, or the company's profit; a **net loss** arises when expenses are greater than revenues. We will discuss the income statement further in Chapter 6 and throughout the book.

### Balance Sheet

A company's **balance sheet** summarizes its financial position *on a given date* (usually the last day of the time period covered by the income statement). It is also called a *statement of financial position*. Exhibit 1-8 shows what kind of information appears on a balance sheet. A balance sheet lists the company's assets, liabilities, and owner's equity on the given date. **Assets** are economic resources that a company owns and that it expects will provide future benefits to the company. **Liabilities** are the company's economic obligations (debts) to its

**EXHIBIT 1-7** **WHAT A COMPANY'S INCOME STATEMENT SHOWS**

**Revenues**

Here's where the company shows what it charged customers for the goods or services provided to them during a specific time period.

**Expenses**

Here's where the company lists the costs of providing the goods and services during that period.

**Net Income**

This is the difference between revenues and expenses.

creditors—people outside the company such as banks and suppliers—and to its employees. The **owner's equity** of a company is the owner's current investment in the assets of the company, which includes the owner's contributions to the company and any earnings (net income) that the owner leaves in (or invests in) the company. A corporation's owners' equity is called **stockholders' equity**. We will discuss the balance sheet further in Chapter 7 and throughout the book.

### Statement of Changes in Owner's Equity

A company's integrated accounting system frequently provides a supporting financial statement, called a **statement of changes in owner's equity**, to explain the amount shown in the owner's equity section of the company's balance sheet. Both the balance sheet and the statement of changes in owner's equity show the owner's investment in the assets of the company on the balance sheet date. However, the statement of changes in owner's equity also summarizes the *changes* that occurred in the owner's investment between the first day and the last day of the time period covered by the company's income statement. Exhibit 1-9 shows the kind of changes in owner's equity that appear on this statement. Net income earned during the period increases the owner's investment in the company's assets (and the assets themselves) as the owner "reinvests" the profit of the company back into the company. Similarly, additional contributions of money by the owner to the company during the time period also increase the owner's investment in the company's assets (and the assets themselves). On the other hand, a net loss, rather than a net income, decreases the owner's investment in the company (and the company's assets), as does the owner's choice to remove (or withdraw) money from the company ("disinvesting" the

**EXHIBIT 1-8** **WHAT A COMPANY'S BALANCE SHEET SHOWS**

**Assets**

Here's where the company lists its economic resources, such as cash, inventories of its products, and equipment it owns.

**Liabilities**

Here's where the company lists its obligations to creditors, such as banks and suppliers, and to employees.

**Owner's Equity**

Here's where the company lists the owner's current investment in the assets of the company.

**EXHIBIT 1-9 WHAT A COMPANY'S STATEMENT OF CHANGES IN OWNER'S EQUITY SHOWS**

**Beginning Owner's Equity**

Here's where the company shows the Owner's Equity amount at the beginning of the income statement period (the last day of the previous income statement period). This amount also appears on the balance sheet on the last day of the previous income statement period.

**+ Net Income**

Here's where the company adds the net income from the period's Income Statement (the profit that the company earned during the income statement period).

**+ Owner's Contributions**

Here's where the company adds any additional contributions to the company that the company's owner made during the income statement period.

**– Withdrawals**

Here's where the company subtracts any withdrawals of cash from the company that the company's owner made during the income statement period.

**Ending Owner's Equity**

Here's where the company shows the resulting Owner's Equity amount that also appears on the company's balance sheet on the last day of the income statement period.

profit from the company). We will discuss the statement of changes in owner's equity further in Chapter 6 and throughout the book.

### Cash Flow Statement

A company's **cash flow statement** summarizes its cash receipts, cash payments, and net change in cash for a specific time period. Exhibit 1-10 shows what kind of information appears in a cash flow statement. The cash receipts and cash payments for operating activities, such as products sold or services performed and the costs of producing the products or services, are summarized in the *cash flows from operating activities* section of the statement. The cash receipts and cash payments for investing activities are summarized in the *cash flows from investing activities* section of the statement. Investing activities include the purchases and sales of assets such as buildings and equipment. The cash receipts and cash payments for financing activities, such as money borrowed from and repaid to banks, are summarized in the *cash flows from financing activities* section of the statement. We will discuss the cash flow statement further in Chapter 8, and throughout the book.

A company may publish its income statement, balance sheet, and cash flow statement (and statement of changes in owner's equity), along with other related financial accounting information, in its **annual report**. Many companies (mostly corporations) do so. We will discuss the content of an annual report in Chapter 10.

## ETHICS IN BUSINESS AND ACCOUNTING

8 What role does ethics play in the business environment?

A company's financial statements are meant to convey information about the company to internal and external users in order to help them make decisions about the company. But if the information in the financial statements does not convey a realistic picture of the results of the company's operations or its financial position, the decisions based on this information can have disastrous consequences.

**EXHIBIT 1-10** **WHAT A COMPANY'S CASH FLOW STATEMENT SHOWS**

**Cash Flows from Operating Activities**

Here's where the company lists the cash it received and paid in selling products or performing services for a specific time period.

**Cash Flows from Investing Activities**

Here's where the company lists the cash it received and paid in buying and selling assets such as equipment and buildings.

**Cash Flows from Financing Activities**

Here's where the company lists the cash it received and paid in obtaining and repaying bank loans and from contributions and withdrawals of cash made by the company's owners.

Consider the fallout from Enron Corporation's 2001 financial statements.[f] On October 1, 2001, Enron Corporation was the seventh-largest company in the United States, employing 21,000 people in more than 40 countries. It was also the largest energy trading company in the United States. *Fortune* magazine had ranked Enron 24th in its "100 Best Companies to Work for in America" in the year 2000.[g] It's stock was trading for about $83 per share. Two weeks later, after reporting incredible profits for its first two quarters (January through June) of 2001, Enron reported a third-quarter (July through September) loss, in part because of adjustments caused by previously misstated profits. But by November 1, JP Morgan Chase and Citigroup's Salomon Smith Barney had attempted to rescue Enron by extending the company an opportunity to borrow $1 billion (above what Enron already owed them). On November 19, Enron publicly acknowledged that its financial statements did not comply with GAAP in at least two areas. This failure resulted in huge misstatements on Enron's financial statements: assets and profits were overstated, and liabilities were understated. On December 2, 2001, Enron declared bankruptcy.

The rapid demise of one of the largest, and what appeared to be one of the most successful, companies in the world to the largest corporate failure in the United States created a wave of economic and emotional effects around the world. Before Enron reported a third-quarter loss, its stock was selling for around $83 per share. After Enron reported its loss, its stock dropped to $0.70 per share—a total drop in market value of almost $60 billion. Most of those who had purchased shares of Enron stock lost money. Many lost hundreds of thousands of dollars! The Enron employees' pension plan, 62 percent of which was Enron stock, lost nearly $2.1 billion dollars, virtually wiping out the retirement savings of most of Enron's employees, many of whom were nearing retirement age. Close to 5,600 Enron employees were laid off from their jobs. Enron left behind approximately $63 billion in debts, with JP Morgan owed $900 million and Citigroup up to $800 million. Many banks around the world also were affected by having lent money to Enron.

In addition to these after-effects, the Justice Department prosecuted the accounting firm Arthur Andersen—Enron's auditor. It claimed that Andersen had interfered with a federal investigation of Enron's collapse by shredding paperwork related to Andersen's audit of Enron. Two Andersen executives—a partner and an in-house attorney—had reminded employees of Andersen's document destruction policy during the time that the Justice Department was investigating Enron's failure, resulting in large-scale shredding of the Enron documents. A jury found Andersen guilty. As a result, Arthur Andersen, a highly respected accounting firm and bastion of integrity, relinquished its accounting license, preventing it from conducting audits. Andersen, a once-thriving company of 28,000 employees shriveled to 200. Ironically, too late for the employees who had lost their jobs, the Supreme Court found that the jurors in this case had received improper instructions, and it rejected the Justice Department's claim, vindicating Arthur Andersen.[h]

Ethical behavior on the part of all of Enron's managers would not have guaranteed the company's success. However, it could have prevented much of the damage suffered by those inside and outside the company, including those who depended on Enron's financial statements to provide them with dependable information about the company.

*Do you think JP Morgan or Citigroup would have lent Enron as much money if Enron had not overstated its net income and assets, and understated its liabilities? Why or why not? What might Enron's employees have done differently if Enron's financial statements had been properly stated?*

Enron was not the first, nor (unfortunately) will it be the last, company to get into trouble for misleading financial reporting. While it seems clear that some of what Enron's managers, and those of some other companies, disclosed on their financial statements was wrong, many business and accounting issues and events in the business environment cannot be interpreted as absolutely right or wrong. Every decision or choice has pros and cons, costs and benefits, and people or institutions who will be affected positively or negatively by the decision. Even in a setting where many issues and events fall between the extremes of right and wrong, it is very important for accountants and businesspeople to maintain high ethical standards. Several groups have established codes of ethics addressing ethical behavior to help accountants and their business associates work their way through the complicated ethical issues associated with business issues and events. These groups include the American Institute of Certified Public Accountants (AICPA), the Institute of Management Accountants (IMA), the International Federation of Accountants (IFAC), and most large companies.

## Professional Organizations' Codes of Ethics

The members of the AICPA adopted a code of professional conduct that guides them in their professional work.[i] It addresses such issues as self-discipline, honorable behavior, moral judgments, the public interest, professionalism, integrity, and technical and ethical standards. The IMA has a code of conduct that is similar to the AICPA's code.[j] It addresses competence, confidentiality, integrity, objectivity, and resolution of ethical conflict.

The IFAC is an independent, worldwide organization. Its stated purpose is to "develop and enhance a coordinated worldwide accountancy profession with harmonized standards." As part of its efforts, it has developed a code of ethics for accountants in each country to use as the basis for founding their own codes of ethics.[k] Because of the wide cultural, language, legal, and social diversity of the nations of the world, the IFAC expects professional accountants in each country to add their own national ethical standards to the code to reflect their national differences, or even to delete some items of the code at their national level. The code addresses objectivity, resolution of ethical conflicts, professional competence, confidentiality, tax practice, cross-border activities, and publicity. It also addresses independence, fees and commissions, activities incompatible with the practice of accountancy, clients' money, relations with other professional accountants, and advertising and solicitation.

## Ethics at the Company Level

Even before the collapse of Enron, many companies developed codes or statements of company and business ethics. For example, **Texas Instruments Incorporated (TI)**, which manufactures microchips, calculators, and other electronic equipment, has several documents containing guidelines for ethical decision making. It even has an ethics office and a director of ethics! The most important ethics document at TI is called *Ethics in the Business of TI.* It was originally published in 1961 and has been periodically revised since then.

The spirit of TI's code of ethics is described by the president and chief executive officer on the inside cover of the publication. "Texas Instruments will conduct its business in accordance with the highest ethical and legal standards. . . . We will always place integrity before shipping, before billings, before profits, before anything. If it comes down to a choice between making a desired profit and doing it right, we don't have a choice. We'll do it right."[1] The code addresses the marketplace, gifts and entertainment, improper use of corporate assets, political contributions, payments in connection with business transactions, conflict of interest, investment in TI stock, TI proprietary information, trade secrets and software of others, transactions with governmental agencies, and disciplinary action, among other subjects.

Although some companies had already developed codes of ethics, the fallout from the collapse of Enron, and from the similar financial misreporting of other companies, inspired Congress to pass the 2002 Sarbanes-Oxley Act. In addition to addressing numerous issues related to corporate financial reporting, the Act also emphasizes the importance of a code of ethics for companies' financial officers (for example, chief financial officers, controllers, and chief accountants). In fact, the Act directed the Securities and Exchange Commission to require corporations to include a statement in their annual reports about whether or not they adopted a code of ethics for their financial officers, and if not, why not.

In our society, we expect people to behave within a range of civilized standards. This expectation allows our society to function with minimal confusion and misunderstanding. Similarly, accounting information developed in an ethical environment allows our economy to function efficiently, and enables users to direct or allocate our resources productively. In both our personal and our business lives, ethics and integrity are our "social glue."

## Framework of the Book

Now that you have been introduced to business and accounting, it is almost time to begin a more in-depth study of the use of accounting information in the business environment. But first we will take a chapter to discuss the types of thinking necessary for one to prosper in this environment. Chapter 2 describes creative and critical thinking, the types of thinking done by people who succeed in accounting and business. In each subsequent chapter you will see examples of creative and critical thinking and will be given the opportunity to practice them.

Beginning in Chapter 3 we will discuss, in more depth, accounting and its use in the management activities of planning, operating, and evaluating, starting with a simple company. Then, in later chapters, we will progress through more complex companies. We will also discuss the use of accounting by decision makers outside the company.

As you read through the book, you will begin to notice the same topics reemerging; but note that each time, a topic will be refined or enhanced by a different company structure, a different type of business, or a different user perspective. You will also notice that we continue to discuss ethical considerations. That's because ethical considerations exist in all aspects of business and accounting.

You will also notice that international issues appear again and again. Many companies operating in the United States have home offices, branches, and subsidiaries in other countries or simply trade with companies in foreign countries. Managers must know the implications of conducting business in foreign countries and with foreign companies. External users of accounting information also must know the effects of these business connections.

## Summary

At the beginning of the chapter we asked you several questions. During the chapter, we asked you to STOP and answer some additional questions to build your knowledge about specific issues. Be sure you answered these additional questions. Below are the questions from the beginning of the chapter, with a brief summary of the key points relating to the answers. Use your thinking skills to expand on these key points to develop more complete answers to the questions and to determine what other questions you have that might lead you to learn more about the issues.

### 1 Why is it necessary to have an understanding of business before trying to learn about accounting?

Accounting involves identifying, measuring, recording, summarizing, and communicating economic information about a company for decision making. It focuses on the resources and activities of companies. Therefore, you need to understand companies and the business environment in which they exist, before trying to learn how to account for their resources and activities.

### 2 What is the role of accounting information within the business environment?

Accounting information helps people inside and outside companies make decisions. It supports management activities by providing managers with quantitative information about their company to aid them in planning, operating, and evaluating the company's activities. Accounting information supports external decision making by providing people outside of the company—such as investors, creditors, stockbrokers, financial analysts, bankers, suppliers, labor unions, customers, and governments—with financial statements containing economic information about the performance of the company.

### 3 What is private enterprise, and what forms does it take?

Companies in the private enterprise system produce goods and services for a profit. These companies can be service, merchandising, or manufacturing companies. Entrepreneurs, or individuals, invest money in companies so that the companies can acquire resources, such as inventory, buildings, and equipment. The companies then use these resources to earn a profit. The three types of business organization are (1) the sole proprietorship, owned by one individual, (2) the partnership, owned by two or more individuals (partners), and (3) the corporation, incorporated as a separate legal entity and owned by numerous stockholders who hold capital stock in the corporation.

### 4 What types of regulations do companies face?

The activities of companies must be regulated because these activities affect us, other companies, the economy, and the environment. All companies, regardless of type, size, or complexity, must contend with regulatory issues. Numerous laws and authorities regulate companies on issues ranging from environmental protection to taxes. Each city, county, state, and country has its own regulations. Owners of companies must learn and comply with the regulations issued by the governments where the companies are located and in the areas in which the companies conduct business.

### 5 What activities contribute to the operations of a company?

Managers strive to make their company successful through setting and achieving the goals of their company, making decisions, and committing the resources of the company to the achievement of these goals. Planning provides the organization and direction for the other activities. Operating involves gathering the necessary resources and employees and implementing the plans. Evaluating measures the actual progress against standards or benchmarks so that problems can be corrected.

### 6 Are there any guidelines for reporting to company managers?

The Institute of Management Accountants publishes a broad set of nonbinding guidelines for management accountants to use in fulfilling their responsibilities. These guidelines provide help for management accountants when they are faced with new situations.

### 7 Are there any guidelines in the United States for reporting to people outside of a company?

So that external users can understand the meaning of accounting information, companies follow agreed-upon principles in their external reports. The FASB, the SEC, and the AICPA contribute to the development of generally accepted accounting principles, the standards or "rules" that many companies must follow.

### 8 What role does ethics play in the business environment?

Since the world is a complex place, where issues are not always clear, decisions must be made in an ethical context with the best available information. Accounting information can be relied on only if it is generated in an ethical environment. Many groups have established codes of ethics.

# Key Terms

**annual report** *(p. 19)*
**assets** *(p. 17)*
**balance sheet** *(p. 17)*
**budgeting** *(p. 14)*
**capital** *(p. 6)*
**cash flow statement** *(p. 19)*
**corporation** *(p. 7)*
**cost analysis or cost accounting** *(p. 14)*
**entrepreneur** *(p. 6)*
**evaluating** *(p. 12)*
**expenses** *(p. 17)*
**external users** *(p. 10)*
**financial accounting** *(p. 15)*
**financial statements** *(p. 17)*
**generally accepted accounting principles (GAAP)** *(p. 16)*
**income statement** *(p. 17)*
**integrated accounting system** *(p. 10)*
**internal users** *(p. 10)*
**liabilities** *(p. 17)*
**management accounting** *(p. 13)*
**manufacturing companies** *(p. 5)*
**merchandising companies** *(p. 4)*
**net income** *(p. 17)*
**net loss** *(p. 17)*
**operating** *(p. 11)*
**owner's equity** *(p. 18)*
**partnership** *(p. 7)*
**partnership agreement** *(p. 7)*
**planning** *(p. 11)*
**profit** *(p. 17)*
**revenues** *(p. 17)*
**service companies** *(p. 4)*
**sole proprietorship** *(p. 7)*
**solvency** *(p. 17)*
**solvent** *(p. 6)*
**statement of changes in owner's equity** *(p. 18)*
**stockholders' equity** *(p. 18)*

# Summary Surfing

Here is an opportunity to gather information on the Internet about real-world issues related to the topics in this chapter. Answer the following questions (for suggestions on how to navigate various organizations' Web site to find the relevant information, see the related discussion in the Preface at the beginning of the book).

- Go to the **Financial Executives Institute** Web site. The FEI's Code of Ethics lists responsibilities that its members have to several groups of people. To what groups is the Code referring? Give an example of a responsibility that members have to each group.
- Go to the **Texas Instruments** Web site. What are the three primary functions of the TI Ethics Office? What does the TI Ethics Committee do?

# Appendix

## The Profession of Accountancy

Perhaps you are wondering what the profession of accountancy is all about. Accountancy has emerged as a profession, alongside other professions such as medicine, law, and architecture. Two characteristics distinguish a profession from an occupation. One is that its members have exclusive technical competence in their field requiring extensive training and specialized study. These members usually demonstrate their initial competence by taking a standardized exam. The second distinguishing characteristic of a profession is that its members adhere to a service ideal (they render a specialized service to the public) and its supporting standards of conduct and ethics. As we discuss in this appendix, the profession of accountancy meets both of these criteria. First of all, the study and the practice of accountancy require a broad understanding of concepts in such areas as business, economics, sociology, psychology, and public administration, as well as an in-depth technical knowledge of specialized accounting areas. Accountants demonstrate their understand-

**EXHIBIT 1-11 THE PROFESSION OF ACCOUNTANCY**

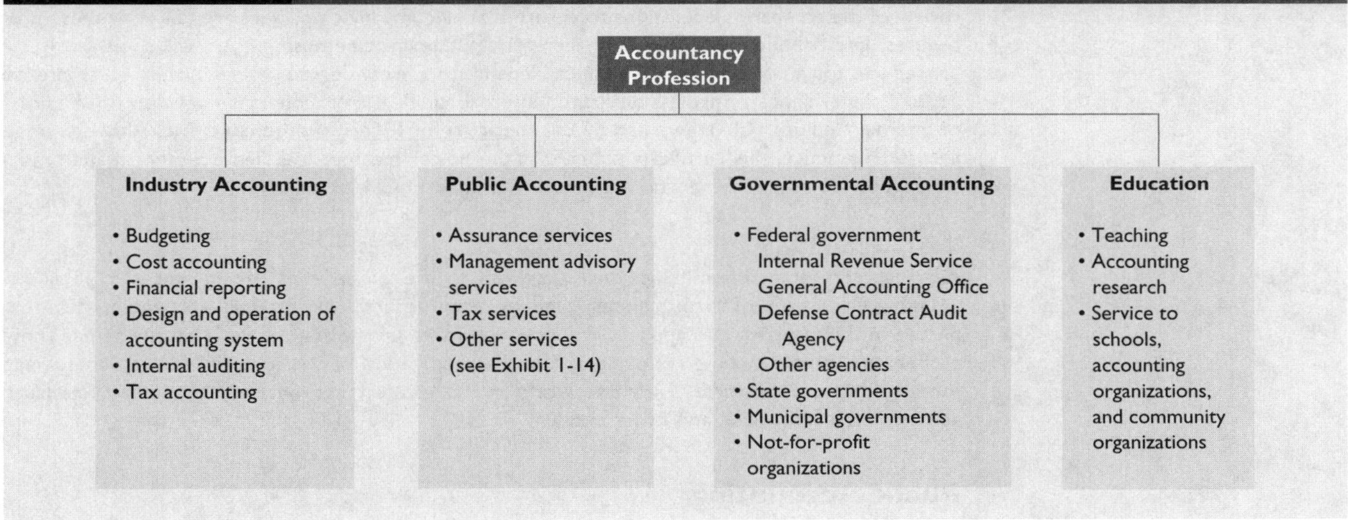


ing of these concepts and their technical accounting knowledge by taking standardized exams such as the CPA Exam and the CMA Exam, which we will discuss later. Secondly, accountants render specialized accounting services in four general areas (or fields) and must comply with specific standards of conduct and ethics (as you read about in the main part of this chapter).

The four general fields of accountancy include (1) industry accounting, (2) public accounting, (3) governmental accounting, and (4) education, each of which has several accounting specialty areas. We summarize them in Exhibit 1-11 and discuss them briefly here.

## Industry Accounting

A company employs industry, or management, accountants to perform its internal (management) accounting activities and to prepare its financial reports. A high-level manager, such as the company's **controller**, usually coordinates these activities. This manager frequently reports directly to a top manager of the organization, such as the **chief financial officer**—an indication of how important the management accounting functions are to the company's operations.

Another indication of the importance of management accounting is the Certificate in Management Accounting (CMA). The CMA is granted to those who meet specific educational and professional standards and who pass a uniform CMA examination, administered twice yearly by the **Institute of Management Accountants**. Although the CMA is not required as a license to practice, accountants holding the CMA are recognized as professional experts in the area of management accounting.

Management accounting activities encompass several areas: budgeting, cost accounting, and financial reporting (which we discussed briefly in this chapter), as well as designing and operating accounting systems, internal auditing, and tax accounting. We discuss the last three of these areas next.

### Design and Operation of an Integrated Accounting System

One duty of the management accountant is to design and operate a company's integrated accounting system, which may be a part of its bigger enterprise resource planning (ERP) system (which we discuss in Chapter 10). This function is sometimes referred to as **general accounting** because of the wide variety of activities involved. These activities include, among others, deciding how much of the accounting system will be computer or manually operated, determining the information needs of different managers and departments, integrating the accounting activities for those departments, and designing accounting procedures, forms, and reports.

### Internal Auditing

One part of the design of an accounting system is establishing good internal control. As we discuss in Chapter 9, **internal control** involves the procedures needed to control or minimize a company's risks (of losses, earnings drops, fraud, fines, scandal, and so forth), to safeguard a company's economic resources, and to promote the efficient and effective operation of its accounting system. Internal auditing is a part of a company's internal control procedures and has as its purpose the review of the company's operations to ensure that all company employees are following these procedures. Internal auditing is becoming increasingly important because, as you will see shortly, the procedures for a company's *external* audit depend, to a great degree, on the quality of its internal control. As evidence of professionalism in internal auditing, an accountant may earn a Certificate of Internal Auditing (CIA), awarded by the **Institute of Internal Auditors, Inc.** Although not a license to practice, this certificate states that the holder has met specified educational and practical experience requirements and has passed the uniform CIA examination.

### Tax Accounting

Although companies often assign their tax work to the tax services department of a public accounting firm, many of them maintain their own tax departments as well. Accountants with expertise in the tax laws that apply to the company make up the staff of these departments. These accountants handle income tax planning and the preparation of the company's state, federal, and foreign income tax returns. They also work on real estate taxes, personal property taxes (such as taxes on inventories), and other taxes.

## Public Accounting

A public accountant is an independent professional who provides accounting services to clients for a fee. Many accountants practice public accounting as individual practitioners or work in local or regional public accounting firms. Others work in large public accounting firms that have offices in most major U.S. and international cities. These firms provide accounting services to large corporations, some of which span the United States as well as the world in their activities.

Most public accountants are **certified public accountants** (CPAs). A CPA has met the requirements of the state in which he or she works, and holds a license to practice accounting in that state. States use licensing as a means of protecting the public interest by helping to ensure that public accountants provide high-quality, professional services. Although the licensing requirements vary from state to state, all CPAs must pass the Uniform CPA Examination. The "CPA exam," which tests the skills and knowledge of entry-level accountants, is a national examination given by the **American Institute of Certified Public Accountants (AICPA)**. Exhibit 1-12 lists the skills and knowledge tested on the CPA exam. In addition to passing the exam, a CPA must have met a state's minimum educational and practical experience requirements to be licensed in that state.

But what do public accountants *do?* Next, we discuss several services that public accountants provide to their client.

### Assurance Services

As a result of the information age, the volume of all types of information has grown, and much of that information is readily available to companies, governments, organizations, and individuals. Since decision makers increasingly rely on such information, they need assurance that the information is valid for the purposes for which they intend to use it. In this regard, "an assurance involves expression of a written or oral conclusion on the reliability and/or relevance of information and/or information systems."[2] Auditing evolved from a need for a specific type of assurance service.

**Auditing** Accounting information is one type of information for which decision makers need assurance. One way a company communicates accounting information is by issuing financial statements. Managers of the company issuing the statements are responsible for preparing these statements. But because of the potential bias of these managers, external users of the financial statements need objective assurance that the statements *fairly* represent the results of the activities of the company. Therefore, both the **New York Stock Exchange** and the **American Stock Exchange**, as well as the **Securities and Exchange Commission**, require that the set of financial statements that certain corporations (those offering equity securities for public sale) issue every year be audited. This audited set of financial statements is called an **annual report**. Similarly, a bank may require a company to provide audited financial statements when the company applies for a loan. For the same

[2]AICPA-sponsored meeting of representatives of small and medium-sized firms, regulators, and scholars.

**EXHIBIT 1-12 CPA EXAM[3]**

| Content (Knowledge) Areas | Skills Needed to Apply Knowledge |
|---|---|
| *Auditing & Attestation*—tests knowledge of auditing procedures, generally accepted auditing standards, and other standards related to attest engagements, and the skills needed to apply that knowledge in those engagements | Ability to communicate |
| *Financial Accounting & Reporting*—tests knowledge of generally accepted accounting principles for business enterprises, not-for-profit organizations, and governmental entities, and the skills needed to apply that knowledge | Ability to perform research |
| *Regulation*—tests knowledge of federal taxation, ethics, professional and legal responsibilities, and business law, and the skills needed to apply that knowledge | Ability to analyze and organize information |
| *Business Environment & Concepts*—tests knowledge of general business environment and business concepts that candidates need to know in order to understand the underlying business reasons for and accounting implications of business transactions, and the skills needed to apply that knowledge | Ability to understand and apply knowledge from diverse areas |
| | Ability to use judgment |

Uniform CPA Examination: Examination Content Specifications, June 14, 2002 (updated Oct. 19, 2005), http://www.cpa-exam.org. Briefing Paper #2, March 2001, Joint AICPA/NASBA Computerization Implementation Committee, pp. 11, 12.

reason, other types of economic entities, such as universities and charitable organizations, also issue audited financial statements. But what does it mean to be audited?

**Auditing** involves the examination, by an *independent* CPA, of a company's accounting records and financial statements, and the company's internal control over its financial reporting. This internal control is a process, designed by the company, to help assure that its financial reporting is reliable. Based on sample evidence gathered in the auditing process, including evidence about the quality and effectiveness of the company's internal controls, the CPA forms and expresses a professional, unbiased opinion about (or *attests* to) the fairness of the accounting information in the company's financial statements. The CPA also expresses an opinion about the effectiveness of the company's internal controls. Auditing plays an important role in society because many external users rely on CPAs' opinions when making decisions about whether to engage in activities with companies, universities, charitable organizations, and other economic entities.

## Other Assurance Services

Recently, because of their clients' needs for assurance about other types of information, public accounting firms have begun to expand their assurance services. In the interest of helping public accounting firms serve their customers, the AICPA, through one of its committees,[14] identified some specific opportunities for these firms to provide assurance services. Exhibit 1-13 summarizes some of these opportunities.

## Management Advisory Services

In addition to auditing departments, many public accounting firms have separate management advisory services departments to conduct special studies to advise non-audit client companies about improving their internal operations and to aid client managers in their various activities. These departments, in part, help to provide some of the assurance services we discussed earlier.

Management advisory services in public accounting firms include the design or improvement of a company's financial accounting system for identifying, measuring, recording, summarizing, and reporting accounting information. These services also may include assistance in areas such as developing cost-control systems, planning manufacturing facilities, and installing computer operations. To provide these services, public accounting firms also must have employees who have a strong understanding of the industries in which their clients operate. Therefore, in addition to hiring accountants, public accounting firms hire people with other specialties—people such as lawyers, industrial engineers, and systems analysts.

[3]AICPA Special Committee on Assurance Services.

**Exhibit 1-13 Opportunities for Providing Assurance Services**

- Assessing whether an entity has identified all its risks and is effectively managing them
- Evaluating whether an entity's performance measurement system contains relevant and reliable measures of its progress toward its goals and objectives
- Assessing whether an entity's integrated information system (or its ERP system) provides reliable information for decision making
- Assessing whether systems used in e-commerce provide appropriate data integrity, security, privacy, and reliability
- Assessing the effectiveness of health care services provided by HMOs, hospitals, doctors, and other providers
- Assessing whether various caregivers are meeting specified goals regarding care for the elderly

### Tax Services

The federal government, governments of other countries, and most state governments require corporations and individuals to file income tax returns and to pay taxes. Because of the high tax rates, complex tax regulations, and special tax incentives today, most companies (and individuals) can benefit from carefully planning their activities to minimize or postpone their tax payments. This is called **tax planning**. Many public accounting firms have separate tax services departments that employ tax professionals who are experts in the various federal, foreign government, and state tax regulations. These tax professionals assist companies and individuals in tax planning. In addition to tax planning, the tax services departments of public accounting firms frequently prepare client corporation or individual income tax returns that reflect the results of these tax-planning activities.

### Other Services

When clients hire an accountant or an accounting firm, they really are not as interested in reports that look good as they are in good advice, sound thinking, and creative answers to difficult problems. Computers, the Internet, and other recent high-tech developments allow accountants to do less "number crunching" and more advising, thinking, and creating. As a result of client demand, both large and small public accounting firms have expanded the types of services they offer their individual, small and medium-sized companies, and large corporate clients. These services can range from asset valuation to creative financing.

For example, one Dallas CPA, a sole practitioner, worked on one of the largest divorce cases in Texas history. He was hired to assign a value to the feuding couple's family-owned baseball card company. Texas is a community property state, and the company had to be sold in the divorce proceedings so the unhappy couple could split the cash received from the sale of the company. By analyzing the company's assets and what they would be worth when sold, and by looking at the company's potential future cash flows and net income, the accountant helped the couple determine the value of the company, which eventually sold for $87.5 million![m]

Accountants who focus on small companies can help their clients find sources of creative financing. Most new companies have difficulty finding capital to pay for their continued growth. Without a long business history, many of these companies don't qualify for traditional bank loans. Accountants can help these companies locate alternative financing sources, such as asset-based lending, leasing, and loans guaranteed by the Small Business Administration. Exhibit 1-14 lists some additional services that public accountants provide to their clients.

## Governmental and Quasi-Governmental Accounting

Certain governmental and quasi-governmental agencies also employ accountants. The Internal Revenue Service, for example, is responsible for the collection of federal income taxes. State revenue agencies also perform similar functions. Administrators of other federal, state, and local government agencies are responsible for the control of both tax revenues and tax expenditures. These agencies hire accountants to provide accounting information for use in the administration of these activities.

| EXHIBIT 1-14 | OTHER SERVICES THAT PUBLIC ACCOUNTANTS PROVIDE FOR THEIR CLIENTS |
|---|---|
| Estate planning | Fraud detection |
| Forensic accounting | Business succession planning |
| Real estate advisory services | Debt restructuring and bankruptcy advising |
| Technology consulting | Business planning |
| Business valuation | Personal financial planning |
| Merger and acquisition assistance | E-commerce advising |
| International accounting | Environmental accounting |

Several other governmental organizations also employ accountants. As we mention in this chapter, the **Securities and Exchange Commission (SEC)** is responsible for overseeing the reported financial statements of certain corporations and has the legal authority to establish accounting regulations for them. The SEC employs accountants to identify appropriate accounting standards and to verify that corporations are following existing regulations. The **General Accounting Office (GAO)** is responsible for cooperating with various agencies of the federal government in the development and operation of their accounting systems to improve the management of these agencies. It also oversees the administration of government contracts and the spending of federal funds. The **Defense Contract Audit Agency (DCAA)** audits all federally funded defense contracts. Its work resembles the audit services of public accounting firms. Other federal and state agencies, such as the **Federal Bureau of Investigation**, the **Environmental Protection Agency**, and the **Federal Communications Commission**, also employ accountants to prepare and use accounting information.

Administrators of federal, state, municipal, and other not-for-profit organizations such as colleges and universities, hospitals, and mental health agencies are responsible for their organizations' efficient and effective operations. The accounting information needed by these organizations is similar to that needed by companies. But because they are not-for-profit organizations financed in part by public funds, these organizations are required to use somewhat different accounting procedures (sometimes called *fund accounting*). These organizations hire accountants to design and operate their accounting systems.

As evidence of professionalism in governmental accounting, an accountant may become a Certified Government Financial Manager (CGFM). A CGFM must have met specified educational and practical experience requirements and must have passed a uniform CGFM exam.

# THE ACCOUNTANT OF THE 21ST CENTURY

In Chapter 2 we discuss the broad skills (communication, interpersonal, and intellectual skills) needed by businesspeople to do business effectively in a changing environment. These same skills, as well as others, also apply to accountants, and make accountants more effective in dealing with their clients. In 1999, the AICPA reframed these broad skills into a set of core competencies that all college graduates entering the *profession of accountancy* should possess, in addition to the traditional technical accounting skills they studied in college. It divided these competencies into three categories: *functional competencies* (technical competencies most closely aligned with the value that accounting professionals add to the business environment), *personal competencies* (individual attributes and values), and *broad business perspective competencies* (relating to an understanding of the internal and external business environment). Exhibit 1-15 lists and describes the competencies in each category.

In order to help accountants acquire the core competencies (or know if they already have these competencies), the **AICPA** also identified the elements (or "sub-competencies") that comprise the competencies, and lists both the competencies and their elements on its Web site. Since 2004, candidates taking the CPA exam have been required to demonstrate their ability to apply many of these competencies and elements in all four sections of the exam (in addition to, and in the context of, the traditional accounting skills typically tested on the exam). This ensures that new accountants "have what it takes" to deliver the best services to their clients and to adapt to the ever-changing business environment.

**EXHIBIT 1-15 AICPA CORE COMPETENCIES***

**FUNCTIONAL COMPETENCIES** relate to the technical competencies, which are most closely aligned with the value contributed by accounting professionals. Functional competencies include:

- Decision Modeling
- Risk Analysis
- Measurement
- Reporting
- Research
- Leverage Technology to Develop and Enhance Functional Competencies

**PERSONAL COMPETENCIES** relate to the attitudes and behaviors of individuals preparing to enter the accounting profession. Developing these personal competencies will enhance the way professional relationships are handled and facilitate individual learning and personal improvement. Personal competencies include:

- Professional Demeanor
- Problem Solving and Decision Making
- Interaction
- Leadership
- Communication
- Project Management
- Leverage Technology to Develop and Enhance Personal Competencies

**BROAD BUSINESS PERSPECTIVE COMPETENCIES** relate to the context in which accounting professionals perform their services. Individuals preparing to enter the accounting profession should consider both the internal and external business environments and how their interactions determine success or failure. They must be conversant with the overall realities of the business environment. Broad business perspective competencies include:

- Strategic/Critical Thinking
- Industry/Sector Perspective
- International/Global Perspective
- Resource Management
- Legal/Regulatory Perspective
- Marketing/Client Focus
- Leverage Technology to Develop and Enhance a Broad Business Perspective

* http://www.aicpa.org/edu/corecomp.htm

## Professional Organizations

A number of *professional* organizations (composed of accounting professionals) exist to facilitate communication among members of the profession, provide professional development opportunities, alert their members to emerging accounting and management issues, and promote ethical conduct. In addition to the Securities and Exchange Commission and the Financial Accounting Standards Board that we mentioned earlier in the chapter, these organizations also influence generally accepted accounting principles (GAAP). Exhibit 1-16 provides a summary of these organizations.

**EXHIBIT 1-16 PROFESSIONAL ORGANIZATIONS THAT INFLUENCE GAAP**

| Web Site | Organization | Description |
|---|---|---|
| http://www.aicpa.org | American Institute of Certified Public Accountants (AICPA) | National professional organization of CPAs. In addition to influencing accounting principles, the AICPA influences auditing standards. The Auditing Standards Board of the AICPA develops auditing standards that govern the way CPAs perform audits. The AICPA also prepares and grades the CPA examination and dispenses the results to the individual states, which then issue licenses to those who have passed the examination and who meet the other qualifications of the state. |
| http://www.fei.org | Financial Executives Institute (FEI) | Organization of financial executives of major corporations and accounting professors in academia. Examples of member executives include chief financial officers, financial vice-presidents, controllers, treasurers, and tax executives. |

*(continued)*

**EXHIBIT 1-16 CONTINUED**

| Web Site | Organization | Description |
|---|---|---|
| http://www.imanet.org | Institute of Management Accountants (IMA) | Organization of management accountants and others interested in management accounting. Besides influencing the practice of management accounting, the IMA prepares and grades the CMA examination. |
| http://aaahq.org/index.cfm | American Accounting Association (AAA) | National professional organization of academic and practicing accountants interested in both the academic and research aspects of accounting. Members of the AAA, many of whom are accounting practitioners, influence accounting standard setting through their research on accounting issues. |

# INTEGRATED BUSINESS AND ACCOUNTING SITUATIONS

**Answer the Following Questions in Your Own Words.**

## Testing Your Knowledge

**1-1** How would you describe private enterprise?

**1-2** What distinguishes a service company from a merchandising or manufacturing company?

**1-3** How is a merchandising company different from a manufacturing company? How are the two types of company the same?

**1-4** What is entrepreneurship?

**1-5** Suppose you were an entrepreneur. Where might you go for business capital?

**1-6** What distinguishes a corporation from a partnership and a sole proprietorship?

**1-7** What types of regulations must companies comply with in different jurisdictions?

**1-8** What is the purpose of an integrated accounting system?

**1-9** Given what you have learned from this chapter, how would you define *accounting?*

**1-10** How would you describe the similarities and differences between management accounting and financial accounting? Why are they different and why are they similar?

**1-11** How do management accounting reports help managers with their activities?

**1-12** What is the purpose of Statements on Management Accounting (SMAs)?

**1-13** What are generally accepted accounting principles?

**1-14** How do financial accounting reports help external users?

**1-15** Why have various business groups found it necessary to establish codes of ethics?

**1-16** (Appendix) What does a company's controller do?

**1-17** (Appendix) What do you know about an accountant who holds a Certificate in Management Accounting (CMA)?

**1-18** (Appendix) What is internal control?

**1-19** (Appendix) What is the purpose of internal auditing?

**1-20** (Appendix) What do you know about an accountant who holds a Certificate of Internal Auditing (CIA)?

**1-21** (Appendix) What are the responsibilities of the accountants who work in a company's tax department?

**1-22** (Appendix) What do you know about an accountant who is a certified public accountant (CPA)?

**1-23** (Appendix) In addition to knowledge of accounting, what other skills and knowledge prepare a college graduate to enter the profession of accountancy?

**1-24** (Appendix) What is an assurance?

**1-25** (Appendix) What is auditing?

**1-26** (Appendix) What do management advisory services include?

**1-27** (Appendix) What tax services does a public accounting firm's tax department perform?

**1-28** (Appendix) In addition to assurance services, tax services, and traditional management advisory services, what other services do accountants perform for their clients?

**1-29** (Appendix) What different types of jobs might a governmental accountant hold?

**1-30** (Appendix) What do you know about an accountant who is a certified government financial manager (CGFM)?

**1-31** (Appendix) What are four professional organizations of accountants and who are their members?

## Applying Your Knowledge

**1-32** How is **American Airlines** an example of a service company? How is **Toyota Motor Corporation** an example of a manufacturing company?

**1-33** How might knowledge of a company's cash receipts and payments affect a bank's decision about whether to loan the company money? What financial statement would the loan officer want to look at to begin to understand the company's cash receipts and payments?

**1-34** What factors would you consider in deciding whether to operate your company as a sole proprietorship, a partnership, or a corporation?

**1-35** Suppose you are Ichabod Cook, CEO of Unlimited Decadence Corporation, maker of candy bars. Unlimited Decadence currently operates in the northeastern United States, and you are considering opening a factory and sales office in California. What questions do you want answered before you proceed with this idea?

**1-36** Refer to 1-35. Suppose, instead, that you are considering opening a factory and sales office in Tokyo. What questions do you want answered before proceeding with *this* idea? How do you explain the similarities and differences in these two sets of questions?

**1-37** What are some examples of company information in which both internal and external users have an interest?

**1-38** Suppose you are a manager of The Foot Note, a small retail store that sells socks. Give an example of information that would help you in each of the management activities of planning, operating, and evaluating the operations of the store.

**1-39** What are generally accepted accounting principles, and how do they affect the accounting reports of companies in the United States? Why might the owner or owners of a company be concerned about a proposed new accounting principle?

**1-40** A friend of yours, Timorous ("Tim," for short) Ghostly, who has never taken an accounting course, has been assigned a short speech in his speech class. In this speech, Tim must describe the financial statements of a company. Tim has come to you for help (with his professor's permission). He says, "Please describe what financial statements are, what the major financial statements are, and what each financial statement includes." Prepare a written response to Tim's request.

**1-41** How do codes of ethics help businesspeople make decisions?

## Making Evaluations

**1-42** Your friend, Vito Guarino (an incredible cook!), plans to open a restaurant when he graduates from college. One evening, while extolling the virtues of linguini to you and some of your other friends, he glances down at your accounting textbook, which is open to Exhibit 1-2. "What kind of a company is a restaurant?" he asks. "How would a restaurant fit into this exhibit?" Everyone in the room waits with great anticipation for your answer and the rationale behind your answer. What are you going to say?

**1-43** You and your cousin, Harvey, have decided to form a partnership and open a landscaping company in town. But before you do, you and Harvey would like to "iron out" a few details about how to handle various aspects of the partnership and then write a partnership agreement outlining these details. What specific issues would you like to see addressed in the partnership agreement before you begin your partnership with Harvey?

**1-44** Suppose you are thinking about whether presidents of companies should be allowed to serve on the FASB. What do you think are the potential benefits of allowing them to serve? What do you think are the potential problems?

**1-45** Read a daily newspaper for the next week. What evidence do you find that supports the need for business codes of ethics?

**1-46** You just nabbed a plum job joining a team of consultants writing an advice column, "Dear Dr. Decisive," for the local newspaper. Yesterday, you received your first letter:

### Dr. Decisive

Dear Dr. Decisive:

Yesterday, my boyfriend and I got into a high-spirited "discussion" about lucky people in business. I say that most successful businesspeople are just plain lucky. They've been in the right place at the right time. He says that these successful people have worked hard preparing themselves for the time when they will be in the right place at the right time. OK, I think we're saying the same thing. He says there is an important difference. Now he won't call me unless I admit I'm wrong (which I'm not) or until you say I'm right.

I'm right, right?

Call me "Lucky."

*Required:* Meet with your Dr. Decisive team and write a response to "Lucky."

## End Notes

[a]U.S. Treasury Department, Internal Revenue Service, *Statistics of Income Bulletin*, Fall 2005, 293, 294, 295.
[b]Ibid.
[c]Ibid.
[d]Ibid.
[e]Institute of Management Accountants, *Statements on Management Accounting: Objectives of Management Accounting,* Statement No. 1B, June 17, 1982.
[f]http://specials.ft.com/enron and http://news.bbc.co.uk
[g]*Fortune* magazine, January 10, 2001, pp. 82–110.
[h]Woellert, L., *BusinessWeek online*, June 1, 2005.
[i]American Institute of Certified Public Accountants, *Code of Professional Conduct,* http://www.aicpa.org.
[j]Institute of Management Accountants, *Statements on Management Accounting: Standards of Ethical Conduct for Management Accountants,* http://www.imanet.org.
[k]International Federation of Accountants, *Code of Ethics for Professional Accountants*, http://www.ifac.org.
[l]Texas Instruments Incorporated, *Ethics in the Business of TI* (1990).
[m]"CPAs Enter New Era," *The Dallas Morning News*, June 12, 2001, 8F.

CHAPTER 2

# Creative and Critical Thinking, Problem Solving, and Their Roles in Business and Accounting

"Creativity can solve almost any problem. The creative act, the defeat of habit by originality, overcomes everything."

—George Lois

1. What factors are causing the business environment and the role of accounting within that environment to change?
2. What skills can people develop to better prepare themselves for problem solving and decision making in the rapidly changing business environment?
3. How can people learn to think creatively and critically?
4. How can creative and critical thinking help people make better business decisions?
5. What are the logical stages in problem solving and decision making?

Have you ever heard the phrase "creative accounting"? People sometimes use it to describe a form of accounting that "sidesteps" generally accepted accounting principles or manipulates accounting information, legally or not. (This type of "accounting" is also sometimes jokingly referred to as "cooking the books.") In this context, "creative accounting" might generate financial accounting reports that benefit the company or division doing the reporting, mislead the reader of the reports, lead to bad decisions by external users, and perhaps result in a substantial fine or jail sentence for the "creative accountant." According to another, more amusing interpretation, this phrase is an oxymoron—a person cannot be creative and also be an accountant. This reading of the phrase is based on caricatures and stereotypes of accountants that usually are not appropriate.

*Compare how a movie might portray a photographer, doctor, or lawyer versus how it might portray an accountant.*

We like to think more positively of creative accounting, to see it as searching for and using innovative solutions to complex management accounting and financial accounting problems. In a constantly evolving business environment, businesspeople, including accountants, face complex, ambiguous, dynamic, and difficult-to-interpret economic events that can cause challenges for which no guidelines, or only sketchy guidelines, exist. These situations present opportunities for companies to grow and change, so accountants and other businesspeople try to anticipate changes in the business environment, to address the associated challenges even before they occur, and to maximize their companies' opportunities to grow and change. But finding creative solutions is just the start in wrestling with the challenges associated with today's economic events. Smart businesspeople must also develop and use their critical thinking skills to identify the *best* solutions to these problems and to make optimum decisions. In fact, recognizing a crucial need for people with more of these skills, accounting firms and other companies are actively recruiting "the best and the brightest" creative and critical thinkers.

## THE CHANGING BUSINESS ENVIRONMENT

Why is the business environment changing so rapidly? As Exhibit 2-1 illustrates, a combination of many interwoven factors in this environment contributes to its complexity and excitement.

**1** What factors are causing the business environment and the role of accounting within that environment to change?

**EXHIBIT 2-1 FACTORS AFFECTING THE COMPLEXITY OF THE BUSINESS ENVIRONMENT**

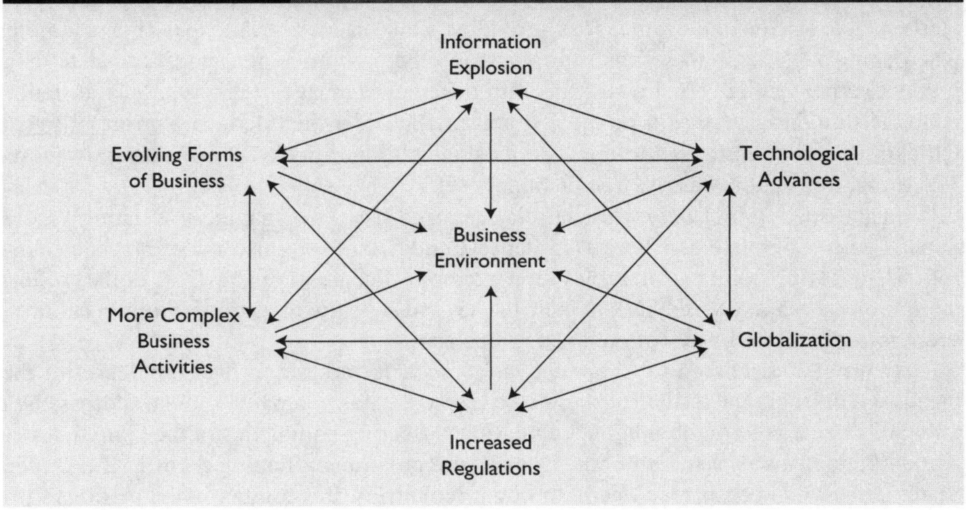

One contributor to the rapidly evolving business environment is the *information explosion.* More information is being generated than ever before, and this information is available to more people than ever. On the information superhighway, networks such as the Internet make available an almost endless list of information that includes library listings, books, journal articles, corporations' financial reports, catalogs, and directories of companies, organizations, and people with similar interests. Since it is impossible to use, let alone understand, all of the available information, businesspeople must be able to filter it to select what is valid, timely, and relevant for making decisions. Furthermore, new discoveries can quickly make old information obsolete or invalid. Because of the amount and accessibility of information, and because new information may replace existing information, company managers must be able to use their creative and critical thinking skills to evaluate and manage this information to their advantage. We will discuss this idea more thoroughly later in the chapter.

Consider how *technological advances* have affected the transmittal of information. Many businesspeople have extended their workday by using cell phones, text-messaging, Blackberries, and Web conferences/online meetings (Webex) to conduct business during commuting time. Fax machines and e-mail now allow us to transmit documents across the world instantly. Computer networks facilitate information transmittal to and from multiple computers. Huge databases, such as airline flight schedules and rate structures, are now stored in computer files and accessed by millions of users around the world. Satellites allow videoconferencing. Rather than traveling to other cities to attend conferences, for example, many businesspeople attend satellite-facilitated teleconferences, sometimes staying in their own offices. This development has made the world more competitive. Companies and individuals who, in the past, had difficulty traveling or communicating around the globe (perhaps because the infrastructures of their countries could not accommodate their needs) have enthusiastically "thrown their hats in the ring." Voicemail now allows messages to be played at "fast-forward" speed so that the listener can hear them in less time! These technological advances allow virtually instant access to current events and up-to-date information.

Technological advances affect not only the products we use and the way business is conducted but also the way the products are manufactured. For example, advanced technologies have allowed the production process in many companies to become fully automated. In many of our factories, computers are used to plan, operate, and monitor manufacturing processes and to make adjustments to these processes as needed. IBM, for example, has a fully automated keyboard assembly factory in Texas capable of operating without human intervention. Robots are now common workers on many production lines.

The *globalization* of business activities and economies is providing more opportunities for companies and individuals to conduct business by creating a larger, more diverse marketplace. At the same time, it is providing new business challenges. For example, when companies begin to sell their products in other countries, they must translate their product names and advertising slogans into different languages. This type of translation is not as straightforward as it might first appear. Consider the dilemma **Kentucky Fried Chicken** faced when it tried to translate its slogan "finger-lickin' good" into Taiwanese. The literal translation was, "Eat your fingers off."[a]

© PHOTOPIA

Do you think this behavior is acceptable in all cultures? Why or why not?

Businesspeople not only must hurdle language barriers (imagine translating "Extra Super-Duper Complete and Pure Decadence Candy Bar") but also must translate transactions involving foreign currencies (for example, Japanese yen to U.S. dollars). Furthermore, as we discussed in Chapter 1, they must learn to negotiate other cultures, economies, laws, and ways of conducting business.

As we also discussed in Chapter 1, another factor adding to the complexity of the business environment is the *increased regulations* that companies must address. Not only are there a growing number of regulations affecting companies in the United States (candy bars probably have a hundred or more regulations affecting them in the United States), but when companies operate in other countries, the number of regulations they face increases substantially with each country in which they conduct their business. This issue has caused many countries to draft agreements among themselves to minimize barriers to free trade. Examples of these agreements include the European Union (EU) of 25 European nations, the North American Free Trade Agreement (NAFTA) among Canada, Mexico, and the United States, the Central American Free Trade Agreement (CAFTA) expanding NAFTA to five Central American nations (Guatemala, El Salvador, Honduras, Costa Rica, and Nicaragua) and the Dominican Republic, and the General Agreement on Tariffs and Trade (GATT), a 145-nation pact that created a World Trade Organization to referee trade disputes among its members.

*More complex business activities* also contribute to the changing business environment. For example, business owners and managers are finding more creative methods of financing their activities, new outlets for investing their excess cash, a larger variety of alternatives for compensating their employees, and more complicated tax laws with which they must comply. In addition, the way companies conduct business is evolving. Where companies used to be "bricks and mortar," they now exist on the Internet. It is now common and convenient for companies to conduct business using **e-commerce**, where companies and consumers buy and sell goods and services over the Internet. E-commerce takes three forms: business-to-business, or B2B (**Cisco Systems**), business-to-consumer, or B2C (**Amazon.com**), or consumer-to-consumer, or C2C (**eBay**).

Finally, *evolving forms of business* are cropping up in the new business environment. For example, numerous variations of the simple business organizations that we discussed in Chapter 1 (sole proprietorships, partnerships, and corporations) now exist. These variations developed in response to the more complex business environment and include such exotic-sounding organizations as general partnerships, limited partnerships, domestic corporations, foreign corporations, nonprofit corporations, professional corporations, business corporations, limited liability corporations, and Subchapter S corporations. Each of these forms of organization has legal advantages and disadvantages that the others don't have, and each addresses a particular aspect of the business environment. A company owner chooses the form of business that most closely meets the company's needs. Furthermore, companies often form temporary alliances with each other (called *joint ventures* or *unincorporated associations*) to accomplish specific tasks or projects.

The factors discussed above not only contribute to the complexity and excitement of the business environment but also challenge the assumptions on which companies and their employees operate. For example, the assumption that a college graduate will go out into the world, pursue a lifelong career, and never return to college is no longer valid. Many people now change careers (careers, not just jobs!) several times before they retire. Often, in order to make a change, they return to college between careers to "retool," or to expand their education to include new skills. Even people who stay in the same career expand their education (through continuing professional education, short courses, conferences, and seminars) to improve their knowledge and abilities.

It is easy to see that a person entering or remaining in this dynamic environment must be dynamic also. In the following sections, we will discuss the characteristics, attitudes, and skills that help people succeed in the business world. While reading these sections, keep in mind that these are attributes and abilities that people learn over a period of time and continue to develop for the rest of their lives (similar to the way athletes learn and improve their athletic skills).

## THE SUCCESSFUL BUSINESSPERSON

Imagine a successful businessperson. Perhaps the person, with sleeves rolled up and hands dirty, is working hard on some project. Or maybe he or she, business-suited and with briefcase in hand, is heading for a meeting. You may have a picture of what this businessperson looks like, but what really determines success is harder to see. It's more a matter of approach than of image.

The successful businessperson thrives on change, seeing it as an opportunity rather than an obstacle. However, treating change as an opportunity is more than just a matter of attitude (more than simply seeing the glass as "half full"). It also involves being *prepared* for the opportunity; the successful businessperson is both willing and *able* to change. Therefore, this person is devoted to lifelong learning, realizing that continuous learning is the only way to keep up with and be prepared for the fast-paced change we described earlier. This means that the businessperson must be willing to read industry or professional journals, attend conferences, and/or take classes to stay up-to-date.

To be able to adapt to change (or "go with the flow"), the successful businessperson develops certain other qualities as well. He or she welcomes others' viewpoints, appreciates differences among people, takes educated and thoughtful risks, anticipates environmental trends and identifies the potential problems and opportunities associated with these trends, and willingly abandons old plans if new information or technology makes them less workable. This doesn't mean that the successful businessperson is a chameleon, changing colors every time the business environment changes, but it does mean that he or she is flexible and adaptable.

## THE ACCOUNTANT OF THE 21ST CENTURY

2 What skills can people develop to better prepare themselves for problem solving and decision making in the rapidly changing business environment?

A successful businessperson in the 21st century will have the characteristics we mentioned above but also will have additional skills and knowledge advanced by the largest accounting firms, the Accounting Education Change Commission, the American Accounting Association, the American Institute of Certified Public Accountants, and the Institute of Management Accountants.[b] These skills include communication, interpersonal, and intellectual skills. Although all businesspeople need these skills in a changing business environment, we will focus specifically on how accountants use these skills in this environment.

### Communication Skills

An accountant's job involves both collecting and communicating information. A key part of collecting information is knowing where to look for it. Although some information may be located in routine places, such as checkbook registers and sales invoices, the accountant must be ready to look beyond the routine. Information may appear in written form (such as documents, written procedures, reports, journals, and reference materials) or in verbal form (such as conversations or presentations).

To gather information from both written and verbal sources, then, an accountant must be a proficient reader and listener. In this case, reading and listening mean more than they appear to at first glance. To be useful, the information gathered must be *relevant* to the decision at hand. The accountant must be able to interpret information, decide whether it is relevant, and then filter out everything else. This means that the accountant cannot be just a casual reader or listener. Rather, the accountant must *analyze* the information he or she reads or hears, actively trying to understand it by considering both its context and its source. Context includes such aspects as the perspective or bias of the information source, how the information was developed, and what assumptions were made in developing the information. To gain this understanding, the accountant must use critical thinking skills, which we will discuss later in the chapter.

Accountants also communicate information. They must be able to present their ideas coherently to people at different levels of the company (all the way up to the chair of the board of directors) and also to people outside the company who have different interests and backgrounds, as well as various levels of accounting and business understanding. These ideas may be presented formally or informally, in written or oral form. An accountant, then, also must be an effective speaker and writer.

## Interpersonal Skills

Although working with numbers may be the most familiar aspect of an accountant's job (have you ever heard accountants referred to as "number crunchers" or "bean counters"?), working with people is just as important. Accountants collect information from some people and communicate it to others. They work on team projects, act as leaders within departments, and also serve on teams that span the entire company. Since accountants advise managers and board members, they must possess the same interpersonal skills that a competent manager or board member possesses. These skills include the ability to lead and influence others, to motivate others, to withstand and resolve conflict, and to organize and delegate tasks.

## Intellectual Skills

The large accounting firms and the AECC recognized that gathering information, interpreting it, and effectively communicating it to others relies on the businessperson's knowledge base and ability to think creatively and critically. Accountants must also have a knowledge base and creative and critical thinking skills that support gathering, interpreting, and communicating information. This knowledge base is grouped into three categories.[c] The first category, **general knowledge**, encompasses knowledge about history and cultures; an ability to interact with people who have dissimilar ideas; a sense of the contrasting economic, political, and social forces in the world and of the magnitude of world issues and ideas; and experience in making value judgments. The second category, **organizational and business knowledge**, includes an understanding of the effects of economic, social, cultural, and psychological forces on companies; an understanding of how companies work; an understanding of methods and strategies for managing change; and an understanding of how technology helps organizations. The third category, **accounting and auditing knowledge**, includes the ability to construct accounting data, as well as the ability to use this data to make decisions, to exercise judgments, to evaluate risks, and to solve problems.

Creative thinking and critical thinking are necessary and complementary skills for successful, efficient problem solving and decision making. However, these skills do not necessarily come naturally. You might be an extremely creative thinker but not a good critical thinker. Similarly, you might be a very capable critical thinker but not a very good creative thinker. Or perhaps you're somewhere between "extremely good" and "just awful" in both skills. Luckily, though, you can continue to improve your creative and critical thinking skills. We will spend the second half of this chapter introducing you to specific creative and critical thinking skills, and we will illustrate their use in solving accounting-related problems throughout the book. According to the largest public accounting firms and the AICPA, then, the accountant must be an analytical thinker and must be able to apply creative and critical thinking to problem solving and decision making within the business world.

# CREATIVE AND CRITICAL THINKING

3 How can people learn to think creatively and critically?

Have you ever tried a sport and performed dreadfully but then, after lessons, practice, and perseverance, found that your skills gradually improved? Improvement begins with awareness; you need to be conscious of your performance, make an effort to improve it, and focus your efforts on an image of what constitutes good performance. A serious tennis player studies tennis. She not only practices but also compares her performance and form with an ideal or with her last game; she reads books and newspaper columns on tennis and tennis form and visualizes herself playing in the different situations they describe;

she watches better tennis players as they play; and she improves by playing against tennis players who are better at the game than she is.

Many serious tennis players also take short lessons that focus on specific skills, such as a defensive lob. Have you seen lessons designed to help thinkers improve specific aspects of their thinking? When we talk about improving our minds, we tend to refer to gaining more knowledge rather than to improving our thinking performance and form. Most of us spend little time monitoring our thinking and comparing it with an ideal. Perhaps this is either because we do not know how to think about thinking or because we do not know what the ideal is.

Most of us tend to consider thinking, like breathing, to be a natural function. We all do it. (After all, isn't thinking supposed to distinguish us from other animals?) However, *creative* and *critical* thinking takes practice, just like tennis. Few people expect to be good at tennis their first time on the court. At first, *bad* tennis seems to be the norm. But with practice aimed at improving and at learning new forms and specific techniques, *better* tennis comes more naturally. In the same way, practicing creative and critical thinking, including new "forms and techniques," makes it more natural. Awareness of our current thinking patterns helps us recognize our strengths and weaknesses; this knowledge gives us a starting point for modifying and improving our thinking performance. We will spend the remainder of the chapter discussing and analyzing the processes (or "forms and techniques") and ideals of creative and critical thinking.

## Creative Thinking

**Creative thinking** is the process of actively generating new ideas to discover solutions to a problem. Effective creative thinking begins with learning to be spontaneous. Letting your thoughts flow freely opens the door to new ideas. Not all of these ideas will be great, but don't try to make that judgment right away. What matters now is generating lots of ideas. Let yourself be spontaneous; you may be surprised at what comes through the door. Like learning a sport, learning to be a creative thinker means developing and nurturing some new skills and attitudes.

### Characteristics of the Creative Thinker

Although some people believe that creativity is a talent that people are born with, some characteristics of creative thinking can be developed. One of these characteristics is inquisitiveness, or a questioning attitude. Inventions and innovations arise from inquisitive people. If you accept, without question, the way things are, it is difficult to recognize problems, and of course, if you do not recognize the existence of a problem, it is difficult to get creative about the solution to that problem. In this sense, creative thinkers are "problem finders." That is, they tend to explore alternative problems before deciding which problem should be addressed. For example, 3M's Post-it notes solved a problem but not the one its inventor started out to address. The problem the inventor was initially trying to solve was how to make a superpermanent adhesive, but each attempt produced an adhesive that didn't stick very well. By using the relatively nonsticky adhesive to solve a different problem—how to attach, to objects and paper, notes that would peel off easily without damaging either—the inventor and his product became an instant success. A good start toward creativity, then, includes an attitude of healthy skepticism that questions existing approaches, practices, techniques, and even the original statement of the problem. If you feel uncomfortable asking questions, remember that no one has all the answers, no matter what anyone may tell you.

Creative individuals strive for both fluency and flexibility in their thinking. **Fluency** refers to the *number* of ideas generated or solutions proposed by the problem solver. **Flexibility** refers to the *spectrum* of ideas generated. When a problem solver is flexible, he or she will probably develop a broad array of ideas for solving a problem, and some of these ideas may be very unconventional.

*Suppose your boss has asked you, the marketing manager, to develop some ideas that will increase sales of a sugarless, fat-free candy bar. Without censoring yourself, how many ideas can you come up with in the next two minutes?*

Creative thinkers are willing to express ideas that are different from everyone else's ideas. They don't censor themselves and their ideas because of what someone else might think (allowing for both fluency and flexibility in their thought processes). They also have patience in their search for solutions to problems. Rather than accept the first workable solution they encounter (limiting their fluency and flexibility), they continue to generate workable solutions. Whereas the desire to find a quick solution often limits fluency and flexibility, patience and relaxation seem to have the opposite effect. In fact, some of the most creative thinking occurs at the least-expected times, such as when people are in the shower or on vacation.

Remember, you can develop and improve the creative thinking characteristics we have just discussed. Exhibit 2-2 lists some questions you can ask yourself when you are trying to think creatively; these questions will help you progress as a creative thinker.

### Strategies of the Creative Thinker

Have you heard of a process called **brainstorming**? It's an example of creative thinking in a group. If you look up *brainstorm* in the dictionary, you will see that one of the definitions refers to "a harebrained idea."[d] Brainstorming generates plenty of these, but it also generates many reasonable ideas, some of which began as "harebrained ideas." In the process of brainstorming, members of a group try to generate as many solutions as possible to a particular problem. For example, maybe your company is trying to cut costs. Brainstorming is one way to generate numerous cost-cutting ideas (probably many more ideas than could be generated by one person thinking alone). In the interest of not inhibiting or censoring anyone in the group, any idea counts during a brainstorming session, no matter how ridiculous (or "harebrained") it may seem on the surface (and participants must be supportive of each other, not judgmental). This guideline improves the spontaneity of the ideas. Remember, even the most ridiculous idea will generate other ideas, some of which may be outstanding. The generation of ideas from other ideas is sometimes called **piggybacking**. The group continues this process until everyone runs out of ideas or until a reasonable amount of time has passed.

Another creative thinking strategy is to draw analogies. **Drawing analogies** involves making connections among facts, ideas, or experiences that are normally considered separately. Discovering these connections often leads to creative solutions to problems; the

**EXHIBIT 2-2 — QUESTIONS FOR CREATIVE THINKERS TO ASK THEMSELVES**

What is it about this idea that stimulates my curiosity?

Can I come up with more ideas?

Can I come up with a greater variety of ideas?

Do I develop ideas independently and not eliminate them from consideration because of social influences?

Do I consider several alternatives before acting?

creative thinker often sees innovative ways of applying a similar solution to two seemingly dissimilar problems. Say, for example, that on your first job you are asked to design a system for keeping track of the company's cash expenditures. You might use your experience keeping track of your own personal expenditures as a starting point for solving this problem, looking for similarities and differences between the company's cash expenditures and your own.

*How many similarities and differences can you think of between how a company might spend its cash and how you spend your cash?*

In some circumstances, you might use a creative thinking strategy called **attribute listing**, which involves listing the characteristics of an object or idea to gain insights into its possible usefulness. The spontaneous, uncensored listing of an object's characteristics can help you do away with preconceived notions that may limit your ability to think creatively. For example, suppose you are asked to list all the possible uses you can think of for your calculator. If you list only mathematical functions, you have not considered all the attributes of the calculator. Did you include its weight, shape, color, hardness, and size? Given these attributes, can you think of other uses for your calculator (maybe a doorstop, a paperweight, a projectile, or even a stalling device that keeps the remote-control addicts in your household from changing stations on the television—until they discover they are holding a calculator)?

Now that you've seen examples of how to generate ideas using creative thinking strategies, we will look at ways of using these ideas to solve problems. This is where critical thinking comes into play.

## Critical Thinking

**Critical thinking** is the process that evaluates the ideas generated by creative thinking. Critical thinking determines if any of the ideas will work, what types of problems they might have, whether they can be improved, and which ones are better than others. To be a successful critical thinker, you have to be in the right frame of mind, use the thought processes and actions necessary for thinking critically, and constantly watch and monitor your thinking (much as the tennis player watches her game).

### Characteristics of the Critical Thinker

Above all, the critical thinker values truth rather than the *appearance* of truth. As you will see, the emotional state, thought processes, and activities involved in thinking critically all help the critical thinker sort out the truth. For example, in looking for the truth, critical thinkers must be independent and objective. Being **independent** means that in the process of evaluating ideas, the critical thinker must rely on his or her own conclusions rather than those of others. This doesn't mean that the critical thinker is a know-it-all—just that he or she doesn't accept the beliefs of others without questioning where those ideas came from, what evidence supports them, and what assumptions were made in developing the ideas.

**Objectivity**, the quality of being unbiased, is a very difficult characteristic to achieve, but one that critical thinkers must have if they value truth. All people select, organize, and interpret information based on their own perceptions, beliefs, and past experiences. Even when we are trying very hard to understand someone else's point of view, we tend to say to ourselves, "Here is how I would feel if I were in that situation . . . therefore, he must feel the same way." We tend to unconsciously impose our own perceptions, beliefs, and past experiences on our understanding of information, ideas, and other people. For this reason, information and understanding are almost automatically biased. Besides being willing to consider new ideas and information, critical thinkers know that they may have limitations that keep them from true understanding. They not only recognize that they may have biases and prejudices but also watch for and try to eliminate these biases from their thinking. By realizing that their viewpoints are a product of their unique experiences, critical thinkers are better able to really listen for and try to understand other viewpoints.

As part of their search for truth and their continual striving toward independent, objective thinking, critical thinkers develop openness to new and different ideas, as well as empathy for other points of view. Have you ever encountered a "know-it-all"? Do you remember feeling frustrated that this person did not listen to your perspective or to your contributions to the conversation? As you have probably experienced, a "know-it-all" assumes that there is no more to learn about a subject. Unfortunately, this assumption blocks that person's receptivity to new information and new perspectives about the subject. How much more could the "know-it-all" learn by keeping an open mind? Furthermore, could this person make better decisions by acknowledging the limits of his or her own knowledge and by making use of all available relevant information?

Critical thinkers also *tolerate ambiguity* and willingly *defer judgment* until they can collect more information and consider and evaluate other solutions. Many problems involve complex issues with multiple interpretations and numerous good solutions. Critical thinkers, like creative thinkers, do not accept the first solution generated as necessarily being the best solution. Rather, they gather multiple solutions and evaluate them against predetermined values or criteria. As you learn about accounting, you will also learn about some of the values and criteria that accountants use for evaluating information and ideas. Critical thinkers also recognize that "good" ideas are often relative rather than absolute (for example, "higher quality," "more probable," and "more objective" ). So even though many ideas may satisfy the critical thinker's values and criteria, some ideas may be better than others.

Finally, critical thinkers *have grit.* Have you ever had an idea that you *knew* was right (after analyzing and evaluating other ideas and viewpoints), but nobody else agreed with you? Grit is what kept you from caving in to the majority opinion. Grit keeps you going when the going gets tough. As we said before, many problems in business are complex and multifaceted. Identifying problems, finding solutions, and overcoming all the obstacles and frustrations along the way takes perseverance.

Just as with creative thinking characteristics, you can develop and improve the critical thinking characteristics we have just discussed. Exhibit 2-3 lists some questions you can ask yourself when you are trying to think critically; these questions will help you improve your critical thinking.

### Strategies of the Critical Thinker

To make sense of the world, to develop solutions to complex problems, to deal with ambiguous issues, and to make decisions, the critical thinker must apply a variety of thinking and reasoning strategies to the thought process. First, the critical thinker must be able

**EXHIBIT 2-3** **QUESTIONS FOR CRITICAL THINKERS TO ASK THEMSELVES**

If an issue is controversial, do I accept my first reaction to it, or do I debate the issue in my head first?

Do I tend to reject new evidence that contradicts my current opinion on a subject, or do I evaluate the new evidence and then decide whether to accept it or reject it?

When I am trying to solve a problem, do I usually accept the first solution that "works," or do I generate multiple solutions and then choose the best one?

When others disagree with me, do I usually listen to them with an open mind and critically evaluate their ideas, or do I try to defend my own ideas?

to define, clearly and precisely, the problem or issue at hand. Without a clear and precise definition of the problem, it is almost impossible to generate the best solution—how could you identify the relevant information for solving it?

Language and clear thinking are directly related. To test thinking for clarity, a critical thinker can ask the following questions about the language used in the reasoning process. Is it specific? Is it precise? Is it accurate? If the language used is not specific, precise, and accurate, chances are that the thinking behind the words is not clear. Consider the following two problem definitions.

1. "Unlimited Decadence Corporation has a problem with high costs."
2. "Many employees at Unlimited Decadence Corporation are making unnecessary end-of-year purchases. They think that if they don't spend the entire amounts budgeted for this year, their departments will be allocated less money to spend next year."

Which of the problem definitions do you think would generate more-focused solutions? Why? Perhaps you chose the second definition because it is clearer and more precise than the first definition. The first problem definition might even lead you down the wrong path. For example, you might spend time looking for overpriced expenditures when the problem at hand is that departments are making *too many* expenditures. We will look more closely at the process of recognizing and defining problems later in this chapter.

After the decision maker recognizes and defines the problem, he or she must identify, gather, and then evaluate the data relevant to the problem at hand. The decision maker must use creative thinking skills to determine what is known about the problem. To make this determination, he or she must first develop ideas about where to locate the data. Sources of data include people familiar with the problem and written material such as reports, documents, memos, and books that contain information about the problem.

Next, the decision maker must use creative thinking skills to determine what additional information and support is needed and is available to solve the problem. After collecting the relevant data and before using it for problem solving and decision making, the decision maker must use critical thinking skills to analyze the data for faulty logic, unsupported assumptions, and emotional appeal. For example, consider the following statement made by a rather disgruntled employee of Unlimited Decadence: "All programmers should have to work regular hours, from 8:00 A.M. to 5:00 P.M., just like everybody else. It isn't fair that the computer programmers can come in late. Sure, they come in during the middle of the night to fix programs when the computer crashes, and they program on into the night when they are 'on a roll,' but we all know it's just a party up there. Mortimer, one of the programmers, is a major party animal. I've been to several parties with him."

Faulty logic can cause you to arrive at a conclusion that isn't warranted. In evaluating the information, the critical thinker must consider the nature of evidence supporting it. How true are the supporting reasons? Do these reasons support the conclusion? In the above example, the decision maker might ask if it is true that night work is just a "party." An untrue assertion can lead a decision maker to the wrong decision, so it is vital to determine, with evidence, that the assertion is valid. The critical thinker also must evaluate the relevance of the evidence used to support arguments or solutions. Does the assertion that Mortimer is a "party animal" at a party necessarily mean that he is a "party animal" at work?

*In this situation, what other questions might a decision maker ask?*

Besides evaluating the relevance (or appropriateness) of the information, the decision maker must also evaluate the credibility of its sources. What do we know about the disgruntled employee? Is he a habitual complainer whose allegations typically don't "hold water"? Is he responsible and normally "on target" with his observations? Is the information provided by this one employee enough to support his own assertion? (By the way, have you checked out the credentials of the authors of this book? Are these credentials relevant to the decision involving whether or not to believe what the authors have written?) Finally, the disgruntled employee has thrown in a dose of emotional appeal: "It isn't *fair*. . . ." Although critical thinkers do not ignore the emotional effects of alternatives, they must consider the alternatives objectively and not be unduly swayed by emotional appeals.

*Do you see any other faulty logic, unsupported assumptions, or emotional appeal in the employee's statement?*

Evidence and reasoning must not only be relevant to the arguments, solutions, and decisions they support but also *consistent* with them. If it is true that the night shift parties all night, does it make sense to have the programmers maintain regular work hours? Would that solve the problem *and* get the work of the company done? If programmers maintained regular working hours, would they be available to fix programs in the middle of the night, and would they be willing to continue a programming streak even though it's 5:00 P.M.? Might another solution work better?

Information and events do not exist in a vacuum. Rather, each of these factors influences and is influenced by the others. Therefore, the critical thinker must synthesize all relevant information, combining it with insights and knowledge to form meaningful patterns in order to gain understanding. Physicians synthesize information when diagnosing an illness based on a patient's symptoms and other information that the physician knows or learns. In business and accounting, the critical thinker also uses symptoms to "diagnose" a problem. The ability to recognize similarities and differences among symptoms and to use other insights and knowledge helps the business decision maker develop meaningful patterns that are useful in synthesizing information.

Critical thinkers use a variety of thinking skills in the problem-solving process. Among these skills is the ability to use logic. **Inductive logic** is reasoning that moves from the specific to the general—from an observation or assumption to a generalized conclusion. An example of a conclusion reached through inductive logic is the following statement: "A recent employee poll reveals that 97 percent of Unlimited Decadence's employees think the company should provide a fitness center for employee use." In arriving at this conclusion, the company surveyed a sample of employees. The results of the survey of *specific* employees were used to generalize about the opinions of *all* the employees. A company's external auditors use inductive logic. Using a sample of the company's transactions and records, the auditor forms an opinion about how fairly the company's financial statements reflect the results of *all* of the company's transactions.

Conversely, **deductive logic** is reasoning that moves from a general statement or assertion to a specific conclusion. Consider the following example of a conclusion reached through deductive logic: "All Unlimited Decadence employees are paid on Fridays. Penelope is an

Is the future rock star trying to use inductive or deductive logic? How did you decide? Do you see any flaws in his logic?

Unlimited Decadence employee. Therefore, Penelope is paid on Fridays." As long as the first two sentences are true, the conclusion is necessarily true. Exhibit 2-4 illustrates the difference between inductive and deductive logic.

Evidence must be relevant for and consistent with arguments, solutions, and decisions, but it also must be logical when it stands alone (without considering the argument, solution, or decision to which it applies). For instance, think back to the example of deductive reasoning regarding Penelope's pay. Try changing the last line of that example so that the reasoning reads: "All Unlimited Decadence employees are paid on Fridays. Penelope is an Unlimited Decadence employee. Therefore, all Unlimited Decadence employees are Penelope." How would you rate the logic of that reasoning on the continuum from logical to illogical? If you ranked it closer to illogical than to logical, does it make sense to use it as evidence of when Penelope is paid?

Finally, in evaluating information, a critical thinker must be sure, within reason, that he or she has considered all relevant information, all points of view, and all workable solutions. Incomplete information leads to less than optimal reasoning, problem solving, and decision making.

A critical thinker measures ideas and problem solutions against ideals or goals closely related to critical thinking characteristics such as those that we described above. Most thinking falls somewhere on a continuum between ideal and imperfect, and many arguments are made and positions defended through the use of thought processes that do not measure up to the ideals. Unfortunately, an unwary thinker may be persuaded by ideas or solutions that are less than ideal.

**EXHIBIT 2-4 INDUCTIVE AND DEDUCTIVE LOGIC**

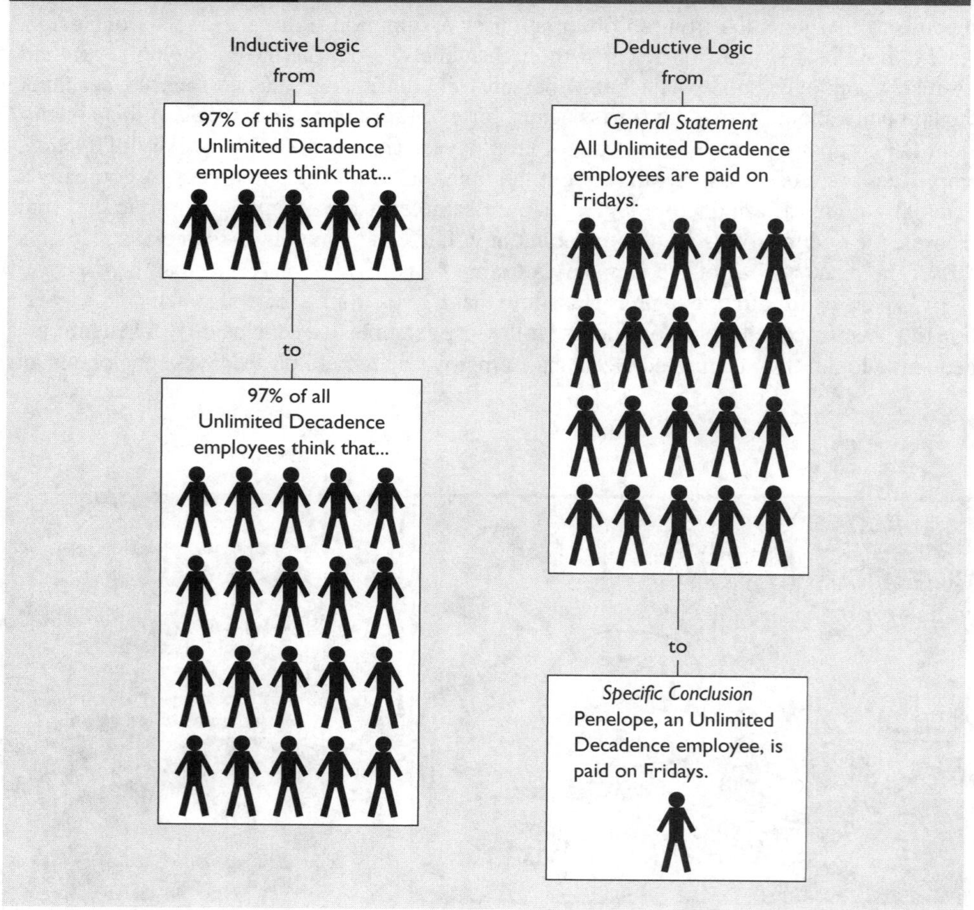
Inductive Logic
from
97% of this sample of Unlimited Decadence employees think that...
to
97% of all Unlimited Decadence employees think that...
Deductive Logic
from
General Statement
All Unlimited Decadence employees are paid on Fridays.
to
Specific Conclusion
Penelope, an Unlimited Decadence employee, is paid on Fridays.

## APPLYING CREATIVE AND CRITICAL THINKING TO BUSINESS DECISIONS

4 How can creative and critical thinking help people make better business decisions?

Every day of our lives, we must solve problems and make decisions ranging from minor issues, like what to have for breakfast, to major issues, like what career to choose. Think about your breakfast decision this morning. To choose what to have for breakfast, you had to gather certain information, such as what type of food you had available to eat, how *much* of this food was available (did you ever pour a bowl of cereal only to find that there wasn't enough milk in the refrigerator?), what type of food you could tolerate in the morning, when your next meal would be, what activities you had planned for the day, the nutritional content of the food, what dishes were clean, and how much time the food would take to prepare. After evaluating all the facts, you were able to make a decision.

A simple problem like choosing what to have for breakfast does not require complex analysis (although you may need a quick shower, first, to wake you up). However, many business problems can involve a jumble of information, opinions, considerations, risks, and alternatives. A systematic method, including creative and critical thinking, is necessary to organize the problem-solving approach and to decide on a solution to the problem. Exhibit 2-5 illustrates the four stages in decision making and the particular impact of creative and critical thinking on each stage. Notice that creative thinking is more important in the earlier stages, while critical thinking is more important in the later stages. We will discuss these stages of decision making in the next four sections.

5 What are the logical stages in problem solving and decision making?

### Recognizing and Defining the Problem

The first stage in solving a problem is the recognition and definition of the problem for which a decision must be made. As we suggested earlier in the chapter, the chances of arriving at a successful solution to a problem are considerably reduced if the decision maker does not have a clear understanding of the problem. An incorrectly defined problem will lead to an unproductive course of action at best and could actually create new problems or make the current problem worse. To fully understand the problem, the decision maker needs to gather the facts surrounding the problem, identify the objectives that would be achieved by solving the problem, and clearly state the problem.

For example, consider the situation facing Basil Doowright, a manager at Unlimited Decadence Corporation. Basil's newly health-conscious boss, Graham Wheatley, has asked if it is possible to manufacture and sell a new, fat-free, sugarless candy bar to be called "Empty Decadence." Basil doesn't want to make a hasty decision, so he uses creative thinking skills to brainstorm a list of questions he has about the idea. Basil's first list looks like this:

1. Why does Wheatley want us to manufacture this new candy bar?
2. When must a decision be made?

**EXHIBIT 2-5 CREATIVE AND CRITICAL THINKING AND FOUR STAGES IN PROBLEM SOLVING AND DECISION MAKING**

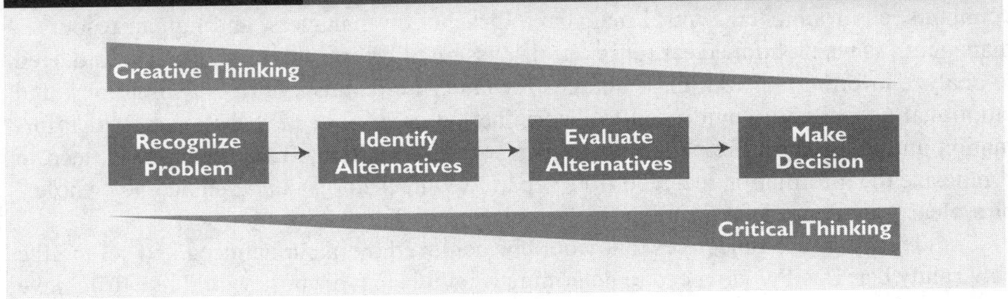

3. Who inside the company would be affected by a decision to manufacture and sell this new candy bar? How would they be affected?
4. Who outside the company would be affected by a decision to manufacture and sell this new candy bar? In what ways would they be affected?
5. How can I break this decision down into smaller parts?
6. What additional information do I need to make a decision?
7. Where can I find additional information?

*Why do you think it is important to know who will be affected by a business decision and how they will be affected?*

Answers to these questions will no doubt lead to further, more probing questions such as the following:

8. Can we manufacture an incredibly delicious, sugarless, fat-free candy bar that meets the company's standards of excellence?
9. How long would it take to develop, market, and manufacture this new candy bar?
10. Who would buy this new candy bar?
11. Will people quit purchasing the popular Pure Decadence candy bar and instead buy the new Empty Decadence candy bar? Or will people who typically avoid buying candy bars be tempted by the fat-free, sugarless qualities of the Empty Decadence, leaving the sales of the Pure Decadence candy bar virtually unaffected, thereby increasing total customers and total sales?
12. What kind of competition would this new candy bar face?
13. At what price could the company sell the new candy bar?
14. What resources would the company need to acquire in order to manufacture this new candy bar? Are these resources available?
15. What would the additional costs be? Does Unlimited Decadence have access to additional financing, if necessary?
16. Would additional people need to be hired? What skills and talents should these people have? What is the probability of finding people with these skills and talents?
17. Would production of the new candy bar force Unlimited Decadence to comply with additional government regulations?
18. Would any of the ingredients, such as sugar substitutes or flavorings, pose health risks?

*In trying to decide whether or not it is possible to manufacture an incredibly delicious, sugarless, fat-free candy bar that meets the company's standards of excellence, what else might you ask?*

Now that Basil has an initial list of questions, he brainstorms about where he might find answers to them. In this case, Basil's sources of information would include such people as suppliers, customers, and potential customers (through market surveys), as well as the company's marketing managers, production managers, chief financial officer and accountants, environmental control managers, distribution managers, and human resources managers. As we mentioned earlier in our discussion of critical thinking, Basil would need to analyze information from these sources for faulty logic, unsupported assumptions, and emotional appeal and would need to determine the credibility of these sources of information and the nature of evidence supporting the information. Basil then would need to synthesize the information received from separate sources into an understandable "whole," or a clear statement of the problem.

In identifying the objectives that would be achieved by manufacturing and selling the new candy bar, Basil would need to determine what it is that his boss would like to achieve by having Unlimited Decadence manufacture the Empty Decadence candy bar. Basil surmises that Wheatley wants to:

1. Satisfy customers who have a need for sweets but not the accompanying calories,
2. Enhance Unlimited Decadence's reputation for being an industry leader and an innovator,
3. Increase the market share (that is, get a greater percentage of all candy sales, perhaps by bringing in people who have a sweet tooth but who haven't been buying Unlimited Decadence products because of the fat and sugar), and
4. Increase profit for the company.

After using creative and critical thinking skills to gather, analyze, and synthesize the facts about the problem and the results that could be achieved by solving the problem (from all perspectives), Basil should have a better understanding of the problem. This understanding will allow Basil to state the problem more clearly and in more detail than he did in the original problem statement, perhaps even allowing for a division of the problem into subproblems. Exhibit 2-6 shows the memo that Basil wrote to Wheatley outlining the problem.

## Identifying Alternative Solutions

After the problem has been clearly defined and stated, the problem solver, using both creative and critical thinking, identifies alternative solutions. Generating numerous alternative solutions makes it more likely that at least one will be workable.

Discussing the problem and possible solutions with other people can help identify alternative solutions. By talking with people who are uninvolved with or unaffected by the

**EXHIBIT 2-6 BASIL'S MEMO OUTLINING THE PROBLEM**

September 24, 2008
TO: Graham Wheatley

FROM: Basil Doowright BD

SUBJECT: Empty Decadence

You asked me if it is possible to manufacture and sell a new, fat-free candy bar to be called "Empty Decadence." I have thought about this for several days and would like to know whether I completely understand the assignment. I presume that you would like Unlimited Decadence to manufacture and sell a new candy bar while at the same time achieving the following objectives:

1. Satisfy customers who have a need for sweets without the accompanying calories,
2. Enhance our reputation as an innovator and industry leader,
3. Increase our market share, and
4. Increase our profit.

Am I on target? I would appreciate your responding in the next day or two. Thanks.

problem or its solution, Basil is likely to get a more objective assessment of the problem or perhaps an entirely new perspective on it. Brainstorming with a group would generate plenty of ideas from which to choose workable solutions. Basil decides to call a meeting, inviting several people from all areas of the company to join a brainstorming team.

After generating a list of ideas, the team must critically evaluate them to identify potentially workable solutions. To be workable, the solutions must fit within the boundaries or limits of the company. For instance, the chief financial officer tells the brainstorming team that the company can borrow only $400,000 to launch the new product; the purchasing officer lists for the team all the available suppliers of ingredients; the production manager reminds the team that Valentine's Day orders will keep managers so preoccupied and production employees so swamped that work on the new product cannot begin until after February 14; and the cleaning crew supervisor informs the team that because the company uses only pure mountain spring water to clean the machines every day, the factory must be located in the mountains. Given this new information, the team comes up with several workable alternatives:

1. Don't manufacture or sell the new Empty Decadence candy bar, and stay with the status quo. (This may be workable, but it may not achieve Wheatley's objectives.)
2. Because $400,000 is not enough to expand the factory, use post-Valentine's Day available space in the current factory to manufacture and sell only a small number of Empty Decadence candy bars to test-market the concept before beginning full-scale production.
3. Drop the Decadent Thunderbolt candy bar product line (which many customers stopped purchasing because it kept them awake at night), and convert the production resources so they can be used for manufacturing the Empty Decadence candy bar. Manufacture and sell a large number of new candy bars (without test-marketing the concept).

*Can you think of other possible alternatives for solving this problem?*

## Weighing the Advantages and Disadvantages of Each Solution

After the team identifies potential workable solutions, Basil must evaluate each of them. Although creative thinking and critical thinking are both useful in developing a list of the advantages and disadvantages of each solution, critical thinking becomes paramount in this stage.

In this example, accounting information is useful in evaluating each solution because each is likely to have different economic effects. Accounting information that is relevant to Basil in weighing the advantages and disadvantages of each solution includes information about the solution's effect on the company's costs, profits, and related income taxes, as well as its effect on the timing of cash receipts and payments. Furthermore, if the Decadent Thunderbolt product line is dropped, Basil must also consider the accompanying change in profits caused by dropping this product line, as well as the change in profits caused by the movement of the Decadent Thunderbolt customers to other candy bars.

After gathering accounting and other information for each alternative, Basil can list the advantages and disadvantages of each alternative. For example, Exhibit 2-7 shows Basil's list of advantages and disadvantages for alternative 2: ". . . manufacture and sell only a small number of Empty Decadence candy bars to test-market the concept before beginning full-scale production." Basil should evaluate the advantages and disadvantages of each workable solution in this way in order to fully understand each alternative solution.

*Can you think of advantages and disadvantages of not manufacturing and selling the new candy bar?*

**EXHIBIT 2-7 BASIL'S LIST OF ADVANTAGES AND DISADVANTAGES FOR MANUFACTURING AND SELLING ONLY A SMALL NUMBER OF EMPTY DECADENCE CANDY BARS**

| Advantages | Disadvantages |
|---|---|
| This alternative will require a smaller initial investment in factory equipment and personnel than would the full-scale production alternative. | A market failure could damage the reputation of the company. |
| With this alternative, Unlimited Decadence has less to lose if the Empty Decadence candy bar does not sell as predicted than it would lose if the full-scale production alternative is implemented and the sales of the Empty Decadence candy bars are less than predicted. | The cost of additions to the factory and personnel could outweigh the money brought into the company through the sale of the Empty Decadence candy bar. |
| Feedback from the test market can be used to improve the Empty Decadence candy bar before it is marketed nationally. | Company employees assigned to produce the Empty Decadence candy bar would be spending time that would otherwise be contributing to the production and sale of well-established candy bars. |
| Positive market response to the Empty Decadence candy bar might open up new sources of financing for further expansion of the factory. | While Unlimited Decadence is test-marketing the Empty Decadence candy bar, the company's competitors could launch a successful full-scale market blitz with a similar candy bar. |
| A new group of customers might be tapped because of the sugarless, low-fat nature of the Empty Decadence candy bar. | |

## Choosing a Solution

The first three stages of the problem-solving process break down the problem in a systematic and detailed manner so that Basil becomes completely familiar with the problem and its possible solutions. After these first three stages, Basil must choose the best solution from among the alternative workable solutions. Basil makes the product decision based, to a great extent, on the accounting information gathered in the previous stage, in which he evaluated the alternatives. However, even after the advantages and the disadvantages of each alternative have been listed and quantified (when possible), the choice of a solution can be difficult. This is because individual advantages and disadvantages weigh differently in the decision and are hard to compare. Not all advantages are equally desirable, and not all disadvantages are equally undesirable. One technique that is useful in ordering the alternatives is to rank them based on their effectiveness in achieving the desired results, and then also to rank them based on their desirability in terms of the company's value system. For example, suppose the company values an innovative image more than one of stability. In this case, the second and third alternatives would rank higher than the first. Another technique that is useful in choosing a solution is to combine the best features of multiple alternative solutions while eliminating some of the disadvantages that each alternative would have if it alone was selected.

Notice that creative and critical thinking are used throughout the problem-solving and decision-making process, although not evenly throughout the process. As we illustrated in Exhibit 2-5, some stages of the process require more of one kind of thinking than the other.

The decision-making process is similar for people who are outside the company and are making decisions about the company. For example, assume Unlimited Decadence applies for a three-year bank loan of $400,000. When this request is made, the banker recognizes that a decision must be made about granting the loan. For the banker, there are many alternatives, including refusing the bank loan, granting a loan of a smaller or greater amount for a shorter or longer time, or granting the loan as requested. The banker must have information concerning the cash in Unlimited Decadence's checking and savings

**EXHIBIT 2-8 ACCOUNTING INFORMATION AND DECISION MAKING**

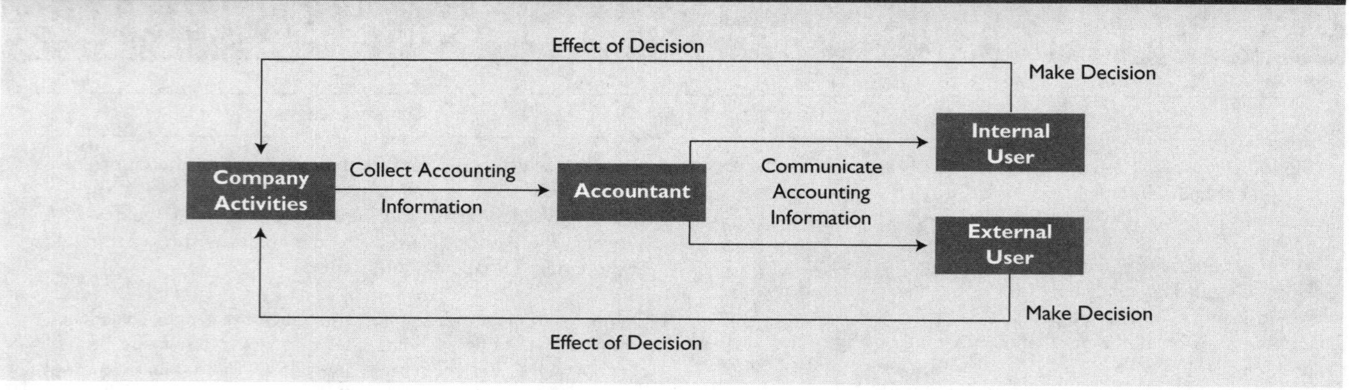


accounts, the cash Unlimited Decadence must spend to pay its bills and the amount it expects to collect from its customers, the timing of these payments and collections, and the way in which the bank loan would be used. By gathering the related accounting information, the banker can evaluate whether Unlimited Decadence needs the bank loan, the appropriate amount and length of time of the loan, and the likelihood that Unlimited Decadence will repay the loan. The banker makes the loan decision, to a great extent, on the basis of accounting information provided by Unlimited Decadence.

### Accounting Information and Decision Making

The role of accounting information in the decision-making process is further illustrated in Exhibit 2-8. As this exhibit illustrates, the accounting information system and decision making are *interactive;* that is, an accountant collects information about a company (locates, gathers, interprets, and organizes relevant information) and communicates this information to both internal and external users to assist them in making decisions. These decisions have an impact on the company's activities, which then have an impact on the company's resulting accounting information (as is reflected when the accounting information accumulation and communication process is repeated again).

For the bank loan and product decisions, you can see that the decisions made by both the internal and the external users will affect the accounting information accumulated and communicated about the company. Before either decision is reached, the information accumulated and communicated will be the information needed to make the decisions, as we discussed earlier. After the decisions are made, regardless of the alternative chosen (whether or not the bank grants a loan to Unlimited Decadence and whether or not Unlimited Decadence manufactures and sells the Empty Decadence candy bar), the result of the decision will affect Unlimited Decadence's future activities and, in turn, result in different accounting information about the company.

## CREATIVE AND CRITICAL THINKING ORIENTATION OF THE BOOK

In the rapidly changing business environment, the businessperson must interpret, evaluate, synthesize, and apply new information and technology. With this new information and technology come new problems, many of which have several reasonable solutions and many of which may not have obvious solutions or any solutions. In this environment, businesspeople and accountants are not operating in a "textbook world," where there are clear-cut, right and wrong answers and where the relevant facts for making decisions are neatly laid out. Therefore, to help you prepare for this challenging environment, throughout this book we will illustrate the use of creative and critical thinking for solving accounting-related problems. Then, in the Integrated Business and Accounting Situations at the ends of the chapters, we will give you the opportunity to enhance your own creative and critical thinking skills. In addition to solving problems that have specific "correct" solutions, we will ask you to make decisions and to solve problems that may have several reasonable solutions or obscure solutions. We will also ask you to interpret, evaluate, and synthesize information and to apply new information to new and different situations. In other words, we will be asking you to think creatively and critically.

## SUMMARY

At the beginning of the chapter we asked you several questions. During the chapter, we asked you to STOP and answer some additional questions to build your knowledge about specific issues. Be sure you answered these additional questions. Below are the questions from the beginning of the chapter, with a brief summary of the key points relating to the answers. Use your creative and critical thinking skills to expand on these key points to develop more complete answers to the questions and to determine what other questions you have that might lead you to learn more about the issues.

### 1 What factors are causing the business environment and the role of accounting within that environment to change?

The business environment is dynamic and is becoming increasingly complex. More information is being generated than ever before, and this information is available to more people than ever before. Technology is advancing rapidly, affecting not only the products we use but also the way the products are manufactured and the way business is conducted. Business activities and economies are becoming globalized, the number of regulations is escalating, business transactions are becoming more complex, and new forms of business are emerging. Because of this dynamic and complex business environment, the successful businessperson must be able to take change in stride, be devoted to lifelong learning, be open to other viewpoints, be tolerant of differences, be willing to take educated and thoughtful risks, be able to anticipate environmental trends and identify the potential problems and opportunities associated with these trends, and be ready to abandon old plans and change course in light of new information.

### 2 What skills can people develop to better prepare themselves for problem solving and decision making in the rapidly changing business environment?

Besides being willing to change, businesspeople can develop skills that better prepare them for problem solving and decision making in this environment. Businesspeople can become broadly proficient in all forms of communication: speaking, writing, listening, and reading. Businesspeople can also develop their interpersonal skills. These skills include the ability to lead and influence others, to motivate others, to withstand and resolve conflict, and to organize and delegate tasks. Intellectual skills are another type of skill that businesspeople can develop. Beyond these skills, a variety of creative and critical thinking skills is needed in a rapidly changing business environment. Among these skills is the ability to use logic.

### 3 How can people learn to think creatively and critically?

People can learn to think creatively and critically first by learning new forms and techniques of thinking and then by practicing these techniques, aiming at improving their decision-making skills. An awareness of their current thinking patterns helps people recognize their strengths and weaknesses; this knowledge gives them a starting point for modifying and improving their thinking performance.

### 4 How can creative and critical thinking help people make better business decisions?

The ideas generated by creative thinking provide the raw materials of the decision-making process. Critical thinking helps decision makers analyze decision alternatives for faulty logic, unsupported assumptions, and emotional appeal. Furthermore, it helps decision makers evaluate the relevance of evidence used to support decision alternatives, the credibility of the sources of evidence, and the consistency of the evidence with the decision alternatives it supports. Finally, creative thinking and critical thinking help decision makers be sure that all relevant information, all points of view, and all workable solutions have been considered.

**5 What are the logical stages in problem solving and decision making?**

Many business problems are difficult and complicated. A systematic approach is necessary to organize the problem and to decide on a solution to the problem. The four stages in problem solving and decision making are (1) recognize the problem, (2) identify alternatives, (3) evaluate the alternatives, and (4) make the decision. The accounting information system plays a big part in the business decision-making process.

## KEY TERMS

**accounting and auditing knowledge** *(p. 39)*
**attribute listing** *(p. 42)*
**brainstorming** *(p. 41)*
**creative thinking** *(p. 40)*
**critical thinking** *(p. 42)*
**deductive logic** *(p. 45)*
**drawing analogies** *(p. 41)*
**e-commerce** *(p. 37)*
**flexibility** *(p. 40)*
**fluency** *(p. 40)*
**general knowledge** *(p. 39)*
**independent** *(p. 42)*
**inductive logic** *(p. 45)*
**objectivity** *(p. 42)*
**organizational and business knowledge** *(p. 39)*
**piggybacking** *(p. 41)*

## SUMMARY SURFING

Here is an opportunity to gather information on the Internet about real-world issues related to the topics in this chapter. Answer the following questions (for suggestions on how to navigate various organizations' Web sites to find the relevant information, see the related discussion in the Preface at the beginning of the book).

- Go to the resources in the **Foundations of Critical Thinking** Web site and look for articles on the fundamentals of critical thinking. Identify the eight elements of reasoning helpful to students in developing their reasoning abilities. List two activities under each guideline. Which guideline(s) seems especially helpful to you?
- Go to the **Creativity Web** Web site to learn about creativity basics and techniques. What are some obstacles to creativity? What are some of the suggestions given to overcome these obstacles?

## INTEGRATED BUSINESS AND ACCOUNTING SITUATIONS

**Answer the Following Questions in Your Own Words.**

### Testing Your Knowledge

**2-1** Describe the factors affecting the business environment and the impact of each of these factors.

**2-2** Think of a recent discovery, technological innovation, world event, regulation, or other factor affecting the business environment (one not mentioned in the chapter). What effect has this factor had on the business environment? What future effect do you think this factor will have on the business environment?

**2-3** What does it mean to be prepared for an opportunity?

**2-4** What are the broad skills, as outlined by the largest public accounting firms, that are necessary for practicing accounting and for effectively conducting business?

**2-5** What is the difference between thinking and critical thinking?

**2-6** How do the creative thinking characteristics of fluency and flexibility complement each other?

**2-7** What are the "ground rules" for brainstorming?

**2-8** How does piggybacking work during a brainstorming session?

**2-9** What is the difference between being independent and being objective?

**2-10** What is the advantage of deferring judgment when making a decision?

**2-11** Why is it important to evaluate the credibility of a source of information?

**2-12** What is the difference between inductive logic and deductive logic?

**2-13** What is the difference between creative thinking and critical thinking? How is each used in decision making and problem solving? How do creative thinking and critical thinking complement each other?

**2-14** How do general knowledge and organizational and business knowledge support creative and critical thinking?

**2-15** Describe the stages of problem solving. What pitfalls might you encounter at each stage?

**2-16** Describe how accounting information is used in each of the stages of problem solving.

## Applying Your Knowledge

**2-17** Suppose you are a manager at Unlimited Decadence Corporation and you receive the following memo from your boss, Max Armstrong: "The results of a survey that I just received indicate that American teenagers will flock to the stores to buy a sugarless, fat-free candy bar. Can we manufacture this type of candy bar? When could we have this product ready for the market?"

*Required:* Before you begin the extensive research necessary for your response to his questions, what would you like to know about the survey? How would the answers to these questions affect what you do next?

**2-18** Consider the following arguments:

(a) "I went over to our supplier's warehouse today and talked with the secretary, who was unbelievably rude! Since he is the only representative of our supplier that I have met, my only conclusion is that everyone who works there must be rude."

(b) "Lyle Biggerstaff, CEO of a large corporation, was able to avoid a lawsuit brought by a customer because he had taped a previous telephone conversation in which the customer both requested unsafe changes in the product and promised not to hold the corporation liable for the consequences of those changes. Given his experience, our company should tape all telephone conversations."

(c) "All purchases over $100 must originate with a purchase order form. Last week, the data-processing manager purchased a $4,000 computer. Therefore, there must have been a purchase order form."

(d) "Almost everyone in the accounting department is a member of the AICPA—the few who are not members either are not ambitious or are careless."

*Required:* Indicate whether each argument is sound and why or why not. If it is not, what would make it sound?

**2-19** Consider the following opposing sides of an issue:
(a) All companies, even those in other countries, should have to follow generally accepted accounting principles.
(b) All companies should not have to follow generally accepted accounting principles.

*Required:* Identify reasons that support each side of the issue.

**2-20** Suppose that your job is beginning to eat into your personal time. During the last six months you have noticed that you have been taking files home with you to work on after supper and on the weekends. Even so, you are having trouble keeping up. After explaining this to your boss, she suggests that you find a way to work more efficiently. Furthermore, she points out that there are many people who would be glad to take over your job.

*Required:* (1) What are some alternative ways to approach your boss? What reasons, information, and evidence might support your point of view?
(2) What reasons, information, and evidence might support your boss's point of view? In what ways might these reasons affect the approach you take in presenting your problem to your boss?

**2-21** You have just landed your dream job working for a gourmet food importer and distributor. Your new boss wants your opinion about whether to open a new branch office in El Paso, Texas. You desperately want to make a good impression on your first assignment and want to be sure you have a good grasp of the situation before you form your opinion.

*Required:* What questions do you want answered before you offer your opinion to your boss? Where might you find the answers to your questions?

**2-22** Suppose your boss has asked you to design a system to keep track of your company's cash expenditures.

*Required:* (1) Before designing this system, what might you want to know that would help you define the problem?
(2) List as many ideas as you can for the design of this system.
(3) What are the advantages and disadvantages of each of your design ideas?

**2-23** Suppose that your brother, the owner of The Last Custard Stand (a specialty dessert shop), has asked you for a substantial loan to help him expand his business.

*Required:* What would you like to know about The Last Custard Stand before you make a decision about whether to loan the company money? How could the answers to each of your questions affect your decision? What accounting information could your brother provide you that could affect your decision?

**2-24** Refer to 2-23. At your request, your brother provides you with the following information:

| | |
|---|---|
| Revenues for 2008 | $80,000 |
| Expenses for 2008 | (65,000) |
| Profit for 2008 | $15,000 |

*Required:* How could this information be presented differently to make it more meaningful for you in reaching your loan decision? What could be added to this particular information to make it more meaningful for you?

**2-25** The office copier has just quit working and is beyond repair. The big question now is what to do with it. Your boss is offering a cash prize for each of the following:
(a) "The longest list of ideas for what to do with the copier
(b) "The most unusual idea
(c) "The widest variety of ideas

*Required:* See if you can win all the cash by providing a written list of your ideas.

**2-26** Your new co-worker just came in and made the following statement: "Every Friday is casual day around here; people wear casual clothes to work on Fridays. Jan, over there, is wearing jeans and a T-shirt today. It must be Friday. TGIF!!!"

*Required:* What's wrong with your co-worker's logic?

## Making Evaluations

**2-27** In this chapter, we discussed the following statement made by a rather disgruntled employee of Unlimited Decadence:

"All programmers should have to work regular hours, from 8:00 A.M. to 5:00 P.M. just like everybody else. It isn't fair that the computer programmers can come in late. Sure, they come in during the middle of the night to fix programs when the computer crashes, and they program on into the night when they are 'on a roll,' but we all know it's just a party up there. Mortimer, one of the programmers, is a major party animal. I've been to several parties with him."

*Required:* Suppose you are this employee's boss. How would you evaluate and respond to this statement? (What faulty logic, unsupported assumptions, or emotional appeals do you see in the statement? Does the employee make any valid points?)

**2-28** Is a business suit the most appropriate article of clothing to wear to a business meeting?

*Required:* Answer the question based on what you believe to be true (answer either "yes," "no," or "not sure"). Explain why you answered the way you did. Now give the reasons and evidence that you believe support your answer (authorities, references, facts, personal experience).

**2-29** Consider, again, the plight of the manager at Unlimited Decadence Corporation, whose boss wants to manufacture and sell the new Empty Decadence candy bar, perhaps using it to replace the Decadent Thunderbolt candy bar. Suppose the accounting department has projected that profit per candy bar will be $0.10 higher for the Decadent Thunderbolt than for the Empty Decadence candy bar. The marketing department predicts that Unlimited Decadence can sell 100,000 Empty Decadence candy bars the first year and then more each year for the next ten years if it drops the Decadent Thunderbolt candy bar. During that same time period, the marketing department forecasts that sales of the Decadent Thunderbolt will be 80,000 candy bars the first year, with sales decreasing slightly after that if the company does not produce the Empty Decadence candy bar. However, if the company produces both candy bars, predicted sales for Empty Decadence will be reduced to 70,000 candy bars the first year, with a slow and steady increase in sales over the next ten years. Predicted sales for the Decadent Thunderbolt will decrease to 65,000 during the first year and decrease slightly each year for the next ten years.

The production department has determined that the new candy bar is possible to manufacture and that the factory can be reconfigured to accommodate the new candy bar while continuing to produce the old candy bar. If Unlimited Decadence drops the Decadent Thunderbolt candy bar, it can convert the equipment so that it can be used to produce the Empty Decadence candy bar. The human resources department is confident that numerous qualified people are available to work if the company wants to produce both candy bars. If the company drops the Decadent Thunderbolt candy bar, those people currently working on the Decadent Thunderbolt candy bar can be easily retrained to work on the Empty Decadence candy bar. The chief financial officer has arranged for financing, if it is needed.

*Required:* (1) Based on the above information, what are the advantages and disadvantages of (a) dropping the Decadent Thunderbolt product line and producing the Empty Decadence candy bar, (b) continuing production of the Decadent Thunderbolt and not producing the Empty Decadence candy bar, (c) producing both the Decadent Thunderbolt and the Empty Decadence candy bars, or (d) producing neither candy bar? How would you decide which alternative is best?
(2) What additional information would make your decision easier?
(3) What other alternative solutions can you think of?

**2-30** The changing business environment provides many challenges for today's businessperson but also opportunities.

*Required:* What opportunities do you see that result from this environment? How would you prepare yourself to take full advantage of these opportunities?

**2-31** Yesterday, you received the letter shown on the following page for your advice column in the local paper:

**DR. DECISIVE**

Dear Dr. Decisive:

Last night my girlfriend and I got into an argument at the Cracked Cuticles concert. I told her that the Cracked Cuticles must be making money because one of the large ticket outlets was sponsoring them and ticket outlets don't sponsor groups that don't make money. We just studied inductive and deductive logic in class, so she commented that I had just used deductive logic. I patiently explained to her that, no, I had just used inductive logic. Now she won't speak to me, let alone go to another concert with me, until you settle this. Help!

Call me "Mr. Right."

*Required:* Meet with your Dr. Decisive team and write a response to "Mr. Right."

## END NOTES

[a]Harry Berkowitz, "Top Firm Slogan Translations a Disaster," *Montreal Gazette,* September 1, 1994.

[b]Arthur Andersen & Co., Arthur Young, Coopers & Lybrand, Deloitte Haskins & Sells, Ernst & Whinney, Peat Marwick Main & Co., Price Waterhouse, and Touche Ross, *Perspectives on Education:Capabilities for Success in the Accounting Profession* (New York, 1989). Accounting Education Change Commission, *Objectives of Education for Accountants,* Position Statement No. 1, September 1990, and Albrecht, W. S. and R. J. Sack, *Accounting Education: Charting the Course Through a Perilous Future,* (American Accounting Association, Sarasota, 2000).

[c]Arthur Andersen & Co. et al., *Perspectives on Education,* 7, 8.

[d]Merriam-Webster Online, http://www.m-w.com/dictionary/brainstorm

PART 2

# Planning in an Entrepreneurial Environment

Chapter 3

## Developing a Business Plan: Cost-Volume-Profit Planning and Analysis

Chapter 4

## Developing a Business Plan: Budgeting

This section includes two chapters that discuss planning for a small company. After reading these chapters, you will be able to:

- *describe what a business plan is and what it contains*
- *prepare various parts of a business plan*
- *understand the differences between variable and fixed costs*
- *use cost-volume-profit analysis in business decisions*
- *prepare a master budget for a retail company*
- *use a master budget in evaluating a company's performance*

CHAPTER 3

# Developing a Business Plan: Cost-Volume-Profit Analysis

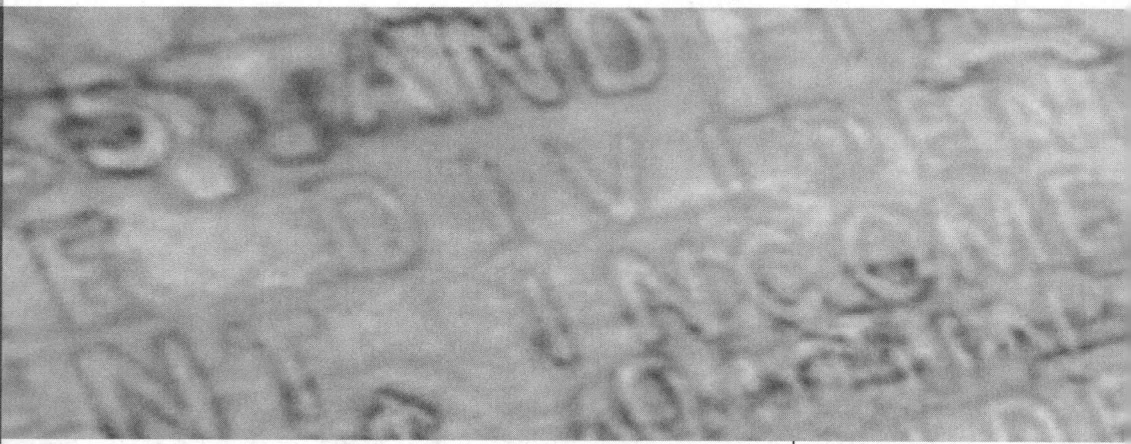

"He who every morning plans the transaction of the day, and follows out that plan, carries a thread that will guide him through the maze of the most busy life. But where no plan is laid, where the disposal of time is surrendered merely to the chance of incidence, chaos will soon reign."

—Victor Hugo

1. Since the future is uncertain and circumstances are likely to change, why should a company bother to plan?
2. What should a company include in its business plan?
3. How does accounting information contribute to the planning process?
4. What must decision makers be able to predict in order to estimate profit at a given sales volume?
5. How can decision makers predict the sales volume necessary for estimated revenues to cover estimated costs?
6. How can decision makers predict the sales volume necessary to achieve a target profit?
7. How can decision makers use accounting information to evaluate alternative plans?

Suppose your sister Anna has hired you, as an employee-advisor, to help her open and run a candy store. Anna, who earned her degree last year with a major in marketing, has an insatiable sweet tooth and has always "hungered" to own a candy store. After long and lively discussions with you about the name of the company, Anna decides to name it "Sweet Temptations." You and Anna arrange to obtain retail space, to purchase display fixtures, supplies, and candy, to hire an employee to sell candy, and to advertise in the newspaper. Now you are ready to open for business. But whoa! Not so fast. Have you thought of everything? If you and Anna want Sweet Temptations to succeed, there are other issues that you must consider before you open your company. Instead of rushing into business when the idea is fresh, first you would be smart to develop a detailed business plan that addresses these issues.

1 Since the future is uncertain and circumstances are likely to change, why should a company bother to plan?

## Planning in a New Company

2 What should a company include in its business plan?

Planning is an ongoing process for successful companies. It begins before a company opens for operations and continues throughout the life of the company. A **business plan** is an evolving report that describes a company's goals and its current plans for achieving those goals. The business plan is used by both internal and external users. A business plan typically includes

1. a description of the company,
2. a marketing plan,
3. an operating plan, and
4. a financial plan.

We will discuss each of these parts in later sections.

A business plan has three main purposes. First, it helps an entrepreneur to visualize and organize the company and its operations. Remember from Chapter 2 how Basil tested the strengths and weaknesses of the proposal to make the Empty Decadence candy bar? Similarly, thinking critically about your hopes for the business and putting a plan on paper will help you and Anna imagine how the plan will work and will help you evaluate the plan, develop new ideas, and refine the plan. By looking at the plan from different points of view, such as those of managers who have responsibility for marketing the company's products or purchasing its inventory of products, you can discover and correct flaws before implementing the plan. Then "paper mistakes" won't become real mistakes!

Second, a business plan serves as a "benchmark," or standard, against which the entrepreneur can later measure the actual performance of a company. You and Anna will be able to evaluate differences between the planned performance of Sweet Temptations, as outlined in its business plan, and its actual performance. Then you will be able to use the results of your evaluation to adjust Sweet Temptations' future activities. For instance, suppose in its first month of business, sales are higher than you and Anna predicted. If you decide that sales will continue at this level, you can use this information to increase Sweet Temptations' future candy purchases.

Third, a business plan helps an entrepreneur obtain the financing that new and growing companies often need. When Anna starts looking for additional funding for Sweet Temptations, potential investors and creditors may request a copy of the company's business plan to help them decide whether or not to invest in Sweet Temptations or to loan it money. For example, as part of its loan-making decisions, **Central Bank** in Jefferson City, Missouri, routinely evaluates the business plans of companies that apply for business loans at the bank.

Investors and creditors, such as Central Bank, have two related concerns when they are making investment and credit decisions. One concern is the level of risk involved with their decisions. **Risk** usually refers to how much uncertainty exists about the future operations of the company. The other concern is the **return**, or money back, that they will receive from their investment and credit decisions. A thorough business plan will provide useful information for helping investors and creditors evaluate their risk and potential return. Now let's look at the parts of a business plan.

## Description of the Company

A business plan usually begins with a description of the company and its basic activities. Details of this description include information about the organization of the company, its product or service, its current and potential customers, its objectives, where it is located, and where it conducts its business.

For example, Sweet Temptations is a new retailing company located in a "high-growth" suburb north of a major metropolitan area. Initially, Sweet Temptations will sell only one kind of candy—boxes of chocolates. You and your sister Anna will expand the "product line" to include other kinds of candy as the company grows. After the sale of chocolates is "up and running," and after you graduate, you plan to join Anna full-time as a partner in the company. You and Anna are eager to begin marketing and operating the company but are waiting to do so until after you finish writing the company's business plan and obtain financing. You realize that writing the plan is helping you to think through the various aspects of the business so that you don't "miss something" important in planning your activities. Exhibit 3-1 illustrates how you might describe Sweet Temptations in its business plan.

The organization of a company and its personnel can have a major influence on the success of a company. Therefore, the description of the company also includes a listing of the important people and the major roles they will play in the company. This listing can include the individuals responsible for starting the company, significant investors who

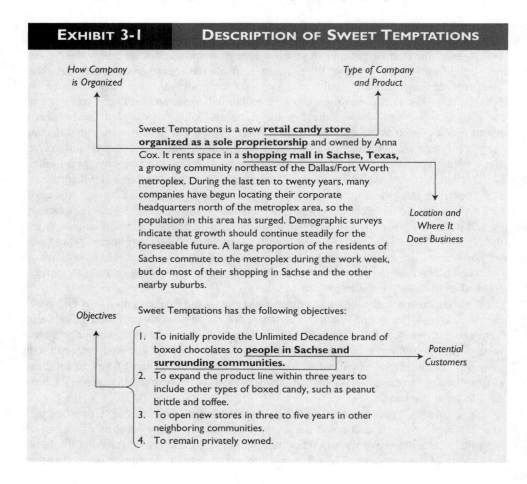

**EXHIBIT 3-1 DESCRIPTION OF SWEET TEMPTATIONS**

*How Company is Organized*

*Type of Company and Product*

Sweet Temptations is a new **retail candy store organized as a sole proprietorship** and owned by Anna Cox. It rents space in a **shopping mall in Sachse, Texas,** a growing community northeast of the Dallas/Fort Worth metroplex. During the last ten to twenty years, many companies have begun locating their corporate headquarters north of the metroplex area, so the population in this area has surged. Demographic surveys indicate that growth should continue steadily for the foreseeable future. A large proportion of the residents of Sachse commute to the metroplex during the work week, but do most of their shopping in Sachse and the other nearby suburbs.

*Location and Where It Does Business*

*Objectives*

Sweet Temptations has the following objectives:

1. To initially provide the Unlimited Decadence brand of boxed chocolates to **people in Sachse and surrounding communities.**
2. To expand the product line within three years to include other types of boxed candy, such as peanut brittle and toffee.
3. To open new stores in three to five years in other neighboring communities.
4. To remain privately owned.

*Potential Customers*

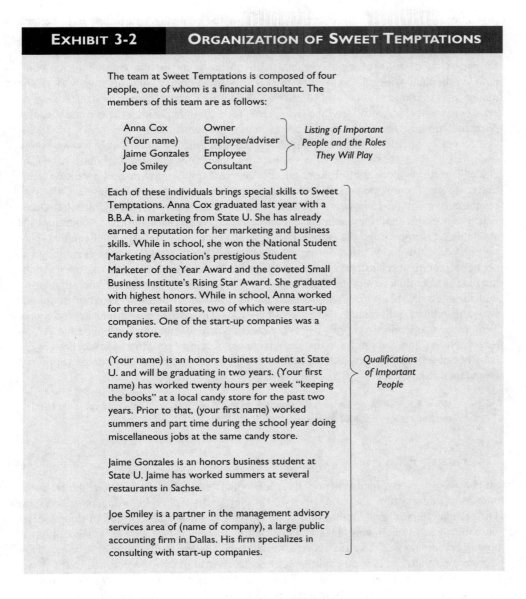

**EXHIBIT 3-2 ORGANIZATION OF SWEET TEMPTATIONS**

The team at Sweet Temptations is composed of four people, one of whom is a financial consultant. The members of this team are as follows:

| | | |
|---|---|---|
| Anna Cox | Owner | *Listing of Important People and the Roles They Will Play* |
| (Your name) | Employee/adviser | |
| Jaime Gonzales | Employee | |
| Joe Smiley | Consultant | |

*Qualifications of Important People:*

Each of these individuals brings special skills to Sweet Temptations. Anna Cox graduated last year with a B.B.A. in marketing from State U. She has already earned a reputation for her marketing and business skills. While in school, she won the National Student Marketing Association's prestigious Student Marketer of the Year Award and the coveted Small Business Institute's Rising Star Award. She graduated with highest honors. While in school, Anna worked for three retail stores, two of which were start-up companies. One of the start-up companies was a candy store.

(Your name) is an honors business student at State U. and will be graduating in two years. (Your first name) has worked twenty hours per week "keeping the books" at a local candy store for the past two years. Prior to that, (your first name) worked summers and part time during the school year doing miscellaneous jobs at the same candy store.

Jaime Gonzales is an honors business student at State U. Jaime has worked summers at several restaurants in Sachse.

Joe Smiley is a partner in the management advisory services area of (name of company), a large public accounting firm in Dallas. His firm specializes in consulting with start-up companies.

also are providing expertise and direction to the company, and influential employees and consultants who have a strong impact on the company. Exhibit 3-2 shows some highlights of how you might discuss Sweet Temptations' organization in its business plan. Notice how this part of the plan highlights the combination of your major in business and Anna's degree in marketing. This part may also contain the company's policies or strategies for selecting, training, and rewarding employees. These issues are particularly important for the long-term success of the company.

## Marketing Plan

The marketing section of a business plan shows how the company will make sales and how it will influence and respond to market conditions. This section receives a lot of attention from investors and creditors because the company's marketing strategy and its ability to implement that strategy can be very important to the company's success.

The marketing section provides evidence of the demand for the company's products or services, including any market research that has been conducted. This section also describes the current and expected competition in the market, as well as relevant government regulations. The marketing section describes how the company will promote, price, and distribute its products (the company's "marketing strategy"), as well as the predicted growth, market share, and sales of its products (its "sales forecast") by period. This information is helpful to the entrepreneur as a starting point for thinking about the company's other activities related to sales, such as timing the purchase of its inventories. The marketing section is also helpful to people outside the company, such as bank loan officers, because it shows how well the entrepreneur has thought through the company's sales potential and how the company will attract and sell to customers.

Sweet Temptations' business plan may be an inch thick! We don't have room to show each part of its plan, so in the next sections we will ask you to think about what to include. The following is a brief description of Sweet Temptations' market conditions. Initially, Sweet Temptations will have a temporary marketing advantage. Currently, community members must drive at least 30 miles to purchase boxes of Unlimited Decadence chocolates (and they actually make the drive!). After evaluating the community's available retail space (and plans for building retail space), you and Anna believe that there will be very little competition during the next several years. However, you eventually expect competing stores to open in the community. In the meantime, part of your marketing plan is to build a reputation for friendly service and quality products. Your advertising will focus on the quality ingredients used in the chocolates. Furthermore, your initial advertising "punch" will include the fact that Unlimited Decadence now produces, and Sweet Temptations sells, mini-versions of "everyone's favorite candy bars" in boxed form. You believe Sweet Temptations has a distinct advantage in selling Unlimited Decadence chocolates because of the already-established good reputation and popularity of the Unlimited Decadence candy bars.

*What information about market conditions facing Sweet Temptations would you include in the marketing section of its business plan?*

## Operating Plan

Since a company is organized to deliver a product or service to a market, the business plan must address how the company will develop and enhance its products or services. The company operations section of a business plan includes a description of the relationships between the company, its suppliers, and its customers, as well as a description of how the company will develop, service, protect, and support its products or services. This section also includes any other influences on the operations of the company. The company operations section of the business plan is important because it helps the entrepreneur think through the details of making the idea work. Also, it helps outside users evaluate the entrepreneur's ability to successfully carry out the idea.

Here is a brief description of Sweet Temptations' operations. Sweet Temptations has a ready supply of chocolates. Unlimited Decadence has no sales agreements with any other candy stores within a 30-mile radius of Sweet Temptations. Furthermore, you know of other potential suppliers—candy manufacturers who have high production standards, quality ingredients, and good reputations in the candy industry. In fact, Anna is now talking with representatives of these companies and visiting their kitchens so that she will have identified and selected other suppliers by the time Sweet Temptations is ready to sell other types of candy.

*What information about Sweet Temptations' operations would you include in its business plan?*

Other influences on the operations of the company might also be described in this section. These other influences might include the availability of employees, concerns of special-interest groups, regulations, the impact of international trade, and the need for patents, trademarks, and licensing agreements.

*If Sweet Temptations' major supplier of chocolates was a company in Brussels, Belgium, rather than Unlimited Decadence Corporation, what additional issues do you think should be included in this section of the business plan? What else do you think managers, owners, creditors, and investors would like to know?*

## Financial Plan

Since Sweet Temptations is a new company, it has no credit history or recent financial statements. Therefore, Anna should also provide a detailed, realistic financial plan in Sweet Temptations' business plan. The purpose of the financial plan section is to identify the company's capital requirements and sources of capital, as well as to describe the company's projected financial performance. For a new company, this section also highlights the company's beginning financial activities, or "start-up" costs.

Here is some information about Sweet Temptations' start-up costs:

> Anna has decided that she will invest $15,000 of her own money as capital to run Sweet Temptations. Based on the rent charged for space in the shopping mall, she has determined that it will cost $1,000 per month to rent store space in the mall. When Sweet Temptations signs a rental contract for the store in December 2007, it will pay six months' rent in advance, totaling $6,000. Based on a supplier's cost quotation, Anna has determined that Sweet Temptations can buy store equipment for $1,800. The supplier will allow Sweet Temptations to make a $1,000 down payment and to sign a note (a legal document, referred to as a *note payable*) for the remaining amount, to be paid later. Based on the purchases budget (which we will discuss in Chapter 4), Sweet Temptations will purchase 360 boxes of chocolates for "inventory" in December 2007 at a cost of $1,620 from Unlimited Decadence. Unlimited Decadence has agreed to allow Sweet Temptations to pay for this inventory in January 2008. Sweet Temptations will also purchase $700 of supplies in December 2007, paying for the supplies at that time.

*What information about Sweet Temptations' start-up costs would you include in the financial section of its business plan?*

### Identifying Capital Requirements

Most companies eventually need additional funding, or **capital**. The financial section of a business plan should include a discussion of the company's capital requirements and potential sources of that capital. For new companies and small companies, this discussion can be the most important part of the business plan. As you may have noticed while reading the business section of your local newspaper, if a company does not have enough capital and sources of capital, it will have a difficult time surviving.

An entrepreneur can determine a company's capital requirements by analyzing two major issues. First, the entrepreneur should decide what resources the company needs, such as buildings, equipment, and furniture. Then, the entrepreneur can estimate how much capital the business will need in order to acquire those resources. Cost quotations, appraisals, and sales agreements are a good starting point for this estimate. Next, the entrepreneur should analyze the company's projected cash receipts and payments to determine whether it will have enough cash to buy the resources and, if not, how much cash the company will need to borrow. Planning capital requirements involves projections, not guarantees, so the entrepreneur must expect and provide for reasonable deviations from plans. Suppose, for example, that cash sales for the month turn out to be less than expected. For "surprises" like this, the entrepreneur should plan to have a "cash buffer," which is extra cash on hand above the projected short-run cash payments of the company. One purpose of this buffer is to protect the company from differences between actual cash

© PHOTOPIA

Significant "start-up" costs for a company.

flows and projected cash flows, and also from unanticipated problems such as having to replace a refrigerated display case sooner than expected. A cash buffer lets the company operate normally through downturns without having to look for financing. It also lets the company take advantage of unexpected opportunities that require cash.

*Can you think of an example of an unexpected opportunity for which an entrepreneur or manager might find a cash buffer to be handy?*

### Sources of Capital

Once the entrepreneur knows the company's capital requirements, potential sources of capital can be identified. Here, the entrepreneur must know both the length of time that the company plans to use the capital before paying it back to creditors or returning it to investors, and the availability of short- and long-term sources of capital. The entrepreneur can determine how long the company will need to use the capital by analyzing the company's projected cash receipts and payments. We will discuss the tools of this analysis more thoroughly in Chapter 4.

**Short-term capital** will be repaid within a year or less. Short-term capital can come from two sources. First, suppliers provide short-term capital to some of their customers through what is called "trade credit." Trade credit involves allowing a customer to purchase inventory "on credit" if the customer agrees to pay soon, usually within 30 days. You and Anna have an arrangement with Unlimited Decadence that will allow Sweet Temptations to buy boxed chocolates on credit and pay Unlimited Decadence 30 days later.

*If Sweet Temptations took longer than 30 days, on the average, to sell its inventory of chocolates, do you think its arrangement with Unlimited Decadence would be valuable? What other questions would you like answered to help you determine the answer to this question?*

Second, financial institutions, such as commercial banks, provide loans to companies, many of which are guaranteed by government agencies such as the **U.S. Small Business Administration**. These institutions require a more formal agreement with a company than do issuers of trade credit. Also, they charge interest on these short-term loans. At some point, Anna may talk with her banker to arrange a small line of credit for Sweet Temptations. A **line of credit** allows a company to borrow money "as needed," with a prearranged, agreed-upon interest rate and a specific payback schedule. We discuss short-term capital more in Chapter 9.

**Long-term capital** will be repaid to creditors or returned to investors after more than a year. Initially, as we mentioned in Chapter 1, companies obtain capital from the owner and from bankers. Sweet Temptations obtained its initial capital from Anna, who invested money from her savings account. Other sources of long-term capital can include friends and relatives, commercial banks, and leasing companies. Many loans are guaranteed by the Small Business Administration or the state's economic-development agency. For example, after being turned down for a bank loan, the owner of **Frosty Factory of America**, a Ruston, Louisiana company that manufactures slush machines for making sorbets and frozen drinks, took his company's business plan to the Louisiana State Economic Development Corporation. After reviewing the plan, the state agency agreed to guarantee 50 percent of the loan. The bank reconsidered and loaned the company $325,000.[a]

*All institutions require a formal agreement with the company about payment dates and interest rates. But suppose Sweet Temptations borrows money from Anna's and your friends and relatives. Do you think it is necessary to have a formal written agreement between these friends and relatives and Sweet Temptations? Why or why not?*

Eventually, as a company grows too large to be financed by the owner and these other sources, it may offer private placements or public offerings. Private placements are securities that are sold directly to private individuals or groups (called *investors*). Public offerings involve issuing bonds or stocks to the public (investors) through securities firms or investment bankers. We will discuss bonds and stocks as a source of long-term capital in Chapters 22 and 24.

For the near future, several of Anna's and your friends and relatives have agreed to lend Sweet Temptations specific amounts of money, as needed. Anna and these friends and relatives have agreed that the interest rate on these loans will match the market interest rate at the time of each loan. Sweet Temptations includes this information in its financial plan.

### Projected Financial Performance

This section of the financial plan projects the company's financial performance. Suppose Anna has assigned you the responsibility of preparing this section of Sweet Temptations' financial plan. Although projecting a company's financial performance involves uncertainty, if you follow some guidelines, the financial performance information will be more dependable.

First, the data that you use should be as reliable as possible. Since Sweet Temptations is a new company, you don't have historical data to use for planning purposes. When you have sketchy data (or no data at all), industry averages found in such sources as *Moody's, Standard & Poor's,* and *Robert Morse Associates* can serve as a guide.

*If you use Moody's, Standard & Poor's, or Robert Morse Associates for industry information, you must be able to identify the industry in which Sweet Temptations is operating. What are some key words that you could use to identify the industry?*

Second, because predicting a company's financial performance is uncertain, you should consider several scenarios. "What if" questions are useful for this type of planning. What if we sell only 800 boxes of chocolates? What if we sell 1,300 boxes of chocolates? The scenarios should be realistic and perhaps should consider the best case, the worst case, and the most probable case.

Third, you should revise your projection as more facts become available. Finally, it is important that the financial plan is consistent with the information in the other sections of the business plan. For example, since the marketing section of Sweet Temptations' business plan refers to the advertising that you plan to do, the financial plan section must show advertising costs.

The financial performance section of the financial plan includes projected financial statements,[1] supported by cost-volume-profit analysis and budgets. Budgets include reports on such items as estimated sales, purchases of inventory, and expenses, as well as estimated cash receipts and payments. In the remainder of this chapter we will discuss cost-volume-profit analysis and its relationship to the projected income statement. In Chapter 4, we will discuss budgets and how they fit into a company's financial plan.

In summary, you have just learned that the business plan shows the direction a company will be taking during the next year. You have also learned that the business plan includes a description of the company, a marketing plan, a description of company operations, and a financial plan. Accountants are most involved with the financial plan, which includes an analysis of predicted costs, sales volumes, and profits. We thus will spend the remainder of this chapter discussing cost-volume-profit analysis and its use in planning.

## COST-VOLUME-PROFIT (C-V-P) PLANNING

3 How does accounting information contribute to the planning process?

Determining if a company will be profitable is difficult before it begins operations. This uncertainty is part of the risk that the entrepreneur takes in starting a business. Although it can be scary, it is also part of the fun. Uncertain profit does not mean that the entrepreneur should disregard any type of analysis before beginning the operations of a company, however. It is possible to take educated risks based on estimations of costs, sales volumes, and profits. The financial plan should include an analysis of these factors. One type of analysis that uses these three factors is called *cost-volume-profit analysis.*

### Cost-Volume-Profit Analysis

**Cost-volume-profit (C-V-P) analysis** shows how profit will be affected by alternative sales volumes, selling prices of products, and various costs of the company. C-V-P analysis sometimes is called "break-even analysis." Entrepreneurs use C-V-P analysis to help them understand how the plans they make will affect profits. This understanding can produce more-informed decisions during the ongoing planning process.

C-V-P analysis is based on a simple profit computation involving revenues and costs. This computation can be shown in an equation or in a graph. Although equations provide precise numbers, C-V-P graphs provide a convenient visual form for presenting the analysis to decision-makers. However, to understand a C-V-P equation or graph, decision makers also must understand how costs behave.

### Cost Behavior

A careful cost analysis considers the activity level of the operation that causes the cost. For example, Unlimited Decadence, a manufacturing company, might measure its activity by using the number of cases of chocolate bars produced or the number of hours worked in producing these cases of chocolate bars. On the other hand, Sweet Temptations, a retail company, might measure its activity by using the number of boxes of chocolates *sold.* The activity level (the number of boxes of candy bars sold) is often referred to as **volume**. The relationship between an activity's cost and its volume helps us determine the cost's behavior pattern.

To understand what C-V-P equations and graphs reveal about a company's potential profitability, let's first look at two cost behavior patterns that describe how most costs behave. These are called *fixed costs* and *variable costs.*

---

[1]The financial plan usually includes a projected balance sheet, but to simplify the discussion in this chapter, we won't discuss the projected balance sheet until Chapter 12.

### Fixed Costs

**Fixed costs** are constant in total for a specific time period; they are *not* affected by differences in volume during that same time period. Managers' annual salaries are usually fixed costs, for instance. For another example, think about the $1,000 monthly rent that Sweet Temptations will pay for its retail space. Sweet Temptations' activity level is its sales volume—the number of boxes of chocolates sold. The rent cost of the retail space will not change as a result of a change in the sales volume, assuming you have planned carefully and have leased enough retail space. Sweet Temptations will pay its monthly rent of $1,000 no matter how many candy bars it sells that month. Since the rent cost does not change as volume changes, it is a fixed cost. The graph in Exhibit 3-3 illustrates the relationship between the rent cost and the sales volume. As you can see, the rent cost will be $1,000 whether Sweet Temptations sells 500 boxes of chocolates or 1,000 boxes.

Note in Exhibit 3-3 that we show a fixed cost as a horizontal straight line on the graph, indicating that the cost will be the same (fixed) over different volume levels. It is important not to be misled about fixed costs. Saying that a cost is "fixed" does not mean that it cannot change from one time period to the next. In the next period, Sweet Temptations could rent more retail space if needed or the landlord could raise the rent when the lease is renewed, causing the rent cost to be higher. To be fixed, a cost must remain constant for a time period in relation to the volume attained *in that same time period.* For example, most companies consider the costs of using their buildings, factories, office equipment, and furniture—called *depreciation*[2]—to be fixed. That is, depreciation costs within a specific time period will not change even if volume changes within that time period.

You have estimated that Sweet Temptations' monthly fixed costs will include the $1,000 rent cost plus $2,050 total salaries for you and Jaime Gonzales (the employee Anna hired to sell candy), $200 consulting costs, $305 advertising costs, $30 supplies costs, $15 depreciation of the store equipment, and $250 telephone and utilities costs.[3] Sweet Temptations' total fixed costs will be the sum of the individual fixed costs, or $3,850.

*What would the graph look like for Sweet Temptations' $3,850 total fixed costs? Why?*

**EXHIBIT 3-3 FIXED COST BEHAVIOR**

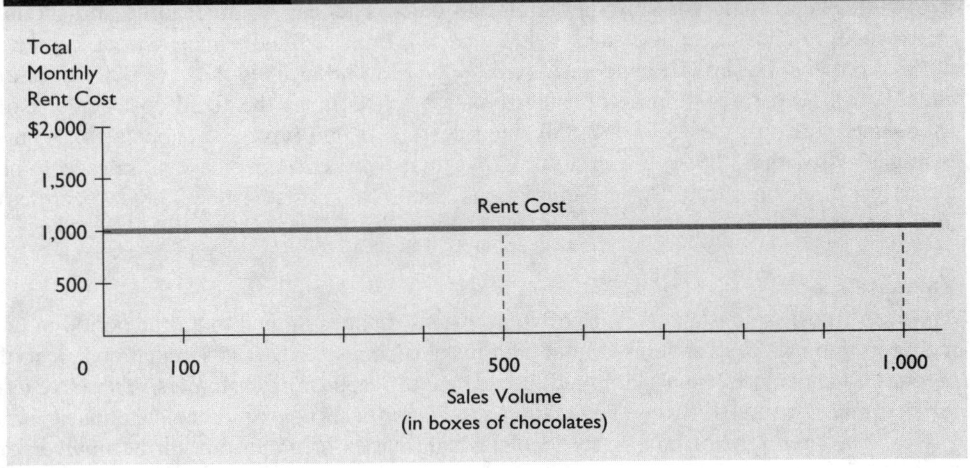


[2]We will discuss in Chapters 5 and 21 how a company determines its depreciation cost. We include a brief discussion here because most companies have some depreciation costs to consider in evaluating their operations.

[3]Some supplies, telephone, and utility costs may have minimum charges, but their total costs are affected by changes in the volume of usage. These costs are called *mixed costs,* which we will discuss in Chapter 11. For simplicity, here we assume they are fixed costs.

If this box of chocolates contained more pieces of candy, would the company's total fixed costs decrease?

Decision makers sometimes state fixed costs as a dollar amount *per unit,* computed by dividing total fixed costs by the volume in units. This can be misleading and should be avoided. For instance, at a sales volume of 500 boxes of chocolates, Sweet Temptations' fixed cost per box of chocolates will be $7.70 ($3,850 fixed costs ÷ 500 boxes of chocolates). At a sales volume of 1,000 boxes of chocolates, the fixed cost per box of chocolates will only be $3.85 ($3,850 fixed costs ÷ 1,000 boxes of chocolates). Comparing $7.70 with $3.85, you might think that total fixed costs decrease as sales volume increases. This is not true! Sweet Temptations' total fixed costs will be $3,850 regardless of the sales volume.

### Variable Costs

A **variable cost** is constant *per unit* of volume, and changes in total in a time period in direct proportion to the change in volume. For instance, consider Sweet Temptations' cost of purchasing chocolates from Unlimited Decadence to resell to its customers. You have estimated that it will cost Sweet Temptations $4.50 for each box of chocolates that it purchases. The *total cost* of boxes of chocolates sold varies in proportion to the *number* of boxes sold. If Sweet Temptations sells 500 boxes of chocolates in January, the total variable cost of these boxes of chocolates sold will be $2,250 (500 boxes of chocolates × $4.50 per box). If the volume doubles to 1,000 boxes of chocolates, the total variable cost of boxes of chocolates sold will also double to $4,500 (1,000 boxes of chocolates × $4.50 per box). It is important to remember that the total variable cost for a time period increases in proportion to volume in that same time period because each unit has the same variable cost.

Exhibit 3-4 shows the estimated total variable costs of boxes of chocolates sold by Sweet Temptations at different sales volumes. Note that total variable costs are shown by a straight line sloping upward from the origin of the graph. This line shows that the total variable cost increases as volume increases. If no boxes of chocolates are sold, the total variable cost will be $0. If 500 boxes of chocolates are sold, the total variable cost will be $2,250. The slope of the line is the rate at which the total variable cost will increase each time Sweet Temptations sells another box of chocolates. This rate is the variable cost per unit of volume, or $4.50 per each additional box of chocolates sold.

*How could rent be a variable cost? If it were a variable cost, how do you think it would affect Sweet Temptations' variable costs line in Exhibit 3-4?*

Because graphs are easy to see, we used them to show Sweet Temptations' fixed and variable costs in Exhibits 3-3 and 3-4. For C-V-P analysis, however, it is often better to use equations because they show more precise numbers. For instance, the equation for the total amount of a variable cost is

Total variable cost = $vX$
where:
$v$ = variable cost per unit sold, and
$X$ = sales volume.

The equation for the variable cost line in Exhibit 3-4 is

Total variable cost of boxes of chocolates sold = $4.50$X$
where:
$X$ = sales volume.

**EXHIBIT 3-4** **VARIABLE COST BEHAVIOR**

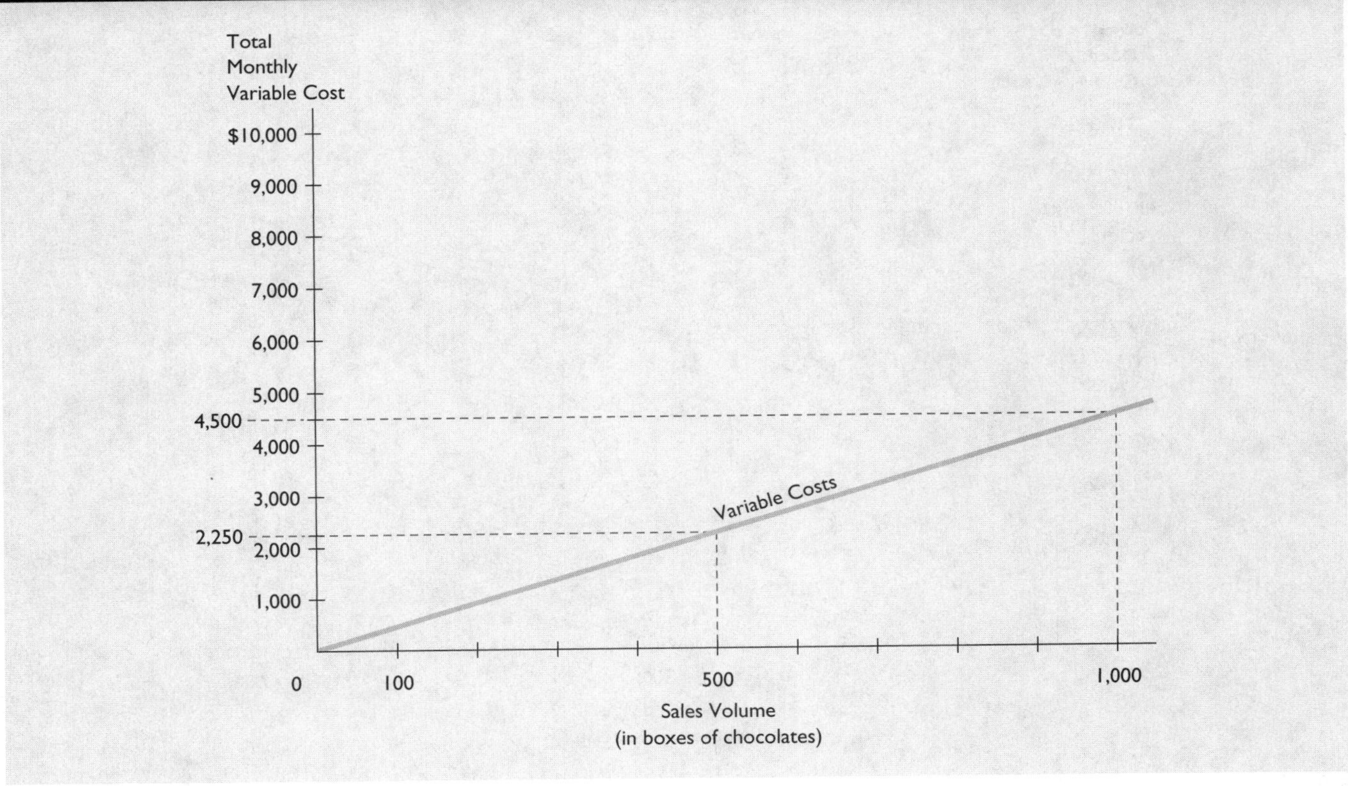

### Total Costs

**Total costs** at any volume are the sum of the fixed costs and the variable costs at that volume. For example, at a sales volume of 500 boxes of chocolates, Sweet Temptations' estimated fixed costs are \$3,850 and its estimated variable costs are \$2,250 (500 × \$4.50), for an estimated total cost of \$6,100 at that volume. At a sales volume of 1,000 boxes of chocolates, estimated fixed costs are \$3,850, estimated variable costs are \$4,500 (1,000 × \$4.50), and the estimated total cost is \$8,350. Exhibit 3-5 illustrates the total cost in relation to sales volume. Notice that if no boxes of chocolates are sold, the total cost will be equal to the fixed costs of \$3,850. As sales increase, the total cost will increase by \$4.50 per box, the amount of the variable cost per box.

The equation for the total cost is

$$\text{Total cost} = f + vX$$

where:

$f$ = total fixed costs,
$v$ = variable cost per unit sold, and
$X$ = sales volume.

The equation for the total cost line in Exhibit 3-5 is

$$\text{Total cost of boxes of chocolates sold} = \$3{,}850 + \$4.50X$$

where:

$X$ = sales volume.

Now that you understand the relationships of volume, fixed costs, and variable costs to the total cost, we can use C-V-P analysis to estimate profit.

**EXHIBIT 3-5** **TOTAL COST BEHAVIOR**

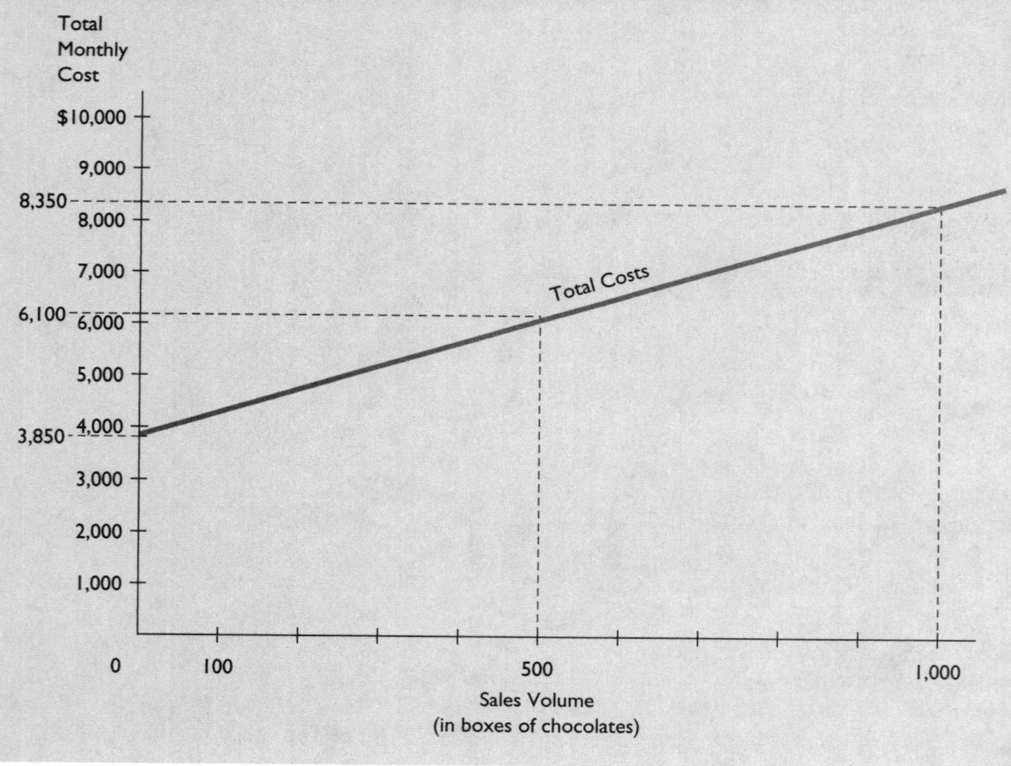

## Profit Computation

According to the marketing plan, Sweet Temptations expects to sell 720 boxes of chocolates at $10 each in January. Exhibit 3-6 shows Sweet Temptations' projected income statement in the format that is presented to external users. This is the same format that we discussed in Chapter 1 and illustrated in Exhibit 1-7. External decision makers find this format understandable and use this form of income statement for their investment and credit decisions. This income statement results from the following equation:

$$\text{Net Income (Profit)} = \text{Revenues} - \text{Expenses}$$

In this equation, revenues (the selling prices of all the boxes of chocolates sold to customers) include cash and credit sales, and expenses (the costs of providing the boxes of chocolates to customers) include the cost of boxes of chocolates sold and the expenses to operate the business.

### Profit Graph

One way of graphing a company's net income (profit) is to show both its revenues and its costs (expenses) on the same graph. Recall that the graph of a company's total costs includes its fixed costs and its variable costs, as we illustrated in Exhibit 3-5 for Sweet Temptations. The graph of a company's revenues is shown by a straight line sloping upward from the origin of the graph. The slope of the line is the rate (selling price per unit) at which the total revenues increase each time the company sells another unit.

The graph in Exhibit 3-7 shows the estimated total revenue line and the estimated total cost line for Sweet Temptations. Note that the total revenue line crosses the total cost line at 700 boxes of chocolates. At this point, the total revenues will be $7,000, and the total costs will be $7,000, so there will be zero profit. The unit sales volume at which a company earns zero profit is called the **break-even point**. Above the break-even unit sales volume, the total revenues of the company are more than its total costs, so there will be a profit. Below the break-even point, the total revenues are less than the total costs, so there will be a loss. For instance, at a sales volume of 720 boxes of chocolates, the graph in Exhibit 3-7 shows that Sweet Temptations will earn a profit of $110 (as we computed

**EXHIBIT 3-6 — PROJECTED INCOME STATEMENT FOR EXTERNAL USERS**

**SWEET TEMPTATIONS**
***Projected Income Statement***
***For the Month Ended January 31, 2008***

| | | |
|---|---|---|
| Revenues: | | |
| Sales revenues | | $7,200 |
| Expenses: | | |
| Cost of boxes of chocolates sold | $3,240 | |
| Rent expense | 1,000 | |
| Salaries expense | 2,050 | |
| Consulting expense | 200 | |
| Advertising expense | 305 | |
| Supplies expense | 30 | |
| Depreciation expense: display cases | 15 | |
| Telephone and utilities expense | 250 | |
| Total expenses | | (7,090) |
| Net income | | $ 110 |

**EXHIBIT 3-7 PROFIT GRAPH FOR SWEET TEMPTATIONS**

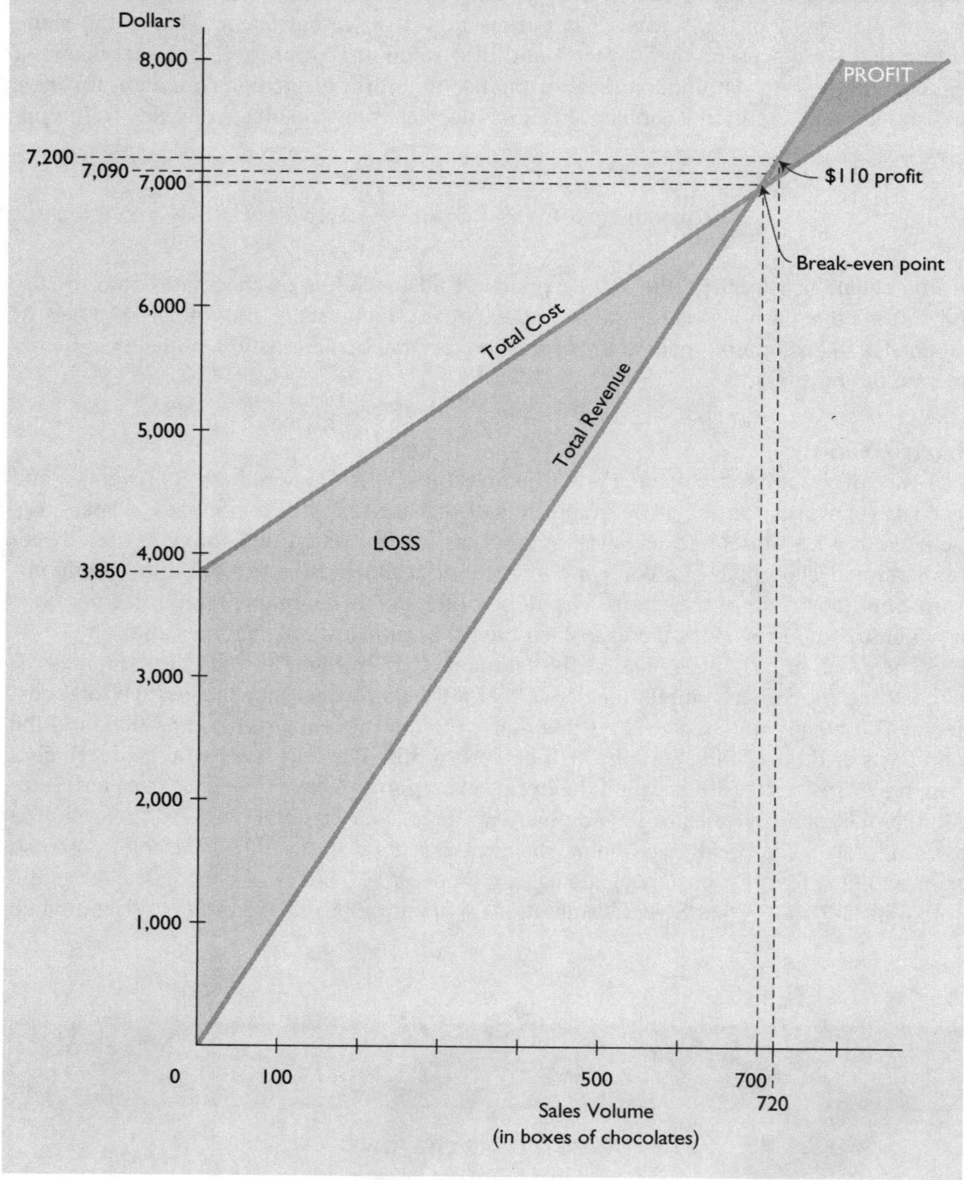


in the income statement in Exhibit 3-6), the difference between the $7,200 estimated total revenue and $7,090 estimated total cost at this volume. Although some decision makers use this type of graph, many others prefer to use a different graph that shows a company's contribution margin, as we discuss next.

### Contribution Margin

To estimate profit at different volume levels, the entrepreneur needs C-V-P information in a form that relates the estimated revenues and estimated variable costs to the estimated fixed costs. Exhibit 3-8 shows an income statement containing the same information as Exhibit 3-6, but in a format that is more useful for the internal decision makers in

**EXHIBIT 3-8** **PROJECTED INCOME STATEMENT FOR INTERNAL USERS (CONTRIBUTION MARGIN APPROACH)**

**SWEET TEMPTATIONS**
***Projected Income Statement***
***For the Month Ended January 31, 2008***

| | | |
|---|---|---|
| Total sales revenues ($10 × 720 boxes of chocolates) | | $7,200 |
| Less total variable costs: | | |
| Cost of boxes of chocolate sold ($4.50 × 720 boxes) | | (3,240) |
| Total contribution margin | | $3,960 |
| Less total fixed costs: | | |
| Rent expense | $1,000 | |
| Salaries expense | 2,050 | |
| Consulting expense | 200 | |
| Advertising expense | 305 | |
| Supplies expense | 30 | |
| Depreciation expense: display cases | 15 | |
| Telephone and utilities expense | 250 | |
| Total fixed costs | | (3,850) |
| Profit | | $ 110 |

performing C-V-P analysis because it shows expenses as variable and fixed. This income statement format is sometimes called the *contribution margin approach.* Notice that, on this income statement, Sweet Temptations first calculates its estimated sales revenue ($7,200) by multiplying the number of boxes of chocolates it expects to sell (720) by the selling price per box ($10). Sweet Temptations next determines the total estimated variable costs of selling the 720 boxes of chocolates ($3,240) by multiplying the number of boxes it expects to sell (720) by the variable cost per box of chocolates ($4.50). These total variable costs are then subtracted from total sales revenue. The $3,960 ($7,200 − $3,240) difference is called the *total contribution margin.*

The **total contribution margin**, at a given sales volume, is the difference between the estimated total sales revenue and the estimated total variable costs. It is the amount of revenue remaining, after subtracting out the total variable costs, that will contribute to "covering" the estimated fixed costs. To compute the estimated profit, we subtract the total estimated fixed costs for the month from the total contribution margin. If the contribution margin is more than the total fixed costs, there will be a profit. If the contribution margin is less than the total fixed costs, there will be a loss. Exhibit 3-8 shows that Sweet Temptations' estimated profit is $110 ($3,960 total contribution margin − $3,850 total fixed costs).

The contribution margin may also be shown on a per-unit basis. The **contribution margin per unit** is the difference between the estimated sales revenue per unit and the estimated variable costs per unit. For Sweet Temptations, the contribution margin per unit is $5.50 ($10 sales revenue − $4.50 variable costs). At 720 units, the total contribution margin will be $3,960 (720 × $5.50), which is the same as shown in Exhibit 3-8. Later, you will see that computing the total contribution margin (by either method described above) is the key to understanding the relationship between profit and sales volume.

Exhibit 3-9 shows what the total contribution margin will be at different unit sales volumes. In this graph, since the contribution margin of one box of chocolates is $5.50, the total contribution margin increases at a rate of $5.50 per box of chocolates sold. For example, at a volume of 500 boxes of chocolates, the contribution margin will be $2,750

**EXHIBIT 3-9** **RELATIONSHIP BETWEEN THE TOTAL CONTRIBUTION MARGIN AND THE UNIT SALES VOLUME**

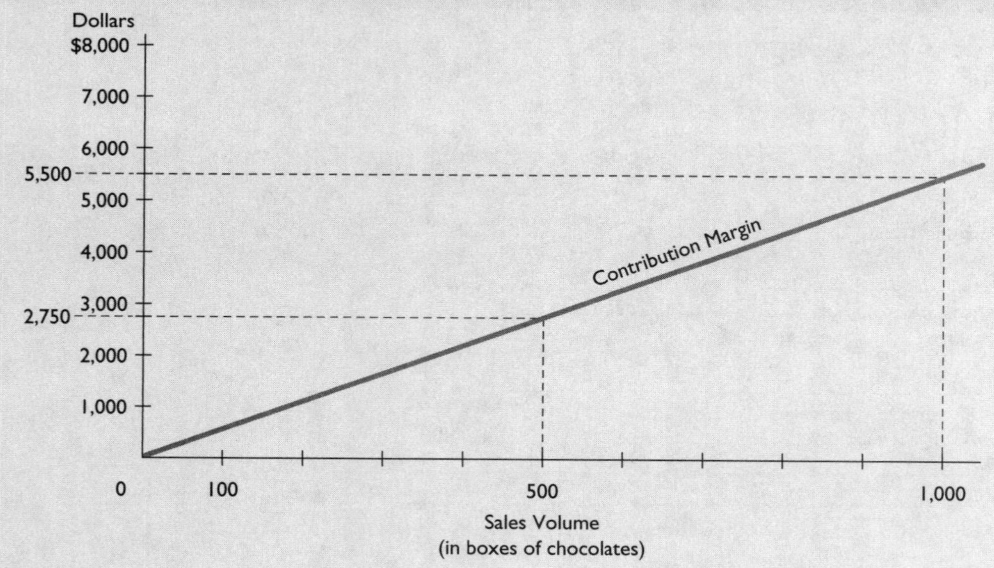


(500 boxes × $5.50). At a volume of 1,000 boxes of chocolates, the contribution margin will be $5,500 (1,000 boxes × $5.50).

*If variable costs were higher per unit, would you expect the contribution margin line in Exhibit 3-9 to be steeper or flatter than it is? Why?*

### Showing C-V-P Relationships

Now that you understand the contribution margin and fixed costs, we can show the estimated profit or loss at different sales volumes in a graph. Exhibit 3-10 shows how sales volume affects the estimated profit (or loss) for Sweet Temptations. Two lines are drawn on this graph. One line shows the estimated total contribution margin at different sales volumes. It is the same line as shown in Exhibit 3-9. The other line shows the $3,850 total estimated fixed costs. The vertical distance between these lines is the estimated profit or loss at the different sales volumes. Remember, estimated profit is the total contribution margin minus the estimated total fixed costs. Note that this graph shows that Sweet Temptations will earn $0 profit if it sells 700 boxes of chocolates; this is its break-even point. Above the break-even unit sales volume (such as at a volume of 1,000 boxes), the total contribution margin ($5,500) is more than the total estimated fixed costs ($3,850), so there would be a profit ($5,500 − $3,850 = $1,650). Below the break-even point (such as at a volume of 500 boxes), the total contribution margin ($2,750) is less than the total estimated fixed costs, so there would be a loss ($2,750 − $3,850 = −$1,100).

*If fixed costs were greater, would you expect Sweet Temptations to break even at a lower sales volume or a higher sales volume? Why?*

### Profit Computation (Equation Form)

In Exhibit 3-10, we show a graph of the C-V-P relationships for Sweet Temptations. Graphs are usually a helpful tool for an entrepreneur (and students!) to see a "picture" of these relationships. Sometimes, however, an entrepreneur (or student) does not need a pic-

**EXHIBIT 3-10 COST-VOLUME-PROFIT RELATIONSHIPS FOR SWEET TEMPTATIONS**

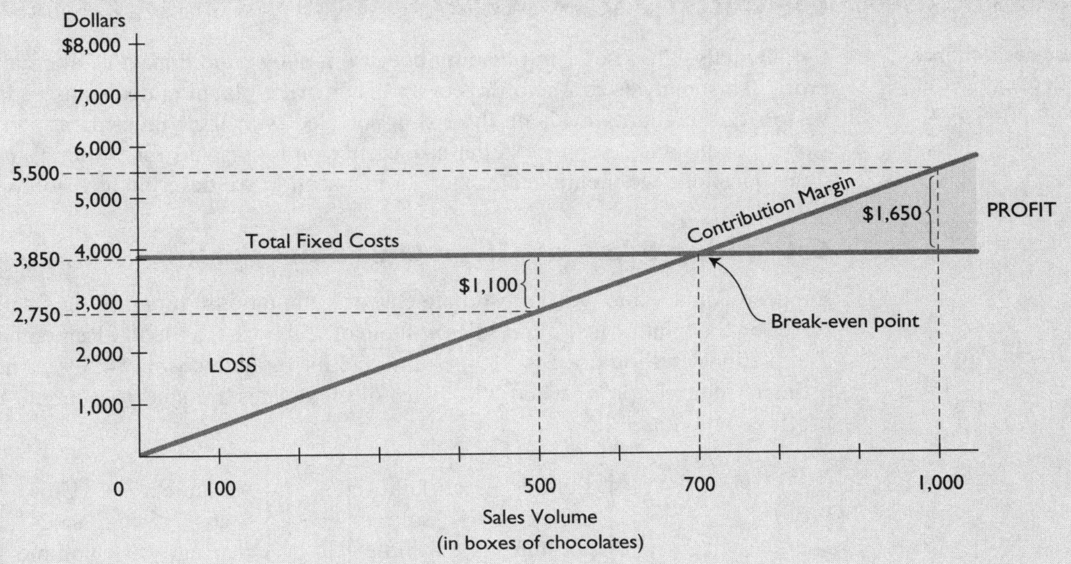


ture to understand the relationships. In this case, using equations may be a better and faster way to understand C-V-P relationships. (You may have already thought of these equations as you studied Exhibit 3-10.) In this section, we look at how to use equations for C-V-P analysis to answer the following questions:

1. How much profit will the company earn at a given unit sales volume?
2. How many units must the company sell to break even?
3. How many units must the company sell to earn a given amount of profit? (The given amount is usually a desired profit that the company uses as a goal.)

In the following discussion, we use Sweet Temptations' revenue and cost information from the projected income statement for internal decision makers, in Exhibit 3-8. We determined the total sales revenue by multiplying the selling price per unit by the estimated sales volume. We determined the total estimated variable costs by multiplying the variable cost per unit by the same sales volume. And we subtracted the total estimated variable and fixed costs from the total estimated sales revenue to determine the estimated profit. We can show this in a "profit equation" as follows:

$$\text{Profit (for a given sales volume)} = \left[\text{Selling price per unit} \times \text{Unit sales volume}\right] - \left[\text{Variable cost per unit} \times \text{Unit sales volume}\right] - \text{Total fixed costs}$$

The profit equation can be used in C-V-P analysis. For Sweet Temptations, for instance, if we use X to stand for a given sales volume of boxes of chocolates, and if we include the estimated selling price and variable cost per unit, the equation is written as follows:

$$\begin{aligned} \text{Profit} &= \$10X - \$4.50X - \$3{,}850 \\ &= (\$10 - \$4.50)X - \$3{,}850 \\ &= \$5.50X - \$3{,}850 \end{aligned}$$

This equation, then, can be used in solving various C-V-P questions for Sweet Temptations.[4]

# USING C-V-P ANALYSIS

**4** What must decision makers be able to predict in order to estimate profit at a given sales volume?

C-V-P analysis is useful in planning because it shows the impact of alternative plans on profit. This analysis can help the entrepreneur make planning decisions and can help investors and creditors evaluate the risk associated with their investment and credit decisions. For instance, suppose Anna has asked you to answer, for Sweet Temptations, the three questions we mentioned earlier. In this section we describe how to do so.

## Estimating Profit at Given Unit Sales Volume

Suppose Anna wants you to estimate Sweet Temptations' monthly profit if it sells 750 boxes of chocolates (i.e., a unit sales volume of 750 boxes) a month. Remember that Sweet Temptations' selling price is $10 per unit and its variable cost is $4.50 per unit. You can estimate monthly profit when 750 boxes of chocolates are sold in a month by using the profit equation as follows:

$$
\begin{aligned}
\text{Profit} &= \left[\begin{matrix}\text{Selling} \\ \text{price} \\ \text{per unit}\end{matrix} \times \begin{matrix}\text{Unit} \\ \text{sales} \\ \text{volume}\end{matrix}\right] - \left[\begin{matrix}\text{Variable} \\ \text{cost} \\ \text{per unit}\end{matrix} \times \begin{matrix}\text{Unit} \\ \text{sales} \\ \text{volume}\end{matrix}\right] - \begin{matrix}\text{Total} \\ \text{fixed} \\ \text{costs}\end{matrix} \\
&= (\$10 \times 750) - (\$4.50 \times 750) - \$3{,}850 \\
&= \$7{,}500 - \$3{,}375 - \$3{,}850 \\
&= \underline{\underline{\$275}}
\end{aligned}
$$

Thus, you can tell Anna that Sweet Temptations will make a monthly profit of $275 if it sells 750 boxes of chocolates a month.

## Finding the Break-Even Point

**5** How can decision makers predict the sales volume necessary for estimated revenues to cover estimated costs?

Suppose Anna wants you to estimate how many boxes of chocolates Sweet Temptations must sell to break even each month. Recall that the break-even point is the unit sales volume that results in zero profit. This occurs when total sales revenue equals total costs (total variable costs plus total fixed costs). To find the break-even point, we start with the profit equation. Remember that the contribution margin per unit is the difference between the sales revenue per unit and the variable costs per unit. With this in mind, we can rearrange the profit equation[5] into a break-even equation as follows:

---

[4]Note in the last line of the equation that the $5.50 is the contribution margin per unit. This can come in handy as a "shortcut" when using the profit equation, so that the equation becomes:

$$
\begin{matrix}\text{Profit} \\ \text{(for a given} \\ \text{sales volume)}\end{matrix} = \left[\begin{matrix}\text{Contribution} \\ \text{margin} \\ \text{per unit}\end{matrix} \times \begin{matrix}\text{Unit} \\ \text{sales} \\ \text{volume}\end{matrix}\right] - \begin{matrix}\text{Total} \\ \text{fixed} \\ \text{costs}\end{matrix}
$$

[5]For those of you who want "proof" of this break-even equation, since the contribution margin per unit is the selling price per unit minus the variable cost per unit, we can substitute the total contribution margin per unit into the profit equation as follows:

$$
\text{Profit} = \left[\begin{matrix}\text{Contribution} \\ \text{margin} \\ \text{per unit}\end{matrix} \times \begin{matrix}\text{Unit} \\ \text{sales} \\ \text{volume}\end{matrix}\right] - \begin{matrix}\text{Total} \\ \text{fixed} \\ \text{costs}\end{matrix}
$$

Since break-even occurs when profit is zero, we can omit the profit, move the total fixed costs to the other side of the equation, and rewrite the equation as follows:

$$
\text{Total fixed costs} = \left[\begin{matrix}\text{Contribution} \\ \text{margin} \\ \text{per unit}\end{matrix} \times \begin{matrix}\text{Unit} \\ \text{sales} \\ \text{volume}\end{matrix}\right]
$$

Finally, we can divide both sides of the equation by the contribution margin per unit to derive the break-even equation:

$$
\frac{\text{Total fixed costs}}{\text{Contribution margin per unit}} = \begin{matrix}\text{Unit sales volume} \\ \text{(to earn zero profit)}\end{matrix}
$$

$$\frac{\text{Unit sales volume}}{\text{(to earn zero profit)}} = \frac{\text{Total fixed costs}}{\text{Contribution margin per unit}}$$

So for Sweet Temptations, you can tell Anna that the break-even point is 700 boxes of chocolates, computed using the break-even equation as follows (letting *X* stand for the unit sales volume):

$$\begin{array}{c}\text{Unit sales volume}\\ \text{(to earn zero profit)}\end{array} = \frac{\$3{,}850 \text{ total fixed costs}}{(\$10 \text{ selling price} - \$4.50 \text{ variable cost}) \text{ per unit}}$$

$$X = \frac{\$3{,}850}{\$5.50}$$

$$X = \underline{\underline{700}} \text{ boxes of chocolates}$$

You can verify the break-even sales volume of 700 boxes of chocolates with the following schedule:

| | |
|---|---|
| Total sales revenue (700 boxes of chocolates @ $10.00 per box) | $7,000 |
| Less: Total variable costs (700 boxes of chocolates @ $4.50 per box) | (3,150) |
| Total contribution margin (700 boxes of chocolates @ $5.50 per box) | $3,850 |
| Less: Total fixed costs | (3,850) |
| Profit | $ 0 |

## Finding the Unit Sales Volume to Achieve a Target Profit

**6** How can decision makers predict the sales volume necessary to achieve a target profit?

Finding the break-even point gives the entrepreneur useful information. However, most entrepreneurs are interested in earning a profit that is high enough to satisfy their goals and the company's goals. A company often states its profit goals at amounts that result in a satisfactory return on the average total assets used in its operations. Since this is an introduction to C-V-P analysis, we will wait to discuss what is meant by "satisfactory return" and "average total assets" until Chapter 11. Here we will assume an amount of profit that is satisfactory. Suppose Anna's goal is that Sweet Temptations earn a profit of $110 per month. How many boxes of chocolates must Sweet Temptations sell per month to earn $110 profit? To answer this question, we slightly modify the break-even equation.

The break-even point is the sales volume at which the total contribution margin is equal to, or "covers," the total fixed costs. Therefore, each additional unit sold above the break-even sales volume increases profit by the contribution margin per unit. Hence, to find the sales volume at which the total contribution margin "covers" both total fixed costs *and* the desired profit, we can modify the break-even equation simply by adding the desired profit to fixed costs, as follows:

$$\begin{array}{c}\text{Unit sales volume}\\ \text{(to earn zero profit)}\end{array} = \frac{\text{Total fixed costs} + \text{Desired profit}}{\text{Contribution margin per unit}}$$

So, if we let *X* stand for the unit sales volume, Sweet Temptations needs to sell 720 boxes of chocolates to earn a profit of $110 a month, computed as follows:

$$X = \frac{\$3{,}850 + \$110}{\$5.50 \text{ per box of chocolates}}$$

$$X = \underline{\underline{720}} \text{ boxes of chocolates}$$

You can verify the $110 profit with the schedule on the following page.

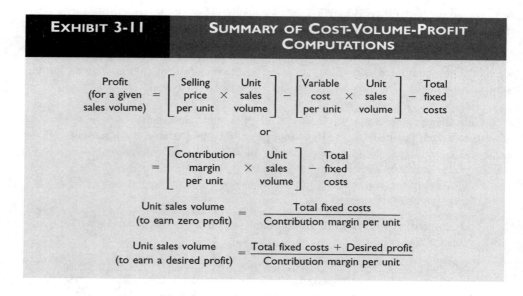

**EXHIBIT 3-11 SUMMARY OF COST-VOLUME-PROFIT COMPUTATIONS**

$$\text{Profit (for a given sales volume)} = \left[\text{Selling price per unit} \times \text{Unit sales volume}\right] - \left[\text{Variable cost per unit} \times \text{Unit sales volume}\right] - \text{Total fixed costs}$$

or

$$= \left[\text{Contribution margin per unit} \times \text{Unit sales volume}\right] - \text{Total fixed costs}$$

$$\text{Unit sales volume (to earn zero profit)} = \frac{\text{Total fixed costs}}{\text{Contribution margin per unit}}$$

$$\text{Unit sales volume (to earn a desired profit)} = \frac{\text{Total fixed costs} + \text{Desired profit}}{\text{Contribution margin per unit}}$$

| | |
|---|---|
| Total sales revenue (720 boxes of chocolates @ $10.00 per box) | $7,200 |
| Less: Total variable costs (720 boxes of chocolates @ $4.50 per box) | (3,240) |
| Total contribution margin (720 boxes of chocolates @ $5.50 per box) | $3,960 |
| Less: Total fixed costs | (3,850) |
| Profit | $ 110 |

Since Anna had included the desired profit of $110 per month in Sweet Temptations' business plan, the income statement for internal decision makers shown in Exhibit 3-8 is an expanded version of the preceding schedule.

## Summary of the C-V-P Analysis Computations

Exhibit 3-11 summarizes the equations that we used in our discussion of C-V-P analysis. Although it may be tempting to try to memorize them, you should strive to understand how these equations relate to one another.

# OTHER PLANNING ISSUES

7 How can decision makers use accounting information to evaluate alternative plans?

Providing answers to the previous three questions showed how C-V-P analysis is useful in planning. There are many other planning issues for which C-V-P analysis provides useful information. For instance, suppose you and Anna are considering alternative plans for Sweet Temptations to raise its monthly profit. These plans include:

1. Raising the selling price of the boxes of chocolates to $11 per box. With this alternative, the variable costs per box of chocolates and the total fixed costs do not change.
2. Purchasing a premium line of chocolates rather than the superior line, thus increasing the variable costs to $4.60 per box. You and Anna are considering this alternative because the improvement in the quality of the chocolate may cause the sales volume of boxes of chocolates to increase. With this change, neither the selling price per unit nor the total fixed costs change.
3. Increasing the total fixed costs by spending $110 more on advertising. With this alternative, the selling price per unit and the variable costs per unit do not change, but the additional advertising may cause an increase in sales volume.

*How would you modify the graph in Exhibit 3-10 to provide information for Plan #1?*

We do not show C-V-P analysis for these three issues at this time because we will discuss similar issues in Chapter 11. We raise these issues here to get you to think about how to use the C-V-P equations or graphs to provide helpful information. The C-V-P analysis for these three alternative plans, however, does not provide all the information you need to make a decision. It is a helpful tool, but it is most effective when used with critical thinking. You must think about the effects each of the alternatives has on your customers.

For instance, each of the alternatives is likely to affect the number of boxes of chocolates that Sweet Temptations can sell. A change in selling price would certainly affect your customers' decisions to purchase boxes of chocolates. A decrease in selling price would bring the boxes of chocolates into the spending range of more people (probably increasing the number of boxes of chocolates you could sell), whereas an increase in selling price may make the boxes of chocolates too expensive for some customers (possibly decreasing the number of boxes of chocolates you could sell). Selling a higher quality of chocolates may attract a different, or additional, group of customers, thus affecting sales volume. Increasing advertising may make more people aware of, and may attract more customers to, Sweet Temptations. Before you make a decision, you should consider how it will affect customers' interest in your product and estimate the probable unit sales volume for each alternative. Then, for whatever sales volume you expect, the analysis can provide a more realistic profit estimate.

## WHAT CAN HAPPEN IF A COMPANY DOESN'T HAVE A BUSINESS PLAN[b]

As the last century ended, many Internet companies were in such a rush to join their apparently wildly successful dot-com peers that they forgot one small detail: a sound business plan. By the end of 2001, more than 519 dot-com companies had failed. Some went bankrupt; others had to make radical adjustments to the way they conducted business, including massive layoffs (98,522 employees in 2000). Some such as Art.com and Wine.com began again with new owners and business plans, and still others simply shut down their Web sites.

A look back on that period reveals that many of those companies needed huge revenue growths just to break even. For example, the revenue of Tickets.com had increased by 38.77% during 2000—but in order to break even, the company's revenue would have had to grow 606.7%! Nineteen companies had an even more grim situation. The worst was E-Loan, whose revenue had increased by 85.24% during 2000—but whose revenue would have had to grow 5,065.2% in order for the company to break even! Both of these companies had failed by the end of 2000.

What happened? Many company owners, in an effort to compete and attract customers, thought they could start out selling their products for less than what they paid for them and then, after increasing their volume of customers, make up the difference later by raising the selling prices of their products. This means that they started out with negative contribution margins, causing them to lose money right from the start on every sale that they made. (And for some companies, even the low selling prices didn't attract enough customers.) Unfortunately, there was no "later," because these companies ran out of capital or attracted an insufficient number of customers to "make a go of it." Additionally, some owners didn't consider the extremely high costs necessary to run and advertise a Web site (particularly the marketing and salary costs), as well as the costs of storing and distributing their companies' products.

A business plan, along with its C-V-P analysis, could have helped the owners of these companies discover the "flaws" in their thinking before their companies got into trouble. With C-V-P analysis it would have been easy for them to confirm that the planned selling prices of their products initially would not have been high enough, *at any volume,* for the companies to break even. Furthermore, a business plan would have focused the owners' attention on the high marketing and salary costs, and the product storage and distribution costs, thereby helping the owners determine the selling prices that would most likely help their companies break even *and* earn desired profits. A business plan also could have helped the owners see the possible effects on their companies' profits of sales predictions that were too optimistic or too pessimistic.

## Business Issues and Values: Waste Not, Want Not

C-V-P accounting information is one factor that influences business decisions, but entrepreneurs also need to consider the nonfinancial effects of their decisions. For example, if the managers of a company are thinking about lowering the company's total costs by omitting toxic waste cleanup around the factory, they must ask questions such as the following: What will be the impact on the environment? What health effects might the employees suffer later? What might be the health impact on the company's neighbors? Legally, can we even consider not cleaning up the toxic waste? Although omitting toxic waste cleanup may reduce total costs dramatically, these managers might consider the other, more-difficult-to-measure costs to be too high. Therefore, after weighing all the factors surrounding the alternatives, the managers may choose a more socially acceptable alternative that results in a less favorable profit.

## Summary

At the beginning of the chapter we asked you several questions. During the chapter, we asked you to STOP and answer some additional questions to build your knowledge about specific issues. Be sure you answered these additional questions. Below are the questions from the beginning of the chapter, with a brief summary of the key points relating to the answers. Use your creative and critical thinking skills to expand on these key points to develop more complete answers to the questions and to determine what other questions you have that might lead you to learn more about the issues.

### 1 Since the future is uncertain and circumstances are likely to change, why should a company bother to plan?

A business plan helps the owners or managers of a company organize the company, serves as a benchmark against which they can evaluate actual company performance, and helps the company obtain financing. The business plan consists of a description of the company, a marketing plan, a description of the company's operations, and a financial plan. Accounting information contributes to the planning process by providing information for C-V-P analysis and by including in the financial plan the effects that estimated revenues, variable costs, and fixed costs have on the company's profits.

### 2 What should a company include in its business plan?

A business plan should include a description of the company, a marketing plan, a description of the operations of the company, and a financial plan. The description should include information about the organization of the company, its products or services, its current and potential customers, its objectives, where it is located, and where it conducts business. The marketing plan shows how the company will make sales and how it will influence and respond to market conditions. The company operations section includes a description of the relationships between the company, its suppliers, and its customers, as well as a description of how the company will develop, service, protect, and support its products or services. The financial plan identifies the company's capital requirements and sources of capital, and describes the company's projected financial performance.

### 3 How does accounting information contribute to the planning process?

Accountants determine how revenues, variable costs, and fixed costs affect profits based on their observations of how costs "behave" and on their estimates of future revenues and costs. By observing cost behavior patterns, accountants are able to classify the costs as fixed or variable, and then to use this classification to predict the amounts of the costs at different activity levels. Accounting information, then, can help decision-makers evaluate alternative plans by using C-V-P analysis to show the profit effect of each plan. C-V-P analysis is a tool that helps managers think critically about the different aspects of each plan.

### 4 What must decision makers be able to predict in order to estimate profit at a given sales volume?

To estimate profit at a given sales volume, decision makers must be able to predict the product's selling price, the costs that the company will incur, and the behavior of those costs (whether they are fixed or variable costs). The fixed costs will not change because of sales volume, but the variable costs will change directly with changes in sales volume.

### 5 How can decision makers predict the sales volume necessary for estimated revenues to cover estimated costs?

To predict the sales volume necessary for estimated revenues to cover estimated costs, decision makers must rearrange the profit equation into the break-even equation. Using what they know about the product's selling price and the behavior of the company's costs, the decision makers can determine the contribution margin per unit of product by subtracting the estimated variable costs per unit from the product's estimated selling price. Then they can substitute the contribution margin and the estimated fixed costs into the equation and solve for the necessary sales volume.

### 6 How can decision makers predict the sales volume necessary to achieve a target profit?

Predicting the sales volume necessary to achieve a target profit is not very different from predicting the sales volume necessary for estimated revenues to cover estimated costs. The only difference is that the decision makers must modify the break-even equation by adding the desired profit to the estimated fixed costs. Then, after substituting the contribution margin and the estimated fixed costs plus the desired profit into the equation, they can solve for the necessary sales volume.

### 7 How can decision makers use accounting information to evaluate alternative plans?

Decision makers can determine how changes in costs and revenues affect the company's profit. Based on accounting information alone, the alternative that leads to the highest profit will be the best solution. However, decision makers should also consider the nonfinancial effects that their decisions may have.

## Key Terms

**break-even point** *(p. 73)*
**business plan** *(p. 61)*
**capital** *(p. 65)*
**contribution margin per unit** *(p. 75)*
**cost-volume-profit (C-V-P) analysis** *(p. 68)*
**fixed costs** *(p. 69)*
**line of credit** *(p. 66)*
**long-term capital** *(p. 67)*
**return** *(p. 61)*
**risk** *(p. 61)*
**short-term capital** *(p. 66)*
**total contribution margin** *(p. 75)*
**total costs** *(p. 72)*
**variable cost** *(p. 70)*
**volume** *(p. 68)*

## Summary Surfing

Here is an opportunity to gather information on the Internet about real-world issues related to the topics in this chapter. Answer the following questions (for suggestions on how to navigate various organizations' Web sites to find the relevant information, see the related discussion in the Preface at the beginning of the book).

- Go to the **SBA (U.S. Small Business Administration)** Web site. What is the mission of the SBA? What percent of all employers are represented by the SBA? What percent of a loan can the SBA guarantee? What is the maximum interest rate allowed?
- Go to the **SBA (U.S. Small Business Administration)** Web site. What are the three elements (identified by roman numerals) of a business plan? Identify a few components under each section. What are the four distinct sections of a business plan? How do these compare with what we discussed in the chapter?

## Integrated Business and Accounting Situations

**Answer the Following Questions in Your Own Words.**

### Testing Your Knowledge

**3-1** Since the future is uncertain and circumstances are likely to change, why should the managers and owners of a company bother to plan?

**3-2** Describe the three main functions of a business plan.

**3-3** Describe the components of a business plan. How does each of these components help an investor, a creditor, and a manager or owner make decisions about a company?

**3-4** Why is it important for a company to have a cash buffer on hand?

**3-5** How can an entrepreneur determine a company's capital requirements?

**3-6** What is the difference between short-term and long-term capital?

**3-7** Explain what cost-volume-profit analysis is.

**3-8** How does cost-volume-profit analysis help entrepreneurs develop their companies' business plans?

**3-9** How can you tell whether a cost is a variable cost or a fixed cost?

**3-10** What is a contribution margin?

**3-11** Explain what it means when a company breaks even.

**3-12** Indicate the effect (increase, decrease, no change, or not enough information) that each of the following situations has on break-even unit sales. If you answer "not enough information," list the information that you need in order to be able to determine the effect.

(a) A retail company purchases price tags to use in place of the stickers it has used in the past.
(b) An athletic equipment store leases more retail space.
(c) A bakery increases its advertising expense.
(d) A merchandiser plans to increase the selling price of its product. To counter potential decreases in sales, the merchandiser also plans to increase the amount of per-product commission that the sales staff earns.

(e) An accounting firm plans to increase its billing rate per hour.
(f) A retail company has found a supplier that will provide the same merchandise its old supplier provided, but at a lower price.
(g) A private college in the Northwest installs air conditioning in its dormitories.
(h) A retail company reduces advertising expenses and increases the commissions of its sales force.
(i) Instead of having its office building cleaned by a cleaning service, a company plans to hire its own cleaning crew.

**3-13** If the total variable cost per unit increases while the selling price per unit, the fixed costs, and the sales volume remain the same, how would you expect the change in variable costs to affect profit? the break-even point?

**3-14** If total fixed costs increase while the selling price per unit, the variable costs per unit, and the sales volume remain the same, how would you expect the change in fixed costs to affect profit? the break-even point?

**3-15** How does the income statement shown in Exhibit 3-8 help internal decision makers perform cost-volume-profit analysis?

## Applying Your Knowledge

**3-16** Imagine that you are going to start your own company. Think about the concept for a minute.

*Required:* What will you call your company? What kind of product or service will you sell? What price will you charge for your product or service? Why? What variable costs and what fixed costs do you think you will incur?

**3-17** Suppose you want to start a company that sells sports equipment.

*Required:* Go to the reference section of your library. What type of information can you find in *Moody's* or *Standard & Poor's* to help you prepare projected financial statements for your company?

**3-18** TLC Company sells a single product, a food basket (containing fruit, cheese, nuts, and other items) that friends and family can purchase for college students who need a little extra TLC. This product, called the Exam-O-Rama, sells for $10 per basket. The variable cost is $6 per basket, and the total fixed cost is $24,000 per year.

*Required:* (1) Draw one graph showing TLC's (a) total revenues and (b) total costs as volume varies. Locate the break-even point on the graph.
(2) What is TLC's profit equation in terms of units sold?
(3) What is TLC's break-even point in units?

**3-19** Bathtub Rings Company sells shower-curtain rings for $1.60 per box. The variable cost is $1.20 per box, and the fixed cost totals $20,000 per year.

*Required:* (1) What is Bathtub Rings' profit equation in terms of boxes of shower-curtain rings sold?
(2) Draw a graph of Bathtub Rings' total contribution margin and total fixed cost as volume varies. Locate the break-even point on this graph.
(3) What is Bathtub Rings' break-even point in units?
(4) What would total profits be if Bathtub Rings sold 500,000 boxes of shower-curtain rings?
(5) How many boxes of shower-curtain rings would Bathtub Rings have to sell to earn $50,000 of profit?

**3-20** Go Figure Company sells small calculators for $12 each. This year, Go Figure's fixed cost totals $110,000. The variable cost per calculator is $7.

*Required:* (1) Compute the break-even point in number of calculators.
(2) Compute the number of calculators required to earn a profit of $70,000.

(3) If the total fixed cost increases to $160,000 next year,
(a) what will Go Figure's break-even point be in number of calculators?
(b) what profit (or loss) will Go Figure have if it sells 30,000 calculators?
(c) how many calculators will Go Figure have to sell to earn a profit of $70,000?

**3-21** Silencer Company sells a single product, mufflers for leaf blowers. The company's profit computation for last year is shown here:

| | |
|---|---|
| Sales revenue (2,000 units @ $25) | $50,000 |
| Less variable costs | (20,000) |
| Contribution margin | $30,000 |
| Less fixed costs | (22,000) |
| Profit | $ 8,000 |

Silencer has decided to increase the price of its product to $30 per muffler. The company believes that if it increases its fixed advertising (selling) cost by $3,400, sales volume next year will be 1,800 mufflers. Variable cost per muffler will be unchanged.

*Required:* (1) Using the above income statement format, show the computation of expected profit for Silencer's operations next year.
(2) How many mufflers would Silencer have to sell to earn as much profit next year as it did last year?
(3) Do you agree with Silencer's decision? Explain why or why not.

**3-22** Rapunzel Company currently sells a single product, shampoo, for $4 per bottle. The variable cost per bottle is $3. Rapunzel's fixed cost totals $6,000.

*Required:* (1) Compute the following amounts for Rapunzel Company:
(a) Contribution margin per bottle of shampoo
(b) Break-even point in bottles of shampoo
(c) The profit that Rapunzel will earn at a sales volume of 25,000 bottles of shampoo
(d) The number of bottles of shampoo that Rapunzel must sell to earn a profit of $16,000
(2) Rapunzel is considering increasing its total fixed cost to $8,000 and then also increasing the selling price of its product to $5. The variable cost per bottle of shampoo would remain unchanged. Repeat the computations from (1), using this new information. Will this decision be a good one for Rapunzel? Why or why not?
(3) Draw a graph with four lines to show the following:
(a) Total contribution margin earned when Rapunzel sells from 0 to 10,000 bottles of shampoo at a selling price of $4 per bottle
(b) Total contribution margin earned when Rapunzel sells from 0 to 10,000 bottles of shampoo at a selling price of $5 per bottle
(c) Rapunzel's fixed cost total of $6,000
(d) Rapunzel's fixed cost total of $8,000
(e) Rapunzel's break-even point in bottles of shampoo before and after the selling price and fixed cost changes
(4) Does the graph support your conclusion in (2) above? If so, how does it support your conclusion? If not, what new or different information did you get from the graph?

**3-23** The Body Shop Equipment Company sells a small, relatively lightweight multipurpose exercise machine. This machine sells for $700. A recent cost analysis shows that The Body Shop's cost structure for the coming year is as follows:

| | |
|---|---|
| Variable cost per unit | $ 325 |
| Total annual fixed costs | 125,000 |

*Required:* (1) Draw a graph that clearly shows (a) total fixed cost, (b) total cost, (c) total sales revenue, and (d) total contribution margin as the sales volume of exercise machines increases. Locate the break-even point on the graph.

(2) Compute the break-even point in number of machines.
(3) How many machines must the Body Shop sell to earn $30,000 of profit per year?
(4) How much profit would be earned at a sales volume of $420,000?
(5) Sean McLean, the owner of the Body Shop Equipment Company, is considering traveling a circuit of gyms and fitness centers around the United States each year to demonstrate the exercise machine, distribute information, and obtain sales contracts. He estimates that this will cost about $6,000 per year. How many additional exercise machines must the company sell per year to cover the cost of this effort?

**3-24** Lady MacBeth Company sells bottles of dry cleaning solvent (spot remover) for $10 each. The variable cost for each bottle is $4. Lady MacBeth's total fixed cost for the year is $3,600.

*Required:* (1) Answer the following questions about the company's break-even point.
(a) How many bottles of spot remover must Lady MacBeth sell to break even?
(b) How would your answer to (1a) change if Lady MacBeth lowered the selling price per bottle by $2? What if, instead, it raised the selling price by $2?
(c) How would your answer to (1a) change if Lady MacBeth raised the variable cost per bottle by $2? What if, instead, it lowered the variable cost by $2?
(d) How would your answer to (1a) change if Lady MacBeth increased the total fixed cost by $60? What if, instead, Lady MacBeth decreased the total fixed cost by $60?

(2) Answer the following questions about the company's profit.
(a) How many bottles must Lady MacBeth sell to earn $4,800 profit?
(b) How would your answer to (2a) change if Lady MacBeth lowered the selling price per bottle by $2?
(c) Suppose that for every $1 the selling price per bottle decreases below its current selling price of $10 per bottle, Lady MacBeth predicts sales volume will increase by 325 bottles. Assume that before lowering the selling price, Lady MacBeth predicts that it can sell exactly 1,400 bottles. Can Lady MacBeth earn $4,800 profit by lowering the selling price per bottle by $2? Explain why or why not.
(d) Suppose that for every $1 the selling price per bottle increases above its current selling price of $10 per bottle, Lady MacBeth predicts sales volume will decrease by 200 bottles. Assume that before raising the selling price, Lady MacBeth predicts that it can sell exactly 1,400 bottles. Can Lady MacBeth earn $4,800 profit by raising the selling price per bottle by $2? Explain why or why not.
(e) How would your answer to (2a) change if Lady MacBeth raised the variable cost per bottle by $2? What if, instead, it lowered the variable cost per bottle by $2?
(f) How would your answer to (2a) change if Lady MacBeth raised the total fixed cost by $60? What if, instead, Lady MacBeth lowered the total fixed cost by $60?

**3-25** The Brickhouse Company is planning to lease a fuel-efficient, hybrid delivery van for its northern sales territory. The leasing company is willing to lease the van under three alternative plans:

Plan A—Brickhouse would pay $0.34 per mile and buy its own gas.
Plan B—Brickhouse would pay $320 per month plus $0.10 per mile and buy its own gas.
Plan C—Brickhouse would pay $960 per month, and the leasing company would pay for all gas.

The leasing company will pay for all repairs and maintenance, insurance, license fees, and so on. Gas should cost $0.06 per mile.

*Required:* Using miles driven as the units of volume, do the following:

(1) Write out the cost equation for the cost of operating the delivery van under each of the three plans.
(2) Graph the three cost equations on the same graph (put cost on the vertical axis and miles driven per month on the horizontal axis).
(3) Determine at what mileage per month the cost of Plan A would equal the cost of Plan B.
(4) Determine at what mileage per month the cost of Plan B would equal the cost of Plan C.
(5) Compute the cost, under each of the three plans, of driving 3,500 miles per month.

**3-26** The Mallory Motors Company sells small electric motors for $2 per motor. Variable costs are $1.20 per unit, and fixed costs total $60,000 per year.

*Required:* (1) Write out Mallory's profit equation in terms of motors sold.
(2) Draw a graph of Mallory's total contribution margin and total fixed cost as volume varies. Locate the break-even point on this graph.
(3) Compute Mallory's break-even point in units.
(4) What total profit would Mallory expect if it sold 500,000 motors?
(5) How many motors would Mallory have to sell to earn $40,000 profit?

**3-27** The Campcraft Company is a small manufacturer of camping trailers. The company manufactures only one model and sells the units for $2,500 each. The variable costs of manufacturing and selling each trailer are $1,900. The total fixed cost amounts to $180,000 per year.

*Required:* (1) Compute Campcraft's contribution margin per trailer.
(2) Compute Campcraft's profit (or loss) at a sales volume of 160 trailers.
(3) Compute the number of units that Campcraft must sell for it to break even.
(4) Compute the number of units that Campcraft must sell for it to earn a profit of $30,000.

**3-28** This year Babco's fixed costs total $110,000. The company sells babushkas for $13 each. The variable cost per babushka is $8.

*Required:* (1) Compute the break-even point in number of babushkas.
(2) Compute the number of babushkas that Babco must sell to earn a profit of $70,000.
(3) If the total fixed cost increases to $150,000 next year,
(a) what will be Babco's break-even point in babushkas?
(b) what profit (or loss) will Babco have if it sells 28,000 babushkas?
(c) how many babushkas will Babco have to sell to earn a profit of $70,000?

**3-29** The Cardiff Company sells a single product for $40 per unit. Its total fixed cost amounts to $360,000 per year, and its variable cost per unit is $34.

*Required:* (1) Compute the following amounts for the Cardiff Company:
(a) Contribution margin per unit
(b) Break-even point in units
(c) The number of units that must be sold to earn $30,000 profit
(2) Repeat all computations in (1), assuming Cardiff decides to increase its selling price per unit to $44. Assume that the total fixed cost and the variable cost per unit remain the same.

## Making Evaluations

**3-30** Suppose your wealthy Aunt Gert gave you and your cousins $10,000 each. Assume for a moment that you are not associated with Sweet Temptations and that you are considering loaning the $10,000 to Sweet Temptations.

*Required:* From the information included in Sweet Temptations' business plan so far, do you think this would be a wise investment on your part? Why or why not? What else would you like to know before making a decision (you don't have to limit your thinking to Sweet Temptations)?

**3-31** Refer to 3-30. What if Aunt Gert instead gave you $100,000 and you were interested in investing it in Sweet Temptations?

*Required:* Would this change your answers to 3-30? Why or why not?

**3-32** Joe Billy Ray Bob's Country and Western Company sells a single product—cowboy hats—for $24 per hat. The total fixed cost is $180,000 per year, and the variable cost per hat is $15.

*Required:* (1) Compute the following amounts for Joe Billy Ray Bob's Country and Western Company:
(a) Contribution margin per hat
(b) Break-even point in hats
(c) The numbers of hats that must be sold to earn $27,000 of profit
(2) Repeat all computations in (1), assuming Joe Billy Ray Bob's decides to increase its selling price per hat to $25. Assume that the total fixed cost and the variable cost per hat remain the same.
(3) Do you agree with Joe Billy Ray Bob's decision to increase its selling price per hat? What other factors should the managers consider in making this decision?

**3-33** The Vend-O-Bait Company operates and services bait vending machines placed in gas stations, motels, and restaurants surrounding a large lake. Vend-O-Bait rents 200 machines from the manufacturer. It also rents the space occupied by the machines at each location where it places the machines. Arnie Bass, the company's owner, has two employees who service the machines. Monthly fixed costs for the company are as follows:

| | |
|---|---|
| Machine rental: | |
| 200 machines × $100 per month | $20,000 |
| Space rental: | |
| 200 locations × $60 per month | 12,000 |
| Employee wages: | |
| 2 employees × $800 per month | 1,600 |
| Other fixed costs | 2,400 |
| Total | $36,000 |

Currently, Vend-O-Bait's only variable costs are the costs of the night crawlers, which it purchases for $1.20 per pack. Vend-O-Bait sells these night crawlers for $1.80 per pack.

*Required:* (1) Answer the following questions:
(a) What is the monthly break-even point (in packs sold)?
(b) Compute Vend-O-Bait's monthly profit at monthly sales volumes of 52,000, 56,000, 64,000, and 68,000 packs, respectively.
(2) Suppose that instead of paying $60 fixed rent per month, Arnie Bass could arrange to pay $0.20 for each pack of night crawlers sold at each location to rent the space occupied by the machines. Repeat all computations in (1).
(3) Would it be desirable for Arnie Bass to try to change his space rental from a fixed cost ($60 per location) to a variable cost ($0.20 per pack sold)? Why or why not?

**3-34** Refer to 3-24. Suppose your boss at Lady MacBeth is considering some alternative plans and would like your input on the following three independent alternatives:
(a) Increase the selling price per bottle by $3
(b) Decrease the variable cost per bottle by $2 by purchasing an equally effective, but less "environmentally friendly," solvent from your supplier
(c) Decrease the total fixed cost by $1,260.

Assume again that Lady MacBeth currently sells bottles of dry cleaning solvent for $10 each, the variable cost for each bottle is $4, and the total fixed cost for the year is $3,600.

*Required:* (1) How many bottles would Lady MacBeth have to sell to break even under each of the alternatives? Using this accounting information alone, write your boss a memo in which you recommend an alternative.

(2) Maybe your boss would like to earn a profit of $4,320. How many bottles would Lady MacBeth have to sell to earn a profit of $4,320 under each of the alternatives? Which of the three alternatives would you recommend to your boss? Is this consistent with your recommendation in (1)? Why or why not? What other issues did you consider when making your recommendation?

**3-35** Japan's **Isuzu Motors Ltd.**, manufacturer of trucks and sports utility vehicles (SUVs), announced several years ago that it planned to eliminate 9,700 jobs (26% of its worldwide work force) over the next three years. Isuzu planned to achieve these job cuts through normal attrition, a freeze on hiring, and an early-retirement program. The company had experienced years of losses but predicted that it would earn a profit as early as the following year.[c]

*Required:* (1) What effect would you expect the decision to have on Isuzu's break-even point? on the number of trucks and SUVs Isuzu would have to sell to earn a desired profit?

(2) What nonfinancial issues do you think Isuzu's owners had to resolve in order to make this decision?

(3) What questions do you think the owners had to answer in order to resolve these issues?

**3-36** Suppose you work for the Miniola Hills Bus Company. The company's 10 buses made a total of 80 trips per day on 310 days last year, for a total of 350,000 miles. Another year like last year will put the company out of business (and you out of a job!). Your boss has come to you for help. Last year, instead of earning a profit, the company lost $102,000, as shown here:

| | | |
|---|---|---|
| Revenue from riders (496,000 @ $0.50) | | $248,000 |
| Less operating costs: | | |
| Depreciation on buses | $100,000 | |
| Garage rent | 20,000 | |
| Licenses, fees, and insurance | 40,000 | |
| Maintenance | 15,000 | |
| Drivers' salaries | 65,000 | |
| Tires | 20,000 | |
| Gasoline and oil | 90,000 | (350,000) |
| Loss | | ($102,000) |

Your boss is considering the following two plans for improving the company's profitability:

(a) Plan A—change the bus routes and reduce the number of trips to 60 per day in order to reduce the number of miles driven

(b) Plan B—sell bus tokens (five for $1.00) and student passes ($2.50 to ride all week) in order to increase the number of riders

*Required:* (1) Write your boss a memo discussing the effect that each of these plans might have on the costs and revenues of the bus company. Identify in your memo any assumptions you have made.

(2) If you were making this decision, what questions would you like answered before making the decision?

**3-37** Yesterday, you received the following letter for your advice column in the local paper:

**DR. DECISIVE**

Dear Dr. Decisive:

What do you think about this situation? My boyfriend refuses to meet me for lunch until I admit I am wrong about this, which I'm NOT. The other day, when we went to lunch at Subs and Floats on campus, he noticed that they had raised the price of BLT subs. He got mad because he thinks the only reason they raised the price was to increase their profit. I told him that, first of all, their profit might not increase and that, second, he was basing his conclusion on some assumptions that might not be true and that if he would just *open up his mind,* he might see how those assumptions are affecting his conclusion. Well, *then* he got mad at *me.* I'm really upset because I know I'm right and because now I have to buy my own lunch. Will you please explain why I'm right? I know he'll listen to you (he reads your column daily). Until you answer, I'll be

"Starving."

*Required:* Meet with your Dr. Decisive team and write a response to "Starving."

## END NOTES

[a]Pete Weaver, "Need a Loan? See Your State," *National Business,* April 1995, 51R.

[b]"What detonated dot-bombs?" *USA Today,* December 4, 2000, 2A,2B; "Dot-coms without plans die," *USA Today,* December 4, 2000, 2B; "Dead and (Mostly) Gone," *Fortune,* December 24, 2001, 46,47.

[c]http://www.cnnfn.cnn.com/news/specials/layoffs, May 28, 2001.

CHAPTER 4

# DEVELOPING A BUSINESS PLAN: BUDGETING

"ADVENTURE IS THE RESULT OF POOR PLANNING."

—COLONEL BLATCHFORD SNELL

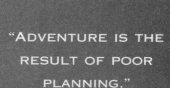

1. How does a budget contribute toward helping a company achieve its goals?
2. Do the activities of a company have a logical order that drives the organization of a budget?
3. What is the structure of the budgeting process, and how does a company begin that process?
4. What are the similarities and differences between a retail company's master budget and a service company's master budget?
5. After a company begins the budgeting process, is there a strategy it can use to complete the budget?
6. How can a manager use a budget to evaluate a company's performance and then use the results of that evaluation to influence the company's plans?

Unless you have been lucky enough to win the lottery, you probably have to budget your money. (Even if you *have* won the lottery, you probably want to budget your money.) Think for a minute about where you get your money. Do you receive cash from a job, a scholarship, financial aid, your parents, or some combination of these sources? Now think about where you spend your money. Most likely you spend it on day-to-day living expenses such as food, rent, utilities, and miscellaneous items, as well as on college-related costs such as tuition, fees, and books. Budgeting helps you to estimate when—and how much—cash will come in, and also helps you figure out when—and how much—cash you will need to pay out. With these estimates, you can plan your activities so that you have enough cash to pay for them.

*Suppose in budgeting your future cash payments, you realize that unless something changes, you will not have enough cash to pay your next car insurance bill. What alternatives do you have to solve this problem?*

Companies must budget their resources too. For most companies, **budgeting** is a formal part of the ongoing planning process and periodically results in a set of related reports called *budgets*. A **budget** is a report that gives a financial description of one part of a company's planned activities for the budget period. For example, a budget might show how many products the company plans to sell during the next year, the dollar amount of these sales, and when the company will collect the cash from these sales. Another budget might show how much cash a company plans to spend during the same year renting business space, employing workers, and advertising its products, and also when the company plans to incur these costs.

## WHY BUDGET?

Budgeting improves the planning, operating, and evaluating processes by helping an entrepreneur

- add discipline, or order, to the planning process,
- recognize and avoid potential operating problems,
- quantify plans, and
- create a "benchmark" for evaluating the company's performance.

1 How does a budget contribute toward helping a company achieve its goals?

THE FAR SIDE® By GARY LARSON

**Early business failures**

How do you think a business plan could have helped this company?

### Budgeting Adds Discipline

Companies survive or fail because of the financial results of their activities. Therefore, *before implementing planning decisions,* effective entrepreneurs carefully think about what will happen as a result of these decisions. That's where budgeting comes in; the more complete and detailed the planning process is, the easier it is for an entrepreneur to foresee what might happen. Budgets add discipline because of their orderliness and detail.

### Budgeting Highlights Potential Problems

Using budgeting to describe a company's plans allows the entrepreneur to uncover potential problems before they occur and to spot omissions or inconsistencies in the plans. For example, you and Anna may plan for Sweet Temptations to sell more boxes of chocolates in February than during other months because of expected Valentine's Day sales. Through the budgeting process, you may discover that unless something changes, Sweet Temptations will not have enough boxes of chocolates on hand in February to fill the expected customer orders. By seeing this problem ahead of time, you and Anna can adjust your purchase plans, perhaps preventing disappointed customers from having to go elsewhere to buy candy.

If you and Anna decide to purchase more chocolates in January and February because of expected increases in sales, Sweet Temptations will also have a higher bill from Unlimited Decadence. You and Anna will need to plan to have enough cash on hand to pay the bill when it is due. This plan will show up in the part of the budget that shows expected *purchases.* The budgeting process helps the entrepreneur see and evaluate how changes in plans affect different parts of a company's operations.

### Budgeting Quantifies Plans

Business plans include the operating activities needed to meet the company's goals. A budget quantifies, or expresses in numbers, these operating activities and goals. For example, most companies have a goal of earning a specific profit for the budget year. This is stated in their business plans. Recall from Chapter 3 that Sweet Temptations included in its business plan a goal of earning a profit of \$110 per month, or \$1,320 (\$110 × 12) during the coming year. The C-V-P analysis included in the business plan in Chapter 3 indicates that to earn this profit, Sweet Temptations must have monthly sales averaging 720 boxes of chocolates, so during the year it must sell at least 8,640 boxes (720 × 12) of chocolates. Sweet Temptations' budget will indicate how many boxes of chocolates it plans to sell each month of the year to meet its profit goal and how many boxes it must purchase each month to support its projected sales.

Budgeting also quantifies the resources that the company expects to use for its planned sales and purchasing activities. For example, if Sweet Temptations must purchase 900 boxes of chocolates to cover its expected sales for any given month, the budget will indicate how much (and when) Sweet Temptations expects to pay for these chocolates.

### Budgeting Creates Benchmarks

Since budgets help quantify plans, an entrepreneur also uses budgets as "benchmarks." The entrepreneur periodically compares the results of the company's actual operating activities with the related budget amounts. These comparisons measure the company's progress toward achieving its goals and help the entrepreneur evaluate how efficiently the company is using its resources. The comparisons also help the entrepreneur focus on what changes should be made, if any, to bring the company's operating activities more in line with its goals. To save time and effort, the entrepreneur uses a management principle known as **management by exception**. Under this principle, the entrepreneur focuses on improving the activities that show significant differences (or exceptions) between budgeted and actual results. These activities have the greatest potential for positively influencing the company's operations.

## Operating Cycles

2 Do the activities of a company have a logical order that drives the organization of a budget?

Earlier, we referred to the operating activities of a company. The operating activities of a company depend on whether it is a retail, service, or manufacturing company because each of these different types of companies has a different operating cycle. In budgeting, a company quantifies its planned activities in relation to its operating cycle. This process is similar to when you prepare your personal budget for the semester. Before we get into the details of budgeting, we will briefly discuss the operating cycles of retail and service companies. We will discuss the operating cycle of a manufacturing company in Chapter 12.

### The Operating Cycle of a Retail Company

A **retail company's operating cycle** is the average time it takes the company to use cash to buy goods for sale (called *inventory*), to sell these goods to customers, and to collect cash from its customers. Sweet Temptations' operating cycle is the time it takes to pay cash to purchase boxes of chocolates from Unlimited Decadence, to sell these chocolates to customers, and to collect the cash from the customers. Unlimited Decadence allows Sweet Temptations to "charge" its purchases of boxes of chocolates. From Sweet Temptations' point of view, these are called *credit purchases* and result in *accounts payable.* Similarly, although most of Sweet Temptations' sales are cash sales, it also allows some of its customers to "charge" their purchases of chocolates. (These purchases are made on "charge accounts" set up directly between the customers and Sweet Temptations; they are not made on charge cards such as VISA or Discover.) From Sweet Temptations' point of view, sales to these customers are called *credit sales* and result in *accounts receivable.*

*From the customers' point of view, what do you think Sweet Temptations' credit sales to them are called?*

Sweet Temptations will pay cash for its accounts payable to Unlimited Decadence within 30 days of the purchases. Similarly, Sweet Temptations will collect cash from customers' accounts receivable within a few days after their purchases of chocolates. We will talk more about how a company decides to extend credit to customers later in this chapter and in Chapter 9.

Exhibit 4-1 shows Sweet Temptations' operating cycle. As you will see later, Sweet Temptations' budgeting process quantifies its operating cycle and its other activities.

## The Operating Cycle of a Service Company

Service companies have a budgeting process that is very similar to that of retail companies. One major difference between these two types of companies, however, involves their operating cycles. A **service company's operating cycle** is the average time it takes the company to use cash to acquire supplies and services, to sell the services to customers, and to collect cash from its customers.

Exhibit 4-2 shows the operating cycle of Hasty Transfer Company, a shipping company hired by Unlimited Decadence to ship its chocolates to Sweet Temptations and other retail companies around the country. This operating cycle may be shorter than that of a retail company because there is no inventory to purchase.

**EXHIBIT 4-1 SWEET TEMPTATIONS' OPERATING CYCLE**

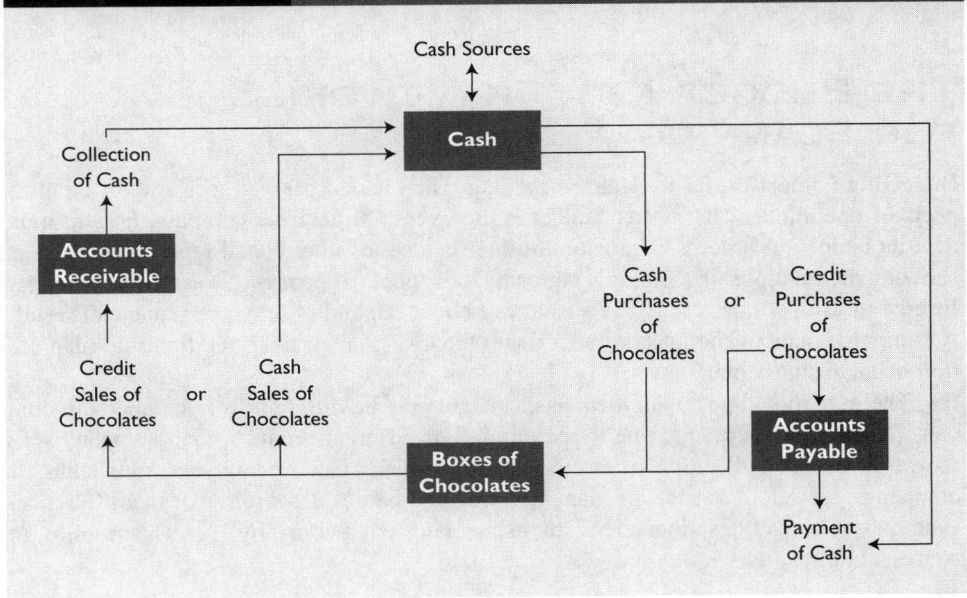

**EXHIBIT 4-2 HASTY TRANSFER'S OPERATING CYCLE**

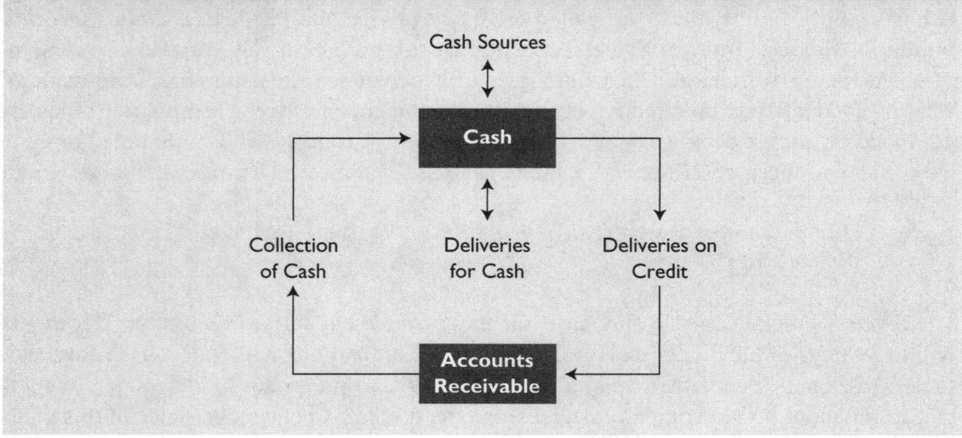


The operating cycle for some service companies can be much longer than the cycle for most retail companies because for these service companies, one service, or job, can take months or years. For example, think about the life of some of the advertising campaigns you have observed recently. For instance, the Energizer Bunny (batteries) and Tony the Tiger (cereal) have been around for years (or decades). Many service companies with long jobs try to shorten their operating cycles by periodically collecting payments from their customers for completed segments of the work. Hasty Transfer's operating cycle, on the other hand, could average only two or three days, since it delivers perishable candy to companies in the same city in which Unlimited Decadence's factory is located and also to companies around the country. The length of Hasty Transfer's operating cycle depends on Hasty's collection policies and when it expects to be paid by its customers. Like Sweet Temptations, Hasty Transfer quantifies its operating cycle and other activities in a budget.

*How long do you think a university's or college's operating cycle is? What are the components of its operating cycle?*

## THE BUDGET AS A FRAMEWORK FOR PLANNING

**3** What is the structure of the budgeting process, and how does a company begin that process?

Budgeting is most useful in decision-making when it is organized to show different aspects of operations. The master budget is the overall structure a company uses to organize its budgeting process. A **master budget** is a set of interrelated reports (or budgets) showing the relationships among a company's (1) goals to be met, (2) activities to be performed in its operating cycle, (3) resources to be used, and (4) expected financial results. A company includes the master budget with the C-V-P analysis in the financial plan section of its business plan.

The individual budgets in the master budget may be different from company to company. These differences are due to the number of different products each company sells, the varying sizes and complexities of the companies and their operations, and whether the companies are retail, service, or manufacturing companies. Regardless of the differences, each master budget describes the relationships between a company's goals, activities, resources, and results.

© PHOTOPIA

The "Tony the Tiger" advertising campaign has been around for decades. Do you think the agency's operating cycle is *that* long?

A master budget for a retail company usually includes the following budgets and projected financial statements:

1. Sales budget
2. Purchases budget
3. Selling expenses budget
4. General and administrative expenses budget
5. Cash budget (projected cash flow statement)
6. Projected income statement
7. Projected balance sheet

A service company's master budget does not include a purchases budget and usually combines the expenses budgets. A manufacturing company's master budget includes additional budgets related to its manufacturing activities.

4 What are the similarities and differences between a retail company's master budget and a service company's master budget?

A company prepares its annual master budget for a year or more into the future. It breaks the master budget down by each budget period—generally by quarter (three-month period). Within each quarter, it shows the budget information on a monthly basis. Some companies develop budgets for each department which they then combine to form a master budget. For example, **JCPenney** might develop budgets for apparel, for housewares, for bed and bath accessories, for optical departments, and for styling salons.

Exhibit 4-3 shows (with arrows) the important relationships among the reports in Sweet Temptations' master budget. Notice that the last budgets prepared in a company's budgeting process are the projected financial statements for the budget period: the cash budget (also called a *projected cash flow statement*), the projected income statement, and the projected balance sheet. The projected financial statements give managers a "preview" of what the company's actual financial statements should look like at the end of the budget period *if everything goes according to plan.* The information for these projected financial statements comes from the other budgets.

We will discuss the nature and the relationships of Sweet Temptations' budgets to illustrate how a retail company plans and describes its operating activities. Since Sweet

**EXHIBIT 4-3 INTERRELATIONSHIPS AMONG BUDGET SCHEDULES IN THE MASTER BUDGET**

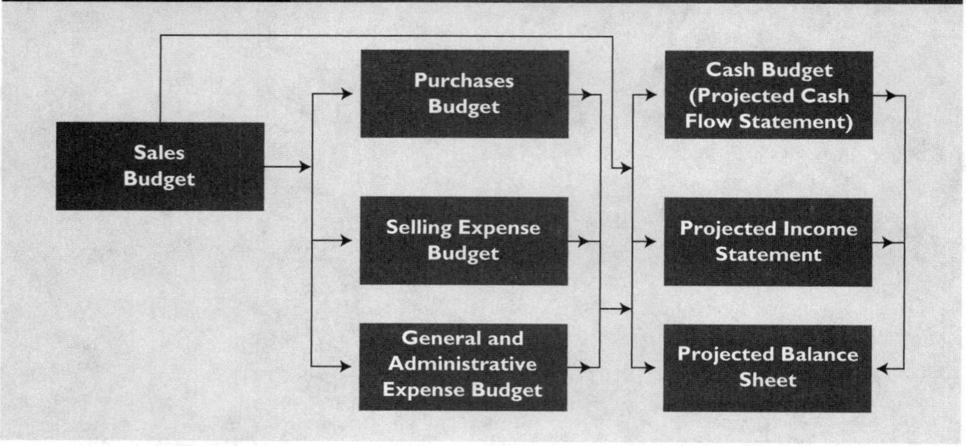


Temptations is a small company, the illustrations will be simple. The larger a company is, the more complex and detailed its budget reports must be to be useful. Often, though, managers of large companies prepare summaries similar to the simpler budgets that we use in this chapter.

When you look at the budgets for Sweet Temptations, try to understand the logic of their development and how they interrelate. As you study the budgets, remember the following "start-up" information from Chapter 3. During December 2007 Anna plans to

- invest $15,000 in Sweet Temptations,
- rent store space for $1,000 per month, paying $6,000 in advance for six months' rent,
- buy $1,800 of store equipment by making a $1,000 down payment and signing a note payable for the remaining amount,
- order 360 boxes of chocolates from Unlimited Decadence for $1,620, to be paid for in January 2008,
- purchase and pay for $700 of supplies.

For each budget, we will also briefly discuss the similar budget for Hasty Transfer, a service company.

## The Sales Budget

5 After a company begins the budgeting process, is there a strategy it can use to complete the budget?

The budgeting process begins with the sales budget because product sales or service contracts affect all the other operating activities of a company. (Without sales of chocolates, why would Sweet Temptations be in business? Without arrangements with Unlimited Decadence and other companies to ship chocolates and other goods, why would Hasty Transfer exist?) A retail company without sales would not need employees, inventory, retail space, store equipment, supplies, advertising, or utilities. As you will soon see, the same is true for a service company. For this reason, the sales budget affects all of the other budgets.

### The Retail Company's Sales Budget

For a retail company, the **sales budget** shows the number of units of inventory that the company expects to sell each month, the related monthly sales revenue, and in which months the company expects to collect cash from these sales. To estimate the number of units of inventory it will sell in each month, a company gathers various types of information, such as past sales data, industry trends, and economic forecasts. If Sweet Temptations were an older company, you and Anna might analyze Sweet Temptations' past sales trends to get an idea about what sales level to expect for the future. However, you should also consider the current economic conditions or circumstances that affect the candy industry.

For example, if the economy has worsened and people are struggling to get food on the table, customers may view the purchase of chocolates as a luxury, and sales may drop, regardless of the level of past sales. On the other hand, if the economy is improving, people may have extra income to spend (extra disposable income), and sales of candy may increase. New findings and breakthroughs also can affect sales. For example, several years ago, **Ross-Abbott Labs** manufactured and helped test a cholesterol-lowering candy bar called a Cardiobar. Volunteers who tested the cardiobars, which come in chocolate and raspberry flavors, lowered their cholesterol level by 33 points! Those who ate look-alike candy bars had no significant change in their cholesterol levels. If Ross-Abbott Labs ever markets the candy bars, their sales may affect the sales of other candy bars already on the market.[a]

*How do you think a well-publicized discovery that sugar is actually good for people would affect your prediction of candy sales for next year?*

Market analysts or consultants are another source of information about the estimated number of products to be sold. Although Anna has a marketing degree, she is busy getting the company "up and running." Therefore, she has hired Joe Smiley (see Exhibit 3-2) to study the market for boxed chocolates in the area north of the metroplex and provide an analysis, including a report on the effect that different prices would have on potential sales of the chocolates. Joe's research should help Anna predict sales during Sweet Temptations' first year of operations. Large companies have additional sources of market information, including their sales forces as well as marketing and advertising specialists. We will discuss the sources in Chapter 12.

After a company has estimated the amount of inventory it expects to sell, it determines its estimated sales revenue by multiplying the number of units of inventory it expects to sell by the unit selling price. After computing its monthly estimated sales revenue, the company determines how much cash it expects to collect each month from sales. If all sales are cash sales, the cash to be collected each month is equal to the sales revenue of that month. For most companies, however, a portion (sometimes substantial) of their sales are credit sales. If a company allows credit sales, its cash collections of accounts receivable will lag behind its sales revenues.

*What do you think is the difference between cash sales and sales revenue? Are they the same thing?*

The credit-granting policy of a company can have a great impact on the length of time between the sale of its product and the collection of cash from that sale. You and Anna would certainly not grant credit to a customer with a poor credit history because there would be a good chance that the customer either will pay you a long time after the sale, pay you only part of the bill, or not pay you at all. Many companies spend a lot of time and effort studying the paying habits of their customers and deciding on an appropriate credit-granting policy. The goal is to shorten the time between sales and collections of cash, and reduce the risk of not being able to collect from their customers. At the same time, companies don't want an overly restrictive credit policy that discourages customers from buying on credit.

*What information about a customer do you think would be helpful in Sweet Temptations' decision of whether or not to grant the customer credit?*

Anna has decided to grant credit to a few nearby companies, hoping they will make numerous purchases. To start, Anna estimates that these credit sales will be about 5 percent of total sales. She has also decided to give these credit customers terms of n/10 ("net 10"), which means that they will pay Sweet Temptations within ten days of when they make credit purchases. Anna selected n/10 because Sweet Temptations is a new company and she does not think it should wait more than ten days to receive cash from its credit customers. Because of this policy, Sweet Temptations will collect roughly two-thirds of each month's credit sales in the month of the sales and the remaining one-third of the credit sales in the following month.

Exhibit 4-4 shows the relationship between Sweet Temptations' January credit sales and its cash collections from these sales. This diagram shows that the sales revenue is earned at the time of the credit sale. However, the cash collection from the credit sale occurs ten days after the sale takes place. As you can see in the exhibit, cash collections from January credit sales occur partly in January and partly in February. For instance, the cash collections from the January 1 credit sales occur on about January 11, and the cash collections from the credit sales on January 31 occur on about February 10.

Exhibit 4-5 shows the sales budget of Sweet Temptations for the first quarter of 2008. The sales amounts are based on Joe Smiley's market analysis. Notice that it shows budgeted sales for each month both in units (boxes of chocolates) and in dollars of sales revenue, and that the monthly sales amounts are added across to show the quarter totals (2,460 units; $24,600 sales revenue). Also notice that the sales budget divides total sales each month between cash sales and credit sales.

*How do you think dividing total monthly sales between cash sales and credit sales helps in the creation of the rest of the sales budget?*

### The Service Company's Sales Budget

The sales budget of a service company is very similar to the sales budget of a retail company, except that the former is selling services rather than products. When Hasty Transfer budgets its sales, it is budgeting sales of delivery services. Expected cash collections from customers depend on Hasty's collection policies. For example, Hasty may expect to be paid by its customers when it picks up merchandise the customers want to ship. On the other hand, Hasty may expect to be paid by its customers only after it delivers the customers' merchandise. Furthermore, Hasty may grant credit to some of its customers—a policy that also will affect the timing of its cash receipts.

**EXHIBIT 4-4 RELATIONSHIP BETWEEN CREDIT SALES AND CASH COLLECTIONS**

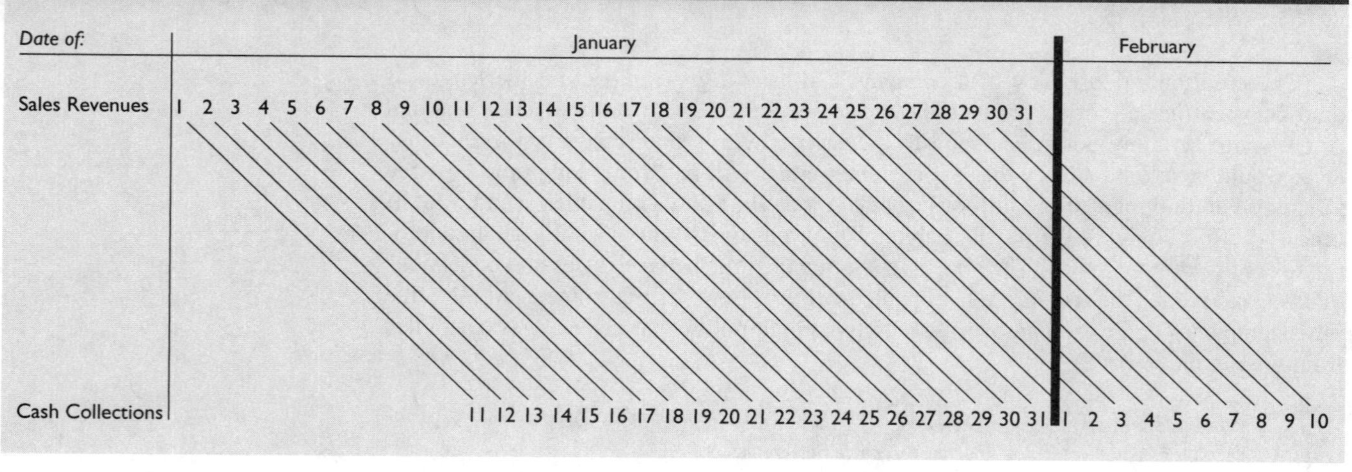

**EXHIBIT 4-5** **SALES BUDGET**

**SWEET TEMPTATIONS**
***Sales Budget***
***First Quarter 2008***

| | January | February | March | Quarter |
|---|---|---|---|---|
| Budgeted total unit sales | | | | |
| (boxes of chocolates) | 720 | 1,200 | 540 | 2,460 |
| Budgeted selling price per box | $ 10 | $ 10 | $ 10 | $ 10 |
| Budgeted total sales revenue | $7,200 | $12,000 | $5,400 | $24,600 |
| Budgeted cash sales | | | | |
| (95% of total sales revenue) | $6,840 | $11,400 | $5,130 | $23,370 |
| Budgeted credit sales | | | | |
| (5% of total sales revenue) | 360 | 600 | 270 | 1,230 |
| Budgeted total sales revenue | $7,200 | $12,000 | $5,400 | $24,600 |
| Expected cash collections: | | | | |
| From cash sales | $6,840 | $11,400 | $5,130 | $23,370 |
| From January credit sales | 240* | 120* | | 360 |
| From February credit sales | | 400* | 200* | 600 |
| From March credit sales | | | 180* | 180 |
| Total cash collections | $7,080 | $11,920 | $5,510 | $24,510 |

*Sweet Temptations estimates that it will collect two-thirds of each month's credit sales during the month of sale. It will collect the remaining one-third in the month following the sale.

*Several years ago, a new airline called Air South began flying from Jacksonville, Florida, to Atlanta, Georgia. The fare for the trip at that time was $19 plus a first-class stamp. How do you think Air South budgeted its cash receipts? How do you think Air South is doing now?*

### Seasonal Sales

Some companies' sales occur evenly throughout the year. Other companies experience *seasonal sales.* That is, these companies' customers purchase the inventory or services more often in some months than in others. The sale of ski apparel is an example of seasonal sales. Although ski shops sell some ski apparel throughout the year, most of their sales occur right before and during ski season. A company offering skiing lessons (a service) may not even be open during the summer. The sale of candy is not as extreme, but it does have some seasonality. For Sweet Temptations, monthly sales differences during its first quarter reflect an expected increase in sales as Valentine's Day approaches.

*What other seasonal effects would you expect for Sweet Temptations?*

## The Retail Company's Purchases Budget

Once a company has estimated (budgeted) its unit sales for each month of the quarter, it can determine the best approach for purchasing the needed inventory. Sweet Temptations expects to sell 2,460 boxes of chocolates this quarter (from the sales budget in Exhibit 4-5). You may be wondering how many of those boxes Sweet Temptations should be ordering now. In making this purchase decision, you should consider several factors.

First, there are the costs of keeping the company's money invested in inventory (rather than investing it somewhere else), of storing and handling inventory, and of paying for insurance and taxes on inventory. Higher inventory levels also increase the risk of theft, damage, and obsolescence. If Sweet Temptations holds too many boxes of chocolates, you and Anna risk either selling chocolates that are not fresh and losing future customers, or having to throw away old chocolates. (Or, with more chocolates around, you may be more tempted to eat the inventory!) Also, there is a physical limit to the number of boxes you can stock in the candy store. For these reasons, some companies use "just-in-time" (JIT) inventory systems, in which they purchase inventory a day before they need it. We will discuss JIT inventory systems in Chapter 18 of Volume 2.

On the other hand, it also can be very expensive not to carry enough inventory. For example, if Sweet Temptations starts running low on chocolates, it may have to pay Hasty Transfer higher shipping costs for rush orders or pay Unlimited Decadence higher costs per box for smaller, last-minute orders. You may also risk alienating customers if you run out of inventory. Every company must plan its own inventory levels, considering the costs of both carrying and not carrying inventory and trying to keep the combined total at the lowest possible amount. We will discuss this planning decision more fully in Chapter 15. Even though the purchases budget does not address all of the above factors, it will help you and Anna make the best purchase decision.

The **purchases budget** shows the purchases (in units) required in each month to make the expected sales (from the sales budget) in that month and to keep inventory at desired levels. It also shows the costs of these purchases and the expected timing and amount of the cash payments for these purchases.

Frequently, companies set desired end-of-month inventory levels at either a constant percentage of the following month's budgeted unit sales or at large enough levels to meet future sales for a specified time. Since many companies base their purchase orders on sales *estimates,* they want to have extra inventory available to sell in case they have underestimated their sales or in case their next shipment of inventory arrives later than expected.

Anna plans to order chocolates from Unlimited Decadence once every month. She has also decided that during any month, Sweet Temptations should have enough candy on hand to cover that month's candy sales and also to have an ending inventory large enough to cover one-half of the next month's sales. For example, projected sales for the first quarter of 2008 (from the sales budget in Exhibit 4-5) and for April (from projections for the second quarter) are as follows:

| | January | February | March | April |
|---|---|---|---|---|
| Budgeted total unit sales (boxes of chocolates) | 720 | 1,200 | 540 | 900 |

Based on Anna's purchasing policy, Sweet Temptations must have enough inventory during January to equal budgeted sales for January plus one-half of budgeted sales for February, or 1,320 boxes of chocolates [720 boxes + ½ (1,200)]. (Then, if Sweet Temptations sells 720 boxes during January, it will have inventory at the end of January equal to half of February's budgeted sales.) Since Sweet Temptations will start business in January with the 360 boxes of chocolates purchased in December (½ of the 720 January budgeted sales), January purchases must be 960 boxes (1,320 total boxes needed − 360 boxes already on hand). Sweet Temptations uses the same calculations to determine each month's purchases of boxes of chocolates. Exhibit 4-6 illustrates how budgeted purchases and budgeted sales are linked together for the first quarter of the year.

*What do you think are the advantages of Anna's plans to order chocolates once per month rather than more often?*

Normally, Sweet Temptations will make purchases during the first week of each month and will receive delivery of the purchases at the beginning of the second week of the month. However, since Sweet Temptations will open for business in January, it must purchase 360 boxes of chocolates in mid-December so that they will be available to sell on

## EXHIBIT 4-6 THE LINK BETWEEN BUDGETED PURCHASES AND BUDGETED SALES

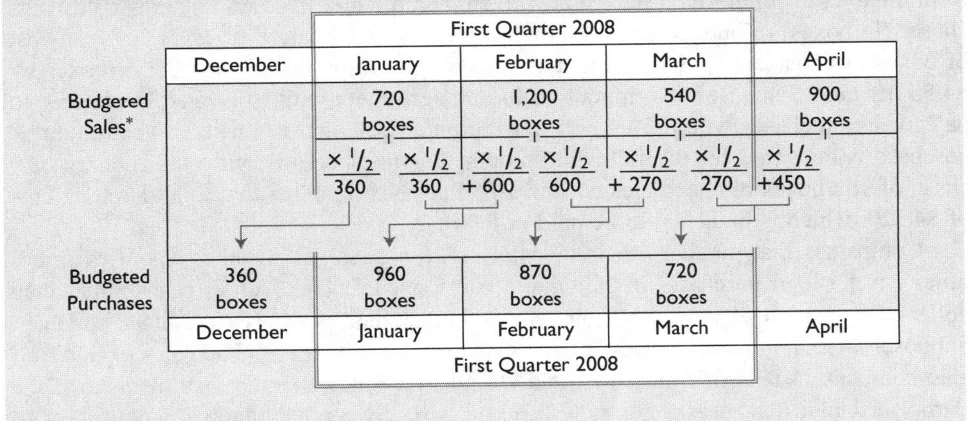


*From Exhibit 4-5, except April, which was estimated as part of second-quarter projections.

the first day of business in January. No sales of chocolates will occur in December, so the amount of chocolates that Sweet Temptations purchases in December will still be in Sweet Temptations' inventory at the end of December (and at the beginning of January).

Exhibit 4-7 shows the purchases budget of Sweet Temptations for the first quarter of 2008. Remember that Sweet Temptations wants to purchase enough boxes of chocolates

## EXHIBIT 4-7 PURCHASES BUDGET

**SWEET TEMPTATIONS**
***Purchases Budget***
***First Quarter 2008***

| | January | February | March | Quarter |
|---|---|---|---|---|
| Budgeted total unit sales (boxes of chocolates) | 720 | 1,200 | 540 | 2,460 |
| Add: Desired ending inventory of boxes of chocolates* | 600 | 270 | 450† | 450‡ |
| Total boxes of chocolates required | 1,320 | 1,470 | 990 | 2,910 |
| Less: Beginning inventory of boxes of chocolates§ | (360)¶ | (600) | (270) | (360)** |
| Budgeted purchases of boxes of chocolates | 960 | 870 | 720 | 2,550 |
| Purchase price per box of chocolates | $ 4.50 | $ 4.50 | $ 4.50 | $ 4.50 |
| Cost of purchases | $4,320 | $3,915 | $3,240 | $ 11,475 |
| Cash payments for purchases | $1,620¶ | $4,320 | $3,915 | $ 9,855 |

*The desired ending inventory is 1/2 of next month's budgeted sales.
†April's budgeted sales are 900 boxes of chocolates.
‡The desired ending inventory at the end of the quarter is the same as the desired ending inventory at the end of March (which is the end of the quarter).
§The beginning inventory is the same as the previous month's ending inventory.
¶360 boxes of chocolates, at a total purchase price of $1,620, ordered in December 2007 to prepare for the start of business.
**The quarter's beginning inventory is the same as December's ending inventory (January's beginning inventory).

each month to meet budgeted sales during the month and to have enough boxes left at the end of the month to cover one-half of the next month's sales. These boxes must come from the inventory on hand at the beginning of the month and from any purchases that the company makes during the month. By subtracting the budgeted beginning inventory from the total inventory required for any given month, you can determine how many purchases (in boxes) to budget for that month. Since purchases are a *variable* cost, the cost of boxes of chocolates purchased is determined by multiplying the number of boxes by $4.50 per unit. Since Sweet Temptations has an agreement with Unlimited Decadence to pay for its purchases within 30 days after the purchases, the payment for each month's purchase is budgeted for the following month. For instance, the budgeted January purchase of 960 boxes of chocolates costing $4.50 per box amounts to a total purchase cost of $4,320, which is budgeted to be paid in February.

Companies that purchase their inventories from suppliers in other countries sometimes pay for their purchases in the other countries' currencies (yen or pesos rather than dollars, for example). These companies should budget their purchases in dollars, however. Suppose, for example, that Sweet Temptations purchased boxes of chocolates from a Belgian company instead of from Unlimited Decadence. Since Belgium is a member of the European Union that uses a currency called a *euro,* Sweet Temptations would have to convert euros to dollars when preparing its purchases budget.

Remember that budgets represent a company's *plans* and are based on estimates. As new information becomes available, the company sometimes changes its plans.

*Suppose that January sales turn out to be 1,010 boxes of chocolates. Should Sweet Temptations change its plans for February and March? What questions should you ask before deciding whether the plans should change, which part of the plans should change, and by how much?*

## The Retail Company's Selling Expenses Budget

To sell its inventory, a retail company must engage in selling activities. The **selling expenses budget** shows the expenses and related cash payments associated with planned selling activities. Examples of selling expenses include salespeople's salaries and commissions, store rent, and advertising. Each of these expenses directly relates to sales.

A selling expenses budget is developed by reviewing past selling expenses (if they are available) and then adjusting them for current plans. It is important for the entrepreneur to understand prior cost behavior patterns when creating a selling expenses budget because some selling expenses are *variable* and change directly with the amount of inventory sold whereas some remain *fixed* regardless of the sales volume. By applying these behavior patterns, the entrepreneur can predict what each selling expense will be at a given estimated sales volume. Sales commissions are an example of variable selling expenses, since total sales commissions increase in direct proportion to increases in sales. Store rent and advertising, on the other hand, are fixed selling expenses, in many cases, because total rent and advertising expenses stay the same as sales increase during the period. In developing a selling expenses budget, the entrepreneur should also be able to distinguish selling expenses from general and administrative expenses. Sometimes fixed expenses must be allocated on a reasonable basis between the two types of expenses.

Exhibit 4-8 shows the selling expenses budget for Sweet Temptations for the first quarter of 2008. The January expenses are the same items listed in Exhibit 3-8 in Chapter 3. These expenses are all *fixed* expenses, so Sweet Temptations expects them to be the same in all three months. (Remember, though, that selling expenses also can be variable expenses.) Not all the *amounts* from Exhibit 3-8 are related to selling activities, however. You and Anna have estimated that three-fourths of each of the following expenses is tied directly to selling activities. The other one-fourth of each expense is tied to the administrative

**EXHIBIT 4-8 SELLING EXPENSES BUDGET**

**SWEET TEMPTATIONS**
***Selling Expenses Budget***
***First Quarter 2008***

| | January | February | March | Quarter |
|---|---|---|---|---|
| Budgeted selling expenses:* | | | | |
| Rent expense | $ 750.00 | $ 750.00 | $ 750.00 | $2,250.00 |
| Salaries expense | 1,537.50 | 1,537.50 | 1,537.50 | 4,612.50 |
| Consulting expense | 150.00 | 150.00 | 150.00 | 450.00 |
| Advertising expense | 305.00 | 305.00 | 305.00 | 915.00 |
| Supplies expense | 22.50 | 22.50 | 22.50 | 67.50 |
| Depreciation expense: | | | | |
| Store equipment | 15.00 | 15.00 | 15.00 | 45.00 |
| Telephone and utilities expense | 187.50 | 187.50 | 187.50 | 562.50 |
| Total budgeted selling expenses | $2,967.50 | $2,967.50 | $2,967.50 | $8,902.50 |
| Budgeted cash payments for selling expenses† | $2,180.00 | $2,180.00 | $2,180.00 | $6,540.00 |

*Exhibit 3-8 shows Sweet Temptations' projected expenses for the month of January. Since these are *fixed* expenses, they are expected to be the same for February and March.
†The $787.50 ($2,967.50 − $2,180) difference between the total budgeted selling expenses and budgeted cash payments for selling expenses each month occurs because the expenses for rent, supplies, and depreciation ($750 + $22.50 + $15) relate to Sweet Temptations' planned December expenditures for rent, supplies, and equipment. They are not counted again as cash payments.

activities of Sweet Temptations and will be included in the general and administrative expenses budget. These expenses are allocated to the selling expenses budget as follows:

| | |
|---|---|
| Rent | $1,000 × 3/4 = $ 750.00 |
| Salaries | $2,050 × 3/4 = $1,537.50 |
| Consulting | $ 200 × 3/4 = $ 150.00 |
| Supplies | $ 30 × 3/4 = $ 22.50 |
| Telephone and utilities | $ 250 × 3/4 = $ 187.50 |

Like the purchases budget, the selling expenses budget includes a schedule of budgeted cash payments for each month in the budget period. The company's payment policies and how they apply to the individual expenses determine the budgeted cash payments.

For now, Sweet Temptations' payment policy is to pay for all of its expenses (except rent, supplies, and depreciation) in the month in which they occur. However, if its policy were to make payments in the month following the expenses, the cash payment schedule of the selling expenses budget would resemble the cash collection schedule illustrated in the sales budget in Exhibit 4-5. Notice that there is a $787.50 ($2,967.50 − $2,180) difference between the budgeted total selling expenses each month and the budgeted monthly cash payments for these expenses. This is because Sweet Temptations expects to pay cash in advance for six months' rent, purchase supplies with cash, and make a cash down payment to buy store equipment in December 2007 to get ready to open for business. The $787.50 ($750 rent expense + $22.50 supplies expense + $15 depreciation expense) monthly expenses related to these planned December cash expenditures are not counted again as planned cash payments in January, February, or March.

## The Retail Company's General and Administrative Expenses Budget

For a retail company, the **general and administrative expenses budget** shows the expenses and related cash payments associated with expected activities other than selling.

**EXHIBIT 4-9** **GENERAL AND ADMINISTRATIVE EXPENSES BUDGET**

**SWEET TEMPTATIONS**
***General and Administrative Expenses Budget***
***First Quarter 2008***

| | January | February | March | Quarter |
|---|---|---|---|---|
| Budgeted general and administrative expenses* | | | | |
| Rent expense | $ 250.00 | $ 250.00 | $ 250.00 | $ 750.00 |
| Salaries expense | 512.50 | 512.50 | 512.50 | 1,537.50 |
| Consulting expense | 50.00 | 50.00 | 50.00 | 150.00 |
| Supplies expense | 7.50 | 7.50 | 7.50 | 22.50 |
| Telephone and utilities expense | 62.50 | 62.50 | 62.50 | 187.50 |
| Total budgeted general and administrative expenses | $ 882.50 | $ 882.50 | $ 882.50 | $2,647.50 |
| Budgeted cash payments for general and administrative expenses† | $ 625.00 | $ 625.00 | $ 625.00 | $1,875.00 |

*Exhibit 3-8 shows Sweet Temptations' projected expenses for the month of January. Since these are fixed expenses, Sweet Temptations expects them to be the same for February and March.
†The $257.50 ($882.50 − $625) difference between the total budgeted general and administrative expenses and the budgeted cash payments for these expenses each month occurs because the monthly expenses ($250 + $7.50) related to the planned December cash expenditures for rent and supplies are not counted again as cash payments.

Examples of general and administrative expenses are secretaries' salaries, consulting charges, and the cost of renting office space. To prepare the general and administrative expenses budget, the entrepreneur reviews past expenses (if they are available), identifies them as fixed or variable, and adjusts them for current plans.

Exhibit 4-9 shows the general and administrative expenses budget for Sweet Temptations for the first quarter of 2008. These expenses are all *fixed* expenses, although general and administrative expenses can also be variable expenses. As we discussed earlier, Sweet Temptations allocates the total of certain monthly expenses between selling activities and general and administrative activities. Recall that you and Anna estimated that one-fourth of each of the expenses is tied directly to administrative activities. The other three-fourths of each is tied to sales activities and appears on the selling expenses budget. These expenses are allocated to the general and administrative expenses budget as follows:

| | |
|---|---|
| Rent | $1,000 × 1/4 = $250.00 |
| Salaries | $2,050 × 1/4 = $512.50 |
| Consulting | $ 200 × 1/4 = $ 50.00 |
| Supplies | $ 30 × 1/4 = $ 7.50 |
| Telephone and utilities | $ 250 × 1/4 = $ 62.50 |

Like the selling expenses budget, the general and administrative expenses budget includes a schedule of budgeted cash payments for each month in the budget period. These cash payments are determined according to the company's payment policies. Sweet Temptations plans to pay for all the expenses listed on the general and administrative expenses budget in the month they occur except for rent and supplies, which it paid for in December.

## The Service Company's Expenses Budget

Service companies do not have a purchases budget for inventory, since they are selling a service rather than a product. Also, they usually do not divide their budgeted expenses into two different budgets, one for selling expenses and one for general and administrative expenses. Instead, in budgeting expenses, service companies simply prepare an *operating expenses* budget.

Remember that our discussion of cost behaviors in Chapter 3 noted that variable costs vary in total in direct proportion to volume. *Volume* can refer to a variety of activities. One measure of volume used by retail companies is number of unit sales. Because they are selling a service, though, service companies are very labor-intensive. Salaries are a major expense for these companies, and many of their other expenses vary with the number of hours that the employees work. Therefore, many service companies use the number of hours that employees work as a measure of volume. Regardless, service companies have many of the same fixed expenses that retail companies have, such as rent and advertising.

## Cash Management and the Cash Budget

The way a company manages its cash can make the difference between success and failure. Cash management involves keeping an eye on the company's cash balance to make sure that

1. there is enough cash on hand to pay for planned operations during the current period,
2. there is a "cash buffer" on hand, and
3. there is not too much cash on hand.

An insufficient cash balance can cause a problem for a company. Without enough cash, a company will have trouble operating at a normal level and paying its bills. In the most extreme case, an entrepreneur will not be able to operate the company at all because it will have gone out of business. Therefore, a good entrepreneur is always looking for long- and short-term financing sources, such as lines of credit at a bank that allow the company to borrow money "as needed" and loan guarantees from government agencies such as the **U.S. Small Business Administration**. A good entrepreneur also watches the company's cash balance to determine when to pay back the financing. We will discuss short-term financing again in Chapter 14 and long-term financing in Chapter 22.

A cash buffer means having some extra cash on hand (or available through a line of credit) to cover normal, but unexpected, events. For example, an unexpected surge in candy sales would cause Sweet Temptations to have to purchase more inventory than planned. A cash buffer would help cover that purchase. A company's insurance policy would usually cover abnormal and unexpected events such as natural disasters or fires.

Too much cash on hand may seem like an odd problem to have because almost everyone would like to have more cash. An excessive cash balance is a problem for a company, though, because this cash balance is not productive. That is, cash earns nothing for the company unless the company invests it internally in profitable projects, or externally in an interest-bearing account or in government or business securities that earn dividends or interest. Therefore, a successful entrepreneur continually watches for good investment opportunities—even short-run opportunities. We will discuss short-term and long-term investments in Chapter 23.

### The Retail Company's Cash Budget (Projected Cash Flow Statement)

The **cash budget** shows the company's expected cash receipts and payments, and how they affect the company's cash balance. The cash budget is very important in cash management. It helps the entrepreneur anticipate cash shortages, thus avoiding the problems of having too little cash on hand to operate and to pay its bills. This budget also helps the company avoid having excess cash that could be better used for profitable projects or investments.

Besides helping the entrepreneur anticipate cash shortages and excesses, the cash budget can also help external users. For example, a potential lender (such as a bank) may want to evaluate the company's cash budget to see how the company plans to use the borrowed cash and to anticipate when the company will have enough cash to repay the loan.

A company's cash budget is similar in many respects to the cash flow statement we discussed in Chapter 1. However, the cash budget shows the cash receipts (inflows) and cash payments (outflows) that the company *expects* as a result of its plans (which is why it sometimes is called a *projected cash flow statement*). On the other hand, a company's cash flow statement reports its *actual* cash receipts and payments. Like the cash flow statement (see Exhibit 1-10), a cash budget may have three sections: it always has an *operating activities* section, and if the company plans for investing or financing activities, the cash budget will have separate *investing activities* and *financing activities* sections.

The **operating activities section** of the cash budget summarizes the cash receipts and payments the company expects as a result of its planned operations. These expected cash flows come from the sales, purchases, and expenses budgets we discussed earlier. This section also shows the net cash inflows (excess of cash receipts over cash payments) or the net cash outflows (excess of cash payments over cash receipts) expected from operations. Adding the net cash inflows to the beginning cash balance (or subtracting the net cash outflows) results in the expected cash balance from operations at the end of the budget period.

The **investing activities section** of the cash budget—if needed—shows the cash payments and receipts the company expects from planned investing activities. A company's investing activities include, for instance, purchases or sales of land, buildings, and equipment, or investments in the stocks and bonds of governments or other companies.

*Why do you think cash receipts from the sale of land, buildings, and equipment, as well as from dividends received on investments, are included in the investing section of the cash budget?*

Although investing activities can occur at any time, companies usually have policies about investing cash balances on hand in excess of a predetermined amount. For instance, based on planned operating activities, Anna has decided that Sweet Temptations should invest any cash on hand in excess of $15,000 in any month.

The **financing activities section** of the cash budget—if needed—shows the cash receipts and payments the company expects from planned financing activities. A company's financing activities include borrowings and repayments of loans, investments by owners, and withdrawals by owners. The cash budget helps a manager decide when financing activities will be necessary. For example, in considering the need for a cash buffer, Anna has decided that Sweet Temptations will begin financing activities when its cash balance drops below $7,000.

Exhibit 4-10 shows Sweet Temptations' cash budget for the first quarter of 2008. Notice that Sweet Temptations' cash budget summarizes the receipts and payments that you saw in the budgets we discussed earlier. The cash receipts amounts come from the sales budget, and the cash payments amounts come from the purchases budget, the selling expenses budget, and the general and administrative expenses budget. The $7,300 beginning cash balance for January (and the quarter) is Sweet Temptations' cash balance at the end of December, assuming preparations for the start of business go according to plan. The ending cash balance for each month is also the beginning cash balance for the next month.

Sweet Temptations has no investment activities planned for this quarter since the expected cash balances in the first three months of 2008 are not more than $15,000. Also, none of the monthly cash balances during the quarter are less than $7,000, so no financing activities are planned during this quarter. Thus, Sweet Temptations' cash budget does not include an investing activities or a financing activities section. We will discuss planned cash flows from both investing and financing activities in Chapter 12.

### The Service Company's Cash Budget (Projected Cash Flow Statement)

The cash budget of a service company is similar to that of a retail company except that the service company reports cash flow information that is obtained from fewer budgets.

**EXHIBIT 4-10** **CASH BUDGET (PROJECTED CASH FLOW STATEMENT)**

**SWEET TEMPTATIONS**
*Cash Budget*
*First Quarter 2008*

| | January | February | March | Quarter |
|---|---|---|---|---|
| Cash flow from operating activities: | | | | |
| Cash receipts from sales* | $7,080.00 | $11,920.00 | $ 5,510.00 | $24,510.00 |
| Cash payments for: | | | | |
| Purchases† | $1,620.00 | $ 4,320.00 | $ 3,915.00 | $ 9,855.00 |
| Selling expenses‡ | 2,180.00 | 2,180.00 | 2,180.00 | 6,540.00 |
| General and administrative expenses§ | 625.00 | 625.00 | 625.00 | 1,875.00 |
| Total payments | $4,425.00 | $ 7,125.00 | $ 6,720.00 | $18,270.00 |
| Net cash inflow (outflow) from operations | $2,655.00 | $ 4,795.00 | $(1,210.00) | $ 6,240.00 |
| Add: Beginning cash balance | 7,300.00 | 9,955.00 | 14,750.00 | 7,300.00 |
| Ending cash balance from operations | $9,955.00 | $14,750.00 | $13,540.00 | $13,540.00 |

*From sales budget (Exhibit 4-5)
†From purchases budget (Exhibit 4-7)
‡From selling expenses budget (Exhibit 4-8)
§From general and administrative expenses budget (Exhibit 4-9)

In Sweet Temptations' cash budget, information came from the sales, purchases, selling expenses, and general and administrative expenses budgets. A service company's cash budget information, on the other hand, would be obtained from its sales budget and its operating expenses budget. Information from these budgets would be used in the same way that a retail company uses its information to prepare the projected financial statements we discuss in the next sections.

## The Projected Income Statement

A **projected income statement** summarizes a company's expected revenues and expenses for the budget period, assuming the company follows its plans. Note that the projected income statement is *not* the same as the cash budget. In Exhibit 4-4, we showed the relationship between sales revenues from credit sales and cash collections from sales. If a company has credit sales, cash receipts occur later than the related sales. The same thing can happen with expenses. Many times, the cash payment for an expense occurs later than the activity that causes the expense. For example, usually employees work before being paid. If the work occurs late in March, the company may not pay the employees until early in April. The projected salaries expense will appear on the projected income statement for the quarter that ends in March (since the work occurred in March), but the projected cash payment will appear on April's cash budget. In other words, timing differences between the operating activities and the related cash receipts and payments cause the differences between the projected income statement and the cash budget. The projected income statement reports on the company's planned operating activities, whereas the cash budget reports on the expected cash receipts and payments related to those activities.

The projected income statement is important because it shows what the company's profit will be if the company follows its plans. At this point in the budgeting process, if the expected profit for the budget period is not satisfactory, the entrepreneur may revise the company's plans to try to increase the profit. In Chapter 3 we discussed how a company uses C-V-P analysis to estimate how some changes in plans will affect its profit. If, as a result of this analysis, the entrepreneur changes the company's plans, then the budgets are changed according to these revised plans.

*What changes do you think an entrepreneur might make in a company's plans to increase its expected profit?*

Exhibit 4-11 shows Sweet Temptations' projected income statement for the first quarter of 2008. Sweet Temptations includes this income statement in its business plan. There are three differences between this statement and the income statement[1] for internal decision-makers that we showed in Exhibit 3-8. First, the income statement in Exhibit 4-11 is for the first *quarter* of 2008. To keep the discussion simple, we showed only the income statement for January in Exhibit 3-8. (If Sweet Temptations had chosen to show an income statement for each month of the first quarter in Exhibit 4-11, the January profits of Exhibits 4-11 and 3-8 would be identical.) Second, in Exhibit 4-11 we group the fixed costs into two categories—selling expenses and general and administrative expenses. In Exhibit 3-8 we listed each expense separately and did not attempt to categorize them. Finally, in Exhibit 4-11 we do not list all the separate expenses because they are shown in the selling expenses and general and administrative expenses budgets.

Notice that the amounts of most of the revenues and expenses in the projected income statement in Exhibit 4-11 come from the budgets we discussed earlier. The variable cost of boxes of candy sold, however, is computed by multiplying the budgeted number of boxes *sold* during the quarter (2,460, from the sales budget in Exhibit 4-5) by Sweet Temptations' cost per box ($4.50, from the purchases budget in Exhibit 4-7). So the cost of boxes of chocolates *sold* that Sweet Temptations listed on its projected income statement is different from the cost of boxes of chocolates *purchased* that Sweet Temptations listed on its purchase budget. This is because the number of boxes sold is different than the number of boxes purchased.

**EXHIBIT 4-11** **PROJECTED INCOME STATEMENT**

**SWEET TEMPTATIONS**
***Projected Income Statement***
***For the Quarter Ended March 31, 2008***

| | | |
|---|---|---|
| Total sales revenue | | $24,600* |
| Less total variable costs | | |
| Cost of boxes of chocolates sold | | (11,070)† |
| Total contribution margin | | $13,530 |
| Less total fixed costs: | | |
| Selling expenses | $8,902.50‡ | |
| General and administrative expenses | 2,647.50§ | |
| Total fixed costs | | (11,550) |
| Profit | | $ 1,980 |

*From the sales budget (Exhibit 4-5).
†The 2,460 budgeted total sales in number of boxes (Exhibit 4-5) times the $4.50 cost per box (Exhibit 4-7).
‡From the selling expenses budget (Exhibit 4-8).
§From the general and administrative expenses budget (Exhibit 4-9).

[1]We could rearrange this income statement so that it would look similar to the income statement for external users that we show in Exhibit 3-8. To save space, we do not include the rearranged income statement in Exhibit 4-11.

### The Projected Balance Sheet

In Chapter 1, we indicated that a balance sheet is a basic financial statement of a company. A balance sheet shows a company's financial position on a particular date. It lists the company's assets, liabilities, and owner's equity. In the same way, a **projected balance sheet** summarizes a company's expected financial position at the end of a budget period, assuming the company follows its plans. Usually, a company includes a projected balance sheet in its master budget. Because preparing a projected balance sheet can be complex, we will wait until Chapter 12 to show one. If we did include a projected balance sheet for Sweet Temptations, it would show what resources (assets) Sweet Temptations expects to have, how much it expects to owe its creditors (liabilities), and what it expects Anna's investment (owner's equity) in the assets of the company to be at the end of the quarter.

## Using the Master Budget in Evaluating the Company's Performance

6 How can a manager use a budget to evaluate a company's performance and then use the results of that evaluation to influence the company's plans?

Managers of all types of companies use budgets as planning tools. Budgeting is also a valuable tool for *evaluating* how a company, division, department, or team actually performed. By analyzing differences between a company's budgeted results and its actual results, a manager can determine where plans went wrong and where to take corrective action next time.

### Finding Differences between Actual and Budgeted Amounts

Comparing budgeted amounts to actual results is an important part of the budgeting process. By using the budgets discussed in this chapter as benchmarks, a manager can evaluate the differences between the actual performance of the company and its planned performance. By understanding *why* the differences occurred, a manager can decide what actions to take for future time periods. For example, Exhibit 4-12 shows a comparison (called a **cost report**) between Sweet Temptations' budgeted and actual expenses for the first quarter of 2008. A large company would usually divide its cost report into selling expenses and general and administrative expenses, and also by division, department, manager, product, or some other identifiable unit. This breakdown is not necessary for Sweet Temptations' cost report, because it has only a few items.

**Exhibit 4-12 Comparison of Actual vs. Budgeted Amounts**

**SWEET TEMPTATIONS COMPANY**
*Cost Report*
*For the Quarter Ended March 31, 2008*

| | Budgeted | Actual | Favorable (Unfavorable) Difference |
|---|---|---|---|
| Rent expense | $ 3,000 | $ 3,000 | — |
| Salaries expense | 6,150 | 6,150 | — |
| Consulting expense | 600 | 600 | — |
| Advertising expense | 915 | 915 | — |
| Supplies expense | 90 | 110 | $(20) |
| Depreciation expense | 45 | 45 | — |
| Telephone and utilities expense | 750 | 800 | (50) |
| | $11,550 | $11,620 | $(70) |

With a quick glance at this cost report, you can see that Sweet Temptations' actual expenses were $70 greater than budgeted expenses in the first quarter of 2008. You can even see that the negative difference between total planned and actual expenses occurs because the telephone and utilities expense as well as the supplies expense were more than expected. However, knowing that there are differences is not enough information for a manager to use in explaining the differences and in planning the next time period's activities. It is at this point in the evaluation process that a manager must use creative and critical thinking skills. A manager can learn about the causes of the differences by asking questions and investigating further. As we discussed in Chapter 2, the answers to these questions will generally lead to additional questions. The cost report gives the manager a starting point from which to begin an investigation.

## Learning Why Differences Occur

While analyzing the difference between the budgeted and the actual telephone and utility expense, Anna might ask herself questions such as the following:

1. Which of the monthly telephone and utility bills were higher or lower than expected?
2. Why were these bills different from what was expected? Was there a difference because Sweet Temptations has just begun operations and Anna had no previous experience to use in estimating what the expenses would be?
3. Did the difference occur because of selling activities or because of general and administrative activities (or both)?
4. What other explanations are there for the differences?

After formulating the questions she wants answered, Anna can devise a strategy to find the answers. Looking for answers will require Anna's creative thinking skills. Suppose she decides to start her investigation by first looking at the monthly telephone and utility bills. If she finds minor differences between planned and actual expenses for all the bills except for the electricity bill, these minor differences can be attributed to her use of estimates. Minor differences from estimates are to be expected, so there would be no need to plan any correcting activities for the future. Suppose, however, that in looking at the electricity bill, Anna discovers that the electric company raised its rate 10 percent since she created the budget. Before planning for the next quarter, Anna must ask another question: Will the same increase be in effect next quarter? If so, Anna will use this information in her future planning and budgeting activities, and the next master budget will include the 10 percent increase in Sweet Temptations' planned electricity expenses.

*What questions do you think Anna should ask about the difference between planned and actual supplies expenses?*

A manager can use information from the master budget to help identify the causes of differences between budgeted and actual expenses, and then to decide what to change in the future. As you just saw, an analysis of the causes of these differences may lead an owner or manager to make changes in future budgets. On the other hand, the same analysis may lead the owner or manager to change future activities rather than future budgets. For example, suppose packaging workers at Unlimited Decadence are working overtime repackaging boxes of chocolates because of a sudden decrease in the quality of purchased packaging materials. Because of this unplanned problem, the actual salary expense for Unlimited Decadence will be higher than its budgeted salary expense. An analysis of the cause of this salary difference may lead the packaging manager to look for a new supplier of packaging materials.

Differences between planned and actual expenses can also be positive differences. For example, Sweet Temptations' telephone and utility expense could have been less than the budgeted expense. Suppose Anna based Sweet Temptations' budgeted telephone and

© PHOTOPIA

Do you think Burger King's estimate of Big King sales affected its estimate of sales of french fries?

utilities expense on a well-publicized planned increase in utility rates. If the state Public Utility Commission later turns down the rate increase, Sweet Temptations' actual expense will be less than the budgeted expense. Anna will use this rate information, which she noticed because of her analysis of the difference between the planned and the actual expenses, for her future planning activities. Unless circumstances change between this budget period and the next budget period, Anna will use the old rate to budget Sweet Temptations' utilities expense.

At other times, differences between planned and actual results can have both positive and negative consequences. Consider when **Burger King** introduced its "Big King" sandwich a few years ago as competition against **McDonald's** "Big Mac" sandwich. In its sales budget, Burger King had estimated that it would sell 1.8 million Big Kings a day. The good news was that the sandwich was so popular at that time that Burger King sold nearly 3 million per day—about 70 percent more than it had expected! The bad news was that since Burger King had budgeted and then made its purchases based on anticipated sales, the *un*anticipated sales quickly caused shortages in Big King sandwiches in many cities, causing Burger King to miss the additional sales.

## Business Issues and Values

The accounting information included in budgets affects and is affected by business decisions. In using this information for decision making, entrepreneurs must also consider other, nonfinancial issues. For example, suppose a small new airline has entered a market dominated by a large, well-established airline. To effectively compete, the new company determines that it must cut costs. A look at the budget shows that one of the largest costs, and an easy one to reduce, is maintenance costs on the fleet. When making the decision about whether to reduce maintenance costs, the entrepreneur would need to consider whether reducing these costs now would drive up future maintenance costs. But more importantly, the entrepreneur would need to consider the safety of the passengers and crew. In this case, the safety concern may outweigh the financial gain resulting from reducing the maintenance costs.

## SUMMARY

At the beginning of the chapter we asked you several questions. During the chapter, we asked you to STOP and answer some additional questions to build your knowledge about specific issues. Be sure you answered these additional questions. Below are the questions from the beginning of the chapter, with a brief summary of the key points relating to the answers. Use your creative and critical thinking skills to expand on these key points to develop more complete answers to the questions and to determine what other questions you have that might lead you to learn more about the issues.

### 1 How does a budget contribute toward helping a company achieve its goals?

A budget helps a company by giving a financial description of the activities planned by the company to help it achieve its goals. It also helps by adding order to the planning process, by providing an opportunity to recognize and avoid potential operating problems, by quantifying plans, and by creating a "benchmark" for evaluating the company's performance.

### 2 Do the activities of a company have a logical order that influences the organization of a budget?

Yes, the operating activities of the company make up what is called the company's *operating cycle.* A company's operating cycle is the average time it takes the company to use cash to buy goods and services, to sell these goods to or perform services for customers, and to collect cash from these customers. The order of activities, and the cash receipts and payments associated with these activities, influence how a company organizes its budget.

### 3 What is the structure of the budgeting process, and how does a company begin that process?

The master budget is the overall structure used for the financial description of a company's plans. It consists of a set of budgets describing planned company activities, the cash receipts or payments that should result from these activities, and the company's projected financial statements (what the financial statements should look like if the planned activities occur). The budgeting process begins with the sales budget because product or service sales affect all other company activities. By gathering various types of information, such as past sales data, knowledge about customer needs, industry trends, economic forecasts, and new technological developments, a company estimates the amount of inventory (or employee time) to be sold in each budget period. Cash collections from sales are planned by examining the company's credit-granting policies. Cash payments for expenses are planned by examining the company's payment policies.

### 4 What are the similarities and differences between a retail company's master budget and a service company's master budget?

For a retail company, the master budget usually includes a sales budget, a purchases budget, a selling expenses budget, a general and administrative expenses budget, a cash budget, a projected income statement, and a projected balance sheet. A service company does not have a purchases budget, and it usually has one operating expenses budget.

### 5 After a company begins the budgeting process, is there a strategy it can use to complete the budget?

Yes. For example, a retail company follows a strategy similar to the following. After budgeting sales, the company plans the amount and timing of inventory purchases. To budget purchases, the company examines the costs associated with inventory purchases and storage as well as the costs of not carrying enough inventory. It also considers its policy on required inventory levels. After budgeting purchases, the company plans the cash payments for inventory purchases by reviewing its payment agreements with suppliers. To budget expenses, the company must first determine the behaviors of these expenses. It budgets fixed expenses by evaluating previous fixed expenses and then adjusting them (if necessary) according to the plans for the coming time period. It budgets variable expenses by first observing what activity causes these expenses to vary and then computing the total expenses by multiplying the cost per unit of activity by the budgeted activity level. For a retail company, the activity level is usually sales. The company budgets the cash payments for these expenses by reviewing the company's policy on the payment of expenses. The information for developing the cash budget comes from the other previously prepared budgets, as does the information for creating the projected income statement.

### 6 How can a manager use a budget to evaluate a company's performance and then use the results of that evaluation to influence the company's plans?

A manager uses a master budget to evaluate a company's performance by comparing the information in the various budgets with the results that occur after the planned activities are implemented. The manager identifies the differences between budgeted and actual results, and learns about the causes of these differences by asking questions and investigating further. Based on these investigations, a manager may adjust the company's activities and plans, as well as its future budgets.

## KEY TERMS

**budget** *(p. 93)*
**budgeting** *(p. 93)*
**cash budget** *(p. 107)*
**cost report** *(p. 111)*
**financing activities section** *(p. 108)*
**general and administrative expenses budget** *(p. 105)*
**investing activities section** *(p. 108)*
**management by exception** *(p. 94)*
**master budget** *(p. 96)*
**operating activities section** *(p. 108)*
**projected balance sheet** *(p. 111)*
**projected income statement** *(p. 109)*
**purchases budget** *(p. 102)*
**retail company's operating cycle** *(p. 94)*
**sales budget** *(p. 98)*
**selling expenses budget** *(p. 104)*
**service company's operating cycle** *(p. 95)*

## SUMMARY SURFING

Here is an opportunity to gather information on the Internet about real-world issues related to the topics in this chapter. Answer the following questions (for suggestions on how to navigate various organizations' Web sites to find the relevant information, see the related discussion in the Preface at the beginning of the book).

- Go to the **CBSC Online Small Business Workshop** Web site. What is a cash flow forecast, and how does it compare with the cash budget that we discussed in the chapter? What are the steps involved in preparing a cash flow forecast? How would preparing the budgets discussed in the chapter help an entrepreneur in preparing a cash flow forecast?
- Go to the **Entrepreneur.com** Web site. How often should a company update its business plan? What are the benefits to a company of keeping its business plan current?

## INTEGRATED BUSINESS AND ACCOUNTING SITUATIONS

**Answer the Following Questions in Your Own Words.**

### Testing Your Knowledge

**4-1** What is it about budgeting that adds discipline to the planning process?

**4-2** If a problem comes to light during the budgeting process, what is the manager likely to do?

**4-3** "Budgeting serves as a benchmark for evaluation." Explain what that means.

**4-4** Describe a master budget. Why might a master budget be different from one company to another?

**4-5** How are the master budgets of a retail company and a service company similar to each other? How are they different from each other?

**4-6** Describe the operating cycle of a retail company. How are the operating cycles of a retail company and a service company similar to and different from each other?

**4-7** Why must the sales budget be developed before any of the other budgets? Where does information for sales forecasts come from?

**4-8** If you just finished budgeting sales for next year, what information would you need to be able to budget cash collections from sales?

**4-9** How does knowing forecasted sales help a manager develop a purchases budget? What else besides forecasted sales would a manager have to know to complete the purchases budget?

**4-10** When developing a selling expenses budget and a general and administrative expenses budget, why do you have to know how expenses behave?

**4-11** Why must you complete all the other budgets before you can develop the cash budget?

**4-12** Why is it important to know about anticipated cash shortages ahead of time?

**4-13** What is a "cash buffer" and what is an example of a circumstance where a company could use one?

**4-14** Why is having too much cash on hand a problem?

**4-15** On the cash budget, why is the beginning cash balance for January the same as the beginning cash balance for the first quarter of the year? Why is the March ending cash balance the same as the first quarter's ending cash balance? How do you determine the first quarter's cash receipts from sales?

**4-16** How is the cash budget similar to a cash flow statement? How are they different from each other?

**4-17** Why is the cash budget not the same as the projected income statement? What items included on the projected income statement are not included on the cash budget?

**4-18** In evaluating a company's performance, why do managers or owners need to learn the causes of differences between actual and budgeted amounts?

## Applying Your Knowledge

**4-19** Jaime's Hat Shop sells hats with college logos on them; the hats sell for $22 each. This year, Jaime's expects to sell 350 hats in May, 300 in June, 400 in July, 800 in August, 1,040 in September, and 750 in October. On average, 25 percent of its customers purchase on credit. Jaime's allows those customers to pay for their purchases the month after they have made their purchases.

*Required:* Prepare a sales budget for Jaime's Hat Shop for the third quarter of this year.

**4-20** Refer to 4-19. Company policy is to plan to end each month with an ending inventory equal to 20 percent of the next month's projected sales. Jaime's pays $8 for each hat that it purchases. Jaime and his supplier have an arrangement that allows Jaime's Hat Shop to pay for each purchase 60 days after the purchase.

*Required:* Prepare a purchases budget for the third quarter of this year for Jaime's Hat Shop.

**4-21** Refer to 4-19. Jaime's ended the second quarter of this year with 60 hats on hand.

*Required:* (1) Notice that Jaime's ended the second quarter with less than 20 percent of projected sales for July. What do you think accounts for the difference?
(2) How many hats should Jaime's purchase in July?

**4-22** Refer to 4-19. Jaime's Hat Shop expects to incur the following expenses for each month of the third quarter of this year:

| | |
|---|---|
| Rent (30% general and administrative, 70% selling) | $1,200 |
| Utilities (30% general and administrative, 70% selling) | 600 |
| Advertising | 400 |
| Salaries (50% general and administrative, 50% selling) | 5,000 |
| Commissions (for each hat sold) | 2 |

In January, Jaime's had prepaid the rent for the whole year. Jaime plans to pay for all the other expenses in the month they occur.

*Required:* (1) Prepare a selling expenses budget for the third quarter of this year.
(2) Prepare a general and administrative expenses budget for the third quarter of this year.

**4-23** Refer to 4-19 through 4-22. Jaime's Hat Shop ended June with a cash balance of $10,343.

*Required:* Prepare a cash budget for the third quarter of this year.

**4-24** Refer to 4-19 through 4-22.

*Required:* Prepare a projected income statement for the third quarter of this year.

**4-25** Mark and Lawanda are partners in a new executive search company called Executive Lost and Found. Executive Lost and Found, which begins operations in December, matches the skills of displaced executives (executives who have been laid off) with the needs of companies looking for top managers. Mark estimates that the employees of Executive Lost and Found will spend 1,000 hours in December, 1,400 hours in January, 1,600 hours in February, and 1,450 hours in March working on filling executive positions for Lost and Found's clients. Executive Lost and Found will bill each of its clients at the end of the month, charging $400 per hour spent working for that client during the month. On average, 50% of the billings for any month will be collected during the following month, 30% during the second month following the billing, and 20% during the third month following the billing.

*Required:* Prepare a sales budget for Executive Lost and Found for the quarter (January through March).

**4-26** Butler Company sells a single product for $6 per unit. Sales estimates (in units) for the last four months of the year are as follows:

| | Units |
|---|---|
| September | 40,000 |
| October | 45,000 |
| November | 35,000 |
| December | 40,000 |

All of Butler's sales are credit sales, and it expects to collect each account receivable 15 days after the related sale. Assume that all months have 30 days.

*Required:* Prepare a sales budget for the last three months of the year, including estimated collections of accounts receivable.

**4-27** The sales budget for Merita Medallion Company shows budgeted sales (in medallions) for December and the first four months of next year:

| | Medallions |
|---|---|
| December | 100,000 |
| January | 40,000 |
| February | 90,000 |
| March | 150,000 |
| April | 50,000 |

*Required:* Prepare a budget for the number of medallions Merita needs to purchase in the first three months of next year for each of the following two *independent* situations:

(1) The company's policy is to have inventory on hand at the end of each month equal to 15% of the following month's sales requirement.

(2) The company's policy is to keep each month's ending inventory to a minimum without letting it fall below 5,000 medallions. Assume that the December 1 inventory has 5,000 medallions and that the company's only supplier is willing to sell a maximum of 125,000 medallions to the company per month.

**4-28** Top Dog Pet Store sells dog food in 20-pound bags for $10 per bag, which it buys from its supplier for $7 per bag. Top Dog estimates that its sales of bags of dog food for the second quarter of the year will be as follows:

| | Bags |
|---|---|
| April | 1,200 |
| May | 1,400 |
| June | 1,500 |

Top Dog's policy is to have bags of dog food on hand at the end of each month equal to 10% of the next month's budgeted sales (bags). It expects to have 120 bags of dog food on hand at the end of March and expects to sell 1,650 bags in July. Top Dog expects its cost of purchases to be $7,770 in March; it pays for its purchases in the following month.

*Required:* (1) Prepare a purchases budget for bags of dog food for the second quarter of this year for Top Dog.

(2) How many bags of dog food did Top Dog expect to sell in March?

**4-29** Blanchar Business Machines estimates its monthly selling expenses as follows:

| | |
|---|---|
| Advertising | $22,000 per month |
| Sales salaries | $18,000 per month |
| Sales calls on customers | $35 per machine |
| Commissions paid to sales personnel | $50 per machine |
| Delivery | $20 per machine |

Assume that Blanchar pays selling expenses in the month after they are incurred. Based on current plans of Blanchar's sales department, monthly sales estimates are as follows: March—80 units, April—90 units, May—100 units, June—120 units.

*Required:* Prepare a selling expense budget for the *second* quarter for Blanchar Business Machines.

**4-30** That Fat Cat Company sells cat food in ten-pound bags for $6.20 per bag. Sales estimates for the first three months of the year are as follows:

| | Bags |
|---|---|
| January | 40,000 |
| February | 35,000 |
| March | 30,000 |

December sales were 30,000 bags of cat food. That Fat Cat's desired ending inventory of cat food each month is 30% of the next month's sales estimate (in bags). All sales are cash sales. That Fat Cat purchases bags of cat food at $4.70 per bag and pays for them the month *after* the purchase. General and administrative expenses total $35,000 per month (including $20,000 depreciation), and That Fat Cat pays for these expenses (except for depreciation) in the same month they are incurred. January's current liabilities (all to be paid in January) total $71,500. The company's cash balance on January 1 is $75,000.

*Required:* Prepare a cash budget for each of the first two months of the year.

**4-31** Refer to 4-30.

*Required:* Prepare a projected income statement for February. How do you explain the differences between the income statement and the cash budget?

## Making Evaluations

**4-32** Suppose you are a banker, and the controller of a small company asks you for a short-term $10,000 loan, due in 120 days. Interest on the loan would be 12%, due when the loan is paid back. To support his request, he gives you the following information from his company's cash budget for the next quarter:

| | January | February | March | Quarter |
|---|---|---|---|---|
| Cash flow from operations: | | | | |
| Cash receipts from sales | $20,000 | $14,400 | $13,600 | $48,000 |
| Cash payments for | | | | |
| Purchases | $15,000 | $10,800 | $10,200 | $36,000 |
| Selling expenses | 3,300 | 3,300 | 3,300 | 9,900 |
| General and administrative expenses | 1,650 | 650 | 650 | 2,950 |
| Total payments | $19,950 | $14,750 | $14,150 | $48,850 |
| Net cash inflow (outflow) from operations | $ 50 | $ (350) | $ (550) | $ (850) |
| Cash flow from investments: | | | | |
| Cash receipt from sale of equipment | | 3,000 | | 3,000 |
| Net cash inflow (outflow) from operations and investments | $ 50 | $ 2,650 | $ (550) | $ 2,150 |
| Add: Beginning cash balance | 4,880 | 4,930 | 7,580 | 4,880 |
| Ending cash balance from operations and investments | $ 4,930 | $ 7,580 | $ 7,030 | $ 7,030 |

*Required:* (1) What is your first reaction?

(2) Before making your decision, what else would you like to know about this company? Can any of what you would like to know be found in any of the company's other budgets or financial statements? What other budgets or statements would you like the owner to provide for you? What information would you hope to get from each of these budgets or statements?

(3) What other information would help you make your decision?

(4) Can you think of any circumstances in which it would be a good idea to loan this company $10,000?

(5) Depending on the information you are able to get, what other alternatives are there to loaning or not loaning this company $10,000?

**4-33** Joe, Billy, Ray, and Bob are business partners who own Joe Billy Ray Bob's Country and Western Wear. Joe Billy Ray Bob's arrangement with all of its clothing suppliers allows it to pay for its merchandise purchases one month after the purchases have been made. About 15% of their customers make purchases on credit. These customers pay for their purchases one month after they have made their purchases. All the partners agree that a bank loan would allow Joe Billy Ray Bob's to revamp the storefront (perhaps causing more customers to want to come inside and shop). The partners are having a disagreement, however, about the cash budget that they plan to include in their loan application package. Joe, Billy, and Bob believe that the budget should be revised to present the bank with the most positive projected cash flows. To accomplish this revision, they are suggesting that on the cash budget, payments for purchases be shown *two* months after the purchases have been made, rather than one month as agreed to by Joe Billy Ray Bob's suppliers. Joe, Billy, and Bob are also suggesting that cash receipts from credit customers be budgeted in the same month as the related sales rather than one month later, even though they expect these customers to wait a month before paying for their purchases. Ray thinks the budget should reflect the partners' actual expectations. The partners have come to you for advice.

*Required:* (1) What ethical issues are involved in this decision?

(2) If the partners make the revisions, what effect will the revisions have on the sales budget? on the purchases budget? on the cash budget?

(3) Who stands to gain and who stands to lose by this budget revision? Is the gain or loss temporary or permanent, short-term or long-term?
(4) How might the bank be hurt by the changed budget? How might the company be hurt by the changed budget?
(5) Since the budget represents a plan of action, how might the changed budget affect the activities of the company during the budget period?
(6) Are there other alternatives to choose from besides changing the budget or not changing the budget?
(7) What do you recommend that the partners do?

**4-34** Assume that a company collects two-thirds of its sales revenue in the month of sale and the remaining one-third in the following month.

*Required:* How much revenue has the company actually earned in the month of the sale? Should the company record revenue on the income statement in the month when it collects the cash or when the work was done to earn the revenue? What reasons do you have for choosing one alternative over the other? (What are your reasons for not choosing the other alternative?)

**4-35** The airline industry is very competitive—management is under constant pressure to improve company profits. Ideas that could improve profits include the following:
(a) Increasing the price of tickets
(b) Reducing the number of flight attendants
(c) Reducing the number of flights on which meals are served
(d) Serving smaller meals or serving snacks instead of meals
(e) Limiting the size of—or eliminating—raises
(f) Reducing the number of baggage handlers

*Required:* For each of these ideas, describe the effect the idea would have on each of the budgets and on the projected financial statements. What other issues should management consider in deciding whether to implement any of these ideas?

**4-36** Bill Morgan is the manager of the sales department of Rise & Shine Company, which sells deluxe bread makers. At the beginning of each month, Bill estimates the total cost of operating the department for the month. At the end of the month he compares the total estimated costs to the total actual costs to determine the difference. If the difference is "small," he doesn't investigate any further because he prefers to spend his time on "more important" issues.

At the beginning of April, Bill estimated that the total operating costs of the sales department would be $60,500. For April, the actual operating costs were $60,400. At the end of April, Bill says, "The sales department is doing pretty well. We came in $100 under budget for the month."

Alice Hoch, the president of the company, has come to you for help. She says, "I am concerned that we are not doing enough analysis of our costs, and I need your help. Start with the sales department and prepare for me a cost report to help me review the costs for April. You can have whatever information you need."

Upon investigation, you find the sales department was expected to sell 500 units (bread makers) in April. Based on these projected sales, its budgeted fixed costs were as follows: advertising, $18,000 and salaries, $25,000, while its budgeted variable costs were $25 commission per unit sold and $10 delivery cost per unit sold. You determine that, during April, 500 units were sold and the sales department spent $19,300 for advertising and $22,600 for salaries. It also paid the $25 commission per unit sold and paid $6,000 for delivering the 500 units.

*Required:* Write a report to the president that (a) includes a cost report for the sales department that compares the budgeted costs to the actual costs for April, (b) identifies the questions you think the president should ask to analyze any differences you find, and (c) suggests some potential answers to the questions.

**4-37** Joe Collagen is the president of a small retail company that sells a skin-smoothing lotion and that has been operating for several years. He keeps meticulous records of his actual operating activities, including monthly sales, purchases, and operating expenses, as well as the related cash receipts and payments. However, Joe has never prepared a master budget for the company. He comes to you for help and says, "My profits have been slowly decreasing and I don't know why. Also, sometimes when I least expect it, the company runs short of cash and I have to invest more into it. I've heard that preparing a master budget is a good thing to do, but I don't know what is involved or where to begin."

*Required:* Prepare a report to the president that (a) explains what budgets and projected financial statements are included in a master budget, and (b) clearly specifies how he would use the information from his previous actual operating activities to develop each of these budgets and the projected income statement.

**4-38** Steve and Tammy are thinking of opening a fitness center with facilities for aerobics, weight training, jogging, and lap swimming as well as diet and injury consultation. They plan to buy land and build their facility near the new shopping mall. They want to employ a director, an assistant director, experts to supervise members in each fitness area, and numerous consulting dietitians and sports medicine professionals. They hope to have the entire facility, including an outdoor all-weather track and an indoor swimming pool, completed by the end of the year. They also believe that it will be important to have the facility fully equipped and staffed before they begin taking memberships. Although their estimates indicate that the fitness center can be profitable if they can establish a growing membership over the first five or six years, many small businesses in town have failed because of "cash flow problems" (excess of cash payments over cash receipts). Before committing themselves to this venture, Steve and Tammy have come to you for advice and for help in preparing a cash budget.

*Required:* Write Steve and Tammy a memo explaining why they might have cash flow problems during their early periods of operations. Show them how they can identify these cash flow problems through careful cash budgeting. Make a few suggestions that might help them reduce such problems if they do decide to open the fitness center.

**4-39** Yesterday, you received the following letter for your advice column in the local paper:

## Dr. Decisive

Dear Dr. Decisive:

Please help my overly compulsive girlfriend, who even reads your column compulsively. She is on the New Housing Committee of her sorority. (They are planning to build a new house.) Last night, after a great movie, she was telling me that her sorority had to take a budget to the bank in order to get a loan. Then she told me about their budget, and I can't BELIEVE how "nit-picky" it is--and I told her so in those words. Well, the movie was terrific, but the evening turned out to be a disaster. We got into a MAJOR fight, and now she says she doesn't want to go out with me next weekend (not that I want to go out with someone so COMPULSIVE next weekend). Here are the details of what I told her:

1. It doesn't matter that her sorority has a problem collecting dues and rent from its members. The members always pay eventually, and that's all the bank needs to know.
2. It doesn't matter that the electric company plans to raise the utility rate it charges. That's the future—

> this is now. Her sorority should budget costs that are real (costs they have already experienced), not costs based on the plans of the electric company.
>
> Please explain to her why you agree with me and why these issues will not affect the bank's decision. Maybe she will realize that her compulsion is EXTREME and then we will be able to go out next weekend. I'm just
>
> "Laid Back."

*Required:* Meet with your Dr. Decisive team and write a response to "Laid Back."

## End Note

[a]"Anti-Cholesterol Cardiobar Takes the Hard out of Arteries," *Columbia Missourian,* November 14, 1995, 2A.

# PART 3

# OPERATING, REPORTING, AND EVALUATING IN AN ENTREPRENEURIAL ENVIRONMENT

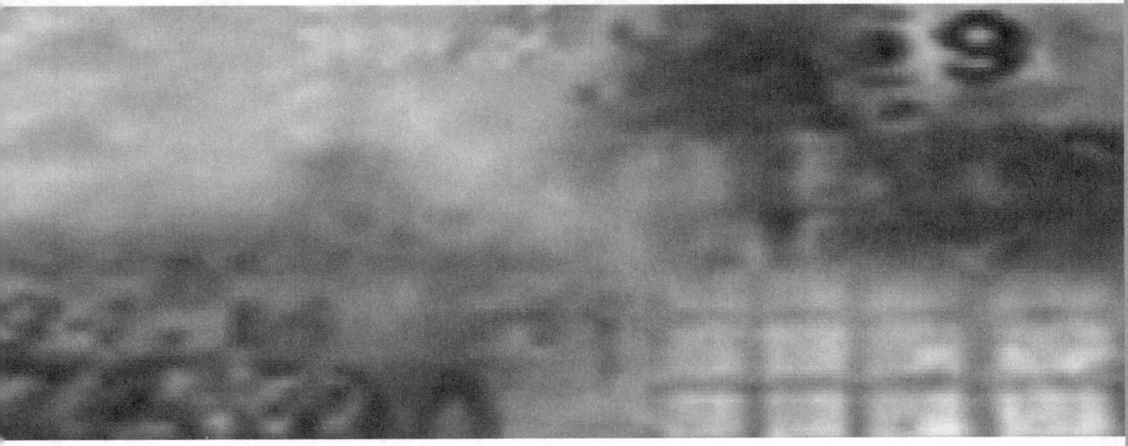

This section consists of five chapters which introduce you to a small company's accounting system and its financial statements, and how to use these financial statements for business decisions. After reading these chapters, you will be able to:

- *understand how a company's accounting system is designed*
- *explain the concepts, principles, and terms used in accounting*
- *account for various business transactions of a company*
- *prepare and use an income statement, balance sheet, and cash flow statement for a company*
- *use ratio analysis to evaluate a company's operating capability, financial flexibility, and profitability*
- *describe how to manage and control a company's working capital*

CHAPTER 5
**THE ACCOUNTING SYSTEM: CONCEPTS AND APPLICATIONS**

CHAPTER 6
**THE INCOME STATEMENT: ITS CONTENT AND USE**

CHAPTER 7
**THE BALANCE SHEET: ITS CONTENT AND USE**

CHAPTER 8
**THE CASH FLOW STATEMENT: ITS CONTENT AND USE**

CHAPTER 9
**MANAGING AND REPORTING WORKING CAPITAL**

CHAPTER 5

# THE ACCOUNTING SYSTEM: CONCEPTS AND APPLICATIONS

"PROFITS ARE THE MECHANISM BY WHICH SOCIETY DECIDES WHAT IT WANTS TO SEE PRODUCED."

—HENRY C. WALLICH

1 Why do managers, investors, creditors, and others need information about a company's operations?

2 What are the basic concepts and terms that help identify the activities that a company's accounting system records?

3 What do users need to know about the accounting equation for a company?

4 Why are at least two effects of each transaction recorded in a company's accounting system?

5 What are revenues and expenses, and how is the accounting equation expanded to record these items?

6 What are the accounting principles and concepts related to net income?

7 Why are end-of-period adjustments necessary?

Do you have a "system" for keeping track of your financial activities? Do you plan your monthly cash receipts and payments by using a budget? When you get your paycheck, do you always review it to be sure you have been paid correctly for the hours that you worked? Do you record every check that you write, and keep a running total of the amount you have in your checkbook? Do you balance your checkbook at the end of each month by comparing it to your bank statement? When you "charge" something on your credit card, do you always check the amount of the receipt before you sign it? Do you keep your credit card receipts and compare them to the charges on your monthly credit card statement before you pay your bill? When you pay your landlord, do you always pay your rent at the beginning of the month? Do you have your bank automatically deduct your car payments from your savings account? Do you pay for your car insurance soon after you get the bill? At the end of each month, do you compare your actual receipts and payments to what you budgeted to see how you stand?

After you graduate, you may want to become a manager of a company. As we discussed in Chapters 3 and 4, accounting methods, such as C-V-P analysis and budgeting, help managers carry out the planning, operating, and evaluating activities of a company. However, managers must also keep track of the company's operations in order to evaluate its performance (and also their own performance as managers). Managers develop and use a company's accounting system for this purpose. For example, a company's accounting system shows managers whether the company sold as many products as it expected and whether it stayed within its budgets.

Managers are not the only people interested in the operations of a company. External users need information about the company's operations to help them decide whether to do business with a company. In this chapter we discuss the role of financial accounting in decision making and explain the basics of the financial accounting process.

## FINANCIAL ACCOUNTING INFORMATION AND DECISION MAKING

Let's return to our discussion of Unlimited Decadence Corporation, the candy bar manufacturer, to see why external users need accounting information. As you can imagine, it takes lots of sugar to make candy bars. Suppose for a moment that you are the president of Sugar Supply Company and that Unlimited Decadence Corporation is considering a purchase of sugar. Unlimited Decadence wants to make bulk purchases on credit and pay for them 30 days later when it has collected money from its candy bar customers.

*As president of Sugar Supply Company, how would you initially react to this request? Why? What facts may change your mind?*

Although your immediate response may be to sell the sugar to Unlimited Decadence, you should think carefully before agreeing to the credit arrangement. Certainly, companies like to make sales. However, increasing sales by extending credit is a good decision only if a company is reasonably sure that its credit customers will pay their bills. If Unlimited Decadence doesn't pay its bills, Sugar Supply Company will have given up some of its resources and have nothing to show for it.

The four-step problem-solving process we discussed in Chapter 2 provides an excellent framework for analyzing this credit decision. You already did the first step—recognizing that the problem is to decide whether to sell sugar to Unlimited Decadence Corporation on credit. You now can take the second step—identifying your company's alternatives. You might decide not to extend credit to Unlimited Decadence, to extend credit under more strict or more lenient terms, or to agree to the original request.

**1** Why do managers, investors, creditors, and others need information about a company's operations?

The third step, evaluating each alternative by weighing its advantages and disadvantages, helps you decide which alternative best helps your company meet its goals of remaining solvent and earning a satisfactory profit. The alternative that you choose will depend, in part, on your company's ability to extend credit and on its existing credit policies. When you perform this step, financial accounting information about Unlimited Decadence plays a big role, helping you determine how good a customer Unlimited Decadence will be.

Exhibit 5-1 shows a simplified income statement and a simplified balance sheet for Unlimited Decadence for the first quarter of 2008.[1] When you analyze these financial statements, you learn from the income statement that during the quarter, Unlimited Decadence earned $18,100,000 of revenues from selling candy bars and made $720,000 net income. From the balance sheet, you learn that on March 31, 2008, Unlimited Decadence had $1,200,000 cash in the bank, inventories of $1,300,000 , and other assets (e.g., trucks, factory, etc.) totaling $16,800,000, and that it owed $3,000,000 to suppliers and $2,000,000 to the bank. Each of these items should affect the specific credit terms, if any, that you are willing to offer. After evaluating the alternatives, you are ready to make a decision about Unlimited Decadence's credit request.

This is just one example of how financial accounting information can help external decision makers choose whether or not to do business with a company. Another example is when a banker studies a company's financial statements to decide the conditions for granting a loan. Businesspeople routinely make decisions like these. In each case, financial statements provide information that is important in solving business problems.

Making good decisions based on information in financial statements assumes that there is agreement about what is included in those statements and how the amounts are

**EXHIBIT 5-1 INCOME STATEMENT AND BALANCE SHEET**

**UNLIMITED DECADENCE**
***Income Statement***
***For Quarter Ended March 31, 2008***
***(in thousands of dollars)***

| | | |
|---|---|---|
| Revenues: | | |
| Sales revenue | | $18,100 |
| Expenses: | | |
| Cost of candy bars sold | $11,500 | |
| Selling expenses | 3,460 | |
| General and administrative expenses | 1,940 | |
| Total expenses | | (16,900) |
| Income before income taxes | | $ 1,200 |
| Income tax expense | | (480) |
| Net Income | | $ 720 |

**UNLIMITED DECADENCE**
***Balance Sheet***
***March 31, 2008***
***(in thousands of dollars)***

| **Assets** | | **Liabilities** | |
|---|---|---|---|
| Cash | $ 1,200 | Accounts payable (suppliers) | $ 3,000 |
| Inventories | 1,300 | Notes payable (bank) | 2,000 |
| Other assets | 16,800 | Total Liabilities | $ 5,000 |
| | | **Stockholders' Equity** | |
| | | Total Stockholders' Equity | $14,300 |
| Total Assets | $19,300 | Total Liabilities and Stockholders' Equity | $19,300 |

[1]For simplicity, we assume here that Unlimited Decadence sells only one type of candy bar. We will relax this assumption in later chapters. Furthermore, Unlimited Decadence Corporation's actual financial statements have many more items, which we don't show here because you have not studied them yet. We will show more complete financial statements in later chapters.

measured. Without agreement on what accounting information the balance sheet, income statement, and cash flow statement should contain, the statements would be essentially useless. If every company defined and measured financial statement items such as assets, liabilities, revenues, and expenses differently, there would be no way to compare one company's information with another's.

*What difficulties do you think would be caused if each state defined traffic laws differently (e.g., laws stipulating on which side of the road to drive) and used different traffic signs?*

The "generally accepted accounting principles" (GAAP) that we mentioned in Chapter 1 were developed to overcome this problem by setting rules for companies to follow when they prepare financial statements. Thus, if you know that a company's financial statements are prepared according to GAAP and you know what rules are included in GAAP, you can confidently use the information in its financial statements for your decision making. The rest of this chapter will give you a basic understanding of the financial accounting process. This process provides the information a company needs for preparing financial statements according to GAAP. Once you have learned some fundamental concepts, we will discuss how the accounting process accumulates and reports information about a company's activities.

## Basic Concepts and Terms Used in Accounting

2 What are the basic concepts and terms that help identify the activities that a company's accounting system records?

Several basic concepts and terms help us identify the activities that a company's accounting process records:

1. Entity concept
2. Transactions
3. Source documents
4. Monetary unit concept
5. Historical cost concept

Each of these items is important for understanding the process of accumulating and reporting information about a company's activities.

### Entity Concept

As you saw in Chapter 1, there are three broad forms of companies—sole proprietorships, partnerships, and corporations. Regardless of a company's form, its accounting records must remain separate from those of its owner, or owners. Even though Anna Cox is the sole proprietor of Sweet Temptations, she doesn't consider her personal assets as belonging to Sweet Temptations, nor does she consider Sweet Temptations' assets to be hers. If Anna owns all or part of several companies, she will keep separate records for each of them. This separation is the basis of the entity concept. An **entity** is considered to be separate from its owners and from any other company. Thus, each company is an entity and has its own accounting system and accounting records. An owner's personal financial activities are *not* included in the accounting records of the company unless this activity has a *direct* effect on the company. For instance, if Anna Cox buys a car only for personal use, its purchase would *not* affect Sweet Temptations' accounting records. On the other hand, if Anna uses personal funds to buy a delivery van to be used in the company, the purchase *would* affect the company's records.

*Why do you think it is important to treat each entity separately?*

Combining company-related items and personal items would make it hard to tell which items are intended for business purposes and which items are for personal use. External users interested in a company's activities would gain little information if you gave them financial statements that included the combined items. With a separate accounting system for a company, it is much easier to identify, measure, and record company activities and to prepare financial statements for the company. Therefore, the financial statements provide more useful information to managers and external users for evaluating the effectiveness of the company's operations.

## Transactions

Recall from Chapter 1 that accounting involves identifying, measuring, recording, summarizing, and communicating a company's economic information for use in decision making. The accounting process usually begins with a business transaction. A **transaction** is an exchange of property or service by a company with another entity. For example, when Unlimited Decadence Corporation purchases sugar, it exchanges cash (or the promise to pay cash) for the ingredients needed to make candy. Many events or activities of a company may be described as transactions. Someone, such as the company's accountant or owner, initially records these transactions based on information from source documents.

## Source Documents

A **source document** is a business record used as evidence that a transaction has occurred. A source document may be a company check, a sales receipt, a bill from a supplier, a bill sent to a customer, a payroll time card, or a log of the miles driven in the company's delivery truck. Although a company's accounting process begins when a transaction occurs, the identification, measurement, and recording of information are based on an analysis of the related source document. For instance, the check that Unlimited Decadence writes to pay for a bulk purchase of sugar shows the date of the transaction, the dollar amount, the name of the company to whom the check was written (called the *payee*), and possibly the reason for the check. Several source documents may be used as evidence of a single transaction. In addition to the canceled check, source documents for Unlimited Decadence's sugar purchase include the sales invoice from the sugar supplier and the report from the loading dock stating that the sugar arrived at Unlimited Decadence's factory.

## Monetary Unit Concept

The source documents for transactions show the value of the exchange in terms that both internal and external users agree on and understand. Since the purpose of recording and analyzing a company's transactions is to understand the company's financial activities, it makes sense to record transactions in terms of money. This idea is known as the **monetary unit concept**. In the United States the monetary unit is the dollar, and therefore U.S.-based companies show their financial statements in dollars. The monetary unit used depends on the national currency of the company's country. For example, **Sony** uses the Japanese yen, while **Volkswagen** and **Benetton** use the European Union euro.

*If a company does business in several countries, what currency do you think it uses to prepare its financial statements? Why? Since* ***Jaguar*** *is owned by* ***Ford****, do you think its financial statements are prepared in British pounds or U.S. dollars?*

## Historical Cost Concept

As we all know, the value of every country's currency changes as a result of inflation. Also, the values of particular goods and services change in the marketplace as supply and demand change. So a company has to decide whether to adjust the recorded amounts to

© SEBASTIAN LASSE/PLUS 49

If Unlimited Decadence purchases a Volkswagen from this dealership in Germany, do you think this candy maker should record the purchase in dollars or euros? Why?

include these types of changes. Under generally accepted accounting principles in the United States, companies generally do *not* record the change in the value of either the currency or the individual goods and services. Instead, they use the historical cost concept or, simply, the cost concept. The **historical cost concept** states that a company records its transactions based on the dollars exchanged (the cost) at the time the transaction occurred. The related source documents show this cost, and the company's accounting records continue to show the *cost* involved in each transaction regardless of whether the *value* of the property or service owned increases (or decreases) or whether the *value* of the currency changes over time. For instance, suppose that a company acquires land for $100,000 and that a year later the value of the land has increased to $130,000. Under the historical cost concept, the company continues to show the land in its accounting records at $100,000, the acquisition cost. However, later in the book you will see that companies do adjust some assets for changes in their values.

*Why do you think most accountants wouldn't want to change the recorded value for the land from $100,000 to $130,000? Why might some want to change?*

In Exhibit 5-2 we combine the entity concept, the monetary unit concept, and the historical cost concept to develop Unlimited Decadence Corporation's balance sheet that we showed in Exhibit 5-1. In this balance sheet, we (a) separate company items from personal items according to the *entity concept*, and (b) use the *monetary unit concept* and the *historical cost concept* to show dollar values for each company-related item.

These three concepts are the foundation of what the accounting process shows. With this in mind, you can see how that process functions. The accountant, or the owner, uses the *entity concept* to separate the activities of a company from the owner's activities, which are not related to the company. The company's *transactions* are identified by analyzing *source documents*. The accountant or owner then enters the transactions into the company's accounting records using *monetary units* based on the *costs* involved in its activities. Every time a company activity occurs, the accountant or owner uses these concepts to help decide the proper way to record that activity. After the economic information about a company's activities is recorded and accumulated, the ultimate goal of the accounting process is to communicate this information in the company's balance sheet, its income statement, and its cash flow statement, each prepared according to GAAP.

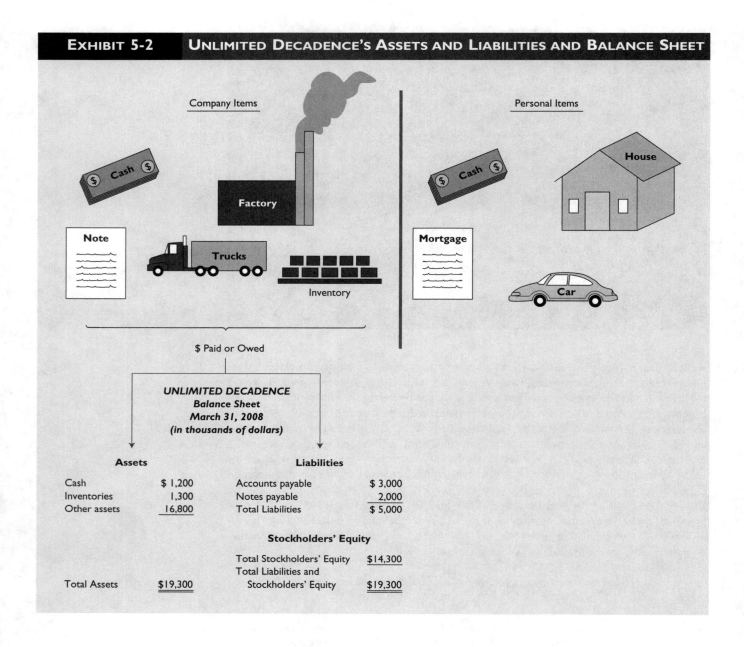

**EXHIBIT 5-2 UNLIMITED DECADENCE'S ASSETS AND LIABILITIES AND BALANCE SHEET**

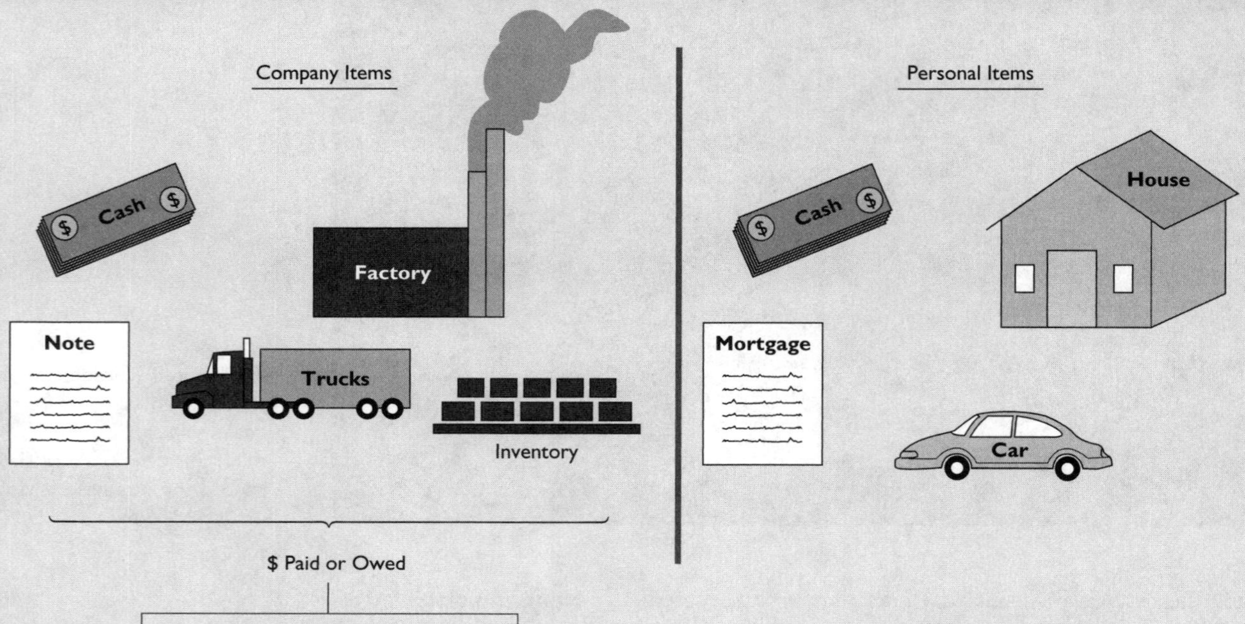


***UNLIMITED DECADENCE***
***Balance Sheet***
***March 31, 2008***
***(in thousands of dollars)***

| Assets | | Liabilities | |
|---|---|---|---|
| Cash | $ 1,200 | Accounts payable | $ 3,000 |
| Inventories | 1,300 | Notes payable | 2,000 |
| Other assets | 16,800 | Total Liabilities | $ 5,000 |
| | | **Stockholders' Equity** | |
| | | Total Stockholders' Equity | $14,300 |
| | | Total Liabilities and | |
| Total Assets | $19,300 | Stockholders' Equity | $19,300 |

# COMPONENTS OF THE ACCOUNTING EQUATION

We can now begin to discuss how the **accounting system** works—the process used to identify, measure, record, and retain information about a company's activities so that the company can prepare its financial statements. This process is based on the three sections of a balance sheet: the asset, liability, and owner's equity sections. Every time a company records the exchange of property or services with another party, the transaction affects at least one of the sections of the balance sheet. So before moving on, consider the following expanded definitions of assets, liabilities, and owner's equity.

## Assets

**Assets** are a company's economic resources that will provide future benefits to the company. A company may own many assets, some of which are physical in nature—such as land, buildings, supplies to be used, and inventory that the company expects to sell to its customers. Other assets do not have physical characteristics but are economic resources because of the legal rights (benefits) they convey to the company. These assets include amounts owed by customers to the company (**accounts receivable**), the right to insurance protection (**prepaid insurance**), and investments made in other companies.

*Can you think of more examples of assets? How do each of these examples meet the definition of assets?*

## Liabilities

**Liabilities** are the economic obligations (debts) of a company. The external parties to whom a company owes the debts are referred to as the **creditors** of the company. Liabilities include amounts owed to suppliers for credit purchases (**accounts payable**) and amounts owed to employees for work they have done (**wages and salaries payable**). Legal documents are often evidence of liabilities. These documents establish a claim (**equity**) by the creditors (the **creditors' equity**) against the assets of a company.

*Can you think of more examples of liabilities? How do each of these examples meet the definition of liabilities?*

## Owner's Equity

The **owner's equity** of a company is the owner's current investment in the assets of the company. (A partnership's balance sheet would refer to **partners' equity**, and a corporation's balance sheet would call this **stockholders' equity**, as you saw in Exhibits 5-1 and 5-2.) The capital invested in the company by the owner, the company's earnings from operations, and the owner's withdrawals of capital from the company all affect owner's equity. For a sole proprietorship, the balance sheet shows the owner's equity by listing the owner's name, the word *capital,* and the amount of the owner's current investment in the company. As you will see later, partners' equity and stockholders' equity appear slightly differently. Owner's equity is sometimes referred to as **residual equity** because creditors have first legal claim to a company's assets. Once the creditors' claims have been satisfied, the owner is entitled to the remainder (residual) of the assets. Sometimes the total of the liabilities (creditors' equity) is combined with the owner's equity, and the result is referred to as the **total equity** of the company.

## Using the Accounting Equation

3 What do users need to know about the accounting equation for a company?

In summary, accountants use the term *assets* to refer to a company's economic resources, and they use the terms *liabilities* and *owner's equity* to describe claims on those resources. All of a company's economic resources are claimed by either creditors or owners. Therefore, the financial accounting system is built on a simple equation:

**Economic Resources = Claims on Economic Resources**

Using the accounting terms you have learned, we can restate the equation:

**Assets = Liabilities + Owner's Equity**

This mathematical expression is known as the basic **accounting equation**. The equality of the assets to the liabilities plus owner's equity is the reason a company's statement of financial position is called a *balance* sheet: the monetary total for the economic resources (assets) of the company must always be *in balance* with the monetary total for the claims (liabilities + owner's equity) on the economic resources. Like the components of any other equation, the components of this equation may be transposed. Another way of showing the equation is shown as follows.

**Assets − Liabilities = Owner's Equity**

In this form of the equation, the left-hand side (i.e., assets minus liabilities) is referred to as **net assets**. This form of the equation also stresses that owner's equity may be thought of as a residual amount. Regardless of what form the equation takes, it must always balance. Because a transaction normally begins the accounting process, a company must record each transaction in a way that maintains this equality. Keeping this equality in mind will help you understand other aspects of the accounting process.

## The Dual Effect of Transactions

4 Why are at least two effects of each transaction recorded in a company's accounting system?

To keep the accounting equation in balance, *a company must make at least two changes in its assets, liabilities, or owner's equity* when it records each transaction. This is called the **dual effect of transactions**. For instance, when an owner invests $20,000 in a company, assets (cash) are increased by $20,000 and owner's equity (owner's capital) is increased by $20,000. This transaction causes two changes—one change in the asset section of the company's balance sheet and one change in the owner's equity section of its balance sheet. Because the left-hand side *and* the right-hand side both increase by the same amount, the accounting equation (assets = liabilities + owner's equity) stays in balance.

The fact that transactions always have a dual effect does not mean that every transaction will affect both sides of the equation—or even two components of the equation. A transaction may affect only one side, by increasing one asset and decreasing another asset by the same amount. For example, assume a company buys office equipment by paying $400 cash. In this case, the asset Office Equipment increases by $400 and the asset Cash decreases by $400. The accounting equation still balances after the company records this transaction because the transaction does not affect the right side of the equation and because the *total* for the asset (left) side of the equation is not changed.

To understand how the accounting equation and the dual effect of transactions provide structure to a company's accounting system, think about these concepts as describing a company's "transaction scales." Exhibit 5-3 shows a set of "transaction scales." Instead

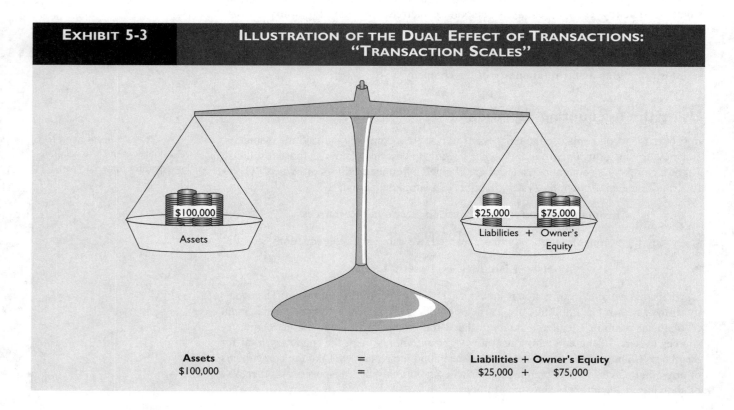

**EXHIBIT 5-3 ILLUSTRATION OF THE DUAL EFFECT OF TRANSACTIONS: "TRANSACTION SCALES"**

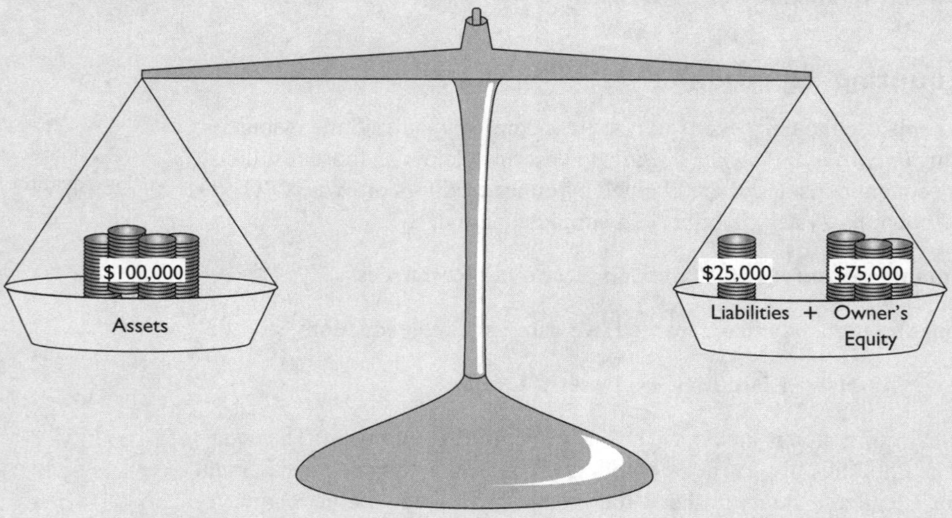


| **Assets** | = | **Liabilities + Owner's Equity** |
|---|---|---|
| $100,000 | = | $25,000 + $75,000 |

of measuring the weight of various objects, using ounces or pounds as measuring units, these scales measure transactions, using dollars (historical cost monetary units). Suppose a company currently has assets of \$100,000, liabilities of \$25,000, and owner's equity of \$75,000. Assume that the company's accountant or owner "places" the company's current economic resources (assets of \$100,000) on the left side of the scales and "places" current claims on those resources (liabilities of \$25,000 + owner's equity of \$75,000) on the right side of the scales. Remember, after each transaction the scales must balance. The dual effect of transactions provides a way to keep the scales in balance as company activities are placed (recorded) on the scales. Note that in Exhibit 5-3 the left side of the scales holds \$100,000 in total assets and the right side holds \$25,000 in liabilities and \$75,000 in owner's equity. The scales balance according to the accounting equation:

| | | | | |
|---|---|---|---|---|
| **Assets** | = | **Liabilities** | + | **Owner's Equity** |
| \$100,000 | = | \$25,000 | + | \$75,000 |

As we stated earlier, regardless of the type of transaction that occurs, the accounting equation, like our set of transaction scales, must always balance. Exhibits 5-4 and 5-5 use

**EXHIBIT 5-4 "TRANSACTION SCALES": INCREASE IN ASSETS AND OWNER'S EQUITY**

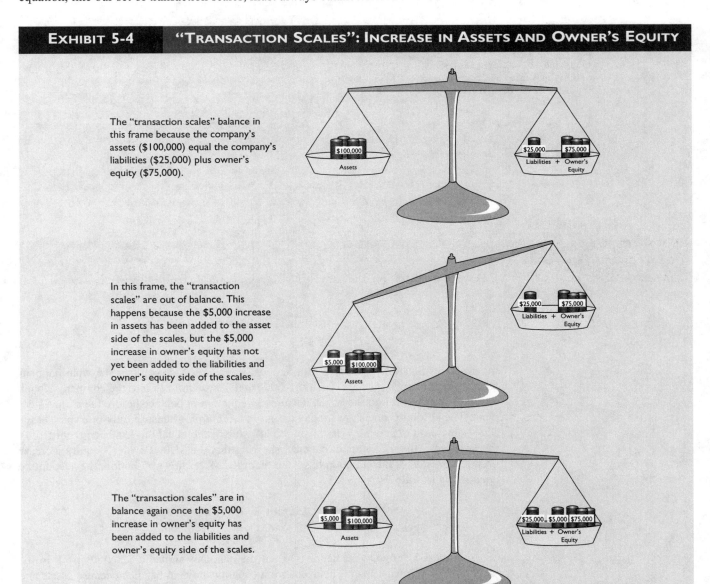

The "transaction scales" balance in this frame because the company's assets (\$100,000) equal the company's liabilities (\$25,000) plus owner's equity (\$75,000).

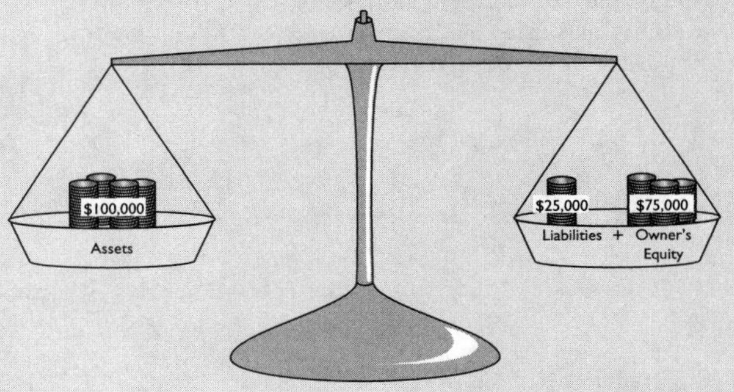


In this frame, the "transaction scales" are out of balance. This happens because the \$5,000 increase in assets has been added to the asset side of the scales, but the \$5,000 increase in owner's equity has not yet been added to the liabilities and owner's equity side of the scales.

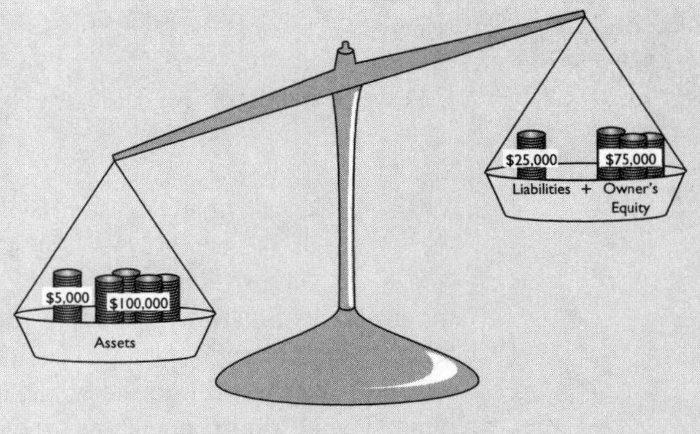


The "transaction scales" are in balance again once the \$5,000 increase in owner's equity has been added to the liabilities and owner's equity side of the scales.

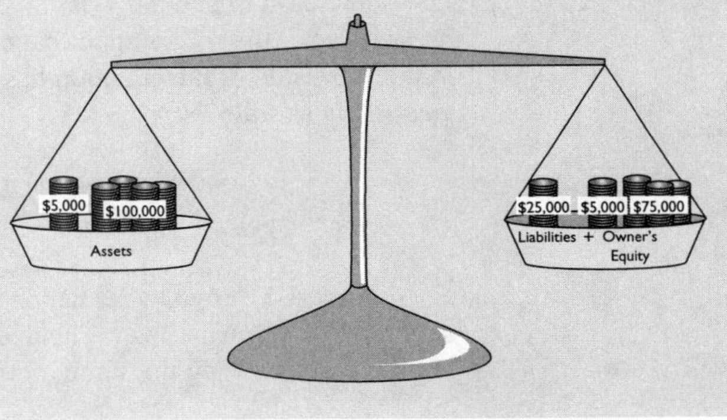

## EXHIBIT 5-5 "TRANSACTION SCALES": DECREASE IN ASSETS AND LIABILITIES

The "transaction scales" balance in this frame because the company's assets ($105,000) equal the company's liabilities ($25,000) plus owner's equity ($80,000).

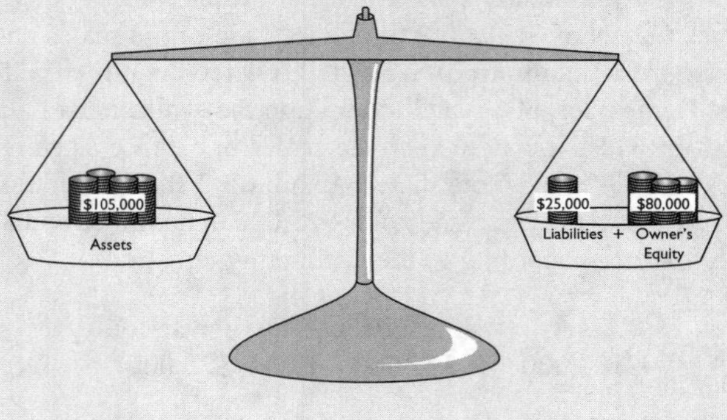


The "transaction scales" do not balance in this frame because, although the $20,000 decrease in assets has been taken off the scales, the liabilities have not yet been changed.

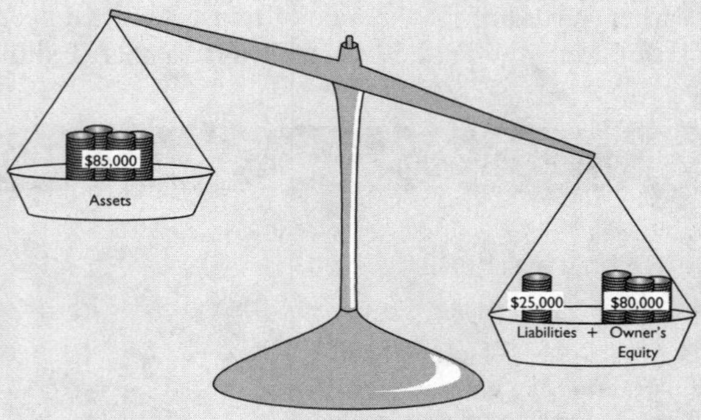


The "transaction scales" are in balance again once the $20,000 decrease in liabilities is removed from the liabilities and owner's equity side of the scales.

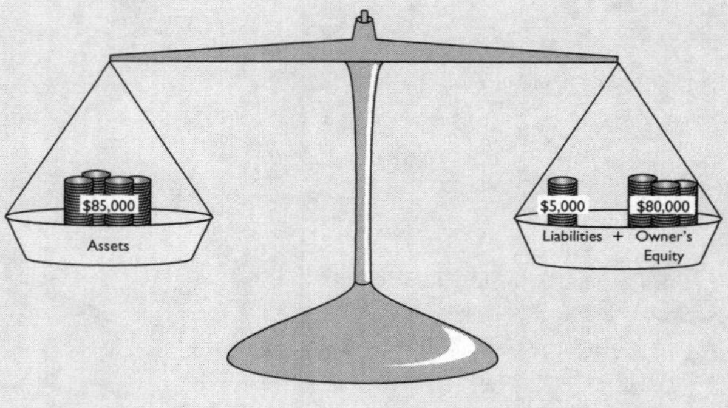


the scales to illustrate two more transactions. In Exhibit 5-4, you can see what happens when the company's owner deposits $5,000 *from personal funds* into the company's bank account. The first frame shows the accounting equation in balance before the owner's deposit. The second frame shows the equation *out of balance* because only one change, the $5,000 increase in company assets on the left side of the equation, has been recorded. In the last frame, the scales again balance, showing that the $5,000 owner's equity increase on the right side of the equation has been recorded. After this transaction, the accounting equation is as follows:

| Assets | = | Liabilities | + | Owner's Equity |
|---|---|---|---|---|
| $105,000 | = | $25,000 | + | $80,000 |

Exhibit 5-5 shows what happens when the company writes a $20,000 check to the bank to pay off a bank loan. The accounting equation stays in balance because assets and liabilities decrease by the same amount:

**Assets = Liabilities + Owner's Equity**
$85,000 = $5,000 + $80,000

*Do you think that companies in other countries use this same structure? Why or why not?*

# Accounting for Transactions to Start a Business

In Chapters 3 and 4 you saw how managers use accounting information to develop a business plan to show potential investors. Managers also use accounting information for internal decision making. C-V-P analysis and budgeting provide accounting information that helps managers answer questions such as the following: How much money does the company need to have on hand to start the business? How much inventory should the company have available? How much money can the company spend to advertise the grand opening of the business? These initial transactions are undertaken for one purpose—so that managers can pursue the goal of earning a satisfactory income (profit) for the owners. The profit goal is met by selling products or services to customers at prices that are higher than the costs of providing the products or services.

Once a company starts operating, it uses financial statements to report to external users about its operations. To prepare these financial statements, the company's accountant or owner identifies transactions and records them in the company's accounting system. This analysis uses the accounting equation and recognizes the dual effect of transactions.

*If you loaned money to a company, how often would you want the company to report on its operations? Why?*

The transactions recorded in the accounting system are the basis for the internal and external reports that the company issues. Therefore, it is very important that the transactions are entered correctly, since they "live on" in the system, sometimes for many years.

With the accounting equation (and the dual effect of transactions) in mind, watch Anna Cox as she analyzes and records the December 2007 transactions involved in starting her business, Sweet Temptations. Note how Anna uses accounting concepts, the accounting equation, and the dual effect of transactions to build an effective accounting system.

## Investing Cash (Transaction 1)

Anna Cox starts her business on December 15, 2007, by writing a $15,000 personal check and depositing it in a checking account she opened for Sweet Temptations. Anna wants to open the candy store to customers on January 2, 2008, so that she can build some customer traffic before people start buying their Valentine candy. This company checking account is separate, of course, from her personal account because of the entity concept.

Anna decides to establish a basic accounting system for Sweet Temptations on a sheet of paper by listing assets, liabilities, and owner's equity as headings of separate columns. Each column is called an **account**—that is, a place a company uses to record and retain information about the effect of its transactions on a specific asset, liability, or owner's equity item. Anna records each transaction by entering the amounts in the appropriate account columns. Anna uses the receipt issued by Sweet Temptations for her check and the bank deposit slip she used to open the company's bank account as source documents for the first transaction. Exhibit 5-6 shows how she records this first transaction.

*Does Anna Cox's personal check serve as a source document for Sweet Temptations? Why or why not?*

**EXHIBIT 5-6** **ANNA INVESTS CASH IN SWEET TEMPTATIONS**

| | | Assets | = | Liabilities | + | Owner's Equity |
|---|---|---|---|---|---|---|
| Trans | Date | Cash | | | | A. Cox, Capital |
| (1) | 12/15/07 | + $15,000 | | | | + $15,000 |
| Balances | | $15,000 | = | | | $15,000 |

Note that Anna makes two $15,000 entries to record the dual effect of the transaction—one to an asset account (Cash) and one to an owner's equity account (A. Cox, Capital)—and that the accounting equation balances because she increases both sides of the equation by the same amount. At the end of each day Anna computes the **balance** of each account—the amount in the account at the beginning of the day plus the increases and minus the decreases recorded in the column that day. In this case, since Anna has recorded only one transaction, Sweet Temptations now has a balance in the Cash account of $15,000 and a balance in the A. Cox, Capital account of $15,000, as we indicate by the "double-lines" under the amounts.

## Prepaying Rent (Transaction 2)

To open Sweet Temptations at the Westwood Mall, Anna signed, in the company's name, a rental agreement with the mall's manager on December 16, 2007. The monthly rent is $1,000, and the agreement requires that rent for six months be paid in advance. Since the space is empty, the mall manager agrees to let Anna begin setting up her business immediately but not to start charging her rent until January 1, 2008. This arrangement works well for Anna because now she can begin purchasing store equipment, supplies, and inventory.

So, on December 16, Anna writes a company check for $6,000 ($1,000 × 6 months) to the Westwood Mall. Sweet Temptations' check and the signed rental agreement are the source documents for the transaction. Exhibit 5-7 shows how Anna records this second transaction.

The benefit of using the mall space for six months to conduct business represents an economic resource, or asset, to Sweet Temptations. As a result, Anna records $6,000 as an increase in a new asset account—Prepaid Rent. Because cash is paid out, she decreases the asset Cash by the total amount paid, $6,000. At the end of the day, she subtracts this amount from the previous amount of Cash to show a new balance, $9,000. Then, she checks the accounting equation to see that it remains in balance. She does this by adding the assets ($9,000 + $6,000) and comparing this $15,000 amount with the to-

**EXHIBIT 5-7** **SWEET TEMPTATIONS PREPAYS RENT**

| | | Assets | | | = | Liabilities | + | Owner's Equity |
|---|---|---|---|---|---|---|---|---|
| Trans | Date | Cash | + | Prepaid Rent | | | | A. Cox, Capital |
| (1) | 12/15/07 | + $15,000 | | | | | | + $15,000 |
| (2) | 12/16/07 | − $ 6,000 | | + $6,000 | | | | |
| Balances | | $ 9,000 | + | $6,000 | = | | | $15,000 |

**EXHIBIT 5-8** **SWEET TEMPTATIONS PURCHASES SUPPLIES WITH CASH**

| | | Assets | | | | | = | Liabilities | + | Owner's Equity |
|---|---|---|---|---|---|---|---|---|---|---|
| Trans | Date | Cash | + | Prepaid Rent | + | Supplies | | | | A. Cox, Capital |
| (1) | 12/15/07 | +$15,000 | | | | | | | | +$15,000 |
| (2) | 12/16/07 | −$ 6,000 | | +$6,000 | | | | | | |
| (3) | 12/17/07 | −$ 700 | | | | +$700 | | | | |
| Balances | | $ 8,300 | + | $6,000 | + | $700 | = | | | $15,000 |

tal of the liabilities ($0) plus owner's equity ($15,000). As you can see, the equation still balances.

*How many changes did Anna make in the accounting equation to record this transaction? Why?*

## Purchasing Supplies with Cash (Transaction 3)

On December 17, 2007, Sweet Temptations purchases $700 of office and store supplies from City Supply Company by writing a check for $700. Anna receives an *invoice* that lists the items purchased, the cost of each item, and the total cost. She uses the invoice as the source document to record this third transaction, as we show in Exhibit 5-8. Because the supplies will be used to conduct business, Anna records them as an asset, Supplies, of $700. Because the purchase is made with cash, she reduces the asset Cash by $700. Note that the changes in these two assets offset each other on the left side of the accounting equation, which thus remains in balance.

## Purchasing Inventory on Credit (Transaction 4)

On December 20, 2007, Sweet Temptations purchases $1,620 of candy (360 boxes of candy for $4.50 each) on credit from Unlimited Decadence Corporation. Sweet Temptations agrees to pay for the candy within 30 days of purchase. An invoice from Unlimited Decadence is the source document for the transaction. Exhibit 5-9 shows how Anna records this fourth transaction. Sweet Temptations needs a way to keep track of the cost of the candy that it buys from manufacturers and has on hand to sell to retail candy customers.

**EXHIBIT 5-9** **SWEET TEMPTATIONS PURCHASES INVENTORY ON CREDIT**

| | | Assets | | | | | | | = | Liabilities | + | Owner's Equity |
|---|---|---|---|---|---|---|---|---|---|---|---|---|
| Trans | Date | Cash | + | Prepaid Rent | + | Supplies | + | Inventory | = | Accounts Payable | + | A. Cox, Capital |
| (1) | 12/15/07 | +$15,000 | | | | | | | | | | +$15,000 |
| (2) | 12/16/07 | −$ 6,000 | | +$6,000 | | | | | | | | |
| (3) | 12/17/07 | −$ 700 | | | | +$700 | | | | | | |
| (4) | 12/20/07 | | | | | | | +$1,620 | | +$1,620 | | |
| Balances | | $ 8,300 | + | $6,000 | + | $700 | + | $1,620 | = | $1,620 | + | $15,000 |

Anna thus adds an account column to assets to record Inventory. She increases Inventory by the cost of the candy, $1,620, but does not reduce Cash because none was paid out. Since Sweet Temptations agrees to pay for the inventory later, it incurs a debt, or a liability. Anna calls the liability Accounts Payable because it is an amount to be paid by the company, and she increases Accounts Payable by $1,620. Note that Unlimited Decadence Corporation, not Anna Cox, finances this increase in Sweet Temptations' assets (economic resources). Unlimited Decadence is now Sweet Temptations' creditor because it has a claim on $1,620 of the candy store's assets. The $1,620 increase in economic resources matches the $1,620 increase in the claims on those resources. So, the left side of the accounting equation and the liability component of the right side both increase by $1,620. The accounting equation balances after the transaction is recorded.

## Purchasing Store Equipment with Cash and Credit (Transaction 5)

On December 29, 2007, Sweet Temptations purchases store equipment from Ace Equipment Company at a cost of $2,200. It pays $1,000 down and signs a note agreeing to pay the remaining $1,200 (plus interest of $24) at the end of three months. Anna uses the invoice, the check, and the note to record this fifth transaction, as we show in Exhibit 5-10. Because the store equipment is an economic resource to be used in the business, Anna increases the asset Store Equipment by the total cost of $2,200. She decreases the asset Cash by the amount paid, $1,000. Since Sweet Temptations incurs a $1,200 liability and issues a legal note, Anna increases the liability Notes Payable by this amount. She does not record any interest now because interest accumulates as time passes, and no time has passed since Sweet Temptations issued the note. This transaction affects two asset accounts and a liability account, but the accounting equation remains in balance.

## Selling Extra Store Equipment on Credit (Transaction 6)

Sweet Temptations obtained a special price on the store equipment by buying a "package," which included an extra computer desk that the company did not need. So on December 30, 2007, Sweet Temptations sells the desk, which cost $400, for that same amount to The Hardware Store, another store in the mall. The Hardware Store agrees to pay for the desk on January 7. Exhibit 5-11 shows how Anna records this sixth transaction. Because Sweet Temptations sells one of its economic resources, Anna decreases the asset Store Equipment by $400, the cost of the desk. Because the amount to be received from The Hardware Store in January is an economic resource for Sweet Temptations, Anna also records an increase of $400 in the asset Accounts Receivable. Again, note the equality of the accounting equation.

**EXHIBIT 5-10** **SWEET TEMPTATIONS PURCHASES STORE EQUIPMENT WITH CASH AND CREDIT**

| | | *Assets* | | | | | | | | | | = | *Liabilities* | | | + | *Owner's Equity* |
|---|---|---|---|---|---|---|---|---|---|---|---|---|---|---|---|---|---|
| **Trans** | **Date** | **Cash** | + | **Prepaid Rent** | + | **Supplies** | + | **Inventory** | + | **Store Equipment** | | = | **Accounts Payable** | + | **Notes Payable** | + | **A. Cox, Capital** |
| (1) | 12/15/07 | + $15,000 | | | | | | | | | | | | | | | + $15,000 |
| (2) | 12/16/07 | − $ 6,000 | | + $6,000 | | | | | | | | | | | | | |
| (3) | 12/17/07 | − $ 700 | | | | + $700 | | | | | | | | | | | |
| (4) | 12/20/07 | | | | | | | + $1,620 | | | | | + $1,620 | | | | |
| (5) | 12/29/07 | − $ 1,000 | | | | | | | | + $2,200 | | | | | + $1,200 | | |
| Balances | | $ 7,300 | + | $6,000 | + | $700 | + | $1,620 | + | $2,200 | | = | $1,620 | + | $1,200 | + | $15,000 |

**EXHIBIT 5-11 SWEET TEMPTATIONS SELLS EXTRA STORE EQUIPMENT ON CREDIT**

| | | *Assets* | | | | | | = | *Liabilities* | + | *Owner's Equity* |
|---|---|---|---|---|---|---|---|---|---|---|---|
| **Trans** | **Date** | **Cash +** | **Prepaid Rent +** | **Supplies +** | **Inventory +** | **Store Equipment +** | **Accounts Receivable** | **=** | **Accounts Payable +** | **Notes Payable +** | **A. Cox, Capital** |
| (1) | 12/15/07 | + $15,000 | | | | | | | | | + $15,000 |
| (2) | 12/16/07 | − $ 6,000 | + $6,000 | | | | | | | | |
| (3) | 12/17/07 | − $ 700 | | + $700 | | | | | | | |
| (4) | 12/20/07 | | | | + $1,620 | | | | + $1,620 | | |
| (5) | 12/29/07 | − $ 1,000 | | | | + $2,200 | | | | + $1,200 | |
| (6) | 12/30/07 | | | | | − $ 400 | + $ 400 | | | | |
| Balances | | $ 7,300 + | $6,000 + | $700 + | $1,620 + | $1,800 + | $ 400 | = | $1,620 + | $1,200 + | $15,000 |

# EXPANDING THE ACCOUNTING EQUATION

5 What are revenues and expenses, and how is the accounting equation expanded to record these items?

Until now, we have focused on how a company records transactions that occur when it is preparing to open for business. You have learned how the accounting equation changes as the company uses its accounting system to record an owner's investment, the purchases of assets with cash and on credit, and the sale of equipment. After the company opens for business, internal and external users of financial statements need income information to evaluate how well the company has been operating. By recording the transactions of its day-to-day operations, a company develops this income information. As you continue reading, keep the accounting equation and the dual effect of transactions in mind.

Anna had no problem using the basic accounting equation to record the start-up transactions in the balance sheet columns. However, she needs to modify the accounting system to record the income-producing transactions, such as sales to customers; these transactions do not fit easily into the equation as it is currently stated.

*If you were Anna, how would you expand Sweet Temptations' accounting system so that you could record revenue and expense transactions? What column headings would you add to the accounting system?*

To modify the accounting system, Anna separates the Owner's Equity part of the equation into two sections. The first, the Owner's Capital account, lets her record transactions relating to her investments and withdrawals of capital from the company. The second section lets her record net income (revenues and expenses). For recording both types of transactions, the equality of the accounting equation is maintained because of the dual effects of transactions. The expanded accounting equation is as follows:

$$\textbf{Assets} = \textbf{Liabilities} + \overbrace{\textbf{Owner's Capital} + \underbrace{\textbf{Net Income}}_{\textbf{Revenues} - \textbf{Expenses}}}^{\textbf{Owner's Equity}}$$

Recall from Chapter 1 that the income of a company is commonly referred to as net income. **Net income** is the excess of revenues over expenses *for a specific time period.* Net income is sometimes called *net profit*, *net earnings*, or simply *earnings*. **Revenues** are the prices a company charged to its customers for goods or services it provided during a specific time period. **Expenses** are the costs of providing the goods or services to customers during the time period.

Anna records revenue and expense transactions by expanding the columns in the simple accounting system she uses. To find out how much net income Sweet Temptations earned over a specific time period (e.g., the month of January), she subtracts the total in the expense column from the total in the revenue column.

We will demonstrate how to use the expanded accounting equation later in the chapter. But first we will discuss various principles and concepts related to net income, since the expanded equation deals with revenues and expenses—the two items that affect net income.

## ACCOUNTING PRINCIPLES AND CONCEPTS RELATED TO NET INCOME

6 What are the accounting principles and concepts related to net income?

Earlier in the chapter we explained several basic concepts and terms used in accounting. Before you learn how a company records its daily transactions to determine net income, it is helpful to know several additional accounting principles and concepts that are part of GAAP.

### Accounting Period

A company typically operates for many years. The company's owner (internal user) needs information about its net income on a regular basis to make operating decisions. External users of financial statement information also need to know about the company's net income on a regular basis to make timely business decisions. Suppliers need this information for granting credit, creditors need this information for renewing bank loans, and investors need this information for providing additional capital.

Given that both internal and external users benefit when a company routinely reports its net income, the question is: How often should a company do so? Earlier we said that net income is the excess of revenues over expenses for a specific time period. An **accounting period** is the time span for which a company reports its revenues and expenses. Most companies base their financial statements on a twelve-month accounting period called a *fiscal year* or a *fiscal period*. The fiscal year is often the same as the *calendar year;* however, a company whose operations are seasonal may use a year that corresponds more closely to its *operating cycle*. For instance, a retail company (such as **Wal-Mart**) may use January 31, 2008 through January 31, 2009 for its fiscal year so that its accounting period will include the purchase and sale of inventory that peaks for the December holiday season. Many companies also compute and report their net income on a quarterly basis. These accounting periods (and others shorter than a year) are referred to as *interim* periods. In this book we often present simplified examples that use one month as the accounting period.

### Earning and Recording Revenues

Revenues result from a company's operating activities that contribute to its earning process. Broadly speaking, every activity of a company contributes to its earning process. More specifically, a company's **earning process** includes purchasing (or producing) inventory, selling the inventory (or services), delivering the inventory (or services), and collecting and paying cash. Although a company *earns* revenues continuously during this process, it generally *records* revenues near or at the end of the earning process.[2] This is because (1) the earning process is complete (the company has made the sale and delivered the product or performed the service) and (2) the prices charged to customers are collectible (accounts receivable) or collected. So we can say that a company **records revenues** during the accounting period in which they are earned and are collectible (or collected).

[2]Construction companies sometimes take several years to complete a project (e.g., an office building). To more fairly report their yearly net income, these companies record a portion of their total revenues each year based on the amount earned during the year.

### Matching Principle

Expenses are subtracted from revenues to calculate net income. Another way of saying this is that the costs used up are *matched* against the prices charged to customers to determine net income. The **matching principle** states that to determine its net income for an accounting period, a company computes the expenses involved in earning the revenues of the period and deducts the total expenses from the total revenues earned in that period. By matching expenses against revenues, a company has a good idea of how much better off it is at the end of an accounting period as a result of its operations during that period.

### Accrual Accounting

Accrual accounting is related to both the recording of revenue and the matching principle. When a company uses **accrual accounting**, it records its revenue and related expense transactions in the same accounting period that it provides goods or services (in the period in which it *earns* the revenue), regardless of whether it receives or pays cash in that period. To accrue means to accumulate. Accrual accounting makes accounting information helpful to external users because it does not let cash receipts and cash payments distort a company's net income. Otherwise, the amount of revenues the company earned during an accounting period could be distorted because the company may have received cash earlier or later than it sold goods or provided services. The amount of expenses could be distorted because the company may have paid cash earlier or later than it incurred (or used up) the related costs.

*Do you think that, by requiring accrual accounting to be used in the preparation of a company's income statement, GAAP implies that the company's cash receipts and payments are not important? Why or why not?*

Under accrual accounting, a company must be certain that it has recorded in each accounting period all revenues that it earned during that period, even if it received no cash during the period. Similarly, at the end of each accounting period, the company must be certain that it has matched all expenses it incurred during the period against the revenues it earned in that same period even if it paid no cash during the period.

**Summary.** How do these concepts relate to a company's accounting system? A company sets up and uses its accounting system based on the *accounting equation* and the *dual effect of transactions*. A company, which is a separate *entity* from its owners, analyzes *source documents* to record its *transactions*. It records the transactions in the accounting system in *monetary units* based on the *historical costs* involved in the company activity. In keeping with *accrual accounting*, a company records its revenue transactions when the revenues are *earned and collectible*, and it records expenses when it incurs the costs. The *matching* principle ensures that all expenses are matched with the revenues they helped earn so that the company can calculate its net income for each *accounting period*.

## RECORDING DAILY OPERATIONS

Here's how Anna uses the expanded accounting equation to record the January 2008 day-to-day operations of the Sweet Temptations candy store at the Westwood Mall.

### Cash Sale (Transaction 1)

On January 2, 2008, Anna Cox opens Sweet Temptations for business. Sweet Temptations sells a total of 30 boxes of candy at $10 a box for cash. For each sale, the cash register tape lists the date, the type and number of boxes of candy sold, and the total dollar amount of the sale. Anna uses the cash register tape as the source document for the 30 cash sales, which total $300. At the end of the day, Anna increases the Revenues column of Owner's Equity by $300. She also increases Cash by this amount. Of course, Sweet

Temptations had to give customers 30 boxes of candy in order to make the $300 in sales. By checking the purchasing records, Anna knows that the candy originally cost Sweet Temptations $135 ($4.50 × 30 boxes) when purchased from Unlimited Decadence Corporation. Because Sweet Temptations no longer owns the candy, Anna decreases Inventory by $135. In addition, because the cost of the candy is a cost of providing the goods that were sold to customers, she increases Expenses by $135.

Exhibit 5-12 shows Sweet Temptations' accounting equation at the close of its first business day, assuming no other transactions occur. The first line in Exhibit 5-12 shows the balances in each of Sweet Temptations' assets, liabilities, and owner's equity accounts at the *start* of its first business day. These balances came from the transactions that Anna recorded in December as she prepared for business (see the balances in Exhibit 5-11). The next line shows how Anna records the cash sale on January 2. Note on this line that Anna shows that the increase in Expenses causes a decrease in Net Income (and therefore Owner's Equity) by putting a minus sign in the column before the increased amount [i.e., |−| + $135] in the Expense column. Note also how the accounting equation remains in balance because of the dual effect of the cash sales transaction. Cash sales will take place every day that Sweet Temptations is open. Although Anna would record these cash sales transactions every day as they occur, to keep things simple in Exhibit 5-20 (later in the chapter), we include a transaction (#13) to represent *all* of the cash sales (770 boxes) that took place from January 3, 2008 through January 31, 2008. These sales total $7,700 ($10 × 770 boxes), so Anna increases both Revenues and Cash by that amount. She also increases Expenses by $3,465 ($4.50 × 770 boxes) and decreases Inventory by that same amount.

*Do you think it is typical to have customers purchase 30 boxes of candy from a small retail store on its first day of business? How could you verify your opinion?*

## Payment for Credit Purchase of Inventory and Additional Inventory Purchase (Transactions 2 and 3)

Recall that Sweet Temptations purchased its beginning inventory on credit from Unlimited Decadence Corporation on December 20, 2007. Anna recorded this transaction as a $1,620 increase in Inventory and a $1,620 increase in Accounts Payable. On January 3, 2008, Anna writes a Sweet Temptations check to Unlimited Decadence as payment for the December 20, 2007, purchase. An invoice from Unlimited Decadence is the source document for the transaction. To show the results of this transaction, Anna decreases the asset Cash by $1,620. Because the company no longer owes Unlimited Decadence for its purchase, she also decreases the liability Accounts Payable by $1,620.

On January 4, 2008, Sweet Temptations purchases 960 boxes of chocolates (at $4.50 per box) on credit from Unlimited Decadence for $4,320. As a result of the purchase, Anna increases Inventory by $4,320, and because the purchase is made on credit, she also increases Accounts Payable by the same amount. Exhibit 5-13 shows the changes in the accounting equation resulting from these two transactions.

*Does this purchase correspond to the expected purchase noted in Sweet Temptations' purchases budget for January, as we discussed in Chapter 4?*

## Credit Sale (Transaction 4)

On January 6, 2008, Sweet Temptations sells 10 boxes of candy for $100 on credit to Bud Salcedo, owner of Bud's Buds flower shop, next door to Sweet Temptations. The sales invoice lists the date, the type of candy sold, the flower shop's name and account number, and the total dollar amount of the sale. Anna assigns each of Sweet Temptations' credit customers a unique account number to help her identify transactions the company has with each of these customers. (This will be particularly useful as the number of credit

## Exhibit 5-12 Sweet Temptations Makes Cash Sales

| | | Assets | | | | | | = Liabilities | | + Owner's Equity | | |
|---|---|---|---|---|---|---|---|---|---|---|---|---|
| | | | | | | | | | | Owner's Capital | + Net Income | |
| Trans | Date | Cash | + Prepaid Rent | + Supplies | + Inventory | + Store Equipment | + Accounts Receivable | = Accounts Payable | + Notes Payable | + A. Cox, Capital | + Revenues | − Expenses |
| Balances | 1/1/08 | $ 7,300 | $6,000 | $700 | $1,620 | $1,800 | $400 | $1,620 | $1,200 | $15,000 | | |
| (1) | 1/2/08 | +$ 300 | | | −$ 135 | | | | | | +$ 300 | +$ 135 |
| Balances | | $ 7,600 | $6,000 | $700 | $1,485 | $1,800 | $400 | $1,620 | $1,200 | $15,000 | $ 300 | $ 135 |

## Exhibit 5-13 Sweet Temptations Pays for Credit Purchases and Makes Additional Credit Purchase of Inventory

| | | Assets | | | | | | = Liabilities | | + Owner's Equity | | |
|---|---|---|---|---|---|---|---|---|---|---|---|---|
| | | | | | | | | | | Owner's Capital | + Net Income | |
| Trans | Date | Cash | + Prepaid Rent | + Supplies | + Inventory | + Store Equipment | + Accounts Receivable | = Accounts Payable | + Notes Payable | + A. Cox, Capital | + Revenues | − Expenses |
| Balances | 1/1/08 | $ 7,300 | $6,000 | $700 | $1,620 | $1,800 | $400 | $1,620 | $1,200 | $15,000 | | |
| (1) | 1/2/08 | +$ 300 | | | −$ 135 | | | | | | +$ 300 | +$ 135 |
| (2) | 1/3/08 | −$ 1,620 | | | | | | −$1,620 | | | | |
| (3) | 1/4/08 | | | | +$4,320 | | | +$4,320 | | | | |
| Balances | | $ 5,980 | $6,000 | $700 | $5,805 | $1,800 | $400 | $4,320 | $1,200 | $15,000 | $ 300 | $ 135 |

## Exhibit 5-14 Sweet Temptations Sells Candy on Credit

| | | Assets | | | | | | = Liabilities | | + Owner's Equity | | |
|---|---|---|---|---|---|---|---|---|---|---|---|---|
| | | | | | | | | | | Owner's Capital | + Net Income | |
| Trans | Date | Cash | + Prepaid Rent | + Supplies | + Inventory | + Store Equipment | + Accounts Receivable | = Accounts Payable | + Notes Payable | + A. Cox, Capital | + Revenues | − Expenses |
| Balances | 1/1/08 | $ 7,300 | $6,000 | $700 | $1,620 | $1,800 | $400 | $1,620 | $1,200 | $15,000 | | |
| (1) | 1/2/08 | +$ 300 | | | −$ 135 | | | | | | +$ 300 | +$ 135 |
| (2) | 1/3/08 | −$ 1,620 | | | | | | −$1,620 | | | | |
| (3) | 1/4/08 | | | | +$4,320 | | | +$4,320 | | | | |
| (4) | 1/6/08 | | | | −$ 45 | | +$100 | | | | +$ 100 | +$ 45 |
| Balances | | $ 5,980 | $6,000 | $700 | $5,760 | $1,800 | $500 | $4,320 | $1,200 | $15,000 | $ 400 | $ 180 |

customers grows.) Having the account number on the sales invoice lets Sweet Temptations keep track of the money each customer owes.

Anna increases the Revenues column of Owner's Equity by $100. Because Sweet Temptations sold the candy on credit instead of receiving cash, Anna increases the asset Accounts Receivable by $100. Remember, Sweet Temptations has to dip into its candy inventory to make the sale. By checking the purchasing records, Anna knows that the boxes originally cost $45. Because the company no longer owns the candy, Anna decreases Inventory by $45. In addition, because the cost of the candy is a cost of providing the goods sold, she increases Expenses by $45. Exhibit 5-14 shows the four changes in the accounting equation from this transaction. The accounting equation remains in balance.

## Receipt of Payment for Credit Sale of Extra Store Equipment (Transaction 5)

Sweet Temptations receives a check for $400 from The Hardware Store on January 7, 2008. The check is to pay for the store equipment that Sweet Temptations sold on credit to The Hardware Store on December 30, 2007. As you can see in Exhibit 5-15, Anna reduces the asset Accounts Receivable by $400 because The Hardware Store has settled its account and no longer owes Sweet Temptations any money. She increases the asset Cash by $400 to show the receipt of the check.

## Withdrawal of Cash by Owner (Transaction 6)

On January 20, 2008, Anna Cox withdraws $50 cash from the business for personal use, writing a $50 check to herself from the Sweet Temptations bank account. She then deposits the check in her personal bank account. The check is the source document for the transaction. A **withdrawal** is a payment from the company to the owner. Thus, it is a disinvestment of assets by the owner. Therefore, as we show in Exhibit 5-16, Anna records a decrease in Cash and a decrease in A. Cox, Capital by the amount of the withdrawal ($50).

*What do you think Anna would record if she took ten boxes of candy instead of cash?*

We will discuss withdrawals again in Chapter 6.

*Can you think of any possible ethical issues involved in withdrawals?*

## Payments for Consulting and Advertising (Transactions 7 and 8)

To prepare for a Valentine's Day grand opening sale, Sweet Temptations hires the Dana Design Group to produce an advertisement. The design group charges $200 and presents the ad on January 25, 2008. Sweet Temptations writes a check for the full amount that day. The receipt received from Dana Design is the source document. As a result of this transaction, Anna increases Expenses by $200 and decreases Cash by $200.

Also on January 25, 2008, Sweet Temptations pays for the advertisement to be published in Westwood Mall's end-of-January promotional flyer. The quarter-page advertisement cost $300. The bill from Westwood Mall's management office is the source document for the transaction. As we show in Exhibit 5-17, to record this transaction, Anna increases Expenses by $300 and decreases Cash by the same amount. Note that the accounting equation remains in balance after these transactions are recorded.

*If Cash was mistakenly decreased by only $100 when the last transaction was recorded, how would you find out that an error was made?*

## EXHIBIT 5-15 SWEET TEMPTATIONS RECEIVES PAYMENT FROM CREDIT SALE OF EXTRA STORE EQUIPMENT

| | | Assets | | | | | | = Liabilities | | + Owner's Equity | | |
|---|---|---|---|---|---|---|---|---|---|---|---|---|
| | | | | | | | | | | Owner's Capital + | Net Income | |
| Trans | Date | Cash + | Prepaid Rent + | Supplies + | Inventory + | Store Equipment + | Accounts Receivable = | Accounts Payable + | Notes Payable + | A. Cox, Capital + | Revenues − | Expenses |
| Balances | 1/1/08 | $ 7,300 | $6,000 | $700 | $1,620 | $1,800 | $400 | $1,620 | $1,200 | $15,000 | | |
| (1) | 1/2/08 | +$ 300 | | | −$ 135 | | | | | | +$ 300 − | +$ 135 |
| (2) | 1/3/08 | −$ 1,620 | | | | | | −$1,620 | | | | |
| (3) | 1/4/08 | | | | +$4,320 | | | +$4,320 | | | | |
| (4) | 1/6/08 | | | | −$ 45 | | +$100 | | | | +$ 100 − | +$ 45 |
| (5) | 1/7/08 | +$ 400 | | | | | −$400 | | | | | |
| Balances | | $ 6,380 + | $6,000 + | $700 + | $5,760 + | $1,800 + | $100 = | $4,320 + | $1,200 + | $15,000 + | $ 400 − | $ 180 |

## EXHIBIT 5-16 ANNA WITHDRAWS CASH FROM SWEET TEMPTATIONS

| | | Assets | | | | | | = Liabilities | | + Owner's Equity | | |
|---|---|---|---|---|---|---|---|---|---|---|---|---|
| | | | | | | | | | | Owner's Capital + | Net Income | |
| Trans | Date | Cash + | Prepaid Rent + | Supplies + | Inventory + | Store Equipment + | Accounts Receivable = | Accounts Payable + | Notes Payable + | A. Cox, Capital + | Revenues − | Expenses |
| Balances | 1/1/08 | $ 7,300 | $6,000 | $700 | $1,620 | $1,800 | $400 | $1,620 | $1,200 | $15,000 | | |
| (1) | 1/2/08 | +$ 300 | | | −$ 135 | | | | | | +$ 300 − | +$ 135 |
| (2) | 1/3/08 | −$ 1,620 | | | | | | −$1,620 | | | | |
| (3) | 1/4/08 | | | | +$4,320 | | | +$4,320 | | | | |
| (4) | 1/6/08 | | | | −$ 45 | | +$100 | | | | +$ 100 − | +$ 45 |
| (5) | 1/7/08 | +$ 400 | | | | | −$400 | | | | | |
| (6) | 1/20/08 | −$ 50 | | | | | | | | −$ 50 | | |
| Balances | | $ 6,330 + | $6,000 + | $700 + | $5,760 + | $1,800 + | $100 = | $4,320 + | $1,200 + | $14,950 + | $ 400 − | $ 180 |

## Exhibit 5-17 Sweet Temptations Pays for Consulting and Advertising

| | | Assets | | | | | | | | | | | = | Liabilities | | | + | Owner's Equity: Owner's Capital | + | Owner's Equity: Net Income | | |
|---|---|---|---|---|---|---|---|---|---|---|---|---|---|---|---|---|---|---|---|---|---|---|
| Trans | Date | Cash | + | Prepaid Rent | + | Supplies | + | Inventory | + | Store Equipment | + | Accounts Receivable | = | Accounts Payable | + | Notes Payable | + | A. Cox, Capital | + | Revenues | − | Expenses |
| Balances | 1/1/08 | $ 7,300 | | $6,000 | | $700 | | $1,620 | | $1,800 | | $400 | | $1,620 | | $1,200 | | $15,000 | | | | |
| (1) | 1/2/08 | +$ 300 | | | | | | −$ 135 | | | | | | | | | | | | +$ 300 | − | +$ 135 |
| (2) | 1/3/08 | −$ 1,620 | | | | | | | | | | | | −$1,620 | | | | | | | | |
| (3) | 1/4/08 | | | | | | | +$4,320 | | | | | | +$4,320 | | | | | | | | |
| (4) | 1/6/08 | | | | | | | −$ 45 | | | | +$100 | | | | | | | | +$ 100 | − | +$ 45 |
| (5) | 1/7/08 | +$ 400 | | | | | | | | | | −$400 | | | | | | | | | | |
| (6) | 1/20/08 | −$ 50 | | | | | | | | | | | | | | | | −$ 50 | | | | |
| (7) | 1/25/08 | −$ 200 | | | | | | | | | | | | | | | | | | | − | +$ 200 |
| (8) | 1/25/08 | −$ 300 | | | | | | | | | | | | | | | | | | | − | +$ 300 |
| Balances | | $ 5,830 | + | $6,000 | + | $700 | + | $5,760 | + | $1,800 | + | $100 | = | $4,320 | + | $1,200 | + | $14,950 | + | $ 400 | − | $ 680 |

## Exhibit 5-18 Sweet Temptations Purchases Another Display Case

| | | Assets | | | | | | | | | | | = | Liabilities | | | + | Owner's Equity: Owner's Capital | + | Owner's Equity: Net Income | | |
|---|---|---|---|---|---|---|---|---|---|---|---|---|---|---|---|---|---|---|---|---|---|---|
| Trans | Date | Cash | + | Prepaid Rent | + | Supplies | + | Inventory | + | Store Equipment | + | Accounts Receivable | = | Accounts Payable | + | Notes Payable | + | A. Cox, Capital | + | Revenues | − | Expenses |
| Balances | 1/1/08 | $ 7,300 | | $6,000 | | $700 | | $1,620 | | $1,800 | | $400 | | $1,620 | | $1,200 | | $15,000 | | | | |
| (1) | 1/2/08 | +$ 300 | | | | | | −$ 135 | | | | | | | | | | | | +$ 300 | − | +$ 135 |
| (2) | 1/3/08 | −$ 1,620 | | | | | | | | | | | | −$1,620 | | | | | | | | |
| (3) | 1/4/08 | | | | | | | +$4,320 | | | | | | +$4,320 | | | | | | | | |
| (4) | 1/6/08 | | | | | | | −$ 45 | | | | +$100 | | | | | | | | +$ 100 | − | +$ 45 |
| (5) | 1/7/08 | +$ 400 | | | | | | | | | | −$400 | | | | | | | | | | |
| (6) | 1/20/08 | −$ 50 | | | | | | | | | | | | | | | | −$ 50 | | | | |
| (7) | 1/25/08 | −$ 200 | | | | | | | | | | | | | | | | | | | − | +$ 200 |
| (8) | 1/25/08 | −$ 300 | | | | | | | | | | | | | | | | | | | − | +$ 300 |
| (9) | 1/25/08 | −$ 200 | | | | | | | | +$ 200 | | | | | | | | | | | | |
| Balances | | $ 5,630 | + | $6,000 | + | $700 | + | $5,760 | + | $2,000 | + | $100 | = | $4,320 | + | $1,200 | + | $14,950 | + | $ 400 | − | $ 680 |

© DAVID BURCH/INDEX STOCK

Do you think Sweet Temptations' location next to Bud's Buds will improve its sales of Valentine candy? Why or why not?

## Acquisition of Store Equipment (Transaction 9)

On January 29, 2008, Sweet Temptations purchases an additional candy display case. Sweet Temptations pays $200 in cash by writing a check. As you can see in Exhibit 5-18, Anna increases Store Equipment by $200 and decreases Cash by the same amount.

## Payment of Salaries (Transaction 10)

Sweet Temptations employs two people (you and Jaime Gonzales) to help stock and sell candy. On January 31, 2008, you both receive checks, totaling $2,050, as payment for your services during January. Your time cards, wage rate schedules, and paychecks are the source documents for the transactions. As you can see in Exhibit 5-19, Anna decreases the asset Cash by $2,050. Because paying an employee's salary is a cost of providing goods and services to customers, she also increases Expenses by the same amount.

## Payment of Telephone and Utilities Bills (Transactions 11 and 12)

On January 31, 2008, Sweet Temptations pays its telephone bill and its utility bill (heat, light, and water) for January. The two checks are written for $60 and $190, respectively. Anna records each transaction separately, using the bills and checks as the source documents. As you can see in Exhibit 5-20, she decreases Cash and increases Expenses for both transactions.

## Summary Cash Sales (Transaction 13)

Exhibit 5-20 also shows the summary transaction, which we discussed earlier, of all the cash sales from January 3 through January 31.

*How many additional boxes of candy did Sweet Temptations sell for cash from January 3 through January 31? Why were Expenses increased by $3,465?*

**EXHIBIT 5-19** SWEET TEMPTATIONS PAYS SALARIES

| | | Assets | | | | | | = Liabilities | | + Owner's Equity: Owner's Capital | + Net Income | |
|---|---|---|---|---|---|---|---|---|---|---|---|---|
| Trans | Date | Cash | + Prepaid Rent | + Supplies | + Inventory | + Store Equipment | + Accounts Receivable | = Accounts Payable | + Notes Payable | + A. Cox, Capital | + Revenues | − Expenses |
| Balances | 1/1/08 | $ 7,300 | $6,000 | $700 | $1,620 | $1,800 | $400 | $1,620 | $1,200 | $15,000 | | |
| (1) | 1/2/08 | +$ 300 | | | −$ 135 | | | | | | +$ 300 | +$ 135 |
| (2) | 1/3/08 | −$ 1,620 | | | | | | −$1,620 | | | | |
| (3) | 1/4/08 | | | | +$4,320 | | | +$4,320 | | | | |
| (4) | 1/6/08 | | | | −$ 45 | | +$100 | | | | +$ 100 | +$ 45 |
| (5) | 1/7/08 | +$ 400 | | | | | −$400 | | | | | |
| (6) | 1/20/08 | −$ 50 | | | | | | | | −$ 50 | | |
| (7) | 1/25/08 | −$ 200 | | | | | | | | | | +$ 200 |
| (8) | 1/25/08 | −$ 300 | | | | | | | | | | +$ 300 |
| (9) | 1/25/08 | −$ 200 | | | | +$ 200 | | | | | | |
| (10) | 1/31/08 | −$ 2,050 | | | | | | | | | | +$2,050 |
| Balances | | $ 3,580 | $6,000 | $700 | $5,760 | $2,000 | $100 | $4,320 | $1,200 | $14,950 | $ 400 | $2,730 |

**EXHIBIT 5-20** SWEET TEMPTATIONS PAYS TELEPHONE AND UTILITY BILLS AND RECORDS SALES FOR JANUARY 3–JANUARY 31

| | | Assets | | | | | | = Liabilities | | + Owner's Equity: Owner's Capital | + Net Income | |
|---|---|---|---|---|---|---|---|---|---|---|---|---|
| Trans | Date | Cash | + Prepaid Rent | + Supplies | + Inventory | + Store Equipment | + Accounts Receivable | = Accounts Payable | + Notes Payable | + A. Cox, Capital | + Revenues | − Expenses |
| Balances | 1/1/08 | $ 7,300 | $6,000 | $700 | $1,620 | $1,800 | $400 | $1,620 | $1,200 | $15,000 | | |
| (1) | 1/2/08 | +$ 300 | | | −$ 135 | | | | | | +$ 300 | +$ 135 |
| (2) | 1/3/08 | −$ 1,620 | | | | | | −$1,620 | | | | |
| (3) | 1/4/08 | | | | +$4,320 | | | +$4,320 | | | | |
| (4) | 1/6/08 | | | | −$ 45 | | +$100 | | | | +$ 100 | +$ 45 |
| (5) | 1/7/08 | +$ 400 | | | | | −$400 | | | | | |
| (6) | 1/20/08 | −$ 50 | | | | | | | | −$ 50 | | |
| (7) | 1/25/08 | −$ 200 | | | | | | | | | | +$ 200 |
| (8) | 1/25/08 | −$ 300 | | | | | | | | | | +$ 300 |
| (9) | 1/25/08 | −$ 200 | | | | +$ 200 | | | | | | |
| (10) | 1/31/08 | −$ 2,050 | | | | | | | | | | +$2,050 |
| (11) | 1/31/08 | −$ 60 | | | | | | | | | | +$ 60 |
| (12) | | −$ 190 | | | | | | | | | | +$ 190 |
| (13) | 1/3/08 thru 1/31/08 | +$ 7,700 | | | −$3,465 | | | | | | +$7,700 | +$3,465 |
| Balances | | $11,030 | $6,000 | $700 | $2,295 | $2,000 | $100 | $4,320 | $1,200 | $14,950 | $8,100 | $6,445 |

# END-OF-PERIOD ADJUSTMENTS

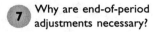

7 Why are end-of-period adjustments necessary?

Remember, revenues are the prices charged to a company's customers for goods or services it provided during the accounting period, and expenses are the costs of providing those goods or services during the period. The net income is the excess of revenues over expenses for the period. To calculate net income for a month, for example, a company counts the dollar totals for all the revenue and expense transactions of that specific month and subtracts the expense total from the revenue total. That is, it matches the expenses against the revenues for the month.

To calculate a company's net income under accrual accounting, the company must make sure that all its revenues and expenses for the accounting period are included in the totals. For Sweet Temptations, Anna can easily verify that the revenue total is correct because every sale is listed on a source document (a sales invoice or a cash register tape), which she used to record each sales transaction. Anna can verify that *most* of Sweet Temptations' expenses are correct because they also have source documents (invoices, utilities bills, and time cards).

*Do you think it sometimes may be difficult to identify when a sale has occurred? Why?*

It is more difficult, however, for a company to make sure that *all* of the expenses it incurred during the month are included in the net income calculation because some of the costs of providing goods or services occur without a source document. Since these expense transactions don't have source documents, there is no "automatic trigger" for recording the transactions. Before calculating its net income, then, a company must analyze its unique expenses (and a few unique revenues, which we will briefly discuss later) to see if it needs to adjust (increase) the total expenses (or revenues) to include those without source documents. These adjustments are called **end-of-period adjustments**.

*What types of expenses can you think of that occur without source documents?*

In general, end-of-period adjustments involve assets that a company had at the beginning of the accounting period but that it used during the period to earn revenues. As assets lose their potential for providing future benefits, they are changed to expenses. Anna must analyze Sweet Temptations' assets to see what additional expenses to record. As you will see, the end-of-period adjustments may also include liabilities that a company owes because of expenses that must be recorded. Let's take a look at the four end-of-period adjustments that Anna makes before calculating Sweet Temptations' net income for January 2008, its first month of operations.

## Supplies Used (Transaction 14)

Recall that on December 17, 2007, Sweet Temptations purchased $700 of supplies from City Supply Company. At this time, Anna increased the asset Supplies by $700 to show the cost of this new asset. Sweet Temptations thus purchased the pens, paper, blank sales invoices, and other items it needed to operate the business.

Because Sweet Temptations operated during January, it used some of these supplies. Thus, at January 31, 2008, the $700 original amount of Supplies is not correct. Anna must adjust the amount to show that since some of the supplies were used, they now are an expense, and only part of the $700 of supplies is still an asset. Anna determines that the office supplies used during January amount to $30. She makes an end-of-period adjustment to increase Expenses by $30 and decrease the asset Supplies by $30, as we show in Exhibit 5-21. When she subtracts the $30 from the $700 original amount, the $670 ending balance is the cost of supplies the company still owns at the end of January. Notice how

**EXHIBIT 5-21** **SWEET TEMPTATIONS MAKES END-OF-PERIOD ADJUSTMENTS**

| | | *Assets* | | | | | | | | | | | = | *Liabilities* | | | + | *Owner's Equity* | | | | |
|---|---|---|---|---|---|---|---|---|---|---|---|---|---|---|---|---|---|---|---|---|---|---|
| | | | | | | | | | | | | | | | | | | *Owner's Capital* | + | *Net Income* | | |
| Trans | Date | Cash | + | Prepaid Rent | + | Supplies | + | Inventory | + | Store Equipment | + | Accounts Receivable | = | Accounts Payable | + | Notes Payable | + | A. Cox, Capital | + | Revenues | − | Expenses |
| Balances | 1/31/08 | $11,030 | | $6,000 | | $700 | | $2,295 | | $2,000 | | $100 | | $4,320 | | $1,200 | | $14,950 | | $8,100 | − | $6,445 |
| (14) | 1/31/08 | | | | | −$ 30 | | | | | | | | | | | | | | | − | +$ 30 |
| (15) | 1/31/08 | | | −$1,000 | | | | | | | | | | | | | | | | | − | +$1,000 |
| (16) | 1/31/08 | | | | | | | | | −$ 15 | | | | | | | | | | | − | +$ 15 |
| (17) | 1/31/08 | | | | | | | | | | | | | | | +$ 8 | | | | | − | +$ 8 |
| Balances | 1/31/08 | $11,030 | + | $5,000 | + | $670 | + | $2,295 | + | $1,985 | + | $100 | = | $4,320 | + | $1,208 | + | $14,950 | + | $8,100 | − | $7,498 |

this adjustment (and each of the following adjustments) maintains the equality of Sweet Temptations' accounting equation and has a dual effect on the equation.

*How do you think Anna determined the amount of supplies used?*

## Expired Rent (Transaction 15)

Recall that Sweet Temptations wrote a check for $6,000 to the Westwood Mall on December 16, 2007, to pay in advance for six months' rent starting on January 1, 2008. At that time Anna recorded a $6,000 asset, Prepaid Rent, to show that Sweet Temptations had purchased the right to use space in the Westwood Mall for six months (January through June) at a price of $1,000 per month. At the end of January, Sweet Temptations has used up one month of Prepaid Rent—for January—because the business occupied the mall space for that entire month. Therefore, Anna must include the cost of the mall space as an expense in the calculation of Sweet Temptations' net income.

Since Sweet Temptations made the $6,000 payment on December 16, 2007, no other source documents relating to the rental of the mall space exist. Although Sweet Temptations has used up one of its six months of rent, the amount listed for Prepaid Rent is still $6,000. Anna must adjust the Prepaid Rent amount to show that only five months of prepaid rent remain. To do so, she increases Expenses for January by $1,000 and reduces Prepaid Rent by the same amount, as we show in Exhibit 5-21. Now Prepaid Rent shows the correct balance of $5,000 ($1,000 × 5) for the remaining five months.

*What adjustment do you think Anna would make at the end of January if Sweet Temptations occupied the rental space for January but did not pay for any rent until February?*

## Depreciation of Store Equipment (Transaction 16)

At the beginning of January the amount for the asset Store Equipment was listed at the cost of $1,800. Sweet Temptations purchased the store equipment because it would help earn revenue. The equipment includes, for instance, display cases, a cash register, and a moving cart. Although Sweet Temptations doesn't expect any equipment to wear out completely after one month or even one year, it does not expect it all to last indefinitely. At some point in the future the display cases will become outdated, the cash register will quit working, and the moving cart will fall apart. At that time the company will decide to sell or dispose of the equipment.

The store equipment provides benefits to the company every period in which it is used. Because Sweet Temptations used the store equipment in January to help earn candy revenue and because the store equipment has a finite life, a portion of the cost of the store equipment is included as an expense in the January net income calculation. **Depreciation** is the part of the cost of a physical asset allocated as an expense to each time period in which the asset is used.

The simplest way to compute depreciation is to divide the cost by the estimated life of the asset. For now, assume that the depreciation for the store equipment is $15 a month. Anna makes an end-of-period adjustment for January's depreciation by increasing Expenses by $15 and decreasing the asset Store Equipment by $15, as we show in Exhibit 5-21.[3] Now store equipment shows the $1,985 remaining cost (called its "book value"). As Sweet Temptations uses the store equipment in each future month, it will record an additional $15 depreciation, which will reduce the book value of the equipment. Therefore, at any point in time the difference between the original cost and the book value is

[3]Sweet Temptations also purchased $200 of additional store equipment late in January. Sweet Temptations will include the depreciation on this store equipment as an expense in later months as it uses the equipment.

the "accumulated depreciation" to date. We will discuss the methods used to calculate depreciation in Chapter 21.

### Accrual of Interest (Transaction 17)

At the end of December 2007, Sweet Temptations purchased store equipment by signing a $1,200 note payable to be paid at the end of three months. Generally, all notes payable also involve the payment of interest for the amount borrowed. This interest is an expense of doing business during the time between the signing of the note and the payment of the note. Sweet Temptations agreed to pay $24 total interest for the note, so that at the end of the three months Sweet Temptations will pay $1,224 ($1,200 + $24). Interest accumulates (*accrues*) over time until it is paid. Since Sweet Temptations owed the note during all of January, Anna must record one month of interest on the note as an expense of doing business during January. Because Sweet Temptations will not pay the interest until it pays the note, it records the January interest as an increase in a liability. For now, assume that the interest is $8 per month ($24 ÷ 3). Anna makes an end-of-period adjustment for the January interest by increasing Expenses by $8 and increasing the liability Notes Payable by $8, as we show in Exhibit 5-21. We will discuss how to compute interest later in the book.

### End-of-Period Revenue Adjustments

There are a few end-of-period adjustments that a company may need to make to ensure that its revenues are correct for the accounting period. Here, we briefly discuss two. First, a company may have a note receivable (asset) that earns interest that the company will collect when it collects the note. At the end of the accounting period, the company must record any interest that has accumulated *(accrued)* by increasing Revenues and increasing the asset Notes Receivable. Second, a company might collect cash in advance from a customer for sales of products that it will deliver to the customer or for services that it will perform for the customer later in the current accounting period or in the next accounting period. In this case, the company has not earned the revenue at the time of the cash collecton. Therefore, it records the receipt by increasing Cash and increasing a liability (sometimes called *Unearned Revenue*). Then, at the end of the current accounting period the company must decrease the Unearned Revenue and increase Revenues for the amount of revenue it has earned during the period. We will discuss end-of-period revenue adjustments more completely in later chapters.

*At the end of January, 2008, what adjustment would Ace Equipment Company make for the $8 interest it has earned on the $1,200 note it received from Sweet Temptations at the end of December, 2007?*

## NET INCOME AND ITS EFFECT ON THE BALANCE SHEET

After recording the results of all the transactions and end-of-period adjustments (shown in Exhibit 5-21, Anna calculates Sweet Temptations' net income for January:

| **Net Income** | = | **Revenues** | − | **Expenses** |
|---|---|---|---|---|
| $602 | = | $8,100 | − | $7,498 |

A company will normally prepare an income statement that lists the various types of revenues and expenses included in net income. For simplicity, in this chapter we use a simple accounting system, which does not help in the preparation of a detailed income statement. In Chapter 6 we will expand the accounting system and show you how to prepare an income statement. Anna can, however, compare the actual net income amount for January with the projected net income that she calculated when she planned Sweet Temptations' operations. In Chapter 3, she calculated a projected net income for Sweet Temptations of $110 for January 2008. Anna should be pleased; by achieving an actual net income of $602, Sweet Temptations has done better than she expected. Later in the book, we will discuss how internal and external users analyze the financial statements of a company to understand how well it did for a specific time period.

To prepare the January 31, 2008 balance sheet for Sweet Temptations, Anna uses the end-of-the-month balances for each asset, liability, and owner's equity account listed in Exhibit 5-21. Exhibit 5-22 shows Sweet Temptations' balance sheet at January 31, 2008.

You should be able to trace the asset and liability amounts directly to the ending balances listed on Exhibit 5-21. The assets on the balance sheet are rearranged, however, to show them in the order of their *liquidity*, or how quickly the assets can be converted to cash or used up. We will discuss liquidity more in later chapters. Also notice that Anna must calculate the balance sheet amount for Owner's Equity (A. Cox, capital) at the end of January. It is the sum of all of the owner's equity items included in Exhibit 5-21:

| | |
|---|---|
| A. Cox, capital | $14,950 |
| Revenues | + 8,100 |
| Expenses | − 7,498 |
| Owner's Equity | $15,552 |

Expressed another way, it is the sum of A. Cox, capital and net income ($14,950 + $602). We will explain how to "update" the balance of the owner's capital account for net income in Chapter 6.

Since Anna is the owner, the net income (revenues minus expenses) is included in her capital amount on the January 31, 2008 balance sheet. Using the total amounts for the asset, liability, and owner's equity sections of Sweet Temptations' balance sheet, we can state the accounting equation on January 31, 2008 as follows:

| **Assets** | = | **Liabilities** | + | **Owner's Equity** |
|---|---|---|---|---|
| $21,080 | = | $5,528 | + | $15,552 |

Because Anna properly recorded Sweet Temptations' transactions, the company's accounting equation is in balance at January 31, 2008.

**EXHIBIT 5-22 SWEET TEMPTATIONS' BALANCE SHEET**

**SWEET TEMPTATIONS**
***Balance Sheet***
***January 31, 2008***

| **Assets** | | **Liabilities** | |
|---|---|---|---|
| Cash | $11,030 | Accounts payable | $ 4,320 |
| Accounts receivable | 100 | Notes payable | 1,208 |
| Inventory | 2,295 | Total Liabilities | $ 5,528 |
| Supplies | 670 | | |
| Prepaid rent | 5,000 | **Owner's Equity** | |
| Store equipment | 1,985 | A. Cox, capital | $15,552* |
| | | Total Owner's Equity | $15,552 |
| Total Assets | $21,080 | Total Liabilities and Owner's Equity | $21,080 |

*$14,950 + $8,100 − $7,498; from Exhibit 5-21.

Just as we expanded the accounting equation to record revenue and expense transactions, we will discuss other changes in the accounting system throughout the book. The changes make it easier to keep track of company activities and increase the usefulness of the accounting system. We will also introduce additional accounting concepts to help you understand why companies make changes to the accounting system. In the next three chapters, we will take a detailed look at three very important outputs of the accounting process—the income statement, the balance sheet, and the cash flow statement. We will also continue to answer questions concerning what accounting is, how accounting works, why accounting is performed, and how accounting information is used for problem-solving and decision-making. We will also discuss how to minimize errors that, among other things, can cause major embarrassments, as we discuss below.

## Business Issues and Values: A Billion Here, a Billion There

In one year, **Fidelity Investments** estimated that it would make a year-end distribution of $4.32 per share to shareholders in its *Magellan Fund.* The company then admitted to an error. Included in a letter sent to shareholders was the following statement: "... The error occurred when the accountant omitted the minus sign on a net capital loss of $1.3 billion and incorrectly treated it as a net capital gain on (a) separate spreadsheet. This meant that the dividend estimate spreadsheet was off by $2.6 billion." The error had no effect on the fund's results or on the shareholders' taxes but was clearly an embarrassment to the company's management!

## Summary

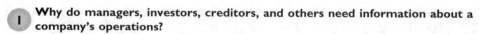

At the beginning of the chapter we asked you several questions. During the chapter, we asked you to STOP and answer some additional questions to build your knowledge about specific issues. Be sure you answered these additional questions. Below are the questions from the beginning of the chapter, with a brief summary of the key points relating to the answers. Use your creative and critical thinking skills to expand on these key points to develop more complete answers to the questions and to determine what other questions you have that might lead you to learn more about the issues.

### 1 Why do managers, investors, creditors, and others need information about a company's operations?

Internal and external users need information about a company's operations to evaluate alternatives. For instance, a manager needs this information to decide which alternative best helps the company meet its goals of remaining solvent and earning a satisfactory profit. A banker also needs this information to decide the conditions for granting a loan.

### 2 What are the basic concepts and terms that help identify the activities that a company's accounting system records?

The basic concepts and terms that help identify the activities that a company's accounting system records are the entity concept (each company is separate from its owners), transactions (exchanges between a company and another entity), source documents (business records as evidence of transactions), the monetary unit concept (transactions are recorded in monetary terms), and the historical cost concept (transactions are recorded based on dollars exchanged).

### 3 What do users need to know about the accounting equation for a company?

Users need to know the accounting equation: Assets = Liabilities + Owner's Equity. They need to know that assets are a company's economic resources, liabilities are a company's debts, and owner's equity is the owner's current investment in the assets of the company.

### 4 Why are at least two effects of each transaction recorded in a company's accounting system?

A company's accounting system is designed so that two effects of each transaction are recorded in order to maintain the equality of the accounting equation. Under the dual effect of transactions, recording a transaction involves at least two changes in the assets, liabilities, and owner's equity of a company.

### 5 What are revenues and expenses, and how is the accounting equation expanded to record these items?

Revenues are the prices a company charged its customers for goods or services provided during an accounting period. Expenses are the costs of providing the goods or services during the period. Net income is the excess of revenues over expenses for the period. The accounting equation is expanded as follows to record revenues and expenses: Assets = Liabilities + [Owner's Capital + (Revenues − Expenses)].

### 6 What are the accounting principles and concepts related to net income?

The accounting principles and concepts related to net income are the accounting period, earning and recording revenues, the matching principle, and accrual accounting. The accounting period is the time span used by a company to report its net income. A company records revenues during the accounting period in which they are earned and collectible. The matching principle states that a company matches the total expenses of an accounting period against the total revenues of the period to determine its net income. Accrual accounting means that a company records its revenues and expenses in the accounting period in which it provides goods or services, regardless of whether it receives or pays cash.

### 7 Why are end-of-period adjustments necessary?

End-of-period adjustments are necessary to record any expenses that a company has incurred (or any revenues that the company has earned) during the accounting period but that it has not yet recorded. Adjustments ensure that these expenses (and revenues) are included in the company's net income calculation.

## KEY TERMS

**account** *(p. 135)*
**accounting equation** *(p. 131)*
**accounting period** *(p. 140)*
**accounting system** *(p. 130)*
**accounts payable** *(p. 131)*
**accounts receivable** *(p. 131)*
**accrual accounting** *(p. 141)*
**assets** *(p. 130)*
**balance** *(p. 136)*
**creditors** *(p. 131)*
**creditors' equity** *(p. 131)*
**depreciation** *(p. 151)*
**dual effect of transactions** *(p. 132)*
**earning process** *(p. 140)*
**end-of-period adjustments** *(p. 149)*
**entity** *(p. 127)*
**equity** *(p. 131)*
**expenses** *(p. 139)*
**historical cost concept** *(p. 129)*
**liabilities** *(p. 131)*
**matching principle** *(p. 141)*
**monetary unit concept** *(p. 128)*
**net assets** *(p. 132)*
**net income** *(p. 139)*
**owner's equity** *(p. 131)*
**partners' equity** *(p. 131)*
**prepaid insurance** *(p. 131)*
**records revenues** *(p. 140)*
**residual equity** *(p. 131)*
**revenues** *(p. 139)*
**source document** *(p. 128)*
**stockholders' equity** *(p. 131)*
**total equity** *(p. 131)*
**transaction** *(p. 128)*
**wages and salaries payable** *(p. 131)*
**withdrawal** *(p. 144)*

# Integrated Business and Accounting Situations

**Answer the Following Questions in Your Own Words.**

## Testing Your Knowledge

**5-1** Why do external users need financial accounting information about a company? How can financial statements help these external users?

**5-2** Why is it important for external users to know that a company's financial statements are prepared according to GAAP?

**5-3** Name and briefly define five concepts and terms that you need to understand to identify the activities that a company's accounting system records.

**5-4** What is the entity concept? How does it affect the accounting for a specific company?

**5-5** What is a transaction? Why is it important in accounting?

**5-6** What is a source document? Why does a company need to prepare source documents?

**5-7** What are the monetary unit and historical cost concepts? How do they affect the recording of transactions?

**5-8** Define assets. Give four examples.

**5-9** Define liabilities. Give two examples.

**5-10** Define owner's equity. What items affect owner's equity?

**5-11** Why is a company's statement of financial condition called a *balance sheet?*

**5-12** What are a company's net assets? How do they relate to owner's equity?

**5-13** What is meant by the dual effect of transactions? How does it relate to the accounting equation?

**5-14** How is the accounting equation used to set up a basic accounting system for a company? What is an *account?* What is an *account balance?*

**5-15** Define revenues, expenses, and net income. How is the accounting equation expanded to record income-related transactions?

**5-16** Name and briefly define four principles and concepts relating to net income.

**5-17** What is an accounting period? What is the usual length of an accounting period?

**5-18** What is a company's earning process, and when does the company record revenues?

**5-19** What is the matching principle? Why is it useful to a company?

**5-20** What is accrual accounting, and why is it important?

**5-21** How do the accounting concepts, principles, and terms discussed in the chapter relate to the accounting system of a company?

**5-22** What are end-of-period adjustments? Why are they needed?

## Applying Your Knowledge

**5-23** Each of the following cases is independent of the others:

| *Case* | *Assets* | *Liabilities* | *Owner's Equity* |
|---|---|---|---|
| 1 | A | $24,000 | $54,000 |
| 2 | $83,000 | B | $42,000 |
| 3 | $98,000 | $32,000 | C |

*Required:* Determine the amounts for A, B, and C.

**5-24** At the beginning of the year, the Thomas Lighting Company had total assets of $78,000 and total liabilities of $22,000. During the year, the total assets increased by $16,000. At the end of the year, owner's equity totaled $64,000.

*Required:* Determine (1) the owner's equity at the beginning of the year and (2) the total liabilities at the end of the year.

**5-25** At the end of the year, a company's total assets are $75,000 and its total owner's equity is $48,000. During the year, the company's liabilities decreased by $11,000 while its assets increased by $7,000.

*Required:* Determine the company's (1) ending total liabilities, (2) beginning total assets, and (3) beginning owner's equity.

**5-26** The following transactions are taken from the records of Phantom Security Company:

| | Assets = Liabilities + Owner's Equity |
|---|---|
| (a) Rex Simpson, the owner, invested $12,000 cash in the business. | |
| (b) Phantom paid $6,000 cash to acquire security equipment. | |
| (c) Phantom received a $7,000 cash loan from Story County Bank. | |

*Required:* Determine the overall effect of each transaction on the assets, liabilities, and owner's equity of Phantom Security Company. Use the symbols *I* for increase, *D* for decrease, and *N* for no change. Also show the related dollar amounts.

**5-27** On August 31, 2008, the Hernandez Engineering Company's accounting records contained the following items (listed in alphabetical order):

| | |
|---|---|
| Accounts payable | $3,700 |
| Accounts receivable | 4,000 |
| Cash | 5,200 |
| L. Hernandez, capital | ? |
| Notes payable | 6,000 |
| Office equipment | 8,900 |
| Office supplies | 600 |
| Prepaid insurance | 800 |

*Required:* Prepare a balance sheet for the Hernandez Engineering Company at August 31, 2008. Insert the correct amount for L. Hernandez, capital.

**5-28** Listed below, in random order, are all the items included in the Ridge Rental Company balance sheet at December 31, 2008:

| | |
|---|---|
| Land | $ 2,200 |
| Accounts receivable | 3,500 |
| Cash | ? |
| Supplies | 900 |
| Accounts payable | 4,600 |
| Building | 19,000 |
| A. Ridge, capital | ? |
| Rental equipment | 6,800 |
| Notes payable | 5,700 |

Total assets on December 31, 2008 are $33,800.

*Required:* Prepare a balance sheet for the Ridge Rental Company on December 31, 2008. Insert the correct amounts for Cash and for A. Ridge, capital.

**5-29** In the chapter, we stated that a transaction is an exchange of property or service by a company with another entity. We also explained that in the recording of a transaction, at least two changes must be made in the assets, liabilities, or owner's equity of a company.

*Required:* In each case on the following page, describe a transaction that will result in the following changes in the contents of a company's balance sheet:

(a) Increase in an asset and increase in a liability
(b) Decrease in an asset and decrease in a liability
(c) Increase in an asset and decrease in another asset
(d) Increase in an asset and increase in owner's equity
(e) Increase in an asset and increase in revenues
(f) Increase in expenses and decrease in an asset

**5-30** Recall from the chapter that we defined a source document as a business record used by a company as evidence that a transaction has occurred.

*Required:* Name the source documents you think a company would use as evidence for each of the transactions listed below.
(a) Receipt of cash from the owner for additional investment in the company
(b) Payment by check to purchase office equipment
(c) Purchase of office supplies on credit
(d) Sale of office equipment at its original purchase price to a local CPA
(e) Purchase of fire and casualty insurance protection
(f) Sale of inventory on credit

**5-31** During October, the Wilson Company incurred the following costs:
(a) At the beginning of the month, the company paid $1,200 to an insurance agency for a two-year comprehensive insurance policy on the company's building.
(b) The company purchased office supplies costing $970 on credit from Bailey's Office Supplies.
(c) The company paid the telephone company $110 for telephone service during October.
(d) The owner withdrew $1,200 for personal use.
(e) The company found that of the $970 of office supplies purchased in (b), only $890 remained at October 31.

*Required:* For each of the preceding items, identify whether it would be recorded as an asset or an expense by the Wilson Company for October. List the dollar amount and explain your reasoning.

**5-32** Gertz Rent-A-Car is in the business of providing customers with quality rental cars at low rates. The company engaged in the following transactions during March:
(a) J. Gertz deposited an additional $1,900 of his personal cash into the company's checking account.
(b) The company collected $1,500 in car rental fees for March.
(c) The company borrowed $7,000 from the 1st National Bank to be repaid in one year.
(d) The company completed arrangements to provide fleet service to a local company for one year, starting in April, and collected $18,000 in advance.

*Required:* For each of the preceding transactions, identify which would be recorded as revenues by Gertz Rent-A-Car for March. List the dollar amount and explain your reasoning.

**5-33** The Slidell Auto Supply Company entered into the following transactions during the month of July:

| *Date* | *Transaction* |
|---|---|
| 7/1 | Joan Slidell, the owner, deposited $12,000 in the company's checking account. |
| 7/11 | Slidell Auto Supply purchased $800 of office supplies from Jips Paper Company, agreeing to pay for half of the supplies on July 31 and the rest of the supplies on August 15. |
| 7/16 | Slidell Auto Supply purchased a three-year fire insurance policy on a building owned by the company, paying $600 cash. |
| 7/31 | Slidell Auto Supply paid Jips Paper Company half the amount owed for the supplies purchased on July 11. |

*Required:* Using the basic accounting equation that we presented in this chapter, record the preceding transactions. Use headings for the specific kinds of assets, liabilities, and owner's equity. Set up your answer in the following form:

| *Date* | *Assets* | = | *Liabilities* | + | *Owner's Equity* |
|---|---|---|---|---|---|

**5-34** Amy Dixon opened the Dixon Travel Agency in January, and the company entered into the following transactions during January:

(a) On January 2, Amy deposited $23,000 in the company's checking account.
(b) To conduct its operations, the company purchased land for $3,000 and a small office building for $15,000 on January 3, paying $18,000 cash.
(c) On January 5, the company purchased $700 of office supplies from City Supply Company, agreeing to pay for half of the supplies on January 15 and the remainder on February 15.
(d) On January 12, the company purchased office equipment from Ace Equipment Company at a cost of $3,000. It paid $1,000 down and signed a note, agreeing to pay the remaining $2,000 at the end of one year.
(e) On January 15, the company paid City Supply Company half the amount owed for the supplies purchased on January 5.
(f) On January 28, Amy decided that the company did not need a desk it had purchased on January 12 for $400. The desk was sold for $400 cash to Chris Watson, an insurance agent, for use in his office.
(g) On January 30, the company collected $900 of commissions for travel arrangements made for customers during January.
(h) On January 31, the company paid Frank Jones $500 for secretarial work done during January.
(i) On January 31, the company received its utilities and phone bill, totaling $120 for January. It will pay for this bill in early February.
(j) On January 31, Amy withdrew $600 from the company for her personal use.

*Required:* (1) Using the accounting system we developed in the chapter, record the preceding transactions.
(2) Prove the equality of the accounting equation at the end of January.
(3) List the source documents that you would normally use in recording each of the transactions.

**5-35** Parsons Fashion Designers was started on June 1. The following transactions of the company occurred during June:

(a) E. Parsons started the business by investing $18,000 cash.
(b) Land and an office building were acquired at a cost of $5,000 and $18,000, respectively. The company paid $6,000 down and signed a note for the remaining balance of $17,000. The note is due in two years.
(c) Design equipment was purchased. The cash price of $2,600 was paid by writing a check to the supplier.
(d) Office supplies totaling $250 were purchased on credit. The amount is due in 30 days.
(e) A one-year fire insurance policy was purchased for $800.
(f) Fashion design commissions (fees) of $1,200 were collected from clients for June.
(g) An assistant's salary of $600 was paid for June.
(h) E. Parsons withdrew $500 from the company for personal use.
(i) Utility bills totaling $150 for June were received and will be paid in early July.

*Required:* (1) Using the accounting system shown in the chapter, record the preceding transactions.
(2) Prove the equality of the accounting equation at the end of June.
(3) List the source documents that you would normally use in recording each of the transactions.

**5-36** L. Snider, a young CPA, started Snider Accounting Services on September 1. During September, the following transactions of the company took place:

(a) On September 1, Snider invested $7,000 to start the business.
(b) On September 1, the company paid $3,000 for one year's rent of office space in advance.
(c) On September 2, office equipment was purchased at a cost of $5,000. A down payment of $1,000 was made, and a $4,000, one-year note was signed for the balance owed.
(d) On September 5, office supplies were purchased for $600 cash.
(e) On September 18, $1,000 was collected from clients for accounting services performed.
(f) On September 28, a $500 salary was paid to an accounting assistant.

(g) On September 29, Snider withdrew $800 for personal use.
(h) On September 30, the company billed clients $1,200 for accounting services performed during the second half of September.
(i) On September 30, the September utility bill of $100 was received; it will be paid in early October.
(j) On September 30, Snider recorded the following adjustments:
1. Rent expense of $250
2. Depreciation of $60 on office equipment
3. Interest expense of $40 on note payable
4. Office supplies used of $50

*Required:* (1) Using the accounting system shown in the chapter, record the preceding items.
(2) Prove the equality of the accounting equation at the end of September.
(3) Calculate the net income of the company for September.
(4) Prepare a balance sheet for the company on September 30.

**5-37** The Johnson Drafting Company was started on March 1 to draw blueprints for building contractors. The following transactions of the company occurred during March:

| *Date* | *Transactions* |
|---|---|
| 3/1 | M. Johnson, the owner, started the business by investing $14,000 cash. |
| 3/2 | Land and a small office building were purchased at a cost of $4,000 and $20,000, respectively. A down payment of $8,000 was made, and a note for $16,000 was signed. The note is due in one year. |
| 3/3 | Cash of $4,800 was paid to purchase computer drafting equipment. |
| 3/8 | Drafting supplies totaling $850 were purchased on credit. The amount is due in early April. |
| 3/15 | The company collected $1,500 from contractors for drafting services performed. |
| 3/28 | M. Johnson withdrew $1,000 for personal use. |
| 3/29 | The company received a $110 utility bill for March, to be paid in April. |
| 3/30 | The company paid $600 in salary to a drafting employee. |
| 3/30 | The company billed contractors $2,000 for drafting services performed during the last half of March. |
| 3/31 | The company recorded the following adjustments:<br>(a) Depreciation of $80 on the office building<br>(b) Depreciation of $100 on computer drafting equipment<br>(c) Interest of $160 on note payable<br>(d) Drafting supplies used of $150 |

*Required:* (1) Using the accounting system shown in the chapter, record the preceding transactions.
(2) Prove the equality of the accounting equation at the end of March.
(3) Calculate the net income of the company for March.
(4) Prepare a balance sheet for the company on March 31.

**5-38** The five transactions that occurred during June, the first month of operations for Brown's Gym, were recorded as follows:

| | | ***Assets*** | | | | | | | | | = | ***Liabilities*** | | | + | ***Owner's Equity*** |
|---|---|---|---|---|---|---|---|---|---|---|---|---|---|---|---|---|
| **Trans** | **Date** | **Cash** | + | **Gym Supplies** | + | **Land** | + | **Building** | + | **Gym Equipment** | = | **Accts. Payable** | + | **Notes Payable** | + | **Tom Brown, Capital** |
| (a) | 6/01 | +$24,000 | | | | | | | | | | | | | | + $24,000 |
| (b) | 6/05 | − 8,000 | | | | + $5,000 | | + $23,000 | | | | | | + $20,000 | | |
| (c) | 6/07 | − 270 | | + $270 | | | | | | | | | | | | |
| (d) | 6/17 | − 4,000 | | | | | | | | + $10,000 | | | | + 6,000 | | |
| (e) | 6/26 | | | + 480 | | | | | | | | + $480 | | | | |
| Balances | 6/30 | $11,730 | + | $750 | + | $5,000 | + | $23,000 | + | $10,000 | = | $480 | + | $26,000 | + | $24,000 |

*Required:* (1) Describe the five transactions that took place during June.
(2) Prepare a balance sheet on June 30.

**5-39** The following transactions were recorded by the Sutton Systems Design Company for May, its first month of operations:

| | | Assets | | | | | | | | | = | Liabilities | | | + | Owner's Equity |
|---|---|---|---|---|---|---|---|---|---|---|---|---|---|---|---|---|
| Trans | Date | Cash | + | Office Supplies | + | Land | + | Building | + | Office Equipment | = | Accts. Payable | + | Notes Payable | + | Steve Sutton, Capital |
| (a) | 5/01 | + $55,000 | | | | | | | | | | | | | | + $55,000 |
| (b) | 5/02 | − 8,000 | | | | + $6,000 | | + $18,000 | | | | | | + $16,000 | | |
| (c) | 5/08 | − 3,500 | | | | | | | | + $7,500 | | | | + 4,000 | | |
| (d) | 5/10 | | | + $1,100 | | | | | | | | + $1,100 | | | | |
| (e) | 5/22 | + 300 | | | | | | | | − 300 | | | | | | |
| Balances | 5/31 | $43,800 | + | $1,100 | + | $6,000 | + | $18,000 | + | $7,200 | = | $1,100 | + | $20,000 | + | $55,000 |

*Required:* (1) Describe the five transactions that took place during May.
(2) Prepare a balance sheet at May 31.

**5-40** At the beginning of July, Patti Dwyer established PD Company by investing $20,000 cash in the business. On July 5, the company purchased land and a building, making a $6,000 down payment (which was 10% of the purchase price) and signing a 10-year mortgage for the balance owed. The land was 20% of the cost, and the building was 80% of the cost. On July 17, the company purchased $3,800 of office equipment on credit, agreeing to pay half the amount owed in 10 days and the remainder in 30 days. On July 27, the company paid the amount due on the office equipment. On July 31, the company sold $900 of the office equipment that it did not need to another company for $900. That company signed a note requiring payment of the $900 at the end of one year.

*Required:* Based on the preceding information, prepare a balance sheet for PD Company on July 31. Show supporting calculations.

## Making Evaluations

**5-41** Your friend Maxine plans to supplement her job salary by running her own company at night and on the weekends. When the company earns enough money so that she can pay for a vacation home in the Caribbean, she plans to pay the bills of the company, sell the company's remaining assets, withdraw all the company's cash, and shut down the company. Since she will be extremely busy with her regular job and with running her new company, she plans to wait until she is ready to shut down the company to prepare a balance sheet, income statement, and cash flow statement. You think this is a bad idea.

*Required:* Do your best to convince Maxine that she should prepare financial statements more often, giving her examples of how doing this can help her and her company.

**5-42** Chris Schandling is a loan officer at the First National Bank in Rochester, Minnesota. One day Nathan Wooten, who owns KidzLand (an indoor playground for young children), comes to the bank to see Chris about getting a $50,000 loan.

*Required:* (1) What types of questions do you think Chris will ask Mr. Wooten? Come up with at least three types of questions.
(2) What types of financial information do you think Chris will ask Mr. Wooten to provide? If Mr. Wooten asks Chris why this financial information is needed, how should Chris respond?
(3) Is it important that KidzLand's financial statements follow GAAP? Why or why not?

**5-43** Andrew Poist works for Nilakanta and Company, a public accounting firm in Florence, South Carolina. On October 4, 2008, Sydney Langston, who started selling decorative, carved-wood duck decoys out of a booth at Cypress Court Mall during the first week in September, comes to see Andrew for some accounting help.

Mr. Langston walks into Andrew's office carrying a small cardboard box. He tells Andrew the following:

"After I retired, I decided I needed something to help keep me busy. I started this little business, 'The Woodshed,' a month ago. It is open only on Fridays when the mall has its Craft Day. I leased the booth for one year. So, every Friday until September 1, 2009, I will display my ducks in the booth and sell them.

I know I should have come to see you before I got started. I just kept putting it off. So, here's what I did. Throughout the month of September I tossed everything having to do with The Woodshed's finances into this box. It has all kinds of documents in it. I have all of my bank deposits for the month, checks I wrote that were paid by my bank, the receipts for the woodworking supplies I bought the day I started, etc. I sorted out some items, like checks I wrote to the grocery store and the electric company. Anyway, it's the first part of October, and I can't figure out how well The Woodshed did in September. Can you?"

"Of course I can," replies Andrew. "I'll have something for you in a couple of days."

Mr. Langston leaves, and Andrew opens the small box. Inside is a small pile of documents:

(a) Five deposit slips from Mr. Langston's checking account. They total $2,300. Andrew notices that on four of the deposit slips, Mr. Langston wrote "Craft Sales." Each one of the deposit dates corresponds to each of the four Fridays in September. On the other deposit slip, which is for $1,300, Mr. Langston wrote "Social Security."

(b) Six canceled checks from Mr. Langston's checking account. They total $3,350. Four checks written to Miranda's Woodworking Supplies Company total $600. One check for $350 was written to Circuit City, and one check for $2,400 was written to Cypress Court Mall Management.

(c) A handwritten schedule that reads as follows:

| | | |
|---|---|---|
| Mallard | $ 60 | sold |
| Grey Goose | $100 | sold |
| Baby Duck | $ 40 | sold |
| Swan | $200 | |
| Donald Duck | $ 70 | sold |
| Large Mallard | $130 | sold |

*Required:* (1) Using the information Mr. Langston supplied to Andrew, calculate your best estimate of the revenues, expenses, and net income for The Woodshed for September 2008.

(2) How could your calculations of revenues, expenses, and net income be misstated? When Andrew meets with Mr. Langston to discuss The Woodshed's operating results for September, what questions should he ask concerning the information Mr. Langston supplied?

**5-44** In this assignment, we are going to chronicle the changes in value and ownership of one asset—a one-acre plot of land on the corner of Cedar Springs Road and McKinney Avenue in Dallas, Texas—from January 2008 through December 2010. Here are the significant events that happened to that plot of land during this time period:

| | |
|---|---|
| *January 4, 2008:* | The land is purchased for $450,000 by Dalton Realty Company. |
| *April 25, 2009:* | Dalton Realty receives a tax assessment notice from the city of Dallas stating that the city now values the land at $510,000 for local tax purposes. |
| *December 12, 2009:* | The land is sold by Dalton Realty Company to Park Cities Development Company for $515,000. Park Cities pays in cash. |
| *May 22, 2010:* | Using the land as collateral (meaning that if Park Cities fails to repay its loan, the bank may get ownership of the land), Park Cities borrows $550,000 from North Carolina National Bank. |
| *June 14, 2010:* | Park Cities rents the land to The Crescent Court office complex for six months. The Crescent Court will store construction equipment on the land while making renovations to its office space. |
| *December 31, 2010:* | Park Cities sells the land to The Crescent Court for $590,000. |

*Required:* When business closes for each day listed below, state (1) which company shows this land in its accounting records as an asset and (2) at what dollar amount the land is shown in that company's accounting records.

| Date | Company showing the land as its asset | Dollar amount shown |
|---|---|---|
| 1-4-08 | | |
| 4-25-09 | | |
| 12-12-09 | | |
| 5-22-10 | | |
| 6-14-10 | | |
| 12-31-10 | | |

**5-45** Five years ago, Linda Monroe became the sole owner of LM Electronics. LM Electronics sells home entertainment centers, car audio equipment, and computers. LM advertises that it sells only the best brands, purchasing its inventory from well-known manufacturers in Japan, Germany, Norway, and the United States. Before opening this company, Linda was the accountant for The Music Warehouse. She understands accounting extremely well and maintains LM Electronics' accounting records according to generally accepted accounting principles.

On Friday morning, September 12, one of Linda's best customers, Sandy Wheeler, purchased a German-made CD player for $600. Linda was excited about making the sale because LM had only recently started carrying this particular brand. Linda filled out the sales invoice, collected the money, and helped Sandy carry the CD player out to her car.

Later that same day, Linda's friend Chris Tucker came into the store, also wanting to purchase a CD player. After browsing through the store, Chris started to leave. Linda stopped him and asked, "Chris, didn't you find a CD player that you would like to own?" Chris responded: "Well, Linda, I saw several items I would love to own, but I hadn't realized how expensive the equipment was. I guess I really can't afford to buy a new CD player."

Except for the deposit of the day's cash sales in the bank, no other activity took place that day at LM Electronics. After the store closed, Linda began thinking about Chris's comment. Early that evening Linda telephoned Chris and said: "Chris, I know you were wanting a new CD player, but if you are interested in saving a bunch of money, I would like to sell you the CD player I use at home. It is about two years old, and it is in great shape. I would sell it to you for $100."

Chris was very excited about Linda's offer. He drove over to Linda's house that same night, gave Linda $100 in cash, and took the CD player home. Linda immediately deposited the $100 in the bank night depository.

*Required:* Given the facts presented above and the information you learned in the chapter, (1) indicate whether you agree or disagree with the following statements and (2) explain each answer (this is the most important part, so think through the following statements carefully).

(a) Linda Monroe sold two CD players on September 12.
(b) LM Electronics sold two CD players on September 12.
(c) LM Electronics should record CD player sales of $700 on September 12.
(d) Linda Monroe should deposit $700 in the bank on September 12.

**5-46** Paul Jenkins is the sole owner of Friendly Pawn Shop. Friendly Pawn Shop buys and sells jewelry, musical instruments, televisions, telephones, and small kitchen appliances. Paul has owned the pawn shop for almost one year, and the shop has developed a reputation as an honest, reliable place for families to buy or sell their used items.

Up until now, Friendly Pawn Shop has bought and sold goods only from retail customers. Paul believes that Friendly Pawn Shop is overstocked with jewelry, and he thinks the shop does not have enough musical instruments to meet the demand that will occur after the new school year starts. Paul believes that the pawn shop needs to sell some jewelry, which cost about $1,500, and replace it with several trumpets, trombones, and flutes.

Friendly Pawn Shop advertises in the newspaper when it wants to buy particular types of used items. This way Paul has the opportunity to inspect the goods before they are purchased, and he has the opportunity to discuss the history of each item with its current owner. In the present situation, however, Paul is considering making a merchandise trade with a wholesale pawnbroker. Although Paul is almost convinced that the trade will be the best way for his company to obtain the musical instruments, he has two major concerns.

First, Paul is concerned about maintaining Friendly Pawn Shop's reputation for reliable merchandise. He knows almost all of his customers, and he has earned their trust. Because Paul does not know where the wholesaler's musical instruments were purchased, he worries that he will be trading good jewelry for inferior-quality musical instruments. He would not find out that the instruments are inferior until the customers told him of their dissatisfaction. Second, Paul does not know how to record the trade in Friendly Pawn Shop's accounting records. He knows that the jewelry he plans to trade cost $1,500 and that he was going to try to sell the jewelry for $4,000. Paul does not know how much the wholesaler paid for the musical instruments or what price to charge his customers for each item.

*Required:* (1) Using the four-step approach you learned earlier in this book, discuss how you think Paul should solve this business problem.
(2) Assuming Friendly Pawn Shop trades the jewelry for the musical instruments owned by the wholesale pawnbroker, discuss how you think this transaction should be recorded in the accounting records. Be sure to include references to the accounting concepts introduced in this chapter.

**5-47** Your friend Jim Wilson is about to prepare the January 31 balance sheet for his new company, Cheap Fun Video Arcade. This is Cheap Fun's first month of operation, and Jim is also going to calculate the first month's net income. He needs to prepare the balance sheet and calculate net income so he can pass the information along to his parents. They loaned him $5,000 so that he could start Cheap Fun.

Although Jim thinks that business is booming, he has a big problem. He does not know enough about accounting to prepare the balance sheet or calculate January's net income. As a matter of fact, Jim had never heard the words "balance sheet" and "net income" until his parents asked him to promise to furnish these statements to them every month before they would agree to loan Jim the $5,000.

Luckily, Jim saves every piece of paper associated with Cheap Fun. He kept copies of all of the business agreements he signed. He deposited all of the money Cheap Fun earned in the company's bank account and retained copies of every deposit slip. Jim also paid every company bill with a check and saved all of the related documents.

*Required:* Assume Jim wants to prepare Cheap Fun's January 31 balance sheet and January's income statement according to generally accepted accounting principles. Describe to Jim, in your own words, how he should organize the information about Cheap Fun's January transactions so that he can prepare a balance sheet and an income statement and keep his promise to his parents.

**5-48** Samson Construction Company is a small company that constructs buildings. Normally, the time for Samson to complete the construction of a building is about six months. At the beginning of this year, Samson signed a contract to build a three-story office building at a selling price of $2,000,000. Samson will collect this amount when it completes construction of the building. Because this is a larger building than it usually builds, Samson expected that it would take two years to complete the construction, at a total cost of $1,400,000. This is the only building that Samson worked on during the year. By the end of the year, construction was on schedule; the office building was half complete and Samson had paid $700,000 costs. At this time Samson's bookkeeper came to Bill Samson, the owner, and said, "Samson Construction Company didn't do very well this year; it had a net loss of $700,000 because its revenue was zero and its expenses were $700,000."

Bill comes to you for advice. He says, "Normally, my company records the revenue and related expenses for constructing a building when it is completed. However, this three-story building will take much longer than usual. My construction crews have already been working on the building for one year and will continue to work on it for another year. My company has paid for one year's worth of salaries, materials, and other costs and will continue to pay for all of these costs incurred next year, so a lot of money will be tied up in the contract and won't be recovered until my company collects the selling price when the building is completed. How and when should my company record the revenue and expenses on this building? Do I really have a $700,000 net loss for the current year?"

*Required:* Prepare a written answer to Bill Samson's questions.

**5-49** Yesterday, you received the following letter for your advice column at the local paper:

## DR. DECISIVE

Dear Dr. Decisive:

My girlfriend went with me and my family to Hawaii last month, and we had a great time. But we have a question that we hope you will answer. Suppose a company has accumulated frequent flier miles (which it hasn't used yet) from plane tickets that it purchased for business trips taken by its employees. Are the company's frequent flier miles an asset or an expense? My girlfriend says they're an asset, but I think they're an expense. We have a bet on your answer. If I lose, I have to take hula lessons. If she loses, she has to take sumo wrestling lessons.

Please help!! I don't look good in a grass skirt.

"Wrestling Fan"

*Required:* Meet with your Dr. Decisive team and write a response to "Wrestling Fan."

CHAPTER 6

# THE INCOME STATEMENT: ITS CONTENT AND USE

"BUSINESS WITHOUT PROFIT IS NOT BUSINESS ANY MORE THAN A PICKLE IS CANDY."

—CHARLES F. ABBOTT

1 Why is a company's income statement important?

2 How are changes in a company's balance sheet and income statement accounts recorded in its accounting system?

3 What are the parts of a retail company's classified income statement, and what do they contain?

4 What is inventory and cost of goods sold, and what inventory systems may be used by a company?

5 What are the main concerns of external decision makers when they use a company's income statement to evaluate its performance?

6 What type of analysis is used by external decision makers to evaluate a company's profitability?

How much did you earn last year working during the summer or during the school year? How did you keep track of your earnings? Did you make enough to cover all of your expenses? Or did your parents have to help you out? If so, what percentage of your expenses did your earnings cover? Companies, like individuals, keep track of their earnings. For instance, for the year ended January 31, 2006, **Wal-Mart** reported $315,654 million of revenues on its income statement. It also reported $240,391 million as the cost of the merchandise that it sold to customers, as well as $64,032 million of various other expenses, so that its net income was $11,231 million. Wal-Mart obtained these numbers from its accounting system. Did Wal-Mart charge customers enough for the merchandise it sold to them compared to what it paid for the merchandise? Did Wal-Mart make enough net income as a percentage of its revenues?

*Overall, do these numbers show that Wal-Mart had a "good" or "bad" year? What other information would you like to have to answer this question?*

In Chapter 5 we looked at the fundamentals of the financial accounting process. You saw how basic accounting concepts, such as the entity concept, the accounting equation, and accrual accounting, provide the framework for the accounting system that a company uses to record its day-to-day activities. The system provides internal users with valuable information that helps managers in their planning, operating, and evaluating activities. The revenue and expense transactions are also the basis of a company's income statement, which shows external users the company's profit (income) for the accounting period.

In this chapter, we discuss the importance of the income statement, expand the accounting system from Chapter 5, describe and present a classified income statement, and show how the income statement helps managers and external users make business decisions.

## Why the Income Statement Is Important

1 Why is a company's income statement important?

A company's income statement plays a key role in the decision making of the users by communicating the company's revenues, expenses, and net income (or net loss) for a specific time period. A company earns income by selling inventory (goods) or by providing services to customers during an accounting period. Recall that revenues are the prices a company charges its customers for the goods or services. Expenses are the costs of providing the goods or services during the period. An income statement is based on the equation we showed in Chapter 5:

**Net Income = Revenues − Expenses**

Companies may use different titles for their income statements, including *statement of income* (**AT&T**, **Rocky Mountain Chocolate Factory, Inc.**), *statement of earnings* (**Black & Decker**, **Eastman Kodak**), or *statement of operations* (**Apple Computer**, **JCPenney**). You may also hear the income statement referred to as a *profit and loss (P&L) statement.*

Recall from Chapter 4 that a company prepares a "projected" income statement for *internal* use as part of its master budget. Exhibit 6-1 shows how internal users (managers) use a company's *projected* income statement and actual income statement in their decision making, as well as how *external* users use a company's *actual* income statement to make economic decisions. We explain the impact of the income statement on users' decisions in the rest of this section.

The income statement summarizes the results of a company's operating activities for a specific accounting period. These operating activities stem from the planning and operating decisions that managers made during the period. Hence, a company's income statement shows the relationship between managers' decisions and the results of those decisions. This information helps both internal and external users evaluate how well the

**EXHIBIT 6-1 USES OF A COMPANY'S INCOME STATEMENT**

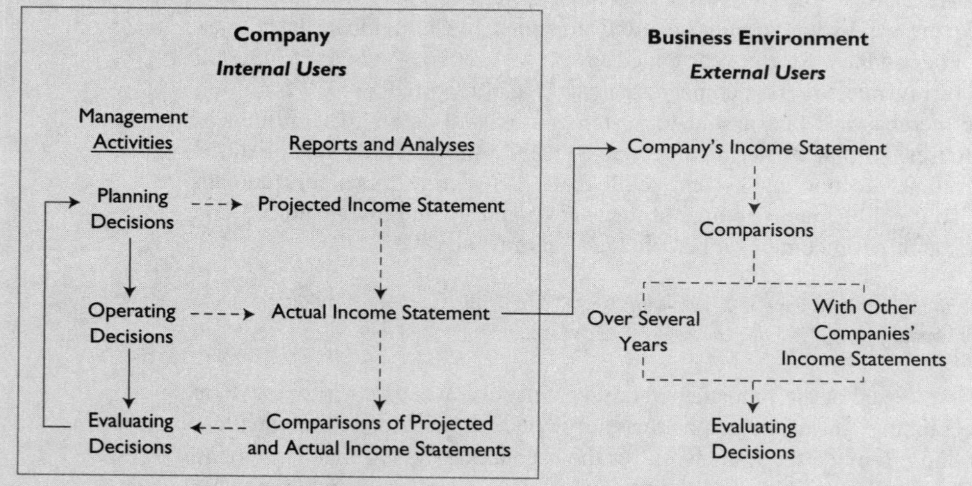


company's managers have "managed" during the period. By comparing a company's income statement information from period to period, users also can evaluate managers' ability over the longer run.

Let's first look at how managers use the income statement for making comparisons. Remember from Chapter 5 that a company keeps track of its activities by using an accounting system based on the accounting equation (Assets = Liabilities + Owner's Equity) and the dual effect of transactions. The accounting system provides the information that managers need to compare actual results with the expected (budgeted) results and to prepare external financial statements. At the end of an accounting period (e.g., one year), a company's income statement will show how well many of its managers' business decisions worked out.

For example, the revenue and expense information shows the results of managers' cost-volume-profit (C-V-P) analysis and budgeting decisions. In Chapter 3, you saw how Anna Cox used C-V-P analysis to develop her business plan. C-V-P analysis showed her how Sweet Temptations could break even and how it could earn a satisfactory profit. Anna calculated that Sweet Temptations needed to sell 700 boxes of candy for $10 a box for the company to break even. In addition to helping managers predict a company's break-even point, C-V-P analysis improves managers' operating decisions such as estimating how much inventory to purchase, what sales price to charge, and what effect on profit to expect from price changes. We determined that if Sweet Temptations was able to sell 720 boxes, it would earn a profit of $110.

Consider the decision that managers must make about what sales price to charge. If Anna sets the price too high, Sweet Temptations risks not selling enough boxes to break even. If she sets the price too low, Sweet Temptations may sell many boxes of candy but may not earn high enough revenues to cover the costs of selling the candy. Later, when the accounting system keeps track of every sale, it records those sales at the prices that the customers actually paid. (Remember that every sale generates a sales invoice to document the transaction and the amount of the sale.) If Anna did a good job of assessing the market and establishing an appropriate price, Sweet Temptations will make sales, will earn revenues high enough to cover its expenses, and will make a profit that it will report on its income statement.

In Chapter 4, we discussed how budgets help managers make plans, control company expenses, and evaluate company performance. If you were the manager of Sweet Temptations, budgeting would allow you to compare your expectations for revenue and expense amounts (reported in the projected income statement) with the actual amounts (reported in the actual income statement). If sales were higher or expenses lower than expected, you could find out what you did right and keep doing it. If, on the other hand, sales were lower or expenses higher than expected, you could analyze your mistakes and try to improve.

*How do you think a company's decision to decrease the price of its product will affect the revenues that it reports on its income statement? How will this decision affect its expenses?*

As valuable as C-V-P analysis and budgets are for internal decision making, companies do not report to external decision makers much of the information they provide. For one thing, companies don't want to reveal specific cost or budget information to their competitors. For another, many companies prepare internal accounting reports daily, so external users may be more confused than helped by the sheer volume of information.

External users need accounting information that lets them compare a company's actual operating performance over several years or with that of other companies. For instance, if the company is a corporation, potential investors and current stockholders use its income statement information to help them decide whether to buy or hold capital stock of the corporation. By comparing the company's current operating performance with that of prior years, they can get a sense of the company's future operating performance. By comparing the company's current operating performance with that of other companies, they can get a sense of whether the company is doing "better" or "worse" than these other companies. Banks and other financial institutions also use a company's income statement in a similar way to evaluate whether or not to give the company a loan. Finally, suppliers also use a company's income statement information. Suppliers do not have the resources to grant credit to all customers. A supplier can compare its customers' income statements to determine which ones might be the best credit risks. Generally accepted accounting principles (GAAP) ensure that all companies calculate and publish financial statement information in a similar, and thus comparable, manner. Thus, understanding GAAP is important to the accountant who prepares financial statements and to the external decision maker who uses these statements to make business decisions.

In Chapter 5 we introduced a simple accounting system, as well as several concepts and terms that form the foundation of GAAP. In this chapter we expand that accounting system, extend our discussion of GAAP as it relates to the income statement, and begin to explain how external users evaluate income statement information for decision making.

## EXPANDED ACCOUNTING SYSTEM

**2** How are changes in a company's balance sheet and income statement accounts recorded in its accounting system?

In Chapter 5 we kept track of Sweet Temptations' transactions using the accounting equation to set up columns for recording amounts for assets, liabilities, and/or owner's equity. We then expanded the accounting equation to include revenue and expense transactions. Adding revenue and expense columns let us keep track of these transactions separately from owner investments and withdrawals. However, a company needs to know more than its total revenues and total expenses. A company must know the total of each of its revenues and the total of each of its expenses for the accounting period so that it can report these items in a useful manner on its income statement for that period. In this chapter we expand the accounting system that we introduced in Chapter 5. We continue to use columns for each asset and liability account. However, we create a separate column under Owner's Equity for *each* revenue account and *each* expense account, while still retaining an owner's capital account column. A company uses these revenue and expense accounts *for only one accounting period* to record the effects of its transactions on its net income, so they are called **temporary accounts**. Asset, liability, and the owner's capital accounts are called **permanent accounts** because they are used *for the life of the company* to record the effects of its transactions on its balance sheet.

By using this expanded accounting system, we show how a company keeps track of the changes in (and balances of) each asset, liability, owner's capital, revenue, and expense account. After showing how a company records a transaction in this accounting system, we also include a marginal note to help you understand the effect of the transaction on the company's financial statements. (We will illustrate how this works in the next section of the chapter.) We use this columnar accounting system because it is easy to see the effects of a company's transactions on its various accounts, accounting equation, and financial statements. You should realize, however, that a real company has many (sometimes hundreds!) different types of assets, liabilities, revenues, and expenses. Imagine how wide the paper would need to be to record transactions involving hundreds of account columns! So a real company uses a computerized accounting system or a more complex manual accounting system involving items you may have heard of, such as "journals," "ledgers," "debits and credits," and different forms of accounts. We illustrate this manual system in Appendix A at the end of Volume 2 of the book.

## THE RETAIL COMPANY'S INCOME STATEMENT

3 What are the parts of a retail company's classified income statement, and what do they contain?

As we discussed earlier, the income statement is an important part of the decision-making process for both internal and external users. It is an expansion of the income equation that we presented earlier:

**Net Income = Revenues − Expenses**

Revenues may be thought of as the "accomplishments" of a company during an accounting period. Revenues are the prices charged to customers and *result in increases in assets (cash or accounts receivable) or decreases in liabilities (unearned revenues)*. Expenses may be thought of as the "efforts" or "sacrifices" made by a company during an accounting period to earn revenue. Expenses are the costs of providing goods and services and *result in decreases in assets or increases in liabilities*.

Keep these definitions in mind while we discuss how a company provides revenue and expense information to external users in its "classified" income statement. Let's return to Sweet Temptations to see how Anna records and reports the results of its first month of operations. To reinforce your understanding of the columnar accounting system, we will show how to record a few revenue and expense transactions. We will also show Sweet Temptations' classified income statement. As you look at this income statement, focus on understanding the income statement sections but also think about how Anna recorded the individual revenue and expense transactions.

The classified income statement of a retail company like Sweet Temptations has two parts: an "operating income" section and an "other items" section. **Operating income** includes all the revenues earned and expenses incurred in the primary operating activities of the company. The operating income section has three subsections: (1) revenues, (2) cost of goods sold, and (3) operating expenses. **Other items** include any revenues and expenses that are not directly related to the primary operations of the company, items such as interest revenue and interest expense. Exhibit 6-2 shows Sweet Temptations' classified income statement for January 2008.

In the next sections, we will discuss various issues related to recording and reporting revenues and expenses. We refer to Exhibit 6-2 to show how Sweet Temptations reports certain items.

## REVENUES

A retail company sells goods to customers either for cash or on credit. When goods are sold on credit, some retail companies offer an incentive for prompt payment. Whether the sales are for cash or on credit, customers sometimes return the goods they purchased. Let's see how companies record these aspects of sales.

**EXHIBIT 6-2** **SWEET TEMPTATIONS' CLASSIFIED INCOME STATEMENT**

**SWEET TEMPTATIONS**
***Income Statement***
***For the Month Ended January 31, 2008***

| | | |
|---|---|---|
| Sales revenues (net) | | $ 8,100 |
| Cost of goods sold | | (3,645) |
| Gross profit | | $ 4,455 |
| Operating expenses (see Exhibit 6-4): | | |
| Selling expenses | $2,961 | |
| General and administrative expenses | 884 | |
| Total operating expenses | | (3,845) |
| Operating income | | $ 610 |
| Other item: | | |
| Interest expense | | (8) |
| Net Income | | $ 602 |

## Sales Revenue

Whether a customer buys goods for cash or on credit, retail companies use a Sales Revenue, or simply Sales, account to record the transaction. Recall from Chapter 5 that the source document for a sale is a sales invoice, or simply an invoice. Some companies that sell only a few products or have a computerized accounting system may use a cash register tape or a credit card receipt as the source document. Exhibit 6-3 shows the sales invoice that Sweet Temptations used for one of its sales. This invoice shows you that on January 6, 2008, Sweet Temptations sold 10 boxes of milk chocolate candy for $10 per box, totaling to a $100 sale. Notice that the invoice also tells you that the invoice number was 0001, that the boxes of milk chocolate had an inventory identification number (ID #) of 0036, that it was a credit sale, and that the credit sale was made to Bud's Buds. It is important that the invoice includes all of the sales information needed to record this transaction.

Anna records the January 6 credit sale by first increasing Accounts Receivable by $100 to show that Bud's Buds owes Sweet Temptations that amount, as we show on the next page. Notice that the beginning balance of accounts receivable was $400; this is the amount owed to Sweet Temptations by The Hardware Store (see Exhibit 5-11). So, Accounts Receivable now has a balance of $500. Anna also increases the Sales Revenue account column under the *Net Income* heading of Owner's Equity by $100 to show that Sweet Temptations earned that amount from the sale. Notice that the previous balance of

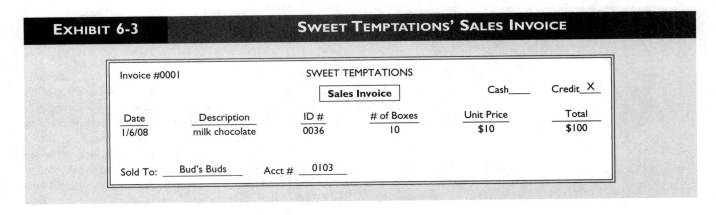

**EXHIBIT 6-3** **SWEET TEMPTATIONS' SALES INVOICE**

Invoice #0001

SWEET TEMPTATIONS

**Sales Invoice**

Cash____ Credit X

| Date | Description | ID # | # of Boxes | Unit Price | Total |
|---|---|---|---|---|---|
| 1/6/08 | milk chocolate | 0036 | 10 | $10 | $100 |

Sold To: Bud's Buds Acct # 0103

sales revenue was $300 due to a sale on January 2, so that Sales Revenue now has a balance of $400.

**FINANCIAL STATEMENT EFFECTS**

Increases assets on ***balance sheet.*** Increases revenues, which increases net income on ***income statement*** (and therefore increases owner's equity on ***balance sheet***).

| Assets | | = | Liabilities | + | Owner's Equity | | |
|---|---|---|---|---|---|---|---|
| | | | | | Net Income | | |
| | | | | | Revenues | − | Expenses |
| Accounts Receivable | | | | | Sales Revenue | | |
| Bal | $400 | | | | $300 | | |
| 1/6/08 | +100 | | | | +100 | | |
| Bal | $500 | | | | $400 | | |

To illustrate how an account balance changes, we showed the beginning and ending balances of both the Accounts Receivable account and the Sales Revenue account. **For simplicity, later in this chapter and future chapters we will include the balance of an account only when it is critical to the discussion.** At first glance, in the previous example it does not appear that Sweet Temptations' accounting equation is in balance. Remember, however, that Sweet Temptations' has many accounts in its accounting system and that we are showing only two of its accounts in this example. Sweet Temptations' accounting equation was in balance before Anna recorded this transaction, as we showed in Exhibit 5-13. What is important to notice is that in the above example, assets (Accounts Receivable) increased by $100 and owner's equity (Sales Revenue) increased by $100. So Sweet Temptations' accounting equation remains in balance after Anna recorded the transaction, as we showed in Exhibit 5-14.

Remember that Sweet Temptations had to dip into its candy inventory to make its sale. Anna uses the inventory identification number from the boxes of candy that Sweet Temptations sold to determine the $45 cost of the candy (10 boxes at $4.50 per box). So Anna records the cost of the sale by first decreasing Inventory by $45, as we show below. Note that the balance of the Inventory account prior to the sale was $5,805 (see Exhibit 5-13) and the balance is $5,760 after the sale. Anna also increases the Cost of Goods Sold account column (an expense) under the *Net Income* heading of Owner's Equity by $45 to show the cost of the boxes of candy that Sweet Temptations sold on January 6. Remember that as cost of goods sold (an expense) *increases,* both net income and owner's equity *decrease*. That is why we include a minus (−) sign in the column in front of the Cost of Goods Sold column. Notice that the previous balance of cost of goods sold was $135 due to the sale on January 2, so that Cost of Goods Sold now has a balance of $180.

**FINANCIAL STATEMENT EFFECTS**

Decreases assets on ***balance sheet.*** Increases cost of goods sold, which decreases net income on ***income statement*** (and therefore decreases owner's equity on ***balance sheet***).

| Assets | | = | Liabilities | + | Owner's Equity | | |
|---|---|---|---|---|---|---|---|
| | | | | | Net Income | | |
| | | | | | Revenues | − | Expenses |
| Inventory | | | | | | | Cost of Goods Sold |
| Bal | $5,805 | | | | | | $135 |
| 1/6/08 | − 45 | | | | | − | + 45 |
| Bal | $5,760 | | | | | − | $180 |

Although we do not show all the account balances in Sweet Temptations' accounting system, notice that the accounting equation continues to remain in balance after Anna records these two transactions because the $55 total increase in assets ($100 increase in Accounts Receivable less $45 decrease in Inventory) is equal to the $55 total increase in owner's equity [$100 increase in Sales Revenue (a revenue) less $45 increase in Cost of Goods Sold (an expense)]. Anna records each sales transaction for January in the same way (except she records cash sales in the Cash account column rather than the Accounts Receivable account column). At the end of the accounting period, she calculates the $8,100 balance in the Sales Revenue account column and Sweet Temptations reports it as revenue on its income statement for January, as we show in Exhibit 6-2. She calculates the $3,645 balance in the Cost of Goods Sold account column and Sweet Temptations reports this as an expense on its income statement.

## How Sales Policies Affect Income Statement Reporting

Companies may have several policies related to the sales of their goods or services. There are three types: discount policies, sales return policies, and sales allowance policies. Companies want to encourage customers to buy their merchandise or services, and sales policies help them do this. A retail company's specific policies will also have an impact on its net sales—the net dollar amount of sales reported on its income statement—because its revenues for an accounting period should include only the prices actually charged to customers for goods sold during the period. In the following sections, we will discuss each of these sales-related policies.

### Discounts

Have you ever taken advantage of a two-for-one special, paid a lower price because you bought a larger quantity of the same item, or used a coupon to get three dollars off the price of your pizza? If so, the company you bought from offered you a discount. A **quantity** (or *trade*) **discount** is a reduction in the sales price of a good or service because of the number of items purchased or because of a sales promotion.

Companies use discounts to attract customers and increase sales. Suppose that in early February, Sweet Temptations puts in its front window a sign that reads, "Valentines Day Special—Buy four or more boxes of chocolates and receive a 10% discount." By using this sales promotion, Sweet Temptations hopes that people walking by will notice the sign, come into the store, and buy candy. In addition, the company hopes that customers who had planned to buy only one or two boxes will instead buy four so that they can get the discount. Anna also hopes the policy will encourage repeat customers.

Before deciding to start a specific quantity discount policy, Sweet Temptations uses C-V-P analysis to determine the discount that will most likely improve company profits. Once a quantity discount policy is set, the company keeps track of the impact the policy has on sales, costs, and profits. However, the company does *not* record quantity discounts in its accounting system.

A company also may decide to offer a discount for early payment on credit sales. A **sales discount** is a percentage reduction of the invoice price if the customer pays the invoice within a specified period. A sales discount is frequently called a **cash discount** because when taken by a customer, the discount reduces the cash received. The sales invoice shows the terms of payment. These terms vary from company to company, although most competing companies have similar credit terms.

Sales (cash) discount terms might read 2/10, n/30 ("two ten, net thirty"). The first number is the percentage discount (2%), and the second number (10) is the number of days in the discount period. The discount period is the time, starting from the date of the invoice, within which the customer must pay the invoice to get the sales discount. The term n/30 means that the total invoice price is due within 30 days of the invoice date. Thus 2/10, n/30 is read as "a 2% discount is allowed if the invoice is paid within 10 days; otherwise, the total amount of the invoice is due within 30 days." If Sweet Temptations makes a $50 sale on credit with terms 2/10, n/30 and the customer pays the invoice within 10 days, the customer would pay $49 [$50 − (0.02 × $50)], and $1 would be the sales discount taken. Sometimes companies offer cash discounts by charging a lower price for cash sales (rather than credit sales). Some gas stations have this policy. A company's accounting system keeps track of sales (cash) discounts by reducing sales revenue by the amount of sales discounts taken when customers pay for their credit purchases.

*How do you think a sales discount taken by a credit customer when paying the account receivable is recorded in the customer's accounting system?*

**Eddie Bauer**
***Customer Service***
***Easy Returns***

If, at any time, you are not completely satisfied with your purchase, simply exchange it or return it to us for a refund.

### Sales Returns and Allowances

When a customer buys merchandise, both the company and the customer assume that it is not damaged and is acceptable to the customer. Occasionally, on checking the merchandise after the purchase, the customer may find that it is damaged, is of inferior quality, or simply is the wrong size or color. Most retail companies have a policy allowing customers to return merchandise. For example, **Eddie Bauer** has a very liberal return policy, as we show in the margin. A **sales return** occurs when a customer returns previously purchased merchandise. The effect of a sales return is to cancel the sale (and the related cost of goods sold).

*Have you ever returned merchandise to a store? Did the customer service representative ask to see your sales receipt? Did you or the customer service representative fill out additional source documents? Why?*

If a customer discovers that merchandise is damaged, a company may offer the customer a sales allowance. A **sales allowance** occurs when a customer agrees to keep the merchandise, and the company refunds a portion of the original sales price.

Although this transaction is not part of our ongoing analysis of Sweet Temptations, assume that one of its customers, Roger Leslie, purchased four boxes of chocolates for $10 per box and paid cash. Remember, each box of candy costs Sweet Temptations $4.50. Anna would have recorded this transaction by increasing both Sweet Temptations' Cash and Sales Revenue by $40 (4 × $10), decreasing Inventory by $18 (4 × $4.50), and increasing Cost of Goods Sold (an expense) by $18.

What would have happened if later that day when Roger opened the candy, he noticed that half of it was melted? If he returned to the store, Anna might have asked him if he wanted to exchange the candy for new boxes, return the candy for a refund, or accept a $20 sales allowance and keep the candy. If the candy still tasted fine, Roger might have decided to accept the sales allowance.

Because Roger paid for the candy with cash, Sweet Temptations would have granted the sales allowance by refunding him $20 cash. Anna would have recorded this sales allowance transaction in Sweet Temptations' accounts as follows:

**FINANCIAL STATEMENT EFFECTS**

Decreases assets on ***balance sheet***. Decreases revenues, which decreases net income on ***income statement*** (and therefore decreases owner's equity on ***balance sheet***).

| **Assets** | = | **Liabilities** | + | **Owner's Equity** | | |
|---|---|---|---|---|---|---|
| | | | | **Net Income** | | |
| | | | | **Revenues** | − | **Expenses** |
| Cash | | | | Sales Revenue | | |
| − $20 | | | | − $20 | | |

If Roger originally purchased the candy on credit, Sweet Temptations would have granted the sales allowance by decreasing Roger's Account Receivable balance, instead of the Cash balance, by $20.

*If Roger returned the candy for a refund, how would you record the transaction?*

Whether a company grants a sales return or a sales allowance, it prepares a source document called a credit memo. (Remember that a source document serves as evidence that a transaction has occurred.) A **credit memo** is a business document that lists the information for a sales return or allowance. It includes the customer's name and address, how the original sale was made (cash or credit), the reason for the sales return or allowance, the items that were returned or on which the allowance was given, and the amount of the return or allowance. The credit memo is the source document used to record the return or allowance. As we will discuss in Chapter 18 of Volume 2, it is also the document used to keep track of "external failure costs," a measure of customer dissatisfaction. The effect of recording sales discounts, sales returns, and sales allowances is to reduce sales revenue (as we will discuss in the next section).

*How can a company's sales return policy help increase profits? Do you think a sales return policy ever can hurt more than it helps? How?*

### Net Sales

At the end of the accounting period, the balance of a company's Sales Revenue account column includes the initial sales revenue, less the sales returns and allowances, and the sales (cash) discounts taken. The balance of the Sales Revenue account is called Sales Revenue (net), or Net Sales, and is reported on the company's income statement.

In January 2008 Sweet Temptations did not allow any cash discounts and did not have any customers return their purchases or ask for an allowance. The company thus reports total sales revenue of $8,100 on its income statement, as we show in Exhibit 6-2. It seems that Sweet Temptations' customers were satisfied with the quality of the candy they bought. In general, the amounts that a company records as sales returns and allowances (and sales discounts) provide useful information about the quality of the company's products (and the effect of its cash discount policy).

*Do you think a company should report to its managers a single net sales amount or both the total sales and the sales returns, allowances, and discounts? To external users? Why?*

## EXPENSES

An old business phrase says, "You have to spend money to make money." But a company should understand that planning and controlling its expenses is an important part of running a business. In the previous section you saw how Sweet Temptations, a retail company, recorded and reported its revenues. In this section we focus on expenses.

### Cost of Goods Sold

4 What is inventory and cost of goods sold, and what inventory systems may be used by a company?

One of the major expenses of a retail company is the cost of the goods (merchandise) that it sells during the accounting period. A classified income statement shows this expense as the **cost of goods sold**.

Although all retail companies report their costs of goods sold, *how* a retail company calculates the amount depends on the type of inventory system it uses. Remember, **inventory** is the merchandise a retail company is holding for resale. A company uses an inventory system to keep track of the inventory it purchases and sells during an accounting period and, thus, the inventory it still owns at the end of the period. Companies use either a perpetual inventory system or a periodic inventory system. Because the type of inventory system that a company uses affects its managers' decisions and the income statement calculations, we briefly discuss the cost of goods sold under each type of system.

#### Perpetual Inventory System

A **perpetual inventory system** keeps a continuous record of the cost of inventory on hand and the cost of inventory sold. Under the perpetual inventory system, when a company purchases an item of inventory, it increases the asset Inventory by the invoice cost of the merchandise plus any freight charges (sometimes called *transportation-in*) it paid to have the inventory delivered. When the company sells merchandise, it records the sale in the usual way. It also reduces Inventory and increases Cost of Goods Sold by the cost of the inventory that it sold. (We illustrated this earlier for one of Sweet Temptations' sales.) So, the company has Inventory and Cost of Goods Sold accounts that are perpetually up-to-date, and the company always knows the physical quantity of inventory it should have on hand.

*Do you think perpetual inventory records could be wrong? What could cause the records to show either too much or too little inventory?*

Because of computer technology, many retail stores use a perpetual inventory system. When you buy something in a store, if the salesperson uses a scanner to record your purchase, the company is using a perpetual inventory system. Computers help stores record sales transactions and keep their perpetual inventory records. For instance, a grocery store uses an optical scanner to read a bar code and record the price of the item into the cash register. The store's computer simultaneously increases Cash (or Accounts Receivable) and Sales Revenue for the item's sales price, reduces Inventory and increases Cost of Goods Sold by the amount of that item's cost, and updates the count of the quantity of inventory on hand. Most department stores use a perpetual inventory system, as do most retail stores that sell a relatively small number of very expensive items, such as automobiles and jewelry.[1]

Whether a company sells expensive jewelry or generic grocery items, the company's perpetual inventory system keeps up-to-date amounts for both Inventory and Cost of Goods Sold. This information helps managers with decisions about day-to-day operations. By monitoring the daily changes in inventory amounts, managers can decide when to make inventory purchases, thus making sure that inventory items are always in stock. Because the cost of goods sold information is current, managers can also compare the revenues and costs of recent sales and estimate the company's profitability. However, managers should evaluate the costs of computerized equipment, employee training, and the other support needed to operate a perpetual inventory system before deciding to use this type of system. In some cases, the benefits may not justify the added costs of keeping perpetual records. As computer technology becomes more affordable and as competition increases, companies typically find that perpetual systems are worth the costs.

At the end of an accounting period, a company includes the balance of its Inventory account on its balance sheet. The company includes the balance of its Cost of Goods Sold account on its income statement. As we illustrated earlier, Sweet Temptations uses a perpetual inventory system. Sweet Temptations also uses the *specific identification method* for determining its cost of goods sold because it identifies the cost of each box of candy sold based on the identification number of the box. At the end of January 2008, its Inventory account has a balance of $2,295, and its Cost of Goods Sold account has a balance of $3,645 from all the purchases and sales transactions recorded in January. We show these account columns below (the amounts are the same as those listed in Exhibit 5-20):

| Inventory | |
|---|---|
| Bal 1/1 | $1,620 |
| 1/2 | − $135 |
| 1/4 | +$4,320 |
| 1/6 | − $45 |
| 1/3–1/31 | −$3,465 |
| Bal 1/31 | $2,295 |

*Cost of inventory purchased*

| Cost of Goods Sold | |
|---|---|
| 1/2 | + $135 |
| 1/6 | + $45 |
| 1/3–1/31 | +$3,465 |
| Bal 1/31 | $3,645 |

*Cost of inventory sold*

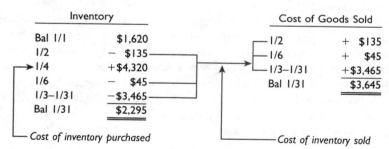

The $3,645 cost of goods sold is reported on the income statement as we show in Exhibit 6-2. The $2,295 ending inventory is reported on the balance sheet shown in Exhibit 5-22. We will discuss perpetual inventory systems in more detail in Chapter 19.

## Periodic Inventory System

A **periodic inventory system** does not keep a continuous record of the inventory on hand and sold, but determines the inventory at the end of each accounting period by physically

[1]In Chapter 19 we will discuss accounting for inventory in more detail. Accounting systems may keep track only of inventory quantities, instead of inventory costs, on a perpetual basis.

© EYEWIRE/GETTY IMAGES

Assuming this person is "taking inventory," what do you suppose is in his notebook?

counting it. Because a periodic inventory system does *not* reduce the Inventory account each time a sale occurs, the *only* time the company knows the cost of its inventory on hand is when it counts the inventory.

Why would a company choose not to keep perpetual inventory records? There are two common reasons. First, many companies that use a periodic inventory system are small enough that they can manage their inventory without perpetual records. Second, many companies sell a high volume of similar, inexpensive goods. Because the items are not expensive, perpetual records are not as important for keeping day-to-day physical control over the inventory. For these reasons, a company may decide that the costs of a perpetual system (i.e., recordkeeping costs, computer hardware and software costs) are not worth the benefits.

Because a company using a periodic system does not keep perpetual records, it must physically count its inventory at year-end. Physically counting the inventory is the only way for the company to determine an accurate inventory amount to be reported in the company's ending balance sheet. Therefore, a company usually counts its inventory immediately after the last working day of its fiscal year.[2] This is a difficult and time-consuming task. Thus, most companies end their fiscal year when inventory levels are likely to be low and business is slow. For example, most department stores take their inventory following the "after Christmas" sales, whereas a ski shop might count its inventory in June.

Perhaps you have noticed a company's advertisement that says something like the following:

**YEAR-END INVENTORY CLEARANCE SALE!!!! WE'D RATHER SELL IT THAN COUNT IT!**

This company is reducing its prices to sell more goods so that it will not have to spend as much time counting inventory. Near the end of the year it is not unusual for a company

[2]A company using a perpetual inventory system also physically counts its inventory at year-end. Even though its accounting records show what *should* be in the inventory, the company takes a physical count to determine its *actual* inventory so it can test the accuracy of its accounting records and estimate the amount of lost or stolen inventory.

to close temporarily, so that it can count its inventory. If you saw the company's sign (like the one in the picture on the previous page) and peeked in the window, you would see people moving from one aisle to the next, counting the merchandise on each shelf.

How does a company using a periodic system know its cost of goods sold? Since the company does not record the cost of the goods sold when each sales transaction takes place, it must *calculate* its cost of goods sold for an accounting period as follows:

| | | Cost of goods available for sale | | | | Cost of goods **not** sold |
|---|---|---|---|---|---|---|
| Cost of Goods Sold | = | Cost of Beginning Inventory | + | Cost of Net Purchases | − | Cost of Ending Inventory |

A company knows the cost of its beginning inventory because the beginning inventory for a new accounting period is the same as the ending inventory for the previous accounting period. A company's cost of net purchases is the dollar amount it recorded during an accounting period for the merchandise it bought for resale. The term **net purchases** is used because the amount of merchandise purchases (invoice cost and transportation-in) is adjusted (reduced) for purchases returns, allowances, and discounts. (These adjustments are similar to the net sales adjustments that we discussed earlier.) A company's **cost of ending inventory** is the dollar amount of merchandise on hand, based on the physical count, at the end of the accounting period.

### Cost of Goods Sold and Gross Profit

Because cost of goods sold is usually a retail company's largest expense, many companies subtract cost of goods sold from net sales to determine **gross profit**. Gross profit is the amount of revenue that a company has "left over" (after recovering the cost of the products it sold) to cover its operating expenses. Sweet Temptations subtracts its $3,645 cost of goods sold from its $8,100 sales revenue (net) to get its $4,455 gross profit, as we showed in Exhibit 6-2.

*Do you think Anna Cox is pleased with Sweet Temptations' gross profit? Why or why not?*

### Operating Expenses

Of course, the cost of goods sold is not the only expense that a retail company incurs. Activities such as having a sales staff, occupying building space, or running advertisements in the newspaper also cost money. These types of expenses are called *operating expenses*. **Operating expenses** are the expenses (other than cost of goods sold) that a company incurs in its day-to-day operations.

A company records its operating expenses in account columns as we discussed earlier. For instance, when Sweet Temptations paid $300 for advertising on January 25, 2008, Anna recorded the transaction as follows:

| Assets | = | Liabilities | + | Owner's Equity | | |
|---|---|---|---|---|---|---|
| | | | | Net Income | | |
| | | | | Revenues | − | Expenses |
| Cash | | | | | | Advertising Expense |
| −$300 | | | | | − | +$300 |

**FINANCIAL STATEMENT EFFECTS**

Decreases assets on ***balance sheet***. Increases operating expenses, which decreases net income on ***income statement*** (and therefore decreases owner's equity on ***balance sheet***).

Notice again that an increase in an expense causes a decrease in owner's equity, as indicated by the minus (−) sign in the column in front of the $300 advertising expense.

Likewise, on January 31, 2008, when Anna prepared the end-of-period adjustment of $15 for depreciation, she recorded the expense as follows:

| Assets | = | Liabilities | + | Owner's Equity | | |
|---|---|---|---|---|---|---|
| | | | | Net Income | | |
| | | | | Revenues | − | Expenses |
| Store Equipment | | | | | | Depreciation Expense |
| Bal $2,000 | | | | | | |
| − $15 | | | | | − | + $15 |
| Bal $1,985 | | | | | − | $15 |

**FINANCIAL STATEMENT EFFECTS**

Decreases assets on ***balance sheet.*** Increases operating expenses, which decreases net income on ***income statement*** (and therefore decreases owner's equity on ***balance sheet***).

Companies refer to the recording of end-of-period adjustments as making **adjusting entries.**

A company may divide its operating expenses section of the income statement into two parts, one for selling expenses and the other for general and administrative expenses. **Selling expenses** are the operating expenses related to the sales activities of a company. Sales activities are activities involved in the actual sale and delivery of merchandise to customers. Selling expenses include such items as sales salaries expense, advertising expense, and delivery expense (sometimes called *transportation-out*) for merchandise sold. **General and administrative expenses** are the operating expenses related to the general management of a company. They include such items as office salaries expense, insurance expense, and office supplies expense.

*Why do you think that companies may report selling expenses separately from general and administrative expenses?*

Some operating expenses involve both sales activities and the general management of a company. Consider utilities, for example. A company keeps telephones at sales desks and office desks, and both sales areas and office spaces are provided with electricity. In these cases, a company allocates part of the total expense to selling expenses and the remainder to general and administrative expenses based on an estimate of how much is used for each activity, as we discussed in Chapter 4.

Exhibit 6-4 shows a detailed schedule of Sweet Temptations' operating expenses for January 2008. Anna developed this schedule from the balances in Sweet Temptations'

**EXHIBIT 6-4 SWEET TEMPTATIONS' OPERATING EXPENSES**

**SWEET TEMPTATIONS**
***Schedule 1: Operating Expenses***
***For Month Ended January 31, 2008***

| | Amount | Chapter 5 Transaction # |
|---|---|---|
| Selling expenses | | |
| Consulting expense | $ 150 | (7) |
| Advertising expense | 300 | (8) |
| Sales salaries expense | 1,537 | (10) |
| Sales telephone expense | 45 | (11) |
| Sales utilities expense | 142 | (12) |
| Sales supplies expense | 22 | (14) |
| Rent expense | 750 | (15) |
| Depreciation expense | 15 | (16) |
| Total selling expenses | $2,961 | |
| General and administrative expenses | | |
| Consulting expense | $ 50 | (7) |
| Office salaries expense | 513 | (10) |
| Office telephone expense | 15 | (11) |
| Office utilities expense | 48 | (12) |
| Office supplies expense | 8 | (14) |
| Rent expense | 250 | (15) |
| Total general and administrative expenses | $ 884 | |

expense accounts at the end of January. These balances are based on all the expense transactions Anna recorded in the accounts during January. Although we do not show these expense accounts here, the amounts she recorded are the same as those in the Expenses column in Exhibits 5-20 and 5-21. For clarity, we have identified the number of the 2008 transaction listed in Chapter 5 that caused each expense. Most of Sweet Temptations' operating expenses are selling expenses. However, Anna estimates that one-quarter of each total for consulting ($200), salaries ($2,050), telephone ($60), utilities ($190), supplies ($30), and rent ($1,000) expenses are general and administrative expenses.[3] Sweet Temptations includes the $2,961 total selling expenses and the $884 total general and administrative expenses on its income statement in Exhibit 6-2. The detailed schedule of expenses is included with its income statement so that users interested in specific types of expenses can get the information they need.

## Operating Income, Other Items, and Net Income

On a company's income statement, the total operating expenses are deducted from gross profit to determine **operating income**. In Exhibit 6-2, Anna adds the total selling expenses to the total general and administrative expenses to determine the $3,845 total operating expenses. She deducts the total operating expenses from the $4,455 gross profit to determine Sweet Temptations' operating income of $610.

The **other items** (sometimes called the *nonoperating income*) section of a company's income statement includes items that are not related to the primary operations of the company. Reported in this section are revenues and expenses related to investing activities or to financing the company's operations (e.g., interest revenue and interest expense), revenues and expenses (called *gains* and *losses*) related to selling property and equipment assets, and incidental revenues and expenses (e.g., miscellaneous rent revenue, losses due to theft or fire). We will discuss these items more fully later in the book. Sweet Temptations includes interest expense of $8 in its *other items* section. This interest expense relates to the note payable that it owed for the entire month of January; the interest was recorded in an adjusting entry (#17) that we showed in Exhibit 5-21.

The total amount of the *other items* (nonoperating income) section is added to (or subtracted from) the operating income to determine a company's net income. The net income of Sweet Temptations (shown in Exhibit 6-2) for the month ended January 31, 2008 is $602, determined by subtracting the $8 other item (interest expense) from the $610 operating income.

## Uses of the Income Statement for Evaluation

To help you understand *how* internal and external decision makers use income statements, we will first briefly review *why* companies prepare financial statements and *what* the statements show. Recall that accounting information helps managers plan, operate, and evaluate company activities. Managers use accounting information on a day-to-day basis to help make decisions (e.g., what type of sales return policy to use or how much inventory to order) to achieve their objective of earning a profit and thereby increasing the company's value. At the end of a specific time period, managers prepare financial statements to report to external users the cumulative results of their day-to-day decisions. By analyzing a company's financial statements, external users can evaluate how well managers' decisions worked and decide whether to do business with the company.

If you are a creditor, a company's financial statements help you decide whether to loan money to the company and, if so, under what loan arrangements (e.g., the interest

[3]For simplicity, the salaries, supplies, and utilities expense allocations are rounded to the nearest dollar.

rate to charge, the amount of time to allow before the loan must be repaid, the restrictions to place on the company's ability to borrow additional money). If you are an investor, a company's financial statements help you estimate the return you may expect on your investment and whether you want to become or continue to be an owner.

*Who else do you think is interested in a company's financial statements? Why?*

5 What are the main concerns of external decision makers when they use a company's income statement to evaluate its performance?

Investors use the income statement to help judge their return on investment, and creditors use it to help make loan decisions. On what do these users base their evaluations? To make their business decisions, financial statement users evaluate a company's risk, operating capability, and financial flexibility. Although these may sound like complicated terms, once we have explained them you will see that they describe the main concerns of most investors and creditors.

When investors or creditors use the income statement to evaluate a company's risk, they are estimating the chances that the company will *not* earn a satisfactory profit or that it will earn a higher-than-expected profit in the future. So **risk** is the uncertainty about the future earnings potential of a company. The greater the chances are that a company will earn a satisfactory profit or will earn a higher-than-expected profit, the less risk there is in investing in that company. As the chances decrease that a company will earn a satisfactory profit or the chances increase that it will earn a lower-than-expected profit, the risk of investing in that company increases. A company's "risk factor" affects the expected investment return that is needed to attract investors and affects the interest rate that creditors charge on that company's loans. The greater the risk, the higher will be the required rate of return and the interest rate.

External users evaluate a company's operating capability and financial flexibility because these factors help determine a company's level of risk. **Operating capability** refers to a company's ability to continue a given level of operations in the future. For example, by comparing a company's current set of financial statements with those of prior years, external users can learn about the company's ability to earn a stable stream of operating income. If the statements show that the company can do this, chances are good that the company will be able to maintain its current level of operations in the future.

**Financial flexibility** refers to a company's ability to adapt to change in the future. External users want to see evidence of financial flexibility because this means that a company will be able to take advantage of business opportunities, such as introducing a new product or building a new warehouse. As you would expect, investors want the company to grow, so they prefer companies that have financial flexibility.

*Do you think your personal financial flexibility is high or low? Why?*

## Business Issues and Values

Have you ever had a part-time job? If so, then you know that many companies depend on part-time employees in their operations. For some companies, part-time employees make up a large percentage of their employee group. By using part-time employees, these companies may significantly enhance their financial flexibility because they can hire and lay off employees quickly. They also avoid having to pay for items such as health insurance and retirement benefits, which companies normally pay for full-time employees. Other companies, though still using some part-time employees to help the companies improve their financial flexibility, have a different view regarding their commitment to their employees. They believe that it is part of their social responsibility to hire, train, and retain full-time employees. Although these companies may have less financial flexibility than those that depend more on part-time employees, some investors and creditors feel that a commitment to full-time employees offsets this limitation.

NEEDED: Part-time receptionist and technician. Office hours 12 noon–8 p.m. Apply in person. NO telephone calls. Horton Animal Hospital–Forum Blvd.

For example, consider Malden Mills, a Lawrence, Massachusetts manufacturer of Polartec and Polar fleece (fabrics in demand by such retailers as **Eddie Bauer** and **L.L. Bean**). When it burned to the ground just before Christmas several years ago, the owner gave every employee a $275 Christmas bonus. Then he announced that all employees would continue to receive full pay and benefits for at least 90 days. His decision was based on the philosophy that "Loyalty and profit go hand in hand! Superior employees produce a superior product, and loyal customers and loyal employees are cut from the same fabric."[a]

## Ratios

6 What type of analysis is used by external decision makers to evaluate a company's profitability?

To evaluate a company's operating performance, managers and external users may perform ratio analysis. **Ratio analysis** consists of computations in which an item on the company's financial statements is divided by another, related item. Although individual users may compute ratios themselves, groups that specialize in financial analysis compute and publish ratios for many companies and industries. The ratios are "benchmarks" used to compare a company's performance with that of previous periods and with that of other companies. There are many commonly computed ratios, which we will discuss in later chapters. As an introduction, here we discuss two that relate to profitability, since profitability affects risk, operating capability, and financial flexibility.

### Profit Margin

One ratio is the *profit margin* (sometimes called the *return on sales*), which is usually expressed as a percentage. A company's **profit margin** is calculated as follows:

$$\text{Profit Margin} = \frac{\text{Net Income}}{\text{Net Sales}}$$

If a company's profit margin is higher than that of previous years or higher than that of other companies, it usually means that the company is doing a better job of controlling its expenses in relation to its sales.

The profit margin of Sweet Temptations for January 2008 is calculated as follows, based on the information in Exhibit 6-2:

$$7.43\% = \frac{\$602}{\$8{,}100}$$

This means that, on average, 7.43 cents of every sales dollar is profit (net income) for Sweet Temptations. Since this is Sweet Temptations' first month of operations, we cannot compare the 7.43% profit margin for January with the profit margin of previous months. However, this profit margin during initial operations is a positive sign.

### Gross Profit Percentage

A second ratio is the *gross profit percentage* (sometimes called the *gross profit margin*), which relates a company's gross profit to its net sales. A company's **gross profit percentage** is calculated as follows:

$$\text{Gross Profit Percentage} = \frac{\text{Gross Profit}}{\text{Net Sales}}$$

A retail company's gross profit generally ranges from 20% to 60% of net sales depending on the types of products it sells or its "pricing" strategy. For example, some companies use a pricing strategy of offering lower selling prices to increase their sales volume, thereby increasing their total gross profit. The gross profit percentage of Sweet Temptations for January 2008 is calculated as follows:

$$55\% = \frac{\$4,455}{\$8,100}$$

This means that, on average, 55 cents of every sales dollar (after the cost of goods sold is subtracted) is left to cover operating expenses and other expenses, and to increase Sweet Temptations' net income. Again, we cannot make comparisons with previous months, but this 55% gross profit margin for January is within the range of a retail company's usual gross profit. This is another positive sign of Sweet Temptations' successful initial operating capability. The managers of a retail company keep a close watch on the company's gross profit because changes in gross profit typically result in large changes in net income.

### Profitability Ratios of Actual Companies

To illustrate ratio analysis, we will use information from the financial statements of two retail companies, **JCPenney Company Inc.** (JCPenney) and **Kohl's Corporation** (Kohl's). Their profit margins[4] for the year ended January 28, 2006 were as follows:

| | *JCPenney* | *Kohl's* |
|---|---|---|
| Profit Margin | 5.8% | 6.3% |

When we compare these two ratios, Kohl's was slightly more successful at generating net income from its sales than was JCPenney.

*Would you expect Kohl's gross profit percentage also to be higher than JCPenney's? Why or why not?*

Now let's compare the gross profit percentages for the two companies.

| | *JCPenney* | *Kohl's* |
|---|---|---|
| Gross Profit Percentage | 39.3% | 35.5% |

Notice that Kohl's had a *lower* gross profit percentage than JCPenney, even though it had a *higher* profit margin. Based on a comparison of these ratios, we can say that JCPenney was more efficient than Kohl's in controlling the costs of merchandise but that Kohl's was more efficient than JCPenney in controlling operating expenses.

*How else might you explain the differences in the ratios of the two companies?*

We will expand the discussion of operating capability and financial flexibility in Chapter 7, adding new ratios for analysis. We also will continue our comparison of JCPenney and Kohl's.

## STATEMENT OF CHANGES IN OWNER'S EQUITY

A company's owner's equity is affected by the owner's investments and withdrawals, as well as by the company's revenue and expense transactions. Although an income statement and its supporting schedules help external users understand the results of revenue and expense activities, the statement and schedules do not include all the activities that

[4]We use well-known corporations in this illustration because the financial statements of most small entrepreneurial companies are not publicly available. For simplicity, we do not show the calculations of the ratios, although the numbers were taken from each company's financial statements. For instance, we calculated JCPenney's profit margin by dividing its net income of $1,088 million by its net sales of $18,781 million. We calculated Kohl's profit margin by dividing its net income of $842 million by its net sales of $13,402 million.

affect owner's equity. A company prepares a supplementary schedule, called a *statement of changes in owner's equity,* for this purpose. The **statement of changes in owner's equity** summarizes the transactions that affected owner's equity during the accounting period. A company presents this statement to "bridge the gap" between its income statement and the amount of owner's capital it reports on its balance sheet.

The schedule begins with the balance in the owner's capital account at the beginning of the accounting period. Then, the total amount of the owner's investments for the accounting period is added because this amount increases the owner's claim on the company's assets. Next, the amount of the company's net income is added because this amount also increases the owner's claim on the company's assets as a result of its operating activities for the accounting period. Finally, the amount of withdrawals that the owner made during the accounting period is subtracted.

Note that the owner's withdrawals are recorded directly in the owner's capital account, as we illustrated in Chapter 5 for Anna's $50 withdrawal in transaction #6 and in Exhibit 5-18. It is important to understand that *withdrawals are not expenses* because they are not the costs of providing goods or services to customers. Withdrawals are recorded as *reductions* of the owner's capital account because they are *dis*investments of assets by the owner. The final amount on a company's statement of changes in owner's equity is the owner's capital balance at the end of the accounting period. The company reports this amount on its ending balance sheet.

By summarizing all the transactions affecting the owner's equity of a company, the statement of changes in owner's equity helps to complete the picture of the company's financial activities for the accounting period. External users find this information helpful in evaluating the changes in the claims on the company's assets, changes that have an impact on its risk, operating capability, and financial flexibility.

*If you saw a large amount of withdrawals reported in a company's statement of changes in owner's equity, how would that affect your evaluation of its risk? Why?*

Exhibit 6-5 shows Sweet Temptations' statement of changes in owner's equity for the month ended January 31, 2008. The $15,000 beginning amount of owner's capital comes from the A. Cox, Capital account (shown in Exhibit 5-6). Anna made no additional investments during the accounting period, so the next item is net income. The $602 net income comes from the income statement in Exhibit 6-2. The $50 of withdrawals comes from the A. Cox, Capital account in Sweet Temptations' accounting records, as we just discussed. The $15,552 ending amount for A. Cox, Capital is the amount reported as owner's equity in Sweet Temptations' January 31, 2008 balance sheet (which is prepared next, and which we showed in Exhibit 5-22).

**EXHIBIT 6-5** **SWEET TEMPTATIONS' STATEMENT OF CHANGES IN OWNER'S EQUITY**

**SWEET TEMPTATIONS**
***Statement of Changes in Owner's Equity***
***For Month Ended January 31, 2008***

| | |
|---|---|
| A. Cox, capital, January 1, 2008 | $15,000 |
| Add: Net income | 602 |
| | $15,602 |
| Less: Withdrawals | (50) |
| A. Cox, capital, January 31, 2008 | $15,552 |

Managers and external users know that a company's income statement and statement of changes in owner's equity do not provide all of the financial information needed for business decisions. Information that is not reported on the company's income statement can have a big impact on its ability to earn profits in the future. In the next chapter, we will discuss how managers, investors, and creditors use the balance sheet in conjunction with the income statement to make business decisions.

## CLOSING THE TEMPORARY ACCOUNTS

Earlier in the chapter we explained that revenue and expense accounts are *temporary accounts* used to accumulate a company's net income amounts for the accounting period. After a company prepares its income statement, statement of changes in owner's equity, balance sheet, and cash flow statement for the accounting period, it prepares "closing entries." **Closing entries** are entries made by a company to transfer the ending balances from its temporary revenue and expense accounts into its permanent account for owner's capital. A company uses closing entries so that when a new accounting period starts, (1) the revenue and expense accounts (temporary accounts) have zero balances because they no longer contain the amounts of any transactions from previous periods, (2) the accounting system keeps the revenue and expense transactions of the current period separate from the revenue and expense transactions of other periods, and (3) the permanent (balance sheet) accounts are up-to-date (net income has been added to the previous balance of the owner's capital account).

We do not illustrate the closing entries for each revenue and expense account because it is too time-consuming and not necessary for your understanding of how a company's accounting system works. To give you an idea of closing entries, however, we will show you a "summary closing entry" for Sweet Temptations. Recall from Exhibit 5-21 that the amounts of the A. Cox, Capital, Revenue, and Expense columns at the end of January 2008 (prior to closing) were $14,950, $8,100, and $7,498, respectively, as we show in the following schedule.

| | Owner's Equity | | | | |
|---|---|---|---|---|---|
| | ***Owner's Capital*** | + | ***Net Income*** | | |
| | A. Cox, Capital | | Revenues | − | Expenses |
| Balances prior to closing | $14,950 | | $8,100 | − | $7,498 |
| Summary closing entry | + $602 | | −$8,100 | − | −$7,498 |
| Balances after closing | $15,552 | | $ 0 | | $ 0 |

Anna prepares the summary closing entry as follows. To decrease the Revenue account column to zero, she subtracts $8,100 from this column. Similarly, to decrease the Expenses column to zero, she subtracts $7,498 from this column. Anna then adds the $602 difference (which is the net income shown in Exhibit 6-2) to the A. Cox, Capital account column. After this summary closing entry, the Revenue and Expense columns both have zero balances and are ready to accumulate the revenue and expense information for February 2008. The A. Cox, Capital account column has a balance of $15,552, which is the amount shown in Exhibit 6-5. We emphasize that this is a "summary closing entry" because in actual closing entries a company would close *each* revenue account and *each* expense account to the owner's capital account. Furthermore, a company's accounting period usually is one year so it would normally prepare its closing entries at the end of the year, rather than at the end of each month.

*Which accounts in Sweet Temptations' accounting system have nonzero balances on February 1, 2008?*

## SUMMARY

At the beginning of the chapter we asked you several questions. During the chapter, we asked you to STOP and answer several additional questions to build your knowledge about specific issues. Be sure you answered these additional questions. Below are the questions from the beginning of the chapter, with a brief summary of the key points relating to the answers. Use your creative and critical thinking skills to expand on these key points to develop more complete answers to the questions and to determine what other questions you have that might lead you to learn more about the issues.

### 1 Why is a company's income statement important?

A company's income statement is important because it summarizes the results (revenues, expenses, and net income) of the company's operating activities for an accounting period. This information is useful in the decision making of both internal and external users because it helps to show how well the company's management has performed during the period and from period to period.

### 2 How are changes in a company's balance sheet and income statement accounts recorded in its accounting system?

Changes in a company's balance sheet accounts are recorded in its accounting system by creating a separate column for *each* asset, liability, and owner's capital account. These accounts are called *permanent accounts* because they are used for the life of the company to record its balance sheet transactions. Changes in a company's income statement accounts are recorded in its accounting system by creating a separate column under Owner's Equity for *each* revenue account and *each* expense account, while still retaining the owner's capital account column. A company uses these revenue and expense accounts to record its net income transactions for only one accounting period, so they are called *temporary accounts*.

### 3 What are the parts of a retail company's classified income statement, and what do they contain?

The classified income statement of a retail company includes two parts, an operating income section and an other items section. The operating income section includes revenues, cost of goods sold, and operating expenses subsections related to a company's primary operating activities. The other items section includes any revenues or expenses that are not directly related to the company's primary operations.

### 4 What is inventory and cost of goods sold, and what inventory systems may be used by a company?

Inventory is the merchandise a retail company is holding for resale. Cost of goods sold is the cost to the company of the merchandise that it sells during the accounting period. A company may use either a perpetual inventory system or a periodic inventory system. A perpetual inventory system keeps a continuous record of the cost of inventory on hand and the cost of inventory sold. A periodic inventory system does not keep a continuous record of the inventory on hand and sold, but uses a physical count to determine the inventory on hand at the end of the accounting period.

### 5 What are the main concerns of external decision makers when they use a company's income statement to evaluate its performance?

When external decision makers use a company's income statement to evaluate its performance, they are concerned about the company's risk, operating capability, and financial flexibility. Risk is uncertainty about the future earnings potential of the company. Operating capability refers to the company's ability to continue a given level of operations. Financial flexibility refers to the company's ability to adapt to change.

### 6 What type of analysis is used by external decision makers to evaluate a company's profitability?

Ratio analysis is used by external users to evaluate a company's profitability. Ratio analysis involves computations in which an item on the company's financial statements is divided by another, related item. The ratios are compared with the company's ratios in previous periods or with other companies' ratios. The ratios used to evaluate a company's profitability include the profit margin (net income divided by net sales) and the gross profit percentage (gross profit divided by net sales).

## KEY TERMS

**adjusting entries** *(p. 179)*
**cash discount** *(p. 173)*
**closing entries** *(p. 185)*
**cost of ending inventory** *(p. 178)*
**cost of goods sold** *(p. 175)*
**credit memo** *(p. 174)*
**financial flexibility** *(p. 181)*
**general and administrative expenses** *(p. 179)*
**gross profit** *(p. 178)*
**gross profit percentage** *(p. 182)*
**inventory** *(p. 175)*
**net purchases** *(p. 178)*
**operating capability** *(p. 181)*
**operating expenses** *(p. 178)*
**operating income** *(pp. 170, 180)*
**other items** *(pp. 170, 180)*
**periodic inventory system** *(p. 176)*
**permanent accounts** *(p. 169)*
**perpetual inventory system** *(p. 175)*
**profit margin** *(p. 182)*
**quantity discount** *(p. 173)*
**ratio analysis** *(p. 182)*
**risk** *(p. 181)*
**sales allowance** *(p. 174)*
**sales discount** *(p. 173)*
**sales return** *(p. 174)*
**selling expenses** *(p. 179)*
**statement of changes in owner's equity** *(p. 184)*
**temporary accounts** *(p. 169)*

## SUMMARY SURFING

Here is an opportunity to gather information on the Internet about real-world issues related to the topics in this chapter (for suggestions on how to navigate various companies' Web sites to find their financial statements and other information, see the related discussion in the Preface at the beginning of the book). Answer the following questions.

- Go to the **JCPenney Company** Web site. Find the company's income statements. Compute the profit margin and the gross profit percentage for the most current year. How do these results compare with the year ended January 28, 2006 ratios we discussed in this chapter?

- Go to the **Kohl's Corporation** Web site. Find the company's income statements. Compute the profit margin and the gross profit percentage for the most current year. How do these results compare with the year ended January 28, 2006 ratios we discussed in this chapter?

## INTEGRATED BUSINESS AND ACCOUNTING SITUATIONS

**Answer the Following Questions in Your Own Words.**

### Testing Your Knowledge

**6-1** Write out the income statement equation, and explain its components.

**6-2** Explain how managers use a company's income statement for decision making.

**6-3** How are changes in a company's income statement accounts recorded in its accounting system?

**6-4** What is the difference between temporary and permanent accounts?

**6-5** Identify the parts and subsections of a retail company's classified income statement. What is included in each part?

**6-6** Explain the difference between a quantity discount and a sales (cash) discount.

**6-7** Explain the difference between a sales return and a sales allowance.

**6-8** What is a perpetual inventory system? How is a company's cost of goods sold determined under this system?

**6-9** What is a periodic inventory system? How is a company's cost of goods sold determined under this system?

**6-10** What are operating expenses? Explain the difference between selling expenses and general and administrative expenses.

**6-11** Explain the meaning of the terms *risk, operating capability,* and *financial flexibility.*

**6-12** What is ratio analysis, and what is it used for?

**6-13** Explain how to compute a company's profit margin. What is this ratio used for?

**6-14** Explain how to compute a company's gross profit percentage. What is this ratio used for?

**6-15** Explain what is included in a company's statement of changes in owner's equity and how the statement is used.

**6-16** What are closing entries and why are they used?

## Applying Your Knowledge

**6-17** On July 1, Drexel's Appliance purchased $5,000 of goods for resale. On July 15, it sold $2,600 of these goods to customers at a selling price of $4,000. The company uses a perpetual inventory system, and all transactions were for cash.

*Required:* Prepare account column entries to record this information.

**6-18** On April 6, Piper Model Shop made a $127 cash sale of merchandise to a customer. The company uses a perpetual inventory system; the merchandise had cost Piper $88. On April 8, the customer was given a sales allowance of $25 cash for a defective model that the customer chose to keep.

*Required:* (1) Prepare account column entries to record this information.
(2) What source documents would be used to record each transaction?

**6-19** The Jardine Tax Services Company was established on January 1 of the current year to help clients with their tax planning and with the preparation of their tax returns. During January, the company entered into the following transactions:

| *Date* | *Transactions* |
|---|---|
| Jan. 2 | D. Jardine set up the company by investing $5,000 in the company's checking account. |
| 3 | The company paid $2,400 in advance for one year's rent of office space. |
| 4 | Office equipment was purchased at a cost of $6,000. A down payment of $1,000 was made, and a $5,000 note payable was signed for the balance owed. The note is due in one year. |
| 7 | Office supplies were purchased for $800 cash. |
| 16 | Fees of $1,700 were collected from clients for tax services provided during the first half of January. |
| 29 | A salary of $700 was paid to the office secretary. |
| 30 | Jardine withdrew $900 for personal use. |
| 31 | The January utility bill of $120 was received; it will be paid in early February. |

31 Clients were billed $2,300 for tax services performed during the second half of January.
31 Jardine recorded the following adjustments:
a. Rent expense for the month
b. Depreciation of $45 on office equipment
c. Interest expense of $50 on the note payable
d. Office supplies used (the office supplies on hand at the end of the month cost $720)

*Required:* (1) Record the preceding transactions in appropriate account columns.
(2) Prepare a classified income statement for the company for January.
(3) Prepare a balance sheet for the company on January 31.
(4) Briefly comment on how well the company did during January.

**6-20** The Salanar Answering Service Company was started on April 1 of the current year to answer the phones of doctors, lawyers, and accountants when they are away from their offices. The following transactions of the company occurred and adjustments were made during April:

*Date* *Transaction*
Apr. 1 P. Salanar started the business by investing $3,000 cash.
2 The company paid cash of $900 in advance for six months' rent of office space.
3 The company purchased telephone equipment costing $5,500, paying $1,500 down and signing a $4,000 note payable for the balance owed.
6 Office supplies totaling $450 were purchased on credit. The amount is due in early May.
15 The company collected $800 from clients for answering services performed during the first half of April.
28 P. Salanar withdrew $600 for personal use.
29 The April $110 utility bill was received; it is to be paid in May.
30 The company paid $300 salary to a part-time employee.
30 Clients were billed $700 for answering services performed during the last half of April.
30 Salanar recorded the following adjustments:
a. Rent expense for April
b. Depreciation of $42 on telephone equipment
c. Interest of $40 on the note payable
d. Office supplies used of $58

*Required:* (1) Record the preceding transactions in appropriate account columns.
(2) Prepare a simple income statement for the company for April.
(3) Prepare a balance sheet for the company on April 30.
(4) Briefly comment on how well the company did during April.

**6-21** The Steed Art Supplies Company sells various art supplies to local artists. The company uses a perpetual inventory system, and the balance of its inventory of art supplies at the beginning of August was $2,500. Its cash balance was $800 and the J. Steed, capital balance was $3,300 at the beginning of August. Steed entered into the following transactions during August:

*Date* *Transactions*
Aug. 1 J. Steed invested another $1,000 cash into the company.
2 Purchased $400 of art supplies for cash.
4 Made a $900 sale of art supplies on credit to P. Tarlet, with terms of n/15; the cost of the inventory sold was $550.
6 Purchased $700 of art supplies on credit from the Rony Company, with terms of n/20.
10 Returned, for credit to its account, $100 of defective art supplies purchased on August 6 from the Rony Company.
12 Made cash sales of $330 to customers; the cost of the inventory sold was $200.
13 Granted a $25 allowance to a customer for damaged inventory sold on August 12.
15 Received payment from P. Tarlet of the amount due for inventory sold on credit on August 4.
25 Paid balance due to the Rony Company for purchase on August 6.

*Required:* (1) Record the preceding transactions in appropriate account columns.

(2) Determine the balances in all the accounts at the end of August.
(3) Compute the gross profit and the gross profit percentage for August.

**6-22** The Kerem Heater Company sells portable heaters and related equipment. The company uses a perpetual inventory system, and its inventory balance at the beginning of November was $2,600. Its cash balance was $1,500, and the B. Kerem, capital balance was $4,100 at the beginning of November. Kerem entered into the following transactions during November:

| *Date* | *Transactions* |
|---|---|
| Nov. 1 | B. Kerem invested another $900 cash into the company. |
| 2 | Made $480 cash sales to customers; the cost of the inventory sold was $280. |
| 3 | Purchased $1,700 of heaters for cash from Jokem Supply Company. |
| 5 | Received $250 cash allowance from Jokem Supply Company for defective inventory purchased on November 3. |
| 6 | Paid $210 for parts and repaired defective heaters purchased from Jokem Supply Company on November 3. |
| 8 | Made a $1,500 sale of heaters on credit to Arvin Nursing Home, with terms of 2/10, n/20; the cost of the inventory sold was $850. |
| 15 | Purchased $1,100 of heaters on credit from Duwell Supplies, with terms of n/15. |
| 18 | Received amount owed by Arvin Nursing Home for heaters purchased on November 8, less the cash discount. |
| 30 | Paid for the inventory purchased from Duwell Supplies on November 15. |

*Required:* (1) Record the preceding transactions in appropriate account columns.
(2) Determine the balances in all the accounts at the end of November.
(3) Compute the gross profit and the gross profit percentage for November.

**6-23** The following information is available for the Arnhold Horn Company for the year:

| | |
|---|---|
| Beginning inventory | $ 45,000 |
| Ending inventory | 50,000 |
| Purchases | 102,000 |
| Purchases returns and allowances | 4,000 |

*Required:* Prepare a schedule that computes the cost of goods sold for the year.

**6-24** The income statement information of the Weeden Furniture Company for 2008 and 2009 is as follows:

| | *2008* | *2009* |
|---|---|---|
| Cost of goods sold | $ *(a)* | $59,300 |
| Interest expense | 600 | 0 |
| Selling expenses | *(b)* | 10,800 |
| Operating income | 21,800 | *(d)* |
| Sales (net) | 96,000 | *(e)* |
| General expenses | 7,900 | *(f)* |
| Net income | *(c)* | 21,600 |
| Interest revenue | 0 | 600 |
| Gross profit | 39,000 | 40,200 |

*Required:* Fill in the blanks lettered (a) through (f). All the necessary information is listed. (*Hint:* It is not necessary to find the answers in alphabetical order.)

**6-25** The following information is taken from the accounts of the Harburn Hobby Shop for the month of October of the current year.

| | |
|---|---|
| Cost of goods sold | $54,000 |
| Sales revenue (net) | 88,000 |
| Selling expenses | 5,000 |
| Interest expense | 1,000 |
| General and administrative expenses | 12,000 |

*Required:* (1) Prepare a classified income statement for Harburn.
(2) Compute Harburn's profit margin.

**6-26** The following information is taken from the accounts of Foile's Music Store for the current year ended December 31.

| | |
|---|---|
| Depreciation expense: office equipment | $ 1,600 |
| Interest revenue | 725 |
| Sales salaries expense | 8,200 |
| Rent expense | 1,800 |
| Depreciation expense: store equipment | 2,400 |
| Sales revenue (net) | 94,200 |
| Office salaries expense | 4,000 |
| Interest expense | 250 |
| Office supplies expense | 600 |
| Cost of goods sold | 59,400 |
| Advertising expense | 360 |

Of the rent expense, 5/6 is applicable to the store and 1/6 is applicable to the office.

*Required:* (1) Prepare a classified income statement for Foile's Music Store for the current year.
(2) Compute the profit margin.
(3) Compute the gross profit percentage. Does this percentage fall near the high or the low end of the range of typical retail companies' gross profit percentages?

**6-27** The December 31, 2008 income statement accounts and other information of Lyon's Hardware are shown below:

| | |
|---|---|
| Advertising expense | $ 4,300 |
| Depreciation expense: store equipment | 1,600 |
| Depreciation expense: building (store) | 3,700 |
| Depreciation expense: office equipment | 2,300 |
| Depreciation expense: building (office) | 1,100 |
| Interest revenue | 1,700 |
| Interest expense | 900 |
| Cost of goods sold | 63,900 |
| Insurance expense | 350 |
| Sales (net) | 102,000 |
| Office supplies expense | 480 |
| Store supplies expense | 800 |
| Sales salaries expense | 5% of net sales |
| Office salaries expense | 2,600 |
| Utilities expense (store) | 1,500 |
| Utilities expense (office) | 400 |

*Required:* (1) Prepare a classified 2008 income statement for Lyon's Hardware.
(2) Compute the profit margin for 2008. If the profit margin for 2007 was 12.5%, what can be said about the 2008 results?

**6-28** Four independent cases related to the owner's equity account of the Cox Company follow:

| *Case* | *L. Cox, Capital May 1* | *Net Income for May* | *Withdrawals in May* | *L. Cox, Capital May 31* |
|---|---|---|---|---|
| 1 | $ A | $2,700 | $1,000 | $25,700 |
| 2 | 37,000 | B | 1,720 | 40,250 |
| 3 | 28,200 | 900 | C | 24,800 |
| 4 | 34,000 | 3,820 | 1,500 | D |

*Required:* Determine the amounts of A, B, C, and D.

**6-29** The beginning balance in the R. Barnum, Capital account on October 1 of the current year, was $23,000. For October, the Barnum Company reported total revenues of $8,000 and total expenses of $4,250. In addition, R. Barnum withdrew $1,400 for his personal use on October 25.

*Required:* Prepare a statement of changes in owner's equity for October for the Barnum Company.

**6-30** Rodgers Company shows the following amounts in its owner's equity accounts at the end of December: B. Rodgers, Capital, $32,200; Revenues, $57,300; Expenses, $42,800.

*Required:* Set up the account balances in account columns and prepare summary closing entries at the end of December.

## Making Evaluations

**6-31** A company engages in many types of activities.

*Required:* For each of the following sets of changes in a company's accounts, give an example of an activity that the company could engage in that would cause these changes and explain why you think the activity would cause these particular changes:

(1) Increase in an asset and decrease in another asset
(2) Increase in an asset and increase in a liability
(3) Increase in an asset and increase in owner's equity
(4) Increase in an asset and increase in a revenue
(5) Decrease in an asset and increase in an expense
(6) Decrease in an asset and decrease in a liability

**6-32** During the current accounting period, the bookkeeper for the Nallen Company made the following errors in the year-end adjustments:

| | *Effect of Error on:* | | | | | |
|---|---|---|---|---|---|---|
| Error | Revenues | Expenses | Net Income | Assets | Liabilities | Owner's Equity |
| Example: Failed to record $200 of salaries owed at the end of the period | N | U $200 | O $200 | N | U $200 | O $200 |
| 1. Failed to adjust prepaid insurance for $400 of expired insurance | | | | | | |
| 2. Failed to record $500 of interest expense that had accrued during the period | | | | | | |
| 3. Inadvertently recorded $300 of annual depreciation twice for the same equipment | | | | | | |
| 4. Failed to record $100 of interest revenue that had accrued during the period | | | | | | |
| 5. Failed to reduce unearned revenues for $600 of revenues that were earned during the period | | | | | | |

*Required:* Assuming that the errors are not discovered, indicate the effect of each error on revenues, expenses, net income, assets, liabilities, and owner's equity at the end of the accounting period. Use the following code: O = Overstated, U = Understated, and N = No effect. Include dollar amounts. Be prepared to explain your answers.

**6-33** Suppose you own a retail company and are considering whether to allow your customers to have quantity discounts, sales discounts, and sales allowances.

*Required:* How do you think quantity discounts, sales discounts, and sales allowances would affect the results of a company's C-V-P analysis and its budgets? Explain what the effects would be. If a company gives quantity discounts, sales discounts, and sales allowances, what information would it need in order to conduct C-V-P analysis and develop budgets? (What questions would you have to ask?)

**6-34** Your friend Allison is planning to open an automobile parts store and has come to you for advice about whether to use a perpetual or a periodic inventory system.

*Required:* Before you advise her, list the questions you would like to ask her. How would the answer to each question help you advise her? Explain to her the advantages and disadvantages of each system.

**6-35** Cara Agee owns a hairstyling shop, Air Hair Company. It is now November 2008, and Cara thinks she might need a bank loan. Her bank has asked Cara to prepare a "projected" income statement and to compute the "projected" profit margin for next year. Although she has never developed this information before, she understands that to do so, she must make a "best guess" of her revenues and expenses for 2009 based on past activities and future estimates. She asks for your help and provides you with the following information.

(a) Styling revenues for 2008 were $70,000. Cara expects these to increase by 10% in 2009.
(b) Air Hair employees are paid a total "base" salary of $30,000 plus 20% of all styling revenues.
(c) Styling supplies used have generally averaged 15% of styling revenues; Cara expects this relationship to be the same in 2009.
(d) Air Hair recently signed a two-year rental agreement on its shop, requiring payments of $400 per month, payable in advance.
(e) The cost of utilities (heat, light, phone) is expected to be 25% of the yearly rent.
(f) Air Hair owns styling equipment that cost $12,000. Depreciation expense for 2009 is estimated to be 1/6 of the cost of this equipment.

*Required:* Prepare a projected income statement for Air Hair Company for 2009 and compute its projected profit margin. Show supporting calculations.

**6-36** The Gray Service Company had a fire and lost some of the accounting records it needed to prepare its 2008 income statement. Stan Gray, the owner, has been able to determine that his capital in the business was $32,000 at the beginning of 2008 and was $33,000 at the end of 2008. During 2008 he withdrew $14,000 from the business. Stan has also been able to remember or determine the following information for 2008.

(a) Cash service revenues were three times the amount of net income; credit service revenues were 40% of cash service revenues.
(b) Rent expense was $500 per month.
(c) The company has one employee, who was paid a salary of $20,000 plus 20% of the service revenues.
(d) The supplies expense was 15% of the total expenses.
(e) The utilities expense was $100 per month for the first nine months of the year and $200 per month during the remaining months of the year due to the cold winter.

Stan also knows that the company owns some service equipment, but he cannot remember the cost or the amount of depreciation expense.

*Required:* Using the preceding information, prepare Gray Service Company's 2008 income statement and compute its profit margin. Show supporting calculations.

**6-37** Your boss has given you last year's income statements of two companies and asked you to recommend one in which your company should invest. The income statements include the following information (in thousands):

| | *Amalgamated Snacks* | *Gourmet Goodies* |
|---|---|---|
| Net sales | $1,360,000 | $2,000 |
| Cost of goods sold | 884,000 | 1,360 |
| Selling expenses | 205,294 | 312 |
| General and administrative expenses | 114,541 | 110 |
| Net income | 156,165 | 218 |

*Required:* Based on this information alone, which company would be the better investment choice? Explain your answer. What other information would you like to have in order to make a more informed decision? How would this information help you recommend the one in which you think your company should invest?

**6-38** A paragraph accompanying recent financial statements of **Dillard's Department Stores Inc.** begins: "Advertising, selling, administrative and general expenses increased as a percentage of sales in [the current year] compared to [last year]. This occurred because of the slower growth rate of sales during the year as compared to prior years."

*Required:* How does the second sentence explain the first? Explain in more detail how this could happen.

**6-39** On January 3, 2009, Ken Harmot agreed to buy the Ace Cleaning Service from Janice Steward. They agreed that the purchase price would be five times the 2008 net income of the company. To determine the price, Janice prepared the following condensed income statement for 2008.

| | |
|---|---|
| Revenues | $ 48,000 |
| Expenses | (36,000) |
| Net Income | $ 12,000 |

Janice said to Ken, "Based on this net income, the purchase price of the company should be $60,000 ($12,000 × 5). Of course, you may look at whatever accounting records you would like." Ken examined the accounting records and found them to be correct, except for several balance sheet accounts. These accounts and their December 31, 2008 balances are as follows: two asset accounts—Prepaid Rent, $3,600; and Equipment, $4,800; and one liability account—Unearned Cleaning Service Revenues, $0.

Ken gathered the following company information related to these accounts. The company was started on January 2, 2006. At that time, the company rented space in a building for its operations and purchased $6,400 of equipment. At that time, the equipment had an estimated life of 8 years, after which it would be worthless. On July 1, 2008, the company paid one year of rent in advance at $300 per month. On September 1, 2008, customers paid $600 in advance for cleaning services to be performed by the company for the next 12 months. Ken asks for your help. He says, "I don't know how these items affect net income, if at all. I want to pay a fair price for the company."

*Required:* (1) Discuss how the 2008 net income of the Ace Cleaning Service was affected, if at all, by each of the items.
(2) Prepare a corrected condensed 2008 income statement.
(3) Compute a fair purchase price for the company.

**6-40** The bookkeeper for Powell Import Service Agency was confused when he prepared the following financial statements.

**POWELL IMPORT SERVICE AGENCY**
***Profit and Expense Statement***
***December 31, 2008***

| | |
|---|---|
| Expenses: | |
| Salaries expense | $ 21,000 |
| Utilities expense | 3,400 |
| Accounts receivable | 1,600 |
| C. Powell, withdrawals | 20,000 |
| Office supplies | 1,500 |
| Total expenses | $(47,500) |
| Revenues: | |
| Service revenues | $ 47,000 |
| Accounts payable | 1,100 |
| Accumulated depreciation: office equipment | 1,800 |
| Total revenues | $ 49,900 |
| Net Revenues | $ 2,400 |

**POWELL IMPORT SERVICE AGENCY**
***Balancing Statement***
***For Year Ended December 31, 2008***

| *Liabilities* | | *Assets* | |
|---|---|---|---|
| Mortgage payable | $27,000 | Building | $44,000 |
| Accumulated depreciation: | | Depreciation expense: | |
| building | 6,400 | building | 1,600 |
| Total Liabilities | $33,400 | Office equipment | 9,700 |
| | | Depreciation expense: | |
| C. Powell, capital[a] | 27,000 | office equipment | 900 |
| Total Liabilities and | | Cash | 4,200 |
| Owner's Equity | $60,400 | Total Assets | $60,400 |

[a]$24,600 beginning capital + $2,400 net revenues

C. Powell asks for your help. He says, "Something is not right! My company had a fantastic year in 2008; I'm sure it made more than $2,400. I don't remember much about accounting, but I do recall that 'accumulated depreciation' should be subtracted from the cost of an asset to determine its book value." You agree based on your understanding of the depreciation discussion in Chapter 5 of this book. After examining the financial statements and related accounting records, you find that, with the exception of office supplies, the *amount* of each item is correct even though the item might be incorrectly listed in the financial statements. You determine that the office supplies used during the year amount to $800 and that the office supplies on hand at the end of the year amount to $700.

*Required:* (1) Review each financial statement and indicate any errors you find.
(2) Prepare a corrected 2008 income statement, statement of changes in owner's equity, and ending balance sheet.
(3) Compute the profit margin for 2008 to verify or refute C. Powell's claim that his company had a fantastic year.

**6-41** Yesterday, the letter shown on the following page arrived for your advice column in the local paper.

## DR. DECISIVE

Dear Dr. Decisive:

I can't believe I am writing to you. In the past, I have always tried to solve my own problems, but now I have one I can't solve on my own. My roommate and I are taking an accounting course together. One night, or maybe I should say very early one morning, we were debating where a bank's interest expense goes on its income statement. I think it should go in the "other items" section, but my roommate thinks it should go in "operating expenses." We could argue about this forever, but neither one of us is willing to give in. My roommate agrees that we will accept your answer. If I win, I don't have to pay my roommate interest on the money I owe him.

"Interested"

*Required:* Meet with your Dr. Decisive team and write a response to "Interested."

# END NOTE

[a]"Mill Owner Keeps Faith with Workers," *Columbia Daily Tribune,* December 22, 1996, sec. A, 1.

CHAPTER 7

# THE BALANCE SHEET: ITS CONTENT AND USE

"THERE ARE BUT TWO WAYS OF PAYING A DEBT: INCREASE INCOME, OR INCREASE THRIFT."

—THOMAS CARLYLE

1. Why is a company's balance sheet important?
2. What do users need to know about a company's classified balance sheet?
3. What is a company's liquidity, and how do users evaluate it?
4. What is a company's financial flexibility, and how do users evaluate it?
5. Why and how do users evaluate a company's profitability?
6. What is a company's operating capability, and how do users evaluate it?

What assets do you own? How do you keep track of them? How much is in your checking account? Savings account? Do you currently have some bills that you need to pay next month? Do you own a car? A computer? A house? What did these assets cost? Did you take out a loan to pay for any of them? Do you still owe money on this loan? If so, what percentage of your total assets is the amount that you owe? Do your assets exceed your debts? Companies also keep track of their assets and debts. For instance, **Wal-Mart** reported $43,824 million of "current" assets, $97,302 million of property and equipment, and $138,187 million of total assets on its January 31, 2006 balance sheet. On this balance sheet, among other amounts, Wal-Mart also reported $48,826 million of "current" liabilities, $26,429 million of long-term debt, and $53,171 of owners' equity. Wal-Mart obtained these numbers from its accounting system. Does Wal-Mart have enough "current" assets on hand to pay its "current" liabilities? Has Wal-Mart taken out too much of a "loan" as long-term debt to pay for its property and equipment?

*Overall, do these numbers show that Wal-Mart was in a "good" or "bad" financial position on this date? What other information would you like to have to answer this question?*

In Chapter 6 you saw how a company's income statement provides managers and external users with important information about its activities. By describing the revenues, expenses, and net income (or net loss) for an accounting period, the income statement helps show whether a company is earning a satisfactory profit. A company's net income (net loss) for an accounting period is the increase (decrease) in owner's equity that resulted from the operating activities of that period. An income statement prepared according to generally accepted accounting principles (GAAP) also enables users to compare financial results from period to period or across companies.

Although the income statement provides useful information for business decision making, managers and external users don't use it alone. They also study the balance sheet. In this chapter, we discuss the importance of the balance sheet. First, we look at the principles, concepts, and accounting methods related to the balance sheet. Second, we describe and present a classified balance sheet. Finally, we explore how managers and external users use a balance sheet to help them make business decisions.

## WHY THE BALANCE SHEET IS IMPORTANT

**1 Why is a company's balance sheet important?**

A balance sheet provides information that helps internal and external users evaluate a company's ability to achieve its primary goals of earning a satisfactory profit and remaining solvent. You may recall that the income statement provides information that is used for similar purposes. The income statement and the balance sheet provide different yet related types of information.

An income statement presents a summary of a company's operating activities for an accounting period: revenues earned, expenses incurred, and the net income that resulted. So, the income statement reports on a company's actions *over a period of time* or, as some say, the "flow of a company's operating activities." The income statement answers questions such as the following: "How much sales revenue did the company earn last year?" "What was the cost of advertising for the year?"

In contrast, a balance sheet presents a company's financial position *on a specific date,* allowing users to "take stock" of a company's assets, liabilities, and owner's equity on that date. Managers and external users need this "financial position" information in order to make business decisions. By examining the balance sheet, users can answer questions such as the following: "What types of resources does the company have available for its operations?" "What are the company's obligations?" They can find out how much money customers owe the company (accounts receivable), see the total dollar amount of the inventory on hand at year-end, and discover how much money the company owes its creditors (accounts payable).

*Some people say that the balance sheet is a "snapshot" of a company's assets, liabilities, and owner's equity on a given date. What do they mean? Do you agree? Why or why not?*

## Why Users Need Both the Balance Sheet and the Income Statement

Remember the creative thinking strategies we discussed in Chapter 2? Let's try a couple of analogies to understand why internal and external users need both the income statement and the balance sheet. You will get the most out of these analogies if you read them actively. In other words, every time you see a question, don't just read ahead, but try to come up with your own answers first. Making analogies really will help you understand accounting—we promise!

Let's say that you want to predict whether your friend Chuck can bake a delicious loaf of bread. What do you need to know to increase your chances of making an accurate prediction? We think you need to know three related items. First, before baking delicious bread, Chuck must have all of the cooking equipment and the ingredients for the bread on hand: flour, butter, yeast, salt, sugar, bread pans, an oven, etc. So, your first question should be, "Does Chuck have everything he needs to bake the bread?" However, even if he has all of the necessary equipment and ingredients, does that mean he can bake delicious bread? Certainly not! The second question you would ask is, "Has he baked delicious bread before?" If the answers to both these questions are yes, it is likely that he can bake a delicious loaf of bread. If the answer to either of these questions is no, then you are much less sure about his ability to bake. Do you agree? The third question (and probably the most important question if you plan on eating his bread) is not as easy to answer. That question is, "Does he still know how to bake?" You won't know the answer to this question until you taste the next loaf out of his oven.

You would follow a similar strategy if you were trying to determine whether a company can earn a satisfactory profit. You want to know if the company has the assets, liabilities, and owner's equity (does it have the "ingredients"?) needed to earn a satisfactory profit (to bake a delicious loaf of bread). You also need to know if the company has been able to use its resources in the past to earn such a profit (has it baked delicious bread before?). Because a company's balance sheet and income statement provide this financial information, analyzing both statements helps you make an informed decision about the

© KARL WEATHERLY/GETTY IMAGES

How do you think these legs would be listed on a sprinter's balance sheet?

company's ability to earn a satisfactory profit (can it still "bake"?). If either financial statement is missing, it is much more difficult to predict how well the company will perform.

For example, to estimate a company's sales revenue for 2008, it is important to know the amount of cash and the amount of inventory available for sale at the beginning of 2008, and the amount of sales revenues in 2007. You would look at the beginning balance sheet to see if the company has sufficient cash to pay for expenses such as advertising, rent, and salaries, and whether it has enough inventory to meet customers' demands for its product. Last year's sales revenue gives an indication of how well a company will perform in the current period. You look at the income statement to find that amount.

Now let's try a sports analogy. Suppose you want to estimate how long it will take a friend, Barb, to run a marathon. What questions would you want answered? You would probably want information about her physical characteristics—things like her age, her height, or her muscle development. These physical characteristics will help you understand her potential running ability. Equally important is information about how well she has used her physical attributes—how long it took her to run her last marathon, when she last ran, and how often she exercises.

When you ask about Barb's physical characteristics, you are "taking stock" of her physical resources, much as an investor analyzes a balance sheet to take stock of a company's financial resources. By learning how well she has used her physical attributes, you are getting information about her past activities that can help you predict her ability to run a fast race. Running a fast race is to sports what earning a satisfactory profit is to business.

*Can you think of any other analogies? What are the goals of the activities in your analogies? What information can help you predict whether the goal will be attained?*

The lesson to be learned from our analogies is this: whenever you try to estimate if a goal can be reached—whether the goal is baking a delicious loaf of bread, running a marathon in a certain amount of time, or earning a satisfactory profit—many different types of related information are helpful. A company's balance sheet is one important source of unique and valuable information for predicting the company's financial performance.

## Cost-Volume-Profit Analysis, Budgeting, and the Balance Sheet

In Chapter 6, we discussed the relationship between cost-volume-profit (C-V-P) analysis, budgeting, and the income statement. Remember that a company's income statement reports on the results of many of its managers' operating decisions. At least in part, the revenue and expense information shows the results of past C-V-P analysis and budgeting decisions.

Balance sheet information also summarizes the results of managers' decisions. For instance, in Chapter 4 we saw how Anna Cox used a sales budget to help her decide how much inventory Sweet Temptations should keep on hand. A company also uses the sales budget to decide how often to purchase inventory and how many units to order. The accounting system keeps track of inventory balances to help the company evaluate these budgeting decisions and report the inventory as an asset on the balance sheet. If the amount of inventory on hand grows at a faster rate than sales from year to year, the company probably overestimated both sales and its need to make inventory purchases. If the amount of inventory on hand is decreasing as a proportion of sales from year to year, the company may have underestimated sales and the need to make additional inventory purchases.[1]

*What other balance sheet information helps you evaluate the budgeting decisions of a company's managers?*

[1]Some companies intentionally minimize the amount of inventory they keep on hand. These companies buy their inventory "just-in-time" to meet their sales. We will discuss this just-in-time philosophy more in Chapter 18.

Remember that financial statements help external users decide if they want to do business with a company. External users are interested in a company's assets, liabilities, and owner's equity because, as we explained in the previous section, these items describe a company's financial characteristics. Because external users may be trying to decide *which* company to do business with, companies prepare balance sheets according to GAAP. Since U.S. companies follow the same set of accounting rules when preparing their financial statements, external users can reliably compare the financial positions of any of these companies as part of their decision-making processes. In the sections that follow, we will briefly review the basic accounting principles that underlie the balance sheet and we will discuss the components of a classified balance sheet.

## THE ACCOUNTING EQUATION AND THE BALANCE SHEET

Recall from Chapter 5 that the financial accounting process is based on a simple equation:

**Economic Resources = Claims on Economic Resources**

Using accounting terminology, we restated the equation as follows:

**Assets = Liabilities + Owner's Equity**

Remember that this mathematical expression is known as the basic **accounting equation** and that the equality of the assets to the liabilities plus owner's equity is the reason a company's statement of financial position is often called a *balance* sheet. The monetary total for the economic resources (assets) of a company must always be *in balance* with the monetary total for the claims to the economic resources (liabilities + owner's equity).

*Do you remember the "transaction scales" we showed in Chapter 5? How did they work?*

The **balance sheet** is a financial statement that reports the types and the monetary amounts of a company's assets, liabilities, and owner's equity on a specific date. A company prepares a balance sheet at the end of each accounting period, although it can prepare a balance sheet at any other time to give a current "snapshot" of the company's financial position. Before preparing a balance sheet, though, the company must be certain that the monetary totals for each of its assets and liabilities and the monetary total for owner's equity are correct. By "correct," we mean that since the date of the last balance sheet, all of the company's transactions and events have been recorded in its accounting system according to GAAP. As we discussed in Chapter 6, we also mean that the balances of the revenue, expense, and owner's withdrawals accounts at the end of the accounting period have been transferred to the owner's capital account.

Exhibit 7-1 shows Sweet Temptations' balance sheet accounts in its accounting system on January 31, 2008 (to save space, we have listed the accounts vertically). The accounts include the correct balance for each of Sweet Temptations' assets, liabilities, and owner's capital (after including the revenue, expense, and withdrawals amounts for January) accounts.

Exhibit 7-2 shows Sweet Temptations' January 31, 2008 balance sheet. By comparing Exhibit 7-2 with Exhibit 7-1, you can see how the balances in the accounts provide the information needed to prepare a balance sheet. Notice that the balance sheet shows the balance for each account. Also notice that the liability and owner's equity items are listed below the assets. This format is called a *report form* of balance sheet (as compared with the *account form,* shown in Exhibit 5-22, which lists the components in an accounting equation format—assets on the left and liabilities and owner's equity on the right). The report form of balance sheet is common because it is easier to show the accounts vertically on a standard sheet of paper.

## EXHIBIT 7-1 SWEET TEMPTATIONS' BALANCE SHEET ACCOUNTS

Assets = Liabilities + Owner's Equity [Owner's Capital + (Revenues − Expenses)]

| Assets | | Liabilities | | Owner's Equity | |
|---|---|---|---|---|---|
| **Cash** | | **Accounts Payable** | | **A. Cox, Capital** | |
| 1/31/08 Bal | $11,030 | 1/31/08 Bal | $4,320 | 1/31/08 Bal | $15,552 |
| **Accounts Receivable** | | **Notes Payable** | | | |
| 1/31/08 Bal | $100 | 1/31/08 Bal | $1,208 | | |
| **Inventory** | | | | | |
| 1/31/08 Bal | $2,295 | | | | |
| **Supplies** | | | | | |
| 1/31/08 Bal | $670 | | | | |
| **Prepaid Rent** | | | | | |
| 1/31/08 Bal | $5,000 | | | | |
| **Store Equipment** | | | | | |
| 1/31/08 Bal | $1,985 | | | | |

## EXHIBIT 7-2 CLASSIFIED BALANCE SHEET

**SWEET TEMPTATIONS**
***Balance Sheet***
***January 31, 2008***

**Assets**

| | | |
|---|---|---|
| Current Assets | | |
| Cash | $11,030 | |
| Accounts receivable | 100 | |
| Inventory | 2,295 | |
| Supplies | 670 | |
| Prepaid rent | 5,000 | |
| Total current assets | | $19,095 |
| Property and Equipment | | |
| Store equipment (net) | $ 1,985 | |
| Total property and equipment | | 1,985 |
| Total Assets | | $21,080 |

**Liabilities**

| | | |
|---|---|---|
| Current Liabilities | | |
| Accounts payable | $ 4,320 | |
| Note payable | 1,208 | |
| Total current liabilities | | $ 5,528 |
| Total Liabilities | | $ 5,528 |

**Owner's Equity**

| | | |
|---|---|---|
| A. Cox, capital | | $15,552 |
| Total Liabilities and Owner's Equity | | $21,080 |

2 What do users need to know about a company's classified balance sheet?

Sweet Temptations' balance sheet is called a **classified balance sheet.** By "classified," we mean that the balance sheet shows subtotals for assets, liabilities, and owner's equity in related groupings. A company decides on the classifications based on the type of business it is in. Later in the chapter, you will see that these groupings make it easier for financial statement users to evaluate a company's performance and to compare its performance with that of other companies.

Notice the way that Sweet Temptations organizes its classified balance sheet. The company adds together the asset groupings to report Total Assets of $21,080 and adds together the liability groupings to report Total Liabilities of $5,528. Finally, it adds the total liabilities to the total owner's equity to report Total Liabilities and Owner's Equity of $21,080. Because Sweet Temptations kept the accounting equation in balance as it recorded its transactions, Total Assets equals Total Liabilities plus Owner's Equity. Let's look at the balance sheet classifications in more detail.

## Assets

**Assets** are a company's economic resources that it expects will provide future benefits to the company. A large company may own hundreds of different types of assets. Some are physical in nature—such as land, buildings, supplies to be used, and inventory that the company expects to sell to its customers. Others do not have physical characteristics but are economic resources because of the legal rights they give to the company. For instance, accounts receivable give the company the right to collect cash in the future.

Think about the different types of assets owned by the grocery store where you shop. We would need several pages to present a complete list, but here are a few examples: cash, accounts receivable, cleaning supplies, grocery carts, storage shelves, forklifts, refrigerators, freezers, bakery equipment, cash registers, the building, the parking lot . . . whew! We'll stop there, but notice that we did *not* even mention any inventory items (groceries) which, of course, are also assets.

*If you work, list the types of assets owned by the company for which you work. If you don't work, talk with someone who does, and find out what types of assets are owned by the company for which he or she works.*

Because Sweet Temptations started with a very small amount of capital, it has only a few assets. This small-company example makes it easier for you to see the basic framework that a company uses in accounting for and reporting its resources. When presenting a classified balance sheet, a small retail candy store, a large grocery store, or almost any other type of retail company uses the same classifications for its assets. Look at the balance sheet for a large retail company, and you will likely find subtotals for current assets, long-term investments, and property and equipment.

### Current Assets

**Current assets** are cash and other assets that the company expects to convert into cash, sell, or use up within one year.[2] Current assets include (1) cash, (2) marketable securities, (3) receivables, (4) inventory, and (5) prepaid items. The current assets section presents these items in the order of their liquidity—that is, according to how quickly they can be converted into cash, sold, or used up. Because companies need cash to pay currently due liabilities, grouping current assets together helps financial statement users evaluate a company's ability to pay its current debts.

*Cash* includes cash on hand (i.e., cash kept in cash registers or the company's safe) and in checking and savings accounts. *Marketable securities,* sometimes called *temporary investments* or *short-term investments,* are items such as government bonds and capital stock of corporations in which the company has temporarily invested (and which the com-

[2]As we discussed in Chapter 4, some companies, such as lumber, distillery, and tobacco companies, have operating cycles of longer than one year, so they use their operating cycle to define current assets.

pany expects to sell within a year). A company usually makes these short-term investments because it has cash it does not need immediately for purchasing inventory or paying liabilities. Instead of just keeping the cash in the bank, the company purchases the marketable securities to earn additional revenue through interest or dividends. Investment companies such as **A G Edwards**, **Merrill Lynch**, and **Charles Schwab** help other companies (and individual investors) buy and sell marketable securities.

*Receivables* include accounts receivable (amounts owed by customers) and notes receivable (and related interest). *Inventory* is goods held for resale. *Prepaid items* such as insurance, rent, office supplies, and store supplies will not be converted into cash but will be used up within one year. Note in Exhibit 7-2 that the current assets for Sweet Temptations on January 31, 2008 total $19,095, consisting of cash ($11,030), accounts receivable ($100), inventory ($2,295), supplies ($670), and prepaid rent ($5,000). Remember, the amount for each current asset listed on Sweet Temptations' balance sheet comes from the related account balance in its accounting system.

Assets that are not classified as current assets are called *noncurrent assets*. The balance sheet shows noncurrent assets, such as long-term investments and property and equipment, in separate categories.

### Long-Term Investments

**Long-term investments** include items such as notes receivable, government bonds, bonds and capital stock of corporations, and other securities. Sometimes these are called *noncurrent marketable securities.* A company must *intend* to hold the investment for more than one year to classify it in the long-term investments section of the balance sheet.

Why would a company purchase a corporation's stock? A company makes investments for many reasons, which we will discuss in more detail later. The most basic reason, however, is because the company believes the investment will increase the company's profit. For example, a company may invest in the stock of a corporation because it expects the price of that stock to increase. If that happens, when the company sells the stock later, it will have a gain, which will increase its net income.

Sweet Temptations has not made any long-term investments. At this early stage of the company's life, Sweet Temptations uses its cash to replenish inventory and meet other basic business needs such as paying salaries, rent, and advertising. Therefore Sweet Temptations shows no long-term investments on its January 31, 2008 balance sheet.

### Property and Equipment

**Property and equipment** includes all the physical, long-term assets used in the operations of a company. Often these assets are referred to as *fixed assets* or *operating assets* because of their relative permanence in the company's operations. Assets that have a physical existence, such as land, buildings, equipment, and furniture, are listed in this category. Land is listed on the balance sheet at its original cost. The remaining fixed assets are listed at their book values. The **book value** of an asset is its original cost minus the related accumulated depreciation. **Accumulated depreciation** is the total amount of depreciation expense recorded over the life of an asset to date; thus, it is the portion of the asset's cost that has been "used up" to earn revenues to date. The book values for fixed assets change from period to period as the company sells and/or buys these assets and as accumulated depreciation increases. The balance sheet thus helps report on related budgeting and operating decisions made by the company's managers. We will discuss accumulated depreciation in detail in Chapter 21 of Volume 2.

You may be wondering how to reconcile the historical cost concept with the reported book value of a company's property and equipment. As a company uses up assets other than property or equipment, the assets that have *not* been used remain on its balance sheet at their historical cost. The assets that *have* been used no longer exist in the company. But when the company uses property or equipment, the asset still exists in the company until the company has finished using it. Every year, the company uses a portion of the asset, but the entire asset still continues to physically exist in the company. What the company reports (the book value) on its balance sheet represents the portion of the property or equipment that the company has not yet used.

Notice in Exhibit 7-2 that Sweet Temptations' store equipment is classified as property and equipment on its balance sheet. Also notice that the store equipment is listed at $1,985 (net). The "(net)" tells the reader that accumulated depreciation has been deducted from the cost (the $1,985 book value consists of the $2,000 cost less $15 accumulated depreciation, as we discussed in Chapter 5). Sweet Temptations does not include any amounts for land or buildings because it rents space in the Westwood Mall and thus does not own such items.

*Sometimes a company has difficulty deciding how to classify its assets. For example, do you think the cars owned by a rental car company are classified as inventory or equipment? Why? Can you think of more examples that present a dilemma?*

## Liabilities

**Liabilities** are the economic obligations (debts) of a company. The external parties to whom the company owes the economic obligations are the company's *creditors.* Legal documents often serve as evidence of liabilities. These documents establish a claim *(equity)* by the creditors (the *creditors' equity*) against the assets of the company.

Companies have many different types of liabilities. For instance, consider the claims that creditors may have on the grocery store's assets we listed earlier. The grocery store probably borrowed money from a bank (by signing a mortgage) to finance its purchases of land and a building. The company also could have obtained the funds used to purchase refrigerators, freezers, baking equipment, and other types of equipment from a bank by signing a long-term (e.g., ten-year) note payable. Most likely, it purchased grocery items from suppliers on credit, resulting in accounts payable. Generally, a company has two types of liabilities—current and noncurrent.

### Current Liabilities

**Current liabilities** are obligations that the company expects to pay within one year by using current assets. Current liabilities include (1) accounts payable and salaries payable, (2) unearned revenues, and (3) short-term notes (and interest) payable. Like current assets, current liabilities are usually listed in the order of their liquidity—that is, how quickly they will be paid.

*Accounts payable* (amounts owed to suppliers) and *salaries payable* (amounts owed to employees) are common examples of obligations to pay for goods and services.

*Unearned revenues* are advance collections from customers for the future delivery of goods or the future performance of services. For instance, if a customer pays a company in advance for rent or for some service, the company owes the customer the future use of the rental space or the service, and it records the liabilities as unearned rent or unearned fees.

Short-term *notes payable* (and related interest owed) are obligations that arise because a company signs a note (legal document) that it will pay within one year. The portion of noncurrent liabilities (discussed next) that the company will pay during the next year is also included in current liabilities.

In Exhibit 7-2, Sweet Temptations' current liabilities total $5,528. Sweet Temptations has two kinds of current liabilities—accounts payable ($4,320) and a short-term note payable ($1,208, which includes the $1,200 borrowed plus $8 accrued interest, as we discussed in Chapter 5). Remember that the amount for each current liability comes from the related account balance in the company's accounting system.

### Noncurrent Liabilities

**Noncurrent liabilities** are obligations that a company does not expect to pay within the next year. Noncurrent liabilities are also called *long-term* liabilities because a company usually won't pay them for several years. This category includes such items as long-term notes payable, mortgages payable, and bonds payable (we will look at these in Chapter 22 of Volume 2 when we discuss corporations). In most cases, a company incurs a long-term liability when it purchases property or equipment because it "finances" the purchase by borrowing the money to buy the item, and then pays back the amount borrowed over a period longer than a year.

The noncurrent liabilities section shows the past financing decisions of the company's managers. The balance sheet for Sweet Temptations in Exhibit 7-2 does not include a noncurrent liabilities section because the company has not yet incurred any long-term debt.

*Is the fact that Sweet Temptations has no long-term liabilities good or bad? Why?*

## Owner's Equity

**Owner's equity** is the owner's current investment in the assets of the company. It is the company's assets less its liabilities. For a sole proprietorship, such as Sweet Temptations, the balance sheet lists the total ending owner's equity in a single *capital* account. The balance sheet shows the owner's equity by listing the owner's name, the word *capital,* and the amount of the current investment. The balance sheets of a partnership and corporation show the owner's equity slightly differently, as we will discuss later in the book. *Residual equity* is a term sometimes used for owner's equity because creditors have first legal claim to a company's assets. Once the creditors' claims have been satisfied, the owner is entitled to the remainder (residual) of the assets.

The ending balance in the account for the owner's capital is affected by the owner's additional investments or withdrawals and by net income. As we discussed in Chapter 6, the company prepares a separate schedule, the statement of changes in owner's equity, to report these items. It also makes closing entries to update the owner's capital account. We show the statement of changes in owner's equity for Sweet Temptations for January 2008 in Exhibit 7-3. Note that we show the $15,552 ending amount of A. Cox, Capital on the balance sheet in Exhibit 7-2. The $21,080 total liabilities and owner's equity ($5,528 total liabilities + $15,552 owner's equity) is equal to the $21,080 total assets.

**EXHIBIT 7-3** **STATEMENT OF CHANGES IN OWNER'S EQUITY**

**SCHEDULE A**
***Sweet Temptations***
***Statement of Changes in Owner's Equity***
***For Month Ended January 31, 2008***

| | |
|---|---|
| A. Cox, capital, January 1, 2008 | $15,000 |
| Add: Net income | 602 |
| | $15,602 |
| Less: Withdrawals | (50) |
| A. Cox, capital, January 31, 2008 | $15,552 |

# USING THE BALANCE SHEET FOR EVALUATION

Remember our bread-baking analogy? We said that without the proper equipment and ingredients, your friend Chuck will have difficulty making delicious bread, no matter how skilled he is. We also noted that the balance sheet informs users of a company's "financial ingredients." Company managers, investors, and creditors are very interested in this information. Without enough resources ("ingredients"), a company will have difficulty remaining solvent and earning a satisfactory profit, no matter how skilled its managers.

However, just having the necessary baking ingredients for the baker is not sufficient. The ingredients must be mixed in the proper proportions at the proper times to improve the chances of baking good bread. Likewise, a company can manage its mix (i.e., types and amounts) of assets, liabilities, and owner's equity to improve its chances of remaining solvent and earning a profit.

A manager is concerned with the company's balance sheet because it is used to evaluate his or her own performance. Also, since external users make investment and credit decisions based in part on balance sheet information, a manager knows that the company's balance sheet affects its ability to get a bank loan or attract new investors.

External users analyze a company's balance sheet to determine whether the company has the right amount and mix of assets, liabilities, and owner's equity to justify making an investment in the company. What they look at in a balance sheet depends on the type of investment they are considering. Short-term creditors are mostly interested in a company's short-term liquidity—whether it can pay current obligations as they are due. Long-term creditors are concerned about whether their interest income is safe and whether the company can continue to earn income and generate cash flows to meet its financial commitments. Investors are concerned about whether they will receive a return on their investment, and how much of a return they will receive. Some potential investors are interested in "solid" companies, that is, companies whose financial statements indicate stable earnings (and, therefore, a steady return). Others want to invest in newer companies that may earn higher income (and, therefore, a higher return) but have more risk.

Notice that in describing the information that external users need from financial statements, we use the words *short-term, long-term, liquidity, stability,* and *risk.* Balance sheet items are classified in a way that help address these needs.

Remember from Chapter 2 that decision making consists of four stages—recognizing the problem, identifying the alternatives, evaluating the alternatives, and making the decision itself. Financial accounting information becomes especially useful when managers and external users want to evaluate the alternatives they have identified. In the next sections, we will discuss a few of the main financial characteristics ("financial ingredients") that managers and external users study when making business decisions. In addition, we will discuss the types of analyses that they use to evaluate a company's performance. Some of these analyses include calculating and evaluating financial statement ratios, which we introduced in Chapter 6. The ratios are "benchmarks" against which decision makers compare a company's performance with its performance in prior periods and with the performance of other companies.

## Evaluating Liquidity

3 What is a company's liquidity, and how do users evaluate it?

**Liquidity** is a measure of how quickly a company can convert its assets into cash to pay its bills. It is an important financial characteristic because to remain solvent, a company must have cash, for instance, to run its operations and pay its liabilities as they become due. The need for adequate liquidity is a major reason a company prepares a cash budget.

External users assess how well a company manages its liquidity by studying its working capital. **Working capital** is a company's current assets minus its current liabilities. The term "working capital" is used because this excess of current assets is the dollar amount of liquid resources a company has to "work with" after it pays all of its short-term debts. Often, users make slightly different computations for the same purpose. The current ratio and the quick (acid-test) ratio are two common indicators of a company's liquidity.

*Given the definition of liquidity, do you think working capital is a good measure of a company's ability to pay its liabilities? Why or why not?*

© PHOTODISC/GETTY IMAGES

When we refer to water as "liquid" and a company as "liquid," do we mean the same thing? How are the meanings similar?

### Current Ratio

The **current ratio** shows the relationship between current assets and current liabilities and is probably the most commonly used indicator of a company's short-run liquidity. It is calculated as follows:

$$\text{Current Ratio} = \frac{\text{Current Assets}}{\text{Current Liabilities}}$$

The current ratio is more useful than working capital for measuring a company's liquidity because the current ratio allows comparisons of different-sized companies.

In the past, as a "rule of thumb," users thought a current ratio of 2.0, or 2 to 1 (signifying that a company has twice the amount of current assets as current liabilities) was satisfactory. If a company's current assets were twice its current debt, creditors generally believed that even if an emergency arose requiring an unexpected use of cash, the company could still pay its short-term debts.

Today, however, users pay more attention to (1) industry structure, (2) the length of a company's operating cycle, and (3) the "mix" of current assets. The mix is the proportion of different items that make up the total current assets. This mix has an effect on how quickly the current assets can be converted into cash. For instance, if a company has a high proportion of prepaid items within its current assets, it may be in a weak liquidity position because prepaid assets are used up rather than being converted into cash. Also, if a company has too *high* a current ratio compared with the ratios of similar companies in the same industry, this may indicate poor management of current assets. For example, maybe the company keeps too much cash on hand rather than investing its excess cash. Finally, the shorter a company's operating cycle, the less likely it is to need a large amount of working capital or as high a current ratio to operate efficiently.

*How do you think the length of a company's operating cycle would affect the amount of working capital it needs or the size of its current ratio?*

Sweet Temptations has working capital of $13,567, calculated by subtracting the $5,528 total current liabilities from the $19,095 total current assets, shown in Exhibit 7-2. The company's current ratio is 3.45 ($19,095 total current assets divided by $5,528 total current liabilities), which would be high for an older company. Because Sweet Temptations is a new company, a high current ratio is good because it indicates a strong ability to pay current debts. Anna Cox will want to keep track of this ratio as she makes decisions about future credit purchases.

### Quick Ratio

The **quick ratio** is a more convincing indicator of a company's short-term debt-paying ability. Short-term lenders often use this ratio when deciding whether to extend credit. The quick ratio uses only the current assets that may be easily converted into cash—referred to as quick assets. *Quick assets* consist of cash, short-term marketable securities, accounts receivable, and short-term notes receivable. The quick ratio excludes inventory because it may not be sold soon and it may be sold on credit; in both cases, inventory cannot be turned into cash as quickly. The quick ratio also excludes prepaid items because they are not convertible into cash. This is why the ratio is sometimes called the *acid-test* ratio. Thus, the quick ratio is calculated as follows:

$$\text{Quick Ratio} = \frac{\text{Quick Assets}}{\text{Current Liabilities}}$$

The quick ratio shows potential liquidity problems when a company has a poor mix of current assets. For instance, the quick ratio will show that a company with a lot of inventory has less liquidity than indicated by its current ratio. The current ratio won't show this because it includes inventory in the numerator. A quick ratio of 1.0, or 1:1 (showing that a company's quick assets and current liabilities are equal) has generally been considered satisfactory, but users also consider the industry structure as well as the length of the company's operating cycle.

*Suppose a company has a quick ratio of 0.5. What do you think of its liquidity? Does your opinion change if you learn that unearned rent revenue amounts to 60 percent of the company's current liabilities? Why or why not?*

Sweet Temptations' quick ratio is 2.01, calculated by dividing Sweet Temptations' $11,130 total quick assets ($11,030 cash + $100 accounts receivable) by its $5,528 total current liabilities. Again, it seems that Sweet Temptations is in a good short-term financial position. Note that Sweet Temptations' quick ratio is about two-thirds of its current ratio because the quick ratio calculation excludes the inventory, supplies, and prepaid rent.

*Why do you think words like "liquid" and "quick" are used in reference to a company's current assets and current liabilities?*

### Liquidity Ratios of Actual Companies

To illustrate ratio analysis, we continue our evaluation of **JCPenney Company Inc.** and **Kohl's Corporation,** which we began in Chapter 6. The companies' current ratios and quick ratios on January 28, 2006 were as follows:

| | *JCPenney* | *Kohl's* |
|---|---|---|
| Current Ratio | 2.43 | 2.44 |
| Quick Ratio | 1.19 | 1.11 |

The current ratios of JCPenney and Kohl's were about the same, but the quick ratio of JCPenney was slightly higher than that of Kohl's. However, both companies' current ratios were higher than the 2.0 "rule of thumb," and both companies' quick ratios were higher than the 1.0 "rule of thumb." This means that JCPenney is less likely to have short-term liquidity concerns than Kohl's, although both are in a sound liquidity position.

## Evaluating Financial Flexibility

4 What is a company's financial flexibility, and how do users evaluate it?

Recall from Chapter 6 that **financial flexibility** is the ability of a company to adapt to change. It is an important financial characteristic because it enables a company to increase or reduce its operating activities as needed. For example, a company with financial flexibility can revise its purchasing plan to take advantage of temporary reductions in wholesale inventory prices. The current ratio and the quick ratio can be used to assess short-term financial flexibility.

Managers, owners, and creditors are also interested in a company's ability to take advantage of major, long-term business opportunities. For a company to be able to purchase additional retail stores, build another manufacturing plant, or adopt new information technologies, it must have enough available resources or must be able to raise additional resources. To assess long-term financial flexibility, financial statement users evaluate a company's debt levels. To do this, they calculate a company's debt ratio.

### Debt Ratio

The **debt ratio** shows the percentage of total assets provided by creditors and is calculated as follows:

$$\text{Debt Ratio} = \frac{\text{Total Liabilities}}{\text{Total Assets}}$$

The higher a company's debt ratio, the lower its financial flexibility. This is because a higher debt ratio indicates that a company may not be able to borrow money (or may need to pay a higher interest rate to borrow money) to adapt to business opportunities. *Creditors* also prefer that a company have a lower debt ratio because if business declines, a lower debt ratio indicates that the company is more likely to be able to pay the interest it owes as well as its other fixed costs. Up to a point, *owners* prefer a higher debt ratio, particularly when the return earned on assets purchased by the company with the borrowed money is higher than the interest the company has to pay to its creditors. We will discuss this in more detail later.

The debt ratio is subtracted from 100% to show the percentage of total assets contributed by the owner. The desired mix between debt and owner's equity depends on the type of business and the country in which the company is located. For example, in Japan, historically investors have preferred a higher debt ratio than is typical for U.S. companies. This is true primarily because Japanese creditors and investors have worked together more closely. (However, in Japan's current economic environment, this relationship may change.)

*Debt ratios vary from industry to industry. What economic factors do you think would account for these differences?*

Sweet Temptations has a debt ratio of 0.26 ($5,528 total liabilities divided by $21,080 total assets). Its debt ratio indicates that most of its assets (74%) are financed by owner's equity. Because Sweet Temptations is new and has no long-term debts, the debt ratio and the current ratio show that it has no immediate problems with solvency or liquidity—that is, it has financial flexibility. If Sweet Temptations decides to expand, creditors will like the fact that, so far, it has relied on Anna's investments and short-term liabilities to finance its operations.

### Debt Ratios of Actual Companies

The debt ratios of JCPenney and Kohl's on January 28, 2006 were as follows:

| | *JCPenney* | *Kohl's* |
|---|---|---|
| Debt Ratio | 67.8% | 34.9% |

Because of its lower proportion of debt, we can conclude that Kohl's relied less on creditors to finance its assets. Therefore, Kohl's had higher financial flexibility because borrowing more money would be easier for the company. Kohl's may also be able to borrow money at a lower interest rate because the lenders may think it has a lower level of risk.

# Relationship Between the Income Statement and the Balance Sheet

Although decision makers find the ratios we just presented—the current ratio, the quick ratio, and the debt ratio—to be very helpful, these ratios do have one limitation: they use only balance sheet information. *It is very important for you to know that many significant business questions can be answered only by analyzing a company's income statement and balance sheet together.* This is the only way to determine whether a company has made a "satisfactory" profit and to calculate other measures of its "operating capability" (which we will discuss later).

*Do you think creditors always need to evaluate a company's balance sheet and income statement before granting a loan? Why or why not?*

Say, for instance, that on its income statement, a company reports that net income for the accounting period is \$5 million. Five million dollars may sound like a lot, but did the company earn a satisfactory profit? You can't tell without comparing the \$5 million with the dollar amount of resources the company used to earn the income (and with the income it earned in each of the last few years). The \$5 million may or may not be satisfactory depending on the size of the company (and how well it has done in prior periods).

Let's say the company reports \$50 million of total assets on its balance sheet at the end of the accounting period. We can divide the company's net income for the period by its total assets (a net income to total assets ratio) and calculate the company's rate of return on assets. Using the dollar amounts given, this company earned a 10% return on assets (\$5 million ÷ \$50 million). Just how satisfied a company's managers, investors, and creditors are with a 10% return on assets depends on how well similar types of companies performed, and on whether this return met or exceeded their expectations. Financial statements work as a *set* of information because, as we noted in the example above, external users need both the income statement and the balance sheet to evaluate a company's performance and financial position.

Exhibit 7-4 illustrates the relationships among the financial statements.[3] Here we show a balance sheet for January 1, 2008, on the far left of the exhibit. This balance sheet reports the resources and claims on resources of a company on the first day of January. It shows the mix of "financial ingredients" that the company had available to work with when starting the accounting period. During the accounting period (2008), the company had many transactions and events affecting assets, liabilities, and owner's equity (owner's investments and withdrawals, revenues and expenses), and all of these transactions and events were recorded in its accounting system. At the end of the accounting period, the company prepares its financial statements. Take some time to study Exhibit 7-4 carefully before you move on; it contains some very important concepts.

The 2008 income statement summarizes how the company used its financial "ingredients" to earn net income and remain solvent. It shows the results of the operating decisions the company's managers made to improve the company's financial position (e.g., how much advertising it used, how much salary expense it incurred, how many sales it made). The year's operating activities, owner's investments, and owner's withdrawals all affect the company's mix of financial resources and the claims to its resources. The 2008 ending balance sheet shows the effects of the net changes.

With the financial information contained in the beginning and ending balance sheets, along with the income statement, you can see what resources the company started with, how it used those resources, and what resources it owns at the end of the accounting period. With this information, you can calculate liquidity, solvency, and performance ratios, as we will discuss in the following section.

[3]The cash flow statement is also a useful financial statement, along with the balance sheet and the income statement. We will discuss this statement in Chapter 8, so we have not included it in our present discussion.

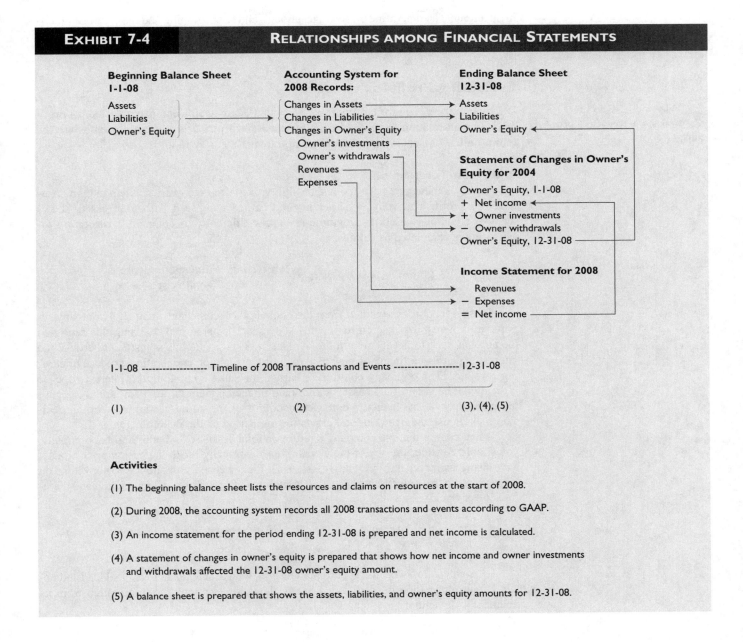

**EXHIBIT 7-4 RELATIONSHIPS AMONG FINANCIAL STATEMENTS**

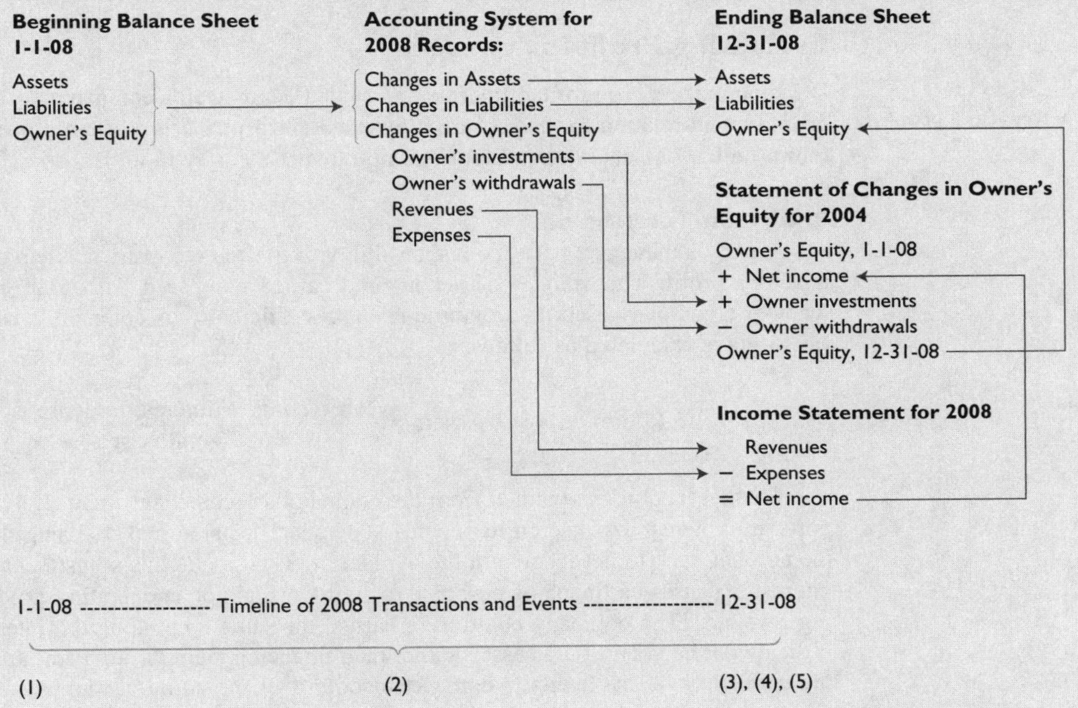


**Activities**

(1) The beginning balance sheet lists the resources and claims on resources at the start of 2008.

(2) During 2008, the accounting system records all 2008 transactions and events according to GAAP.

(3) An income statement for the period ending 12-31-08 is prepared and net income is calculated.

(4) A statement of changes in owner's equity is prepared that shows how net income and owner investments and withdrawals affected the 12-31-08 owner's equity amount.

(5) A balance sheet is prepared that shows the assets, liabilities, and owner's equity amounts for 12-31-08.

## EVALUATIONS USING THE BALANCE SHEET AND THE INCOME STATEMENT

A company's managers, investors, and creditors use information from its income statement and balance sheet to calculate ratios for measuring the company's financial success. The numerator of each ratio is an income statement amount showing the "flow" into or out of the company (e.g., net income, net credit sales, cost of goods sold) *during* the accounting period. The denominator of each ratio is a balance sheet amount showing the "resources" used to obtain the "flow." Some of these ratios use an *average* figure for the denominator. This is because balance sheet amounts are measured at a *point in time* (the beginning and the end of the accounting period). By using an average amount for the accounting period (average total assets, average owner's equity, average inventory) in the denominator, the balance sheet amount "covers" the same time period as the income statement amount. To determine the average amount, add the beginning and the ending amounts together and then divide by 2. We will discuss some common ratios and their calculations in the following sections.

## Evaluating Profitability

5 Why and how do users evaluate a company's profitability?

Decision makers use profitability ratios to evaluate how well a company has met its profit objectives in relation to the resources invested. Two of these profitability ratios are the return on total assets ratio and the return on owner's equity ratio.

### Return on Total Assets

A company's managers have the responsibility to use the company's assets to earn a satisfactory profit. The amount of net income earned compared with total assets shows whether a company used its economic resources efficiently. A company's **return on total assets** is calculated as follows:

$$\text{Return on Total Assets} = \frac{\text{Net Income} + \text{Interest Expense}}{\text{Average Total Assets}}$$

The net income is obtained from the company's income statement. If a company reports any interest expense on its income statement, decision makers using this ratio add the amount back to net income in the numerator. They make this adjustment because the interest expense is a financing cost paid to creditors and not an operating expense of earning revenue. (The company could have earned the same income before interest expense if the owner had contributed assets rather than financing them through creditors.) Because the company uses its assets to earn net income over the entire accounting period, decision makers use the *average* total assets for the period as the denominator.

When comparing one company's return on total assets with that of another company, you should consider the age of the assets of each company. With increasing prices today, a company using recently purchased assets (at higher costs) will show a lower return on these assets. Also, older assets have higher amounts of accumulated depreciation and therefore lower book values.

*Do you think companies' liabilities affect how their return on total assets ratios are interpreted? Why or why not?*

Let's calculate Sweet Temptations' return on total assets for January 2008. Listed below is the information needed to make the calculation (we took the information from its financial statements):

| | |
|---|---|
| Net income for January 2008: | $ 602 |
| Interest expense for January 2008 | 8 |
| Total assets, January 1, 2008 | 17,820 |
| Total assets, January 31, 2008 | 21,080 |

The return on total assets ratio of Sweet Temptations for January 2008 is calculated as follows:

$$3.14\% = \frac{\$602 + \$8}{[(\$17{,}820 + \$21{,}080)/2]}$$

Although this 3.14% return on assets for Sweet Temptations seems low, remember that it is for one month and not for an entire year, as is typical. (Multiplying the ratio by 12 [months] gives an estimate of Sweet Temptations' ratio for the year.) If Sweet Temptations can keep up January's level of income for the rest of the year, it is likely to earn a satisfactory rate of return on its assets for 2008.

### Return on Owner's Equity

A company's managers also have the responsibility to earn a satisfactory return on the owner's investment in the company. Dividing net income by the *average* owner's equity shows the company's return (in percentage terms) to the owner—resulting from all of the company's activities during the accounting period. A company's **return on owner's equity** is calculated as follows:

$$\text{Return on Owner's Equity} = \frac{\text{Net Income}}{\text{Average Owner's Equity}}$$

Note that in contrast to the return on total assets ratio, the return on owner's equity ratio does not add interest expense back to net income. This is because net income is a measure of a company's profits available to owners *after* incurring the financial cost related to creditors.

We can calculate Sweet Temptations' return on owner's equity for January 2008 by taking the information listed below from its financial statements:

| | |
|---|---|
| Net income for January 2008 | $ 602 |
| A. Cox, capital, January 1, 2008 | 15,000 |
| A. Cox, capital, January 31, 2008 | 15,552 |

The return on owner's equity ratio of Sweet Temptations for January 2008 is calculated as follows:

$$3.94\% = \frac{\$602}{[(\$15{,}000 + \$15{,}552)/2]}$$

Sweet Temptations' 3.94% return on owner's equity for January 2008 is low, but again it is for only one month. (Multiplying the ratio by 12 gives an estimate of Sweet Temptations' ratio for the year.) Also, Sweet Temptations' return on owner's equity is higher than its return on total assets. This shows users that the company has benefited from using debt to help finance its assets.

### Profitability Ratios of Actual Companies

The ratios used to evaluate the profitability of JCPenney and Kohl's for the year ended January 28, 2006 were as follows:

| | *JCPenney* | *Kohl's* |
|---|---|---|
| Return on Total Assets | 9.5% | 10.7% |
| Return on Owners' Equity | 24.5% | 15.3% |

How do you think Ernie's plan would boost his company's return-on-assets ratio? Do you think it is a good idea? Why or why not?

Based on Kohl's higher return on total assets, we can say that Kohl's used its economic resources more efficiently than JCPenney. However, based on JCPenney's higher return on owner's equity, we can say that it earned a more satisfactory profit for its owners than did Kohl's.

6 What is a company's operating capability, and how do users evaluate it?

## Evaluating Operating Capability

Recall from Chapter 6 that **operating capability** refers to a company's ability to sustain a given level of operations. Information about a company's operating capability is important in evaluating how well it is maintaining its operating level, and in predicting future changes in its operating activity. The current ratio helps predict a company's ability to continue to purchase inventory. If a company's current ratio is less than 2.0, investors may worry that the company's operations won't generate enough cash to replenish inventory. The debt ratio helps evaluate whether a company has the resources to replace property and equipment.

In this section we discuss how evaluating the level of a company's activities can provide insights into its operating capability. This is done through activity ratios, used to show the length of the parts of the company's operating cycle. This knowledge lets users evaluate the liquidity of selected current assets. Recall that a retail company's operating cycle is the length of time it takes to invest cash in inventory, make credit sales, and convert the receivables into cash. Two common activity ratios are the (1) inventory turnover and (2) accounts receivable turnover.

### Inventory Turnover

A company purchases, sells, and replaces inventory throughout its accounting period. Dividing the company's cost of goods sold (from its income statement) for the period by the average inventory (from its beginning and ending balance sheets) shows the number of times the company *turns over* (or sells) the inventory during that period. A company's **inventory turnover** is calculated as follows:

$$\text{Inventory Turnover} = \frac{\text{Cost of Goods Sold}}{\text{Average Inventory}}$$

As a general rule, the higher the inventory turnover, the more efficient the company is in its purchasing and sales activities and the less cash it needs to invest in inventory. A company with a higher turnover generally purchases its inventory more often and in smaller amounts than it would if it had a lower inventory turnover. It is also less likely to have obsolete inventory (because it holds on to its inventory for only a short time before selling it). These efficiencies "free up" a company's cash—it needs less cash and can invest excess cash in other earnings activities. However, a company's inventory turnover can be too high. If a company's inventory turnover is too high, the company may not be keeping enough inventory on hand to meet customer demand, and it may be missing out on additional sales.

Let's calculate Sweet Temptations' inventory turnover for January 2008. Listed below is the information needed to make the calculation (we took the information from its financial statements):

| | |
|---|---|
| Cost of goods sold for January 2008 | $3,645 |
| Inventory, January 1, 2008 | 1,620 |
| Inventory, January 31, 2008 | 2,295 |

We can calculate Sweet Temptations' inventory turnover ratio for January 2008 as follows:

$$1.86 \text{ times} = \frac{\$3,645}{[(\$1,620 + \$2,295)/2]}$$

This ratio shows that Sweet Temptations turned over its inventory almost two times in January. (To estimate Sweet Temptations' inventory turnover for the year, assuming every month has the same rate of turnover, multiply the January turnover by 12.) Since Sweet Temptations is a candy store, this turnover is a good sign that Sweet Temptations is operating efficiently (who wants to buy old candy?). Over the next few months, Anna should continue to monitor Sweet Temptations' inventory turnover to see if she needs to make any changes in its purchasing budget.

Users sometimes want a different measure of how efficient a company is in its inventory activities—how long it takes a company to sell its inventory. This measure is called the **number of days in the selling period.** Dividing the number of operating days in a company's business year (a company that does business seven days a week has 365 days in its business year) by its inventory turnover shows the number of days in its selling period, as follows:

$$\text{Number of Days in Selling Period} = \frac{\text{Number of Days in Business Year}}{\text{Inventory Turnover}}$$

This ratio estimates the average time (in days) it takes the company to sell its inventory. Because we are calculating these ratios for Sweet Temptations for only one month, we use 30 days (the number of days Sweet Temptations was open in January, excluding New Year's Day) as the numerator. With that in mind, the number of days in its selling period is calculated as follows:

$$16.13 \text{ days} = \frac{30}{1.86}$$

This ratio tells us that in January, Sweet Temptations sold its inventory about every 16 days. To evaluate how well it is managing its inventory, we should compare these results with how long a box of candy stays "fresh," with Sweet Temptations' ratio in previous years (if it were not a new company), and with other companies' performances.

*What do you think Anna should do if a box of candy stays "fresh" about two weeks?*

### Accounts Receivable Turnover

If a company sells inventory on credit, it must collect the accounts receivable from the sales to complete its operating cycle. Dividing a company's net credit sales for the period (from its income statement) by its average accounts receivable (from its beginning and ending balance sheets) shows how many times the average receivable turns over (is collected) each period. A company's **accounts receivable turnover** is calculated as follows:

$$\text{Accounts Receivable Turnover} = \frac{\text{Net Credit Sales}}{\text{Average Accounts Receivable}}$$

The accounts receivable turnover measures how efficiently a company collects cash from its credit customers. Users prefer to see a higher turnover, which shows that the company has less cash tied up in accounts receivable, collects this cash faster, and usually has fewer customers who don't pay.

The amount of net *credit* sales is the best amount to use as the numerator. This is the number that managers use when making this calculation. However, since companies don't give a breakdown between credit and cash sales on their income statements, external users must calculate the ratio using total net sales. Because using total net sales increases the numerator (unless all sales are credit sales), this calculation will overestimate the number of times a company's accounts receivable turns over.

Users often divide a company's accounts receivable turnover into the number of days in the business year to show the **number of days in the collection period,** as follows:

$$\text{Number of Days in Collection Period} = \frac{\text{Number of Days in Business Year}}{\text{Accounts Receivable Turnover}}$$

The number of days in a company's collection period is the average time it takes the company to collect its accounts receivable. By comparing a company's average collection period with the days in its credit terms (i.e., 2/10, n/30), a user can see how aggressive the company is in collecting overdue accounts. The user can also compare this number with the ratios for past years and with those of other companies. Because Sweet Temptations made only one credit sale in January, we do not calculate these accounts receivable ratios here. To estimate the number of days in a company's operating cycle, a user can add together the number of days in the company's selling period and the number of days in its collection period.

*Is a company's operating cycle always the same, or can a company control the length of its operating cycle? What, if anything, can be done to control the length of the operating cycle?*

### Operating Capability Ratios of Actual Companies

The ratios used to evaluate the operating capability of JCPenney and Kohl's for the year ended January 28, 2006 were as follows:

| | *JCPenney* | *Kohl's* |
|---|---|---|
| Inventory Turnover | 3.6 | 4.1 |
| Accounts Receivable Turnover | 69.0 | 8.8 |

Kohl's higher inventory turnover shows that it took less time to sell its inventory than did JCPenney, indicating that Kohl's was more efficient in managing its inventory. However, JCPenney was more efficient in collecting its cash from credit customers than was Kohl's, as shown by its higher accounts receivable turnover.[4]

## Limitations of the Income Statement and the Balance Sheet

In Chapters 5 and 6 you saw that a company's accounting system is based on several important accounting concepts and principles. The concepts and principles were created to ensure that companies' accounting systems provide useful, reliable, and relevant information to their managers and other interested parties.

*The key concepts and principles are the entity concept, the monetary unit concept, the historical cost concept, the accounting period concept, the matching principle, and accrual accounting. In your own words, describe why each of these is important.*

These concepts and principles guide accountants as they analyze company activities, record transactions, make adjustments, and prepare a company's income statement and balance sheet. Yet even though we have seen how concepts and principles help to build a useful accounting system, they also set limits on the types of information the financial statements provide. These limits restrict the usefulness of the information. For example, the historical cost concept requires that the asset Land be reported on a company's balance sheet at its original cost. So if a company purchased land in 1983 for $10,000, its

[4]However, care must be taken when comparing the two companies' ratios. JCPenney "sells" a significant amount of its accounts receivable to a finance company, which results in lower average accounts receivable and therefore a higher accounts receivable turnover.

2008 ending balance sheet will list "Land $10,000," no matter how much the land is currently worth. In 2008, the land may be worth much more than $10,000. Thus, the balance sheet doesn't always show each asset's current value. But if the company has no intention of selling an asset, the current value may not be relevant.

Another limitation of the income statement and the balance sheet is that they do not provide much information about a company's cash management because they are based on accrual accounting. Hence, investors and creditors also need a financial statement that provides a summary of a company's cash flows during an accounting period. Thus, a company prepares and reports a third financial statement—the cash flow statement, which we will discuss in Chapter 8.

*What do a company's balance sheet and income statement reveal about its management of cash? What else would an investor or creditor want to know?*

## Business Issues and Values

Recall that assets are a company's economic resources that it expects will provide future benefits to the company. As we mentioned above, in accordance with GAAP, companies record assets at their historical cost and do not change these amounts for changes in their values. One of the major economic resources of many companies is their employees. A company that has a loyal, well-trained employee group has a valuable "asset" that may increase in value over time because of additional training and job satisfaction. This employee group makes very important contributions to the company's ability to earn profits. (Do you continue to shop at a store where the employees are rude?) But because of the historical cost concept, the company cannot report this economic resource as an asset on the balance sheet it issues to external users. However, some companies that take pride in the quality of their employees do prepare internal reports that include measures of their employees' values; their managers use these reports for internal decision making.

*Does "investing" in its employees worsen a company's reported performance in the current year?*

## SUMMARY

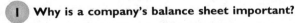

At the beginning of the chapter we asked you several questions. During the chapter, we asked you to STOP and answer some additional questions to build your knowledge about specific issues. Be sure you answered these additional questions. Below are the questions from the beginning of the chapter, with a brief summary of the key points relating to the answers. Use your creative and critical thinking skills to expand on these key points to develop more complete answers to the questions and to determine what other questions you have that might lead you to learn more about the issues.

### 1 Why is a company's balance sheet important?

A company's balance sheet is important because this statement provides internal and external users with information to help evaluate the company's ability to achieve its primary goals of earning a satisfactory profit and remaining solvent. A balance sheet provides information about a company's economic resources and the claims on those resources (its financial position) on a specific date.

### 2 What do users need to know about a company's classified balance sheet?

Users need to know that a company's classified balance sheet shows important subtotals, in related groupings, for the assets, liabilities, and owner's equity of the company. The groupings include current assets and noncurrent assets, as well as current liabilities and noncurrent liabilities.

Current assets are cash and other assets that a company expects to convert into cash, sell, or use up within one year. Current assets include cash, marketable securities, receivables, inventory, and prepaid items. Noncurrent assets are assets other than current assets; these include items such as long-term investments, as well as property and equipment. Current liabilities are obligations that a company expects to pay within one year by using current assets. Current liabilities include accounts payable and salaries payable, unearned revenues, and short-term notes (and interest) payable. Noncurrent liabilities are obligations that a company does not expect to pay within the next year; these include items such as long-term notes payable, mortgages payable, and bonds payable.

### 3 What is a company's liquidity, and how do users evaluate it?

A company's liquidity is a measure of how quickly it can convert its current assets into cash to pay its current liabilities as they become due. Users evaluate a company's liquidity by studying its working capital (current assets minus current liabilities), current ratio (current assets divided by current liabilities), and quick (acid-test) ratio (quick assets divided by current liabilities).

### 4 What is a company's financial flexibility, and how do users evaluate it?

A company's financial flexibility is its ability to adapt to change. Measures of a company's financial flexibility are used to assess whether the company can increase or reduce its operating activities as needed. Users study a company's current ratio and quick ratio to evaluate its short-term financial flexibility. They study a company's debt ratio (total liabilities divided by total assets) to evaluate its long-term financial flexibility.

### 5 Why and how do users evaluate a company's profitability?

Users evaluate a company's profitability to determine how well it has met its profit objectives in relation to the resources invested. They study a company's return on total assets [(net income plus interest expense) divided by average total assets] and return on owner's equity (net income divided by average owner's equity) ratios to evaluate a company's profitability.

### 6 What is a company's operating capability, and how do users evaluate it?

A company's operating capability is its ability to sustain a given level of operations. Measures of a company's operating capability are used to assess how well the company is maintaining its operating level and to predict future changes in its operating activity. Users study a company's activity ratios to determine the length of the parts of the company's operating cycle. These ratios include the inventory turnover (cost of goods sold divided by average inventory) and the accounts receivable turnover (net credit sales divided by average accounts receivable).

## KEY TERMS

**accounting equation** *(p. 200)*
**accounts receivable turnover** *(p. 215)*
**accumulated depreciation** *(p. 203)*
**assets** *(p. 202)*
**balance sheet** *(p. 200)*
**book value** *(p. 203)*
**classified balance sheet** *(p. 202)*
**current assets** *(p. 202)*
**current liabilities** *(p. 204)*
**current ratio** *(p. 207)*
**debt ratio** *(p. 209)*
**financial flexibility** *(p. 208)*
**inventory turnover** *(p. 214)*
**liabilities** *(p. 204)*
**liquidity** *(p. 206)*
**long-term investments** *(p. 203)*
**noncurrent liabilities** *(p. 204)*
**number of days in the collection period** *(p. 216)*
**number of days in the selling period** *(p. 215)*
**operating capability** *(p. 214)*
**owner's equity** *(p. 205)*
**property and equipment** *(p. 203)*
**quick ratio** *(p. 208)*
**return on owner's equity** *(p. 213)*
**return on total assets** *(p. 212)*
**working capital** *(p. 206)*

## SUMMARY SURFING

Here is an opportunity to gather information on the Internet about real-world issues related to the topics in this chapter (for suggestions on how to navigate various companies' Web sites to find their financial statements and other information, see the related discussion in the Preface at the beginning of the book). Answer the following questions.

- Go to the **JCPenney Company** Web site. Find the appropriate financial statement(s). Compute the current ratio, quick ratio, debt ratio, return on owners' equity, and inventory turnover for the most current year. How do these results compare with the January 28, 2006 ratios we discussed in this chapter?
- Go to the **Kohl's Corporation** Web site. Find the appropriate financial statements. Compute the current ratio, quick ratio, debt ratio, return on owners' equity, and inventory turnover for the most current year. How do these results compare with the January 28, 2006 ratios we discussed in this chapter?

## INTEGRATED BUSINESS AND ACCOUNTING SITUATIONS

**Answer the Following Questions in Your Own Words.**

### Testing Your Knowledge

**7-1** What is a balance sheet, and what types of questions can a user answer by studying the balance sheet?

**7-2** What is the accounting equation, and how does it relate to the balance sheet of a company?

**7-3** What is the difference between an account form and a report form of balance sheet?

**7-4** Explain what is meant by a *classified* balance sheet, and identify the major groupings of assets and liabilities.

**7-5** Explain the meaning of the term *current assets*.

**7-6** Identify and briefly explain the major current assets.

**7-7** What are long-term investments? Give several examples.

**7-8** What is property and equipment? At what amount is each item of property and equipment listed on the balance sheet?

**7-9** Explain the meaning of the term *current liabilities*.

**7-10** Identify and briefly explain the major current liabilities.

**7-11** What are noncurrent liabilities? Give several examples.

**7-12** What is owner's equity, and why is it sometimes called *residual equity*?

**7-13** What is meant by the term *liquidity*, and why is it important?

**7-14** Explain how to compute the current ratio and what it is used for.

**7-15** Explain how to compute the quick ratio and what it is used for.

**7-16** What is meant by the term *financial flexibility*, and why is it important?

**7-17** Explain how to compute the debt ratio and what it is used for.

**7-18** Explain how to compute a company's return on total assets and what it is used for.

**7-19** Explain how to compute a company's return on owner's equity and how it relates to the return on total assets.

**7-20** What is meant by the term *operating capability,* and why is information about it important?

**7-21** Explain how to compute a company's inventory turnover. Is a high inventory turnover good or bad? Why?

**7-22** Explain how to compute a company's accounts receivable turnover. What is a "good" accounts receivable turnover? Why?

## Applying Your Knowledge

**7-23** In each of the following situations, the total increase or decrease for one component of the accounting equation is missing:
(a) Assets increased by $10,400; liabilities increased by $3,200.
(b) Liabilities decreased by $2,000; owner's equity increased by $10,000.
(c) Assets decreased by $6,200; owner's equity decreased by $13,500.
(d) Owner's equity increased by $27,500; liabilities decreased by $5,715.
(e) Assets increased by $12,600; owner's equity decreased by $25,750.

*Required:* Using Assets: $60,000 = Liabilities: $20,000 + Owner's Equity: $40,000 as the beginning accounting equation for each of the preceding situations, determine (1) the total increase or decrease for the missing component of the equation and (2) the amount of each component in the *ending* accounting equation. Treat each situation independently.

**7-24** The total increase or decrease for one component of the accounting equation is missing in each situation that follows:
(a) Assets decreased by $10,000; liabilities decreased by $6,500.
(b) Owner's equity decreased by $15,750; assets decreased by $7,500.
(c) Liabilities increased by $1,000; owner's equity decreased by $5,000.
(d) Owner's equity increased by $18,000; assets increased by $9,650.

*Required:* Using Assets: $45,000 = Liabilities: $15,000 + Owner's Equity: $30,000 as the beginning accounting equation for each of the preceding situations, determine (1) the total increase or decrease for the missing component of the equation and (2) the amount of each component in the *ending* accounting equation. Treat each situation separately.

**7-25** Listed below are the balances of selected accounts of the Watson Company at the end of the current year:

| | |
|---|---|
| Equipment | $18,500 |
| Prepaid insurance | 2,600 |
| Notes payable (due in 30 days) | 7,100 |
| Cash | 3,900 |
| Land | 11,700 |
| Accounts receivable (net) | 10,200 |
| Inventory | 24,400 |
| Mortgage payable (due next year) | 33,000 |
| Notes receivable (due in 60 days) | 4,000 |
| Marketable securities (short-term) | 6,300 |
| Buildings (net) | 74,000 |
| Notes receivable (due in 2 years) | 5,600 |

*Required:* Prepare the current assets section of the Watson Company's balance sheet.

**7-26** Listed below are the balances of selected accounts of the Chriswat Company at the end of the current year:

| | |
|---|---|
| Notes receivable (due in 3 years) | $14,200 |
| Accounts payable | 18,300 |
| Bonds payable (due in 5 years) | 46,000 |
| Land | 13,500 |
| Marketable securities (short-term) | 6,400 |
| Salaries payable | 5,700 |

| | |
|---|---|
| Notes payable (due in 6 months) | 8,000 |
| Mortgage payable (due next year) | 4,600 |
| Unearned rent revenue (6 months) | 2,400 |
| Notes payable (due in 2 years) | 10,000 |
| Mortgage payable (due in 5 years) | 18,000 |

*Required:* Prepare the current liabilities section of the Chriswat Company at the end of the current year.

**7-27** A classified balance sheet contains the following sections:

A. Current assets
B. Long-term investments
C. Property and equipment
D. Current liabilities
E. Noncurrent liabilities
F. Owner's equity

*Required:* The following is a list of accounts. Using the letters A through F, indicate in which section each account is shown.

_____ 1. Land
_____ 2. Accounts payable
_____ 3. A. Smith, capital
_____ 4. Cash
_____ 5. Bonds payable
_____ 6. Equipment
_____ 7. Accounts receivable
_____ 8. Unearned revenue
_____ 9. Mortgage payable (due in 4 years)
_____ 10. Salaries payable
_____ 11. Marketable securities (short-term)
_____ 12. Notes receivable (due in 2 years)
_____ 13. Buildings
_____ 14. Notes payable (due in 9 months)
_____ 15. Prepaid insurance
_____ 16. Inventory

**7-28** The following is an alphabetical list of the accounts of Swenson Stores on December 31, 2008:

Accounts payable
Accounts receivable
Administrative expenses
Bonds payable (due 2018)
Buildings (net)
Cash
Cost of goods sold
Equipment (net)
Mortgage payable (10 equal annual payments)
Notes payable (due in 6 months)
Notes payable (due in 4 years)
Notes receivable (due in 8 months)
Notes receivable (due in 3 years)
Office supplies
General expenses
Interest expense
Interest payable (current)
Interest receivable (current)
Interest revenue
Inventory
Investment in government bonds (due 2019)
Land
Prepaid insurance
Salaries payable
Sales
Selling expenses
T. Swenson, capital
Temporary investments in securities

*Required:* Prepare a December 31, 2008 classified balance sheet (without amounts) for Swenson Stores.

**7-29** The financial statement information of the Leon Appraisal Company for 2008 and 2009 is as follows:

| | *2008* | *2009* |
|---|---|---|
| Assets, 12/31 | $ (a) | $308,900 |
| Expenses | 47,400 | 51,600 |
| Net income | (b) | 39,700 |
| Liabilities, 12/31 | 153,500 | (e) |
| Leon, capital, 1/1 | (c) | 115,200 |
| Revenues | 83,600 | (f) |
| Leon, withdrawals | 24,000 | (g) |
| Leon, capital, 12/31 | (d) | 124,900 |

*Required:* Fill in the blanks lettered (a) through (g). All the information is listed. (*Hint:* It is not necessary to calculate your answers in alphabetical order.)

**7-30** The financial statement information of the Charles Adjusting Company for 2008 and 2009 is shown on the following page.

| | *2008* | *2009* |
|---|---|---|
| Charles, capital, 12/31 | $ 83,500 | $ (d) |
| Charles, withdrawals | (a) | 24,000 |
| Revenues | (b) | 65,000 |
| Charles, capital, 1/1 | 69,400 | (e) |
| Liabilities, 12/31 | (c) | 116,800 |
| Net income | 24,100 | (f) |
| Charles, additional investments | 8,000 | (g) |
| Expenses | 35,200 | 39,800 |
| Assets, 12/31 | 184,500 | 211,500 |

*Required:* Fill in the blanks lettered (a) through (g). All the information is listed. (*Hint:* It is not necessary to calculate your answers in alphabetical order.)

**7-31** The balance sheet information at the end of 2008 and 2009 for the Decatur Medical Equipment Company is as follows:

| | *2008* | *2009* |
|---|---|---|
| Current assets | $ (a) | $ 27,000 |
| Noncurrent liabilities | (b) | 34,900 |
| Long-term investments | 19,200 | 22,500 |
| Davis, capital | 81,900 | (d) |
| Total liabilities | (c) | (e) |
| Current liabilities | 14,500 | 12,300 |
| Total assets | 130,200 | (f) |
| Property and equipment (net) | 85,700 | 93,100 |

*Required:* Fill in the blanks labeled (a) through (f). All the necessary information is provided. (*Hint:* It is not necessary to calculate your answers in alphabetical order.)

**7-32** The balance sheet information at the end of 2008 and 2009 for Columbia Electronics is as follows:

| | *2008* | *2009* |
|---|---|---|
| Bevis, capital | $ 83,500 | $ 88,700 |
| Current liabilities | (a) | 9,800 |
| Property and equipment (net) | (b) | 87,500 |
| Current assets | 18,500 | (e) |
| Long-term liabilities | (c) | 30,200 |
| Total assets | (d) | (f) |
| Working capital | 9,300 | 10,200 |
| Long-term investments | 23,700 | (g) |
| Total liabilities | 38,100 | (h) |

*Required:* Fill in the blanks labeled (a) through (h). All the necessary information is provided. (*Hint:* It is not necessary to calculate your answers in alphabetical order.)

**7-33** The following items and their corresponding amounts appeared in the accounting records of the Office Equipment Specialists Company on December 31, 2008:

| | |
|---|---|
| Accounts receivable | $ 4,900 |
| Accounts payable | 2,900 |
| Building (net) | 24,000 |
| Cash | 1,400 |
| Delivery equipment (net) | 10,000 |
| Inventory | 7,500 |
| J. Jenlon, capital | 35,400 |
| Mortgage payable (due 9/1/2010) | 29,000 |
| Marketable securities | 2,000 |
| Notes payable (due 10/1/2009) | 10,000 |
| Office supplies | 2,600 |
| Land | 6,000 |
| Notes receivable (due 12/31/2010 ) | 7,000 |
| Office equipment (net) | 6,400 |
| Prepaid insurance | 1,700 |

| | |
|---|---|
| Notes payable (due 12/31/2012) | 11,000 |
| Interest payable (due 10/1/2009) | 1,000 |
| Unearned revenue | 3,000 |
| Investment in government bonds (due 12/31/2017) | 20,000 |
| Salaries payable | 1,200 |

*Required:* (1) Prepare a classified balance sheet for the Office Equipment Specialists Company on December 31, 2008.

(2) The Office Equipment Specialists Company is applying for a short-term loan at a local bank. If you were the banker, would you grant the company a loan? Explain your decision using what you learned in this chapter about evaluating a company's liquidity.

**7-34** The following accounts and account balances were listed in the accounting records of the Rigons Lighting Company on December 31, 2008:

| | |
|---|---|
| Salaries payable | $ 1,100 |
| Accounts receivable | 11,300 |
| Investment in government bonds (due 12/31/2012) | 30,000 |
| Accounts payable | 7,700 |
| Unearned revenue | 1,000 |
| Building (net) | 37,000 |
| Interest payable (due 9/1/2009) | 200 |
| Cash | 6,100 |
| Notes payable (due 12/31/2010) | 15,000 |
| Store equipment (net) | 14,000 |
| Prepaid insurance | 900 |
| Office equipment (net) | 9,600 |
| Inventory | 13,200 |
| Notes receivable (due 12/31/2011) | 8,000 |
| P. Rigons, capital | 85,300 |
| Land | 4,000 |
| Mortgage payable (due 7/1/2010) | 22,500 |
| Office and store supplies | 2,700 |
| Marketable securities | 3,000 |
| Notes payable (due 9/1/2009) | 7,000 |

*Required:* (1) Prepare a classified balance sheet for the Rigons Lighting Company on December 31, 2008.

(2) The Rigons Lighting Company is applying for a $2,000 short-term loan at a local bank. If you were the banker, would you grant a loan to the company? Explain your decision using what you learned in this chapter about evaluating a company's liquidity.

**7-35** Taylor Machines Company has the following condensed balance sheet on December 31, 2008:

| | | | |
|---|---|---|---|
| Current assets | $ 13,400 | Current liabilities | $ 6,800 |
| Noncurrent assets | 91,200 | Noncurrent liabilities | 36,700 |
| | | Total Liabilities | $ 43,500 |
| | | T. Taylor, capital | 61,100 |
| Total Assets | $104,600 | Total Liabilities and Owner's Equity | $104,600 |

The company's quick assets are 60% of its current assets.

*Required:* Compute the company's working capital and its current, quick, and debt ratios at the end of 2008.

**7-36** Simpson Company reported net income of $78,200 for 2009. Interest expense of $4,800 was deducted in the calculation of this net income. The following schedule shows other information about the company's capital structure:

| | *12/31/2008* | *12/31/2009* |
|---|---|---|
| Total Assets | $670,000 | $730,000 |
| Total Owner's Equity | 415,000 | 465,000 |

*Required:* (1) Compute the return on total assets for 2009.
(2) Compute the return on owner's equity for 2009.
(3) Compute the debt ratio at the end of 2009. How does this compare with the debt ratio at the end of 2008?

**7-37** Parket Company began 2008 with accounts receivable of $32,000 and inventory of $40,000. During 2008, the company made total net sales of $600,000, of which 70% were credit sales. The company's cost of goods sold averaged 60% of total net sales during 2008. Parket was open for business each day of the year, and at the end of the year it had accounts receivable of $36,000 and inventory of $60,000.

*Required:* (1) Compute the inventory turnover and the number of days in the selling period for 2008.
(2) Compute the accounts receivable turnover and the number of days in the collection period for 2008.
(3) What is your estimate of the number of days in the company's operating cycle during 2008?

## Making Evaluations

**7-38** A friend of yours makes this statement: "Accumulated depreciation and depreciation expense are the same thing, since they both measure the portion of the cost of an asset that has been 'used up' to earn revenues."

*Required:* Do you agree or disagree with your friend's statement? Support your answer.

**7-39** Many long-term loans are payable over a period of time. For example, when a company takes out a mortgage to finance a building, it pays off a fraction of that mortgage every month.

*Required:* What criteria would you use to decide whether to classify the mortgage as a current liability or a long-term liability, and how would you classify the mortgage?

**7-40** In this chapter, we said that the quick ratio is a better measure of liquidity than is the current ratio because the quick ratio includes only those current assets that may be easily converted to cash.

*Required:* What is the quick ratio? Do you think this is the best possible measure of liquidity? If so, defend your answer. If not, design a better measure and defend it.

**7-41** On March 8, 2008, Peter Bailey started his own company by depositing $10,000 in the Bailey Company checking account at the local bank. On March 14, 2008, the Bailey Company checkbook was stolen. During that period of time, the Bailey Company had entered into several transactions, but unfortunately, it had not set up an accounting system for recording the transactions. Bailey did save numerous source documents, however, which had been put into an old shoebox.

In the shoebox is a fire insurance policy dated March 13, 2008, on a building owned by the Bailey Company. Listed on the policy was an amount of $300 for one year of insurance. "Paid in Full" had been stamped on the policy by the insurance agent. Also included in the box was a deed for land and a building at 800 East Main. The deed was dated March 10, 2008, and showed an amount of $40,000 (of which $8,000 was for the land). The deed indicated that a down payment had been made by the Bailey Company and that a mortgage was signed by the company for the balance owed.

The shoebox also contained an invoice dated March 12, 2008, from the Ace Office Equipment Company for $600 of office equipment sold to the Bailey Company. The invoice indicates that the amount is to be paid at the end of the month. A $34,000 mortgage, dated March 10, 2008, and signed by the Bailey Company, for the purchase of land and a building is also included in the shoebox. Finally, a 30-day, $4,000 note receivable is in the shoebox. It is dated March 15, 2008, and is issued to the Bailey Company by the Ret Company for "one-half of the land located at 800 East Main."

The Bailey Company has asked for your help in preparing a classified balance sheet as of March 15, 2008. Peter Bailey indicates that company checks have been issued for all cash payments. Bailey has called its bank. The bank's records indicate that the Bailey Company's checking account balance is $9,500, consisting of a $10,000 deposit, a $200 canceled check made out to the Finley Office Supply Company, and a $300 canceled check made out to the Patz Insurance Agency.

You notice that the Bailey Company has numerous office supplies on hand. Peter Bailey states that a company check was issued on March 8, 2008, to purchase the supplies but that none of the supplies had been used.

*Required:* Based on the preceding information, prepare a classified balance sheet for the Bailey Company on March 15, 2008. Show supporting calculations.

**7-42** The following items appear (in millions) on the January 28, 2006 financial statements of **Target Corporation**:

| | |
|---|---|
| Accounts receivable | $ 5,666 |
| Inventory | 5,838 |
| Sales (net) | 51,271 |
| Cost of goods sold | 34,927 |

On January 29, 2005, Target had accounts receivable of $5,069M and inventory of $5,384M. Suppose that in February 2006, Target wants to arrange with its supplier to pay for merchandise 90 days after the purchase.

*Required:* Based on the above information, would you, as a supplier, feel confident about the ability of Target to pay you in 90 days? Justify your answer. If you were making the decision to grant Target credit, what other information would you like to know about Target Corporation?

**7-43** Bart Brock is thinking about starting his own company, BB's. At the beginning of October 2008, he plans to invest $16,000 into the business. During October the company will purchase land, a small building to house the business, some office equipment, and some supplies. Bart has found land and a building that would be suitable for the company. The purchase price of both the land and the building is $60,000. Bart estimates that the cost of the land is 15% of the total price and the building is 85% of the total price. Bart wants the company to "finance" this purchase through its bank. The bank would require BB's to make a 20% down payment and would also require the company to sign a mortgage for the balance. Bart has determined that there is too much land, however, so that if BB's purchased the land and building, it would sell one-quarter of the land to another company to use as a parking lot. The other company has agreed to buy the land at a price equal to the cost paid by BB's and to sign a note requiring payment of this cost at the end of two years. Bart has found some used office equipment that could be purchased by BB's for $1,800 on credit, to be paid in 60 days. He also expects that BB's will need $800 of office supplies, which the company would purchase with cash. Before the bank will lend BB's the money to buy the land and building, it has requested a "projected" balance sheet for the company, along with a "projected" current ratio and debt ratio as of October 31, 2008, based on the preceding plans. Bart Brock has asked for your help.

*Required:* (1) Using the preceding information, prepare a projected balance sheet, current ratio, and debt ratio for BB's as of October 31, 2008. Show supporting calculations.
(2) Basing your decision solely on this information, if you were the banker would you give BB's the loan? What other information would help you make your decision?

**7-44** Today is January 1, 2009. Last night you were at a New Year's Eve party at which you ran into a long-lost friend, Art Washet, who is the owner of Washet Company. In a conversation, Art mentioned that his company would like to borrow $5,000 from you now and repay you $6,000 at the end of two years. You told him to stop by your house today with his financial records. He has just dropped off the following balance sheet, along with his accounting records:

**WASHET COMPANY**
***Balance Sheet***
***For Year Ended December 31, 2008***

| | | | |
|---|---|---|---|
| Working capital | $ 11,100 | Noncurrent liabilities | $ 9,400 |
| Other assets | 93,900 | Owner's equity | 95,600 |
| Total | $105,000 | Total | $105,000 |

Your analysis of these items and the accounting records reveals the following information (the amounts in parentheses indicate deductions from each item):

(a) Working capital consists of the following:

| | |
|---|---|
| Equipment (net) | $ 14,000 |
| Land | 10,000 |
| Accounts due to suppliers | (28,000) |
| Inventory, including office supplies of $3,700 | 34,700 |
| Salaries owed to employees | (2,600) |
| Note owed to bank (due June 1, 2009) | (17,000) |
| | $ 11,100 |

(b) Other assets include the following:

| | |
|---|---|
| Cash | $ 6,000 |
| Prepaid insurance | 1,900 |
| Buildings (net) | 46,000 |
| Long-term investment in government bonds | 30,000 |
| A. Washet, withdrawals | 10,000 |
| | $ 93,900 |

(c) Noncurrent liabilities consist of the following:

| | |
|---|---|
| Mortgage payable (due March 1, 2013) | 33,000 |
| Accounts due from customers | (16,600) |
| Notes receivable (due December 31, 2011) | (7,000) |
| | $ 9,400 |

(c) Owner's equity includes the following:

| | |
|---|---|
| A. Washet, capital | $104,900 |
| Securities held as a temporary investment | (11,000) |
| Interest payable (due with note on June 1, 2009) | 1,700 |
| | $ 95,600 |

*Required:* (1) Using your analysis, prepare a properly classified December 31, 2008 balance sheet (report form) for Washet Company.
(2) Compute the current ratio and the quick ratio for the company on December 31, 2008. Basing your decision solely on this information, would you loan $5,000 to the company?

**7-45** Ray Young owns and operates a repair service called Ray's Rapid Repairs. It is the end of the year, and his bookkeeper has recently resigned to move to a warmer climate. Knowing only a little about accounting, Ray prepared the following financial statements, based on the ending balances in the company's accounts on December 31, 2008:

**RAY'S RAPID REPAIRS**
***Income Statement***
***For Year Ended December 31, 2008***

| | | |
|---|---|---|
| Repair service revenues | | $ 29,000 |
| Operating expenses: | | |
| Rent expense | $ 3,200 | |
| Salaries expense | 9,900 | |
| Utilities expense | 1,100 | |
| R. Young, withdrawals | 16,000 | |
| Total operating expenses | | (30,200) |
| Net Loss | | $ (1,200) |

**RAY'S RAPID REPAIRS**
***Balance Sheet***
***December 31, 2008***

| *Assets* | | *Liabilities and Owner's Equity* | |
|---|---|---|---|
| Cash | $ 1,500 | Accounts payable | $ 2,600 |
| Repair supplies | 2,400 | Note payable (due 1/1/11) | 10,000 |
| Repair equipment | 15,000 | Total Liabilities | $12,600 |
| | | R. Young, capital[a] | 6,300 |
| Total Assets | $18,900 | Total Liabilities and Owner's Equity | $18,900 |

[a]Beginning capital − net loss

Ray is upset and says to you, "I don't know how I could have had a net loss in 2008. Maybe I did something wrong when I made out these financial statements. Could you help me? My business has been good in 2008. In these times of high prices, people have been getting their appliances and other items repaired by me instead of buying new ones. I used to have to rent my repair equipment, but business was so good that I purchased $15,000 of repair equipment at the beginning of the year. I know this equipment will last 10 years even though it won't be worth anything at the end of that time. I did have to sign a note for $10,000 of the purchase price, but the amount (plus $1,200 annual interest) will not be due until the beginning of 2011. I still have to rent my repair shop, but I paid $3,200 for two years of rent in advance at the beginning of 2008, so I am OK there. And besides, I just counted my repair supplies, and I have $1,100 of supplies left from 2008 which I can use in 2009."

He continues: "I'm not too worried about my cash balance. I know that customers owe me $700 for repair work I just completed in 2008. These are good customers and always pay, but I never tell my bookkeeper about this until I collect the cash. I am sure I will collect in 2009, and that will also make 2009 revenues look good. In fact, it will almost offset the $600 I just collected in advance (and recorded as a revenue) from a customer for repair work I said I would do in 2009. I still have to write a check to pay my bookkeeper for his last month's salary, but he was my only employee in 2008. In 2009 I am going to hire someone only on a part-time basis to keep my accounting records. You can have the job, if you can determine whether the net loss is correct and, if not, what it should be and what I am doing wrong."

*Required:* (1) Set up the following account columns: under *Assets:* Accounts Receivable, Repair Supplies, Prepaid Rent, and Repair Equipment; under *Liabilities:* Unearned Revenues, Salaries Payable, and Note Payable; under *Owner's Equity* (*Revenues*): Repair Service Revenues; and (*Expenses*): Depreciation Expense, Interest Expense, Rent Expense, Supplies Expense, and Salaries Expense. Enter any balances for these accounts shown on the financial statements.

(2) Using the accounts from (1), prepare any year-end adjustments you think are appropriate for 2008. Show any supporting calculations. Compute the ending balance of each account.

(3) Prepare a corrected 2008 income statement, statement of changes in owner's equity, and ending classified balance sheet (report form).

(4) Write a brief report to Ray Young, summarizing your suggestions for improving his accounting practices.

**7-46** The following are a condensed 2008 income statement and a December 31, 2008 balance sheet for Murf Company:

**MURF COMPANY**
***Income Statement***
***For Year Ended December 31, 2008***

| | |
|---|---|
| Sales (net) | $154,000 |
| Cost of goods sold | (91,300) |
| Gross profit | $ 62,700 |
| Operating expenses | (47,300) |
| Interest expense | (2,800) |
| Net Income | $ 12,600 |

**MURF COMPANY**
***Balance Sheet***
***December 31, 2008***

| | |
|---|---|
| Cash | $ 3,200 |
| Marketable securities (short-term) | 2,100 |
| Accounts receivable | 7,370 |
| Inventory | 9,650 |
| Property and equipment (net) | 97,680 |
| Total Assets | $120,000 |
| Current liabilities | $ 12,400 |
| Note payable (due 12/31/13) | 35,000 |
| Total Liabilities | $ 47,400 |
| S. Murf, capital | 72,600 |
| Total Liabilities and Owner's Equity | $120,000 |

On January 1, 2008, the accounts receivable were $6,050, the inventory was $10,950, the total assets were $110,000, and the owner's capital was $62,600. The company makes 60% of its net sales on credit and operates on a 300-day business year. At the end of 2007, the following ratio results were computed, based on the company's financial statements for 2007:

| | |
|---|---|
| (a) Current | 2.0 |
| (b) Quick | 1.3 |
| (c) Debt | 43.3% |
| (d) Inventory Turnover | 8.5 times (35.3 days) |
| (e) Accounts Receivable Turnover | 13.6 times (22.1 days) |
| (f) Gross Profit Percentage | 39.2% |
| (g) Profit Margin | 7.8% |
| (h) Return on Total Assets | 12.4% |
| (i) Return on Owner's Equity | 17.0% |

The company has hired you to update its ratio results and compare its performance in 2008 with that in 2007.

*Required:* (1) Compute the preceding ratios for 2008.
(2) Write a short report that compares the company's performance in 2008 with that in 2007 regarding its liquidity, financial flexibility, operating capability, and profitability.

**7-47** Yesterday, you received the letter shown below for your advice column in the local paper:

## Dr. Decisive

Dear Dr. Decisive:

I always read your column and think you do a good job settling squabbles. Here's one for you. I took my accounting book home over the break, and one of my parents (let's just call him "Dad") started to look through it. Soon he encountered a statement he didn't agree with, and the squabble began. Here's the statement: "If a company has a higher return on owner's equity than its return on total assets, this shows users that the company has benefited from using debt to help finance its assets." Dad says that a company will always have a higher return on owner's equity than it will have on total assets because owner's equity is always going to be smaller than total assets. I say that Dad is not correct. I think that sometimes a company can have a return on owner's equity that is lower than its return on total assets. His logic doesn't take into account the fact that when a company has debt, it also has interest, and that interest expense affects the company's return on assets but not its return on owner's equity. But when I challenge Dad, we always end up arguing. And every time we talk, the same subject comes up. Please help, and please show us with numbers! I need some peace and quiet.

"Enough Already"

*Required:* Meet with your Dr. Decisive team and write a response to "Enough Already."

CHAPTER 8

# THE CASH FLOW STATEMENT: ITS CONTENT AND USE

"THE USE OF MONEY IS ALL THE ADVANTAGE THERE IS IN HAVING IT."

—BENJAMIN FRANKLIN

1. Why is a company's cash flow statement important?
2. What are the types of transactions that may cause cash inflows and cash outflows for a company?
3. What do users need to know about a company's cash flow statement?
4. How does a company report the cash flows from its operating activities on its cash flow statement under the direct method?
5. How do users combine the changes in a company's current assets and current liabilities with its revenues and expenses for the accounting period to determine the company's operating cash flows?
6. Why do internal and external users study a company's cash flow statement in conjunction with its income statement and balance sheet?
7. What cash flow ratios are used to evaluate a company's performance?

How much cash do you currently have in your checking and savings accounts? Where did you get it? Did you get it from working at your job? Was this enough to finance your activities? Or did you have to borrow money from your parents or the bank during the last year? If you borrowed money, did you agree to pay it back this year, next year, or several years from now? If you agreed to pay back some of the loans this year, how much did you pay back? Did you invest in any stock this year? Did you buy a computer or car this year? If so, how much did you pay for these items? Just like individuals, companies must pay close attention to where they got their cash and where they spent it. For the year ended January 31, 2006, **Wal-Mart** reported cash inflows from its operating activities of $17,633 million, cash payments for its investing activities of $14,183 million, and cash payments for its financing activities of $2,422 million. Wal-Mart obtained these numbers from its accounting system. Did Wal-Mart collect "enough" cash from its operating activities during the year? Did Wal-Mart invest the "right amount" of cash?

*Overall, do these numbers show that Wal-Mart managed its cash "well" or "poorly" during the year? What additional information would you like to have to answer this question?*

In Chapters 6 and 7 we studied two major financial statements: the income statement, which summarizes the results of a company's operating activities during an accounting period, and the balance sheet, which shows the financial position of a company on a specific date. Together, these statements provide managers, investors, and creditors with information about a company's operating performance and financial condition.

However, as we mentioned in Chapter 7, there are some limits to how well a company's income statement and balance sheet can measure and report its activities and financial position. In this chapter we discuss how a company uses a third financial statement, the cash flow statement, to summarize its cash activities during an accounting period. More specifically, we (1) discuss why the cash flow statement is important, (2) define the components of the cash flow statement, (3) describe how the cash flow statement is used in evaluating a company, and (4) analyze the relationships between the cash flow statement and the cash budget, the income statement, and the balance sheet.

There are many issues involving the cash flow statement. In this chapter we focus on the basics. We will discuss other, more advanced topics in later chapters.

# WHY THE CASH FLOW STATEMENT IS IMPORTANT

1 Why is a company's cash flow statement important?

A cash flow statement shows the changes in a company's cash during an accounting period by listing the cash inflows and outflows from its operating, investing, and financing activities during the period. The cash flow statement primarily provides information about a company's ability to remain solvent (meet its obligations) and to grow. It summarizes the "flow" of *cash* activities during an accounting period and provides information that cannot be obtained by studying the company's income statement or balance sheet. So, analyzing the cash flow statement provides answers to the following questions: "How much cash was provided or used by the company's operating activities?" "How much cash did the company receive or spend in investing or financing activities?" Managers and others study a company's cash flows because the company cannot survive if it does not have enough cash to operate on a day-to-day basis and if it does not pay its debts when they are due.

What do you think this button means?

*What do a company's balance sheet and income statement show about its management of cash? What else do you think an investor or creditor would want to know?*

# UNDERSTANDING CASH FLOW TRANSACTIONS

To use a company's cash flow statement for evaluating its performance, you first must understand how the company's accounting system provides the cash flow information. Remember that a company's accounting system records all its transactions and is based on the *accrual* accounting concept.

A company's **cash flow statement** shows the inflows (receipts) and outflows (payments) of cash during an accounting period, explaining how its beginning cash balance changed to its ending cash balance because of transactions that resulted in increases and decreases in cash. A company's beginning cash balance is the amount of cash listed on its balance sheet at the end of the last accounting period (which is also the balance sheet for the beginning of the current period). A company's ending cash balance is the amount of cash listed on its balance sheet at the end of the current accounting period. "*Cash inflows*" is another way of saying "transactions that resulted in *increases* in cash." "*Cash outflows*" is another way of saying "transactions that resulted in *decreases* in cash." Without a cash flow statement, all that external users would know about a company's cash would be the beginning and ending cash balances. Thus the balance sheet and the cash flow statement are related. The equation in Exhibit 8-1 shows this relationship and uses Sweet Temptations as an example.

Recall that in Chapter 5, you learned how a company uses account columns in its accounting system to record increases and decreases in cash (as well as in other assets, liabilities, and owner's equity). For every transaction involving cash, the company records the effect on cash in its Cash account column. An internal manager can look at this account and see all the transactions that caused inflows and outflows of cash during an accounting period. However, not all managers have the desire (or need) to look at detailed records. And the external user, of course, cannot look at the company's accounts. Therefore, both need the cash flow statement.

## Cash Inflows and Outflows

2 What are the types of transactions that may cause cash inflows and cash outflows for a company?

To understand the cash flow statement, you need to know the kinds of transactions that cause a company's cash inflows and outflows. Inflows of cash occur, for example, when a company receives cash from selling inventory or receives cash from issuing a note or when an owner invests cash in the company. So, we can say that a company's cash inflows are caused by certain decreases in assets (other than cash), increases in liabilities, and increases in owner's equity during an accounting period.

*Does the preceding sentence make sense? How can a decrease in an asset other than cash cause a cash inflow?*

Outflows of cash occur, for example, when a company pays cash to purchase inventory or pays cash to reduce a note payable or when the owner withdraws cash from the company. So, we can say that a company's cash outflows are caused by certain increases in assets (other than cash), decreases in liabilities, and decreases in owner's equity during the accounting pe-

**EXHIBIT 8-1 CASH ACCOUNT AND CASH FLOWS**

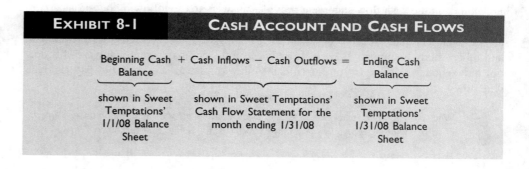

| Beginning Cash Balance | + Cash Inflows − Cash Outflows = | Ending Cash Balance |
|---|---|---|
| shown in Sweet Temptations' 1/1/08 Balance Sheet | shown in Sweet Temptations' Cash Flow Statement for the month ending 1/31/08 | shown in Sweet Temptations' 1/31/08 Balance Sheet |

riod. We summarize these cash inflows and outflows in Exhibit 8-2. We show the categories in a Cash account to remind you that these activities are recorded in the accounting system.

In the following two sections we will discuss the types of transactions that may result in either a cash inflow or a cash outflow. To illustrate these transactions, we provide six examples for a hypothetical company. (We will discuss Sweet Temptations' cash transactions later in the chapter.) For these examples, we assume the company has a beginning cash balance of $2,000. By analyzing the changes in the cash balance, you can better understand how each transaction affects cash.

### Inflows (Receipts) of Cash

As we mentioned earlier, there are three types of transactions that may cause a company's cash inflows. One type of transaction that may cause cash inflows involves *decreases in assets other than cash.* A decrease in an asset (other than cash) causes an inflow (increase) of cash when cash is received in exchange for the asset. This type of cash inflow occurs when a company collects an account receivable or sells property and equipment.

For example, assume that the company's account balances for Cash and Accounts Receivable are $2,000 and $800, respectively. If the company collects $200 from a customer for a previous credit sale, it records this transaction in its accounting system as follows:

| | Assets | | = | Liabilities | + | Owner's Equity |
|---|---|---|---|---|---|---|
| | Cash | Accounts Receivable | | | | |
| Beg Bal | $2,000 | $800 | | | | |
| | + 200 ←→ | − 200 | | | | |
| End Bal | $2,200 | $600 | | | | |

Notice that the $200 decrease in the asset Accounts Receivable resulted in a $200 increase in Cash. Also, if a company sells property or equipment for cash, Property and Equipment decreases and Cash increases.

A second type of transaction that may cause cash inflows involves *increases in liabilities.* An increase in a liability causes an inflow (increase) of cash when a company receives cash in exchange for the liability. For example, assume that the company's account balances for Cash and Notes Payable are $2,200 and $1,500, respectively. If the company borrows $4,000 from a bank, it records this transaction as follows:

| | Assets | = | Liabilities | + | Owner's Equity |
|---|---|---|---|---|---|
| | Cash | | Notes Payable | | |
| Beg Bal | $2,200 | | $1,500 | | |
| | +$4,000 ←→ | | +$4,000 | | |
| End Bal | $6,200 | | $5,500 | | |

The cash balance increases from $2,200 to $6,200 as a result of the $4,000 increase in a liability.

**EXHIBIT 8-2** **BALANCE SHEET ACCOUNTS AND CASH FLOWS**

**Cash**

Beginning Cash Balance
+ *Cash Inflows (Receipts)*
1. Decreases in assets other than cash
2. Increases in liabilities
3. Increases in owner's equity

− *Cash Outflows (Payments)*
1. Increases in assets other than cash
2. Decreases in liabilities
3. Decreases in owner's equity

Ending Cash Balance

A third type of transaction that may cause cash inflows involves *increases in owner's equity*. Owner's equity increases mainly because of additional investments by owners and net income. An additional investment causes an inflow (increase) of cash because the owner has used cash from personal sources to increase his or her investment in the company. Net income is slightly more complicated because the cash inflows and outflows for operating activities are usually not equal to the revenues and expenses included in net income. This is because net income is based on the accrual concept, whereas here we are concerned with cash flows. We will discuss revenues, expenses, and net income, and their effects on cash flows later in the chapter.

In this example, assume the company's account balances for Cash and Owner's Capital are $6,200 and $50,000, respectively. If the owner invests an additional $1,000 in the company, the company records this transaction in its accounting system as follows:

| | **Assets** | = | **Liabilities** | + | **Owner's Equity** |
|---|---|---|---|---|---|
| | Cash | | | | Owner's Capital |
| Beg Bal | $6,200 | | | | $50,000 |
| | +$1,000 ← | | → | | +$ 1,000 |
| End Bal | $7,200 | | | | $51,000 |

The cash balance increases from $6,200 to $7,200 as a result of the $1,000 increase in owner's equity.

*Stop and think of additional examples of each type of transaction that causes cash inflows. How would these transactions affect the company's accounts?*

## Outflows (Payments) of Cash

As we mentioned earlier, there also are three types of transactions that may cause a company's cash outflows. Instead of separately showing the accounts to explain each type, in this section we discuss the transactions and show the results of these transactions in Exhibit 8-3.

One type of transaction that may cause cash outflows involves *increases in assets other than cash.* An increase in an asset (other than cash) causes an outflow (decrease) of cash when a company pays cash for the asset. When the company pays $50 to purchase store supplies, this type of transaction occurs. See Transaction 1 in Exhibit 8-3.

A second type of transaction that may cause cash outflows involves *decreases in liabilities.* A decrease in a liability causes an outflow (decrease) of cash when a company uses cash to pay the debt. When the company pays $500 to reduce its note payable, this type of transaction occurs. See Transaction 2 in Exhibit 8-3.

A third type of transaction that may cause cash outflows involves *decreases in owner's equity.* For example, owner's equity decreases because of the owner's withdrawals. When the owner withdraws $300 from the company, this type of transaction occurs. See Transaction 3 in Exhibit 8-3.

*Think of additional examples of each type of transaction that causes cash outflows. How would each of these transactions affect the company's accounts? If you're having trouble, don't move on. You need to understand this before you continue.*

**EXHIBIT 8-3** **OUTFLOWS OF CASH**

| | **Assets** | | = | **Liabilities** | + | **Owner's Equity** |
|---|---|---|---|---|---|---|
| | Cash | Store Supplies | | Notes Payable | | Owner's Capital |
| Beg Bal | $7,200 | $2,200 | | $4,000 | | $51,000 |
| Trans. 1 | −$ 50 ↔ | +$ 50 | | | | |
| Trans. 2 | −$ 500 ← | | | → −$ 500 | | |
| Trans. 3 | −$ 300 ← | | | | | → −$ 300 |
| End Bal | $6,350 | $2,250 | | $3,500 | | $50,700 |

# THE ORGANIZATION OF THE CASH FLOW STATEMENT

Now that you know where to find information about cash transactions, you also need to know the best way to present this information in a company's cash flow statement. This is a challenging task. Think about trying to develop a report that summarizes the cash you received and paid out during the last month or year!

**3** What do users need to know about a company's cash flow statement?

*How would you summarize your cash flows for last month? Imagine getting out your checkbook and summarizing all of the deposits and payments in a useful manner. Were any of the deposits related to student loans? Did you buy any durable goods (a television or a telephone)?*

The cash flow statement shows a company's cash flows in three sections according to the *type* of activity that caused the increase or decrease in cash. The three sections are (1) cash flows from operating activities, (2) cash flows from investing activities, and (3) cash flows from financing activities. **Operating activities** include the primary activities of buying, selling, and delivering goods for sale, as well as providing services. They also include the activities that support the primary activities, such as administrative activities. **Investing activities** include lending money and collecting on the loans, investing in other companies, and buying and selling property and equipment. **Financing activities** include obtaining capital from the owner and providing the owner with a return on the investment, as well as obtaining capital from creditors and repaying the amounts borrowed. Exhibit 8-4 lists examples of the cash inflows and cash outflows from each type of activity.

For each type of cash activity, notice that the *net* cash flow provided by that type of activity is calculated by subtracting the cash outflows from the cash inflows. So, we can

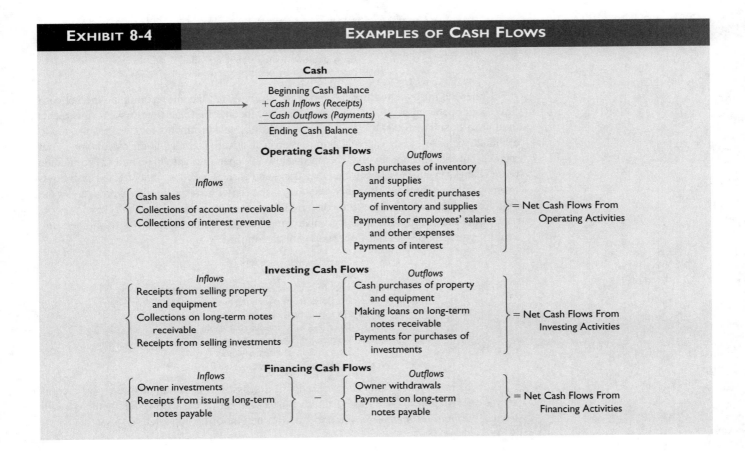

**EXHIBIT 8-4** **EXAMPLES OF CASH FLOWS**

**Cash**

Beginning Cash Balance
+ *Cash Inflows (Receipts)*
− *Cash Outflows (Payments)*

Ending Cash Balance

**Operating Cash Flows**

| *Inflows* | | *Outflows* | |
|---|---|---|---|
| Cash sales<br>Collections of accounts receivable<br>Collections of interest revenue | − | Cash purchases of inventory and supplies<br>Payments of credit purchases of inventory and supplies<br>Payments for employees' salaries and other expenses<br>Payments of interest | = Net Cash Flows From Operating Activities |

**Investing Cash Flows**

| *Inflows* | | *Outflows* | |
|---|---|---|---|
| Receipts from selling property and equipment<br>Collections on long-term notes receivable<br>Receipts from selling investments | − | Cash purchases of property and equipment<br>Making loans on long-term notes receivable<br>Payments for purchases of investments | = Net Cash Flows From Investing Activities |

**Financing Cash Flows**

| *Inflows* | | *Outflows* | |
|---|---|---|---|
| Owner investments<br>Receipts from issuing long-term notes payable | − | Owner withdrawals<br>Payments on long-term notes payable | = Net Cash Flows From Financing Activities |

restate the link between the cash balances shown in a company's beginning and ending balance sheets and its cash flow statement as follows:

Beginning Cash Balance (1/1/08)
+ or − Net Cash Flows From Operating Activities
+ or − Net Cash Flows From Investing Activities
+ or − Net Cash Flows From Financing Activities
= Ending Cash Balance (1/31/08)

## Net Cash Flows from Operating Activities

4 How does a company report the cash flows from its operating activities on its cash flow statement under the direct method?

There are two methods of calculating and reporting a company's net cash flows from operating activities. One method is called the direct method. The other is called the indirect method. A company using the **direct method** subtracts the operating cash outflows from the operating cash inflows to determine the net cash provided by (or used in) operating activities. Under the direct method, a company may report operating cash inflows in as many as three categories: (1) collections from customers, (2) collections of interest, and (3) other operating receipts. It may report operating cash outflows in as many as four categories: (1) payments to suppliers, (2) payments to employees, (3) payments of interest, and (4) other operating payments. Using the direct method, a company organizes the cash flows from operating activities section of its cash flow statement as follows:

*Cash Flows From Operating Activities*
Cash Inflows:
Collections from customers
Collections of interest
Other operating receipts
Cash inflows From operating activities
Cash Outflows:
Payments to suppliers
Payments to employees
Payments of interest
Other operating payments
Cash outflows for operating activities
Net cash provided by operating activities

Under the **indirect method**, a company adjusts its net income to compute the net cash flow from operating activities. That is, it lists net income first and then makes adjustments (additions or subtractions) to net income. It makes these adjustments for two reasons: (1) to eliminate expenses, such as depreciation expense, that were included in the calculation of net income but that did not involve a cash outflow for operating activities, and (2) to include those changes in current assets (other than cash) and current liabilities that affected cash flows from operating activities differently than they affected net income. In other words, under the indirect method, income flows are converted from an *accrual* basis to a *cash* basis.

Under the indirect method, a company might organize the cash flows from operating activities section of its cash flow statement as follows:

*Cash Flows From Operating Activities*
Net income
Adjustments for differences between net income and cash flows from operating activities:
Add: Depreciation expense
Decrease in accounts receivable
Less: Decrease in accounts payable
Decrease in salaries payable
Net cash provided by operating activities

For the main part of this chapter, we will discuss how to calculate and report a company's operating cash flows using the *direct method* on its cash flow statement. We will discuss the *indirect method* in the appendix at the end of this chapter.

# PREPARING THE CASH FLOW STATEMENT

To explain how to prepare the cash flow statement, we now turn to Sweet Temptations' January 2008 activities. This is the same set of transactions we used in Chapters 5, 6, and 7 (see Exhibit 5-20). Exhibit 8-5 shows the Cash account, which kept track of the company's January 2008 cash transactions. Notice that we show two columns of information on each side of the Cash account. The inside columns provide a brief explanation of each transaction recorded in the account. We then use the explanations to classify the items according to the type of cash flow activity. The outer columns label each item as an operating, investing, or financing cash inflow or cash outflow. As Exhibit 8-5 shows,

**EXHIBIT 8-5** **SWEET TEMPTATIONS' CASH ACCOUNT**

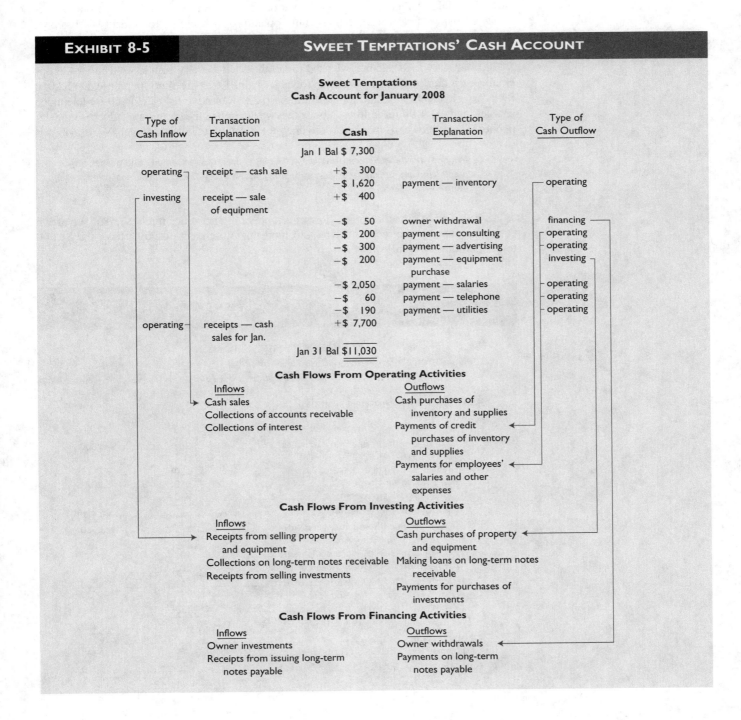

**Sweet Temptations**
**Cash Account for January 2008**

| Type of Cash Inflow | Transaction Explanation | Cash | Transaction Explanation | Type of Cash Outflow |
|---|---|---|---|---|
| | | Jan 1 Bal $ 7,300 | | |
| operating | receipt — cash sale | +$ 300 | | |
| | | −$ 1,620 | payment — inventory | operating |
| investing | receipt — sale of equipment | +$ 400 | | |
| | | −$ 50 | owner withdrawal | financing |
| | | −$ 200 | payment — consulting | operating |
| | | −$ 300 | payment — advertising | operating |
| | | −$ 200 | payment — equipment purchase | investing |
| | | −$ 2,050 | payment — salaries | operating |
| | | −$ 60 | payment — telephone | operating |
| | | −$ 190 | payment — utilities | operating |
| operating | receipts — cash sales for Jan. | +$ 7,700 | | |
| | | Jan 31 Bal $11,030 | | |

**Cash Flows From Operating Activities**

| Inflows | Outflows |
|---|---|
| Cash sales | Cash purchases of inventory and supplies |
| Collections of accounts receivable | Payments of credit purchases of inventory and supplies |
| Collections of interest | Payments for employees' salaries and other expenses |

**Cash Flows From Investing Activities**

| Inflows | Outflows |
|---|---|
| Receipts from selling property and equipment | Cash purchases of property and equipment |
| Collections on long-term notes receivable | Making loans on long-term notes receivable |
| Receipts from selling investments | Payments for purchases of investments |

**Cash Flows From Financing Activities**

| Inflows | Outflows |
|---|---|
| Owner investments | Owner withdrawals |
| Receipts from issuing long-term notes payable | Payments on long-term notes payable |

we determined the type of cash flow activity for each item by comparing the item explanations with the more general descriptions of activities that we presented in Exhibit 8-4.

Exhibit 8-6 shows Sweet Temptations' cash flow statement for the month ending January 31, 2008. The statement shows a summary of the company's cash flows by category of activity. In the following two sections, we will use Sweet Temptations' Cash account to explain the information that each section of Sweet Temptations' cash flow statement provides.

## Cash Flows From Operating Activities

The cash flows from operating activities section of a company's cash flow statement provides financial statement users with information about its ability to obtain cash from its day-to-day activities. Sweet Temptations' only operating cash *inflow* for January is listed as "Collections from customers" in Exhibit 8-6 and totals $8,000. In Exhibit 8-7 we show that the $8,000 is the sum of two items in the Cash account: (1) a cash sale of $300 and (2) a $7,700 summary cash sale that we used for all the other January cash sales. The $4,420 operating cash *outflows* consist of the following: (1) a $1,620 inventory purchase, (2) $2,050 for salary payments, (3) $200 for consulting, (4) $300 for advertising, (5) $60 for telephone charges, and (6) $190 for utilities. Notice that we combined the consulting, advertising, telephone, and utilities cash payments into an "other" category of operating cash outflows.

*Why do you think we combined the consulting, advertising, telephone, and utilities payments? In summarizing your personal cash flows, would you combine certain categories of items? Why or why not?*

Sweet Temptations' net cash flows from operating activities totals $3,580. We arrive at this amount by subtracting the $4,420 total operating cash outflows from the $8,000 total operating cash inflows.

**EXHIBIT 8-6 SWEET TEMPTATIONS' CASH FLOW STATEMENT**

**SWEET TEMPTATIONS**
***Cash Flow Statement***
***For Month Ended January 31, 2008***

| | | |
|---|---|---|
| Cash Flows From Operating Activities | | |
| Cash Inflows: | | |
| Collections from customers | $ 8,000 | |
| Cash inflows from operating activities | | $ 8,000 |
| Cash Outflows: | | |
| Payments to suppliers | $(1,620) | |
| Payments to employees | (2,050) | |
| Other operating payments | (750) | |
| Cash outflows for operating activities | | (4,420) |
| Net cash provided by operating activities | | $ 3,580 |
| Cash Flows From Investing Activities | | |
| Receipt from sale of store equipment | $ 400 | |
| Payment for purchase of store equipment | (200) | |
| Net cash provided by investing activities | | 200 |
| Cash Flows From Financing Activities | | |
| Withdrawals by owner | $ (50) | |
| Net cash used for financing activities | | (50) |
| Net Increase in Cash | | $ 3,730 |
| Cash, January 1, 2008 | | 7,300 |
| Cash, January 31, 2008 | | $11,030 |

## EXHIBIT 8-7 EXPLANATION OF CASH FLOW STATEMENT (OPERATING ACTIVITIES)

**Cash Account for January 2008**

| Type of Cash Inflow | Transaction Explanation | Cash | Transaction Explanation | Type of Cash Outflow |
|---|---|---|---|---|
| | | Jan 1 Bal $ 7,300 | | |
| operating | receipt — cash sale | +$ 300 | | |
| | | −$ 1,620 | payment — inventory | operating |
| investing | receipt — sale of equipment | +$ 400 | | |
| | | −$ 50 | owner withdrawal | financing |
| | | −$ 200 | payment — consulting | operating |
| | | −$ 300 | payment — advertising | operating |
| | | −$ 200 | payment — equipment purchase | investing |
| | | −$ 2,050 | payment — salaries | operating |
| | | −$ 60 | payment — telephone | operating |
| | | −$ 190 | payment — utilities | operating |
| operating | receipts — cash sales for Jan. | +$ 7,700 | | |
| | | Jan 31 Bal $11,030 | | |

Cash Flow Statement (Operating Activities only)
For Month Ended January 31, 2008

| | | |
|---|---|---|
| Cash Flows From Operating Activities | | |
| Cash Inflows: | | |
| Collections from customers | $ 8,000 | |
| Cash inflows from operating activities | | $8,000 |
| Cash Outflows: | | |
| Payments to suppliers | $(1,620) | |
| Payments to employees | (2,050) | |
| Other operating payments | (750) | |
| Cash outflows for operating activities | | (4,420) |
| Net cash provided by operating activities | | $3,580 |

(1) $300 cash sale made on January 2, 2008 plus $7,700 summary item representing all other January cash sales equals $8,000 in receipts from customers.

(2) $1,620 check written on January 3, 2008 to pay Unlimited Decadence for an inventory purchase made on credit in December 2007.

(3) On January 30, 2008 checks totaling $2,050 were written to you and Jaime Gonzales in payment for working in January.

(4) The $750 total for other operating expenses includes $200 paid to a promotion consultant, $300 for the advertisement in Westwood Mall's January promotional flyer, $60 for telephone charges, and $190 for utilities.

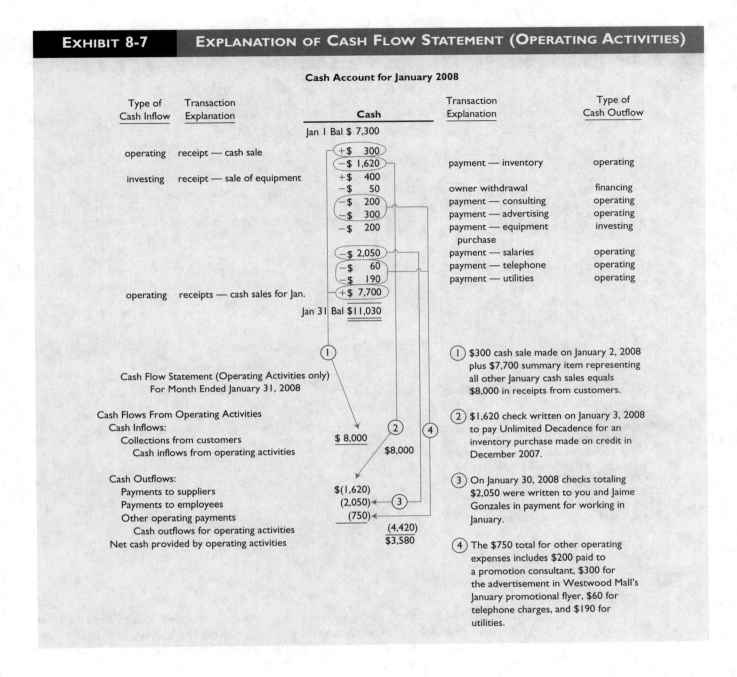

## Cash Flows From Investing and Financing Activities

Exhibit 8-8 shows that Sweet Temptations' $200 net cash provided by investing activities during January 2008 consisted of two items. A $400 investing cash *inflow* resulted from the sale of store equipment. A $200 investing cash *outflow* resulted from a purchase of store equipment. Sweet Temptations' $50 net cash outflow for financing activities consisted of one item, Anna Cox's $50 withdrawal.

## Reconciliation of Cash Balances

At the bottom of Exhibit 8-8, we also show the net increase in cash, and we "reconcile" the beginning cash balance to the ending cash balance. The $3,730 net increase in cash

**EXHIBIT 8-8**

**EXPLANATION OF CASH FLOW STATEMENT (INVESTING AND FINANCING ACTIVITIES)**

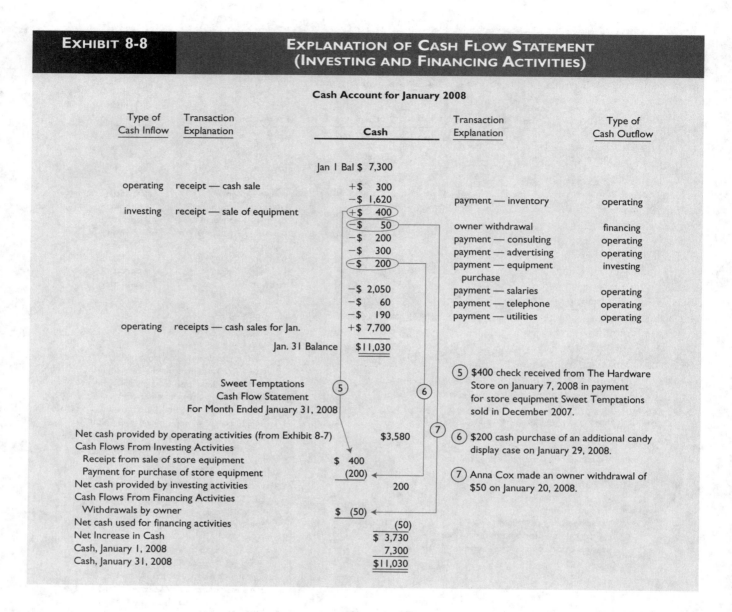

**Cash Account for January 2008**

| Type of Cash Inflow | Transaction Explanation | Cash | Transaction Explanation | Type of Cash Outflow |
|---|---|---|---|---|
| | | Jan 1 Bal $ 7,300 | | |
| operating | receipt — cash sale | +$ 300 | | |
| | | −$ 1,620 | payment — inventory | operating |
| investing | receipt — sale of equipment | +$ 400 | | |
| | | −$ 50 | owner withdrawal | financing |
| | | −$ 200 | payment — consulting | operating |
| | | −$ 300 | payment — advertising | operating |
| | | −$ 200 | payment — equipment purchase | investing |
| | | −$ 2,050 | payment — salaries | operating |
| | | −$ 60 | payment — telephone | operating |
| | | −$ 190 | payment — utilities | operating |
| operating | receipts — cash sales for Jan. | +$ 7,700 | | |
| | Jan. 31 Balance | $11,030 | | |

Sweet Temptations
Cash Flow Statement
For Month Ended January 31, 2008

| | | |
|---|---|---|
| Net cash provided by operating activities (from Exhibit 8-7) | | $3,580 |
| Cash Flows From Investing Activities | | |
| Receipt from sale of store equipment (5) | $ 400 | |
| Payment for purchase of store equipment (6) | (200) | |
| Net cash provided by investing activities | | 200 |
| Cash Flows From Financing Activities | | |
| Withdrawals by owner (7) | $ (50) | |
| Net cash used for financing activities | | (50) |
| Net Increase in Cash | | $ 3,730 |
| Cash, January 1, 2008 | | 7,300 |
| Cash, January 31, 2008 | | $11,030 |

(5) $400 check received from The Hardware Store on January 7, 2008 in payment for store equipment Sweet Temptations sold in December 2007.

(6) $200 cash purchase of an additional candy display case on January 29, 2008.

(7) Anna Cox made an owner withdrawal of $50 on January 20, 2008.

is determined by adding the $3,580 net cash provided by operating activities and the $200 net cash provided by investing activities, and subtracting the $50 net cash used for financing activities. We add this $3,730 increase in cash to the $7,300 January 1, 2008 cash balance to show the $11,030 January 31, 2008 cash balance. This $11,030 cash balance is the same amount we showed in Sweet Temptations' January 31, 2008 balance sheet in Exhibit 7-2.

## EXPANDED DISCUSSION OF CALCULATIONS FOR THE DIRECT METHOD

A company does not always prepare its cash flow statement each month. Usually, a company will prepare its cash flow statement each quarter or each year. When a cash flow statement is not prepared for a long time, the company may have hundreds of entries in its Cash account. In this case, it is very time-consuming to analyze each entry to see whether it involved a cash inflow or outflow from an operating, investing, or financing activity. Furthermore, sometimes an external user (e.g., bank) evaluating a company's performance may have the company's income statement and balance sheet but not its cash flow statement. In these cases, the company or external user may use a "shortcut" approach to preparing a cash flow statement. This approach involves analyzing the company's income statement amounts and the changes in its balance sheet amounts to determine the change in cash. In later chapters, we will study how to analyze the changes in balance sheet amounts to determine the cash inflows and cash outflows from investing and financing activities. In this chapter, we focus on determining the cash inflows and cash outflows from operating activities.

To understand how to determine a company's operating cash flows, remember how a company operates. Recall that a company's **operating cycle** is the average time required to pay for inventory, sell the inventory, and collect on the sales. To begin its operating cycle, a company buys inventory for cash or on credit (increasing accounts payable). When a company makes cash or credit sales during the current accounting period, it increases cash (or accounts receivable) and revenues, and increases cost of goods sold and reduces inventory. It increases other expenses and either decreases cash or increases liabilities (e.g., salaries payable) for the expenses. When the company collects its accounts receivable, it increases cash and decreases accounts receivable. When it pays its accounts payable, it decreases cash and decreases accounts payable. This collection of accounts receivable and payment of accounts payable may occur weeks or even months later in the next accounting period. When the company records all of these transactions, it always keeps the accounting equation in balance and maintains the dual effect of transactions.

5 How do users combine the changes in a company's current assets and current liabilities with its revenues and expenses for the accounting period to determine the company's operating cash flows?

To determine its cash inflows and outflows from operating activities, a company can analyze its income statement accounts and the changes in its balance sheet accounts related to its day-to-day operations (i.e., current assets and current liabilities). The reason a company does this analysis relates to accrual accounting, which we discussed in Chapter 5. Under **accrual accounting**, a company records its revenue and related expense transactions in the same accounting period that it provides goods or services, regardless of whether it receives or pays cash in that period. Thus, the analysis for the operating cash flows involves "converting" accrual accounting information to operating cash flow information. From our earlier discussion, recall that a company must report several types of cash inflows and outflows from operating activities. To keep this discussion simple, we will focus on determining the collections from customers, the payments to employees, and the payments to suppliers. These are the major operating cash flows.

## Collections from Customers

To determine a company's collections from customers during the accounting period, recall that it can make sales for cash or for credit. So its Sales Revenue account includes both cash and credit sales. Its Accounts Receivable account (a current asset) includes increases due to the credit sales and decreases due to collections of accounts receivable. So, if the Accounts Receivable account balance *decreases* during the accounting period, this means that *more* cash was collected (from current and previous credit sales) than the amount of current credit sales that were made. Or, if the Accounts Receivable account balance *increases* during the accounting period, this means that *less* cash was collected than the amount of credit sales. By taking the balance in its Sales Revenue account and adding to it the decrease in Accounts Receivable (or subtracting the increase in Accounts Receivable), a company can determine its cash collections from customers during the accounting period.

The upper part of Exhibit 8-9 shows how to calculate a company's cash collected from customers. In this example, assume that a company made cash sales of $30,000 and credit sales of $40,000 during its *first* year of operations and collected $35,000 of the related accounts receivable. At the end of the year its Sales Revenue account shows a balance of $70,000, and its Accounts Receivable account shows an increase of $5,000 above its balance at the beginning of the year. The $65,000 cash collected from customers is determined by subtracting the $5,000 increase in Accounts Receivable from the $70,000 in

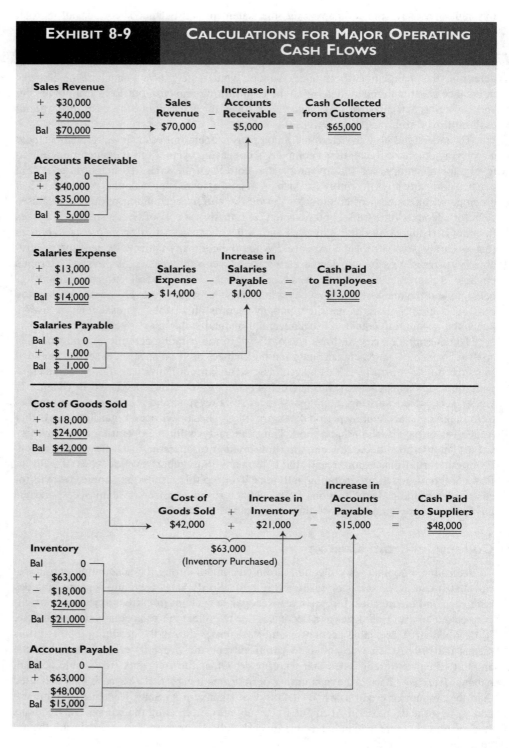

**EXHIBIT 8-9** **CALCULATIONS FOR MAJOR OPERATING CASH FLOWS**

**Sales Revenue**
+ $30,000
+ $40,000
Bal $70,000

**Accounts Receivable**
Bal $ 0
+ $40,000
− $35,000
Bal $ 5,000

| Sales Revenue | − | Increase in Accounts Receivable | = | Cash Collected from Customers |
|---|---|---|---|---|
| $70,000 | − | $5,000 | = | $65,000 |

**Salaries Expense**
+ $13,000
+ $ 1,000
Bal $14,000

**Salaries Payable**
Bal $ 0
+ $ 1,000
Bal $ 1,000

| Salaries Expense | − | Increase in Salaries Payable | = | Cash Paid to Employees |
|---|---|---|---|---|
| $14,000 | − | $1,000 | = | $13,000 |

**Cost of Goods Sold**
+ $18,000
+ $24,000
Bal $42,000

| Cost of Goods Sold | + | Increase in Inventory | − | Increase in Accounts Payable | = | Cash Paid to Suppliers |
|---|---|---|---|---|---|---|
| $42,000 | + | $21,000 | − | $15,000 | = | $48,000 |

$63,000 (Inventory Purchased)

**Inventory**
Bal 0
+ $63,000
− $18,000
− $24,000
Bal $21,000

**Accounts Payable**
Bal 0
+ $63,000
− $48,000
Bal $15,000

Sales Revenue. (You can confirm the $65,000 cash collected by adding the cash sale of $30,000 to the accounts receivable collection of $35,000.)

## Payments to Employees

To determine a company's payments to employees, recall that its Salaries Expense account includes the amount of salaries earned by employees during this period. This amount includes both salaries that were paid to employees and salaries that were recorded as owed to employees at the end of the period for work they did during the accounting period. The Salaries Payable account (a current liability) includes increases due to salaries owed to employees at the end of the current accounting period and decreases due to payments of employees' salaries from the previous accounting period. So, if the Salaries Payable account balance *decreases* during the period, this means that *more* cash was paid this period for salaries than employees earned this period. Or, if the Salaries Payable account balance *increases* during the period, this means that *less* cash was paid this period for salaries than employees earned this period. By taking the balance in the Salaries Expense account and adding the decrease in Salaries Payable (or subtracting the increase in Salaries Payable), a company can determine the cash it paid to employees during the accounting period.

The middle part of Exhibit 8-9 shows how to calculate the cash payments to employees. In this example, assume that the company paid salaries of $13,000 and recorded salaries owed of $1,000 at the end of its first year of operations. At year-end, the Salaries Expense account shows a balance of $14,000, and its Salaries Payable account shows an increase of $1,000. The $13,000 cash paid to employees is determined by subtracting the $1,000 increase in Salaries Payable from the $14,000 in Salaries Expense.

*Using this analysis, how would you determine the amount of interest that was paid during the year?*

## Payments to Suppliers

The calculations of the cash collected from customers and paid to employees each involved one income statement account and one balance sheet account. The calculation of the cash paid to suppliers is slightly more complicated because it involves one income statement account and two balance sheet accounts. To determine a company's payments to suppliers, recall that its Cost of Goods Sold account includes the cost of inventory sold to customers during the accounting period. The Inventory account (a current asset) includes entries for both the purchase and the sale of inventory. So, if the Inventory account *increases* during the accounting period, this means that more inventory was purchased than sold. If it *decreases,* more inventory was sold than purchased. The inventory was purchased either by paying cash or using credit. The Accounts Payable account (a current liability) includes increases due to credit purchases of inventory and decreases due to payments of accounts payable. So, if the Accounts Payable account balance *decreases* during the accounting period, this means that *more* cash was paid (for current and previous credit purchases) than the amount of credit purchases of inventory that were made during the current period. Or, if the Accounts Payable account balance *increases* during the period, this means that *less* cash was paid than the amount of credit purchases of inventory.

Because the cost of inventory (both cash and credit) "flows" into the Inventory account at the time of purchase and flows out at the time of sale (and into the Cost of Goods Sold account), two calculations must be made to determine the cash paid to suppliers for inventory. First, the total amount of inventory purchased must be determined. This is done by adding the increase in the Inventory account to (or subtracting the decrease from) the balance in the Cost of Goods Sold account. Then, the impact of the credit purchases must be eliminated. This is done by adding the decrease in Accounts Payable to (or subtracting the increase in Accounts Payable from) the total amount of inventory purchased. The end result is the cash paid to suppliers during the accounting period.

The lower part of Exhibit 8-9 shows how to calculate the cash paid to suppliers. In this example, assume that the cost of goods sold related to the cash sales and credit sales were $18,000 and $24,000, respectively, so that the Cost of Goods Sold account shows a balance of $42,000. The Inventory account shows an increase of $21,000 during the year. The Accounts Payable account shows an increase of $15,000. The $63,000 total amount

**EXHIBIT 8-10 CALCULATIONS FOR ALL OPERATING CASH FLOWS**

| Income Statement Amounts | Adjustments | | Cash Flows From Operating Activities | Net Operating Cash Flows |
|---|---|---|---|---|
| Sales revenue | + Decrease in accounts receivable<br>or<br>− Increase in accounts receivable | = | Collections from customers | Cash Inflows From Operating Activities |
| Interest revenue | + Decrease in interest receivable<br>or<br>− Increase in interest receivable | = | Collections of interest | |
| Other revenues | + Increase in unearned revenues*<br>or<br>− Decrease in unearned revenues* | = | Other operating receipts | |
| Cost of goods sold | + Increase in inventory<br>or<br>− Decrease in inventory<br>+ Decrease in accounts payable<br>or<br>− Increase in accounts payable | = | Payments to suppliers | Cash Outflows For Operating Activities |
| Salaries expense | + Decrease in salaries payable<br>or<br>− Increase in salaries payable | = | Payments to employees | |
| Interest expense | + Decrease in interest payable<br>or<br>− Increase in interest payable | = | Payments of interest | |
| Other expenses | + Increase in prepaid expenses<br>or<br>− Decrease in prepaid expenses<br>− Depreciation† | = | Other operating payments | |

*Unless related to normal sales; then the adjustment is made to sales revenue
†Unless listed as separate item on income statement

of inventory purchased is determined by adding the $21,000 increase in Inventory to the $42,000 in Cost of Goods Sold. The $48,000 cash paid to suppliers is determined by subtracting the $15,000 increase in Accounts Payable from the $63,000 total amount of inventory purchased.

For the sake of discussion, we used a simple example that had only a few numbers in each balance sheet account. To some of you, it may appear that our analysis could have been shortened even more. In reality, balance sheet accounts may have many numbers in them, and for external users, only the balances (from the beginning and ending balance sheets) are known. So, the method we explained will work under complex or simple circumstances. We also explained how to calculate only three operating cash flows. The analysis used for calculating other operating cash flows is the same. We show a diagram of the calculations for all operating cash flows in Exhibit 8-10 and provide an example later in the chapter.

## ANALYSIS OF THE CASH FLOW STATEMENT

Financial statement users think that cash flows are a critical part of a company's ability to remain solvent. A comment from a bank executive sums up why evaluating a company's cash flows is important: "A bank lends cash to its customers, collects interest from them, and requires the customers to repay the loan in cash. It's all about cash."[a]

By reviewing a company's cash flow statement, external users can see how a company obtained and used its cash. Because a company summarizes its cash flows by operating, investing, and financing activities, users can compare the amounts in each section of the statement to see if important changes have occurred. External users can evaluate the company's need for additional cash to pay for its existing operations or for the expansion of its operations. They can also evaluate the ability of the company to make interest payments and to pay off debt when it comes due. A comparison with the cash flows of other companies also can show, for instance, that the company is obtaining a greater proportion of its cash from investing activities than are similar companies. This situation may indicate a problem with the company's net cash flows from operating activities. One possible explanation is that the company is selling a relatively large portion of its assets to get the cash it needs for operations. If it does not replace the assets, the company may hamper its ability to obtain cash from operations in the future. For example, suppose you owned a lawn-mowing business, and because your company was short on cash, you sold several of the company's lawn mowers for cash. Would the company be able to mow as many lawns after the sale as it could before the sale?

Managers are able to use the information in the cash flow statement in much the same way as do external users. They can determine whether the net cash flow from operating activities is large enough to finance existing operations, whether excess cash from operating activities may be sufficient to finance expansion projects, or whether additional cash must be obtained from external parties.

6 Why do internal and external users study a company's cash flow statement in conjunction with its income statement and balance sheet?

In addition, both managers and external users use the cash flow statement in conjunction with the balance sheet and the income statement to help evaluate a company. All three financial statements help users analyze three important company characteristics: (1) liquidity and solvency, (2) ability to make property and equipment purchases, and (3) cash flow returns (which we discuss later).

Financial statement users assess a company's *liquidity* and *solvency* to see whether a company is generating enough cash to pay its debts. Recall from Chapter 7 that liquidity refers to how quickly a company can convert its assets to cash to pay its bills. In that chapter, we showed you how decision makers use the current assets and current liabilities sections of the balance sheet to calculate the current ratio and the quick ratio. Solvency refers to a company's ability to pay its long-term debts as they come due. The debt ratio is calculated from balance sheet information to help assess solvency.

© TOM STEWART/CORBIS

What are the operating cash flows related to this student's lawn mowing activities?

These balance sheet ratios are important in assessing a company's liquidity and solvency. However, they focus on the relationship between a company's assets and liabilities without regard for a company's ability to generate the cash needed to pay its debts. By showing a company's sources and uses of cash, the cash flow statement provides additional information about a company's management of cash.

In addition to paying its debts, a company must have enough property and equipment to continue earning a satisfactory profit. For example, Sweet Temptations may need to have cash available to buy additional equipment. If, for instance, an Unlimited Decadence frozen candy bar becomes quite popular, Sweet Temptations must be able to purchase refrigerated display cases. Assessing a company's ability to make these types of purchases helps decision makers determine how well a company can continue to perform.

It is unlikely that a company can continue to be successful unless it can obtain most of its cash from its operating activities. Thus, financial statement users want to know whether or not the cash the company received from selling goods or services is more than the cash it paid to provide the goods or services. External users can compare the company's net cash flow from operating activities for a given year with that year's income from operations to assess how well its operating activities provide cash.

A company's ability to generate enough cash to remain in business and earn a satisfactory profit can also be studied by computing its **cash flow returns**. By "cash flow returns," we mean the company's cash flows divided by the dollar amount of its assets or owner's equity. This is similar to the return on total assets or the return on owner's equity calculations we discussed in Chapter 7. We will discuss each of these evaluations in the following sections.

## Relationship between the Cash Flow Statement and the Cash Budget

Remember from Chapter 4 that a cash budget gives a description of the company's planned cash activities. Also recall that one purpose of a budget is to provide a benchmark for the evaluation of a company's performance. One way managers evaluate their company's operating performance for an accounting period is by comparing the information from the operating activities section of the company's cash flow statement with the projected operating cash flows in its cash budget.

Listed below is a comparison of the January 2008 cash budget information for Sweet Temptations (from Exhibit 4-10) and the actual cash flow from operations information for January.

| Item | Budget | Actual | Effect of Difference on Cash Balance |
|---|---|---|---|
| Cash receipts from sales | $7,080 | $8,000 | +$920 |
| Cash paid to suppliers | (1,620) | (1,620) | 0 |
| Cash paid to employees | (2,050) | (2,050) | 0 |
| Cash paid for other operating items | (755) | (750) | + 5 |
| Net cash provided by operations | $2,655 | $3,580 | +$925 |

As you can see, Sweet Temptations did an excellent job of following its January operating cash budget. Cash receipts from sales were $920 greater than budgeted, and cash paid for other operating items was $5 less than budgeted. Hence, Sweet Temptations ended January with $925 more cash than it expected. Because Sweet Temptations is so small, it was able to anticipate its operating cash outflows (payments) almost exactly. More difficult to anticipate, however, is the amount of operating cash inflow for January. The cash flow information for sales reinforces our conclusion that Sweet Temptations had a successful first month of operations.

*How do you think this comparison will affect the cash budget for the next period? Why?*

In the remainder of this chapter, we will discuss some additional, more specific ways that managers and external decision makers use the cash flow statement to evaluate a company's performance.

## Relationship between the Cash Flow Statement and the Income Statement

The income statement and the cash flow statement are related because both report on a company's activities during an accounting period. The difference between the two is that the income statement reports on activities using accrual accounting whereas the cash flow statement reports only on cash activities. Because of the differences in the way these statements measure income and cash flows and because of the type of information that results from these differences, managers, investors, and creditors are interested in both measures of operating performance.

### Operating Cash Flow Margin

7 What cash flow ratios are used to evaluate a company's performance?

We explained in Chapter 6 that a company's profit margin (net income ÷ net sales) is an important measure of profitability. Information from the cash flow statement is used to calculate an additional profitability (and liquidity) measure. The operating cash flow margin is calculated as follows:

$$\text{Operating Cash Flow Margin} = \frac{\text{Net Cash Flow Provided by Operating Activities}}{\text{Net Sales}}$$

This ratio describes how much net cash the company generated from each dollar of net sales. It is similar to a profit margin measure, but in this case the higher the ratio, the better the company is at generating cash from operating activities and the greater is its liquidity.

For example, Exhibit 8-6 shows that in January, Sweet Temptations' net cash provided by operating activities was $3,580. Its net sales for January were $8,100 (see Exhibit 6-2). Therefore, its operating cash flow margin was 0.44 ($3,580 ÷ $8,100). This means that Sweet Temptations generated $0.44 net cash for each dollar of its net sales.

*What do you think causes the difference between the amount of Sweet Temptations' net sales and the net amount of cash it generated from its net sales?*

**REL Consultancy Group** specializes in helping companies improve their working capital and cash flow positions. Every year REL compiles and publishes a survey on the working capital efficiency of over 1,000 companies. One of the key ratios that REL computes is what it calls the *cash-conversion efficiency (CCE) ratio,* which is calculated in the same way as the operating cash flow margin we just discussed. REL considers the CCE ratio to be very important in evaluating a company's cash flow (and liquidity) performance, and its annual survey provides "benchmarks" to help a company compare its performance with other companies.[b]

### Operating Cash Flow Margins of Actual Companies

To illustrate ratio analysis, we continue our evaluation of **JCPenney Company Inc.** and **Kohl's Corporation**, discussed in Chapters 6 and 7. The companies' operating cash flow margins for 2005 were as follows:

| | *JCPenney* | *Kohl's* |
|---|---|---|
| Operating Cash Flow Margin | 7.1% | 6.6% |

Notice that JCPenney was more efficient than Kohl's at generating cash from sales, indicating that JCPenney had more liquidity for the year ended January 28, 2006.

*In Chapter 6, Kohl's profit margin was higher than that of JCPenney. Why do you think* JCPenney's *operating cash flow margin is higher than that of Kohl's?*

## Relationship between the Cash Flow Statement and the Balance Sheet

The balance sheet is related to the cash flow statement in much the same way as it is related to the income statement. Recall from Chapter 7 that a company's balance sheet shows the "stock" of its resources at a specific date and that the company's income statement shows the "flow" of its operating activities for an accounting period. Further, remember that a company's income statement and balance sheet are used together to assess how well the company performed given its level of resources. Because net cash flow from operating activities provides an alternative measure ("flow") of company performance, it also can be used with balance sheet information to assess how well a company performed given its resources.

### Cash Return Ratios

Two ratios used to assess a company's cash flow performance in relation to its resources are (1) the cash return on total assets and (2) the cash return on owner's equity. These ratios are calculated as follows:

$$\text{Cash Return on Total Assets} = \frac{\begin{array}{c}\text{Net Cash Flow Provided} \\ \text{by Operating Activities}\end{array} + \begin{array}{c}\text{Interest} \\ \text{Paid}\end{array}}{\text{Average Total Assets}}$$

$$\text{Cash Return on Owner's Equity} = \frac{\begin{array}{c}\text{Net Cash Flow Provided} \\ \text{by Operating Activities}\end{array}}{\text{Average Owner's Equity}}$$

A company's cash return on total assets measures how well the company is using its resources to generate net cash from operating activities. Interest payments are added back in the numerator because they are returns to the creditors who loan the company money to purchase some of the assets. Exhibit 8-6 shows that in January, Sweet Temptations' net cash provided by operating activities was $3,580. Its average total assets for January were $19,450. ([$17,820 total assets on January 1 + $21,080 total assets on January 31] divided by 2—see Exhibit 7-2.) Therefore, its cash return on total assets was 18.4 percent ($3,580 ÷ $19,450). Notice that we did not add back interest payments in the numerator because Sweet Temptations made no interest payments in January. A cash return on total assets of 18.4 percent means that every dollar Sweet Temptations had invested in assets in January generated net cash from Sweet Temptations' operating activities of 18.4 cents.

A company's cash return on owner's equity measures how much net cash from operating activities the company generated with each dollar of owner's capital. Sweet Temptations' average owner's equity during January was $15,276. ([$15,000 owner's equity on January 1 + $15,552 owner's equity on January 31] divided by 2—see Exhibit 7-2.) Its cash return on owner's equity was 23.4 percent ($3,580 net cash flow from operating activities ÷ $15,276). This means that each dollar of Anna Cox's capital generated net cash from operating activities of 23.4 cents.

The two cash return ratios are used much the same as are the return on total assets and return on owner's equity ratios discussed in Chapter 7. These cash return ratios help managers and external users assess whether or not the company is generating enough cash from its operating activities.

### Cash Return Ratios of Actual Companies

The ratios used to evaluate the cash returns of JCPenney and Kohl's for the year ended January 28, 2006 were as follows:

| | *JCPenney* | *Kohl's* |
|---|---|---|
| Cash Return on Total Assets | 11.3% | 11.1% |
| Cash Return on Owners' Equity | 30.2% | 16.0% |

These ratios indicate that JCPenny generated slightly more cash for each dollar of assets and much more cash for each dollar of owners' equity than did Kohl's.

*In chapter 7, Kohl's return on total assets was higher than that of JCPenney. Why do you think JCPenney's cash return on total assets is higher than Kohl's?*

### Interrelationship of Financial Statements

In Chapters 6, 7, and 8 we introduced the major financial statements of a company and began to show how decision makers use the information in these financial statements. These decision makers understand the interrelationship between the various items on a company's financial statements. We show two examples in the following diagram.

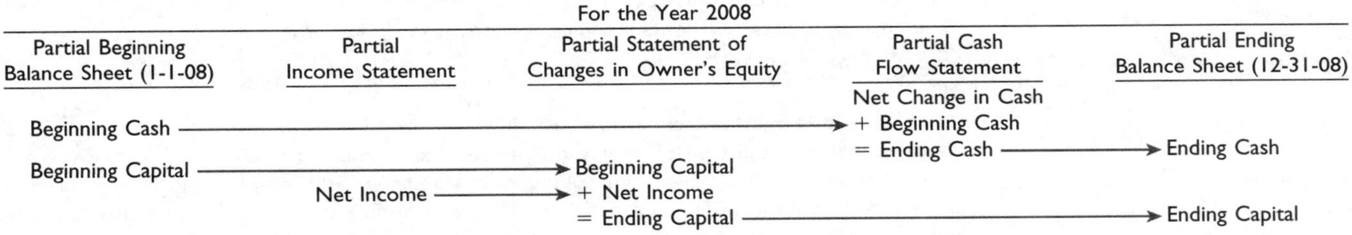


We have only scratched the surface regarding how managers, investors, and creditors use accounting information to make business decisions. In Chapter 9 we will discuss specific uses of accounting information for cash management, inventory control, and debt management, just to name a few topics.

## Business Issues and Values

As the end of an accounting period approaches, an entrepreneur may notice that unless something changes, the company's net cash flows for the period will not be as high as planned. In an effort to remedy this less-than-happy realization, the owner may postpone payments to the company's suppliers and employees. The effect is to reduce the cash payments from operations for the period and, therefore, to increase the company's net cash flows from operating activities. The company's operating cash flow margin, cash return on total assets, and cash return on owner's equity will all be higher than they would have been if the company had not postponed payments to suppliers and employees. But although this action may make the company "look better" in the short run, it has some negative effects. External users of the company's cash flow statement might think that the company is more liquid (and healthier) than it really is, perhaps leading them to make ill-informed decisions about the company. A more immediate effect is the reduced cash flows of the suppliers and employees. In deciding whether to take actions such as this, managers and owners must look "beyond the numbers" and consider all the "stakeholders" in the decision. In other words, managers must consider who will be affected by the different decision alternatives (in this case the company, the external users, the employees, and the suppliers, at a minimum) and how the alternatives will affect these people.

## SUMMARY

At the beginning of the chapter we asked you several questions. During the chapter, we asked you to STOP and answer some additional questions to build your knowledge about specific issues. Be sure you answered these additional questions. Below are the questions from the beginning of the chapter, with a brief summary of the key points relating to the answers. Use your creative and critical thinking skills to expand on these key points to develop more complete answers to the questions and to determine what other questions you have that might lead you to learn more about the issues.

### 1 Why is a company's cash flow statement important?

A company's cash flow statement is important because it summarizes the changes in the company's cash by listing the cash inflows and cash outflows from its operating, investing, and financing activities during an accounting period. This information cannot be obtained from the company's income statement or balance sheet. The information is useful to decision makers in evaluating the company's solvency and liquidity.

### 2 What are the types of transactions that may cause cash inflows and cash outflows for a company?

The types of transactions that may cause cash inflows (receipts) for a company are decreases in its assets other than cash, increases in its liabilities, and increases in its owner's equity. The types of transactions that may cause cash outflows (payments) for a company are increases in its assets other than cash, decreases in its liabilities, and decreases in its owner's equity.

### 3 What do users need to know about a company's cash flow statement?

Users need to know that a company's cash flow statement shows its cash inflows and cash outflows according to the type of activity that caused the increase or decrease in cash. There are three sections: the cash flows from operating activities, the cash flows from investing activities, and the cash flows from financing activities. The net cash flows from each section are summed, and the total increase (decrease) in cash is added to (subtracted from) the beginning cash balance to determine the ending cash balance.

### 4 How does a company report the cash flows from its operating activities on its cash flow statement under the direct method?

Under the direct method, a company reports its cash flows from operating activities in two parts: operating cash inflows and operating cash outflows. A company may report as many as three categories of operating cash inflows (e.g., collections from customers) and as many as four categories of operating cash outflows (e.g., payments to suppliers).

### 5 How do users combine the changes in a company's current assets and current liabilities with its revenues and expenses for the accounting period to determine the company's operating cash flows?

The change in accounts receivable is combined with the sales revenue to determine the collections from customers. The change in salaries payable is combined with the salaries expense to determine the payments to employees. The change in inventory and the change in accounts payable are combined with the cost of goods sold to determine the payments to suppliers.

### 6 Why do internal and external users study a company's cash flow statement in conjunction with its income statement and balance sheet?

Internal and external users study a company's cash flow statement in conjunction with its income statement and balance sheet to evaluate the company's liquidity and solvency, its ability to purchase property and equipment, and its cash flow returns.

### 7 What cash flow ratios are used to evaluate a company's performance?

The operating cash flow margin (net cash flow from operating activities divided by net sales) is used to evaluate a company's profitability (and liquidity). The cash return on total assets ([net cash flow from operating activities + interest paid] divided by average total assets) and the cash return on owner's equity (net cash flow from operating activities divided by average owner's equity) are used to evaluate a company's performance in relation to its available resources.

## KEY TERMS

**accrual accounting** *(p. 241)*
**cash flow returns** *(p. 246)*
**cash flow statement** *(p. 232)*
**direct method** *(p. 236)*
**financing activities** *(p. 235)*
**indirect method** *(p. 236)*
**investing activities** *(p. 235)*
**operating activities** *(p. 235)*
**operating cycle** *(p. 241)*

## APPENDIX

### Indirect Method for Reporting Cash Flows from Operating Activities

As we mentioned in the chapter, there are two methods of computing and reporting a company's cash flows from operating activities on its cash flow statement—the direct method and the indirect method. In the chapter, we discussed and illustrated the direct method because it is conceptually sound, easier to understand, and more closely follows how a company analyzes its forecasted operating cash flows in its cash budget. In this appendix, we explain the indirect method because it is the method that most companies use in the cash flow statements they present to external users.[1] Under the **indirect method**, a company determines its net cash provided by operating activities *indirectly* by converting its net income to operating cash flows. It does this by adding amounts to and subtracting amounts from its net income to compute its net cash flow from operating activities. We will discuss how a company does this later in this section. First, we need to briefly review a company's operating cycle.

In the chapter, we discussed how each part of a company's operating cycle affects both its net income and its operating cash flows. We explained that each may be affected differently, however, because of differences between when the company *records* revenues and expenses and when it *receives* or *pays* cash. We illustrated these differences as they related to changes in current assets (accounts receivable and inventory) and changes in current liabilities (accounts payable and salaries payable).

Also, changes in some noncurrent assets (property and equipment) affect the company's net income but do not result in an operating cash inflow or outflow. For instance, when the company records depreciation for equipment, it increases depreciation expense and decreases the equipment's book value. Although depreciation expense decreases net income (and a noncurrent asset), there is no operating cash outflow.

Since most companies use the indirect method in the cash flow statements they present to external users, you (as an external user) need to understand how the changes in each of a company's current assets and current liabilities, as well as its depreciation expense, affect its net cash flows from operating activities under this method. To help you understand the indirect method, we use an example that compares the direct method and the indirect method.

[1]Companies have the option of using either the direct method or the indirect method. However, if a company uses the direct method, it must provide much more additional information. As a result, most companies continue to use the indirect method.

## REVIEW OF DIRECT METHOD

As we discussed in the chapter, under the direct method a company subtracts its operating cash outflows from its operating cash inflows to determine the net cash provided by (or used in) operating activities. A company's operating cash inflows may include: (1) collections from customers, (2) collections of interest, and (3) other operating receipts. The operating cash outflows may include: (1) payments to suppliers, (2) payments to employees, (3) payments of interest, and (4) other operating payments[2]. A company computes its operating cash inflows and operating cash outflows based on an analysis like the one we used in Exhibit 8-9. To understand this method, suppose that Frank's Cookies, a retail company, shows the following income statement information for the current year:

| | | |
|---|---|---|
| Sales | | $360,000 |
| Cost of goods sold | | (150,000) |
| Gross profit | | $210,000 |
| Operating expenses | | |
| Salaries expense | $70,000 | |
| Depreciation expense | 30,000 | |
| Other operating expenses | 56,000 | |
| Total operating expenses | | (156,000) |
| Net income | | $ 54,000 |

A comparison of the company's balance sheets at the beginning of the year and the end of the year show the following changes in its current assets and current liabilities:

Accounts receivable decreased by $15,000
Inventory increased by $20,000
Accounts payable increased by $13,000
Salaries payable decreased by $4,000

Under the direct method, Frank's Cookies reports its cash flows from operating activities on the cash flow statement as follows:

| | | |
|---|---|---|
| *Cash Flows from Operating Activities:* | | |
| Cash Inflows: | | |
| Collections from customers | $ 375,000 | |
| Cash inflows from operating activities | | $375,000 |
| Cash Outflows: | | |
| Payments to suppliers | $(157,000) | |
| Payments to employees | (74,000) | |
| Other operating payments | (56,000) | |
| Cash outflows for operating activities | | (287,000) |
| Net cash provided by operating activities | | $ 88,000 |

Next we provide a schedule that shows how Frank's Cookies calculated each of the preceding amounts, followed by an explanation of each calculation.

| Income Statement Amount | | | Balance Sheet Change | | | Cash Flow |
|---|---|---|---|---|---|---|
| Sales revenue | $360,000 | + | Decrease in accounts receivable | $15,000 | = | $375,000 |
| Cost of goods sold | (150,000) | + | Increase in inventory | (20,000) | | |
| | | − | Increase in accounts payable | 13,000 | = | (157,000) |
| Salaries expense | (70,000) | + | Decrease in salaries payable | (4,000) | = | (74,000) |
| Depreciation expense | (30,000) | | Not included | | | |
| Other operating payments | (56,000) | | No change | | | (56,000) |
| Income flow | $ 54,000 | | Operating cash flow | | | $ 88,000 |

Because accounts receivable *decreased* between the beginning and the end of the year, we know that the company's cash collections this year were *more* than its sales revenue. So, part of

[2]If a company is a corporation, it also reports its payments of income taxes (under both the direct and indirect methods) as we discuss in Chapter 22.

the cash collected from customers was for sales the company made to them *last* year. Therefore, we compute the $375,000 cash received from customers by adding the decrease in accounts receivable ($15,000) to this year's sales revenue ($360,000). This is the only cash receipt, so that the cash inflows from operating activities were $375,000.

Because inventory *increased* between the beginning and the end of the year, we know that the company purchased *more* inventory than it sold. Therefore, we compute the purchases of $170,000 by adding the increase in inventory ($20,000) to the cost of goods sold ($150,000). Because accounts payable *increased* between the beginning and the end of the year, we know that the company paid for *less* inventory than it purchased. Therefore, we compute the $157,000 cash paid to suppliers by subtracting the increase in accounts payable ($13,000) from the purchases ($170,000). Because salaries payable *decreased* between the beginning and the end of the year, we know that the company paid its employees *more* than they earned this year (and more than the company recorded as an expense). In other words, part of the payments to employees was for work they did *last* year. Therefore, we compute the $74,000 cash paid to employees by adding the decrease in salaries payable ($4,000) to the salaries expense ($70,000).

For simplicity, we assume that all of the $56,000 other operating expenses were paid in cash. So, the $375,000 cash inflows from operating activities less the $287,000 cash outflows for operating activities ($157,000 payments to suppliers + $74,000 payments to employees + $56,000 other operating payments) results in $88,000 net cash provided by operating activities of Frank's Cookies for the current year. Note that the $30,000 depreciation expense is *not* included because it did not involve a cash flow. Note also that we did not introduce any new concepts here. We just used summary amounts from Frank's Cookies' income statement and balance sheet (which were provided to external users), rather than having internal information about transactions.

The direct method has the advantages of being easy to understand and similar to the upper part of the cash budget that we discussed in Chapter 4. External users have criticized the method, however, because it does not "tie" the net income that a company reports on its income statement to the net cash provided by operating activities that the company reports on its cash flow statement. Also, the direct method does not show how the changes in the parts (i.e., current assets and current liabilities) of a company's operating cycle affected its operating cash flows.

## ILLUSTRATION OF INDIRECT METHOD

When a company uses the indirect method to report the net cash provided by operating activities on its cash flow statement, the two criticisms of the direct method are resolved. Under the indirect method, a company adjusts its net income to the net cash provided by operating activities. To do this, it lists net income first and then makes adjustments (additions or subtractions) to the net income (1) to include any changes in the current assets (other than cash) and current liabilities involved in the company's operating cycle that affected cash flows differently than they affected net income, and (2) to eliminate amounts that were included in its net income but that did not involve an operating cash flow. In other words, under the indirect method, a company's income flows are converted from an *accrual* basis to a *cash* basis.

*Would you expect that a typical company's net cash flow from operating activities would be greater or less than its net income? Explain your answer.*

We use Frank's Cookies' income statement and balance sheet information, shown earlier, to illustrate the indirect method. The company reports its net cash flow from operating activities under the indirect method on its cash flow statement as follows:

| | |
|---|---|
| *Cash Flows from Operating Activities* | |
| Net income | $54,000 |
| Adjustments for differences between net income and cash flows from operating activities: | |
| Add: Decrease in accounts receivable | 15,000 |
| Increase in accounts payable | 13,000 |
| Depreciation expense | 30,000 |
| Less: Increase in inventory | (20,000) |
| Decrease in salaries payable | (4,000) |
| Net cash provided by operating activities | $88,000 |

First, note that the net cash provided by operating activities ($88,000) is the same under both the direct and the indirect methods. Now, why did we make each adjustment to convert net income to the net cash provided by operating activities? We will discuss these adjustments as they relate to sales revenue, cost of goods sold, expenses, and noncash items. First, as we discussed earlier, since accounts receivable decreased by $15,000, we know that the company's cash collections were more than its sales revenue, so it must have collected some accounts receivable related to sales from the previous period. Since the current sales of $360,000 are lower than the amount of cash that the company collected, its net income of $54,000 is lower than it would have been if the company had counted the amount of cash it collected this period from sales of the previous period. Therefore, we add the $15,000 decrease in accounts receivable to net income as one step in computing the net cash provided by operating activities. Also note that adding the decrease in accounts receivable to sales revenue (the direct method) has the same effect as adding the decrease to net income (the indirect method).

Next, because inventory increased by $20,000, we know that the company purchased more inventory than it sold. So the cost of goods sold is not the same as the amount of inventory that the company purchased. Since the cost of goods sold is subtracted from sales in computing income, we *subtract* the increase in inventory from the net income to show the additional outflow from purchasing more inventory. However, because accounts payable increased by $13,000, we know that the company paid for less inventory than it purchased. Therefore, we *add* the increase in accounts payable to net income to compute the net cash inflow. Remember that a *lower* cash *outflow* means that the *net* cash *inflow* is *higher*. Also note that (1) adding the increase in inventory to cost of goods sold (the direct method) has the same effect as subtracting the increase from net income (the indirect method), and (2) subtracting the increase in accounts payable from purchases (the direct method) has the same effect as adding the increase to net income (the indirect method).

*Does this make sense? Why does adding the increase in inventory to cost of goods sold have the same effect as subtracting the increase from net income?*

Because salaries payable decreased by $4,000, we know that the company paid its employees more than it recorded as an expense, so we subtract the decrease in salaries payable from net income to compute the net cash inflow. Note that adding the decrease in salaries payable to salaries expense (the direct method) has the same effect as subtracting the decrease from net income (the indirect method).

*Explain how to adjust net income for an increase in salaries payable.*

Since all of the company's other operating expenses were paid in cash, it does not have any changes in other current assets (such as prepaid rent) or other current liabilities (such as interest payable). If it did have changes in these accounts, we would also need to adjust net income for these changes.

Next, we add the $30,000 depreciation expense to the net income because it was subtracted to determine net income but there was no cash outflow. Thus, by making these adjustments, we converted Frank's Cookies' $54,000 net income to its $88,000 net cash provided by operating activities. To help you understand the effect of various items on the net cash provided by operating activities under the indirect method, we show the common adjustments[3] to net income in Exhibit 8-11.

*If a company uses the indirect method in its cash flow statement, would you be able to compute its operating cash flows under the direct method?*

## Steps to Complete under the Indirect Method

Based on the previous example, we can identify six steps that a company completes under the indirect method to compute the net cash provided by operating activities that it reports on its cash flow statement:

[3]We will discuss other less common or more complex adjustments as they apply to specific topics in later chapters.

**EXHIBIT 8-11** **ADJUSTMENTS TO CONVERT NET INCOME TO NET CASH PROVIDED BY OPERATING ACTIVITIES**

Net Income

Plus

Decrease in accounts receivable
Decrease in inventory
Decreases in other current assets related to operating activities
Increase in accounts payable
Increase in salaries payable
Increases in other current liabilities related to operating activities
Depreciation expense

Minus

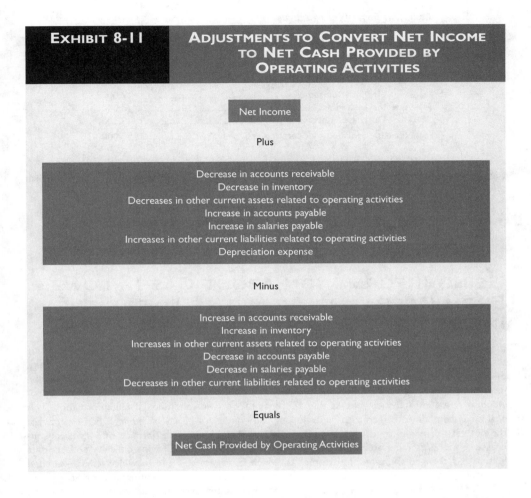

Increase in accounts receivable
Increase in inventory
Increases in other current assets related to operating activities
Decrease in accounts payable
Decrease in salaries payable
Decreases in other current liabilities related to operating activities

Equals

Net Cash Provided by Operating Activities

1. Compute the increase or decrease during the year in each current asset and current liability account
2. List the company's net income first in the cash flows from operating activities section
3. *Add* the *decrease* in each current *asset* and the *increase* in each current *liability* to the net income
4. *Subtract* the *increase* in each current *asset* and the *decrease* in each current *liability* from the net income
5. *Add* the depreciation *expense* on the company's property and equipment assets to the net income
6. Compute the net cash provided by (or used in) operating activities

To illustrate, we assume that Symes Syrup Company earned net income of $36,000 for 2008. It included depreciation expense of $17,000 in the operating expenses deducted from sales revenue to determine this net income. Step 1 involves determining the changes in the current assets and current liabilities. A review of the 2008 ending and beginning balance sheets for Symes Syrup Company shows the following current assets and current liabilities:

| | **Balances** | | **Changes** |
|---|---|---|---|
| **Accounts** | **12/31/2008** | **12/31/2007** | **(Step 1)** |
| Accounts receivable | $14,000 | $10,000 | $4,000 |
| Inventory | 20,000 | 28,500 | (8,500) |
| Accounts payable | 11,500 | 21,000 | (9,500) |
| Salaries payable | 6,000 | 4,000 | 2,000 |

Based on this information, the cash flows from operating activities section of Symes Syrup Company's 2008 cash flow statement follows (Steps 2–6 are listed in parentheses before the items):

| | |
|---|---|
| *Cash Flows from Operating Activities* | |
| (2) Net income | $36,000 |
| Adjustments for differences between net income and cash flows from operating activities: | |
| (3) Add: Decrease in inventory | 8,500 |
| Increase in salaries payable | 2,000 |
| (5) Depreciation expense | 17,000 |
| (4) Less: Increase in accounts receivable | (4,000) |
| Decrease in accounts payable | (9,500) |
| (6) Net cash provided by operating activities | $50,000 |

Symes Syrup Company would include this section with the cash flows from investing activities and the cash flows from financing activities sections (not discussed here) to complete its cash flow statement for 2008.

*If a company uses the direct method in its cash flow statement, would you be able to compute its operating cash flows under the indirect method?*

# Using Information about Cash Flows From Operating Activities Under the Indirect Method

If a company reports its net cash flows from operating activities on its cash flow statement using the indirect method, an external user can calculate the ratios we discussed in the chapter (e.g., operating cash flow margin) to evaluate the company's performance. In addition, a user may be interested in looking at the difference between the company's net income and its net cash provided by operating activities because this difference may provide additional useful information. This analysis is sometimes referred to as evaluating the company's *quality of earnings*. For example, if the net cash provided by operating activities is less than net income because of a significant increase in accounts receivable, this may indicate that the company is having difficulty collecting its bills or has changed the type of customer to which it makes sales and to which it has extended its credit terms. As another example, if the net cash provided by operating activities is greater than net income because of a significant increase in accounts payable, this may indicate that the company is having difficulty paying its bills, or is delaying payment so much that it may damage its relationships with its suppliers.

Since a company may use either the direct or the indirect method to report its net cash provided by operating activities, a user may have difficulty comparing two companies that use different methods. Fortunately, when a company uses the direct method, it must also disclose the results of the indirect method in the notes to its financial statements. When a company uses the indirect method, it must disclose its payments for interest. However, the company has no obligation to report the other operating cash inflows or outflows. Many users find the direct method easier to understand. So when a company uses the indirect method, a user may want to compute the cash flows under the direct method, using the logic that we discussed earlier in the chapter.

## Summary Surfing

Here is an opportunity to gather information on the Internet about real-world issues related to the topics in this chapter (for suggestions on how to navigate various companies' Web sites to find their financial statements and other information, see the related discussion in the Preface at the beginning of the book). Answer the following questions.

- Go to the **EMC Corporation** Web site. What kinds of services does EMC provide its customers? Find EMC's statements of cash flows. How much cash did EMC receive from customers for the most current year? How much cash did EMC pay to suppliers and employees during the most current year? Find EMC's balance sheets. What is EMC's cash return on owners' (stockholders') equity for the most current year?

- Go to the **Tech Data Corporation** Web site. What kinds of products and services does Tech Data Corp. provide and where does it do business? Find Tech Data Corp.'s statement of cash flows. How much cash did the company receive from customers during the most current year? How much cash did the company pay to its suppliers and employees for the current year? How does the company's net cash provided by operating activities for the current year compare to the previous year? Find the company's balance sheets. What was the company's cash return on total assets for the most current year?

# INTEGRATED BUSINESS AND ACCOUNTING SITUATIONS

**Answer the Following Questions in Your Own Words.**

## Testing Your Knowledge

**8-1** What is a cash flow statement, and what types of questions can a user answer by studying a company's cash flow statement?

**8-2** Write out a cash flow equation that links the beginning and the ending cash balances.

**8-3** What three types of transactions related to balance sheet items may cause cash inflows? Give an example of each.

**8-4** What three types of transactions related to balance sheet items may cause cash outflows? Give an example of each.

**8-5** Identify the three sections of a company's cash flow statement, and briefly explain what is included in each section.

**8-6** How is the net cash provided by operating activities determined under the direct method?

**8-7** What are the three categories of operating cash inflows under the direct method?

**8-8** What are the four categories of operating cash outflows under the direct method?

**8-9** Describe how to compute a company's collections from customers during an accounting period, based on an analysis of its income statement and its beginning and ending balance sheets.

**8-10** Describe how to compute a company's payments to employees during an accounting period, based on an analysis of its income statement and its beginning and ending balance sheets.

**8-11** Describe how to compute a company's payments to suppliers during an accounting period, based on an analysis of its income statement and its beginning and ending balance sheets.

**8-12** How is the operating cash flow margin of a company computed, and what does it describe?

**8-13** How is the cash return on total assets of a company computed, and what does it measure?

**8-14** How is the cash return on owner's equity of a company computed, and what does it measure?

**8-15** (Appendix) How does a company determine its net cash provided by operating activities under the indirect method?

**8-16** (Appendix) Identify the steps a company completes under the indirect method to compute its net cash provided by operating activities.

## Applying Your Knowledge

**8-17** The following are several transactions and activities of a company:
(a) Receipt from sale of building
(b) Withdrawal by owner
(c) Decrease in accounts receivable
(d) Payment for purchase of investment
(e) Receipt from issuance of long-term note payable
(f) Payment for purchase of inventory

*Required:* Indicate in which section of the company's cash flow statement each of the preceding items would appear. Also indicate whether each would be an inflow or an outflow.

**8-18** The following are several transactions and activities of a company:
(a) Cash sales
(b) Decrease in accounts payable
(c) Payment for purchase of equipment
(d) Investment by owner
(e) Payment of long-term note payable
(f) Receipt from selling investment

*Required:* Indicate in which section of the company's cash flow statement each of the preceding items would appear. Also indicate whether each would be an inflow or an outflow.

**8-19** The following is selected information taken from the Cash account of the Wilson Book Company for May:
(a) Cash sales, $10,000
(b) Payment of interest, $600
(c) Payment for inventory, $1,000
(d) Collection of accounts receivable, $2,000
(e) Payments to employees, $5,000
(f) Collection of interest, $500

*Required:* Using the direct method, prepare the cash flows from operating activities section of the Wilson Book Company's cash flow statement for May.

**8-20** Rocky Shoe Company has the following information in its Cash account for August:
(a) Paid employees, $4,500
(b) Paid suppliers, $2,000
(c) Made cash sales of $11,000
(d) Collected $800 interest
(e) Paid $500 interest
(f) Collected $5,000 of accounts receivable

*Required:* Using the direct method, prepare the cash flows from operating activities section of Rocky Shoe Company's cash flow statement for August.

**8-21** The following is a list of items to be included in the cash flow statement of the Brockman Lawn Sprinklers Company for the current year:
(a) Payment for purchase of trenching equipment, $6,000
(b) Payments to suppliers, $3,200
(c) Receipt from sale of land, $1,000
(d) Collections from customers, $15,800
(e) Withdrawals by owner, $2,500
(f) Receipt from issuance of note payable, $4,000
(g) Payments to employees, $5,600
(h) Beginning cash balance, $1,200

*Required:* (1) Prepare the company's cash flow statement.
(2) If net sales were $69,000, compute the company's operating cash flow margin.

**8-22** The items to be included in the Garcia Hardware Company's cash flow statement for the current year are as follows:

(a) Investment by owner, $3,000
(b) Payments to employees, $8,100
(c) Receipt from sale of investments, $1,300
(d) Ending cash balance, $7,300
(e) Payments for inventory, $6,000
(f) Cash collected from customers, $17,400
(g) Withdrawals by owner, $1,800
(h) Payment for purchase of warehouse, $9,200
(i) Payment of interest, $500

*Required:* (1) Prepare the company's cash flow statement.
(2) If the average owner's equity was $15,500, compute the company's cash return on owner's equity. What is your evaluation if last year the company's cash return was 17.2%?

**8-23** An analysis of the Toney Company's Cash account for September shows the following entries:

(a) Beginning cash balance, $800
(b) Collections from customers, $21,500
(c) Payment for purchase of storage shed, $9,500
(d) Investment by owner, $5,000
(e) Payment to suppliers, $12,800
(f) Collection of interest, $600
(g) Receipt from sale of equipment, $2,100
(h) Payments of employees' salaries, $4,500
(i) Payment of interest on loan, $700
(j) Ending cash balance, $2,500

*Required:* Prepare the company's cash flow statement for September.

**8-24** The Leone Company's Cash account shows the following entries for June:

(a) Beginning cash balance, $400
(b) Receipt from issuance of note, $10,000
(c) Payment of interest on loan, $900
(d) Payment for purchase of sales fixtures, $1,800
(e) Collections from customers, $33,400
(f) Owner withdrawal, $4,000
(g) Payment of employees' wages, $7,000
(h) Payment for delivery van, $12,000
(i) Payments to suppliers, $16,200
(j) Ending cash balance, $1,900

*Required:* Prepare the company's cash flow statement for June.

**8-25** Among other items, the Kelly Company's income statement for the year shows sales revenue of $78,000, cost of goods sold of $46,300, and salaries expense of $21,200. An analysis of its beginning and ending balance sheets for the year shows an increase in accounts receivable of $2,900, a decrease in inventory of $7,100, a decrease in accounts payable of $5,600, and a decrease in salaries payable of $2,800.

*Required:* Determine the company's collections from customers, payments to suppliers, and payments to employees for the year.

**8-26** While reviewing the Taber Company's income statement for the year, you find that it had sales of $81,500, cost of goods sold of $50,000, and wages expense of $30,200. A review of its beginning and ending balance sheets shows a decrease in accounts receivable of $3,400, an increase in inventory of $4,500, an increase in wages payable of $3,300, and an increase in accounts payable of $7,800.

*Required:* Determine the company's collections from customers, payments to suppliers, and payments to employees for the year.

**8-27** Frey Company's 2008 cash flow statement, as developed by its bookkeeper, is as follows:

**FREY COMPANY**
***Cash Flow Statement***
***December 31, 2008***

| | | |
|---|---|---|
| Cash Inflows: | | |
| Receipt from sale of equipment | $ 1,500 | |
| Collections from customers | 50,800 | |
| Receipt from issuance of note payable | 5,900 | |
| Total inflows | | $58,200 |
| Cash Outflows: | | |
| Payments to employees | $24,300 | |
| Withdrawals by owner | 5,000 | |
| Payment to purchase land | 8,000 | |
| Payments to suppliers | 19,400 | |
| Total outflows | | 56,700 |
| Increase in Cash | | $ 1,500 |
| Cash, January 1, 2008 | | 4,400 |
| Cash, December 31, 2008 | | $ 5,900 |

You determine that the *amounts* of the items listed on the statement are correct but are incorrectly classified.

*Required:* Prepare a correct 2008 cash flow statement for Frey Company.

**8-28** The cash flow statement information of the Fairview Flowers Shop for 2008 is as follows:

| | |
|---|---|
| Net cash provided by operating activities | $18,000 |
| Cash, January 1, 2008 | 8,500 |
| Receipt from sale of equipment | 6,400 |
| Owner withdrawals | 25,000 |
| Net cash used for investing activities | (a) |
| Cash paid to employees | 9,200 |
| Cash, December 31, 2008 | (b) |
| Cash received from customers | 44,300 |
| Receipt from issuance of note payable | (c) |
| Net cash used for financing activities | 5,000 |
| Cash paid to suppliers | (d) |
| Payment to purchase building | 23,000 |
| Net decrease in cash | (e) |

*Required:* Fill in the blanks lettered (a) through (e). All the necessary information is listed. (*Hint:* It is not necessary to calculate your answers in alphabetical order.)

**8-29** The cash flow statement information of the Bray Tire Company for 2008 is as follows:

| | |
|---|---|
| Net increase in cash | $ (a) |
| Cash received from customers | 60,200 |
| Receipt from sale of land | 5,000 |
| Cash, January 1, 2008 | (b) |
| Net cash used for investing activities | 7,800 |
| Cash paid to suppliers | 25,900 |
| Net cash provided by operating activities | (c) |
| Cash, December 31, 2008 | 11,000 |
| Payment to purchase equipment | (d) |
| Cash paid to employees | 19,100 |
| Net cash used for financing activities | (e) |
| Receipt from issuance of note payable | 10,000 |
| Owner withdrawals | 16,000 |

*Required:* Fill in the blanks labeled (a) through (e). All the necessary information is listed. (*Hint:* It is not necessary to calculate your answers in alphabetical order.)

**8-30** Welch Raskits Company has asked for your assistance in preparing its cash flow statement for 2008. Among other items, its 2008 income statement shows sales revenue (net) of $67,500, cost of goods sold of $36,000, and salaries expense of $18,400. You analyze its 2008 beginning and ending balance sheets and find a beginning cash balance of $8,100, an increase in accounts receivable of $6,800, an increase in inventory of $2,200, an increase in accounts payable of $4,600, and a decrease in salaries payable of $2,100. Further investigation shows that the owner withdrew $12,000 and that the company sold land for $5,500, issued a note payable for $8,000, and purchased a van for $14,800.

*Required:* (1) Using your findings, prepare the company's 2008 cash flow statement.
(2) Compute the company's 2008 operating cash flow margin. If the company's operating cash flow margin was 10.1% in 2007, what is your evaluation of the company's liquidity in 2008?

**8-31** You have been hired by Seeser Flappits Company to prepare its 2008 cash flow statement. The company provides you with its 2008 income statement as follows:

| | | |
|---|---|---|
| Sales (net) | | $56,600 |
| Cost of goods sold | | (31,400) |
| Gross profit | | $25,200 |
| Salaries expense | $19,200 | |
| Depreciation expense | 2,800 | |
| Other expenses (all cash) | 1,000 | |
| Total operating expenses | | (23,000) |
| Net Income | | $ 2,200 |

You determine that these numbers are correct. You review the company's 2008 beginning and ending balance sheets and find that the cash balance was $1,900 on January 1, 2008, and $5,100 on December 31, 2008. In addition, you find the following changes:

| | |
|---|---|
| Accounts receivable | $4,200 decrease |
| Inventory | 5,600 decrease |
| Accounts payable | 2,500 decrease |
| Salaries payable | 1,200 increase |

Furthermore, you determine that during 2008, the company sold equipment for $4,800, purchased land for $13,000, and issued a note payable for $7,500, all for cash. The owner also withdrew $9,600. After all these changes, the company had average total assets of $74,000 for 2008.

*Required:* (1) Using your findings, prepare the company's 2008 cash flow statement (use the direct method for operating cash flows).
(2) Compute the company's 2008 cash return on total assets.

**8-32** In 2008, Franklin Fibers Company had net cash provided by operating activities of $9,400. A review of its 2008 financial statements shows that the company had net income of $9,000, average total assets of $93,800, and average owner's equity of $50,000. Included in the net income were sales (net) of $77,000 and interest expense (all cash) of $600.

*Required:* Using the preceding information, for 2008 compute the company's (1) operating cash flow margin, (2) cash return on total assets, and (3) cash return on owner's equity.

**8-33** Nibbets Baskets Company had net cash provided by operating activities of $4,300 for 2008. The company's income statement showed sales (net) of $40,000, interest expense of $400, and net income of $4,000. Its 2008 beginning balance sheet listed total assets of $42,000 and owner's equity of $18,000, and its 2008 ending balance sheet listed total assets of $48,000 and owner's equity of $22,000. Interest payable decreased by $100 during the year.

*Required:* Using the preceding information, compute the company's (1) operating cash flow margin, (2) profit margin, (3) cash return on total assets, (4) return on total assets, (5) cash return on owner's equity, and (6) return on owner's equity.

**8-34** (Appendix) The following information is taken from the accounting records of Tilder Company for the current year:

Net income, $17,000
Increase in inventory, $4,600
Decrease in accounts receivable, $8,500
Depreciation expense, $10,000
Decrease in salaries payable, $1,000
Increase in accounts payable, $6,200

*Required:* Using the indirect method, prepare the cash flows from operating activities section of Tilder's cash flow statement for the current year.

**8-35** (Appendix) In the current year, Faldo Company earned net income of $61,000. Included in the computation of net income was $12,500 of depreciation expense. During the year, the company had the following changes in its current assets and current liabilities:

| Increases | Decreases |
|---|---|
| Accounts receivable, $5,700 | Inventory, $7,400 |
| Salaries payable, $3,000 | Accounts payable, $9,600 |

*Required:* (1) Using the indirect method, prepare the cash flows from operating activities section of Faldo's cash flow statement for the current year.
(2) What does your answer to (1) reveal compared with Faldo's net income?

**8-36** (Appendix) During the current year, Woods Company earned net income of $56,000. Depreciation expense of $11,000 was included in the computation of net income. Woods' accounting records show the following beginning and ending balances in its current assets and current liabilities for the year:

| Account | Ending Balance | Beginning Balance |
|---|---|---|
| Accounts receivable | $56,700 | $37,200 |
| Inventory | 34,400 | 43,100 |
| Prepaid rent | 2,000 | 0 |
| Accounts payable | 25,600 | 33,000 |
| Salaries payable | 1,300 | 0 |

*Required:* (1) Using the indirect method, prepare the cash flows from operating activities section of Woods' cash flow statement for the current year.
(2) What does your answer to (1) reveal compared with the company's net income?

## Making Evaluations

**8-37** Now that you have begun studying accounting, it seems as though *everyone* is coming to you for advice. Just yesterday, your mother's friend Juanita asked you to explain the following sentences that appear in the notes to recent financial statements of **Dillard Department Stores**: "[This year], the Company generated $299.1 million in cash from operating activities, as compared to $395.3 million [last year] and $314.5 million [the year before that]. The primary reason for the decrease [this year] was an increase in merchandise inventories." Since you didn't have time to explain it then (or to get your thoughts together), you asked Juanita if you could mail her an explanation.

*Required:* Write Juanita that note, being careful to use language that she can understand (since she has never had an accounting course).

**8-38** The owner of Roadkill Recycling Company (a company that publishes "kitchen-tested" recipes) has come to your bank for a loan. He states, "In each of the last two years our cash has gone down. This year we need to increase our cash by $8,000 so that we have a $20,000 cash balance at year end. We have never borrowed any money on a long-term basis and are reluctant to do so. However, we definitely need to purchase some new, more advanced equipment to replace the old equipment we are selling this year. We also want to invest in the stock market. Given our expected net income and the money we will receive from our depreciation expense, I estimate we will have to borrow $11,000, based on the following schedule."

*Schedule of Cash Flows for the Year 2009*

| | | |
|---|---|---|
| Inflows of cash: | | |
| Collections from customers | | $ 35,000 |
| Collections of interest | | 2,000 |
| Other operating receipts | | 4,000 |
| Receipt from sale of old equipment | | 8,000 |
| Depreciation expense | | 6,000 |
| Bank loan (estimated) | | 11,000 |
| Total inflows | | $ 66,000 |
| Outflows of cash: | | |
| Purchase of equipment | $(20,000) | |
| Salaries | (28,000) | |
| Other operating payments | (3,000) | |
| Payments to suppliers | (7,000) | |
| Total outflows | | (58,000) |
| Increase in Cash | | $ 8,000 |

The owner explains that the company will purchase $5,000 of office furniture from him. The payment of $5,000 from the company to him for the office equipment was not included in the schedule of cash flows because it would involve only a transaction between the company and him and would be of no interest to "outsiders." The owner also states that if his figures are "off a little bit," the most the company wants to borrow is $16,000. You determine that the amounts he has listed for each item are correct, except the bank loan.

*Required:* (1) Prepare a projected cash flow statement (using the direct method for operating cash flows) that shows the necessary bank loan for Roadkill Recycling Company to increase cash by $8,000.
(2) Explain to the owner why his $11,000 estimate of the bank loan is incorrect.
(3) Suggest ways to reduce the necessary bank loan and still increase cash.
(4) Make a list of questions you would like the owner to answer before you decide whether or not to make a loan to Roadkill Recycling Company.

**8-39** Your friend Basil Nutt has come to you for advice. He says, "I don't understand it. My company, Nutts and More, had a net income of $4,300 in 2008, so I expected the balance in the company's cash account to go up. But the cash went down from $8,000 to $800! The company is almost broke, and it didn't buy any equipment, and I didn't make any withdrawals. The company used its cash only for operating activities. Help me figure out what is going on."

You study the company's accounting records and find that it prepared an income statement and a balance sheet. The company's 2008 income statement is as follows:

| | | |
|---|---|---|
| Sales | | $72,300 |
| Cost of goods sold | | (40,000) |
| Gross profit | | $32,300 |
| Salaries expense | $18,000 | |
| Depreciation expense | 4,100 | |
| Other expenses (all cash) | 5,900 | |
| Total operating expenses | | (28,000) |
| Net Income | | $ 4,300 |

You determine that the income statement is correct. You also find that during 2008, the company's accounts receivable increased by $6,300, its inventory increased by $7,300, its accounts payable decreased by $3,000, and its salaries payable increased by $1,000.

*Required:* Prepare for Basil Nutt a report (using the direct method) that explains why his company's cash decreased during 2008.

**8-40** The following are pairs of ratios related to the income statement, the cash flow statement, and the balance sheet:

| | | |
|---|---|---|
| (1) Profit Margin | *and* | Operating Cash Flow Margin |
| (2) Return on Total Assets | *and* | Cash Return on Total Assets |
| (3) Return on Owner's Equity | *and* | Cash Return on Owner's Equity |

*Required:* For each of the preceding pairs of ratios, explain the similarities and the differences between the two ratios in the pair. In your discussion, be sure to include an explanation of the *interpretation* of each ratio.

**8-41** Suppose, at a party last weekend, your friend LaQuinta mentioned to you, in confidence, that her company was in the middle of a big scandal. It seems that the company needed a loan in order to enter into a top-secret marketing effort. In preparing the financial statements necessary for securing the loan, the company's bookkeeper noticed that cash flows from operations had been declining over the past five years, although total cash flows had been increasing. Apparently afraid that the bank would turn down the company's request for a loan if it saw the company's decreasing trend in cash flows from operations, he decided to reclassify cash receipts from the sale of equipment as collections from customers.

*Required:* (1) What do you think the bookkeeper hoped to accomplish by making the reclassification?
(2) Who do you think might be affected by this decision, and how might they be affected?
(3) If you were the company's owner, how would you have reacted to the bookkeeper's "help"?

**8-42** On January 1, 2008, Paula Randolph opened a boutique called P.R.'s Boutique. At that time she deposited $30,000 cash in the company's checking account. Paula then immediately wrote company checks to purchase $7,000 of inventory and $16,000 of store equipment, and to pay two years' rent in advance for store space. Paula estimated that the store equipment would last ten years and would then be worthless. During the year, the boutique appeared to operate successfully. Paula did not know anything about accounting, although she did keep an accurate company checkbook. The company checkbook showed the following summarized items on December 31, 2008:

| | |
|---|---|
| Payment for store equipment | $16,000 |
| Payment for two years' rent of store space | 2,400 |
| Payments for purchases of inventory* | 23,000 |
| Receipts from cash sales | 39,000 |
| Payments for operating expenses | 12,000 |
| Withdrawals of cash for personal use | 11,000 |

*Including $7,000 beginning inventory

On December 31, 2008, Paula asks for your assistance. She says, "The ending cash balance in the company checkbook is $4,600. Since my initial investment was $30,000, the company seems to have had a net loss of $25,400. Something must be wrong. I am sure the company did better than that. Please find out what the company's earnings were for 2008, why the cash went down so much during 2008, and what its financial position is at the end of 2008. Also, for what the company sold in 2008, how does its profit percentage compare with its operating cash intake percentage?"

You agree to help Paula. She tells you that the company used a periodic inventory system during 2008, that she has just finished "taking inventory," and that the cost of the 2008 ending inventory is $9,000. She has kept copies of invoices made out to customers who purchased merchandise on credit. These uncollected invoices total $12,000. Paula also has a file of unpaid invoices from suppliers for purchases of inventory. These unpaid invoices add up to $8,000. Just as you begin your calculations, Paula says, "Oh yes, $10,000 of the payments for operating expenses were employees' salaries. I also owe my employees $700 of salaries that they have earned this week."

*Required:* (1) Prepare a 2008 income statement, a 2008 cash flow statement (using the direct method for operating activities), and a December 31, 2008 balance sheet for P.R.'s Boutique. Include explanations for all amounts shown.

(2) Answer Paula's question about the comparison of the "profit percentage" with the "operating cash intake percentage."

**8-43** Jay Ryan owns "Jay's Skateboard Shop," which he opened on April 1, 2008. At that time Jay invested $20,000 cash into the company. With this money, the shop immediately purchased store equipment for $8,000. Jay estimated that this equipment would last ten years and would have no value after that time. The shop also purchased $6,000 of inventory for cash and paid $1,800 for one year of store rent in advance. During the year, the shop was open for business six days a week. Over the nine-month period in 2008, Jay withdrew $1,000 per month for his personal expenses. He used a periodic inventory system, employed one part-time helper, and paid the shop's bills by company check. For most of the year the shop made only cash sales and paid for purchases before the goods were shipped from the shop's supplier. However, near the end of the year the shop began to sell items on credit to a few "responsible customers." Jay kept a small notebook of the amounts of these credit sales. They totaled $3,000 at the end of 2008, and none had been collected yet. Because the shop was such a good customer, its suppliers allowed the shop to purchase $4,000 of inventory on credit near the end of 2008. The shop had not yet paid for these purchases at the end of 2008. At the end of 2008, Jay wanted to know how well the shop was doing, so he prepared the following "income statement."

*Income Statement for 2008*

| | | |
|---|---|---|
| Cash receipts: | | |
| Cash sales | | $ 36,000 |
| Cash payments: | | |
| Salary to part-time help | $ 3,200 | |
| Cash purchases of inventory | 20,000 | |
| Rent expense | 1,800 | |
| Utilities expense | 1,300 | |
| Withdrawals | 9,000 | (35,300) |
| Net Income | | $ 700 |

Jay did not feel comfortable with this information and came to you, a small-business consultant, for help. He said, "The shop shows net income of $700, but there is $12,700 in the company's checking account, so cash went down by $7,300. I don't understand. I just "took inventory," and it amounts to $5,000 (including the credit purchases), but the shop owes $400 of salary to my employee. I want to know how much the shop earned in 2008, what were its cash flows in 2008, and where the shop stands financially at the end of 2008. I also am interested in the return ratios on my investment in the company over the last nine months. Finally, I need a recommendation about my accounting system. Please prepare a report for me that answers these questions."

*Required:* Prepare for Jay a report that includes an income statement and a cash flow statement (using the direct method for operating cash flows) for the nine months ended December 31, 2008, and a balance sheet on December 31, 2008, for his shop. Include explanations for all amounts shown, as well as a discussion that answers Jay's questions and that recommends an accounting system.

**8-44** Ava Mendleson operates a small fabric shop. She has been earning a satisfactory profit but is short of cash. Following is an accurate but unclassified balance sheet of the store on December 31, 2007.

**MENDLESON'S FABRIC SHOP**
***Balance Sheet***
***December 31, 2007***

| | |
|---|---|
| Cash | $ 2,500 |
| Store equipment (net) | 6,400 |
| Inventory | 9,500 |
| Accounts receivable | 3,000 |
| Total Assets | $21,400 |
| Accounts payable | $ 4,500 |
| Ava Mendleson, capital | 16,900 |
| Total Liabilities and Owner's Equity | $21,400 |

On January 2, 2008, Ava went to her bank to get a loan for her company. The bank agreed to loan her $5,000 under the following conditions. First, the note payable would be a three-year note, so that the company would repay $5,000 plus $1,500 interest on December 31, 2010. Second, she must prepare a "forecasted" classified income statement for 2008 that shows that the company expects to earn a net income of at least $11,000 and that it will have "satisfactory" profit margin and return ratios. Third, she must prepare a "forecasted" cash flow statement for 2008 that shows that the company expects to have cash on hand at the end of 2008 of at least $10,000 (including the cash from the bank loan) and that it will have "satisfactory" operating cash flow ratios. Finally, she must prepare a "forecasted" classified balance sheet as of December 31, 2008, that shows a current ratio of at least 3.0 and a debt ratio of no more than 40%.

Ava has never prepared any forecasted financial statements. She understands, however, that they are prepared using the best estimates she can make, based on the store's previous operations and her future expectations. Ava has come to you for help, having gathered the following information:

(a) Sales for 2008 are expected to be $80,000. Of these, half will be cash sales, and half will be credit sales. There are no cash discounts. Of the credit sales, 10% will not be collected until 2009. The accounts receivable on December 31, 2007 will be collected in 2008.
(b) Purchases of inventory for 2008 are expected to be $50,000. All purchases are on credit; there are no cash discounts. Of the purchases, 12% will not be paid until 2010. The accounts payable on December 31, 2007 will be paid in 2008.
(c) Sales returns and purchases returns are expected to be insignificant.
(d) The company's gross profit percentage has been 40% of sales, and this rate is expected in 2008.
(e) The store rents space in a local mall. The rent is $200 per month; the rent for the whole year is due on January 6, 2008.
(f) The store equipment that originally cost $8,000 has a 10-year estimated life, after which it is expected to have no value.
(g) Ava pays her one salesperson a basic salary of $7,000 per year, plus 10% of gross sales. The total salary for 2008 will be paid in cash by the end of the year.
(h) Ava expects to withdraw $8,000 during 2008 to cover her personal living expenses.
(i) Other operating expenses are expected to be $1,600 in 2008; these will be paid in cash by the end of the year.

You determine that the information Ava has gathered is "reasonable" and includes her best estimates.

*Required:* (1) Prepare a forecasted classified income statement for 2008. Show supporting calculations.
(2) Prepare a forecasted cash flow statement for 2008. Use the direct method for operating cash flows. Show supporting calculations.
(3) Prepare a forecasted classified balance sheet as of December 31, 2008. Show supporting calculations.
(4) Compute the applicable ratios and briefly discuss whether the company has met the bank's conditions.

**8-45** (Appendix) Refer to the information in **8-31** for the Seeser Flappits Company. In addition to this information, you find the following average ratio results in 2008 for similar companies in the same industry:

| | |
|---|---|
| Operating cash flow margin: | 10.1% |
| Cash return on total assets: | 15.7% |

*Required:* (1) Using the indirect method for operating cash flows, prepare Seeser Flappits Company's 2008 cash flow statement.
(2) Compute the company's (a) operating cash flow margin, and (b) cash return on total assets. Briefly evaluate how well the company is doing in 2008, compared to similar companies in the same industry.
(3) Now consider how the decrease in accounts receivable and decrease in inventory affected the company's ratio results. Reevaluate your answers to (2).

**8-46** Yesterday, you received the following letter for your advice column in the local paper:

**DR. DECISIVE**

Dear Dr. Decisive:

My mom and I haven't had a major disagreement since I was 16, but now we can't see eye-to-eye (and it isn't even about my social life!). It all started from a comment that her friend made when visiting us the other day. The comment was something like this: "I don't know how to interpret the financial reports my accountant gave me the other day for my shop. I do know this—the shop had a huge profit last year, but it ended up with less cash this year than it did last year." Well, of course, that led to a discussion between my mom and her friend, but I just couldn't leave well enough alone. I thought they were "barking up the wrong tree," so I had to interject my two cents. Here's the issue: is it possible for a company to have a positive cash flow from operations in the same year that it has a net loss or to have a negative cash flow from operations in the same year that it has a net income? I think it isn't possible. Income and cash flows may be different, but they will both be either positive or negative. Mom disagrees. In fact, she disagrees so strongly that she says if you say I am right, she will raise the amount of the monthly check she sends me. In the meantime, I am . . .

"Knowledge Rich, But Cash Poor"

*Required:* Meet with your Dr. Decisive team and write a response to "Knowledge Rich, But Cash Poor."

# END NOTES

[a]R. A. (Bob) Hammerschmidt Jr., President and CEO, Southwest Missouri Region, *Commerce Bank*, July 17, 2001.

[b]See, for instance, "Work It Out: The 2001 Working Capital Survey," *CFO Magazine*, August, 2002 and "Capital Ideas: The 2005 Working Capital Survey," *CFO Magazine*, September 1, 2005.

CHAPTER 9

# MANAGING AND REPORTING WORKING CAPITAL

"MOST PEOPLE HAVE WRONG-MINDED IDEAS ABOUT WHY COMPANIES FAIL. THEY THINK IT'S BECAUSE OF A LACK OF MONEY. IN MOST CASES, IT HAS VERY LITTLE TO DO WITH THAT."

—MICHAEL E. GERBER,
AUTHOR AND
BUSINESS CONSULTANT

1. What is working capital, and why is its management important?
2. How can managers control cash receipts in a small company?
3. How can managers control cash payments in a small company?
4. What is a bank reconciliation, and what are the causes of the difference between a company's cash balance in its accounting records and its cash balance on its bank statement?
5. How can managers control accounts receivable in a small company?
6. How can managers control inventory in a small company?
7. How can managers control accounts payable in a small company?

How do you protect your cash? Do you organize your money in your wallet so that 1-dollar bills are in front and larger denominations are behind? Do you keep a jar of "change" to pay for small items? At your apartment or dorm room, do you store your wallet in a "secret" place? When you get your paycheck, do you examine the "pay stub" to be sure you were paid the right amount and that the deductions are correct? Do you have a checking account or savings account? Do you earn interest on the balance you keep in the account? Do you immediately deposit your paycheck in this checking or savings account? Do you record each check that you write in your check register? Do you reconcile your checkbook each time you get a bank statement? Have any of your friends asked you to lend them money? Did you consider the likelihood they would pay you back before you decided whether to lend them the money? If you lent them money, did you make them sign an agreement to pay you back? When you pay for several items at a store by using your credit card, do you examine the receipt to make sure the store has not overcharged you? These are all ways that individuals might keep "control" over their cash, amounts owed to them, and amounts they owe. To be successful, companies also need sound controls over their cash, accounts receivable, and accounts payable.

According to Michael E. Gerber, accounting issues are the basis for three of the top ten reasons why small companies fail. These three are (1) a lack of management systems, such as financial controls, (2) a lack of financial planning and review, and (3) an inadequate level of financial resources.[a] The third reason can be interpreted to mean "a lack of money." The first two reasons, however, focus on managing a company's financial resources.

Often, it is difficult for a new company to keep an adequate amount of financial resources. Because so many companies start with very little cash, a relatively new term, *bootstrapping*, describes how these companies operate under such tight financial constraints. The term is taken from an old phrase about being self-reliant: these companies are "pulling themselves up by their bootstraps." Some very successful companies, for example **Dell Computer Corporation** and **Joe Boxer Company**, started business with very limited resources. These companies were able to manage their resources effectively and grow into sizable businesses.

In this chapter, we build on the knowledge you gained in previous chapters. We take a closer look at how companies manage and report four important balance sheet items: cash, accounts receivable, inventory, and accounts payable. As you will learn, how a company manages these items affects its cash flows, financial performance, and financial reporting. More specifically, we define *working capital,* discuss its importance, examine its major components, and explain how managers and external users evaluate it. We believe that through proper short-term financial management, many small companies can increase their likelihood of success.

## WORKING CAPITAL

1 What is working capital, and why is its management important?

A company's **working capital** is the excess of its current assets over its current liabilities. That is, working capital is current assets minus current liabilities.

*Why do you think this amount is called "working" capital? Why do you think a company is concerned with its working capital?*

Recall that the current asset section of a company's balance sheet includes assets that the company expects to convert into cash, sell, or use up within one year. The current liability section includes liabilities that it expects to pay within one year by using current assets. The term *working capital* represents the *net* resources that managers have to *work* with (manage) in the company's day-to-day operations. Exhibit 9-1 shows Sweet Temptations' balance sheets for December 31, 2009 and December 31, 2008. We have assumed that Sweet Temptations has operated for two years and has recorded all its transactions correctly. We highlight the current sections of the balance sheet and calculate Sweet Temptations' working capital at the bottom of Exhibit 9-1. Note that the amount of the current liabilities (accounts payable) is subtracted from the total amount for the current assets (cash, accounts

**EXHIBIT 9-1 SWEET TEMPTATIONS' BALANCE SHEETS**

**SWEET TEMPTATIONS**
***Comparative Balance Sheets***
***December 31, 2009 and 2008***

| **Assets** | December 31, 2009 | | December 31, 2008 | |
|---|---|---|---|---|
| Current Assets | | | | |
| Cash | $ 5,818 | | $ 5,014 | |
| Accounts receivable (net) | 7,340 | | 8,808 | |
| Inventory | 1,570 | | 1,300 | |
| Total current assets | | $14,728 | | $15,122 |
| Property and Equipment | | | | |
| Store equipment (net) | $13,500 | | $10,420 | |
| Total property and equipment | | 13,500 | | 10,420 |
| Total Assets | | $28,228 | | $25,542 |
| **Liabilities** | | | | |
| Current Liabilities | | | | |
| Accounts payable | $ 7,540 | | $ 7,731 | |
| Total current liabilities | | $ 7,540 | | $ 7,731 |
| Noncurrent Liabilities | | | | |
| Notes payable | $ 5,000 | | $ 5,000 | |
| Total noncurrent liabilities | | 5,000 | | 5,000 |
| Total Liabilities | | $12,540 | | $12,731 |
| **Owner's Equity** | | | | |
| A. Cox, capital | | $15,688 | | $12,811 |
| Total Liabilities and Owner's Equity | | $28,228 | | $25,542 |

Working Capital = Current Assets − Current Liabilities
12/31/2009 Working Capital = $14,728 − $7,540 = $7,188
12/31/2008 Working Capital = $15,122 − $7,731 = $7,391

receivable, and inventory) to calculate working capital. Changes in any of these four items affect Sweet Temptations' working capital. Decisions that managers make regarding any of these items are considered part of *working capital management.* Other terms for working capital management are *operating capital management* and *short-term financial management.*

*How much working capital do you need in your personal life? Why?*

Companies manage working capital because they want to keep an appropriate amount on hand. But what is an *appropriate* amount of working capital for a company? An appropriate amount is enough working capital to finance its day-to-day operating activities plus an extra amount in case something unexpected happens. For instance, the extra amount may enable the company to buy inventory when it is offered at a reduced price or to cover the lost cash when a customer doesn't pay its account. If a company has too little working capital, it risks not having enough liquidity. If it has too much, the company risks not putting its resources to their best use. In summary, companies manage working capital to keep an appropriate balance between (1) having enough working capital to operate and to handle unexpected needs for cash, inventory, or short-term credit and (2) having so much excess cash, inventory, or available credit that profitability is reduced.

Keeping the right amount of working capital requires careful planning and monitoring. For instance, the timing of inventory purchases usually does not coincide with the timing of sales. Thus, at any given time a company may find itself with either too little or too much inventory. Cash receipts usually do not coincide with the company's need to use its cash. So, a company may have excess cash sitting idly in its checking account, or it may need additional short-term financing.

The fact that customers have some control over when they make their payments affects a company's management of cash collections from its accounts receivables. The longer customers take to pay, the longer the company must wait between the time when it purchased inventory and the time when it receives cash from the sale. The company can manage this aspect of working capital by setting policies that encourage early payment of accounts receivable.

On the other hand, the company must also manage the payments of its obligations. It should make these payments on time, as well as take advantage of purchases discounts available from its suppliers.

Managing working capital affects all aspects of a company's operating activities. Exhibit 9-2 shows a time line of Sweet Temptations' (ST) operating activities. The top half of the exhibit shows Sweet Temptations' transactions with its supplier, Unlimited Decadence (UD). These consist of ST purchasing chocolates (increasing inventory) on credit (increasing accounts payable), paying invoices as they come due (decreasing cash and accounts payable), and monitoring inventory to determine when to restock (not shown).

How can a company encourage its customers to pay their bills more quickly?

**EXHIBIT 9-2** **WORKING CAPITAL FLOWS**

**Purchasing and Cash Payments**

1. ST purchases boxes of chocolates from UD on credit.
2. ST waits until almost the invoice due date to process cash payment.
3. ST sends check for payment.
4. UD processes receipt and deposits ST's check; ST's bank deducts check from its checking account.

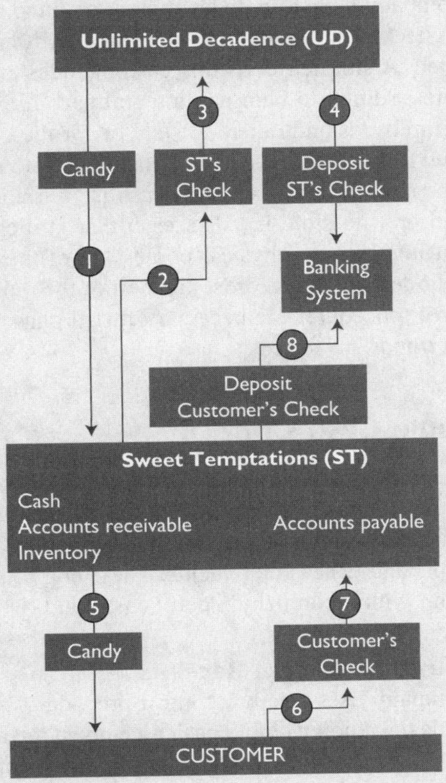


**Sales and Cash Receipts**

5. ST sells boxes of chocolates to a customer on credit.
6. Customer waits until almost the due date to process cash payment.
7. Customer sends check for payment to ST.
8. ST processes receipt and deposits the customer's check with other daily receipts in its checking account.

*Why do you think Sweet Temptations waits until almost the invoice due date to process its cash payment to Unlimited Decadence?*

The bottom half of Exhibit 9-2 shows Sweet Temptations' transactions with its customers. These consist of Sweet Temptations making candy sales (decreasing inventory) on credit (increasing accounts receivable) or for cash (not shown), and of credit customers mailing payments based on the credit terms of the sales (decreasing accounts receivable). When Sweet Temptations receives customers' payments, it deposits the checks in the bank (increasing cash). These deposits are then available to make cash payments.

Managers control each aspect of the operating cycle to ensure that operating activities are performed in accordance with company objectives. As you will see, they do this by establishing an internal control structure. An **internal control structure** is a set of policies and procedures that directs how employees should perform a company's activities.

The reporting by a company of the amount of each current asset and current liability on its balance sheet provides external users with information about the company's ability to keep an appropriate level and mix of working capital. In turn, this reporting helps managers and users evaluate the company's liquidity.

To put this another way, working capital is to a company what water is to a plant. If the plant does not have enough water, it will not grow. Eventually, it will wither and die. If the plant receives too much water, it will drown. Just as plants need the right amount of water in order to grow, companies need the right amount of working capital to achieve desired levels of profitability and liquidity. In the following sections we will discuss how a company manages and reports its working capital items—cash, accounts receivable, inventory, and accounts payable.

# CASH

A company's **cash** includes money on hand, deposits in checking and savings accounts, and checks and credit card invoices that it has received from customers but not yet deposited. A simple rule is that cash includes anything that a bank will accept as a deposit.

In addition to being an integral part of a business, cash is also the most likely asset for employees and others to steal or for the company to misplace. For example, cash received from customers in a retail store has no identification marks that have been recorded by the store. Therefore, when cash is "missing" it is very difficult to prove the cash was stolen or who stole it. Also, cash that is illegally transferred from a company bank account involves no physical possession of the cash by the thief, and if the thief can conceal or destroy the records, the theft of the money may not be traceable. Although internal control procedures are necessary for all phases of a company's business, they are usually most important for cash.

## Simple Cash Controls

For any size company, the best way to prevent both intentional and unintentional losses is to hire competent and trustworthy personnel and to establish cash controls. Next, we discuss two categories of simple cash controls. These are internal controls over (1) cash receipts and (2) cash payments. These controls apply to all cash transactions except those dealing with a company's petty cash fund, which we will discuss later in the chapter.

### Controls over Cash Receipts

2 How can managers control cash receipts in a small company?

A company uses internal control procedures for cash receipts to ensure that it properly records the amounts of all cash receipts in the accounting system and to protect them from being lost or stolen. Cash receipts from a company's operating activities result from cash sales and from collections of accounts receivable mailed in by its customers.

*How might an employee steal from his or her employer when working at a company's cash register?*

For cash sales, a company should use three control procedures. The most important control procedure is the proper use of a cash register. Managers should make sure that a prenumbered sales receipt is completed for every sale and that the salespeople ring up each sale on the register. In most companies, the cash register produces the receipt as well as a tape containing a chronological list of all sales transactions rung up on the register. This step is important because it is the first place that sales get entered into the accounting system. The fact that customers expect to receive a copy of the receipt helps ensure that each sale is entered. As a customer, you may have been part of a company's cash controls without even knowing it. At many **Sbarro Pizza** franchises, for example, there is a sign near the cash register that reads,

**Dear Customer: If we fail to give you a receipt, let us know and your next meal is free!**

This added control increases the likelihood that salespeople will enter all sales into the cash register, and it signals to company employees the importance of this activity.

*Could an employee at Sbarro's still take money from the company? How?*

© PHOTODISC

How can this customer help QuickTrip keep control of the cash in this register?

Second, when a check is accepted for payment, the salesperson should make sure that the customer has proper identification in order to minimize the likelihood that the check will "bounce." Even this procedure is not always adequate. For instance, in Vail, Colorado (and in other ski areas), retail and service companies must be especially careful in accepting checks at the end of the ski season because some customers close out their accounts when they leave.

Third, at the end of each salesperson's work shift, the employee should match the total of the amounts collected (cash plus checks and credit card sales) against the total of the cash register tape and report any difference between the two totals to a supervisor.

Some companies (e.g., **QuikTrip**) use a fourth control procedure for cash sales. These companies remove the "big bills" from cash registers even during one employee's shift. For example, if more than five 20-dollar bills are in the register, the employee inserts the excess bills through a slot into a locked safe that is kept behind the counter. Only the store manager knows the combination to the safe.

A company should use three control procedures to safeguard collections of cash from accounts receivable. First, either the owner-manager or an employee who does not handle accounting records should open the mail. This control procedure is called *separation of duties.* Separating the duties of handling accounting records and opening the mail prevents an employee from stealing undeposited checks *and* covering up the theft by making a fictitious entry in the accounting records. Second, immediately after opening the mail, the employee should list all of the checks received. Later, if a customer claims to have previously paid a bill, the company can review the list. You may be wondering what happens if the customer *did* pay the bill but the receipt is not listed because the employee stole the undeposited check. In this case, the customer's canceled check (from the customer's bank) may help the company discover that its employee stole the check. Third, while opening the mail, the employee should restrictively endorse each incoming check for deposit in the company's bank account. At Sweet Temptations, this is done by stamping "for deposit only—Sweet Temptations" on the back of each check. If a check is lost or stolen, the endorsement makes it more difficult to cash the check illegally.

*Why do you think an owner might be interested in not recording all cash receipts?*

Finally, a company should adopt one additional procedure to help it safeguard the cash collected from both its cash sales and its accounts receivable. It should deposit all cash receipts intact daily. This means that at the end of the day, the company should take all of its cash (everything included in our definition of cash), fill out a deposit slip, and make a bank deposit. These daily bank deposits aid in two ways. First, keeping a substantial amount of cash at the company overnight is taking an unnecessary risk of theft. By depositing all cash receipts on a daily basis, the company does not leave cash unattended overnight. Second, the bank's deposit records show the company's cash receipts for each day. When the company receives its monthly bank statement, the company can check the daily bank deposits listed in the bank statement against its Cash account to determine that it deposited all its recorded cash receipts in the bank and that it properly recorded all bank deposits in its Cash account.

### Controls over Cash Payments

3 How can managers control cash payments in a small company?

The basic rule for good internal control over cash payments is to have all payments made by check. A very small company that the owner operates may have little need for any additional internal control procedures. The owner purchases items, signs checks for payment, and pays employees by check. As the company grows, two more controls over cash payments can provide added security over cash. First, the company should pay only for approved purchases that are supported by proper documents. The proper documents generally include an approved copy of the company's purchase order providing evidence that the company actually ordered the items (which we will discuss in detail later in the chapter), a freight receipt showing evidence that the company received the items it ordered, and the supplier's invoice. This procedure reduces the chances that the company will pay either for items that it did not want to purchase or for items that it has not received. Second, immediately after writing the check for payment, the owner should stamp "PAID" on the supporting documents. Canceling the documents in this way prevents the company from paying for items more than once.

*Why do you think an employee might want to deceive the company about its cash payments? Why do you think an owner might be interested in not recording all cash payments?*

## Bank Reconciliation

Despite all of the procedures used to control the receipts and payments of cash, errors in a company's records can still occur. Since the bank also keeps a record of the company's cash balance, the company can use both sets of records to determine what its correct cash balance should be. However, the time when the company records its receipts and payments differs from the time when the bank records them. Therefore, a company uses a bank reconciliation to determine the accuracy of the balance in its Cash account. In this section, we discuss what a bank reconciliation is, why it is necessary, and how it is performed.

*Do you reconcile your bank statement every month? What risks do you take if you don't reconcile the statement?*

A company's bank independently keeps track of the company's cash balance. Each month the bank sends the company a **bank statement** that summarizes the company's banking activities (e.g., deposits, paid checks) during the month. A company uses its bank statement, along with its cash records, to prepare a bank reconciliation.

When a company uses the internal control procedures of depositing daily receipts and paying only by check, the ending balance in its Cash account should be the same as the bank's ending cash balance for the company's checking account, except for a few items.

(We will discuss the various causes of the difference between the two balances below.) A company prepares a **bank reconciliation** to analyze the difference between the ending cash balance in its accounting records and the ending cash balance reported by the bank in the bank statement. Through this process, the company learns what changes, if any, it needs to make in its Cash account balance. This enables the company to report the correct cash balance on its balance sheet.

4 What is a bank reconciliation, and what are the causes of the difference between a company's cash balance in its accounting records and its cash balance on its bank statement?

Exhibit 9-3 summarizes the causes of the difference between the ending cash balance listed on the bank statement and the ending cash balance listed in the company's records. The causes include (1) deposits in transit, (2) outstanding checks, (3) deposits made directly by the bank, (4) charges made directly by the bank, and (5) errors.

*Which of the five listed items are most important when you reconcile your bank account?*

## EXHIBIT 9-3 CAUSES OF DIFFERENCE IN CASH BALANCES

1. *Deposits in Transit.* A **deposit in transit** is a cash receipt that the company has added to its Cash account but that the bank has not included in the cash balance reported on the bank statement. When a company receives a check, it records an increase to its Cash account. As illustrated in Exhibit 9-2, a short period of time may pass before the company deposits the check and the bank records it. At the end of each month the company may have deposits in transit (either cash or checks) that cause the deposits recorded in the company's Cash account to be greater than deposits reported on the bank statement.

2. *Outstanding Checks.* An **outstanding check** is a check that the company has written and deducted from its Cash account but that the bank has not deducted from the cash balance reported on the bank statement because the check has not yet "cleared" the bank. As illustrated in Exhibit 9-2, a period of time is necessary for the check to be received by the payee (the company to whom the check is written), deposited in the payee's bank, and forwarded to the company's bank (physically or electronically) for subtraction from the company's bank balance. Therefore, at the end of each month a company usually has some outstanding checks that cause the cash payments recorded in its Cash account to be more than the cancelled checks itemized on the bank statement.

3. *Deposits Made Directly by the Bank.* Many checking accounts earn interest on the balance in the account. For these accounts, the bank increases the company's cash balance in the bank's records by the amount of interest the company earned on its checking account; the bank lists this amount on the bank statement. This causes deposits listed on the bank statement to be greater than the deposits listed in the company's Cash account. The company is informed of the amount of interest when it receives the bank statement.

4. *Charges Made Directly by the Bank.* A bank frequently imposes a service charge for a depositor's checking account and deducts this charge directly from the bank account. Banks also charge for the cost of printing checks, according to an agreed price, and for the cost of stopping payment on checks. The company is informed of the amount of the charge when it receives the bank statement showing the amount of the deduction.

When the company receives a customer's check, it adds the amount to its Cash account and deposits the check in its bank account for collection. The company's bank occasionally is unable to collect the amount of the customer's check. That is, the customer's check has "bounced." A customer's check that has "bounced" is called an **NSF (not sufficient funds) check**. Because the bank did not receive money for the customer's check, it lists the check as an NSF check on the bank statement. Although the bank usually informs the company immediately of each NSF check, there may be some NSF checks that are included in the bank statement and that the company has not recorded.

At the end of the month, the bank lists any service charges and NSF checks as deductions on the bank statement—deductions not yet listed in the company's Cash account.

5. *Errors.* Despite the internal control procedures established by the bank and the company, errors may arise in either the bank's records or the company's records. The company may not discover these errors until it prepares the bank reconciliation. For example, a bank may include a deposit or a check in the wrong depositor's account or may make an error in recording an amount. Or, a company may record a check for an incorrect amount or may forget to record a check.

### The Structure of a Bank Reconciliation

Exhibit 9-4 shows a common way to structure a bank reconciliation. Notice that the reconciliation has two sections: an upper section starting with the bank's record of the company's ending cash balance, and a lower section starting with the company's record of its cash balance. It is logical to set up these two sections because the purpose of the bank reconciliation is to determine the company's correct ending cash balance. By adjusting the cash balance in each section for the amounts that either are missing or are made in error, the company is able to determine its reconciled (correct) ending cash balance.

For example, in the upper section, a deposit in transit is added to the ending cash balance from the bank statement because this deposit represents a cash increase that the bank has not yet added to the company's checking account. In the lower section, a service charge made by the bank is subtracted from the ending balance in the company's Cash account because this charge represents a cash decrease that the company has not yet recorded.

The bank reconciliation is complete when the ending reconciled cash balances calculated in these two sections are the same. This ending reconciled cash balance is the correct cash balance that the company includes in its ending balance sheet. This form of bank reconciliation acts as another type of internal control over cash because it enables a company to identify errors in its cash-recording process and to know its correct cash balance at the end of each month.

### Preparing a Bank Reconciliation

When you prepare a bank reconciliation, keep in mind that you are doing it to determine the correct ending cash balance to be shown on the company's balance sheet. The cash balance at the end of the month is correct if it includes *all* of the company's transactions and events that affected cash. As you work through the upper section of the reconciliation, ask yourself, "What cash transactions (e.g., checks written and deposits made) have taken place that the bank doesn't know about?" In the lower section ask yourself, "What is not included in calculating the company's ending cash balance but should be (e.g., bank service charges, interest earned)?" Keep these questions in mind as you work through the reconciliation until the reconciled balances are the same.

To prepare a bank reconciliation, you need two sets of items: (1) the bank statement for the month being reconciled, along with all of the items returned with the statement, and (2) the company's cash records. With these items, you can work through a reconciliation in a step-by-step manner. Exhibit 9-5 summarizes the eight steps to follow in preparing a bank reconciliation.

In the following section, we illustrate the reconciliation process by preparing Sweet Temptations' December 31, 2009 bank reconciliation.

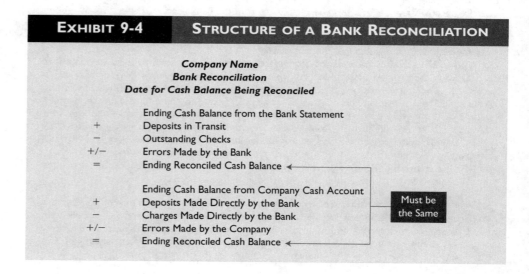

**EXHIBIT 9-4 STRUCTURE OF A BANK RECONCILIATION**

***Company Name***
***Bank Reconciliation***
***Date for Cash Balance Being Reconciled***

| | | |
|---|---|---|
| | Ending Cash Balance from the Bank Statement | |
| + | Deposits in Transit | |
| − | Outstanding Checks | |
| +/− | Errors Made by the Bank | |
| = | Ending Reconciled Cash Balance | ← Must be the Same |
| | Ending Cash Balance from Company Cash Account | |
| + | Deposits Made Directly by the Bank | |
| − | Charges Made Directly by the Bank | |
| +/− | Errors Made by the Company | |
| = | Ending Reconciled Cash Balance | ← Must be the Same |

## Exhibit 9-5 Steps in Preparing a Bank Reconciliation

1. *Set up the proper form for the bank reconciliation.* Fill in the information you already know (e.g., ending unadjusted cash balances from the bank statement and the Cash account).

2. *Look for deposits in transit.* Compare the increases in cash listed in the company's Cash account with the deposits shown on the bank statement. Check to see if any increase in the company's Cash account is not listed as a deposit on the bank statement. For any deposit in transit, add the amount to the ending cash balance from the bank statement listed on the reconciliation.

3. *Look for outstanding checks.* Compare the decreases in cash listed on the company's Cash account with the paid checks shown on the bank statement. Identify any decrease that is shown in the company's Cash account during the month but that is not matched with a corresponding check deduction on the bank statement. Starting from the company's records, trace each decrease to its check listing on the bank statement. Subtract the amounts of the outstanding checks from the ending cash balance from the bank statement listed on the bank reconciliation.

4. *Identify any deposits that were made directly by the bank but that are not included as increases in the company's Cash account.* Look through the bank statement for bank deposits that the company has not recorded as increases in its Cash account. Usually, these deposits are for interest earned on the company's checking account balance. Add these deposits to the balance of the company's Cash account listed on the bank reconciliation.

5. *Identify any charges that were made directly by the bank but that are not included as decreases in cash on the company's records.* Look through the bank statement for bank charges that the company has not recorded as decreases in its Cash account. Usually, these charges result from bank services such as printing checks or handling the company's own NSF checks. Deduct these charges from the balance of the company's Cash account listed on the bank reconciliation.

6. *Determine the effect of any errors.* While completing steps 1 through 5, you may discover that the bank or the company (or both) made an error during the processing of the cash transactions. If you find a bank error, contact the bank to get the error corrected in the company's checking account, and correct the amount of the error in the upper section of the bank reconciliation. If the company made an error, correct the amount of the error in the lower section of the reconciliation.

7. *Complete the bank reconciliation.* After you have finished steps 1 through 6, complete the reconciliation. Include the date and amount for any deposit in transit, and list the check numbers for any outstanding checks. This improves documentation and makes the reconciliation easier for others to understand. Describe any bank charges or error corrections in sufficient detail so that these activities can be recorded properly in the company's accounting records. At this point, the reconciled (correct) cash balances in both sections of the reconciliation should be the same. If not, trace back through the process carefully to locate any mistakes (e.g., outstanding checks you failed to include, math errors, etc.).

8. *Adjust the balance of the company's Cash account to agree with the corrected cash balance.* The lower section of a completed reconciliation answers the question "What is not included in the company's ending cash balance but should be?" The last step in preparing a reconciliation is to record these items in the company's Cash account (and the other related accounts). This recording changes the company's cash balance from the amount listed at the top of the lower section of the bank reconciliation to the correct ending amount.

### Sweet Temptations' Bank Reconciliation

Exhibit 9-6 on the following two pages shows several documents: Sweet Temptations' Cash account (for illustrative purposes, we show the increases in the left column and decreases in the right column) for December, the December bank statement the company received from First National Bank, and the completed bank reconciliation. Exhibit 9-6 also summarizes Steps 1 through 7 from Exhibit 9-5 that Anna Cox followed to prepare the reconciliation. We use an arrow and a number to trace each step on the documents.

## EXHIBIT 9-6 SWEET TEMPTATIONS' BANK RECONCILIATION

**Steps to Complete Bank Reconciliation**

*Step 1.* Anna transferred the $5,465 cash balance from the bank statement and the $5,812.75 balance from Sweet Temptations' Cash account to the reconciliation. Next, she completed the upper section of the reconciliation.

*Step 2.* Anna compared the increases in the Cash account with the bank deposits and found that the December 31 increase of $786.00 was not listed on the bank statement. She entered $786.00 on the reconciliation as a deposit in transit.

*Step 3.* Anna compared the bank statement's listing of checks and Sweet Temptations' record of decreases in its Cash account and found that all but two of the decreases (check #948 for $347.00 and check #950 for $121.00) were deducted on the current month's bank statement. She subtracted these outstanding checks from the ending cash balance of the bank statement in the reconciliation. After completing the upper section of the bank reconciliation, Anna calculated the reconciled ending cash balance to be $5,783.00.

*Step 4.* Anna began completing the lower section of Sweet Temptation's reconciliation. Anna reviewed the deposits listed in the bank statement and found that Sweet Temptations had not recorded a $12.25 bank deposit for interest earned as an increase in its Cash account. She added the $12.25 deposit to the company's ending balance on the reconciliation.

*Step 5.* Anna reviewed the charges on the bank statement and found that Sweet Temptations had not recorded a $15.00 bank service charge (for printed checks) as a decrease in its Cash account. She subtracted the $15.00 charge from the company's ending cash balance on the reconciliation.

*Step 6.* When Anna compared the decreases in Sweet Temptations' Cash account with the bank statement in Step 3, she also found that Sweet Temptations had incorrectly recorded check #942 (in payment of an account payable) in its records for $136 instead of $163. Because the amount that Sweet Temptations should have recorded is $27.00 more than the amount that it did record ($163.00 − $136.00), Anna subtracted $27.00 from the company's ending cash balance on the reconciliation.

*Step 7.* After completing the lower section of the reconciliation, Anna calculated the reconciled ending cash balance to be $5,783.00. Anna also observed that the reconciled balances shown in the upper and lower sections of the bank reconciliation are the same. This indicates that she completed the bank reconciliation properly.

**Cash**

Beg Bal. 12/1/2009 $3,238.48

| Increases | | Decreases | | |
|---|---|---|---|---|
| Date | Amount | Date | Ch# | Amount |
| Dec. 1 | $142.25 | Dec. 1 | 939 | $287.94 |
| Dec. 3 | 155.21 | Dec. 3 | 940 | 34.51 |
| Dec. 3 | 142.15 | Dec. 3 | 941 | 26.79 |
| Dec. 4 | 154.45 | Dec. 8 | 942 | 136.00 |
| Dec. 5 | 198.00 | Dec. 8 | 943 | 593.15 |
| Dec. 6 | 98.66 | Dec. 10 | 944 | 385.00 |
| Dec. 8 | 190.23 | Dec. 10 | 945 | 190.12 |
| Dec. 10 | 163.65 | Dec. 14 | 946 | 489.57 |
| Dec. 10 | 187.04 | Dec. 24 | 947 | 452.18 |
| Dec. 11 | 156.55 | Dec. 24 | 948 | 347.00 |
| Dec. 12 | 177.91 | Dec. 28 | 949 | 1,904.78 |
| Dec. 13 | 217.87 | Dec. 29 | 950 | 121.00 |
| Dec. 15 | 313.57 | | | |
| Dec. 15 | 293.32 | | | |
| Dec. 17 | 336.58 | | | |
| Dec. 18 | 387.22 | | | |
| Dec. 19 | 441.10 | | | |
| Dec. 20 | 457.16 | | | |
| Dec. 22 | 451.82 | | | |
| Dec. 22 | 591.78 | | | |
| Dec. 24 | 458.25 | | | |
| Dec. 27 | 287.35 | | | |
| Dec. 28 | 335.76 | | | |
| Dec. 29 | 418.43 | | | |
| Dec. 31 | 786.00 | | | |

End Bal. 12/31/2009 Before Reconciliation $5,812.75

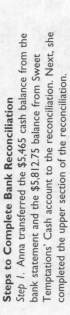

SWEET TEMPTATIONS
WESTWOOD MALL #117
SACHSE, TX 75665-0117

First National Bank
7th and Grand
Sachse, TX 75662-3443
Phone (214) 555-9800
Member FDIC

NO. 137-187-8

| | | | | |
|---|---|---|---|---|
| Beginning balance December 1, 2009 | | | | $ 3,158.48 |
| Deposits and other additions: | | | | |
| Deposits: | | | | |
| Dec. 3 | $101.00 | | | |
| Dec. 3 | 142.25 | Dec. 17 | $313.57 | |
| Dec. 3 | 155.21 | Dec. 17 | 293.32 | |
| Dec. 3 | 142.15 | Dec. 17 | 336.58 | |
| Dec. 4 | 154.45 | Dec. 19 | 387.22 | |

1 2 3 6

**EXHIBIT 9-6 CONTINUED**

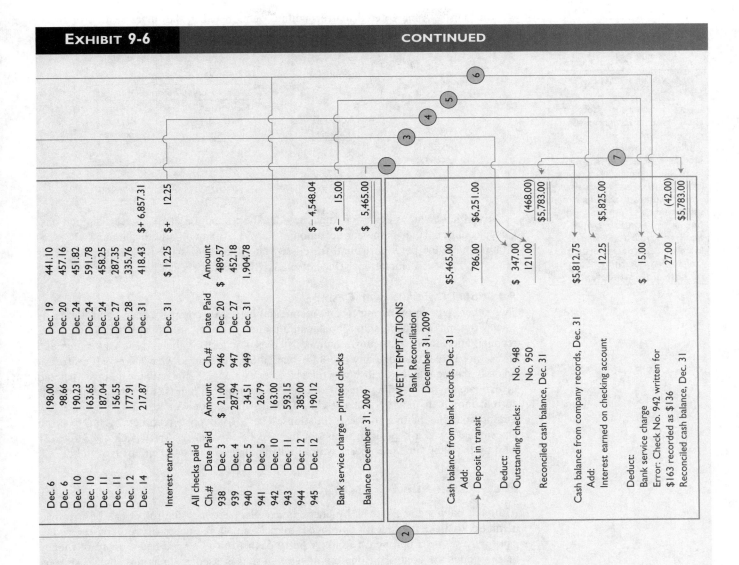

| | | | | |
|---|---|---|---|---|
| Dec. 6 | 198.00 | Dec. 19 | 441.10 | |
| Dec. 6 | 98.66 | Dec. 20 | 457.16 | |
| Dec. 10 | 190.23 | Dec. 24 | 451.82 | |
| Dec. 10 | 163.65 | Dec. 24 | 591.78 | |
| Dec. 11 | 187.04 | Dec. 24 | 458.25 | |
| Dec. 11 | 156.55 | Dec. 27 | 287.35 | |
| Dec. 12 | 177.91 | Dec. 28 | 335.76 | |
| Dec. 14 | 217.87 | Dec. 31 | 418.43 | $+ 6,857.31 |
| Interest earned: | | Dec. 31 | $ 12.25 | $+ 12.25 |

All checks paid

| Ch.# | Date Paid | Amount | Ch.# | Date Paid | Amount | |
|---|---|---|---|---|---|---|
| 938 | Dec. 3 | $ 21.00 | 946 | Dec. 20 | $ 489.57 | |
| 939 | Dec. 4 | 287.94 | 947 | Dec. 27 | 452.18 | |
| 940 | Dec. 5 | 34.51 | 949 | Dec. 31 | 1,904.78 | |
| 941 | Dec. 5 | 26.79 | | | | |
| 942 | Dec. 10 | 163.00 | | | | |
| 943 | Dec. 11 | 593.15 | | | | |
| 944 | Dec. 12 | 385.00 | | | | |
| 945 | Dec. 12 | 190.12 | | | | $− 4,548.04 |

| | |
|---|---|
| Bank service charge – printed checks | $− 15.00 |
| Balance December 31, 2009 | $ 5,465.00 |

SWEET TEMPTATIONS
Bank Reconciliation
December 31, 2009

| | | | |
|---|---|---|---|
| Cash balance from bank records, Dec. 31 | | $5,465.00 | |
| Add: | | | |
| Deposit in transit | | 786.00 | $6,251.00 |
| Deduct: | | | |
| Outstanding checks: | No. 948 | $ 347.00 | |
| | No. 950 | 121.00 | (468.00) |
| Reconciled cash balance, Dec. 31 | | | $5,783.00 |
| Cash balance from company records, Dec. 31 | | $5,812.75 | |
| Add: | | | |
| Interest earned on checking account | | 12.25 | $5,825.00 |
| Deduct: | | | |
| Bank service charge | | $ 15.00 | |
| Error: Check No. 942 written for $163 recorded as $136 | | 27.00 | (42.00) |
| Reconciled cash balance, Dec. 31 | | | $5,783.00 |

(Callouts 1–7 link bank statement items to reconciliation lines.)

In Step 8, Anna entered the reconciling items listed in the lower section of Sweet Temptations' bank reconciliation (interest earned, bank service charge, and correction of error) into the company's accounting records on December 31, 2009, as follows:

| Assets | = | Liabilities | + | Owner's Equity | | |
|---|---|---|---|---|---|---|
| | | | | Net Income | | |
| | | | | Revenues | − | Expenses |
| Cash | | Accounts Payable | | Interest Revenue | | Banking Expense |
| +$12.25 | | | | +$12.25 | | |
| −$15.00 | | | | | − | +$15.00 |
| −$27.00 | | −$27.00 | | | | |
| −$29.75 | | −$27.00 | | +$12.25 | − | +$15.00 |

**FINANCIAL STATEMENT EFFECTS**

Decreases current assets and total assets, and decreases current liabilities and total liabilities on ***balance sheet***. Increases other items, which increases net income. Also increases operating expenses, which decreases net income on ***income statement*** (and therefore decreases owner's equity on ***balance sheet***). Increases and decreases cash flows from operating activities on ***cash flow statement***.

Exhibit 9-7 shows that after Anna recorded the reconciling items, Sweet Temptations' Cash account balance is the correct amount: $5,783. Anna will add this amount to the total amount in the petty cash fund (discussed later) and will show the combined total as "Cash" on Sweet Temptations' December 31, 2009 balance sheet.

### Additional Controls over Cash

Two other steps in preparing a bank reconciliation help a company keep control over its cash. First, the company should make sure that any deposit in transit listed on the bank reconciliation for the *previous* month is listed as a deposit on the current bank statement. If it is not listed, the company should investigate to determine what happened to the deposit. It may be that the deposit was misplaced or even stolen. Second, the company should investigate any outstanding check from the *previous* month that is still outstanding for the current month. It may be that the check was misplaced or was lost in the mail. Sweet Temptations has neither of these situations. The $101 deposit recorded by the bank on December 1 was a deposit in transit at the end of November. And check #938 for $21 paid by the bank on December 1 was an outstanding check at the end of November.

## Petty Cash Fund

Although paying for all items by check is excellent internal control, it can be inconvenient. So, to make it easier for employees to make small, but necessary, purchases, a company may set up a petty cash fund. A **petty cash fund** is a specified amount of money that is under the control of one employee and that is used for making small cash payments for the company. A company uses a petty cash fund because some payments can be made only with "currency" or because writing checks for small amounts (e.g., for postage) would be cumbersome. There is less control over these expenditures, but the amounts involved are so small that an employee probably will not be tempted to steal.

*What items do you always pay for with "currency"?*

To start a petty cash fund, a company gives an employee an amount of money, say $50, to be kept at the company. Usually the employee keeps the money locked in his or her desk drawer. Each time a payment is made from the fund, the employee makes a record of the payment and keeps a written receipt. At any time, the total of the receipts plus the remaining cash should equal the amount (in this case, $50) that was originally given to the employee. When the fund gets low or on the date of its balance sheet, the company replenishes the fund to the original amount and uses the receipts to record the various cash transactions in its accounting system. For each receipt, the company records an increase in the related expense (or asset) account (e.g., postage expense, office supplies) and a decrease in its Cash account. This ensures that all of the petty cash payments are included in the amounts reported in the company's financial statements.

**EXHIBIT 9-7 ADJUSTMENTS FROM BANK RECONCILIATION**

**Cash**

Beg Bal. 12/1/2009 $3,238.48

| Increases | | Decreases | | |
|---|---|---|---|---|
| Date | Amount | Date | Ch# | Amount |
| Dec. 1 | $142.25 | Dec. 1 | 939 | $ 287.94 |
| Dec. 3 | 155.21 | Dec. 3 | 940 | 34.51 |
| Dec. 3 | 142.15 | Dec. 3 | 941 | 26.79 |
| Dec. 4 | 154.45 | Dec. 8 | 942 | 136.00 |
| Dec. 5 | 198.00 | Dec. 8 | 943 | 593.15 |
| Dec. 6 | 98.66 | Dec. 10 | 944 | 385.00 |
| Dec. 8 | 190.23 | Dec. 10 | 945 | 190.12 |
| Dec. 10 | 163.65 | Dec. 14 | 946 | 489.57 |
| Dec. 10 | 187.04 | Dec. 24 | 947 | 452.18 |
| Dec. 11 | 156.55 | Dec. 24 | 948 | 347.00 |
| Dec. 12 | 177.91 | Dec. 28 | 949 | 1,904.78 |
| Dec. 13 | 217.87 | Dec. 29 | 950 | 121.00 |
| Dec. 15 | 313.57 | | | |
| Dec. 15 | 293.32 | | | |
| Dec. 17 | 336.58 | | | |
| Dec. 18 | 387.22 | | | |
| Dec. 19 | 441.10 | | | |
| Dec. 20 | 457.16 | | | |
| Dec. 22 | 451.82 | | | |
| Dec. 22 | 591.78 | | | |
| Dec. 24 | 458.25 | | | |
| Dec. 27 | 287.35 | | | |
| Dec. 28 | 335.76 | | | |
| Dec. 29 | 418.43 | | | |
| Dec. 31 | 786.00 | | | |

| | |
|---|---|
| Ending Bal. 12/31/2009 Before Reconciliation | $5,812.75 |
| Adjustments to company records based on bank reconciliation: | |
| Interest earned | +12.25 |
| Bank service charge | −15.00 |
| Correct error for check no. 942 | −27.00 |
| Reconciled Cash Bal 12/31/2009 | $5,783.00 |

Sweet Temptations keeps a petty cash fund totaling $35. As we will discuss next, Anna adds this amount to Sweet Temptations' ending reconciled cash balance for its checking account so that Sweet Temptations shows its total cash on its balance sheet.

## Reporting the Cash Balance on the Balance Sheet

Cash is usually the first asset listed on the balance sheet because it is the most liquid current asset. Recall that Cash includes money on hand, deposits in checking and savings accounts, and checks and credit card receipts that a company has received but not yet deposited. As we discussed in the previous sections, a company's accounting system keeps track of these items separately. When reporting Cash on its balance sheet, a company must combine the balances of each of these items.

Sweet Temptations' total cash balance at December 31, 2009 consists of two items:

| | |
|---|---|
| 1. The December 31 reconciled cash balance in its checking account | $5,783.00 |
| 2. The amount in its petty cash fund | 35.00 |
| Total cash balance on December 31, 2009 | $5,818.00 |

Notice that Sweet Temptations shows this amount as Cash on its December 31, 2009 balance sheet in Exhibit 9-1.

A company that sells on credit cannot manage its cash without managing its accounts receivable. We will discuss the management of accounts receivable next.

*Have you ever applied for credit? What steps did you have to go through? Why do you think you had to go through that process in order to get credit?*

## Accounts Receivable

**Accounts receivable** are the amounts owed to a company by customers from previous credit sales. The company intends to collect these amounts in cash. Companies make sales on credit for three basic reasons. The first reason is that selling on credit may be more convenient than selling for cash. For example, when a company is selling goods that must be shipped, it is common for the purchaser to pay for the goods after receiving them. Between the time that the purchaser receives the goods and the time that the seller collects the payment, the seller has extended credit to the purchaser. The second reason a company makes credit sales is that managers believe that offering credit will encourage customers to buy items that they might not otherwise purchase. This is common in retail sales, when the customer may not have enough cash to make the purchase. The third reason a company makes credit sales is to signal product quality. By allowing customers to pay after receiving, seeing, and using the goods, a company shows that it is confident in the quality of the goods.

*Do credit card sales result in accounts receivable? Some? All? None?*

Credit sales using accounts receivable are not the same as "credit card sales." If you use a credit card to pay for goods that are sold to you, it is the credit card company (e.g., **VISA, Mastercard, Discover**) that is extending credit to you, not the company that sold you the goods. A retail store deposits its credit card receipts into its checking account just as it does its cash receipts. Because of this, credit card sales receipts are sometimes referred to as "instant cash."

© AP/WIDE WORLD PHOTOS

Who is extending credit in this transaction?

### The Decision to Extend Credit

If accounts receivable increase a company's sales, why not automatically decide to grant all customers credit? The decision is not automatic because accounts receivable also have two disadvantages. One disadvantage of credit sales is that having accounts receivable requires significant management effort. Managers must make credit investigations, prepare and send bills, and encourage payments from the customers. All of these activities involve a cost to the company in money and in employee time. The second disadvantage is that when a company makes credit sales, there is always the chance that the purchaser will not pay. However, just because a company has some uncollectible accounts ("bad debts"), it does not mean that the company should not make credit sales. If, given the additional revenues and costs of managing accounts receivable, the company's profits are increased by extending credit, then credit sales help the company achieve its goals. A company uses a form of cost-volume-profit (C-V-P) analysis for this evaluation. We will explain more about a company's decision to extend credit in Chapter 13. In this chapter, we focus on managing and reporting the accounts receivable for a small company.

## Simple Controls over Accounts Receivable

*Has anyone ever asked to borrow money from you? If they did, what factors affected your decision? Will you deal with the next situation in the same way? Why or why not?*

5 How can managers control accounts receivable in a small company?

Accounts receivable provide a greater increase in profit if credit sales are monitored properly. Internal controls over accounts receivable focus on procedures that help maximize the increase in profit from granting credit. For a small company, such as Sweet Temptations, three control procedures should be used with accounts receivable.

First, before extending credit, a company should determine that a customer is likely to pay. The risk of not collecting customers' accounts is greatly reduced if a company extends credit only to customers who have a history of being financially responsible. But how does a company decide if a customer is creditworthy? And how much credit should a company extend?

*Some companies grant credit "on the spot" with no credit checks. Why would a company do this? What problems could the company later encounter?*

To answer these questions, a company asks each potential credit customer to complete a credit application (similar to the one you would fill out for a car loan). Normally, a credit application requests that the applicant provide the following information: (1) the name of the applicant's employer and the applicant's income, (2) the name of the applicant's bank, his or her bank account numbers, and the balances in his or her accounts, (3) a list of assets, (4) credit card account numbers and amounts owed, and (5) a list of other debts. The company will contact the applicant's employer, bank, and credit card companies to verify the application information and ask questions about the applicant's credit history. If the applicant has been financially responsible (i.e., earns a minimum level of income, has not issued many NSF checks, and has made bank and credit card payments in a timely manner), the company approves the application. The amount of credit that it approves depends on the applicant's income, amounts of other debt, and the specific results of the company's investigation. Credit sales should be made only to customers whose credit it has approved.

Second, a company should monitor the accounts receivable balances of its customers. Recall from Chapter 6 that credit customers agree to accept certain payment terms. Common credit terms are "2/10, net/30." Under this arrangement the customer agrees that a 2 percent cash discount will be granted if it makes payment within 10 days and that, if it does not make payment then, the full amount is due in 30 days. To monitor customer credit effectively, a company needs to have an accounting system that is able to keep track of each customer's credit activity. The company also needs to have an organized collection effort. It should mail monthly statements to customers and should consider payments not received in 30 days (in this case) to be past due. It should send personalized letters to customers whose accounts become past due and should deny them additional credit until it collects the past-due amounts. If accounts become very overdue, say 90 days or more, the company can use telephone calls to encourage payments. At some point, it may consider an overdue account to be uncollectible and may decide not to make any further effort to collect the account or to turn it over to a collection agency.

Third, a company should monitor its total accounts receivable balance. If the balance increases, the company should investigate the reasons for the increase. If the increase resulted from an increase in credit sales from creditworthy customers, the company will continue with its standard collection efforts. However, if the increase resulted from a slowdown in cash collections, the company should reexamine its credit and collection policies to try to solve the problem.

Regardless of the collection effort made by a company, it can expect that some of its accounts receivable will not be collectible. The point of the collection effort is to improve the percentage of accounts receivable that *are* collected. Most financial statement users know that some of a company's accounts receivable are not collectible. In the next section, we will discuss how a company includes this information when reporting the amount of its accounts receivable on its balance sheet.

*Would you rather know the amount you are owed or the amount you expect to receive? Why?*

## Accounts Receivable Balance

The amount of accounts receivable that a company reports on its balance sheet is the amount of cash it expects to receive from customers as payments for previous credit sales. The words "expects to receive" reflect the fact that the company may not collect all of its accounts receivable. So, the amount a company shows on its balance sheet as accounts receivable is the total owed by customers (the "gross" amount) less an amount that it expects to be uncollectible. GAAP refers to this amount as the *net realizable value* of accounts receivable.

A company shows its accounts receivable at their net realizable value because, as part of an analysis of its liquidity, financial statement users are concerned with the company's ability to turn accounts receivable into cash. As you learned in Chapter 8, predicting a company's cash flows helps external users make business decisions.

The gross amount of the total accounts receivable at year-end is calculated by adding all of the individual customers' balances. However, the dollar amount of accounts receivable that are uncollectible requires an estimate. This is because the company doesn't know which customers won't pay. (If, at the time of the credit sale, the company thought a particular customer would not pay for the goods, it would not have granted the credit!)

Given the uncertainties of collecting accounts receivable, how does a company estimate the amount that it expects will be uncollectible? In general, a company bases this estimate on its past experience with collections. Using the company's history as a guide, it either calculates the estimate as a percentage of credit sales (e.g., 1 percent of credit sales) or bases the estimate on an "aging analysis" of the accounts receivable (i.e., the older a receivable is, the more likely it is to be uncollectible). We will discuss specific types of estimation methods in Chapter 13.

To inform financial statement users that a company is showing its accounts receivable at the net realizable value, the company places the word "net" after accounts receivable on the balance sheet: Accounts receivable (net).

Sweet Temptations shows its accounts receivable on its December 31, 2009 balance sheet (Exhibit 9-1) as follows:

| | |
|---|---|
| Accounts receivable (net) | $7,340 |

To determine this net amount, Sweet Temptations calculated its dollar estimate of uncollectible accounts receivable and subtracted it from the total amount of accounts receivable listed in the accounting records. Assuming Sweet Temptations' gross accounts receivable are $7,874 (the company's accounting system keeps track of this amount), we can determine that its estimated uncollectible accounts receivable at December 31, 2009 are $534 ($7,874 − $7,340).

Many companies' accounts receivable result from selling inventory on credit. We will discuss inventory management in the next section.

# INVENTORY

*Why do companies sometimes sell their goods for 50 percent off the retail price? Why do they advertise that they are having an inventory reduction sale? Should this affect the way they account for their inventory?*

A company's **inventory** is the merchandise being held for resale. In Chapter 6, we discussed how a company uses either a perpetual inventory system or a periodic inventory system to keep track of its merchandise. That discussion focused on the calculation of a company's cost of goods sold. Remember that the cost of goods sold is the cost a company has incurred for the merchandise (goods) it has sold to customers during the accounting period. The company includes the cost of goods sold as an expense on its income statement. In this section, we focus on the calculation of a company's ending inventory.

Accounting for, controlling, and reporting on inventory are important for several reasons. First, selling inventory is the primary way a retail or manufacturing company gets cash from operating activities (and earns a profit). If the amount of inventory is too low, the company could have future difficulties providing the cash it will need for operations. Second, a company usually expects to turn over its inventory (purchase it, sell it, and replace it with newly purchased inventory) several times during the year. If inventory sales slow down, investors and creditors may become concerned about the company's ability to continue to sell the inventory at a satisfactory profit. Third, storing inventory is expensive due to storage space, utilities, and insurance costs. Finally, inventory can be stolen and/or can become obsolete. For these reasons, a company must effectively account for, control, and report on its inventory.

## Simple Inventory Controls

6 How can managers control inventory in a small company?

A company should establish several simple internal controls that will help safeguard its inventory and improve record-keeping. First, it should control the ordering and acceptance of inventory deliveries. In a small company, the owner is usually the only person who places orders for inventory. But even in a small company, the owner should place orders using a purchase order. A **purchase order** is a document authorizing a supplier to ship the items listed on the document at a specific price. It is signed by an authorized person in the company. Use of purchase orders helps ensure that purchasing activities are efficient and that no unauthorized person can purchase inventory.

A company should keep a list of the purchase orders or copies of the purchase orders where employees can have access to them. Employees receiving inventory need to know what has been ordered because they should accept only approved orders. In addition, employees should check the quantity and condition of every order received. If, on further inspection, an employee finds that the order was not filled properly (e.g., the wrong boxes of chocolates are received) or that the goods are damaged (e.g., the chocolates melted), the supplier should be notified immediately.

*Think about the last time you went shopping. What physical controls over inventory did you notice?*

Second, a company should establish physical controls over inventory while the inventory is being held for sale. One physical control involves restricting access to inventory. You have probably seen signs on certain company doors that state:

**FOR EMPLOYEES ONLY**

Companies post the signs to help keep customers out of storage areas. Other controls include locked display cases, magnetic security devices, and camera surveillance systems.

Finally, to make sure that inventory records are accurate, a company should periodically take a physical count of its inventory. Whether a company uses a perpetual or a periodic inventory system (discussed in Chapter 6), by physically counting inventory the company can determine the accuracy of its inventory records and can estimate losses from theft, breakage, or spoilage. Almost all companies count inventory at least once a year. Many companies count inventory after closing on the date of their year-end balance sheet. By counting inventory at the end of the fiscal year, a company can use the inventory count to help determine the dollar amount of inventory that it will show on its balance sheet and the cost of goods sold that it will show on its income statement.

Recall that Sweet Temptations uses a perpetual inventory system, so it keeps a running balance of its inventory and cost of goods sold in its accounting records. To verify the accuracy of these balances, Anna Cox and an employee spent two hours counting the boxes of chocolates in Sweet Temptations' inventory after it closed on December 31, 2009. When they were finished, Anna calculated that Sweet Temptations owned 274 boxes of Unlimited Decadence chocolates at year-end.

## Determining the Cost of Ending Inventory

A company shows its inventory on its ending balance sheet as a *dollar amount.* So, after the company has counted the number of units in its ending inventory, it must determine the appropriate unit *cost* for each item. How does a company figure out the cost of each inventory item? To answer that question, we need to explain two things: (1) the relationship among cost of goods available for sale, cost of goods sold, and year-end inventory, and (2) the concept of cost flows.

### Cost of Goods Available for Sale, Sold, and Held in Inventory

At the start of any month, a company has a certain number of inventory items available for sale—its beginning-of-the-month inventory. For example, say Sweet Temptations starts the month of December 2009 with 590 boxes of chocolates. During the month, a company like Sweet Temptations sells some of its inventory and makes purchases to restock for additional sales. Ideally, at the end of the month, one of two things has happened to all of the items that were available for sale during the month. Either the goods were sold *or* the goods remain in inventory. If Sweet Temptations purchases an additional 300 boxes of chocolates during December and sells 616 boxes, 274 boxes remain in inventory on December 31. Remember that the year-end physical count of inventory was 274 boxes. These calculations for the month of December can be summarized as follows:

| | | |
|---|---|---|
| | Beginning inventory for December | 590 boxes |
| + | December purchases | 300 boxes |
| = | Goods available for sale during December | 890 boxes |
| − | Goods sold during December | (616) boxes |
| = | Goods in inventory on December 31, 2009 | 274 boxes |

As we discussed in earlier chapters, when Sweet Temptations prepares its financial statements for the month, it includes the *cost* of the goods sold during the month in the monthly income statement and the *cost* of the ending inventory in the month-end balance sheet, based on its perpetual inventory records. For December, Sweet Temptations' Cost of Goods Sold account shows a balance of $3,399.75, and its Inventory account shows an ending balance of $1,570.25. To arrive at these amounts, Sweet Temptations converted the number of boxes of candy purchased, sold, and on hand to dollar amounts. Sweet Temptations recorded these dollar amounts in its Inventory and Cost of Goods Sold accounts, as we illustrated in Chapter 6.

Exhibit 9-8 shows the December inventory information for Sweet Temptations.[1] Notice that Sweet Temptations' beginning inventory cost $5.50 per box. The purchase it

[1]Normally, when a company takes a physical inventory at the end of its fiscal year, it calculates its units and costs of goods available for sale for the entire year. For simplicity, we illustrate Sweet Temptations' inventory information for only one month.

**EXHIBIT 9-8 SWEET TEMPTATIONS' INVENTORY INFORMATION**

| | | |
|---|---|---|
| Beg. Inventory, Dec. 1 | 590 boxes @ $5.50 per box = | $3,245 |
| December 13 purchase | 300 boxes @ $5.75 per box = | 1,725 |
| Cost of goods available for sale | 890 boxes | $4,970 |
| Sales during December | (616) boxes | |
| End. Inventory, Dec. 31 | 274 boxes | |

made on December 13 cost $5.75 per box. Since the unit costs of the inventory changed during the month, Sweet Temptations had to decide which cost to assign to the boxes it sold and which cost to assign to the boxes left in inventory. For example, should it assign all of the boxes a cost of $5.50 or all a cost of $5.75? Or should it use both costs and, if so, to which boxes should it assign $5.50 and to which ones $5.75? Or should it use the average of both costs?

A company must have a *method* for deciding how to calculate the dollar amounts for inventory and cost of goods sold, and it may use one of several methods to determine these dollar amounts. However, the company should use its chosen method consistently from year to year, unless a different method would better reflect the company's operations, so that users of its financial statements can compare its performance from year to year. Here, we discuss the specific identification method. We will discuss other methods in Chapter 19.

### Specific Identification Method

The **specific identification method** allocates costs to cost of goods sold and to ending inventory by assigning to each unit sold and to each unit in ending inventory the cost to the company of purchasing that particular unit. Under this method a company keeps track of the cost of each inventory item separately. Usually, it does this tracking through a computer system or through an inventory coding system. For example, on every box of chocolates that Sweet Temptations receives from Unlimited Decadence, the date the chocolates were made is stamped on the bottom. Because Unlimited Decadence sends its chocolates out freshly made, Sweet Temptations can use this date to tell which shipment a box came from and the exact cost of the box.[2] Many companies have *point of sale* cash register systems that scan the inventory codes to keep track of the costs of inventory sold and inventory on hand.

For example, say that on December 21 a customer purchases three boxes of chocolates for $12 per box and pays in cash. As Anna rings up the sale, she notes on the sales receipt that two boxes are dated 11-29-2009 and one box is dated 12-13-2009. From Exhibit 9-8 we can see that the boxes dated 11-29-2009 cost $5.50 per box and the box dated 12-13-2009 cost $5.75. When she records this sale, Anna increases the Cash and Sales accounts by $36 ($12 × 3 boxes). She also decreases the Inventory account and increases the separate expense account—Cost of Goods Sold—by $16.75, the exact cost of the items sold ($5.50 + $5.50 + $5.75).

**FINANCIAL STATEMENT EFFECTS**

Increases current assets and total assets on ***balance sheet***. Increases revenues, which increases net income on ***income statement*** (and therefore increases owner's equity on ***balance sheet***). Increases cash flows from operating activities on ***cash flow statement***.

**FINANCIAL STATEMENT EFFECTS**

Decreases current assets and total assets on ***balance sheet***. Increases expenses (cost of goods sold), which decreases net income on ***income statement*** (and therefore decreases owner's equity on ***balance sheet***).

The inventory amount that Sweet Temptations shows on its December 31, 2009 balance sheet is calculated from the results of the physical inventory count. (This amount should be the same as the amount that it shows in its accounting records.) Recall that 274 boxes remained in inventory on December 31. Under the specific identification method, in addition to counting the inventory, Anna and her employee must keep track of the boxes according to the stamped dates. Exhibit 9-9 shows Anna's inventory count instructions, the results of the count, and the year-end inventory and cost of goods sold calculations.

[2]Although we did not mention it in Chapter 6, we used the specific identification method in our earlier inventory discussion.

## EXHIBIT 9-9 SWEET TEMPTATIONS' YEAR-END INVENTORY CALCULATION

**The Inventory Count**

After Sweet Temptations closes on the evening of December 31, 2009, Anna and one employee spend two hours counting the company's inventory. Anna tells her employee how the count will work: "You and I will count all of the items independently of each other. I will follow along right behind you. We will count one section of the store at a time. Both of us will mark our findings on inventory count sheets, noting separately the number of boxes dated 11-29-2009 and the number dated 12-13-2009. We have to count these boxes separately because we purchased them at different prices and we value inventory using the specific identification method. After we finish each section of the store, we will compare our results to see that we agree on the count. If the numbers don't match, we will recount the section. After we count all of the inventory, we will compute a total for the number of boxes dated 11-29-2009 and 12-13-2009."

**The Results of the Inventory Count**

Sweet Temptations' inventory count ran smoothly. After compiling all of the inventory count sheets, Anna concluded that the year-end inventory consisted of the following:

253 boxes of chocolates dated 12-13-2009
21 boxes of chocolates dated 11-29-2009

**December 31, 2009 Inventory Calculation**

| | |
|---|---|
| 253 boxes @ \$5.75 = | \$1,454.75 |
| 21 boxes @ \$5.50 = | 115.50 |
| Ending inventory | \$1,570.25 |

**December Cost of Goods Sold Calculation**

| | |
|---|---|
| Cost of goods available for sale (Exhibit 9-8) | \$4,970.00 |
| − Ending inventory | (1,570.25) |
| Cost of goods sold | \$3,399.75 |

*As a manager, would you "allow" customers to select any box of chocolates from the shelves?*

Because Sweet Temptations' physical inventory count of 274 boxes is the same as the calculation of its ending inventory from its inventory records of beginning inventory, purchases, and sales shown earlier, the \$1,570.25 cost of the ending inventory calculated in Exhibit 9-9 is the same as the amount in its Inventory account. Furthermore, the \$3,399.75 cost of goods sold calculated in Exhibit 9-9 is the same as the amount in its Cost of Goods Sold account. So, by taking a physical count, Sweet Temptations has verified that the amounts in its accounting records are correct.

Now suppose that Anna and her employee counted 253 boxes of chocolates dated 12-13-2009 but only 17 boxes dated 11-29-2009. In this case, 4 boxes of chocolates are missing, and the cost of the ending inventory is \$1,548.25 [(253 × \$5.75) + (17 × \$5.50)]. Anna should try to find out why these boxes are missing. For instance, they may have been given away as "free samples," stolen (or eaten by the employees), or thrown away because they were stale. Whatever the reason, she should adjust the accounting records by increasing the Cost of Goods Sold account and decreasing the Inventory account by \$22 (4 × \$5.50) for the missing boxes.

**FINANCIAL STATEMENT EFFECTS**

Decreases current assets and total assets on ***balance sheet***. Increases expenses (cost of goods sold), which decreases net income on ***income statement*** (and therefore decreases owner's equity on ***balance sheet***).

*Suppose that the year-end count of inventory is less than the accounting records show as ending inventory because Anna threw away stale boxes of chocolates. How might this information affect Anna's future decisions?*

# ACCOUNTS PAYABLE

As we explained earlier in the chapter, companies often sell on credit to customers. These credit sales result in accounts receivable. Similarly, companies often make purchases on credit, which result in the liability accounts payable. **Accounts payable** are the amounts that a company owes to its suppliers for previous credit purchases of inventory and supplies. The reasons for purchasing on credit are similar to the reasons for selling on credit. The first reason is that purchasing on credit is often more convenient than purchasing with cash. The second reason for purchasing on credit is to delay paying for purchases and, by doing so, to obtain a short-term "loan" from the supplier. Many companies, particularly small companies, are often short of cash and find it difficult to pay for their purchases immediately. Managers of these companies, therefore, try to delay payment until their companies receive the cash from the eventual sale of their products; they then use this cash to pay the amounts their companies owe. This delay is the reason many suppliers offer their customers cash discounts for prompt payment.

## Simple Controls over Accounts Payable

7 How can managers control accounts payable in a small company?

A company's accounts payable represent promises to pay the amounts due to other businesses. As is the case with accounts receivable, a company needs controls over accounts payable. Controls over accounts payable should focus on three primary concerns. The first concern involves the ability of employees to obligate the company to an account payable. Giving too many employees the authority to place orders for company purchases makes it more difficult for managers to coordinate and monitor credit purchases, and makes it easier for untrustworthy employees to obligate the company for personal expenditures. In response to this concern, a company should limit the number of employees who have the authority to make company purchases. In a small company, this authority may be given only to the owner. Larger companies usually have a purchasing department that controls all company purchases.

Second, once a company incurs an account payable, the company is concerned that it makes each payment at the appropriate time and that the *supplier* records each payment properly. A company monitors the timeliness of its payments by having an employee keep track of the credit terms of each account payable. If cash discounts are available, the company should take advantage of the cash savings by making the payment within the cash discount period. A company makes sure that the supplier records its payments properly by checking the supplier's monthly statements. If the payment is not recorded properly, an employee should investigate the discrepancy and perhaps contact the supplier.

Finally, managers, investors, and creditors are concerned about a company's total dollar amount of accounts payable because, in the very near future, the company will need to use its cash to pay these liabilities. If the accounts payable are large relative to the company's current assets, the company may experience liquidity problems.

Managers will investigate relatively large increases in accounts payable. If the increase is a result of planned increases in inventory, they assume that increased sales will provide the cash needed to pay the liabilities. If the increase is a result of cash flow problems, managers may postpone purchases of inventory and/or property and equipment, or may contact suppliers to try to arrange an extension of the credit terms.

## Accounts Payable Balance

The amount of accounts payable that a company owes on the balance sheet date is listed in the current liabilities section of the ending balance sheet. A company calculates this amount by summing the accounts payable owed to individual suppliers. As Exhibit 9-1 shows, on December 31, 2009, Sweet Temptations' total accounts payable is $7,540.

## BUSINESS ISSUES AND VALUES

*Has anyone ever forgotten to repay you for money that he or she borrowed? Has it ever been difficult for you to pay off a debt? How should a company handle these situations? What factors should it consider when developing policies concerning late payments by its customers or to its suppliers?*

We started the chapter by stating that managing working capital effectively is an important part of financial management. This is especially true for new companies that have a relatively small amount of capital and may be prone to liquidity problems. But how aggressive should a company be in managing its working capital? When trying to collect accounts receivable payments, some companies repeatedly telephone customers at their offices and homes. On the other hand, when trying to hold off paying their own debts, some companies continue to tell suppliers that "the check is in the mail" when it really is not.

The ethics of aggressive working capital management has been questioned by some business leaders and critics. Instead of being seen as conscientious, a company that uses aggressive collection efforts can be viewed as intimidating and harassing. A company that signs a purchase agreement, even though it knows that it will make suppliers wait an additional 30 or 60 days before paying for the goods, can be viewed as untrustworthy, not as a shrewd financial planner. What do you think? We will continue to discuss these types of issues in future chapters when we examine corporations.

## SUMMARY

At the beginning of the chapter we asked you several questions. During the chapter, we asked you to STOP and answer some additional questions to build your knowledge about specific issues. Be sure you answered these additional questions. Below are the questions from the beginning of the chapter, with a brief summary of the key points relating to the answers. Use your creative and critical thinking skills to expand on these key points to develop more complete answers to the questions and to determine what other questions you have that might lead you to learn more about the issues.

### 1 What is working capital, and why is its management important?

Working capital is current assets minus current liabilities. A company needs to manage its working capital so that it keeps an appropriate balance between having enough to conduct its operations and to handle unexpected needs, and having too much so that profitability is reduced.

### 2 How can managers control cash receipts in a small company?

Managers can control cash receipts by requiring the proper use of a cash register, separating the duties of receiving and processing collections of accounts receivable, and depositing receipts every day.

### 3 How can managers control cash payments in a small company?

Managers can control cash payments by paying all bills by check, paying only for approved purchases supported by source documents, and immediately stamping "paid" on the supporting documents after payment.

### 4 What is a bank reconciliation, and what are the causes of the difference between a company's cash balance in its accounting records and its cash balance on its bank statement?

A bank reconciliation is an analysis that a company uses to resolve the difference between the cash balance in its accounting records and the cash balance reported by the bank on its bank statement. The causes of the difference are deposits in transit, outstanding checks, deposits made directly by the bank, charges made directly by the bank, and errors.

### 5 How can managers control accounts receivable in a small company?

Managers can control accounts receivable by evaluating a customer's ability to pay before extending credit, monitoring the accounts receivable balance of each customer, and monitoring the total accounts receivable balance.

### 6 How can managers control inventory in a small company?

Managers can control inventory by establishing policies for ordering and accepting inventory, establishing physical controls over inventory being held for sale, and taking a periodic physical count of the inventory.

### 7 How can managers control accounts payable in a small company?

Managers can control accounts payable by coordinating and monitoring credit purchases, making payments at the appropriate time, and monitoring the total accounts payable balance.

## KEY TERMS

**accounts payable** *(p. 289)*
**accounts receivable** *(p. 282)*
**bank reconciliation** *(p. 275)*
**bank statement** *(p. 274)*
**cash** *(p. 272)*
**deposit in transit** *(p. 275)*
**internal control structure** *(p. 272)*
**inventory** *(p. 285)*
**NSF (not sufficient funds) check** *(p. 275)*
**outstanding check** *(p. 275)*
**petty cash fund** *(p. 280)*
**purchase order** *(p. 285)*
**specific identification method** *(p. 287)*
**working capital** *(p. 269)*

## SUMMARY SURFING

Here is an opportunity to gather information on the Internet about real-world issues related to the topics in this chapter (for suggestions on how to navigate various companies' Web sites to find their financial statements and other information, see the related discussion in the Preface at the beginning of the book). Answer the following questions.

- Go to the **SBA** (U.S. Small Business Administration) **OnLine Library** Web site. Click on *Publications*. Under **STARTUP** *Financial Management Series* click on 1. *Understanding Cash Flow FM-4* and open the article. How does the article define "working capital cash conversion cycle"? What are some suggestions for (a) more efficient collections, (b) more efficient payments, (c) more efficient management of accounts receivable, (d) more efficient inventory management, and (e) purchasing goods on more favorable terms?

## INTEGRATED BUSINESS AND ACCOUNTING SITUATIONS

**Answer the Following Questions in Your Own Words.**

### Testing Your Knowledge

**9-1** What is a company's working capital, and what is included in its two components?

**9-2** Why does a company manage its working capital?

**9-3** Define *cash* for a company.

**9-4** Briefly discuss the controls over cash sales.

**9-5** Briefly discuss the controls over collections of cash from accounts receivable.

**9-6** Briefly discuss the controls over cash payments.

**9-7** What is a bank reconciliation?

**9-8** Identify the causes of the difference between the ending cash balance in a company's records and the ending cash balance reported on its bank statement.

**9-9** Briefly explain what is meant by the terms *deposits in transit* and *outstanding checks.*

**9-10** Briefly explain what are included in deposits made directly by the bank and charges made directly by the bank.

**9-11** Prepare an outline of a bank reconciliation for a company.

**9-12** Briefly explain what a petty cash fund is and how it works.

**9-13** Why do companies make sales on credit?

**9-14** Briefly discuss the controls over accounts receivable.

**9-15** Briefly explain how a company reports its accounts receivable on its ending balance sheet.

**9-16** Why is accounting for, controlling, and reporting of inventory important?

**9-17** Briefly discuss the controls over inventory.

**9-18** Briefly explain how the specific identification method works for determining inventory costs.

**9-19** Evaluate this statement: "My company uses a perpetual inventory system, so it doesn't need to take a periodic physical inventory."

**9-20** Briefly discuss the controls over accounts payable.

## Applying Your Knowledge

**9-21** The following are several internal control weaknesses of a small retail company in regard to its cash receipts and accounts receivable:

(a) Sales invoices are not prenumbered.
(b) Receipts from daily sales are deposited every Tuesday and Thursday evening.
(c) One employee is responsible for depositing customer checks from collections of accounts receivable and for recording their receipt in the accounts.
(d) For credit sales on terms of 2/10, net/30, customers are allowed, for convenience, the discount if payment is received within 20 days.
(e) A money box is used instead of a cash register to store both the sales invoices and the cash from the sales.
(f) Credit sales of a large dollar amount can be approved by any sales employee.
(g) When customers write checks for payment, only the identification of customers who look "untrustworthy" is verified.

*Required:* (1) For each internal control weakness, explain how the weakness might result in a loss of the company's assets.
(2) For each internal control weakness, explain what action should be taken to correct the weakness.

**9-22** The following are several internal control weaknesses of a retail company in regard to its cash payments, accounts payable, and inventory:

(a) The inventory of gold jewelry for sale is kept in unlocked display cases.
(b) One employee is responsible for ordering inventory and writing checks.
(c) Some purchases are made by phone, and no purchase order is written up.
(d) The company takes a physical inventory every two years.
(e) Employees are allowed to bring coats, bags, and purses into working areas.
(f) Inventory received at the loading dock is rushed immediately to the sales floor before it is counted.

(g) When inventory is low, any sales employee can prepare a purchase order and mail it to the supplier.
(h) For efficiency, the company pays invoices on credit purchases once a month, even if it has to forgo any cash discounts for prompt payment.

*Required:* (1) For each internal control weakness, explain how the weakness might result in a loss of the company's assets.
(2) For each internal control weakness, explain what action should be taken to correct the weakness.

**9-23** A company is preparing its bank reconciliation and discovers the following items:
(a) Outstanding checks
(b) Deposits in transit
(c) Deposits made directly by the bank
(d) Charges made directly by the bank
(e) The bank's erroneous underrecording of a deposit
(f) The company's erroneous underrecording of a check it wrote

*Required:* Indicate how each of these items would be used to adjust (1) the company's cash balance or (2) the bank balance to calculate the reconciled cash balance.

**9-24** At the end of March, the Elbert Company records showed a cash balance of $7,027. When comparing the March 31 bank statement with the company's Cash account, the company discovered that deposits in transit were $725, outstanding checks totaled $862, bank service charges were $28, and NSF checks totaled $175.

*Required:* (1) Compute the March 31 reconciled cash balance of the Elbert Company.
(2) Compute the cash balance listed on the March 31 bank statement.

**9-25** At the end of September, the Bross Bicycle Company's records showed a cash balance of $3,513. When comparing the September 30 bank statement, which showed a cash balance of $1,860, with the company's Cash account, the company discovered that outstanding checks were $462, bank service charges were $23, and NSF checks totaled $89.

*Required:* (1) Compute the September 30 reconciled cash balance of the Bross Bicycle Company.
(2) Compute the September deposits in transit.

**9-26** The following five situations (columns 1–5) are independent:

| | 1 | 2 | 3 | 4 | 5 |
|---|---|---|---|---|---|
| Ending balance in the company's checking account | (a) | $2,000 | $4,000 | $12,000 | $3,000 |
| Deposits made directly by the bank | $ 200 | (b) | 500 | 450 | 200 |
| Deposits in transit | 700 | 800 | (c) | 500 | 900 |
| Outstanding checks | 450 | 1,200 | 600 | (d) | 1,000 |
| Ending cash balance from bank statement | 6,000 | 3,000 | 4,100 | 12,000 | (e) |

*Required:* Compute each of the unknown amounts, items (a) through (e).

**9-27** An examination of the accounting records and the bank statement of the Evans Company at March 31 provides the following information:
(a) The Cash account has a balance of $6,351.98.
(b) The bank statement shows a bank balance of $3,941.83.
(c) The March 31 cash receipts of $3,260.95 were deposited in the bank at the end of that day but were not recorded by the bank until April 1.
(d) Checks issued and mailed in March but not included among the checks listed as paid on the bank statement were as follows:

| | |
|---|---|
| Check No. 706 | $869.38 |
| Check No. 717 | 212.00 |

(e) A bank service charge of $30 for March was deducted on the bank statement.
(f) A check received from a customer for $185 in payment of his account and deposited by the Evans Company was returned marked "NSF" with the bank statement.
(g) Interest of $20.42 earned on the company's checking account was added on the bank statement.
(h) The Evans Company discovered that Check No. 701, which was correctly written as $562 for the March rent, was recorded as $526 in the company's accounts.

*Required:* (1) Prepare a bank reconciliation on March 31.
(2) Record the appropriate adjustments in the company's accounts. Compute the ending balance in the Cash account.

**9-28** You have been asked to help the Rancher Company prepare its bank reconciliation. You examine the company's accounting records and its bank statement at May 31, and find the following information:
(a) The Cash account has a balance of $7,753.24.
(b) The bank statement shows a bank balance of $3,783.04.
(c) The May 31 cash receipts of $4,926.18 were deposited in the bank at the end of that day but were not recorded by the bank until June 1.
(d) Checks issued and mailed in May but not included among the checks listed as paid on the bank statement were as follows:

| | |
|---|---|
| Check No. 949 | $518.65 |
| Check No. 957 | 699.95 |

(e) A bank service charge of $27 for May was deducted on the bank statement.
(f) A check received from a customer for $241 in payment of her account and deposited by the Rancher Company was returned marked "NSF" with the bank statement.
(g) Interest of $25.18 earned on the company's checking account was added on the bank statement.
(h) The Rancher Company discovered that Check No. 941, which was correctly written as $647.21 for the May utility bill, was recorded as $627.41 in the company's accounts.

*Required:* (1) Prepare a bank reconciliation on May 31.
(2) Record the appropriate adjustments in the company's accounts. Compute the ending balance in the Cash account.

**9-29** The Huron Company keeps a petty cash fund of $80. On June 30 the fund contained cash of $36.87 and the following petty cash receipts:

| | |
|---|---|
| Office supplies | $10.00 |
| Postage | 27.48 |
| Miscellaneous | 5.65 |

*Required:* (1) If the company's fiscal year ends June 30, should the petty cash fund be replenished on June 30? Why?
(2) How much cash is needed to replenish the petty cash fund?
(3) Prepare entries in the company's accounts to record the petty cash payments.

**9-30** On December 31, the Bighorn Condominium Management Company had a balance of $70 in its petty cash fund, a reconciled balance of $1,283 in its checking account, and a $4,627 balance in its savings account.

*Required:* Show how the company would report its cash on its December 31 balance sheet.

**9-31** The Snow-Be-Gone Company sells one type of snowblower and uses the perpetual inventory system. At the beginning of January, the company had a balance in its Cash account of $2,100 and an inventory of 8 units (snowblowers) costing $100 each. During January, it made the following purchases and sales of inventory:

| | | |
|---|---|---|
| Jan. 5 | Purchases | 4 units @ $102 per unit |
| 12 | Sales | 11 units @ $150 per unit |
| 18 | Purchases | 12 units @ $104 per unit |
| 25 | Purchases | 6 units @ $103 per unit |
| 29 | Sales | 13 units @ $150 per unit |

All purchases and sales were for cash. The company uses "bar codes" to verify each sale. For the sales on January 12, 8 were units from the beginning inventory, and 3 were units purchased on January 5. For the sales on January 29, 9 were units purchased on January 18, and 4 were units purchased on January 25.

*Required:* (1) Record the beginning balances in the Cash and Inventory accounts. Using account columns, record the purchases and sales transactions during January and compute the ending balances of all the accounts you used.

(2) Assume that the company counted its inventory at the end of January and determined that it had 6 snowblowers on hand. Prove that the ending balance in the Inventory account that you computed in (1) is correct.

(3) Compute the company's gross profit.

**9-32** The Kvam Lawn Mower Store sells one type of lawn mower at a price of $200 per unit. On June 1, it had an $800 accounts receivable balance and a $600 accounts payable balance, as well as an inventory of 10 mowers costing $120 each. During June, its purchases and sales of mowers were as follows:

| | Purchases | Sales |
|---|---|---|
| June 8 | 7 mowers @ $125 each | |
| 15 | | 11 mowers |
| 21 | 6 mowers @ $121 each | |
| 26 | 4 mowers @ $124 each | |
| 30 | | 8 mowers |

All purchases and sales were on credit. No payments or collections were made during June. The company has a perpetual inventory system and uses "bar codes" to verify each sale. For the June 15 sales, 8 were mowers from the beginning inventory, and 3 were mowers purchased on June 8. For the June 30 sales, 2 were mowers from the beginning inventory, 5 were mowers purchased on June 21, and 1 was a mower purchased on June 26.

*Required:* (1) Record the beginning balances in the Accounts Receivable, Inventory, and Accounts Payable accounts. Using account columns, record the purchases and sales transactions during June and compute the ending balances of all the accounts you used.

(2) Assume that the company counted its inventory at the close of business on June 30 and determined that it had 8 mowers in stock. Prove that the ending balance in the Inventory account that you computed in (1) is correct.

(3) Compute the company's gross profit percentage for June. How does this compare with its gross profit percentage of 40.8% for May? What might account for the difference?

**9-33** The Bugs-Be-Gone Company sells two types of screen doors. Model A, which sells for $30, is the basic screen door, and Model B, which sells for $50, is the deluxe screen door that features removable glass panels so that it can be turned into a storm door during the winter. At the beginning of July, the company had a balance in its Cash account of $1,600 and an inventory consisting of 12 units of Model A costing $20 each and 15 units of Model B costing $35 each. During July, it made the following purchases and sales of inventory:

| | | Model A | Model B |
|---|---|---|---|
| July 6 | Sales | 8 units @ $30 each | 10 units @ $50 each |
| 13 | Purchases | 9 units @ $19 each | 10 units @ $36 each |
| 20 | Sales | 10 units @ $30 each | 12 units @ $50 each |
| 24 | Purchases | 7 units @ $21 each | 6 units @ $37 each |
| 29 | Sales | 7 units @ $30 each | 3 units @ $50 each |

All purchases and sales are for cash. The company has a perpetual inventory system, using "bar codes" to verify each sale. For the July 20 sales, 3 units of Model A were from the beginning inventory, and 7 were units purchased on July 13; 5 units of Model B were from the beginning inventory, and 7 were units purchased on July 13. For the July 29 sales, 1 unit of Model A was purchased on July 13, and 6 were units purchased on July 24; 1 unit of Model B was purchased on July 13, and 2 were units purchased on July 24.

On July 31, the company counted its inventory and determined that it had 3 units of Model A and 6 units of Model B on hand. However, 1 of the 3 units of Model A was run over by a customer's truck and had to be thrown away. This unit had been in the beginning inventory.

*Required:* (1) Record the beginning balances in the Cash and Inventory accounts. Using account columns (use one account column for inventory), record the purchases and sales transactions during July and compute the ending balances of all the accounts you used.

(2) Record the disposal of the damaged unit and prove the accuracy of the ending balance in the Inventory account.

(3) Compute the gross profit percentage. How was this affected by the damaged inventory?

(4) Do you think your work would have been easier if you had used two inventory accounts in (1)? How do you think a company with many items of inventory keeps track of these items under a perpetual inventory system?

## Making Evaluations

**9-34** Your younger brother, always bursting with curiosity, recently purchased a fishing rod from a catalog. While he was filling out the order form, he noticed the warning: "Don't Send Cash!" So, after pointing it out to you, he asked, "Does it seem odd to you that a company wouldn't appreciate receiving cash? You're taking accounting. Don't they teach you in there that companies need cash? Why would they say such a thing?"

*Required:* Tell your brother why you think the company puts this warning in its catalogs, give him some examples of what might happen if customers paid for their purchases with cash, and explain how checks and credit cards might prevent this from happening.

**9-35** Sam Lewis has been operating a "full service" service station for several years. Although he occasionally has employed students part-time, he has collected the cash and checks for gas and repair work himself. He now has decided to open a second "full service" service station and put himself more in the role of a manager. He will hire employees to run the service stations and to pump gas and do repair work.

*Required:* How should Sam Lewis implement internal control procedures over cash receipts for the service stations?

**9-36** Your dad's friend Frank was over for dinner the other night, and discussion turned to his business, Frank's Franks, which is responsible for street-corner vending of hotdogs, pretzels, beer, and soda. It's a small company, with an office downtown and four vending carts located in different areas of downtown. When you asked Frank what kind of internal controls his company has in place, Frank said, "We don't have a formal system of internal controls—don't need them. My employees are family members and friends, and I trust them completely! Now when the business grows, and I have to hire strangers, then I'll think about those controls. But now, the company's profitable, and I'm happy." After Frank left, you talked to your dad about what you had learned in accounting, and asked whether he thought Frank would appreciate hearing about it. Your dad assured you that Frank would be open to your suggestions.

*Required:* Write a letter to Frank explaining how you think his company would benefit from a system of internal controls, even though he trusts his employees. Also describe specific controls that Frank could use in his particular business.

**9-37** Your friend Ruby Johnson works as a cashier in an upscale restaurant located in a business center that includes a bank. She works the late shift, and since the restaurant caters to the convention crowd, she generally doesn't leave work until 2:00 or 2:30 in the morning. One day, when you were having lunch with her, she began complaining about one aspect of her job: "My boss is a real stickler for procedures. Even though it's really late when the last customer leaves, and even though we are exhausted, we still have to follow *procedure.* Before the host and I can leave, we have to count the money in the register and match it against the register tape and match both amounts against the dollar total of the checks the customers paid. And, as if that's not enough, we have to make sure that every check number is accounted for. Every night the manager writes down the numbers of the checks each waitperson has been given to use that night for taking customer orders. At the end of the night, the waitpeople give the cashier all the checks they didn't use. If any money is missing, guess who takes the blame and has to make up the difference? Anyway, after we count the money, we have to put the money and the tape in a deposit bag, walk it across the parking lot to the bank, and deposit it in the bank's night-deposit box, *even though there is a safe right under the cash register!* Like we're not sitting ducks for anybody who wants to rob us. I don't understand why she would risk our lives like that. Furthermore, the boss unlocks the part of the register that contains a copy of the tape that we took to the bank, and uses that tape to enter the day's cash receipts amount into the accounting system. Like she really trusts me so much that she has to keep the tape copy under lock and key. What a jerk!" Now that you are taking accounting, you have a little better insight into why the boss is so interested in these procedures.

*Required:* Explain to Ruby what's going on before she does something rash, like quit her job.

**9-38** The Anibonita Company is a retail store with three sales departments. It also has a small accounting department, a purchasing department, and a receiving department. All inventory is kept in the sales departments. When the inventory for a specific item is low, the manager of the sales department that sells the item notifies the purchasing department, which then orders the merchandise. All purchases are on credit. Anibonita pays the freight charges on all its purchases after being notified of the cost by the freight company. When the inventory is delivered, it is inspected and checked in by the receiving department and then sent to the sales department, where it is placed on the sales shelves. After notification that the ordered inventory has been received, the accounting department records the purchase. Upon receipt of the supplier's invoice or the freight bill, the accounting department verifies the invoice (or freight bill) against the purchase order and the receiving report before making payment.

*Required:* Briefly explain the internal controls that the Anibonita Company uses for its purchasing process. Include in your discussion what source documents it probably uses.

**9-39** The JeBean Company makes only sales on credit. All JeBean's customers order through the mail. The company has a small accounting department, a credit department, an inventory department, and a shipping department. After approval of an order by the credit department, the merchandise is assembled in the inventory department and then sent to the shipping department. The shipping department packs the merchandise in cardboard boxes; then it is picked up by the freight company and shipped to the customer. The JeBean Company pays for freight charges on all items shipped to customers after being notified of the cost by the freight company. After verification of shipment, the accounting department mails an invoice to the customer and records the sale. On receipt of the customer's check, the accounting department records the collection.

*Required:* Briefly explain the internal controls that the JeBean Company uses for its sales process. Include in your discussion what source documents it probably uses.

**9-40** Oliver Bauer, owner of Bauer's Retail Store, has been very careful to establish good internal control over inventory purchases for his store. The store has several employees, and since Ollie cannot devote as much time as he would like to running the store, he has entrusted a longtime employee with the task of purchasing inventory. This employee has worked for Ollie for 15 years and knows all of the store's suppliers. Whenever inventory must be purchased, the employee prepares a purchase order and mails it to the supplier. When a rush order is needed, the employee occasionally calls in the order and does not prepare a purchase order. This procedure is acceptable to the suppliers because they know the employee. When the merchandise is received from the supplier, this employee carefully checks in each item to verify the correct quantity and quality. This job is usually done at night after the store is closed, thus allowing the employee to help with sales to customers during regular working hours. After checking in the items, the employee initials the copy of the supplier invoice received with the merchandise, staples the copy to the purchase order (if there is one), records the purchase in the company's accounts, and prepares a check for payment. Oliver Bauer examines the source documents (purchase order and initialed invoice) at this point and signs the check, and the employee records the payment. Ollie has become concerned about the store's gross profit, which has been steadily decreasing even though he has heard customers complaining that the store's selling prices are too high. He has a discussion with the employee, who says, "I'm doing my best to hold down costs. I will continue to do my purchasing job as efficiently as possible—even though I am overworked. However, I think you should hire another salesperson and spend more on advertising. This will increase your sales and, in turn, your gross profit."

*Required:* Why do you think the gross profit of the store has gone down? Prepare for Oliver Bauer a report that summarizes any internal control weaknesses existing in the inventory purchasing procedure and explain what the result might be. Make suggestions for improving any weaknesses you uncover.

**9-41** In the chapter, we mentioned that if Sweet Temptations came up short four boxes of candy, it should increase its Cost of Goods Sold account and decrease its Inventory account by the cost of those boxes. Suppose Anna wanted to keep a record of candy shortages in the accounting system.

*Required:* Design a way that Sweet Temptations' accounting system could be changed to accommodate Anna's request.

**9-42** Suppose that one of your company's largest customers has written an NSF check for $9,734 and your boss has just found out about it. This morning he comes flying into your office (with smoke coming out of his ears) and demands to know how this NSF check will affect specific accounts in the company's financial statements. You examine the bank statement that came in the morning's mail and notice that, not only has the customer written an NSF check, but the bank has charged you a fee of $75 for processing this check.

*Required:* List the accounts that will be affected by this turn of events, and indicate by how much they will be affected. What do you think should happen next?

**9-43** You are a consultant for several companies. The following are several independent situations you have discovered, each of which may or may not have one or more internal control weaknesses. The names of the companies have been changed to protect the innocent.

(a) In Company A, one employee is responsible for counting and recording all the receipts (remittances) received in the mail from customers paying their accounts. Customers usually pay by check, but they occasionally mail cash. Every day, after the mail is delivered, this employee opens the envelopes containing payments by customers. She carefully counts all remittances and places the checks and cash in a bag. She then lists the amount of each check or cash received and the customer's name on a sheet of paper. After totaling the cash and checks received, she records the receipts in the company's accounts, endorses the checks in the company's name, and deposits the checks and cash in the bank.

(b) Company B has purchased several programmable calculators for use by the office and sales employees. So that these hand calculators will be available to any employee who needs one, they are kept in an unlocked storage cabinet in the office. Anyone who takes and uses a calculator "signs out" the calculator by writing his or her name on a sheet of paper posted near the cabinet. When the calculator is returned, the employee crosses out his or her name on the sheet.

(c) Company C owns a van for deliveries of sales to customers. No mileage is kept of the deliveries, although all gas and oil receipts are carefully checked before being paid. To advertise the store, Company C printed two signs with the store's name and hung one on each side of the van. These signs are easily removable so that the van can be periodically cleaned without damaging the signs. The company allows employees to borrow the van at night or on the weekends if they need the van for personal hauling. No mileage is kept of the personal hauling, but the employee who borrowed the van must fill the gas tank before returning the van.

(d) Employee Y is in charge of employee records for Company D. Whenever a new employee is hired, the new employee's name, address, salary, and other relevant information are properly recorded. Every payday, all employees are paid by check. At this time Employee Y makes out each employee's check, signs it, and gives it to each employee. After distributing the paychecks, Employee Y makes an entry in the company's accounts, increasing Salaries Expense and decreasing Cash for the total amount of the salary checks.

(e) To reduce paperwork, Company E places orders for purchases of inventory from suppliers by phone. No purchase order is prepared. When the goods arrive at the company, they are immediately brought to the sales floor. An employee then authorizes payment based on the supplier's invoice, writes and signs a check, and mails payment to the supplier. Another employee uses the paid invoice to record the purchase and payment in the company's accounts.

(f) All sales made by Company F, whether they are for cash or on account, are "rung up" on a single cash register. Employee X is responsible for collecting the cash receipts from sales and the customer charge slips at the end of each day. The employee carefully counts the cash, preparing a "cash receipts" slip for the total. Employee X sums the amount on the cash receipts slip and the customer charge slips, and compares this total with the total sales on the cash register tape to verify the total sales for the day. The cash register tape is then discarded, and the cash is deposited in the bank. The cash receipts slip and the customer charge slips are turned over to a different employee, who records the cash and credit sales in the company's accounts.

*Required:* (1) List the internal control weakness or weaknesses you find in each of the preceding independent situations. If no weakness can be found, explain why the internal control is good.

(2) In each situation in which there is an internal control weakness, describe how you would remedy the situation to improve the internal control.

**9-44** Yesterday, you received the letter shown on the following page for your advice column in the local paper:

## DR. DECISIVE

Dear Dr. Decisive:

Well, this takes the cake! I thought my boss was a little on the shady side, and now I'm pretty convinced, but some of my friends think I'm wrong. What do you think? Here's some background. My company uses the specific identification method to assign costs to inventory and cost of goods sold. Well, this year our inventory consisted of two batches of goods. We paid $6.00 per unit for each inventory item in the old batch and $6.75 for each item in the batch we purchased this year. As it turned out, most of the inventory items we sold this year came out of the new batch (the $6.75 ones). The effect was that our cost of goods sold for the year is higher than it would have been if we had sold the old batch of items before we sold items from the new batch.

(Are you following me?) So my attitude is, "Well, que sera sera." Well, that's not my boss's attitude. This morning he came into my office and actually asked me to "recost" the inventory and cost of goods sold assuming that we sold the items in the old batch first and then sold items from the new batch. But we didn't!! Of course, his method would make the cost of goods sold that we report in our income statement lower and our net income higher. So the company would look better. But something about this really galls me. My friends say: "So what? What difference does it make?" Help! You can call me

"Ethical Ethyl" (or not)

*Required:* Meet with your Dr. Decisive team and write a response to "Ethical Ethyl."

## END NOTE

[a]Interview with Michael E. Gerber by Maria Shao, *Des Moines Register*, February 14, 1994, 15-B.

# PART 4

# PLANNING IN A CORPORATE ENVIRONMENT

CHAPTER 10
**INTRODUCTION TO CORPORATIONS: STRUCTURES, REPORTS, AND ANALYSES**

CHAPTER 11
**DEVELOPING A BUSINESS PLAN FOR A MANUFACTURING COMPANY: COST-VOLUME-PROFIT PLANNING AND ANALYSIS**

CHAPTER 12
**DEVELOPING A BUSINESS PLAN FOR A MANUFACTURING COMPANY: BUDGETING**

This section consists of three chapters which introduce you to corporations and how planning in large companies differs from planning in small companies. After reading these chapters, you will be able to:

- *explain the organizational structure of a corporation*
- *describe the unique features of a corporation's financial statements*
- *understand the differences between variable, fixed, and mixed costs*
- *use multiple product cost-volume-profit analysis in business decisions*
- *prepare a master budget for a manufacturing company*
- *use a master budget in the evaluation of a large company's responsibility centers*

CHAPTER 10

# INTRODUCTION TO CORPORATIONS: STRUCTURES, REPORTS, AND ANALYSES

"WHEN SOMETHING GOES WRONG IN A LARGE CORPORATION, YOU BLAME THE BUREAUCRACY. WHEN SOMETHING GOES WRONG IN YOUR SMALL COMPANY, THERE IS NO ONE TO BLAME BUT YOURSELF."

—UNKNOWN

1. What are the three most common forms of business organizations and their basic characteristics?
2. What are the qualities that make accounting information about large corporations useful for decision making?
3. What do users need to know about the stockholders' equity section of a corporation's balance sheet and about its income statement?
4. How does a corporation provide information to external users?
5. How do users perform intracompany and intercompany analyses?
6. What is percentage analysis, and what are its three types?

In its 2005 annual report, **Johnson & Johnson Corporation** indicates that it has 115,600 employees and 230 operating companies in 57 countries (a large company!). It also reports that it is organized on the principle of "decentralized" management, and that its Executive Committee is the principal management group responsible for the operations and allocation of the company's resources in its consumer, pharmaceutical, and medical devices and diagnostics businesses. Besides its Chief Executive Officer, Johnson & Johnson has 11 vice-presidents responsible for such areas as advertising, human resources, finance, technical resources, legal, government policy, information, public affairs, corporate development, diversity, worldwide operations and science and technology.

Starting with this chapter, we begin to study how accounting information helps managers, investors, and creditors of larger companies make business decisions. There are many similarities in how small and large companies operate. Both use cost-volume-profit (C-V-P) analysis, budgeting, and a GAAP-based accounting system. But, in part because large companies are more complex, there are many differences in the ways these companies make decisions and use accounting information. Large companies have a more formal and well-defined organizational and decision-making structure. In a small company, the owner-manager decides when to order additional inventory, to which customers to extend credit, or how to get the resources needed to expand. A large company usually has entire departments that deal with each of these issues. Large companies also usually have a complex ownership structure.

© AP/WIDE WORLD PHOTOS

Do you think Target Corporation has an entire department responsible for ordering inventory, or do you think a store manager has that responsibility?

As we mentioned in Chapter 1, there are three main forms of business organizations: sole proprietorships, partnerships, and corporations. Corporations generally are larger than sole proprietorships or partnerships. In fact, although fewer than 20 percent of U.S. companies are corporations, they make nearly 90 percent of all U.S. sales.

Most large retail or manufacturing companies are corporations. As a result of incorporating, companies must follow additional laws and regulations. And although companies of all sizes face complicated business decisions, such as determining whether to rent or buy equipment, larger companies are more likely to do so.

In this chapter, we introduce several aspects of the environment in which larger corporations operate. First, we explain the legal forms and characteristics of different business organizations. Second, we discuss the structure of large corporations. Third, we discuss the qualities that make accounting information about large corporations useful for decision making. Fourth, we focus on the unique aspects of financial reporting for large corporations. Finally, we discuss what financial information about corporations external decision makers use and how they use it.

## FORMS OF BUSINESS ORGANIZATIONS

I What are the three most common forms of business organizations and their basic characteristics?

Think about the following names of companies:

**ATI Technologies, Incorporated**
**Target Corporation**
**Ernst & Young LLP**
**Triple R Technologies, LP**
**Delta Electronics, Incorporated**
**General Motors Corporation**
**Underwriters Laboratories Incorporated**

Did you notice several words the names have in common? Five of the companies include either "corporation" or "incorporated" in their name. Two companies include the letters "LP" or "LLP" in their title. Why do companies include these designations in their names? These designations reveal a company's form of organization. The word *corporation,* or *incorporated,* indicates that the company is a separate legal entity known as a corporation. The "P" in LP and LLP stands for *partnership.* (We will discuss the L and LL later.)

Choosing a company's legal form is an important decision for the company's owners to make. For example, as a company owner, this decision determines how laws and regulations affect your personal responsibility to pay the company's debts. When choosing among legal forms, you need to know the characteristics and advantages and disadvantages of each. Once you select a legal form and start operating your company, laws and regulations specific to your type of company will affect some of your business decisions. In this section we discuss the three most common forms of business organizations: sole proprietorships, partnerships, and corporations. In addition, we explain how some aspects of these forms have been combined to create three other forms: limited partnerships, limited liability partnerships, and Subchapter S corporations.

## Sole Proprietorships

A **sole proprietorship** is a company owned by one person who is the sole investor of capital into the company. Because Anna Cox is the only investor in Sweet Temptations, this company is an example of a sole proprietorship. In general, sole proprietorships are small companies that focus either on selling merchandise or on performing a service. Many of the small shops you see downtown are sole proprietorships.

Usually, the owner of a sole proprietorship also manages the company. The owner makes the company's important decisions, such as when to purchase equipment, how much debt to incur, and to which customers to extend credit. In the United States, tax laws and regulations require each owner of a sole proprietorship to report and pay taxes on his or her company's taxable income. The company's taxable income is included in the owner's individual income tax return; there is no separate income tax return for a sole proprietorship. So, the owner adds the income from the sole proprietorship to his or her other sources of income, such as wages earned from other jobs and interest received from bank deposits. In the case of Sweet Temptations, Anna Cox includes with her personal income tax return a schedule that reports Sweet Temptations' taxable income. She includes this amount in her total personal taxable income. Anna calculates her personal income tax liability based on all her sources of income. In addition to income taxes, individuals who operate a sole proprietorship must pay self-employment taxes. These taxes are similar to social security taxes, and the owner also calculates and reports them on his or her individual tax return.

U.S. laws state that an owner of a sole proprietorship must assume personal responsibility for the debts incurred by the company. This requirement is referred to as **unlimited liability**. Unlimited liability may be a problem for the owner of a sole proprietorship because if the company cannot pay its debts, the company's creditors may force the owner to use his or her personal assets to pay them. So, if the sole proprietorship becomes insolvent, the owner may lose *more than* the amount of capital he or she invested in the company. Thus, unlimited liability adds additional financial risk for the owner of a sole proprietorship.

The life of a sole proprietorship is linked directly to its individual owner. Basically, a sole proprietorship ceases to exist when the owner decides to stop operating as a sole proprietor. If the owner of a sole proprietorship decides to sell the company, the owner's sole proprietorship dissolves, and the new owner or owners must choose the new company's form of business organization. Because of these characteristics, a sole proprietorship is said to have a **limited life**.

## Partnerships

*Have you ever shared the purchase and use of an item with someone? Maybe you share a computer or an apartment. How do you decide how much money each contributes? How do you split the costs of software, rent, or insurance?*

By definition, a sole proprietorship is owned by only one person. What if two or three people come up with a great business idea and want to start a company? What if the owner of a sole proprietorship wants someone else to invest in her company? One option is for the individuals to operate their company as a partnership. A **partnership** is a company owned by two or more individuals who each invest capital into the company.

Individuals must make many decisions before starting a partnership. These decisions include the following:

1. The dollar amount each partner will invest
2. The percentage of the partnership each individual will own
3. How to allocate and distribute partnership income to each partner
4. How business decisions will be made
5. The steps to be taken if a partner withdraws from the partnership or if a new partner is added

To limit disagreements, partners should always sign a contract, called a **partnership agreement**, before their company begins operations. This is a good idea even if partners are best friends or close relatives. This agreement specifies the terms of the formation, operation, and termination of the partnership. It defines the nature of the business, the types and number of partners, the capital contributions required of each partner, the duties of each partner, the conditions for admission or withdrawal of a partner, the method of allocating income to each partner, and the distribution of assets when the partnership is terminated.[1]

© PHOTOPIA

What should be included in the partnership agreement for this law firm?

## Characteristics of Partnerships

*What concerns would you have about joining a partnership? Why?*

Partnerships have many characteristics that are similar to those of sole proprietorships. Each partner is required by tax laws and regulations to report his or her share of the partnership's income on his or her individual income tax return. Laws and regulations regarding unlimited liability also apply to partnerships. In addition, a partnership has a **limited life**. It terminates whenever the partners change (i.e., when a partner leaves the partnership or when a new partner is added).

Of course, there is a basic difference between partnerships and sole proprietorships in that a partnership requires two or more owners. Several partnership characteristics relate to the co-ownership feature. To understand these characteristics, assume that Anna Cox invites her friend, Sanjeev Patal, to form Sweet Temptations as a partnership. If Sanjeev is like most other people, the first thing he would think is "What would I be getting myself into?" Because of a partnership's legal and business characteristics, he may be getting into more than he thinks. One important characteristic to know is that all the partners jointly own all the assets owned by a partnership; this is called **joint ownership**. Therefore, if Sanjeev contributes his property to the partnership, it no longer belongs to him alone.

Before entering a partnership, you should also know that each partner is an agent of the partnership. An **agent** is a person who has the authority to act for another. Thus a partner has the power to enter into and bind the partnership—and, therefore, all the partners—to any contract within the scope of the business. For example, either Anna or Sanjeev can bind the partnership to contracts for purchasing inventory, hiring employees, leasing a building, purchasing fixtures, or borrowing money. All of these activities are within the normal scope of a retail candy business.

[1]If a partnership does not have a formal agreement about how to operate, its partners resolve any disputes by referring to the Uniform Partnership Act. The Uniform Partnership Act, a set of laws adopted by most states, governs the formation, operation, and liquidation of a partnership in the absence of a partnership agreement.

The fact that each partner can obligate the partnership to honor contracts affects the unlimited liability requirements. **Unlimited liability** for a partnership means that each partner is liable for *all* the debts of the partnership. A creditor's claim is on the partnership, but if there are not enough assets to pay the debt, *each* partner's personal assets may be used to pay the debt. The only personal assets that are excluded are a partner's assets protected by bankruptcy laws, such as a personal residence. If one of the partners uses personal assets to pay the debts of the partnership, that partner has a right to claim a share of the payment from the other partners.

*Given the partnership characteristics we just discussed, if you were about to form a partnership, what specific items would you want to include in your partnership agreement?*

### Partnership Equity

Accounting for the owners' equity of a partnership differs from accounting for the owner's equity of a sole proprietorship (and a corporation). Company transactions that do not affect owners' equity are recorded in the same way regardless of the organizational form. But because a partnership's ownership is divided among the partners, its accounting system has a *Capital* account for each partner in which it records the partner's investments, withdrawals, and share of the partnership's net income.

A partnership's net income is computed in the same way as is the net income for a sole proprietorship. However, because there is more than one owner in a partnership, the net income must be allocated to each partner. Before their company begins operations, the partners need to decide how to split the partnership's net income among themselves and list this allocation in the partnership agreement. Two factors that usually affect the distribution of income among partners are (1) the dollar amount of capital contributed by each partner and (2) the dollar value of the time each partner spends working for the partnership. These factors are important because the portion of net income allocated to each partner represents the return on his or her investment of capital or time. A partnership includes a schedule at the bottom of its income statement that shows how, and how much, net income is allocated to each partner.

## Corporations

Recall that Unlimited Decadence is a corporation that manufactures candy bars and sells them to companies like Sweet Temptations. Although a corporation is made up of individual owners, the law treats it as a separate "being." A **corporation** is a separate legal entity that is independent of its owners and is run by a board of directors. Hence, it has a *continuous* life beyond that of any particular owner. Therefore, it has a number of advantages. Because of the legal separation of the owners and the company, ownership in a corporation may be easily passed from one individual to another. Briefly, here's how it works. In exchange for contributing capital to the corporation, owners of a corporation receive shares of the corporation's *capital stock.* Hence, they are called **stockholders** (or *shareholders*). These shares of stock are the "ownership units" of the corporation and are *transferable.* That is, the current stockholders can transfer or sell their shares to new owners. As we discuss later, the capital stock of many corporations sells on organized stock markets such as the **New York Stock Exchange**, the **American Stock Exchange**, the **Tokyo Stock Exchange**, the **London Stock Exchange**, and the **NASDAQ Stock Market, Inc.** So stockholders of these corporations can sell their shares to new owners more easily.

Because a corporation is a separate legal entity, a stockholder has no personal liability for the corporation's debts. Therefore each stockholder's liability is limited to his or her investment. Corporations tend to be larger than sole proprietorships and partnerships, so to operate, they need more capital invested by owners. Since transferring ownership is easy and since stockholders have *limited liability,* corporations can usually attract a large number of *diverse investors* and the large amounts of capital needed to operate. Corporations also can attract *top-quality managers* to operate the different departments, so stockholders are not involved in the corporations' operating decisions.

There also are several disadvantages of a corporation. As a separate legal entity, a corporation must pay federal and state income taxes on its taxable income. It reports this income on an income tax return for corporations. The maximum federal income tax rate for corporations is currently 35 percent, but since many of them also pay state income taxes, it is not unusual for the combined income taxes to be more than 40 percent of a corporation's taxable income. If some, or all, of the after-tax income of the corporation (the other 60 percent of the corporation's taxable income) is distributed to stockholders as dividends, the stockholders again may be taxed on this personal income. This is referred to as **double taxation**.

*Why do you think this is called double taxation? Is the stockholder taxed twice? Why or why not?*

As we discussed earlier in this chapter, for a sole proprietorship or a partnership, the owners may have to use personal assets to pay the company's debts. However, since the owners (stockholders) of a corporation have limited liability, a corporation (particularly a smaller one) may find it more difficult to borrow money. Since the creditors can't go to the owners for payment, they may think there is more risk of not being paid.

Corporations also are subject to *more government regulation.* For instance, the federal and state governments have laws to protect creditors and owners. For example, the laws of the state in which it is incorporated usually limit the payment of dividends by a corporation. Since creditors cannot go to the owners of a corporation for payment of its debts, limiting the corporation's dividend payments is a way of protecting creditors—the corporation may have more resources with which to pay its debts. In addition, if a corporation's capital stock is traded in the stock market, the corporation must file specified reports with the Securities and Exchange Commission.

However, the advantages of a corporation usually exceed the disadvantages when a business grows to a reasonable size. Exhibit 10-1 summarizes the characteristics of each type of business organization.

**EXHIBIT 10-1** **GENERAL CHARACTERISTICS OF EACH FORM OF BUSINESS ORGANIZATION**

| Characteristics | Sole Proprietorships | Partnerships | Corporations |
|---|---|---|---|
| ***Number of owner(s)*** | Single owner | Two or more owners (partners) | Usually many owners (stockholders) |
| ***Size of businesses*** | Small | Most are small; some professional partnerships (e.g., law firms) have several hundred partners. | Many are very large; some may have stock traded on an exchange. |
| ***Examples of businesses that typically have this legal form*** | Small retail shops; local service or repair shops; single practitioners such as CPAs, lawyers, doctors | Law firms; CPA firms; real estate agencies; family-owned businesses | Manufacturing companies; multinational companies; retail store chains; fast-food chains |
| ***Who makes business decisions*** | Owner | Depends on partnership agreement. Small partnerships will have all partners involved in business decisions; large partnerships will have managing partners. Partners are agents. | Decided by board of directors. Large corporations are managed by business professionals who often own little or no stock. |
| ***Liability of owner(s)*** | Unlimited | Unlimited | Limited |
| ***Life of organization*** | Limited | Limited | Continuous |

### Other Legal Forms of Business Organizations

Remember the company names we listed at the start of this section? Two companies had the letters LP or LLP in their names (Triple R Technologies, LP and Ernst & Young LLP). The initials "LP" stand for *limited partnership,* and the initials "LLP" stand for *limited liability partnership.* Both types of partnerships were created by law to reduce the unlimited liability of partners.

Why should the government pass laws limiting a partner's liability? In the case of limited partnerships, the laws were enacted to protect partners who are not active in the management of a large partnership, so that they won't lose more money than they invested. In a limited partnership, only certain partners (usually the partners who originally set up the partnership) have unlimited liability. These partners are called *general partners.* Other investors (called *limited partners*) in a limited partnership do not have unlimited liability. Instead of having all their personal assets at risk, limited partners may lose only the amount of money they invested in the limited partnership.

In recent years, laws have been passed that allow large public accounting firms and other types of partnerships to become limited liability partnerships. The CPA profession actively lobbied the U.S. Congress and state legislatures to enact legislation allowing limited liability partnerships. These types of partnerships limit, to a prescribed amount, *each* partner's risk of losing his or her personal assets as a result of ownership in an LLP.

Another form of business organization, a Subchapter S corporation, is available to small businesses. A Subchapter S corporation maintains the attractive features of corporate ownership. The distinctive feature of these corporations is that the owners—not the corporation—pay income taxes on corporate income. Thus, owners of a Subchapter S corporation are not subject to double taxation.

In the sections that follow, we will make general statements about the characteristics of corporations. Because corporations are subject to state laws, which may differ, these general statements may not always be entirely accurate. However, the general overview will help you understand what you need to know for later discussions.

## STARTING A CORPORATION

To operate as a corporation in the United States, a company must be incorporated in one of the states. **Incorporation** is the process of filing the required documents and obtaining permission from a state to operate as a corporation. The state-approved documents are called **articles of incorporation**.

After the state approves the incorporation, the individuals who filed for incorporation meet to complete several important tasks. First, they distribute among themselves the first issuance of capital stock. (As holders of the company's stock, these individuals have the right to vote on major corporate policies and decisions.) Then they (the stockholders) decide on, among other things, (1) a set of rules (bylaws) to regulate the corporation's operations, (2) a board of directors to plan and oversee the corporation's long-range objectives, and (3) a team of people to serve in top management positions.

Not all corporations are huge companies like **3M** or **Exxon**. Some corporations are small companies that are owned by one person or a few people. The owners of small companies set them up as corporations because the owners want the legal benefits of incorporation, primarily limited liability. If a corporation is owned by a small number of investors, it is called a **closely held corporation**. The stock of a closely held corporation may not be purchased by the general public, and the board of directors places restrictions on the selling of stock by current stockholders. Generally, closely held corporations are relatively small, although some, such as **Hallmark Corporation** (the company that makes Hallmark greeting cards) and **Mars Inc.** (the company that manufactures M&Ms, the Snickers candy bar, Whiskas pet food, and Uncle Ben's rice), are very large multinational companies.

A typical trading day on the New York Stock Exchange.

**Publicly held corporations** sell their stock to the general public, and generally there are no restrictions on the selling of stock by current stockholders. After a corporation sells its stock to the public in what is called an **initial public offering** (or IPO), the stock begins to trade in a secondary equity market. The **secondary equity market** is where investors buy the stock of corporations from other investors rather than from the corporations. This means that the corporations have already issued this stock. In these secondary markets, the stock is traded between new and current stockholders, so the corporation is not involved in the trade.

Today, the secondary equity market is well established and plays an important role in the global economy. The New York, American, Tokyo, and London Stock Exchanges, as well as NASDAQ, are just a few of the national organizations in the secondary equity market, and they trade the stocks of thousands of corporations. For example, on an average day, the New York Stock Exchange (NYSE) trades over 1,602 million shares of stock.[a] By contacting a stockbroker, you can purchase stock in companies such as **Tootsie Roll Industries** or **Matsushita Electric**.

*Assume you plan to invest $1,000. Think of three publicly held corporations. Which would you invest in? Why? What factors would influence your decision?*

## The Organizational Structure of Large Corporations

*Do you think the size of a company affects how it interacts with its customers? employees? suppliers? If so, why?*

After the incorporation process is completed, a corporation begins operations. Recall that companies are created to achieve two specific goals: to earn a satisfactory profit by providing services or products to customers and to remain solvent. To accomplish these goals, each company must be organized into a structure that makes clear the jobs and working relationships of the employees of that company. This structure shows who is responsible for each task, whether it is an individual or a work team, and who reports to whom.

In a small company, the structure may be simple. The owner makes all of the important business decisions, and all of the company's employees report directly to the owner. This is consistent with our discussion in Chapter 9 of working capital controls. However, as a company grows (e.g., hires more employees, opens additional stores, uses more suppliers), the owner will have more difficulty managing all of the company's activities. Also, the owner may not have the desire, or ability, to manage a larger organization. Eventually, the owner delegates some of these responsibilities to other managers. At this point, the small company starts to become a large company and may incorporate.

The organizational structure of a large corporation can be divided logically in a number of ways, such as by type of customer, by type of product, by geographical location, or by function. Whatever the organization, however, almost all large companies have functional areas involving the management of resources and activities related to marketing, production, human resources, finance, and distribution. All large companies also have an information technology component, but its personnel generally work in each functional area. In most companies, the **marketing** function is responsible for managing activities and resources to identify consumer needs, analyze consumer behavior, evaluate customer satisfaction, and promote the company's products. The **production** function is responsible for managing people and equipment to convert materials, components, and parts into products that the company will sell to customers. The **human resources** function is responsible for managing the company's employee-related activities, such as recruiting, hiring, training, and compensating employees, as well as providing a safe workplace. The **finance** function manages the company's capital requirements for both the short and the long term. This involves locating sources of capital and investing excess cash inside or outside of the United States. This function is also responsible for managing accounting activities. The **distribution** function is responsible for managing physical distribution systems to move products through the company and to customers. Exhibit 10-2 summarizes the management responsibilities within each function. The management of a corporation uses accounting information to identify, estimate, control, and report the costs of the marketing, production, human resources, finance, and distribution functions.

## Enterprise Resource Planning Systems

In Chapter 1, we discussed an *integrated accounting system* in which accounting information about a company's activities is identified, measured, recorded, and accumulated so that it can be communicated in an accounting report. We pointed out that the managers of a company use the information in the accounting reports from the integrated accounting system to help them make decisions. Many corporations are now "reengineering" their operations by installing **enterprise resource planning (ERP) systems**, of which the integrated accounting system is one part. Unlimited Decadance uses an ERP system. The goal of an ERP system is to help all the functional areas of a company run smoothly in an integrated manner. An ERP system involves computer software that is "multi-functional." That is, the software records and stores many different types of data (e.g., units, quanti-

**Exhibit 10-2 Management Functional Areas**

| Marketing | Production | Human Resources | Finance | Distribution |
|---|---|---|---|---|
| Identifying consumer needs<br>Analyzing consumer behavior<br>Evaluating customer satisfaction<br>Promoting products | Converting materials into products<br>Overseeing purchasing<br>Controlling manufacturing | Recruiting, hiring, training, terminating employees<br>Compensating employees<br>Providing safe working conditions | Locating cash resources<br>Investing excess cash<br>Accounting | Moving products from company to customer<br>Moving products within company<br>Protecting inventory<br>Processing orders |

ties, times, prices, names, pay rates, and addresses, to name a few) that can be used to create a **data warehouse**. Each data entry is "coded"; that is, codes (letters and/or numbers) are assigned to similar entries. For instance, in the integrated accounting component of Unlimited Decadence's ERP system, a $1,000 cash sale and a $400 credit sale might be coded within its Sales Revenues account column as CA +1,000 and CR +400, respectively. Other information that might be coded with these sales include product numbers identifying the products sold and customer numbers identifying the customers who purchased the items. The software is "integrated" so that a manager who is in the process of making a decision can perform *data mining* to extract useful information from the data warehouse. For instance, a marketing manager might "mine" the data warehouse to identify when, what, and to whom credit sales were made, including the characteristics of the products sold (which can be mined using the product numbers) and the types of customers who purchased them (which can be mined using the customer numbers). Companies like **SAP** and **Oracle** are developing and improving ERP systems to help the managers in a corporation's marketing, production, human resources, finance, and distribution functions use this computer technology to improve their decisions. For instance, Exhibit 10-3 shows a diagram of the Operations Management framework of an ERP system. The operating activities of a company are depicted at the top of the diagram and include purchasing, manufacturing, warehousing, promotion, and sales activities. The boxes at the bottom of the diagram illustrate how different "resources" (including information) of a corporation's operations "interact" with each other. For instance, the middle box shows the capital resources component. The corporation's finance function must manage the acquisition of capital resources to help obtain materials resources and human resources. The materials resources component (the left box) is managed by the corporation's distribution function. The distribution function, for instance, must manage the materials resources within the corporation for manufacturing its products, storing the products in the warehouse, and delivering the products to its customers. The human resources component (the right box) is managed by the corporation's human resources function. The human resources component hires employees so that, for instance, the production function can manage the purchase of materials and labor to manufacture the company's products, and the marketing function can manage the activities needed to promote the products. Together, the various functional areas interact with each other to allow the corporation to operate as efficiently as possible. We will discuss how corporations are reengineering various aspects of their operations relating to accounting in later chapters.

**EXHIBIT 10-3** **ERP OPERATIONS MANAGEMENT**

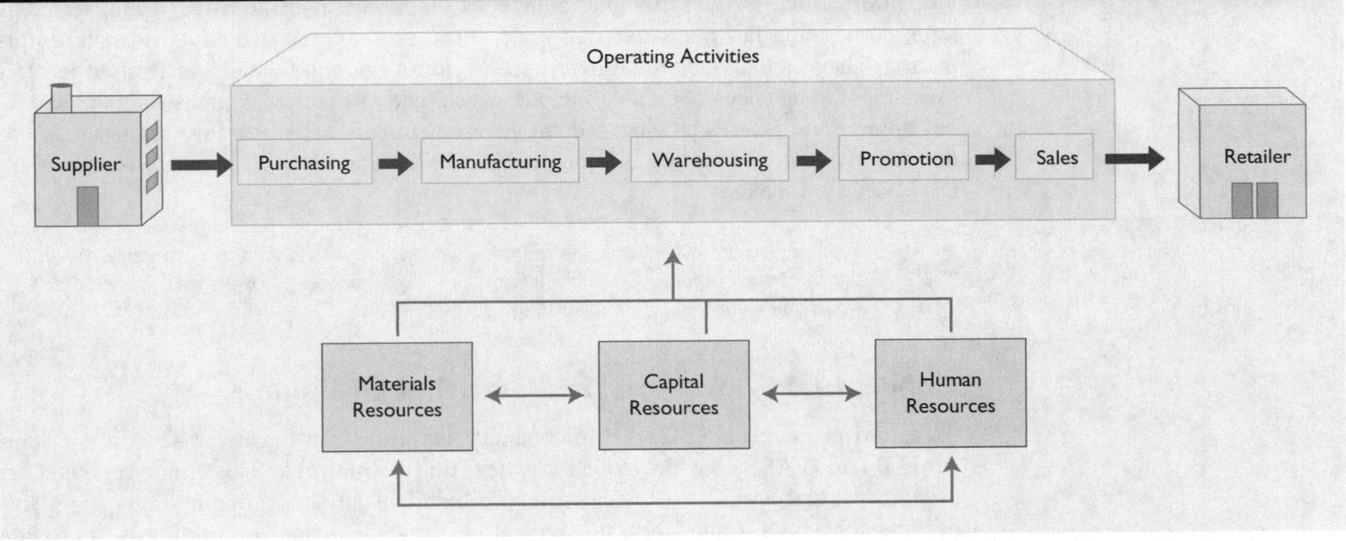

## E-Business

Many large corporations, and some smaller ones, engage in e-business. Companies involved in **e-business** use the Internet to conduct transactions electronically. Most of these transactions involve online selling or purchasing. You are probably most familiar with *e-catalog stores,* where a customer can purchase an item from a company online through its Web site. For instance, **LandsEnd.com**, **Amazon.com**, and **Wilsonsports.com** sell clothing, books, and sporting goods, respectively, over the Internet. These and many other e-business companies also promote their products and services on the Internet, as you have noticed if you use a commercial Internet online service like **AOL.com**.

But e-business is not limited to retail companies selling online to consumers. Many e-business retailers, manufacturers, and suppliers establish "linked" online purchasing/selling relationships with each other. This allows each of the linked companies to have access to the other companies' inventory systems. So, for instance, when a retailer runs low on a particular inventory item, its system is programmed to automatically place an order with the manufacturer, which then produces sufficient quantities of the item in a timely manner for the retailer. Also, the manufacturer's system is programmed to place orders with its suppliers to provide the materials to the manufacturer for producing the inventory items.

Whether an e-business company sells only to consumers or is linked in its purchasing/selling function to other companies, the company's ERP system must be able to "interface" with its e-business system. This interface enables the company's managers to effectively and efficiently run its operations. We will discuss various e-business activities in later chapters.

## Qualities of Useful Accounting Information

Given the size, complexity, and wide dispersion of ownership of large corporations, summarizing and reporting useful accounting information to internal and external users is a challenging task. In later chapters, we will discuss how managers develop and use tools such as cost-volume-profit (C-V-P) analysis and master budgeting for internal decision making in large corporations. In the remainder of this chapter, we focus on financial reporting for external decision making. Two of the major advantages of the corporate form of organization—the ease of transferring ownership and the ability to attract large amounts of capital—have a significant effect on financial reporting.

As a small sole proprietorship, Sweet Temptations uses its financial reporting to provide information to Anna Cox and to the bank that makes loans to Sweet Temptations. A large corporation has many external users who also are interested in its financial information. They include individual investors, stockbrokers, and financial analysts who offer investment assistance. They also include consultants, bankers, suppliers, employees, labor unions, and local, state, and federal governments. In this section we discuss many of the qualities that accounting information should have in order to be useful to these external decision makers.

*Suppose you are a banker trying to decide whether to grant a loan to a company. When the company provides its financial information to you for your decision, what qualities would you want that information to have?*

### Conceptual Framework and Decision Usefulness

As an aid in establishing GAAP for financial reporting, the Financial Accounting Standards Board (FASB) has developed a **conceptual framework**. This framework is a set of concepts that provides a logical structure for financial accounting and reporting. Under this conceptual framework, the general objective of financial reporting is to provide useful information for external users in their decision making. Therefore, in the United States, *improving external decision making* is the primary purpose of financial accounting information. Other countries may have other objectives for financial accounting information, such as satisfying government requirements for computing income taxes, demonstrating compliance with the government's economic plan, or monitoring social responsibility activities.

To be useful for external decision making, financial accounting information must be relevant and reliable. Closely related to relevance and reliability are materiality and validity. We show these qualities of useful information in Exhibit 10-4. Although these concepts apply to financial reporting, they are equally applicable to management accounting information used for internal decision making.

2 What are the qualities that make accounting information about large corporations useful for decision making?

## Relevant Accounting Information

Accounting information is **relevant** when it has the capacity to influence a user's decision. For example, suppose Second National Bank is considering whether to loan Unlimited Decadence money to be used for the purchase of new production equipment. The amount of cash in Unlimited Decadence's checking and savings accounts and the cash it expects to collect from sales and to pay its suppliers are relevant for the banker's decision.

*If you were buying a new car, what information about the car would be relevant to you?*

## Reliable Accounting Information

Even if information is relevant, users must have confidence that the information they are using for decision making is reliable. Accounting information is **reliable** when it is capable of being verified. Reliability does not always mean certainty. For example, Unlimited Decadence may be able to reliably *estimate* how many of its credit sales will not be collectible if there has been a uniform pattern of uncollectibility in the past. Source documents such as invoices, cash receipts, and canceled checks play an important part in verifying the reliability of accounting information.

*If you have a checking account, how do you verify the ending balance on your monthly bank statement? Do you consider the information reliable? Why or why not?*

## Materiality

Materiality is like relevance because both concepts relate to influencing a user of accounting information. Accounting information is **material** when the monetary amount is large enough to make a difference in a user's decision. Only material accounting information

**EXHIBIT 10-4 QUALITIES OF USEFUL ACCOUNTING INFORMATION**

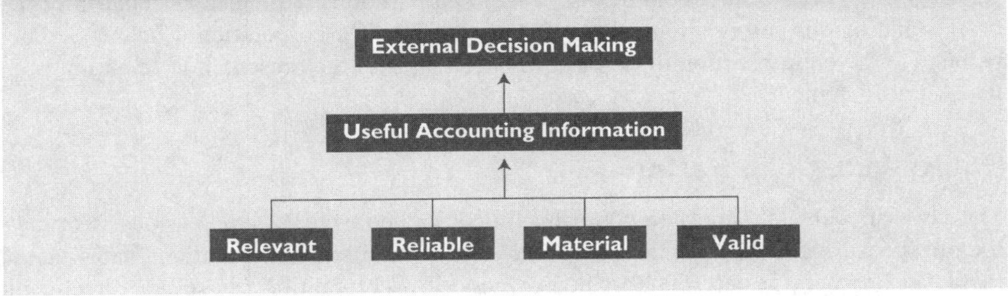

© AFP/CORBIS

What dollar amount do you think would be material for Tiger Woods?

should be accumulated and communicated to users. Materiality is relative, however. A $1,000 purchase may be material to you but may be only a "drop in the bucket" to someone like Britney Spears or Tiger Woods. Similarly, what is material accounting information for Sweet Temptations may not be material for a company like Unlimited Decadence because of their different sizes.

Many users consider that an item *is not* material if its dollar amount is less than 5% and *is* material if the dollar amount is more than 10%. But the question here is, 5% or 10% of what? If an item is related to the income statement, then a user could use net income, gross profit, or some other summary amount (or even a single item) as the basis for comparison. So, for instance, if an income statement item is 12% of a company's net income, a user would generally consider the item to be material relative to net income. If another item is 3% of sales, the user would generally consider the item to be immaterial relative to sales. If an item is related to the balance sheet, then a user could use total assets, total liabilities, total owners' equity, or a summary amount such as current assets or working capital (or even a single item) as a basis for comparison. Furthermore, a user must decide whether an amount between 5% and 10% is, or is not, material. So you should understand that materiality is a concept that involves significant judgment and critical thinking.

*How much would you consider as a material difference in prices in purchasing a new mountain bike? a new car?*

### Valid Accounting Information

Validity is closely related to reliability. Accounting information is **valid** when it shows a realistic picture of what it is meant to represent. To be valid, accounting information must realistically portray the results of a company's activities and financial position. Valid accounting information is like a good videotape or snapshot from a camera that does not distort the real picture (unlike your driver's license photo).

Keep these qualities in mind as you consider how to accumulate and use financial and management accounting information. We now turn to financial reporting for large corporations.

## Unique Features of a Corporation's Financial Statements

3 What do users need to know about the stockholders' equity section of a corporation's balance sheet and about its income statement?

Financial statements for corporations follow the same structure that we discussed in earlier chapters and illustrated with Sweet Temptations. A corporation's balance sheet shows the dollar amounts of its assets, liabilities, and owners' equity on a specific date. Its income statement reports revenues, expenses, and net income for a specific period of time. The cash flow statement shows the corporation's cash receipts and payments from operating, investing, and financing activities for a specific period. Like Sweet Temptations, corporations prepare these financial statements according to GAAP.

However, the size and complexity of large corporations requires additional information. Some of this information relates to two aspects of a corporation's financial statements: (1) the equity section of its balance sheet, and (2) the presentation of earnings on its income statement.

### Equity in a Corporation

The laws of each state apply to companies incorporated in that state. Various state laws require special accounting procedures for the owners' equity of a corporation. States passed these laws to help protect the absentee owners of a corporation (those not directly involved in the management of the company) as well as its creditors.

### Corporate Capital Structure

The owners' equity of a corporation is called **stockholders' equity** because the owners of a corporation are called *stockholders*. Usually there are many stockholders of a corporation, and frequent changes in ownership can occur; as a result, maintaining separate capital accounts for each owner would be impractical. Instead, the stockholders' equity on a corporation's balance sheet is usually separated into two sections: contributed capital and retained earnings.[2] This division of stockholders' equity is required by state laws.

The **contributed capital** section shows the total investments made by stockholders in the corporation. As we will discuss in the next section, this section usually consists of two parts—capital stock and additional paid-in capital. The **retained earnings** reports the corporation's total lifetime net income that has been reinvested in the corporation and not distributed to stockholders as dividends.

Because stockholders' equity on a corporation's balance sheet consists of two sections, a corporation expands its accounting system to record information for these sections. So, under the accounting equation, it expands the stockholders' equity component to include (1) the permanent balance sheet sections of Contributed Capital and Retained Earnings and (2) the temporary revenue and expense accounts that comprise its current-year net income, as follows:

| **Assets** | = | **Liabilities** | + | **Stockholders' Equity** | |
|---|---|---|---|---|---|
| | | | | ***Permanent Sections*** | ***Net Income*** |
| | | | | Contributed Capital + Retained Earnings | Revenues − Expenses |

In this accounting system, a corporation records transactions in account columns in the same manner as a sole proprietorship (as we discussed earlier in the book), except for contributed capital and retained earnings transactions (as we will discuss later in this chapter and the book).

### Capital Stock and Legal Capital

**Capital stock** refers to the ownership units in the corporation. There are two types of capital stock: common stock and preferred stock. If a corporation issues only one type of stock, this is called **common stock**. If a corporation also issues another type of stock, that stock is called **preferred stock**. The differences between common stock and preferred stock involve stockholders' rights, and we will discuss these differences in Chapter 24. Here we focus on common stock.

A corporation may issue common stock for cash. It also may trade stock for an asset such as land or equipment. When an investor buys stock from the corporation, the corporation records the issuance (selling) price using both a Common Stock account and an Additional Paid-in Capital account. To protect creditors, state laws require corporations to keep in the company a minimum amount of the capital contributed by the owners. This is called *legal capital*. Usually, **legal capital** is a monetary amount per share of common stock, called the **par value**. The par value is stated in the articles of incorporation and is printed on each stock certificate. The par value of a share of common stock is often set very low—perhaps $10, $2, or even less per share—and has *no* relationship to the value of the stock. The total legal capital of a corporation is determined by multiplying the par value per share by the number of shares issued. Generally, states require companies to keep track of legal capital, so each time a corporation issues common stock, *it records the par value (legal capital) in the Common Stock account.*

### Additional Paid-In Capital

The total dollar amount the corporation receives from selling its stock is called the **market value** of the stock. Corporations normally sell common stock at a market value much

[2]A corporation may also have a stockholders' equity section called "accumulated other comprehensive income." We will discuss this section in Chapter 23 of Volume 2.

higher than the par value. So, legal capital is usually only a small part of the total selling price. When a corporation sells common stock, in addition to recording the par value in a Common Stock account it also records the excess of the market value over the par value. The excess value it receives is called *additional paid-in capital.* **Additional paid-in capital** is the difference between the selling price and the par value in each stock transaction and is recorded in an Additional Paid-in Capital account.

Now that you have this background, we can explain how the accounting system keeps track of one kind of common stock transaction—common stock issued for cash. We will explain other kinds of common stock transactions in Chapter 24 of Volume 2.

### Common Stock Sold for Cash

To understand the issuance of common stock, assume that Unlimited Decadence Corporation sells 30,000 shares of its $3 par value common stock for $16 per share. It records the transaction as follows:

**FINANCIAL STATEMENT EFFECTS**

Increases current assets and total assets, increases contributed capital and total stockholders' equity on ***balance sheet.*** Increase cash flows from financing activities on ***cash flow statement.***

| Assets | = | Liabilities | + | Stockholders' Equity | |
|---|---|---|---|---|---|
| | | | | *Contributed Capital* | |
| Cash | | | | Common Stock | Additional Paid-in Capital |
| +$480,000 | | | | +$90,000 | +$390,000 |

As a result of this transaction, Unlimited Decadence increases assets (cash) by $480,000 (30,000 × $16), the total amount of capital invested in the corporation. Because Unlimited Decadence received the $480,000 from investors, it also increases stockholders' equity by $480,000 in the following manner. To adhere to state laws, Unlimited Decadence increases its common stock account by the $90,000 (30,000 shares × $3) par value (legal capital), and increases additional paid-in capital by the $390,000 difference between the total selling price and the total par value ($480,000 − $90,000 = $390,000).

### Stockholders' Equity Section of Balance Sheet

As we said earlier, the stockholders' equity section of a corporation's balance sheet has two parts: (1) contributed capital and (2) retained earnings. Contributed capital includes common stock (the legal value) and additional paid-in capital, and shows the total capital invested in the corporation by its owners.

Exhibit 10-5 shows the stockholders' equity of Unlimited Decadence's balance sheet at December 31, 2008. As of this date, the stockholders of Unlimited Decadence have invested $8,140,000 in the corporation in exchange for 1,200,000 shares of common stock. Unlimited Decadence's common stock totals $3,600,000 ($3 par value × 1,200,000 shares), and additional paid-in capital totals $4,540,000 ($8,140,000 − $3,600,000). Because these numbers are large, Unlimited Decadence shows the amounts on its balance sheet in thousands of dollars. This is a common practice of many large corporations. Many corporations are so large that they show their balance sheet amounts in *millions* of dollars!

**EXHIBIT 10-5 UNLIMITED DECADENCE CORPORATION**

**STOCKHOLDERS' EQUITY SECTION OF BALANCE SHEET**
***December 31, 2008***
***(in thousands of dollars)***

| | |
|---|---|
| Stockholders' Equity | |
| Contributed capital | |
| Common stock, 1,200,000 shares issued ($3 par value) | $ 3,600 |
| Additional paid-in capital | 4,540 |
| Contributed capital | $ 8,140 |
| Retained earnings | 9,060 |
| Total stockholders' equity | $17,200 |

The **retained earnings** reported in a corporation's stockholders' equity is the amount of its lifetime net income that has been reinvested in the corporation to date.[3] As we show in Exhibit 10-5, at December 31, 2008, the retained earnings for Unlimited Decadence is $9,060,000. The total stockholders' equity of Unlimited Decadence is $17,200,000, the sum of the $8,140,000 contributed capital and the $9,060,000 retained earnings.

## Corporate Earnings

*When investors are evaluating a corporation, should they be concerned with how the corporation earned its net income? Do you think every dollar of income a corporation earns is equally important to investors? Why or why not?*

The income statement of a corporation may contain several sections. Each section helps financial statement users better understand how a corporation earned its net income. Generally, a corporation will show separately (1) the earnings that resulted from its "continuing" operations, (2) the earnings that resulted from other, "nonrecurring" activities, and (3) the earnings per share of common stock. The nonrecurring earnings might include the income or loss from "discontinued operations" (such as **PepsiCo, Inc.**'s earnings from **Pizza Hut**, **Taco Bell**, and **KFC** in the year that it sold them) and any income or loss from "extraordinary" events (such as a tornado). We will discuss these nonrecurring items in Chapter 24.[4] Here, we discuss the two most common sections—income from continuing operations and earnings per share. Unlimited Decadence's income statement for the year ended December 31, 2008 (shown in Exhibit 10-6)[5] illustrates how the company reported these two sections (it did not have any nonrecurring earnings).

**EXHIBIT 10-6 UNLIMITED DECADENCE CORPORATION**

**INCOME STATEMENT**

***For Year Ended December 31, 2008***

***(in thousands of dollars)***

| | | |
|---|---|---|
| Sales (net) | | $72,800 |
| Cost of goods sold | | (46,500) |
| Gross profit | | $26,300 |
| Operating expenses | | |
| Selling expenses | $13,840 | |
| General and administrative expenses | 7,670 | |
| Total operating expenses | | (21,510) |
| Operating income | | $ 4,790 |
| Other items | | |
| Interest revenue | $ 320 | |
| Interest expense | (210) | |
| Nonoperating income | | 110 |
| Pretax income from continuing operations | | $ 4,900 |
| Income tax expense | | (1,960) |
| Net income | | $ 2,940 |
| Earnings per share | | $ 2.45 |

[3]In its closing entries (which we discussed in Chapter 6), a corporation closes its revenue and expense accounts to its Retained Earnings account.

[4]A corporation may also have "other comprehensive income," which we will also discuss in both Chapter 23 and Chapter 24.

[5]For simplicity, we assume here that Unlimited Decadence sells only one type of candy bar. We will relax this assumption in Chapter 11.

### Income from Continuing Operations

**Income from continuing operations** reports a corporation's revenues and expenses that resulted from its ongoing operations. For Unlimited Decadence, this section reports the revenues and expenses from the manufacture and sale of candy bars.

This section includes **operating income**, which is determined by subtracting cost of goods sold from net sales to obtain gross profit, and then by deducting the selling expenses and the general and administrative expenses. As we show in Exhibit 10-6, the operating income of Unlimited Decadence for 2008 is $4,790,000. (Remember, the numbers shown are rounded to the nearest thousand dollars.)

Income from continuing operations also includes nonoperating income, in a section called **other items**. These other (nonoperating) items include revenues and expenses that frequently occur in a corporation but do not relate specifically to its primary operating activities. Interest expense, interest revenue, and gains (or losses) are common examples of other items. The amounts of the other items are summed to determine the nonoperating income (or loss). Under other items, Unlimited Decadence reports $320,000 of interest revenue and $210,000 of interest expense, so that its nonoperating income is $110,000.

Since we have not previously discussed gains and losses, we briefly discuss them here. **Gains (losses)** are increases (decreases) in a corporation's income (and therefore its stockholders' equity) that result from transactions unrelated to providing goods and services. The rules for recording gains (losses) in a corporation's accounting system are the same as the rules for recording revenues (expenses). When a corporation has a gain or loss, it expands the net income section of its owners' equity in its accounting system as follows:

| Assets | = | Liabilities | + | Stockholders' Equity | | |
|---|---|---|---|---|---|---|
| | | | | Net Income | | |
| | | | | Revenues (Gains) | − | Expenses (Losses) |

For instance, suppose a corporation owns land that cost $8,000. If it sells the land for $10,000, it records a $2,000 gain ($10,000 selling price − $8,000 cost) as follows:

| Assets | | = | Liabilities | + | Stockholders' Equity | | |
|---|---|---|---|---|---|---|---|
| | | | | | Net Income | | |
| | | | | | Revenues (Gains) | − | Expenses (Losses) |
| Cash | Land | | | | Gain on Sale of Land | | |
| +$10,000 | −$8,000 | | | | +$2,000 | | |

**FINANCIAL STATEMENT EFFECTS**

Increases current assets, decreases property and equipment, and increases total assets on ***balance sheet.*** Increases gains (in "other items"), which increases net income on ***income statement*** (and therefore increases total stockholders' equity on ***balance sheet***). Increases cash flows from investing activities on ***cash flow statement.***

The corporation would report the $2,000 gain in the other items section of its income statement. We will discuss gains and losses more later in the book.

A corporation's operating income is added to the nonoperating income to determine its pretax income from continuing operations. For Unlimited Decadence, the $4,790,000 operating income is added to the $110,000 nonoperating income to determine its $4,900,000 pretax income from continuing operations.

As we discussed earlier, corporations must pay income taxes on their earnings. **Income tax expense** is listed separately within this section. Unlimited Decadence is subject to a 40 percent income tax rate on its pretax (taxable) income, so its income tax expense is $1,960,000 ($4,900,000 × 0.40). This amount is subtracted from the pretax income from continuing operations to get the company's $2,940,000 income from continuing operations.

If Unlimited Decadence had nonrecurring earnings, it would report these items (and the related income tax expense) below income from continuing operations. Because Unlimited Decadence had no nonrecurring earnings during 2008, the income from continuing operations is called *net income.*

### Earnings Per Share

A corporation's net income is earned for all the corporation's stockholders. Because the common stock for most large corporations is owned by many stockholders, it is useful to report a corporation's net income on a per-share basis. **Earnings per share (EPS)** is the amount of net income earned for each share of common stock. In its simplest form, earnings per share is computed by dividing the corporation's net income for the accounting period by the average number of shares of common stock owned by all of the corporation's stockholders during the period.

All corporations must report earnings per share on their income statements, and it is the last item they show. On its income statement in Exhibit 10-6, Unlimited Decadence shows earnings per share of $2.45. We can prove that this amount is correct by dividing the company's net income by the number of shares of common stock[6] reported in the stockholders' equity section of its balance sheet:

$$\text{Earnings Per Share} = \frac{\text{Net Income}}{\text{Average Number of Common Shares}} = \frac{\$2{,}940{,}000}{1{,}200{,}000} = \underline{\underline{\$2.45}}$$

If a corporation has several sections on its income statement or if the number of shares that stockholders own changes during the year, the calculation of earnings per share is more complicated. We will discuss this calculation in Chapter 24.

## Financial Information Used in Decision Making

External users analyze the financial statements of a company to determine how well the company is achieving its two primary goals—remaining solvent and earning a satisfactory profit. In the case of a small company, owners and creditors can also discuss the company's financial performance with its managers. However, in a large corporation, this is usually not possible.

If investors and creditors in a large corporation are given few or no opportunities to ask its managers about its operations or plans, how do they get the information they need to make business decisions? Individuals investing in large corporations must rely on publicly available information when making their investment decisions. **Publicly available information** is any information released to the public; it may come directly from the corporation or from secondary sources.

### Information Reported by Corporations

Much of the information that investors and creditors use to evaluate a corporation comes directly from the corporation. Corporations use four methods to supply information about themselves to external users: (1) annual reports, (2) Securities and Exchange Commission (SEC) reports, (3) interim financial statements, and (4) media releases.

4 How does a corporation provide information to external users?

#### Annual Reports

Corporations publish their annual financial statements as part of their **annual report**. In addition to the current year's financial statements, most corporations include the financial statements of the previous two years. These are called **comparative financial statements** and are included to help external users in their analyses. A corporation's annual report is always published in hard copy; it may also be available on the corporation's Web site.

In addition to the financial statements, a corporation's annual report also includes notes to the financial statements, an internal control report, an audit report, financial highlights or a summary, and management's discussion and analysis of the corporation's performance. In a study commissioned by **Potlatch Corp.**, a San Francisco-based paper manufacturer, a

[6] The number of shares of common stock owned by all of Unlimited Decadence's stockholders was 1,200,000 for the entire year, so the average number is also 1,200,000.

majority of portfolio managers and securities analysts ranked annual reports as the most important documents that a company produces, including documents on computer disks and on-line services.

**Notes to the financial statements** inform external users of the company's accounting policies and of important financial information that is not reported in the financial statements. For example, a note may inform users of a lawsuit against the company. **Molson Coors Brewing Company**'s 2005 notes mentioned a lawsuit that the city of Denver has brought against it as a "potential responsible party" in regard to pollution-control issues. Although, in 2005, the lawsuit had not resulted in an additional liability for Coors, information about the lawsuit was relevant to users of its financial statements. Investors and creditors should analyze the notes to a company's financial statements before making their investment and credit decisions.

Each publicly-held corporation is required to include a report about its internal control over financial reporting in its annual report. In this context, internal control refers to the corporation's process for providing reasonable assurance that its accounting system reports reliable information in its financial statements. This report is typically called **Management's Report on Internal Control over Financial Reporting**. In this report, the management of the corporation states that it has evaluated the corporation's internal control process for financial reporting and states its conclusions about the effectiveness of this process.

Because financial statements are so important, the Securities and Exchange Commission requires publicly-held corporations to issue audited financial statements. Banks also may require a small company to provide its audited financial statements when applying for a loan. **Auditing** involves the examination of a company's accounting records and financial statements by an independent certified public accountant (CPA). It also involves the examination by the CPA of the internal control surrounding the company's financial reporting. These examinations enable the CPA to attest to: (1) the effectiveness of the internal

A wide variety of users are interested in the information contained in a company's annual report.

control by the company over its financial reporting, (2) the fairness of management's report about that effectiveness, and (3) the fairness of the accounting information in the company's financial statements.

During an audit, an auditor must communicate with a company's managers to gain a better understanding of the company's internal control, accounting system, and transactions. This relationship creates the possibility that the auditor will not maintain independence from the company's managers, which would reduce the reliability of the company's financial statements. To help facilitate auditor independence, most companies have audit committees. An **audit committee** is a part of a company's board of directors, and the committee's members usually are "outside directors" (not officers or employees of the company). The primary responsibility of the audit committee is to oversee the financial reporting process of the company and the involvement of both the company's managers and its auditor in that process. As part of this oversight, the company's audit committee generally selects the auditor for the company, and then acts as a "liaison" between the auditor and the company's managers. Although the specific duties of an audit committee vary from company to company, generally the audit committee of a company oversees the company's internal control structure, helps select the company's accounting policies, reviews the company's financial statements, and oversees the audit. A company will often mention in its annual report that it has an audit committee, which enhances the credibility of its financial statements.

A corporation's annual report includes an **audit report** in which the auditor (CPA) expresses three opinions regarding whether:

1. The company's management has fairly stated its evaluation that the company maintained effective internal control over its financial reporting,
2. The company did maintain effective internal control over its financial reporting, and
3. The company's financial statements present fairly the financial position of the company and the results of its operations and cash flows in conformity with accounting principles generally accepted in the United States of America.

Exhibit 10-7 shows the audit report (partial) for the 2005 annual report of the **Hershey Company**. (For simplicity, we have omitted three paragraphs relating to a discussion of auditing standards and the internal control process.) Note that KPMG (the CPA firm that conducted the audit) expressed the three opinions discussed above.

An audit report is important to external users because it provides a measure of assurance that they can rely on the information presented in the financial statements. In Exhibit 10-7, the CPA firm **KPMG LLP** is telling investors that it believes that Hershey Company maintained effective internal control over its financial reporting, and that its financial statements are fair in that they comply with all applicable accounting standards. This type of audit report is referred to as an *unqualified* or *clean* opinion. Around 90 percent of all audit reports are unqualified. If the company's audited financial statements did not comply with GAAP, the auditor would disclose this in the audit report to warn users.

Companies also include 5-, 10-, or 15-year summaries of key data from their financial statements in their annual report. These are titled **Financial Highlights** or **Financial Summaries**. Some companies merely list revenues, net income, total assets, and other key figures for recent years. Others use such items as graphs, pie charts, and ratio comparisons. As we show in Exhibit 10-8, **Intel Corporation** used bar graphs in its 2005 annual report to illustrate how its net revenue and return on average stockholders' equity have changed over time.

Have you ever handed in a report and wanted the opportunity to explain what you think the report means? When a corporation releases its financial statements to the public, the corporation's managers want to provide their own analysis of its performance and financial condition. As part of the annual report, managers will include sections titled **Management's Discussion and Analysis** (MD&A) and **Letter to Shareholders**. In these sections, managers comment on how well (or poorly) the corporation performed over the past year, specifically in regard to its liquidity, capital, and results of operations. Usually

**EXHIBIT 10-7** **HERSHEY COMPANY (PARTIAL) AUDIT REPORT**

**Report of Independent Registered Public Accounting Firm**

**The Board of Directors and Stockholders**
**The Hershey Company:**

We have audited management's assessment, included in the accompanying Management Report on Internal Control Over Financial Reporting, that The Hershey Company and subsidiaries (the "Company") maintained effective internal control over financial reporting as of December 31, 2005, based on criteria established in Internal Control-Integrated Framework issued by the Committee of Sponsoring Organizations of the Treadway Commission (COSO). The Company's management is responsible for maintaining effective internal control over financial reporting and for its assessment of the effectiveness of internal control over financial reporting. Our responsibility is to express an opinion on management's assessment and an opinion on the effectiveness of the Company's internal control over financial reporting based on our audit.

.
.
.

In our opinion, management's assessment that the Company maintained effective internal control over financial reporting as of December 31, 2005, is fairly stated, in all material respects based on criteria established in Internal Control-Integrated Framework issued by COSO. Also in our opinion, the Company maintained, in all material respects, effective internal control over financial reporting as of December 31, 2005, based on criteria established in Internal Control-Integrated Framework issued by COSO.

We also have audited, in accordance with the standards of the Public Company Accounting Oversight Board (United States), the consolidated balance sheets of the Company as of December 31, 2005 and 2004, and the related consolidated statements of income, cash flows and stockholders' equity for each of the years in the three-year period ended December 31, 2005, and our report dated February 27, 2006 expressed an unqualified opinion on those consolidated financial statements.

**KPMG LLP**

New York, New York
February 27, 2006

these sections include a discussion about industry and market trends. Managers also discuss their plans for improvement. External users find this information useful because it explains how the corporation's current and planned operations are viewed "through the eyes of management."

In **The Campbell's Soup Company** annual report for 2005, Mr. Douglas Conant, President and CEO, used a straightforward approach to comment on the company's performance. His letter to shareholders stated: "I am pleased to report that our company has delivered a year of quality growth, surpassing the financial goals we set for ourselves. . . . This is an important step in fulfilling our mission to build the world's most extraordinary food company." His letter then detailed Campbell's strategy to improve its performance. Investors, creditors, and other interested parties certainly considered the president's comments as they made business decisions regarding Campbell.

*If you were a Campbell Soup Company stockholder, what do you think your response would have been to Mr. Conant's comment? Why do you think you would have reacted that way?*

### Securities and Exchange Commission (SEC) Reports

In addition to distributing annual reports to the public, corporations file reports with the SEC that are also available to the public. A company offering stock for public sale must file a

**EXHIBIT 10-8** **INTEL CORPORATION: BAR GRAPHS INCLUDED IN ITS 2005 ANNUAL REPORT**

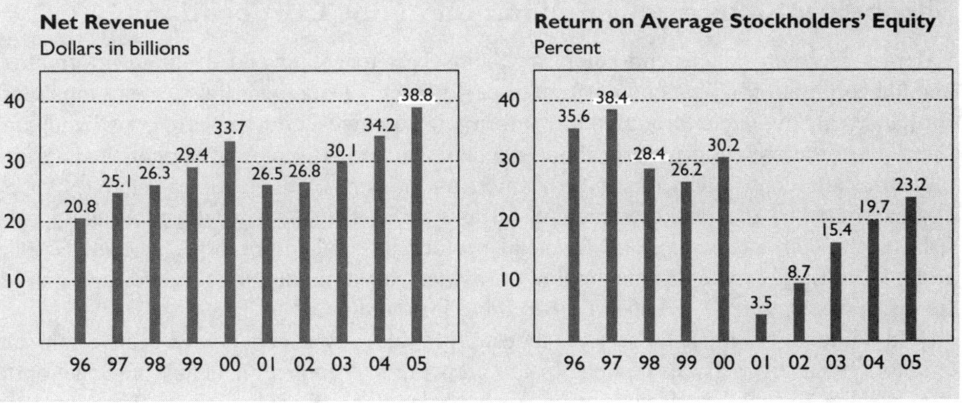


registration statement with the SEC and must provide potential investors with a "prospectus" containing most of the same information given the SEC. The **prospectus** typically contains the corporation's financial reports and other information, such as a description of the stock to be sold, the offering price, and how the cash received from the sale will be used.

Corporations that have their stock traded on any of the national stock exchanges, such as the New York Stock Exchange, must also file annual 10-K reports with the SEC. A **10-K report** includes the corporation's annual report and other information such as officers' names, salaries, and stock ownership. Corporations file these forms electronically with the SEC. For any company with revenues greater than $1.2 billion, the company's "chief executive" and "chief financial officer" both must "certify" that the company's annual report in the 10-K is both complete and accurate. This certification enhances the credibility of the company's financial statements. Companies' 10-K reports are located in the SEC's Electronic Data Gathering, Analysis, and Retrieval System (commonly known as *EDGAR*). When making business decisions, investors use information in these documents and other SEC filings.

### Interim Financial Statements

Companies normally use one year as their accounting period, but many companies also prepare interim financial statements. In fact, corporations registered with the SEC *must* provide external users with interim financial statements (called a *10-Q report*). **Interim financial statements** are financial statements prepared for a period of less than one year. It is most common for corporations to issue interim financial statements on a quarterly basis (every three months). These are published at the end of each quarter, and the quarterly results are also included in the corporation's annual report.

By issuing interim financial statements, corporations provide investors and creditors with new information to use to reevaluate their business decisions (such as whether or not to sell stock purchased in an earlier period) on a more frequent basis.

### Media Releases

Corporations also release important financial information in a more timely manner through press conferences and interviews with the media. Research by accounting professors has shown that corporate announcements of earnings, changes in dividend policies, major contracts with the government, and other important business activities affect investors' business decisions and result in changes in a corporation's stock price.

*Suppose Unlimited Decadence announced that last quarter's earnings were double its earnings in the same quarter the previous year. How do you think this announcement would affect Unlimited Decadence's stock price? Why?*

## Secondary Sources of Information about Corporations

External users do not depend solely on themselves to gather and evaluate information about a corporation's financial position or performance. Data regarding corporations' performances are available through many information services, both in "hard copy" and "on-line." Furthermore, information about standard industries is regularly published. These industries are identified by their North American Industry Classification System (NAICS) code assigned by the U.S. government. Firms such as **Dun & Bradstreet** annually publish statistics about the average financial performance of corporations in each NAICS code. Increasingly, computer technology provides vast amounts of data regarding market trends, industry trends, and specific corporate information.

In addition, the financial services industry provides investment advice to investors and creditors. Financial services companies use corporations' publicly available information to evaluate the financial performance of these corporations. Stockbrokerage firms, such as **A. G. Edwards** and **Morgan Stanley**, closely follow market and industry trends and the performance of individual corporations in order to give advice to their clients. These firms provide services to thousands of investors by making purchases and sales of stock for them.

# ANALYSIS OF FINANCIAL INFORMATION

5 How do users perform intracompany and intercompany analyses?

How do individuals and financial services firms evaluate a corporation's operating performance and financial condition? Basically, there are two approaches. One approach is to compare the corporation's current operating results and financial position with its past performance or with its expected performance. This approach is called **intracompany analysis**. One reason that external users perform intracompany analysis is to help determine *trends* in a corporation's financial performance. In other words, investors and creditors use trends to evaluate whether the corporation's performance is stable, improving, or declining.

*What trends in a corporation's performance do you think are most important? Why?*

External users will probably want answers to the following questions about Unlimited Decadence: (1) Did Unlimited Decadence's sales increase over sales in the prior year? If so, what was the percentage growth? (2) Did Unlimited Decadence's net income change from that of the prior year? If so, what was the percentage growth or decline? (3) Is Unlimited Decadence's current ratio continuing to improve over the ratios of prior years? (4) Are Unlimited Decadence's sales growing at a higher rate than its operating expenses?

External users also use intracompany analysis to investigate whether a corporation is meeting *its* performance expectations. Investors and creditors learn about corporate performance expectations from annual reports, media releases, and financial analysts who study corporations' performances. With this data, they can answer important questions about Unlimited Decadence: (1) Did Unlimited Decadence meet the sales projections it disclosed in its prior year's annual report? (2) Did Unlimited Decadence's net income reach the level that financial analysts had predicted? (3) Did Unlimited Decadence make the capital expenditures it announced at earlier meetings? (4) What is the relationship between Unlimited Decadence's earnings and its stock price?

A second approach to analyzing a corporation's financial performance is known as intercompany analysis. **Intercompany analysis** involves comparing a company's operating results and financial position with that of competing companies, industry averages, or averages in related industries. For example, investors and creditors might want to compare

Unlimited Decadence's operating results and financial position with those of **Hershey Company** or with the averages of all companies in the confectionary industry. They may perform intercompany analyses for a single period or for several past periods.

6 What is percentage analysis, and what are its three types?

Companies are of many sizes, and their sizes change from year to year. Because of these size differences, intracompany and intercompany analyses are easier to conduct and to interpret if percentage analysis is used. **Percentage analysis** involves converting financial statement information from dollars to percentages. For example, suppose that Unlimited Decadence's sales increased by $2,800,000—from $70,000,000 in 2007 to $72,800,000 in 2008. At the same time, a competing company's sales also increased by $2,800,000—from $35,000,000 to $37,800,000. Since both companies' sales increased by the same dollar amount, it might be tempting to think they performed equally well. But instead of evaluating the yearly change in each company's sales only as a dollar increase of $2,800,000, think of the change as a 4% ($2,800,000 ÷ $70,000,000) increase in Unlimited Decadence's sales and an 8% ($2,800,000 ÷ $35,000,000) increase in the competitor's sales. Thinking of the change in each company's sales as a *percentage change* leads to a different conclusion. Percentage analyses are especially useful when making intercompany comparisons.

There are three basic types of percentage analyses: ratio analysis, horizontal analysis, and vertical analysis. Recall that **ratio analysis** involves dividing an item on the financial statements by another related item (for example, net income divided by aver-age owner's equity). We used ratio analyses in Chapters 6 through 8 to perform intracompany analysis for Sweet Temptations, and to perform intercompany analysis of JCPenney and Kohl's.

**Horizontal analysis** shows the changes in a company's operating results over time in percentages as well as in dollar amounts. Unlimited Decadence's yearly sales change that we talked about earlier is an example of horizontal analysis. **Vertical analysis** shows each item in a financial statement of a given period or date both as a percentage of another item on that statement (for example, every item on the income statement stated as a percentage of sales, or every asset stated as a percentage of total assets) and as a dollar amount. Investors and creditors use each of these types of analyses to help evaluate a corporation's performance.

## BUSINESS ISSUES AND VALUES

*Should society expect corporations to do more than comply with laws and regulations, try to remain solvent, and earn a satisfactory profit for the owners? If so, what else should society expect? If not, what impact can this have on society?*

Large corporations have the same basic goals as small companies—to remain solvent and to earn a satisfactory profit for the owners. Our society has placed limits on what companies, both large and small, can do to meet these goals. These limits may be formal laws or regulations, such as those controlling misleading advertising, product safety, and management fraud. Other limits are not laws or regulations but are norms about what society expects from the business community. For example, society expects companies to treat employees, investors, and creditors fairly, support the local economy, and "give back" some of their profits by supporting local and national charities.

There is a continuing debate over how large corporations should balance these sometimes conflicting expectations. How much severance pay should corporations offer employees who are terminated? How much profit should corporations give back to the local community?

For large corporations, these questions are difficult, in part because managers usually do not own the corporation. For example, the question of supporting charities is difficult to answer because the managers of a corporation are spending the stockholders' (not their own) resources on charities that it decides to support. How would you like someone else deciding where your donations to charity should go? On the other hand, through a corporation's identification with the charity, this support may help it increase customer loyalty and improve overall financial performance. Throughout the book we will discuss how accounting plays a role in shaping these types of corporate decisions.

## SUMMARY

At the beginning of the chapter we asked you several questions. During the chapter, we asked you to STOP and answer some other questions to build your knowledge about specific issues. Be sure you answered these additional questions. Below are the questions from the beginning of the chapter, with a brief summary of the key points relating to the answers. Use your creative and critical thinking skills to expand on these key points to develop more complete answers to the questions and to determine what other questions you have that might lead you to learn more about the issues.

### 1 What are the three most common forms of business organizations and their basic characteristics?

The three most common forms of business organizations are sole proprietorships, partnerships, and corporations. A sole proprietorship is usually small, has a limited life, and is owned by one person who has unlimited liability. A partnership is owned by two or more people (called *partners*) who have unlimited liability; it can be large or small, is usually governed by a partnership agreement, and has a limited life. A corporation is a legal entity incorporated in one of the states. It is usually large and usually has many owners (called *stockholders*) who have limited liability. A corporation may have many managers, is subject to income taxes and other government regulations, and has an unlimited life.

### 2 What are the qualities that make accounting information about large corporations useful for decision making?

To be useful for decision making, accounting information must be relevant, reliable, material, and valid. Relevant information has the capacity to affect a user's decision. Reliable information is capable of being verified. Information is material when the dollar amount is large enough to make a difference in a decision. Information is valid when it shows a realistic picture of what it is meant to represent.

### 3 What do users need to know about the stockholders' equity section of a corporation's balance sheet and about its income statement?

The stockholders' equity section of a corporation's balance sheet is divided into two sections: contributed capital and retained earnings. Contributed capital includes the par value (legal capital) of the common stock as well as additional paid-in capital. Retained earnings reports the total lifetime net income that has been reinvested into the corporation and not distributed to stockholders as dividends. A corporation's income statement differs from the income statement of other types of companies because the former includes income from both continuing operations and nonrecurring earnings. Since corporations are subject to income taxes, a corporation's income statement also includes income tax expense. Finally, a corporation reports earnings per share on its income statement.

### 4 How does a corporation provide information to external users?

A corporation provides information to external users through its annual report, Securities and Exchange Commission (SEC) reports, interim financial statements, and media releases. A corporation's annual report includes its financial statements, related notes, audit report, financial highlights, management's discussion and analysis, and other information. SEC reports include a registration statement and an annual 10-K report. A corporation usually issues interim financial statements quarterly. Media releases provide information related to important business activities.

### 5 How do users perform intracompany and intercompany analyses?

Users perform intracompany analysis by comparing a corporation's current operations and financial position with its past results and expected results. They perform intercompany analysis by comparing a corporation's performance with the performance of competing companies, and with industry averages or averages in related industries.

### 6 What is percentage analysis, and what are its three types?

Percentage analysis involves converting financial statement information from dollars to percentages. There are three types of percentage analysis: ratio analysis, horizontal analysis, and vertical analysis. Ratio analysis involves dividing a financial statement item by another related item. Horizonal analysis shows the changes in a company's operating results over time as percentages. Vertical analysis shows the items on a financial statement of a given period or date as percentages of another item on that statement.

## KEY TERMS

**additional paid-in capital** *(p. 316)*
**agent** *(p. 305)*
**annual report** *(p. 319)*
**articles of incorporation** *(p. 308)*
**auditing** *(p. 320)*
**audit committee** *(p. 321)*
**audit report** *(p. 321)*
**capital stock** *(p. 315)*
**closely held corporation** *(p. 308)*
**common stock** *(p. 315)*
**comparative financial statements** *(p. 319)*
**conceptual framework** *(p. 312)*
**contributed capital** *(p. 315)*
**corporation** *(p. 306)*
**data warehouse** *(p. 311)*
**distribution** *(p. 310)*
**double taxation** *(p. 307)*
**e-business** *(p. 312)*
**earnings per share (EPS)** *(p. 319)*
**enterprise resource planning (ERP) systems** *(p. 310)*
**finance** *(p. 310)*
**Financial Highlights** *(p. 321)*
**Financial Summaries** *(p. 321)*
**gains** *(p. 318)*
**horizontal analysis** *(p. 325)*
**human resources** *(p. 310)*
**income from continuing operations** *(p. 318)*
**income tax expense** *(p. 318)*
**incorporation** *(p. 308)*
**initial public offering** *(p. 309)*
**intercompany analysis** *(p. 324)*
**intracompany analysis** *(p. 324)*
**interim financial statements** *(p. 323)*
**joint ownership** *(p. 305)*
**legal capital** *(p. 315)*
**Letter to Shareholders** *(p. 321)*
**limited life** *(pp. 304, 305)*
**losses** *(p. 318)*
**Management's Discussion and Analysis** *(p. 321)*
**marketing** *(p. 310)*
**market value** *(p. 315)*
**material** *(p. 313)*
**notes to the financial statements** *(p. 320)*
**operating income** *(p. 318)*
**other items** *(p. 318)*
**par value** *(p. 315)*
**partnership** *(p. 305)*
**partnership agreement** *(p. 305)*
**percentage analysis** *(p. 325)*
**preferred stock** *(p. 315)*
**production** *(p. 310)*
**prospectus** *(p. 323)*
**publicly available information** *(p. 319)*
**publicly held corporation** *(p. 309)*
**ratio analysis** *(p. 325)*
**relevant** *(p. 313)*
**reliable** *(p. 313)*
**retained earnings** *(pp. 315, 317)*
**secondary equity market** *(p. 309)*
**sole proprietorship** *(p. 304)*
**stockholders** *(p. 306)*
**stockholders' equity** *(p. 315)*
**10-K report** *(p. 323)*
**unlimited liability** *(p. 304)*
**valid** *(p. 314)*
**vertical analysis** *(p. 325)*

## SUMMARY SURFING

Here is an opportunity to gather information on the Internet about real-world issues related to the topics in this chapter (for suggestions on how to navigate various companies' Web sites to find their financial statements and other information, see the related discussion in the Preface at the beginning of the book). Answer the following questions.

- Go to the **TI** (Texas Instruments) Web site. Find the company's balance sheets. What types of stock does TI have? What is the par value per share of common stock, and how many shares were issued at the end of the most current year? What were the amounts of its retained earnings and its total stockholders' equity on December 31 of the most current year?

- Go to the **Intel Corporation** Web site. Find the company's income statements. What was Intel's net income for the most current year, and how does this compare with its income in the previous year? What was Intel's earnings per share for the most current year, and how does this compare with its earnings per share in the previous year? Find the Management's discussion and analysis of financial condition and results of operations. By what percent did Intel's net revenues increase or decrease from the previous year to the most current year, and what were the reasons for this change?

# INTEGRATED BUSINESS AND ACCOUNTING SITUATIONS

**Answer the Following Questions in Your Own Words.**

## Testing Your Knowledge

**10-1** What is a sole proprietorship? What is meant by the terms *unlimited liability* and *limited life* as they apply to a sole proprietorship?

**10-2** What is a partnership? What is meant by the terms *limited life, joint ownership, agent,* and *unlimited liability* as they apply to a partnership?

**10-3** What is included in a partnership agreement?

**10-4** What is a corporation? What is meant by the terms *capital stock, limited liability,* and *double taxation* as they apply to a corporation?

**10-5** What is the secondary equity market? Name three organizations that are part of the secondary equity market.

**10-6** Name the typical functional areas of a large corporation. How is accounting information used to manage these functions?

**10-7** What is an enterprise resource planning (ERP) system and how does it relate to a data warehouse and data mining?

**10-8** What is the FASB's conceptual framework, and what is the primary purpose of financial accounting information?

**10-9** What is relevant accounting information, and how does it relate to materiality?

**10-10** What is reliable accounting information, and how does it relate to validity?

**10-11** What is the owners' equity of a corporation called, and into what two sections is it separated on a corporation's balance sheet?

**10-12** What is included in contributed capital and retained earnings on a corporation's balance sheet?

**10-13** What amounts are included in a corporation's common stock and additional paid-in capital accounts?

**10-14** What is reported in the income from continuing operations section of a corporation's income statement?

**10-15** What is the last item shown on a corporation's income statement, and how is it computed?

**10-16** What is included in a corporation's annual report?

**10-17** What are the three opinions that an auditor expresses in an audit report? Why is an audit report important to external users?

**10-18** What is included in the management's discussion and analysis (MD&A) section of a corporation's annual report?

**10-19** What is the difference between intracompany analysis and intercompany analysis?

**10-20** What is the difference between horizontal analysis and vertical analysis?

## Applying Your Knowledge

**10-21** Companies have different forms of organization.

*Required:* Discuss the differences among sole proprietorships, partnerships, and corporations regarding ownership, decision making, income taxes, the responsibility of owners for the company's debts, and the life of the company.

**10-22** Suppose you were starting a new business with a friend. Your friend and you have agreed that he will invest most of the capital and that you will do most of the work. You will invest some cash and a two-year-old truck, which will be used as a delivery vehicle in the business.

*Required:* Briefly discuss what information you would include in the partnership agreement for the new company. Be as specific as possible.

**10-23** At the end of 2008, before allocating net income, the Simon and Art partnership had total owners' equity of $100,000, consisting of Simon, capital: $60,000, and Art, capital: $40,000. During 2008 the partnership earned net income of $35,000. The partnership agreement specifies that net income is to be allocated according to three factors as follows: (a) first, each partner is to be allocated a share of net income equal to 10% of her capital amount, (b) second, Simon is to be allocated a salary of $8,000, and Art is to be allocated a salary of $12,000 as a share of net income, and (c) the remaining net income is to be allocated 60% to Simon and 40% to Art.

*Required:* (1) Prepare a schedule that allocates the net income to Simon and Art according to the partnership agreement. (*Hint:* The salaries paid to the partners are used only to allocate the net income; they are not included as salaries expense on the income statement.)
(2) Explain why you think factors (a) and (b) for allocating net income were included in the partnership agreement.

**10-24** During 2008, the Fame and Fortune partnership had sales revenue of $200,000, cost of goods sold of $120,000, and operating expenses of $25,000. At the end of 2008, before allocating net income, the A. Fame, Capital account had a balance of $140,000, and the B. Fortune, Capital account had a balance of $70,000. In reviewing the partnership agreement, you find that annual net income is to be allocated to each partner based on three factors. (a) First, A. Fame is to be allocated a salary of $5,000, and B. Fortune is to be allocated a salary of $20,000 as a share of net income. (b) Second, each partner is to be allocated a share of net income equal to 10% of his capital account balance. (c) Third, the remaining net income is to be allocated 2/3 to A. Fame and 1/3 to B. Fortune.

*Required:* (1) Prepare a 2008 income statement for the Fame and Fortune partnership. At the bottom of the income statement, include a schedule that allocates the net income to each partner based on the factors in the partnership agreement. (*Hint:* The salaries paid to the partners are used only to allocate the net income; they are not included as salaries expense on the income statement.)
(2) Explain why you think factors (a) and (b) for allocating net income were included in the partnership agreement.

**10-25** One way to logically divide the organization structure of a large corporation is by function.

*Required:* Identify the typical functional areas of a corporation, and briefly discuss what activities are performed in each area. Briefly explain how managers would use accounting information in the operations of these functional areas.

**10-26** A friend of yours has recently completed a course in bookkeeping at his high school. He has been browsing through this chapter of your book and noticed the term "conceptual framework." He says, "We never had a conceptual framework in our bookkeeping class. What is this framework anyhow? Please tell me about the qualities of useful accounting information, and define each one."

*Required:* Prepare a written response to your friend's question.

**10-27** Ryland Carpet Corporation sells 10,000 shares of its common stock for $10 per share.

*Required:* (1) Using account columns, show how Ryland Carpet Corporation would record this transaction under each of the following independent assumptions:
(a) The stock has a par value of $2 per share.
(b) The stock has a par value of $5 per share.
(c) The stock has a par value of $7 per share.
(2) If you were a stockholder of Ryland Carpet Corporation, which par value would you prefer? Why?

**10-28** Tiger Corporation previously had issued 10,000 shares of its $2 par value common stock for $15 per share. On December 28, 2008, it sells another 5,000 shares to investors for $20 per share.

*Required:* (1) Using account columns, (a) enter the balances in the applicable accounts for the common stock that had previously been issued and (b) record the sale of the 5,000 shares of common stock on December 28, 2008.
(2) Prepare the contributed capital section of Tiger Corporation's December 31, 2008 balance sheet.

**10-29** On December 29, 2008, Lion Corporation sells 4,000 shares of its common stock with a $5 par value to investors for $25 per share. This is the only sale of common stock during 2008. Before 2008, the corporation had issued 12,000 shares of this common stock for $21 per share. At the end of 2008, the corporation had retained earnings of $124,000.

*Required:* (1) Using account columns, (a) enter the balances in the Common Stock and Additional Paid-in Capital accounts at the beginning of 2008 and (b) record the sale of the 4,000 shares of common stock on December 29, 2008.
(2) Prepare the stockholders' equity section of Lion Corporation's December 31, 2008 balance sheet.

**10-30** During all of 2008, stockholders of the Planet Pluto Corporation owned 15,000 shares of its $3 par value common stock. They had purchased this stock from the corporation for $29 per share. At the end of 2008, the Planet Pluto Corporation had an ending balance of $247,000 in its retained earnings account.

*Required:* Prepare the stockholders' equity section of the Planet Pluto Corporation's December 31, 2008 balance sheet.

**10-31** The stockholders of Riglets Corporation owned 10,000 shares of its $5 par value common stock during all of this year. The corporation is subject to a 40% income tax rate. The corporation's balance sheet information at the end of this year and its income statement information for this year are as follows:

| | |
|---|---|
| Common stock, $5 par value | $ (a) |
| Gross profit | 113,000 |
| Pretax income from continuing operations | (b) |
| Operating expenses | 33,000 |
| Total contributed capital | 228,000 |
| Income tax expense | (c) |
| Retained earnings | 181,000 |
| Net income | 48,000 |
| Additional paid-in capital | (d) |
| Earnings per share | (e) |
| Cost of goods sold | (f) |
| Sales (net) | 240,000 |
| Total stockholders' equity | (g) |

*Required:* Fill in the blanks lettered (a) through (g). All the necessary information is listed. (*Hint:* It is not necessary to calculate your answers in alphabetical order.)

**10-32** Braiden Corporation is subject to a 40% income tax rate. During all of this year, stockholders owned 20,000 shares of its $2 par value common stock. The corporation's income statement information for this year and its balance sheet information at the end of this year are as follows:

| | |
|---|---|
| Sales (net) | $311,000 |
| Net income | (a) |
| Total stockholders' equity | 500,000 |
| Operating expenses | (b) |
| Additional paid-in capital | 198,000 |
| Income tax expense | (c) |
| Common stock, $2 par value | (d) |
| Pretax income from continuing operations | (e) |
| Earnings per share | 3.15 |
| Total contributed capital | (f) |
| Gross profit | 147,000 |
| Retained earnings | (g) |
| Cost of goods sold | 164,000 |

*Required:* Fill in the blanks lettered (a) through (g). All the necessary information is listed. (*Hint:* It is not necessary to calculate your answers in alphabetical order.)

**10-33** Ringland Glass Corporation showed the following balances in its income statement accounts at the end of 2008:

| | |
|---|---|
| Interest expense | $ 1,400 |
| Sales (net) | 585,000 |
| Selling expenses | 54,200 |
| Interest revenue | 3,200 |
| Cost of goods sold | 350,700 |
| General expenses | 31,900 |

The corporation pays income taxes at a rate of 40%. It had average stockholders' equity during 2008 of $500,000, and stockholders owned 30,000 shares of its common stock during all of 2008.

*Required:* (1) Prepare a 2008 income statement for Ringland Glass Corporation.
(2) Compute the return on owners' (stockholders') equity of Ringland Glass Corporation for 2008. How does this compare with the industry average of 14.8%?

**10-34** The stockholders of Buffalo Chips Corporation owned 40,000 shares of its common stock during all of 2008. The corporation pays income taxes at a rate of 40% and had the following balances in its income statement accounts at the end of 2008:

| | |
|---|---|
| Administrative expenses | $ 67,400 |
| Cost of goods sold | 302,000 |
| Interest expense | 3,500 |
| Interest revenue | 1,700 |
| Sales (net) | 563,800 |
| Selling expenses | 40,600 |

*Required:* (1) Prepare a 2008 income statement for Buffalo Chips Corporation.
(2) Compute the profit margin of Buffalo Chips Corporation for 2008. How does this compare with the industry average of 17.4%?

**10-35** On July 1, 2008, Kelly Corporation sold for $15,000 an acre of land that it was not using in its operations. Kelly had purchased the land four years ago for $9,000. In other transactions during 2008, Kelly incurred $1,500 interest expense.

*Required:* (1) Using account columns, record the sale of the land by Kelly.
(2) Prepare the Other Items section of Kelly's 2008 income statement.

**10-36** Stockholders of the Tomar Export Corporation owned 5,000 shares of common stock during all of this year. The corporation listed the following items in its financial statements on December 31 of this year:

| | |
|---|---|
| Net income | $ 12,000 |
| Current assets | 15,000 |
| Average stockholders' equity | 70,000 |
| Cost of goods sold | 72,000 |
| Total liabilities | 26,000 |
| Net sales | 100,000 |
| Current liabilities | 6,000 |
| Average inventory | 9,000 |
| Total assets | 100,000 |

*Required:* Using the preceding information, compute the following ratios of the Tomar Export Corporation for this year: (1) earnings per share, (2) gross profit percentage, (3) profit margin, (4) return on owners' (stockholders') equity, (5) current ratio, (6) inventory turnover, and (7) debt ratio.

**10-37** Taboue Cutlery Corporation showed the following income statement information for the years 2008 and 2009:

**TABOUE CUTLERY CORPORATION**

***Comparative Income Statements***

***For Years Ended December 31***

| | | | Year-to-Year Increase (Decrease) | |
|---|---|---|---|---|
| | **2008** | **2009** | **Amount** | **Percent** |
| Sales (net) | $60,000 | $65,000 | $ (a) | (b) % |
| Cost of goods sold | (33,600) | (c) | (d) | (e) |
| Gross profit | $26,400 | $27,950 | $ (f) | (g) |
| Operating expenses | (h) | (19,050) | 400 | (i) |
| Pretax operating income | $ (j) | $ 8,900 | $1,150 | (k) |
| Income tax expense | (3,100) | (3,560) | (l) | (m) |
| Net Income | $ 4,650 | $ (n) | $ (o) | (p) |
| Number of common shares issued | (q) | 2,700 | (r) | 12.6 |
| Earnings per share | $ 1.94 | $ 1.98 | $ (s) | (t) |

*Required:* (1) Determine the appropriate percentages and amounts for the blanks lettered (a) through (t). Round to the nearest tenth of a percent.
(2) Did you just do horizontal or vertical analysis? Briefly comment on what your analysis reveals.

**10-38** The Clovland Corporation presents the following comparative income statements for 2008 and 2009:

**CLOVLAND CORPORATION**

***Comparative Income Statements***

***For Years Ended December 31***

| | **2008** | **2009** |
|---|---|---|
| Sales (net) | $90,000 | $108,000 |
| Cost of goods sold | (45,000) | (60,000) |
| Gross profit | $45,000 | $ 48,000 |
| Operating expenses | (20,000) | (22,000) |
| Pretax operating income | $25,000 | $ 26,000 |
| Income tax expense | (10,000) | (10,400) |
| Net Income | $15,000 | $ 15,600 |
| Number of common shares | 6,800 | 7,000 |
| Earnings per share | $ 2.21 | $ 2.23 |

*Required:* (1) Based on the preceding information, prepare a horizontal analysis for the years 2008 and 2009. (*Hint:* To the right of the income statements, add an *Amount* column and a *Percent* column as in 10-37.)

(2) Calculate the corporation's profit margin for each year. What is this ratio generally used for, and what does it indicate for the Clovland Corporation?

**10-39** The Anton Electronics Corporation presents the following income statement for 2008:

**ANTON ELECTRONICS CORPORATION**
***Income Statement***
***For Year Ended December 31, 2008***

| | |
|---|---|
| Sales (net) | $140,000 |
| Cost of goods sold | (81,340) |
| Gross profit | $ 58,660 |
| Operating expenses | (28,560) |
| Pretax operating income | $ 30,100 |
| Income tax expense | (12,100) |
| Net Income | $ 18,000 |
| Earnings per share | $ 3.20 |

In addition, the average inventory for 2008 was $10,000.

*Required:* (1) Based on the preceding information, prepare a vertical analysis of the income statement for 2008. (*Hint:* To the right of the income statement, add a *Percent* column, and assign 100% to net sales.)

(2) Compute the corporation's inventory turnover for 2008, and briefly explain what this ratio tells you about a company.

## Making Evaluations

**10-40** A recent annual report of **Toys "R" Us** contained the following information in the section called "Report of Management": ". . . Management has established a system of internal controls to provide reasonable assurance that assets are maintained and accounted for in accordance with its policies and that transactions are recorded accurately on the company's books and records. . . . The company has distributed to key employees its policies for conducting business affairs in a lawful and ethical manner. . . . The financial statements of the company have been audited by Ernst & Young LLP, independent auditors, in accordance with auditing standards generally accepted in the United States, including a review of financial reporting matters and internal controls to the extent necessary to express an opinion on the . . . financial statements."

*Required:* Suppose you were using these financial statements to make a decision about investing in Toys "R" Us. Would this information help you make your decision? If so, how would it help? If not, why do you think Toys "R" Us includes the information with its financial statements?

**10-41** You have a close friend from high school who is attending college in another state. You see each other at holidays, and in between visits you correspond on a regular basis by e-mail. Here is the latest e-mail you received from your friend:

From: HT246@UA.EDU <friend>

To: Ace@AAU.EDU <you>

Subject: HELP!!!

Hey, how's it going? Sorry I don't have time to chat. I need some help. I'm taking a personal finance course. In this course, I estimate how much my annual income will be after I graduate, establish a personal monthly budget, and decide how to invest my monthly savings. As part of this, I must select a real-life corporation to invest in.

I estimated my annual income to be $75,000 (hey, you know me—I think positive), so I have a lot of savings to invest. Here's where you come in. I am having trouble getting started with the part of the assignment where I pick a real-life corporation to invest in. Luckily, dear friend, I remembered that you are taking this accounting course.

Remember how I helped you out when you were taking Poli Sci? Now it's return-the-favor time. Tell me what you know about (1) the kinds of information I need to decide whether a corporation is a good investment, (2) where I can get the information, and (3) how to analyze the information once I get it.

By the way, the assignment is due day after tomorrow, so don't send back 20 pages of techno-jargon I can't even understand. Just send what you think is most important, and tell me in words I can understand. Thanks a bunch.

*Required:* Using the material presented in this chapter, write an e-mail message back to your friend. Make sure you respond specifically to the three items he needs help with.

**10-42** Below are condensed income statements of **Dell Computer Corporation** for fiscal years 2006 and 2005.

| | Fiscal Year Ended | |
|---|---|---|
| *(in millions, except earnings per share)* | **February 3, 2006** | **January 28, 2005** |
| Net revenue | $55,908 | $49,205 |
| Cost of revenue | 45,958 | 40,190 |
| Gross margin | $ 9,950 | $ 9,015 |
| Operating expenses: | | |
| Selling, general, and administrative | 5,140 | 4,298 |
| Research, development, and engineering | 463 | 463 |
| Total operating expenses | $ 5,603 | $ 4,761 |
| Operating income | $ 4,347 | $ 4,254 |
| Investment and other income, net | 227 | 191 |
| Income before income taxes | $ 4,574 | $ 4,445 |
| Provision for income taxes | 1,002 | 1,402 |
| Net Income | $ 3,572 | $ 3,043 |
| Earnings per common share: | $ 1.49 | $ 1.21 |

*Required:* (1) Based on the preceding information, prepare a horizontal analysis for the fiscal years 2006 and 2005. (*Hint:* To the right of the income statements, add an *Amount* column and a *Percent* column as in 10-37.)

(2) For each year, compute (a) the gross profit percentage and (b) the profit margin.

(3) Briefly explain what your results from (1) and (2) tell you about Dell's change in its profitability, and why this change took place.

**10-43** Below are condensed comparative balance sheets of **Dell Computer Corporation** for the fiscal years ended February 3, 2006 and January 28, 2005.

| *(in millions)* | **February 3, 2006** | **January 28, 2005** |
|---|---|---|
| **Assets** | | |
| Current assets: | | |
| Cash and cash equivalents | $ 7,042 | $ 4,747 |
| Short-term investments | 2,016 | 5,060 |
| Receivables, net | 5,452 | 4,548 |
| Inventories | 576 | 459 |
| Other | 2,620 | 2,083 |
| Total current assets | $17,706 | $16,897 |
| Property, plant, and equipment, net | 2,005 | 1,691 |
| Investments | 2,691 | 4,294 |
| Other noncurrent assets | 707 | 333 |
| Total assets | $23,109 | $23,215 |

**Liabilities and Stockholders' Equity**

| | | |
|---|---|---|
| Current liabilities: | | |
| Accounts payable | $ 9,840 | $ 8,895 |
| Accured and other | 6,087 | 5,241 |
| Total current liabilities | $15,927 | $14,136 |
| Long-term debt | 504 | 505 |
| Other non-current liabilities | 2,549 | 2,089 |
| Total liabilities | $18,980 | $16,730 |
| Total stockholders' equity | 4,129 | 6,485 |
| Total liabilities and stockholders' equity | $23,109 | $23,215 |

*Required:* (1) Based on the preceding information, prepare a vertical analysis of each balance sheet. (*Hint:* To the right of each column, add a *Percent* column and assign 100% to total assets, as well as to total liabilities and stockholders' equity.)

(2) For each year, compute the (a) current ratio and (b) debt ratio.

(3) Briefly explain what your results from (1) and (2) tell you about Dell's liquidity and financial flexibility.

**10-44** Refer to the income statements and balance sheets for the **Dell Computer Corporation** in 10-42 and 10-43. In addition to this information, you determine that at the end of fiscal year 2004, Dell had receivables (net) of $3,635 million, inventories of $327 million, total assets of $19,311 million, and total stockholders' equity of $6,280 million.

*Required:* (1) For each fiscal year (2006 and 2005), compute the (a) accounts receivable turnover (for simplicity, assume all Dell's net revenue is from credit sales), (b) inventory turnover, (c) return on owners' (stockholders') equity, and (d) return on total assets (assume that Dell has interest expense of $28 million in fiscal year 2006 and $16 million in fiscal year 2005).

(2) Briefly explain what your results from (1) tell you about the change in (a) Dell's operating capability and (b) Dell's profitability.

(3) Explain whether you are using intercompany analysis or intracompany analysis.

**10-45** In this chapter, we described how investors and creditors obtain information about publicly held corporations, and we began our coverage of the stockholders' equity section of a corporation's balance sheet and a corporation's income statement. Read the following item that appeared on May 16 of a recent year, on the first page of the Money section of *USA Today:*

> TOY SALES: The world's largest toy retailer, hurt by weak video game sales, said [yesterday] that its first-quarter net income slipped 51%. **Toys "R" Us** net income fell to $18.4 million, or 7 cents a share, from $37.58 million, or 13 cents a share, a year earlier. Revenue was up slightly, at $1.49 billion, compared with $1.46 billion in the year-ago quarter. Revenue for stores open at least a year fell 10%. Toys "R" Us stock dropped 1⅛ to $26 in heavy trading. The company has 618 toy stores in the USA, 300 international toy stores and 206 Kids "R" Us children's clothing stores.

*Required:* Respond to the following questions:

(1) In what month does the annual accounting period for Toys "R" Us end? How did you figure that out? Why would Toys "R" Us end its accounting period then?

(2) How many shares of stock do you think are owned by Toys "R" Us investors at the end of the first quarter of the year? How did you calculate that number?

(3) What was the market value of Toys "R" Us stock on the morning of May 15? What about on the morning of May 16? Explain why you think this change occurred.

(4) Assume you had purchased 500 shares of Toys "R" Us stock on May 15 of the previous year for $24 a share. How would you evaluate your investment's performance? As an investor, what specific information in the newspaper item would concern you the most? Why?

**10-46** Almost everyone has eaten at **McDonald's**. Big Macs and Quarter Pounders are part of many people's weekly diet. At last count, McDonald's serves over 50 million people per day. McDonald's Corporation is known not only for its fast food but also for its corporate social responsibility efforts. We have listed several social responsibility activities that McDonald's Corporation decided to undertake:

(a) McDonald's decided to sponsor Ronald McDonald Houses, where families with hospitalized children can stay near the hospital for free.
(b) McDonald's decided to become a major contributor to Jerry Lewis's fund-raising campaign to fight muscular dystrophy.
(c) McDonald's decided to employ physically and/or mentally challenged adults who find it more difficult to get jobs.
(d) Although McDonald's believed that styrofoam containers helped to maintain the quality of its food, it decided to reduce its use of styrofoam containers in response to news reports about the dangers of fluorocarbons and in response to pressures applied by nonprofit environmental groups.

In each of these cases, McDonald's senior executives probably consulted managers from some or all of the functional areas (marketing, production, human resources, finance, distribution) before making their decision.

*Required:* Answer the following questions. Think through your answers carefully so that you can defend the conclusions you reach.

(1) For each of the four activities listed above, list the questions you would ask to determine whether McDonald's decision to undertake this activity helps or hinders the corporation's ability to meet its basic objectives of remaining solvent and earning a satisfactory profit.
(2) For each of the four activities, analyze what functional areas will be affected and how they will be affected. Then, assuming you are the finance manager, use your analysis to write McDonald's senior executives a memo explaining the impact of activities (a) and (d) on your functional area.
(3) Now, think back through your answers to (1) and (2) with one thing in mind—information from other functional areas. More specifically, brainstorm about information that the other functional areas could provide that would improve your ability to answer questions (1) and (2). Use the knowledge you have gained about costs, profits, budgeting, and reporting to help formulate your answer.

**10-47** In this chapter, we said that individuals investing in large corporations must rely on publicly available information when making their investment decisions. But some individuals may have more than just publicly available information. Consider the following situation.

Suppose you and your mom were playing golf with two of her business "cronies." While waiting to tee off at the eighth hole, one of them, the chief financial officer of her company, mentioned ("off the record") that her company had just finished the development of a new product that would "blow the socks off" the health care industry. Although she was not at liberty to discuss the product (it won't be released until early next year), she speculated that once the product was released, the company stock price would "skyrocket." She also mentioned that she intended to purchase a large number of shares of the company's stock (which is being traded on the New York Stock Exchange) later in the day, and to sell them after the product was released.

WHOA!!! This could be an opportunity for you to invest the $2,000 your wealthy Aunt Bertha gave you for your birthday. Also, your boss, coworkers, and friends might like to know about this opportunity.

*Required:* (1) What are the relevant facts for your decision?
(2) Are there any ethical issues involved in your decision?
(3) Who has a stake in your decision (who stands to gain and who stands to lose), and how might your decision affect these stakeholders?
(4) What do you think you should do? Why?
(5) Do you see any ethical issues in the chief financial officer's discussion and decision?
(6) Who are the stakeholders in her discussion and decision?
(7) Suppose that when you got home after the golf game, your mom asked you what you thought of the conversation at the eighth hole. How would you answer her?
(8) What do you think should happen to "level the playing field"?

**10-48** Yesterday, you received the following letter for your advice column at the local paper:

## DR. DECISIVE

Dear Dr. Decisive:

I am having a crisis with my professional life right now and could use an objective opinion. Please help! I have been working for a partnership for ten years (let's just call it "Seedman and Seedman") and have built up a strong relationship with the company's customers. I am currently earning a salary of $42,000. But last week I received from one of Seedman and Seedman's competitors a job offer (unsolicited) that included a salary of $50,000. The offer is tempting, but I like my current job. So, I met with the Seedmans to see if they could increase my salary to match the offer. Well, I wasn't prepared for their response. They offered me a share of the partnership!! But here's where it gets complicated. In order to join the partnership, I would contribute $25,000 cash but would be paid no salary until the end of the year. Then, after the net income of the partnership was determined for each year, it would be allocated as follows. First, I would be allocated a salary of $38,000, Sadie Seedman would be allocated a salary of $42,000, and Johnny Seedman would be allocated a salary of $38,000. The remaining net income (after we withdrew our salaries) would be assigned to our individual capital accounts. Sadie's share would be 50%, Johnny's 30%, and mine 20%. (If I become a partner, we could call ourselves Seedman, Seedman, and Seedling—I'd be the seedling.) If I take the other job, I plan to invest $25,000 in the stock of a high-tech company in my city.

What do you see as the advantages and disadvantages of each of my alternatives?

"Seedling"

*Required:* Get together with your Dr. Decisive consulting team and write a response to "Seedling."

## END NOTE

[a]*NYSE Overview statistics* (http://www.nysedata.com, July, 2006).

# CHAPTER 11

# DEVELOPING A BUSINESS PLAN FOR A MANUFACTURING COMPANY: COST-VOLUME-PROFIT PLANNING AND ANALYSIS

"WE SHOULD ALL BE CONCERNED ABOUT THE FUTURE BECAUSE WE WILL HAVE TO SPEND THE REST OF OUR LIVES THERE."

—CHARLES KETTERING

1. How does the fact that a manufacturing company makes the products it sells affect its business plan?
2. How does a manufacturing company determine the cost of the goods that it manufactures?
3. Why are standard costs useful in controlling a company's operations?
4. How do manufacturing costs affect cost-volume-profit analysis?
5. What is the effect of multiple products on cost-volume-profit analysis?
6. How does a manufacturing company use cost-volume-profit analysis for its planning?

Have you ever read the ingredients in a candy bar and then wondered how these ingredients were combined to form the candy bar? It is the manufacturing process that precisely mixes these ingredients and performs the other activities necessary to form and package a tasty candy bar. This process involves a combination of materials (ingredients), employees who work in the factory, and manufacturing activities. To succeed, a manufacturing company must plan all these aspects of its manufacturing processes.

Earlier in this book, we discussed many aspects of planning that apply to entrepreneurial service and retail companies. Now we will expand our discussion to include additional aspects of planning that apply to larger companies and specifically to manufacturing companies. Recall from our early discussion in Chapter 1 that the fact that manufacturing companies *make* the products they sell to their customers distinguishes them from service and retail companies. As you will see, although the planning processes of all types of companies are basically the same, this characteristic of a manufacturing company influences its planning processes and its business plan.

## A Manufacturing Company's Business Plan

1 How does the fact that a manufacturing company makes the products it sells affect its business plan?

Like the entrepreneurs we discussed in Chapter 3, a manufacturing company's managers use its business plan to help them plan their company's activities, visualize the results of implementing their plans, carry out the company's plans, and later evaluate how well the company performed. A company may decide to share its business plan with potential investors and creditors. If so, they can use the company's business plan to help them learn as much as they can about the company, its plans, and how it operates so that they can make decisions about whether to invest in or lend money to the company.

A manufacturing company's business plan has much in common with the business plans of retail and service companies and contains the same components that we discussed in Chapter 3. However, since a manufacturing company makes the products that it sells, its business plan contains an additional component useful to internal and external decision makers—the production plan. The production plan has considerable impact on the other sections of the business plan, particularly the financial plan, which we will discuss later in this chapter.

© LISA KRANTZ/SYRACUSE NEWSPAPER/THE IMAGE WORKS

How does the production and sale of these candies fit into this corporation's business plan?

## The Production Plan

The production plan included in a manufacturing company's business plan describes how the company plans to efficiently produce its goods while maintaining a desired level of product quality. It also describes the company's plans for achieving specific levels of productivity through the use of materials, labor, equipment, and facilities. For example, **Techknits, Inc.**, a sweater manufacturer in New York, purchased computerized looms to improve its production. So Techknits would have described in its production plan how it planned to complete orders for sweaters faster and more efficiently than it did previously. For example, the company planned to use these looms 24 hours a day. Whereas previously one person was needed per manual loom, after the purchase of the computerized loom, one person would be able to run four computerized looms.[a] Techknits also would have explained that with this process, it would be able to turn out 60,000 sweaters a week. A company's production plan also describes the raw materials that make up the company's products, the company's production processes, and the finished products.

### The Raw Materials

**Raw materials** are the materials, ingredients, and parts that make up a company's products. They also include materials that the company needs for production but that do not become a part of the products, such as production supplies and grease for lubricating machine parts. For example, some of the raw materials that Unlimited Decadence uses in manufacturing one of its candy bars include cocoa nibs, cocoa liqueur, sugar and other sweeteners, cocoa butter, milk products, emulsifiers, and paper (for packaging the candy bars). When Unlimited Decadence lists its raw materials in this section, it specifies any criteria that these materials must meet (such as standards or grades of cocoa). It also indicates which of them are perishable and how quickly they perish.

A company also lists its raw materials suppliers in this section. This list includes such information as the company's major suppliers and alternative suppliers, as well as a comparison of these suppliers' characteristics such as quality, delivery time and method, dependability, cost, and payment methods and schedules.

Another aspect of raw materials that a company describes in this section is the way it handles the raw materials once it receives them from its suppliers. This description includes the company's delivery inspection procedures, warehousing, and security for the raw materials. Since Unlimited Decadence's candy bar ingredients are perishable, Unlimited Decadence follows special procedures to ensure that fresh, quality raw materials go into its candy bars. In this section of its production plan, Unlimited Decadence describes how it inspects incoming raw materials for grade (percent defective) and for freedom from bugs and other contamination. Unlimited Decadence also describes unique aspects of its raw materials storage, including regulated temperature, humidity, and exposure to air.

*Picture the movement of ingredients from the warehouse of the supplier to that of Unlimited Decadence. If you were a manager at Unlimited Decadence, at what point or points in this movement would you want the ingredients to be inspected for grade, freedom from bugs, and other contamination? What is your rationale?*

### The Production Processes

This section typically includes a description of the employees, facilities, and equipment necessary for the manufacture of a company's products. Here, the company describes the sequence of production steps necessary to manufacture its products and how the raw materials flow through this sequence. For example, Exhibit 11-1 lists the production steps necessary to manufacture Unlimited Decadence's Darkly Decadent candy bar. A company also describes the employees needed for each of the steps,

**EXHIBIT 11-1 PRODUCTION STEPS NECESSARY TO MANUFACTURE THE DARKLY DECADENT CANDY BAR**

(1) Preparing ingredients—pulverizing cocoa nibs, grinding sugar
(2) Mixing ingredients—producing chocolate paste of a rough texture and plastic consistency
(3) Refining chocolate paste—smoothing texture of paste
(4) Conching chocolate paste—dispersing sugar and milk solids in liquid fat
(5) Tempering chocolate paste—stabilizing chocolate, causing good color and texture
(6) Molding candy bars—shaping candy bars
(7) Wrapping candy bars—packaging candy bars

including what their skills must be, the availability of employees with these skills, how much time they will be spending on each product, and how much this time will cost the company.

*__Fairchild of California__, a sofa manufacturer near Los Angeles, has employed 100 highly skilled immigrant workers to produce sofas at wages ranging from $9 to $13 per hour (depending on how many sofas each employee worked on in an hour).[b] What information about these employees do you think Fairchild would have included in this section of its business plan?*

A company also lists in this section all the equipment and facilities it uses or plans to use in the production process, as well as the costs associated with the use of the equipment and facilities. These associated costs include mortgage, rent, utilities, maintenance, and insurance payments. The diagram in Exhibit 11-2 illustrates the equipment that Unlimited Decadence uses to manufacture the Darkly Decadent candy bar and other candy bars. Notice that it uses an electronic control panel to regulate and automate the production process. For example, the control panel dictates how much of each ingredient is fed into the mixer from the hoppers. Since the proportion of ingredients is different for each type of candy bar, Unlimited Decadence programs different formulas into the control panel; the formulas determine the mix of ingredients for each type of candy bar. The control panel also monitors such production variables as temperature and candy density, and it adjusts the production process when these variables deviate from the acceptable range of values.

*__Spangler Candy Co.__ in Bryan, Ohio, a manufacturer of candy canes, would describe in its production processes section its partially automated factory, which doubles Spangler's output by automatically wrapping the canes in a thin plastic film, packing them in boxes of twelve (in tiny cradles to keep them from breaking), and bundling the boxes into cases. Before automation, Spangler hand-packaged the candy canes. It also would describe the costs associated with this automation, including the cost of the 215,000-square-foot warehouse where it stores the millions and millions of candy canes from February, when it begins candy cane production, until they are sold during the holiday season.[c] Can you think of any other costs that might be associated with this automated factory?*

Another aspect of production that a company addresses in this section is the regulations with which it must comply and the permits and licenses that it must maintain. For example, manufacturers in California, like those in other states, must follow national rules for clean air. In most states, regulators dictate how companies must meet these rules. However, in California, regulators allow companies to determine how they will comply with these rules. These companies include their clean air plans in this section of their business plans.[d] Recall from our discussion of regulations in Chapter 1 that these regulations, permits, and licenses also include such items as operating permits, certification and inspection licenses, state and local building codes, and recycling systems.

**EXHIBIT 11-2 EQUIPMENT NECESSARY TO MANUFACTURE THE DARKLY DECADENT CANDY BAR**

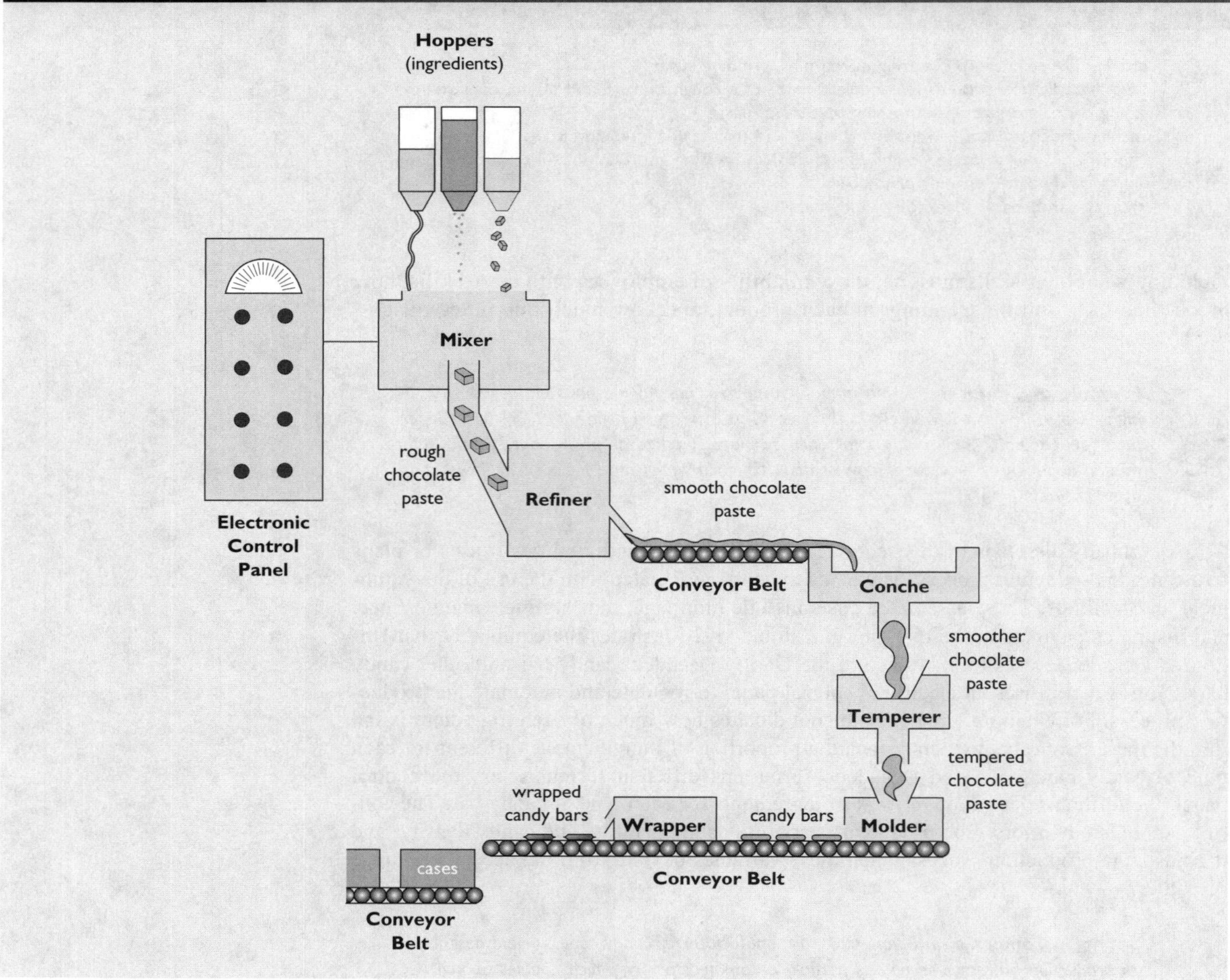


## The Finished Products

Virtually all manufacturing companies have some form of product inspection that occurs during the production process to ensure a quality finished product. In this section of the production plan, a company describes where in the production process this quality inspection occurs, the inspection criteria that it uses, and how it handles defective products. Since Unlimited Decadence manufactures a food product, it also discusses sanitation and pest control in this section. Regardless of the rigorous inspection procedures that a company may have, it should still have procedures in place for handling defective products that reach its customers and should describe these procedures in this section. These procedures may include warranties, guarantees, and repair and replacement policies.

A company also describes in this section how it protects, stores, and keeps track of its finished products before selling them, and how it transports them to its customers (it includes names of carriers and alternative carriers, as well as carrier reliability, delivery schedules, shipping fees, and payment schedules). If the company's products require

© GREGORY EDWARDS/INTERNATIONAL STOCK

As a potential investor or creditor, would you have an interest in this company's clean air plan?

special shipping accommodations, such as a regulated temperature, the company describes these conditions in this section of the business plan.

By including a production plan in its business plan, a manufacturing company gives potential investors and creditors vital information about how well it can execute its production plans, meet its sales orders, stay in business, pay back its loans, and provide a return to its investors. These same production plan details give managers a plan of action and a benchmark against which to later measure the company's actual production performance.

### The Financial Plan

As we mentioned earlier, the production plan influences a company's financial plan. This influence not only results from the unique production function of a manufacturing company, but is also a direct reflection of how accounting in a manufacturing company differs from that in a retail or service company. As we will discuss later in this chapter and in the next chapter, these differences add some new dimensions to both the cost-volume-profit (C-V-P) analysis and the budgeting of a manufacturing company. Before we look at these dimensions, however, we will first explore some of the ways that accounting differs between a manufacturing company and its retail and service counterparts.

## MANUFACTURING COSTS

2 How does a manufacturing company determine the cost of the goods that it manufactures?

A major difference between the accounting of a manufacturing company and that of a retail company is the way in which a manufacturing company accounts for inventories and cost of goods sold. As you know, a retail company has one type of inventory—goods available (ready) for sale. When it sells these goods, the retail company moves the cost of these goods from its inventory account into its cost of goods sold account. Since a manufacturing company *makes* the goods that it sells, it has *three* types of inventories: (1) the raw materials it uses either directly or indirectly in manufacturing its products, called **raw materials inventory**, (2) the products that it has started manufacturing but that are not yet complete, called **goods-in-process inventory** (also called *work-in-process inventory*), and (3) finished products that are ready to be sold, called **finished goods inventory**. Raw materials inventory and goods-in-process inventory are unique to manufacturing companies. However, a manufacturing company's finished goods inventory is the equivalent of the inventory of a retail company. Both of these inventories contain goods that are ready to be sold.

Since a manufacturing company makes the products it sells rather than purchasing them in a form ready for sale, determining the cost of the three inventories is more complex than is determining the cost of the one inventory of a retail company. For example, the cost of a retail company's inventory is usually the sum of the inventory's invoice price and shipping costs. On the other hand, the cost of a manufacturing company's finished goods inventory is the sum of all of the costs of manufacturing that inventory.

In a simple manufacturing process, three elements, or production inputs, contribute to the cost of manufacturing a product: the cost of direct materials, the cost of direct labor, and the cost of factory overhead. The sum of the costs of these three elements eventually becomes the cost of the manufactured products. Then, as each product is sold, its cost (composed of the costs of direct materials, direct labor, and factory overhead) becomes part of the total cost of goods sold. Exhibit 11-3 shows the relationships among these cost elements, the manufacturing process, the three inventories, and the cost of goods sold for Unlimited Decadence. We will discuss these elements and relationships next.

## Direct Materials

**Direct materials** are the raw materials that physically become part of a manufactured product. In other words, direct materials are the raw materials and parts from which the product is made. Think again about that list of ingredients on the wrapper of a candy bar. These ingredients are the direct materials from which that candy bar was made. Now consider the Girl Scout cookies made at the Little Brownie Bakery in Louisville, Kentucky.[e] The direct materials the company uses each week to make the cookies include:

- 21 truckloads of flour (875,000 pounds)
- 3.5 truckloads of sugar (650,000 pounds)
- 7 truckloads of shortening (300,000 pounds)
- 115,000 pounds of peanut butter
- 45,000 pounds of cocoa
- 72,000 pounds of toasted coconut
- 475,000 pounds of chocolate coating

Direct materials include materials the company acquires from natural sources, such as the honey that Unlimited Decadence includes in some of its candy bars. Direct materials also include processed or manufactured products that the company purchases from other companies, such as the milk products that Unlimited Decadence purchases from Mo-o-oving Milk Products and the corn syrups that it purchases from Corn Syrups Are Us. The direct materials of many manufacturing companies also include parts or components that they purchase from other companies. For example, the microchips inside your computer were probably manufactured by a different company from the one that manufactured your computer. Since direct materials become a part of the finished product, a company includes their costs in the cost of the finished product.

## Direct Labor

Unless a factory is fully automated, factory employees help convert or assemble the direct materials into a finished product. **Direct labor** is the labor of the employees who work with the direct materials to convert or assemble them into the finished product. For example, when Unlimited Decadence manufactures some of its candy bars, the labor of all the employees who operate the equipment that prepares the candy bar ingredients, mixes the ingredients, refines and tempers the chocolate paste, forms the candy bars, and packages the candy bars is direct labor. The Little Brownie Bakery employs 900 people

**EXHIBIT 11-3 RELATIONSHIPS AMONG MANUFACTURING COST ELEMENTS OF UNLIMITED DECADENCE**

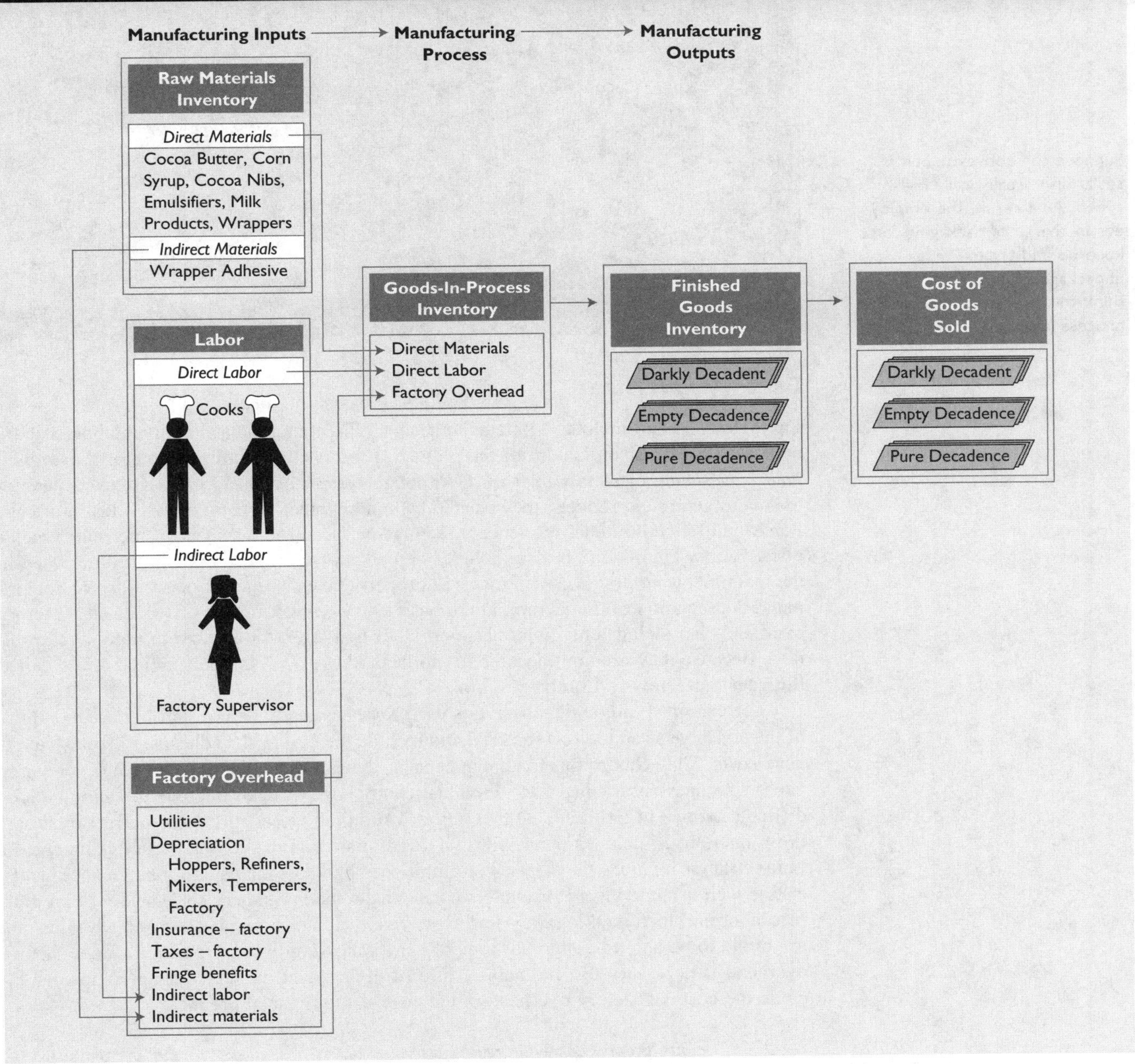

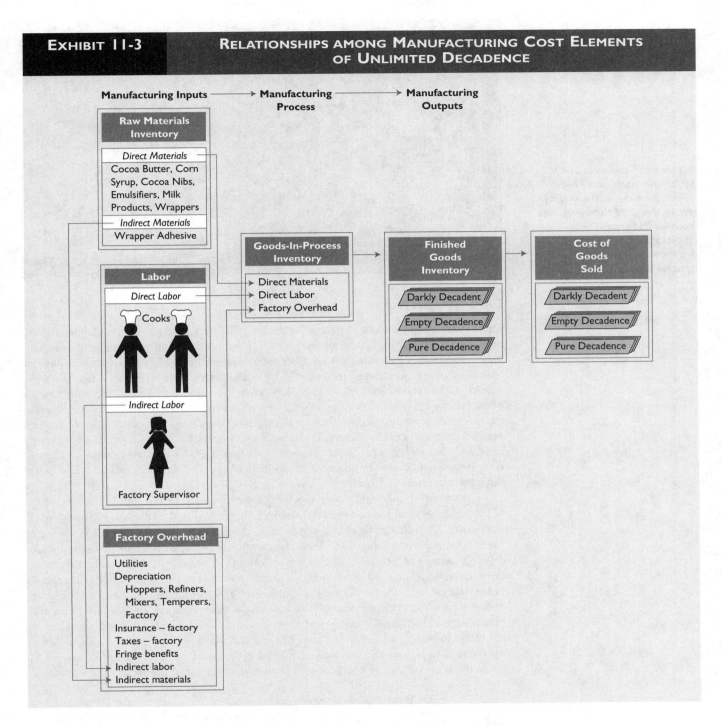

to convert the direct materials into Girl Scout cookies.[f] The cost of the direct labor is the wages earned by these employees. Since direct labor is the labor necessary to convert or assemble direct materials into a finished product, manufacturing companies include the cost of direct labor in the cost of the finished product. Since labor in some countries is cheaper than that in the United States, some U.S. manufacturing companies ship direct materials to those countries to be assembled. By doing this, the companies save on direct labor costs.

*Do you think the cost of shipping the direct materials to other countries and back should be included in the cost of the finished product? Why or why not?*

© PHOTOFEST

Suppose the conveyor belt is set at an unrealistically high speed. As a result, the employees in charge of packaging can't keep up and try to "hide" the unpackaged candy. Do you think this candy manufacturing process has any "hidden" costs?

## Factory Overhead

**Factory overhead** includes all items, other than direct materials and direct labor, that are necessary for the manufacture of the product. Factory overhead is often called *manufacturing overhead,* or simply *overhead.* Although factory overhead items are necessary for the manufacture of products, they usually cannot be traced directly to individual products. For example, Unlimited Decadence's factory overhead includes repair and maintenance of its factory equipment. It also includes depreciation of this equipment, utilities used in the manufacturing process, insurance and property taxes on the factory and factory equipment, depreciation of the factory, and other factory costs. Unlimited Decadence's factory overhead also includes raw materials and labor that are not traceable to individual products. Because they are not traceable to products, these raw materials and labor are called **indirect materials** and **indirect labor**.

For example, although adhesive is used for each candy bar wrapper, managers think of the adhesive as an indirect material and include the cost of the adhesive in factory overhead costs. They choose this treatment because the amount and cost of adhesive per candy bar is so small that tracing it to individual candy bars, or even to cases of candy bars, is difficult. Notice in Exhibit 11-3 that before Unlimited Decadence uses indirect materials in production, it includes them with the direct materials in the raw materials inventory. Indirect labor includes the salaries of employees like custodians and maintenance workers, as well as supervisors. Managers consider the factory supervisor's salary to be indirect labor and include this salary in factory overhead costs because her job activities are too broad to be able to assign portions of her salary to individual products. Since factory overhead is necessary for the manufacture of the product, manufacturing companies include the costs of factory overhead in the cost of the finished product.

*The Little Brownie Bakery has quality control employees who make sure that the Girl Scout cookies meet size, weight, percent coating, moisture, and baking specifications. The bakery also has five metal detectors through which the cookies must pass.*[g] *Would the quality control employees and the metal detectors be a part of the bakery's overhead? Why, or why not?*

Notice that all of the overhead costs relate to what goes on in the factory. Factory overhead does not include selling costs, general and administrative costs, or other costs that we discussed earlier in the book. Although we discussed salaries, utilities, and depreciation expenses in previous chapters, these expenses did not occur in the factory and, therefore, did not relate to the manufacturing process. Since both manufacturing companies and retail companies have selling and administrative activities, the two types of companies treat these items in exactly the same way.

A manufacturing company includes manufacturing costs (direct materials, direct labor, and factory overhead) in the cost of its manufactured products and, therefore, in the cost of its inventories. Then, as the company sells its products, it transfers these costs from finished goods inventory to cost of goods sold. A retail company shows the cost of its products on hand (the invoice price and transportation costs) on its balance sheet as inventory and then as it sells these products, it transfers these costs from inventory to cost of goods sold. Exhibit 11-4 shows selling expenses, and general and administrative expenses for a retail company, and how a retail company (Sweet Temptations) shows these expenses on its income statement. It also shows selling expenses, and general and administrative expenses, as well as the manufacturing costs for a manufacturing company, and how a manufacturing company (Unlimited Decadence) shows these items on its income statement. However, note that cost of goods sold includes only the cost of inventory sold, and not the total manufacturing cost for inventory produced.

*Since products have three types of inputs—direct materials, direct labor, and factory overhead—why do you think candy bar labels list only the candy bars' ingredients?*

## EXHIBIT 11-4 RELATIONSHIP OF COSTS TO THE INCOME STATEMENTS OF A RETAIL COMPANY AND A MANUFACTURING COMPANY

**Retail Company Costs***

**Sales Office**

Selling expenses
- Advertising
- Sales salaries and commissions
- Promotional efforts
- Shipping

Insurance for sales branches (or selling space)
Property taxes for sales branches (or selling space)
Depr. of sales branch offices (or selling space), display fixtures, etc.
Utilities for sales branches (or selling space)

**Administrative Offices**

General and administrative expenses
- Accounting salaries
- Administrative salaries

Insurance for office building and equipment (or administrative space and equipment)
Property taxes for office buildings (or administrative space)
Depreciation of office buildings and equipment (or administrative space and equipment)
Utilities for office buildings

*A retail company shows the cost of its products on hand on its balance sheet as inventory and then transfers these costs from inventory to cost of goods sold as it sells its products.

***Sweet Temptations†***
***Income Statement***
***For Month Ended January 31, 2008***

| | | |
|---|---|---|
| Sales revenue (net) | | $ 8,100 |
| Cost of goods sold | | (3,645) |
| Gross profit | | $ 4,455 |
| Operating expenses | | |
| → Selling expenses | $ 2,961 | |
| → General and administrative expenses | 884 | |
| Total operating expenses | | (3,845) |
| Operating income | | $ 610 |
| Other item: | | |
| Interest expense | | (8) |
| Net income | | $ 602 |

†Exhibit 6-2

## STANDARD COSTS

A knowledge of how many direct materials, how many hours of direct labor, and approximately how much overhead should go into the manufacture of each product gives managers information with which to plan the materials, labor, and overhead necessary for expected levels of production. It also gives managers a benchmark against which to measure the actual usage of each of these production inputs in the manufacture of the product. Similarly, a knowledge of what the *costs* of these production inputs should be gives managers information with which to plan production costs and cash flows, and also gives them a benchmark against which to measure the actual costs of manufacturing each product. The accounting system supplies managers with standard costs and actual costs of materials, labor, and overhead to aid them in planning and controlling the operations of the company.

### What Are Standard Costs?

**Standard costs** are the costs that *should* be incurred in performing an activity or producing a product under a given set of planned operating conditions. Management accountants, engineers, and others involved in a manufacturing activity establish the standard costs, or predetermined costs, of that activity based on a careful study of the manufac-

**EXHIBIT 11-4 (CONTINUED)**

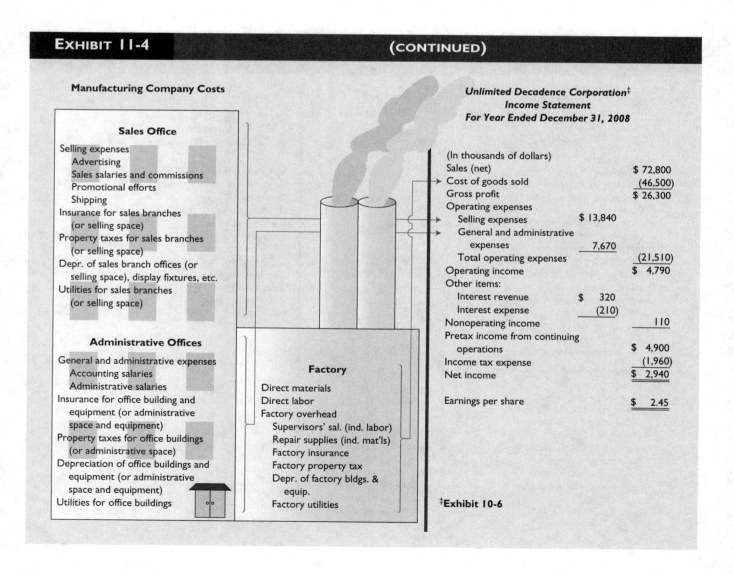

**Manufacturing Company Costs**

**Sales Office**

Selling expenses
- Advertising
- Sales salaries and commissions
- Promotional efforts
- Shipping

Insurance for sales branches (or selling space)
Property taxes for sales branches (or selling space)
Depr. of sales branch offices (or selling space), display fixtures, etc.
Utilities for sales branches (or selling space)

**Administrative Offices**

General and administrative expenses
- Accounting salaries
- Administrative salaries

Insurance for office building and equipment (or administrative space and equipment)
Property taxes for office buildings (or administrative space)
Depreciation of office buildings and equipment (or administrative space and equipment)
Utilities for office buildings

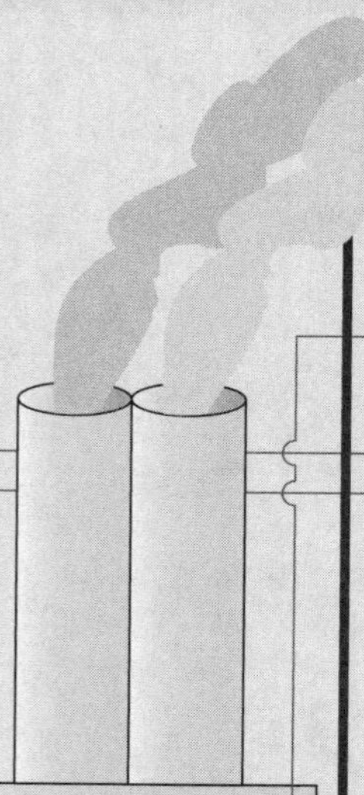

**Factory**

Direct materials
Direct labor
Factory overhead
- Supervisors' sal. (ind. labor)
- Repair supplies (ind. mat'ls)
- Factory insurance
- Factory property tax
- Depr. of factory bldgs. & equip.
- Factory utilities

***Unlimited Decadence Corporation*‡**
***Income Statement***
***For Year Ended December 31, 2008***

| (In thousands of dollars) | | |
|---|---|---|
| Sales (net) | | $ 72,800 |
| Cost of goods sold | | (46,500) |
| Gross profit | | $ 26,300 |
| Operating expenses | | |
| Selling expenses | $ 13,840 | |
| General and administrative expenses | 7,670 | |
| Total operating expenses | | (21,510) |
| Operating income | | $ 4,790 |
| Other items: | | |
| Interest revenue | $ 320 | |
| Interest expense | (210) | |
| Nonoperating income | | 110 |
| Pretax income from continuing operations | | $ 4,900 |
| Income tax expense | | (1,960) |
| Net income | | $ 2,940 |
| Earnings per share | | $ 2.45 |

‡Exhibit 10-6

turing process. Many factors can influence these costs, so in setting standards, the group must assume that a certain set of conditions exists. For example, Unlimited Decadence bases the standard direct labor costs in its factory on the assumption that the company has direct materials of the proper specification (for example, dark chocolate versus milk chocolate) and quality entering the process as needed, equipment adjusted properly for the particular candy bar being manufactured, cooks who have the proper training and experience and who earn the normal wage rate, and so forth. The standard costs are the costs that managers expect the company to incur when these conditions exist. Together, these costs become the standard cost for each manufactured product.

*If direct materials do not meet the company's specifications or quality requirements, how might using these materials affect direct labor costs? Why would maladjusted manufacturing equipment affect direct labor costs?*

## Uses of Standard Costs and Variances

**3** Why are standard costs useful in controlling a company's operations?

One reason that standards are useful in planning is that they aid in the development of budgets, as you will see in the next chapter. Later in this chapter you will see how the standard costs for direct materials, direct labor, and factory overhead become part of a manufacturing company's variable costs.

Standards also are a valuable source of information for decision making. If they reflect current operating conditions, standard costs provide a more reliable basis for estimating costs than do actual past costs, which may reflect abnormal conditions or past inefficiencies. It is also normally less time-consuming and costly to develop cost estimates from standard costs than to perform an analysis of actual past costs each time a decision is required.

The most valuable use of standard costs, however, is in controlling company operations. Standard costs provide the benchmark against which managers compare actual costs to help them evaluate an activity. As we said earlier, the standard cost is the amount of cost that *should* be incurred if the planned conditions under which an activity is to be performed actually exist when the activity is performed. If the actual cost incurred differs from the standard cost, one or more of the planned conditions must not have existed. This difference between a standard cost and an actual cost is called a **variance**. Reporting a variance provides a *signal* that an operating problem (such as a machine being out of adjustment) is occurring and may require managers' attention. If actual costs do not differ from standard costs, managers assume that no operating problems are occurring and that no special attention is needed. In other words, timely *feedback* of variance information helps managers implement the *management by exception* principle that we discussed in Chapter 4. We will talk more about analyzing variances in Chapter 17 of Volume 2.

## Standards for Manufacturing Costs

You might be wondering how a company determines its standard costs. Managers establish standard costs for each manufactured product (or *output* of the manufacturing process). Remember, a company uses three inputs (direct materials, direct labor, and factory overhead) to manufacture a product, and the costs of these inputs become costs of its manufactured products. Therefore, to establish the standard cost of each product *output* of the manufacturing process, managers must first determine two standards for each *input* to the manufacturing process: a quantity standard and a price standard.

### Quantity Standard

A **quantity standard** is the *amount* of an input that the company should use to produce a unit of product in its manufacturing process. Examples of quantity standards for direct materials and direct labor are the 10 pounds of cocoa beans and the 30 minutes of direct labor that Unlimited Decadence expects to use to produce one case of Darkly Decadent candy bars.

#### Price Standard

A **price standard** is the *cost* that the company should incur to acquire one unit of input for its manufacturing process. Examples of price standards are the expected cost per pound of the cocoa beans that Unlimited Decadence uses to produce a case of Darkly Decadent candy bars, and the expected cost per hour for the wages of the cooks who produce a case of Darkly Decadent candy bars. We will discuss quantity standards and price standards more in Chapter 17.

## COST-VOLUME-PROFIT ANALYSIS

4 How do manufacturing costs affect cost-volume-profit analysis?

One of the most common forms of analysis in which managers use cost estimates based on standards is cost-volume-profit (C-V-P) analysis, or break-even analysis. Recall from our discussion in Chapter 3 about C-V-P analysis in retail companies that this is a tool that managers use to evaluate how changes in sales volume, selling prices of products, variable costs per unit, and total fixed costs affect a company's profit. Managers in manufacturing companies use the same type of analysis.

### Behaviors of Manufacturing Costs

As in C-V-P analysis for a retail company, the first step in C-V-P analysis for a manufacturing company is to identify the behaviors of the company's costs. Remember, a manufacturing company has three additional costs over those of a retail company: the manufacturing costs of direct materials, direct labor, and factory overhead. Like the other costs, these can ultimately be classified as variable or fixed costs.

#### Variable Manufacturing Costs

We just discussed how managers develop standard quantities and costs for the inputs into the production process. Since the standard quantity of direct materials and direct labor are for one unit of product, the total quantity of direct materials and direct labor that should be used in manufacturing the company's products will increase as the level of production increases. For example, assume that the standard amount of cocoa beans used to produce a case (unit) of Darkly Decadent chocolate bars is 10 pounds. If Unlimited Decadence plans to produce 25 cases of Darkly Decadent candy bars, it expects to use 250 pounds of cocoa beans (10 pounds of cocoa beans per case × 25 cases). If it plans to produce 30 cases, it expects to use 300 pounds of cocoa beans (10 pounds of cocoa beans per case × 30 cases).

Since companies develop standard costs for each unit of input, the total cost of production input increases as the quantity of direct materials and direct labor increases. If Unlimited Decadence's standard cost per pound of cocoa beans is $0.45, the cost of the cocoa beans it expects to use in producing 25 cases of Darkly Decadent candy bars is $112.50 ($0.45 per pound × 10 pounds per case × 25 cases). If it plans to produce 30 cases of the candy bar, the cost of cocoa beans it expects to use is $135 ($0.45 per pound × 10 pounds per case × 30 cases).

A **variable manufacturing cost** is constant for each unit produced but varies in total in direct proportion to the volume produced. Since the costs of direct material and direct labor are constant for each unit produced and since the total costs of direct materials and direct labor increase as total production increases, we classify these costs as variable manufacturing costs.

We also classify some (but not all) factory overhead costs as variable costs. For example, as we mentioned earlier, Unlimited Decadence classifies the adhesive used to close the candy bar wrappers as factory overhead rather than direct material because tracing this adhesive to any particular product is difficult. Since the amount of adhesive used increases as the production of cases of candy bars increases, the total cost of the adhesive increases as the production of cases of candy bars increases. We classify the adhesive's cost, then, as a variable manufacturing cost.

### Fixed Manufacturing Costs

We classify all factory overhead costs that are not affected in total by changes in the volume of production within a specific period as fixed costs. At Unlimited Decadence, for example, the factory supervisor's salary, the depreciation on factory machines, and the property tax on the factory are all fixed costs.

### Mixed Manufacturing Costs

**Mixed costs** (sometimes called *semivariable costs*) are costs that behave as would the sum of a fixed cost and a variable cost. That is, mixed costs have a fixed cost component and a variable cost component.

For example, suppose that the local power company charges Unlimited Decadence a constant amount, say \$0.10, for each kilowatt hour (kwh) of electricity it uses. If the amount of electricity that Unlimited Decadence uses for factory lighting remains constant each year regardless of the volume of production (say at 420,000 kwh per month), the power cost for this use is fixed at \$42,000 per month (420,000 kwh × \$0.10 per kwh). The amount of electricity required by the equipment used in production, however, is directly proportional to the number of cases of candy bars produced (the volume). Normally, the power cost for this use varies in proportion to the number of cases of candy bars produced. Suppose, for the sake of illustration, that we know it takes 0.5 kwh of electricity for each case of candy bars produced. The total power cost is a mixed cost because it equals the sum of a fixed component of \$42,000 (from factory lighting) and a variable component (from equipment use) that increases at a rate of \$0.05 per case of candy bars produced (\$0.10 per kwh × 0.5 kwh per case of candy bars).

The general cost equation for the total amount of a mixed cost is as follows:

$$\text{Total mixed cost} = \mathrm{F} + \mathrm{v}X$$

where:

$\mathrm{F}$ = The fixed component
$\mathrm{v}$ = The rate at which the variable component increases per unit of volume
$X$ = The volume

*This equation should look familiar to you. In Chapter 3 we used this same equation for total costs. What is the difference between total costs and a mixed cost?*

The cost equation describing Unlimited Decadence's total power cost for one year is as follows:

$$\text{Total power cost} = \$42{,}000 + \$0.05X$$

where:

$X$ = The number of cases of candy bars produced per year

Thus, the total power cost is \$242,000 at a production volume of 4,000,000 cases of candy bars [\$42,000 + \$0.05(4,000,000)]. At a production volume of 4,800,000 cases of candy bars, the total power cost would be \$282,000 [\$42,000 + \$0.05 (4,800,000)].

Exhibit 11-5 shows a graph of the mixed cost we just described. Notice that a mixed cost increases in a straight line. In other words, the mixed cost increases at a constant rate equal to the rate of its variable component (\$0.05 per case of candy bars produced) as volume increases. However, unlike a variable cost, it intersects the vertical (cost) axis above the origin at an amount equal to its fixed cost component (\$42,000).

Managers often separate the fixed and variable components of mixed costs and treat them independently. The fixed components of mixed costs are grouped with (and treated like) other fixed costs, and the variable components are grouped with (and treated like) variable costs. This is how we will treat them in this chapter.

**EXHIBIT 11-5** **GRAPH OF A MIXED COST (TOTAL POWER COST)**

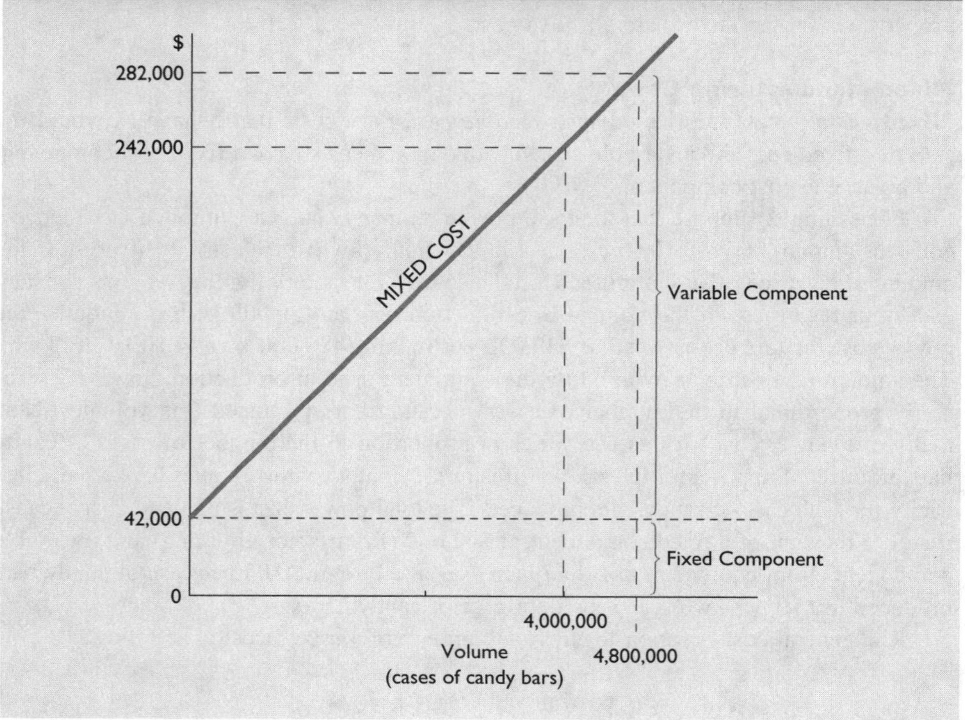


### Estimating Costs

So far, we have treated variable, fixed, and mixed costs as if they are linear; if we graphed them, they would form a straight line. However, many factors other than volume can also affect costs. In reality, costs do not always behave linearly, although they *approximate* that behavior. For example, assume that Unlimited Decadence's electric bills for the factory and for candy bar production for the last six years were the following:

| Year | Volume (cases) | Total Power Cost |
|---|---|---|
| 1 | 2,800,000 | $182,000 |
| 2 | 3,000,000 | 198,700 |
| 3 | 3,500,000 | 208,200 |
| 4 | 4,000,000 | 255,100 |
| 5 | 4,620,000 | 268,900 |
| 6 | 5,000,000 | 292,000 |

We can visualize the behavior of these costs by plotting them on a graph, as we show in Exhibit 11-6. This pattern of points on a graph is called a **scatter diagram**. Although the points on the scatter diagram don't form a straight line, they approximate one.

If we visualize a straight line that runs through these points and that best represents the pattern of the points, this line would intersect the vertical axis above the origin of the graph, just as would a mixed cost. Therefore, for the total power cost, we can assume a mixed behavior pattern that would be represented by the equation for a mixed cost. We then can solve the equation by estimating the fixed component and the variable component. One way to do this is by observing where the line intersects the vertical axis (the fixed cost) and how much the line increases for every unit change in volume (the variable cost). However, visually drawing the line through the scatter diagram is not very pre-

**EXHIBIT 11-6 UNLIMITED DECADENCE'S ELECTRIC BILLS AND PRODUCTION FOR THE LAST SIX YEARS**

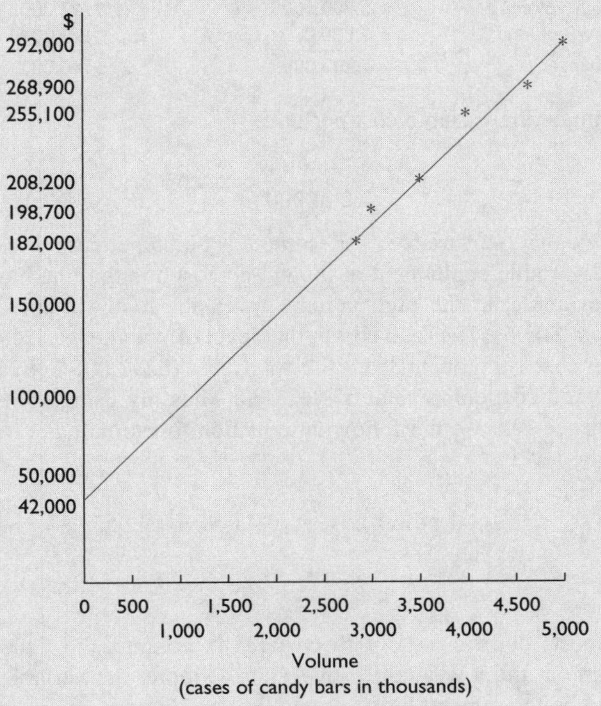

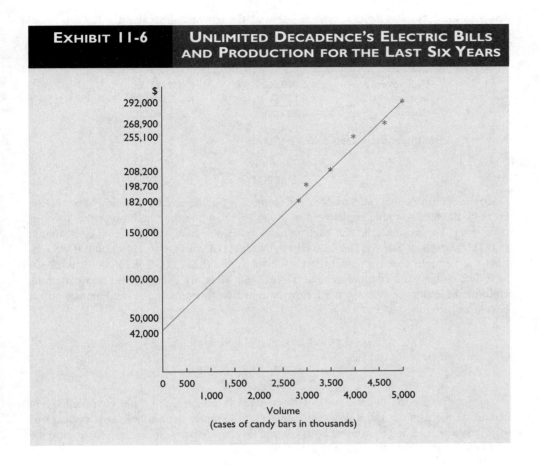

cise; if you drew a line through the points and compared your line with that of one of your classmates, you would likely see two different lines. Another method that managers often use to give a quick, shorthand estimate of fixed and variable costs is called the *high-low method*.

### The High-Low Method

The **high-low method** assumes that any change that occurs in total costs when volume changes from the lowest volume level to the highest volume level must be due to the total variable cost change that occurs with that volume increase. (Remember, fixed costs don't change with volume.) Therefore, the variable cost per unit of volume can be estimated with the following equation:

$$v = \frac{\text{Cost change from lowest to highest volume}}{\text{Volume change from lowest to highest volume}}$$

where:

$v$ = The variable cost per unit of volume

Going back to Unlimited Decadence's power cost and volume data for the last six years, we can figure the volume and corresponding cost changes from the lowest to the highest volume levels as follows. Since it is a change in volume that causes the total variable cost to increase or decrease, we first identify the highest and the lowest volume levels. The difference between these volume levels is the volume change from the lowest to the highest volume. Next, we identify the total cost at each volume level. The difference between these costs is the cost change—that is, the increase in total variable costs—that occurred as a result of the change in volume.

| | Volume (cases) | Total Power Cost |
|---|---|---|
| High volume | 5,000,000 | $292,000 |
| Low volume | 2,800,000 | 182,000 |
| Change | 2,200,000 | $110,000 |

Now we can estimate the variable cost per unit:

$$v = \frac{\$110{,}000}{2{,}200{,}000} = \$0.05$$

Once we determine that the variable cost estimate is $0.05 per case of candy bars, we can estimate the total variable component of the mixed cost at either the high or the low volume level. For example, at the high volume level, the total variable cost is $250,000 (5,000,000 cases × $0.05). The total cost at that level of volume was $292,000. If we subtract the variable cost component from the total cost ($292,000 − $250,000), what we have left is the fixed cost component of $42,000. Thus, by using the high-low method, Unlimited Decadence can use the following equation to estimate the total annual power cost at any volume level:

$$\text{Total power cost} = \$42{,}000 + \$0.05X$$

where:

$$X = \text{Volume}$$

Since fixed costs don't change with changes in volume, the fixed cost component should be the same at the low volume level. Furthermore, the variable cost per case of candy bars should be the same at both volume levels. We can test this by substituting the low volume level into the above equation:

$$\text{Total power cost} = \$42{,}000 + \$0.05(2{,}800{,}000) = \$182{,}000$$

As expected, the $182,000 we computed equals the $182,000 total cost measured at the low volume level of 2,800,000 cases.

It is important to be careful when studying past cost data to establish future cost behavior patterns. In making the analysis, you should be able to answer *yes* to the following questions before using this method:

- Were conditions essentially the same in all the periods the data represent?
- Will the same conditions continue to exist in the future, so that the cost behavior patterns will remain the same?
- Does the computed cost pattern make sense?

It is important that similar conditions existed in the time periods from which the data were obtained because abnormal conditions would distort the data and, consequently, the estimates made from the data. Suppose, for example, that during one of the years from which we obtained Unlimited Decadence's power costs, Unlimited Decadence had to add supplemental heat from electric furnaces in the factory because of an unusually cold winter. If that year happened to be the high- or low-activity year, the high-low method would produce a distorted result because of the abnormally high power cost during that year.

We also must expect that the conditions on which we are basing our estimates will continue. Otherwise, we can't count on the cost behavior patterns to stay the same. If, for example, the power company adds a surcharge or if Unlimited Decadence increases its lighting requirements, these changed conditions will also change the cost equation.

Finally, the resulting cost pattern must make sense. (Is it reasonable?) For instance, using the high-low method to estimate the relationship between sales volume and depreciation of factory equipment would give misleading results; sales volume and the depreciation of factory equipment are not directly related.

The high-low method allows decision-makers to quickly estimate the fixed and variable components of mixed costs. However, it is not the most precise method. Statistical methods such as regression analysis, which you may learn about in another class, provide more accurate results but are not as convenient. Even with these methods, however, careless interpretation can lead to misleading results. Furthermore, even the most precise estimates apply only within a certain range of volumes.

### Relevant Range

Each time a management accountant prepares an analysis that involves cost estimates for a manager's decision, the requirements of the decision determine a range of volumes over which the estimates must be especially accurate. For example, if Unlimited Decadence expects to produce between 3,500,000 and 6,000,000 cases of candy bars each year and wants to decide whether or not to change its manufacturing process, cost estimates for both the existing process and the alternative process over that specific range (3,500,000 to 6,000,000 cases) would be useful in making the decision. The company would not be helped by knowing which process is less expensive to operate when producing below 3,500,000 candy bars, nor would the company care about comparing manufacturing costs for volumes above 6,000,000 candy bars. Only the range of volumes from 3,500,000 to 6,000,000 is relevant (useful) to the decision.

The **relevant range** is the range of volumes over which cost estimates are needed for a particular use and over which observed cost behaviors are expected to remain stable. The relevant range concept is extremely important because by focusing on the range of volumes for which cost estimates should be accurate, a management accountant can make cost estimates that are useful for decision making. Decision makers will be able to ignore cost behavior patterns outside of the relevant range. Furthermore, if the management accountant states the relevant range whenever providing cost estimates, potential users of the estimates will be alerted to the range of volumes over which the estimates are reliable.

Some costs do not fit the fixed, variable, or mixed cost behavior patterns we described. They may vary, but not in a straight line over all possible volumes. For example, Unlimited Decadence may pay less for each tub of cocoa butter that it purchases above a certain volume level than it pays for each tub that it purchases below that volume level. Other costs may be fixed over a wide range of volumes but increase abruptly to a higher amount if the upper limit of that volume range is exceeded. For example, once Unlimited Decadence's production of candy bars reaches a certain level, the capacity of its mixers will be reached. To exceed that level of production, Unlimited Decadence will need to purchase an additional mixer. When this occurs, Unlimited Decadence's fixed depreciation cost for mixers will jump by the amount of the new mixer's depreciation. Exhibit 11-7 presents graphs of these two cost behavior patterns.

Despite these potential cost behavior patterns, the management accountant must determine only how the costs behave within the relevant range, and in most cases, these costs fit one of the three common behavior patterns. For example, the behavior patterns shown in the graphs in Exhibit 11-7 might be estimated within the relevant range as a variable cost and a fixed cost, as we show in Exhibit 11-8.

**EXHIBIT 11-7 GRAPHS OF COSTS THAT ARE NOT FIXED, VARIABLE, OR MIXED**

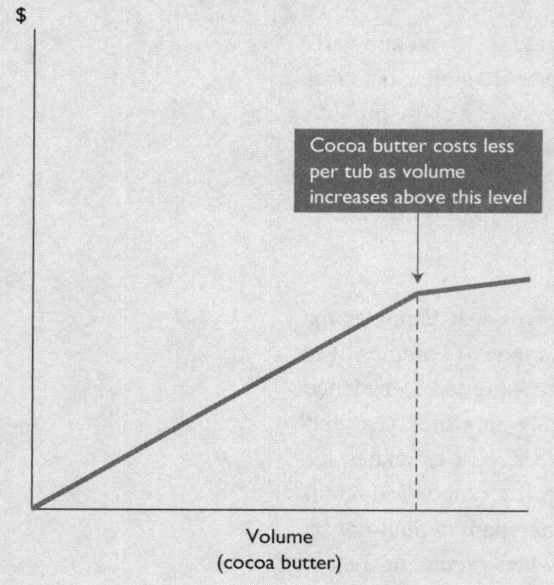


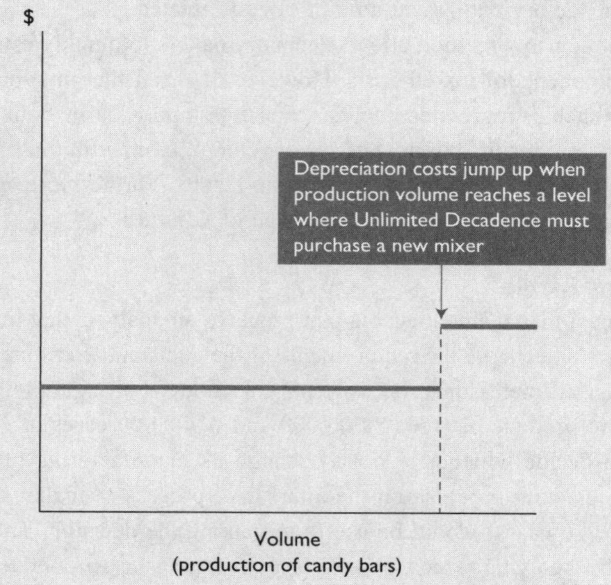


## C-V-P Computations Using the Profit Equation (Multiple Products)

5 What is the effect of multiple products on cost-volume-profit analysis?

Remember from our discussion in Chapter 3 that C-V-P analysis is an examination of how profit is affected by changes in the sales volume, in the selling prices of products, and in the various costs of the company. Decision makers use C-V-P analysis to gain an

**EXHIBIT 11-8 RELEVANT RANGE OF COSTS THAT ARE NOT FIXED, VARIABLE, OR MIXED**

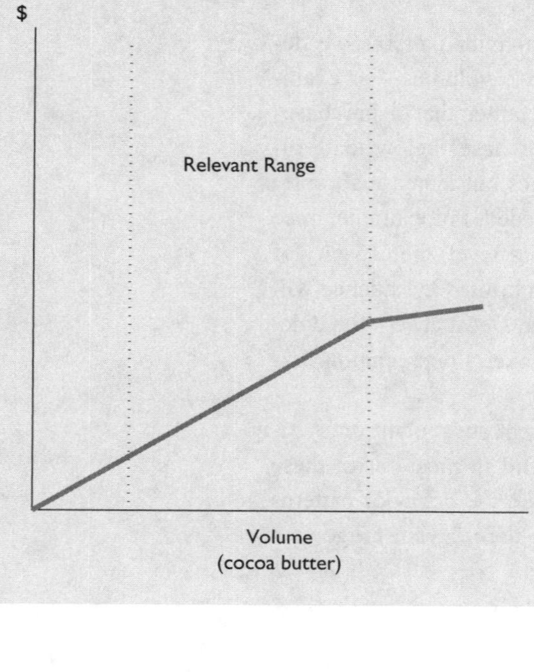


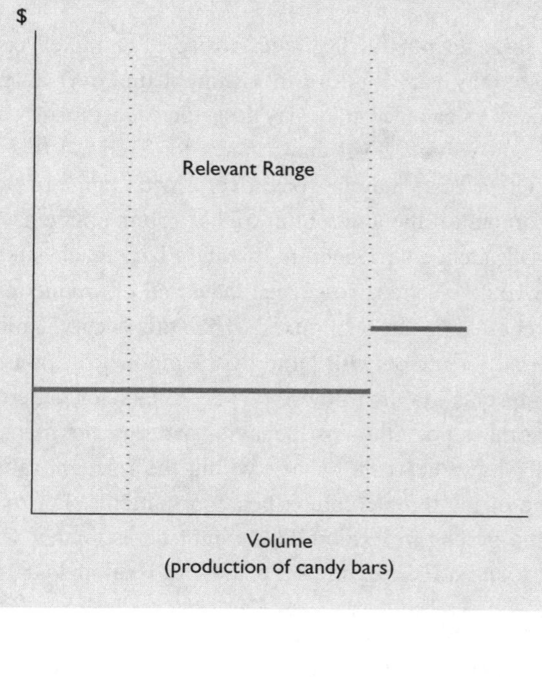

understanding of the profit impact of plans that they are making. This understanding can produce more informed decisions during the planning process.

When a manufacturing company produces and sells only one product, its C-V-P computations are the same as those that Sweet Temptations used in Chapter 3, with sales volume measured in units of that product. However, most companies sell several products. When these companies (manufacturing and retail companies) perform a C-V-P analysis of their overall operations, they must consider the relative sales volumes of their different products.

This doesn't mean that the single-product analysis we described in Chapter 3 is not useful, however. Managers can use a single-product analysis to study the relationship of the cost, volume, and profit of one of a company's products as long as they can separate the costs and the sales revenues of that product from the costs and revenues caused by the production and sales of other products.

Next, we will discuss C-V-P analysis in companies that sell more than one product. Our discussion assumes that you remember single-product C-V-P analysis from Chapter 3. A brief review, on your part, of the concepts and computations in Chapter 3 will help you understand the following discussion. To keep the computations simple, we will use an example involving two products, but *the procedure we are about to describe can be used with any number of products.*

### Contribution Margin for a Given Product Sales Mix

Managers can apply the single-product form of analysis to any *group* of a company's products if they know the product sales mix and the costs and sales revenues of the individual products within that group of products. The **product sales mix** is the relative proportion of units of the different products sold. In C-V-P analysis when there is more than one product, the product sales mix is considered to be one "unit." For example, if Unlimited Decadence has typically sold five cases of Darkly Decadent candy bars for every one case of Pure Decadence candy bars sold, this combination of cases of candy bars is considered to be one "unit." (Visualize a basket containing five cases of Darkly Decadent candy bars and one case of Pure Decadence candy bars.) As long as Unlimited Decadence plans to continue to sell the Darkly Decadent and Pure Decadence candy bars in that proportion, we can say that it has the same product sales mix as it had in the past.

Suppose that Unlimited Decadence estimates that its fixed costs will be $24,800,000 in the coming year and that its product sales mix will be five cases of Darkly Decadent candy bars sold for every one case of Pure Decadence candy bars. Cases of Darkly Decadent candy bars will sell for $16, require $11 of variable cost, and earn a contribution margin of $5. Cases of Pure Decadence candy bars will sell for $20 each, require $14 of variable cost, and earn a contribution margin of $6. Thus, the sales revenue, variable cost, and contribution margin per "unit" (5 cases of Darkly Decadent candy bars and 1 case of Pure Decadence candy bars) will be $100, $69, and $31, respectively. The sales revenue per "unit" is computed as follows:

Selling price per "unit" = ($16 per case of Darkly Decadent candy bars ×
5 cases of Darkly Decadent candy bars) +
($20 per case of Pure Decadence candy bars ×
1 case of Pure Decadence candy bars)
= $100

The variable cost per "unit" is computed as follows:

Variable cost per "unit" = ($11 per case of Darkly Decadent candy bars ×
5 cases of Darkly Decadent candy bars) +
($14 per case of Pure Decadence candy bars ×
1 case of Pure Decadence candy bars)
= $69

Therefore, the contribution margin per unit is $31 ($100 selling price per "unit" – $69 variable cost per "unit"). We summarize this information in the following schedule:

| | Darkly Decadent Candy Bars | | Pure Decadence Candy Bars | | Total per "Unit" |
|---|---|---|---|---|---|
| Selling price/case | $16 | | $20 | | |
| Variable cost/case | (11) | | (14) | | |
| Contribution margin/case | $ 5 | | $ 6 | | |
| Expected sales mix (cases) | 5 | | 1 | | |
| Sales revenue | $80 | + | $20 | = | $100 |
| Less: variable cost | (55) | + | (14) | = | (69) |
| Contribution margin | $25 | + | $ 6 | = | $ 31 |

## Finding the Break-Even Point

We can calculate the break-even point in units of product sales mix by beginning with the same equation that we used in calculating the break-even point for one product:

$$\text{Unit sales volume (to earn zero profit)} = \frac{\text{Total fixed cost}}{\text{Contribution margin per unit}}$$

However, keep in mind that when Unlimited Decadence uses this equation, its contribution margin per unit represents a "unit" that now consists of five cases of Darkly Decadent candy bars and one case of Pure Decadence candy bars. Since fixed costs are $24,800,000, Unlimited Decadence can find the break-even point expressed as "units" of sales volume by dividing the $24,800,000 total fixed cost by the $31 contribution margin per "unit." We can write this in equation form as follows:

$$\text{Break-even point (in "units")} = \frac{\text{Total fixed cost}}{\text{Contribution margin per "unit"}}$$

$$= \frac{\$24{,}800{,}000}{\$31}$$

$$= \underline{\underline{800{,}000}} \text{ "units"}$$

To break even, Unlimited Decadence would have to sell 800,000 "units," composed of 4,000,000 cases of Darkly Decadent candy bars (800,000 × 5 cases of Darkly Decadent candy bars) and 800,000 cases of Pure Decadence candy bars (800,000 × 1 case of Pure Decadence candy bars).

We can verify the break-even "unit" sales volume of 800,000 "units" that we just computed for Unlimited Decadence with the following profit computation:

| | | |
|---|---|---|
| Sales revenue: | | |
| Cases of Darkly Decadent candy bars (4,000,000 cases @ $16 per case) | $64,000,000 | |
| Cases of Pure Decadence candy bars (800,000 cases @ $20 per case) | 16,000,000 | |
| Total sales revenue | | $80,000,000 |
| Less variable costs: | | |
| Cases of Darkly Decadent candy bars (4,000,000 cases @ $11 per case) | $44,000,000 | |
| Cases of Pure Decadence candy bars (800,000 cases @ $14 per case) | 11,200,000 | |
| Total variable cost | | (55,200,000) |
| Total contribution margin | | $24,800,000 |
| Less total fixed cost | | (24,800,000) |
| Profit | | $ 0 |

Note in this computation that total sales revenue ($80,000,000) equals total cost ($55,200,000 variable + $24,800,000 fixed). Also note that total contribution margin equals total fixed cost ($24,800,000). In either case, profit equals $0.

### Finding the Unit Sales Volume to Achieve a Target Pretax Profit

A company often states its profit goal at an amount that results in a satisfactory rate of return on owner's equity. Remember, the return on owner's equity measures how effectively managers have earned income on the amount the owners invested in the company.

In Chapter 7, in our discussion of entrepreneurial companies, we calculated the return on owner's equity as follows:

$$\text{Return on owner's equity} = \frac{\text{Net income}}{\text{Average owner's equity}}$$

The calculation is similar for a corporation, but with two differences. One difference is that the denominator is stockholders' equity. The other difference is caused by the fact that a corporation pays income taxes and deducts the amount of its income tax expense on its income statement to determine its net income. Since the return on stockholders' equity measures a company's efficiency in earning income on the stockholders' investment, and since income taxes are a tax *on* that income, both internal and external users are interested in the return *after* income taxes. The calculation then becomes as follows:

$$\text{Return on stockholders' equity} = \frac{\text{Income after taxes}}{\text{Average stockholders' equity}}$$

But since internal users usually can't control the income tax expense imposed by the U.S. government, they are interested in what pretax income (profit) the company must earn to achieve its targeted after-tax income. For example, assume Unlimited Decadence estimates that its average stockholders' equity for the coming year will be $18,000,000, and assume that its managers would like it to earn a return on stockholders' equity of 18%, the industry average for confectioners. To achieve this return on stockholders' equity, Unlimited Decadence will have to earn $3,240,000 income after taxes ($18,000,000 × 18%). Suppose, then, that you want to know how many units Unlimited Decadence will have to sell to earn this desired after-tax income. To use the C-V-P equations, you must first convert the desired after-tax income to pretax income, using the following equation:[1]

$$\text{Pretax income} = \frac{\text{After-tax income}}{(1 - \text{Tax rate})}$$

If we assume that Unlimited Decadence is subject to a 40 percent income tax rate, it must earn $5,400,000 [$3,240,000 ÷ (1 − 0.40)] pretax income to achieve a $3,240,000 after-tax income. The computation to determine the "unit" sales volume to achieve this target pretax income is as follows:

$$\begin{array}{c}\text{"Unit" sales volume needed to} \\ \text{earn a desired pretax income}\end{array} = \frac{\text{Total fixed cost} + \text{Desired pretax income}}{\text{Contribution margin per "unit"}}$$

$$\begin{array}{c}\text{"Unit" sales volume needed to} \\ \text{earn \$5,400,00 pretax income}\end{array} = \frac{\text{\$24,800,000 fixed cost} + \text{\$5,400,000 pretax income}}{\text{\$31}}$$

$$= \underline{\underline{974{,}194}} \text{ "units" (rounded)}$$

[1]Recall that we use the following formula to compute after-tax income:

$$\text{After-tax Income} = \text{Pretax Income} - \text{Income Tax Expense}$$

Income tax expense is computed with the following formula:

$$\text{Income Tax Expense} = \text{Pretax Income} \times \text{Tax Rate}$$

We can substitute the second formula into the first formula, yielding the following revised formula for after-tax income:

$$\text{After-tax Income} = \text{Pretax Income} - (\text{Pretax Income} \times \text{Tax Rate})$$

Then, by eliminating pretax income from each of the two terms on the right side of the equation, we can restate the equation as follows:

$$\text{After-tax Income} = \text{Pretax Income} \times (1 - \text{Tax Rate})$$

Then we can find pretax income by isolating it on one side of the equation:

$$\text{Pretax Income} = \frac{\text{After-tax Income}}{(1 - \text{Tax Rate})}$$

Therefore, at a sales mix of five cases of Darkly Decadent candy bars and one case of Pure Decadence candy bars per "unit," Unlimited Decadence will have to sell 4,870,970 cases of Darkly Decadent candy bars (974,194 × 5 cases of Darkly Decadent candy bars) and 974,194 cases of Pure Decadence candy bars (974,194 × 1 case of Pure Decadence candy bars) to earn a pretax income of $5,400,000.

### Finding the Dollar Sales Volume to Achieve a Target Pretax Profit

When a company sells more than one product, it is often easier to represent sales volume in dollars instead of units. Earlier, we said that Unlimited Decadence would break even if it sold 800,000 "units," composed of 4,000,000 cases of Darkly Decadent candy bars and 800,000 cases of Pure Decadence candy bars. Since Darkly Decadent candy bars sell for $16 per case and Pure Decadence candy bars sell for $20 per case, Unlimited Decadence would break even when its sales revenue was $80,000,000 [(4,000,000 cases of Darkly Decadent candy bars × $16) + (800,000 cases of Pure Decadence candy bars × $20)].

A more direct way to find the dollar sales volume to achieve a desired profit is to use the company's contribution margin percentage. The *contribution margin percentage* is the ratio of the contribution margin to sales revenue or, stated another way, the contribution margin as a percentage of sales revenue. Since the contribution margin of one "unit" of Unlimited Decadence's product sales mix is $31 and the sales revenue of this "unit" is $100, its contribution margin percentage is 31% ($31 ÷ $100). We could say, then, that the contribution margin is 31% of sales revenue for this product sales mix.

Since break-even occurs when

$$\text{Contribution margin} = \text{Fixed costs},$$

we could also say that it occurs when

$$\text{Sales revenue} \times \text{Contribution margin percentage} = \text{Fixed costs}.$$

Therefore, Unlimited Decadence could compute its break-even point (in sales dollars) as shown here:

$$\text{Break-even point (in dollars)} = \frac{\text{Total fixed cost}}{\text{Contribution margin percentage}}$$

$$= \frac{\$24{,}800{,}000}{31\%}$$

$$= \underline{\underline{\$80{,}000{,}000}}$$

Similarly, it could compute the total dollar sales volume needed to earn a desired amount of pretax income. For example, if managers want Unlimited Decadence to earn $5,400,000 pretax income, sales will have to be $97,419,355. The computation is as follows:

$$\begin{array}{l}\text{Dollar sales volume}\\ \text{needed to earn a}\\ \text{desired pretax income}\end{array} = \frac{\text{Total fixed cost} + \text{Desired pretax income}}{\text{Contribution margin percentage}}$$

$$\begin{array}{l}\text{Dollar sales volume}\\ \text{needed to earn}\\ \$5{,}400{,}000\text{ desired}\\ \text{pretax income}\end{array} = \frac{\$24{,}800{,}000\text{ Fixed cost} + \$5{,}400{,}000\text{ Pretax income}}{31\%}$$

$$= \underline{\underline{\$97{,}419{,}355}}$$

*How can you verify the dollar sales volumes needed to break even and to earn a pretax profit of $5,400,000?*

### What If the Company Changed Its Product Sales Mix?

Remember that Unlimited Decadence's contribution margin percentage is 31% only if its product sales mix is five cases of Darkly Decadent candy bars and one case of Pure Decadence candy bars. Consider what will happen if sales of cases of Darkly Decadent candy bars change relative to sales of Pure Decadence candy bars so that Unlimited Decadence sells three cases of Darkly Decadent candy bars for every four cases of Pure Decadence candy bars. The new contribution margin percentage will be 30.47%, shown as follows:

| | Darkly Decadent Candy Bars | | Pure Decadence Candy Bars | | Total per "Unit" |
|---|---|---|---|---|---|
| Selling price/case | $16 | | $20 | | |
| Variable cost/case | (11) | | (14) | | |
| Contribution margin/case | $ 5 | | $ 6 | | |
| Expected sales mix (cases) | 3 | | 4 | | |
| Sales revenue | $48 | + | $80 | = | $128 |
| Less: variable costs | (33) | + | (56) | = | (89) |
| Contribution margin | $15 | + | $24 | = | $ 39 |
| Contribution margin percentage ($39/$128) | | | | | 30.47% (rounded) |

With this new product sales mix, the dollar sales volume will have to be $99,113,883 [($24,800,000 fixed cost + $5,400,000 income before taxes) ÷ 30.47%] to earn a profit of $5,400,000 before income taxes. Furthermore, with the new product sales mix, total dollar sales volume will have to be $81,391,533 ($24,800,000 total fixed cost ÷ 30.47%) for Unlimited Decadence to break even.

## Applications of C-V-P Analysis in a Manufacturing Environment

6 How does a manufacturing company use cost-volume-profit analysis for its planning?

So far, we have described fixed and variable costs as they relate to changes in sales. However, costs do not always vary with sales. They may vary with production, number of hours worked by employees, or some other measure of operating activity. Manufacturing companies incur costs to produce the products as they manufacture them. For this reason, managers of manufacturing companies usually classify the behavior of production costs based on whether or not these costs vary with the level of *production.*

As in a service or retail company, C-V-P analysis in a manufacturing company is useful in planning because it shows the potential impact of alternative plans on profit. The analysis can help managers make planning decisions and help investors and creditors evaluate the risk associated with their investment and credit decisions. In the following discussion, we illustrate how C-V-P analysis in a manufacturing company can show the potential profit impact of alternative plans.

Suppose that Unlimited Decadence is considering manufacturing the new fat-free, sugarless candy bar (to be called "Empty Decadence") that we discussed in Chapter 2. Marketing thinks it can sell 450,000 cases of these candy bars at $20 per case during the first year on the market. Purchasing has located suppliers for the sweetener and for the fat substitute. Together, all the direct materials for a case of Empty Decadence candy bars will cost $4. The production department expects to hire two new cooks to produce the Empty Decadence candy bars and has set a standard of 45 minutes of direct labor for every case of these candy bars. The human resources department expects the pay rate for these cooks to be $12 per hour. The production department estimates that variable overhead costs will increase by $0.50 per case of Empty Decadence candy bars. Marketing expects variable selling and administrative costs to increase by $1.00 because of the sale of this new product. There is currently space in the factory to manufacture the Empty Decadence candy bar, but Unlimited Decadence will need to purchase new equipment to process the sweetener and the fat substitute. The finance department has located financing for the new equipment.

The production department expects depreciation and insurance on this equipment, together with the additional advertising expense, to add $1,188,000 to Unlimited Decadence's fixed costs.

Unlimited Decadence must decide whether to manufacture the Empty Decadence candy bar. Recall from Chapter 2 that there are numerous questions that Unlimited Decadence's managers should answer before they make a decision. Furthermore, there may be more than two alternatives (manufacturing or not manufacturing) to solving this issue. However, assume that Unlimited Decadence's managers are very interested in adding this new product and are gathering product information that will help them make their decision. C-V-P analysis will contribute useful information for evaluating this decision.

Managers first may want to know whether the revenue from sales of the Empty Decadence candy bar will even cover the additional costs of producing it, or whether it will "break even." We can calculate the contribution margin of each case of Empty Decadence candy bars as follows:

| | | |
|---|---|---|
| Sales revenue per case | | $20.00 |
| Variable costs per case | | |
| Direct materials | $4.00 | |
| Direct labor ($12/hour × 3/4 hour) | 9.00 | |
| Additional variable overhead | 0.50 | |
| Additional variable selling and administrative costs | 1.00 | (14.50) |
| Contribution margin per case | | $ 5.50 |

Now we can calculate the break-even point for the Empty Decadence candy bar:

$$\text{Break-even unit sales} = \frac{\text{Additional fixed costs}}{\text{Contribution margin per unit}}$$

$$= \frac{\$1{,}188{,}000}{\$5.50}$$

$$= \underline{\underline{216{,}000}} \text{ cases}$$

Unlimited Decadence will need to sell 216,000 cases of Empty Decadence candy bars in order for this line of candy bars to break even. Each case sold above the break-even point will cause Unlimited Decadence's profit to increase by $5.50. So, at the predicted sales level of 450,000 cases, Unlimited Decadence should earn $1,287,000 additional profit [(450,000 cases − 216,000 cases) × $5.50] on sales of the Empty Decadence candy bar.

Based on this information alone, it seems like a good idea to manufacture this new candy bar. The manager of the purchasing department, though, thinks that there is a possibility that the costs of the sweetener and the fat substitute (both direct materials) may increase in the next few months. It would be useful to know how much these costs can increase before the Empty Decadence line of candy bars will "lose money," or not be able to earn enough revenue to cover its costs. We know that costs can increase until they equal revenues, or until Empty Decadence "breaks even" at predicted sales of 450,000 cases (assuming that the marketing department's estimates are correct and that the selling price of a case of Empty Decadence candy bars doesn't change). So, we use the same formula:

$$\text{Break-even unit sales} = \frac{\text{Additional fixed costs}}{\text{Contribution margin per unit}}$$

$$450{,}000 = \frac{\$1{,}188{,}000}{X}$$

$$X = \underline{\underline{\$2.64}}$$

The contribution margin per case can decrease to $2.64 before the Empty Decadence product line will break even. If it decreases more than that, the Empty Decadence product line will lose money. In other words, the contribution margin can decrease by $2.86 (the old contribution margin of $5.50 minus the new contribution margin of $2.64). Therefore, if the only factors that change are the costs of the sweetener and the fat substitute, the direct materials can increase by $2.86 from $4.00 to $6.86 per case without the Empty Decadence product line generating a loss. We can verify this as follows:

| | | |
|---|---|---|
| Sales revenue per case | | $20.00 |
| Variable costs per case | | |
| Direct materials ($4.00 + $2.86) | $6.86 | |
| Direct labor ($12/hour × 3/4 hour) | 9.00 | |
| Additional variable overhead | 0.50 | |
| Additional variable selling and administrative costs | 1.00 | (17.36) |
| Contribution margin per case | | $ 2.64 |

If Unlimited Decadence sells 450,000 cases, each will contribute $2.64, for a total contribution margin of $1,188,000, just enough to cover the additional fixed costs.

But what if marketing overestimates sales of the Empty Decadence candy bar? How much below its sales estimate can Unlimited Decadence's actual sales be before it loses money, if the costs of the sweetener and fat substitute do not change? The amount that sales (in units) can decrease without a loss, or the difference between the estimated sales volume and the break-even sales volume, is called the **margin of safety**. Managers use the margin of safety as a measure of the risk of a new plan. The higher the margin of safety is, the lower is the risk.

At the current cost estimate, break-even sales is 216,000 cases of Empty Decadence candy bars. That means that the margin of safety is 234,000 cases (450,000 cases − 216,000 cases). Sales could drop 234,000 cases below the estimate before Empty Decadence would experience a loss.

Notice that in making this calculation, we considered only the revenues and costs attributable to the Empty Decadence candy bar. Isolating these costs and revenues gives managers a clearer picture of the expected effect of adding the Empty Decadence candy bar. However, Unlimited Decadence must also consider the other effects of adding this product. For example, will the manufacture and sale of the Empty Decadence candy bar cause the sales of Unlimited Decadence's other candy bars to decrease? If so, it is possible that even though the sale of the Empty Decadence candy bar will probably generate a profit for the candy bar, *total income* for Unlimited Decadence may decrease. The decrease in the sales of other candy bars could be larger than the increase generated by the sale of the Empty Decadence candy bar. (On the other hand, maybe it would be better for Unlimited Decadence to introduce this new product before its competition does!) Wherever possible, when deciding whether to introduce a new product, managers should consider quantitative information about how the new product would affect the profits generated by the company's other products.

### Summary of the C-V-P Analysis Computations for Multiple Products

Exhibit 11-9 summarizes the profit, break-even point, and sales volume computations used in our discussion of C-V-P analysis with multiple products. As in Chapter 3, we present these computations as equations that can be used to answer the basic questions that occur frequently in C-V-P analysis. Although it may be tempting to try to commit them all to memory, you should instead strive to understand how these equations relate to one another and how managers can use the answers found by applying these formulas in certain types of decision making.

## Business Issues and Values

To make smart decisions, managers must combine the results of C-V-P analysis with other factors. For example, many factors other than C-V-P analysis influence Unlimited

**EXHIBIT 11-9 SUMMARY OF COST-VOLUME-PROFIT COMPUTATIONS**

$$\text{Contribution Margin per ``Unit'' for Two Products, A and B} = \left[\text{Contribution Margin of Product A} \times \text{Number of Product A in Product Sales Mix}\right] + \left[\text{Contribution Margin of Product B} \times \text{Number of Product B in Product Sales Mix}\right]$$

$$\text{``Unit'' Sales Volume to Earn Zero Profit} = \frac{\text{Total Fixed Cost}}{\text{Contribution Margin per ``Unit''}}$$

$$\text{``Unit'' Sales Volume Needed to Earn a Desired Pretax Income} = \frac{\text{Total Fixed Cost} + \text{Desired Pretax Income}}{\text{Contribution Margin per ``Unit''}}$$

$$\text{Contribution Margin Percentage per ``Unit''} = \frac{\text{Contribution Margin per ``Unit''}}{\text{Sales Revenue per ``Unit''}}$$

$$\text{Break-even Point (in dollars)} = \frac{\text{Total Fixed Cost}}{\text{Contribution Margin Percentage per ``Unit''}}$$

$$\text{Pretax Income} = \frac{\text{After-tax Income}}{(1 - \text{Tax Rate})}$$

$$\text{Dollar Sales Volume Needed to Earn a Desired Pretax Income} = \frac{\text{Total Fixed Cost} + \text{Desired Pretax Income}}{\text{Contribution Margin Percentage}}$$

Decadence's decision about whether to manufacture and sell the Empty Decadence candy bar; one of these factors is the hiring of the two new cooks. How much responsibility does Unlimited Decadence have when it hires new employees? Perhaps the two cooks will have to quit their secure jobs in order to work for Unlimited Decadence. Given the fact that it may be difficult for them to return to their old jobs, how sure should Unlimited Decadence be that its new product will succeed before it hires new employees? What if the two cooks are currently unemployed? Should that make a difference in Unlimited Decadence's decision?

Another factor that influences this decision is the presence or absence of health risks associated with the sweetener and fat substitute used in the Empty Decadence candy bar. Unlimited Decadence prides itself on its concern for its customers and would like to maintain its reputation of producing quality candy bars. Therefore, even if C-V-P analysis indicates that the Empty Decadence candy bar should be produced, the presence of health risks (if any) in the sweetener or fat substitute may cause managers to delay production until the company can locate safer alternatives.

Another example of other factors that companies must consider is the raising of the minimum wage. For example, periodically, Congress raises the minimum wage. While this change in policy positively affects millions of minimum-wage earners, it also affects the decisions of the companies that hire these workers because an increase in the minimum wage causes companies' variable costs to increase. For instance, the owners of fast-food franchises typically hire minimum-wage workers to staff their restaurants. The fast-food industry is a "low margin" industry, which means that the average contribution margin of restaurants in this industry is low relative to that of companies in other industries. An increase in the minimum wage causes the already low contribution margins of these companies to drop lower. So companies faced with raising the wages of their minimum-wage employees must make a difficult decision, with alternatives such as accepting lower profits, reducing staff, or raising prices. Using their critical thinking skills, managers and owners of these companies might ask the following questions when making this decision: Would accepting lower profits threaten the long-term solvency of the company? If the company raises prices, will competitors also raise prices, keeping competition about the same within the industry? Will raising prices hurt the industry as a whole? (In other words, will people eat at home more often?) If competitors don't raise prices, will the company lose customers?

A more difficult issue for these companies is the effect of reducing staff. In many of these restaurants, workers are already assigned multiple tasks. How many employees can a fast-food restaurant lay off without hurting quality, service, productivity, and morale? Furthermore, in many cases, the poorest, least-skilled workers would be the first to be laid off; the more versatile, multiskilled individuals would keep their jobs but would perhaps be assigned more duties. How much responsibility do the restaurants have to these employees and to the neighborhoods in which they conduct business and from which they hire their workers? Clearly, the answers to these questions are not as clear-cut as the results of C-V-P analysis alone.

*Can you think of any other factors that the managers of Unlimited Decadence should consider when deciding whether to produce Empty Decadence candy bars?*

## SUMMARY

At the beginning of the chapter we asked you several questions. During the chapter, we asked you to STOP and answer some additional questions to build your knowledge about specific issues. Be sure you answered these additional questions. Below are the questions from the beginning of the chapter, with a brief summary of the key points relating to the answers. Use your creative and critical thinking skills to expand on these key points to develop more complete answers to the questions and to determine what other questions you have that might lead you to learn more about the issues.

### 1 How does the fact that a manufacturing company makes the products it sells affect its business plan?

A manufacturing company's business plan has much in common with the plans of retail and service companies. However, because a manufacturing company makes the products it sells, its business plan also includes a production plan, which affects other parts of the business plan, particularly the financial plan. The production plan describes how a company intends to manufacture and maintain the quality of the products it will sell. The plan describes the raw materials that the company will use in manufacturing its product. A description of the production process specifies how these raw materials will be converted into finished products. The production plan also describes where the company intends to store the finished products before it sells them.

### 2 How does a manufacturing company determine the cost of the goods that it manufactures?

Managers of a manufacturing company determine the cost of the goods that it manufactures by adding together the direct materials costs, the direct labor costs, and the factory overhead costs that it incurs in manufacturing its products. To determine the direct materials costs, managers must know how much of each raw material went into the company's products and multiply the amount of raw materials by their costs. To determine the direct labor costs, managers must know how much of each type of direct labor was necessary to manufacture the company's products and multiply the number of hours of each type of direct labor by the appropriate wages per hour. To determine the factory overhead costs, managers must add together the costs of each type of factory overhead.

### 3 Why are standard costs useful in controlling a company's operations?

A manufacturing company uses standard costs as a way of controlling its production. By measuring actual costs against standard costs (what the costs actually were against what the costs should have been), the managers of a company can evaluate its activities. They can determine which activities caused costs to be too high or too low and decide whether to change those activities. A company develops standards for each manufactured product by determining price and quantity standards for each input to its manufacturing process.

### 4 How do manufacturing costs affect cost-volume-profit analysis?

Managers of manufacturing companies treat manufacturing costs like other costs when performing cost-volume-profit analysis. Like other costs, manufacturing costs can be classified as fixed or variable costs. So, managers add the variable manufacturing costs to the other variable costs and add the fixed manufacturing costs to the other fixed costs when performing cost-volume-profit analysis.

### 5 What is the effect of multiple products on cost-volume-profit analysis?

C-V-P analysis is similar for a company that sells only one product and for a company that sells multiple products. With multiple products, however, managers must know the product sales mix and the costs and sales revenues of the group of products being analyzed. The C-V-P calculation for a company with multiple products results in the number of "units" of product mix that the company must sell to break even or earn a desired profit. The managers then must convert the number of "units" of product mix to the number of units of individual products. Managers may find dollar sales volume to be more useful than unit sales volume in determining the level of sales necessary to achieve a desired profit.

### 6 How does a manufacturing company use cost-volume-profit analysis for its planning?

C-V-P analysis helps the managers of a manufacturing company make planning decisions by showing the potential impact of alternative plans on profit. These alternative plans might include changing suppliers of direct materials, hiring production workers, buying new equipment, adding or dropping a product line, raising or lowering product costs or selling prices, or changing the planned sales volume on some of its products (and therefore also changing the planned production of those products).

## KEY TERMS

**direct labor** *(p. 344)*
**direct materials** *(p. 344)*
**factory overhead** *(p. 346)*
**finished goods inventory** *(p. 343)*
**goods-in-process inventory** *(p. 343)*
**high-low method** *(p. 353)*
**indirect labor** *(p. 346)*
**indirect materials** *(p. 346)*
**margin of safety** *(p. 363)*
**mixed costs** *(p. 351)*
**price standard** *(p. 350)*
**product sales mix** *(p. 357)*
**quantity standard** *(p. 349)*
**raw materials** *(p. 340)*
**raw materials inventory** *(p. 343)*
**relevant range** *(p. 355)*
**scatter diagram** *(p. 352)*
**standard costs** *(p. 348)*
**variable manufacturing cost** *(p. 350)*
**variance** *(p. 349)*

## SUMMARY SURFING

Here is an opportunity to gather information on the Internet about real-world issues related to the topics in this chapter (for suggestions on how to navigate various organizations' Web sites to find the relevant information, see the related discussion in the Preface at the beginning of the book). Answer the following questions.

- Go to the **CCH Business Owners Toolkit** Web site. You should find a case study for a manufacturing company's business plan. What business plan components are represented? Identify Breakaway Bicycle Company's direct materials costs and direct labor costs.

- Go to the **Quicken.com Small Business** Web site. Suppose you are interested in starting a small business. You should find tools and services for writing a business plan, containing sample business plans. Find Morningstar Bakery's business plan. Calculate its break-even point. Does it match Morningstar's break-even analysis?

## INTEGRATED BUSINESS AND ACCOUNTING SITUATIONS

**Answer the Following Questions in Your Own Words.**

### Testing Your Knowledge

**11-1** Describe the purpose of the production plan.

**11-2** Describe how raw materials in a manufacturing company are different from the goods that a retail company sells.

**11-3** What type of information about raw materials does a manufacturing company include in its production plan?

**11-4** What type of information about labor does a manufacturing company include in its production plan?

**11-5** What type of information about equipment and facilities does a manufacturing company include in its production plan?

**11-6** What type of information about finished products does a manufacturing company include in its business plan?

**11-7** Describe the three types of inventories in a manufacturing company.

**11-8** Describe the three types of production input. Give an example of each type of input for a company that builds houses.

**11-9** Describe the difference between direct and indirect materials.

**11-10** Describe the difference between direct and indirect labor.

**11-11** How do you know if a cost should be classified as a factory overhead cost?

**11-12** Define *standard costs,* and describe how managers use them.

**11-13** What is a variance? How do managers use variance information?

**11-14** What is the difference between a price standard and a quantity standard?

**11-15** Describe a mixed cost and how it behaves.

**11-16** Describe three methods that can be used to estimate the components of a mixed cost. What are the advantages and disadvantages of each?

**11-17** What is a relevant range? How is C-V-P analysis affected by this concept? Why would it be useful for users of cost estimates to know the relevant range?

**11-18** What is the difference between C-V-P analysis with one product and C-V-P analysis with multiple products?

**11-19** Explain what is meant by a company's product sales mix. Give an example.

**11-20** What happens to the results of C-V-P analysis if a company's product sales mix changes? Why does this happen?

**11-21** How is a contribution margin for a product sales mix different from a contribution margin for one product?

**11-22** How does a desired return on stockholders' equity help managers determine the company's target profit?

**11-23** How do income taxes affect C-V-P analysis?

## Applying Your Knowledge

**11-24** Visit your favorite grocery store and select a packaged product.

*Required:* What raw materials went into the production of that product?

**11-25** Think about how decision makers use a business plan.

*Required:* Why do you think it is important to include information about a manufacturing company's suppliers in its production plan?

**11-26** Suppose you work for a company called Split Decisions and the boss has selected you to develop the production steps necessary to manufacture a banana split.

*Required:* Describe the sequence of the production steps and how the raw materials flow through this sequence.

**11-27** Western Brands produces western accessories. It manufactures one product, a bolo tie, from a thin 36-inch strip of leather, 1/3-inch wide, and four fancy brass rings. The leather strip is threaded through two of the rings, which act as a clasp. The remaining two rings are sewn onto the ends of the leather strip.

Western Brands purchases leather strips in 72-inch lengths that are 2 inches wide for $4.80 each and cuts them to 1/3-inch widths and then 36-inch lengths. Brass rings cost $9.60 per dozen. It takes two people 5 minutes each to produce one bolo tie. Each person earns $6 per hour.

*Required:* (1) What is the cost, per tie, of the direct materials?
(2) What is the cost, per tie, of the direct labor?
(3) What are the total direct costs for 500 ties?

**11-28** The utility costs and production levels for The Cat's Pajamas for the last four months were as follows:

| Month | Production Levels (pairs of pajamas) | Cost |
|---|---|---|
| 1 | 1,700 | $1,280 |
| 2 | 2,600 | 1,600 |
| 3 | 3,200 | 1,970 |
| 4 | 2,900 | 1,680 |

*Required:* (1) Assuming the utility cost is a mixed cost, use the high-low method with the above data to determine the variable cost per pair of pajamas and the total fixed cost per month.
(2) If 3,150 pairs of pajamas are manufactured, what should the utility cost be?

**11-29** Western Brands has estimated its factory overhead costs for the next year at two production volumes, 100,000 and 200,000. These estimates are shown below.

| | *Factory Overhead Costs* | |
|---|---|---|
| | **100,000 ties** | **200,000 ties** |
| Depreciation on factory equipment | $ 5,000 | $ 5,000 |
| Factory rent | 30,000 | 30,000 |
| Factory supervisor's salary | 45,000 | 45,000 |
| Maintenance of factory equipment | 1,920 | 2,240 |
| Factory utilities | 7,000 | 14,000 |
| Factory supplies | 3,000 | 6,000 |

*Required:* Estimate total factory overhead at a production level of 140,000 ties.

**11-30** A company with multiple products has a break-even point of 5,000 "units."

*Required:* Explain the preceding sentence.

**11-31** Bathtub Rings Corporation manufactures shower curtains that sell for $5.00 each and cost $3.48 to produce. It also manufactures shower-curtain rings that sell for $1.60 per box and cost $1.22 per box to produce. Fixed costs total $30,000 per year. Bathtub Rings sells five shower curtains for every two boxes of shower-curtain rings that it sells.

*Required:* (1) How many of each product must Bathtub Rings sell to break even?
(2) How many of each product must Bathtub Rings sell to earn a pretax income of $49,800?
(3) How many of each product must Bathtub Rings sell to earn an after-tax income of $49,800 if the income tax rate is 30%?

**11-32** Refer to 11-31.

*Required:* (1) Compute Bathtub Rings' contribution margin percentage per "unit."
(2) Compute Bathtub Rings' break-even point in sales dollars.
(3) What total pretax income (loss) would Bathtub Rings have if its total sales revenue amounted to $216,000?

**11-33** Sí, Your Dinner! Mexican Food Company manufactures three strengths of salsa: Lightweight, Hot Stuff, and Burn Your Tongue. The selling prices and manufacturing costs of these salsas are as follows:

| | **Lightweight** | **Hot Stuff** | **Burn Your Tongue** |
|---|---|---|---|
| Selling price per jar | $3.00 | $4.00 | $6.00 |
| Manufacturing cost per jar | 2.00 | 2.00 | 4.50 |

For every 9 jars sold, 3 are Lightweight, 2 are Hot Stuff, and 4 are Burn Your Tongue.

*Required:* (1) What is the contribution margin percentage per "unit"?
(2) By how much would profits change if a $1,000 advertising campaign increased the sales of Lightweight salsa by 900 jars but left sales of the other salsas unchanged?
(3) Sales are currently $9,430, and fixed costs total $2,125.
(a) How many jars of Lightweight salsa were sold?
(b) How many jars of Burn Your Tongue salsa were sold?
(c) What is the current pretax income?
(4) If the sales mix changes to 3 jars of Lightweight, 3 of Hot Stuff, and 4 of Burn Your Tongue, what would be the new contribution margin percentage?

**11-34** The Grandma Corporation manufactures two products—cookies and candy. Cookies have a contribution margin of $4 per box, and candy has a contribution margin of $5 per bag. Grandma's total fixed cost is currently $450,000. Grandma expects to sell two boxes of cookies for every three bags of candy sold. Boxes of cookies and bags of candy each sell for $10.

*Required:* (1) Compute the contribution margin percentage per "unit."
(2) At the current product mix, what total dollar sales volume is required for Grandma to earn a pretax income of $217,000?

**11-35** Greco Manufacturing Corporation produces two products—olives and baklava. Olives require $3 of variable costs per jar and sell for $5 per jar. Baklava has variable costs of $5 per box and sells for $10. Greco's total fixed costs amount to $72,250. This year Greco sold 30,000 jars of olives and 5,000 boxes of baklava. Greco believes that consumer tastes will shift dramatically next year. Although it expects total dollar sales volume to be the same as this year's sales volume, the product mix will change, so that one-third of the units sold will be boxes of baklava.

*Required:* (1) Compute Greco's pretax income for *this* year.
(2) At what dollar sales volume would Greco have broken even for *this* year?
(3) Compute Greco's expected pretax income for *next* year assuming total dollar sales volume does not change.
(4) Why does Greco expect more pretax income next year than it earned this year when the total dollar sales volume is expected to be the same? Explain.

**11-36** The Boston Company (a sole proprietorship) expects to operate at a loss next year on its two products, as shown here:

| | Commons | Not So Commons | Total |
|---|---|---|---|
| Production and sales (units) | 100,000 | 20,000 | 120,000 |
| Sales revenue | $200,000 | $100,000 | $300,000 |
| Variable costs | (140,000) | (40,000) | (180,000) |
| Contribution margin | $ 60,000 | $ 60,000 | $120,000 |
| Less: Fixed costs | | | (172,240) |
| Loss | | | $ (52,240) |

Boston has two plans that it believes will improve its profit (reduce its loss) next year:

Plan A—to spend $53,000 on advertising to increase the number of *Not So Commons* sold without affecting the number of *Commons* sold

Plan B—to reduce the selling price of *Not So Commons* from $5 per unit to $4 per unit; this plan should change the product mix so that one *Not So Common* is sold for every two *Commons*

*Required:* (1) If Boston follows neither of the two plans, so that its product mix is one *Not So Common* sold for each five *Commons* sold, what must total dollar sales volume be for the company to break even?

(2) If Boston follows Plan A, how many *Not So Commons* must it sell next year to break even? (The number of *Commons* sold will still be 100,000.)

(3) If Boston follows Plan B, what total dollar sales volume is required for it to break even?

(4) Compare your answers to (1) and (3). Explain the result obtained from this comparison.

**11-37** Professional Robotics Corporation manufactures three different robots in its "domestic servants" line. Sales information for this line of product is given below:

| | Butler | Maid | Bartender |
|---|---|---|---|
| Selling price per unit | $3,000 | $2,500 | $4,000 |
| Variable cost per unit | 750 | 750 | 1,300 |
| Expected sales mix | 1 | 3 | 4 |

Fixed costs are $2,500,000.

*Required:* (1) What is Professional Robotics' break-even point, in "units" of sales mix?

(2) To break even, how many Butlers, Maids, and Bartenders must Professional Robotics sell?

(3) Suppose Professional Robotics' sales during the year were $4,800,000. Assuming a normal sales mix, how many units of each product were sold? What was Professional Robotics' pretax income?

(4) Assuming a normal sales mix and an income tax rate of 40%, how many Butlers, Maids, and Bartenders must Professional Robotics sell to earn an after-tax profit of $198,000?

## Making Evaluations

**11-38** Suppose you and your brother Noah, a veterinary medicine major, want to open a pet store. After long deliberations and lively discussion about the name of the corporation, you agree to name it Noah's Bark. You arrange to obtain retail space, to purchase supplies and pets, and to advertise in the newspaper. Now you are almost ready to open for business. But first you want to analyze how your plans will affect profit.

You and Noah plan to sell Labrador retrievers for $350 each, and you estimate that total fixed costs for Noah's Bark will be $6,375 ($2,000 rent, $4,000 salaries, and $375 advertising). The cost to you of purchasing the Labrador retriever puppies is $120 each. On average, you spend $60 to feed each puppy before it is sold and $30 per puppy on miscellaneous items such as dipping and grooming supplies.

*Required:* (1) How many dogs must Noah's Bark sell to break even?
(2) How much pretax income will Noah's Bark earn if it sells 750 dogs?
(3) How many dogs must Noah's Bark sell to earn $14,000 pretax income?
(4) What must dollar sales be to break even?
(5) What must dollar sales be to earn $14,065 pretax income?

Suppose you and your brother believe that if the selling price does not change, Noah's Bark will be able to sell 200 Labrador retrievers next year. At that unit sales volume, profit is expected to be $21,625 ([$140 contribution margin per dog × 200 dogs] − $6,375 total fixed costs). However, you are considering three alternative plans (only one of which will be followed) that you believe may allow Noah's Bark to earn even more than $21,625. These plans are as follows:

(a) Raise the selling price of the dogs to $450 per dog. With this alternative, variable costs per dog and total fixed costs do not change.
(b) Purchase only those Labrador retrievers that are descendants of American Kennel Club (AKC) ribbon winners, thus increasing the variable cost to $240 (these dogs can be purchased for $150 each). You are considering this alternative because you think the perceived improvement in the purity of the breed will increase the sales volume of dogs. With this change, neither the selling price per dog nor the total fixed cost changes.
(c) Increase total fixed costs by spending $1,000 more on advertising. With this alternative, the selling price per dog and the variable costs per dog do not change.

*Required:* (6) Basing your decision on C-V-P results alone, which plan should you choose? Why?
(7) What other factors might you want to consider in making this choice?

**11-39** Suppose that after Noah's Bark (in 11-38) has been in business for a year, you and your brother Noah decide to sell beagles in addition to Labrador retrievers. Each beagle sells for $150, requires $60 of variable cost, and earns a contribution margin of $90. Each Labrador retriever still sells for $350, requires $210 of variable cost, and earns a contribution margin of $140. The contribution margin earned by Noah's Bark in the second year of business from beagles, from Labrador retrievers, and in total is shown here:

| | Labrador Retrievers | Beagles | Total |
|---|---|---|---|
| Sales (dogs) | 600 | 200 | 800 |
| Sales revenue | $210,000 | $30,000 | $240,000 |
| Less variable costs | (126,000) | (12,000) | (138,000) |
| Contribution margin | $ 84,000 | $18,000 | $102,000 |

Assume that fixed costs for Noah's Bark are now $76,500 per year.

*Required:* (1) Compute the break-even point (in sales dollars).
(2) What must sales be (in dollars) for Noah's Bark to earn $30,000 pretax income?
(3) What is the break-even point in beagles and Labs?
(4) How many beagles and Labs must Noah's Bark sell to earn a pretax income of $30,000?
(5) How many beagles and Labs must it sell to earn a net income of $30,000? The income tax rate is 40%.

Suppose you and your brother are considering three independent alternative plans (only one of which will be followed) that you believe may raise the company's income. These plans are as follows:

(a) Raise the selling price of the Labs to $450 per dog. With this alternative, variable costs per dog and total fixed costs do not change.
(b) Purchase only those Labrador retrievers that are descendants of American Kennel Club (AKC) ribbon winners, thus increasing the variable cost to $240 (these dogs can be purchased for $150 each). You are considering this alternative because you think the perceived improvement in the purity of the breed will increase the sales volume of dogs. With this change, neither the selling price per unit nor the total fixed cost changes.

(c) Increase total fixed costs by spending $1,000 more on advertising. With this alternative, the selling price per unit and the variable costs per unit do not change.

*Required:* (6) Based on C-V-P analysis alone, which plan should you choose? Why?
(7) What other factors might you want to consider in making this choice?

**11-40** Lucas Air Service, a sole proprietorship, provides charter flights on weekdays only. Earl Lucas, the owner, is thinking of offering flying lessons on weekends. He has always protected his weekends for family time and will give up his family weekends only if he can earn at least $12,000 per year extra. Estimates of demand for lessons suggest that, weather permitting, he could teach a full six-lesson day every Saturday and Sunday for the entire year.

Earl's large plane could be used for about half of the lessons. He would borrow a smaller plane, owned by his friend Pat, for the other half. Fuel and maintenance would run about $45 per flying lesson with the large plane. With the small plane, fuel would cost $25 per lesson, and Earl would pay Pat $75 per day when he used the small plane regardless of how many lessons he gave in it.

Earl plans to use the large plane for advanced students and to charge them $85 for a lesson. He would use the small plane for beginners and charge them $75 per lesson. Each weekend day that Earl opens for flight lessons he will incur $35 for the salary of his receptionist, utilities, and other expenses to keep his office open.

*Required:* (1) Prepare a schedule showing the daily profit if
(a) Earl gives from 1 to 6 advanced lessons only
(b) Earl gives from 1 to 6 beginner lessons only
(c) Earl offers both types of lessons on a given day for a total of 6 lessons (make the profit computation for only two situations: the situation where Earl gives 3 lessons of each type and the situation where Earl gives 4 advanced lessons and 2 beginner lessons).
(2) Is it more or less profitable for Earl to give 4 advanced lessons and 2 beginner lessons each day than to give 3 lessons of each kind each day?
(3) If Earl gives 3 flight lessons of each type each day, how much profit could he earn if he gives lessons for 90 days?
(4) How much profit could Earl earn if he gives 6 advanced lessons in the large plane for each of 45 days and 6 beginner lessons in the small plane for each of 45 days?
(5) How much profit could Earl earn if he gives 6 advanced lessons in the large plane for each of 60 days and 6 beginner lessons in the small plane for each of 30 days?
(6) Explain why the mix of two-thirds advanced and one-third beginner lessons seems better than the mix of half advanced and half beginner lessons in the case where only advanced or only beginner lessons are scheduled on a given day.

**11-41** Golden Chocolate Inc. of Brooklyn, a manufacturer of chocolate bars, learned that a Connecticut child suffered a mild allergic reaction to the nuts in its candy bar. The wafer in the chocolate bar contains ground hazelnuts, but the candy bar's label didn't include nuts in its list of ingredients.[h] Suppose you have been hired to advise Golden Chocolates about how to respond to this situation and how to prevent related potential problems.

*Required:* Assume Candace Sugarbaker is the company president. Write her a memo making a recommendation or recommendations. For each recommendation, describe the effect you think it will have on Golden Chocolate's sales, fixed costs, variable costs, and break-even point. Include any other factors you think Golden's managers should consider when they make this decision.

**11-42** The National Fishing Heritage Center in Grimsby, a port in northeastern England, is luring a record number of visitors (up 27 percent from last year) with some very fishy techniques: Scratch 'n' Sniff leaflets; Whiff You Were Here postcards; and "Smelloons"—balloons filled with fresh-fishy odors. Scents include "Hint of Haddock," "Compressed Cod," and "Sentiment of Seaweed."[i] The center views this effort as a major success.

*Required:* Working with your class team, identify the changes in fixed and variable costs caused by this tourist campaign. Besides the increase in visitors, what criteria would you use to measure the success of this effort? What questions would you ask to help you determine its success?

**11-43** Chico, Maria, Elaina, and Juan are taking a year off from school to form a partnership to develop the commercial potential of a cleaning solvent they accidentally discovered in their college chemistry lab. In liquid form, their product can remove grease stains from clothing and can launder shop towels so that they appear like new. In solid form (actually a buttery consistency), it can make a mechanic's hands look like those of a baby in two minutes, and as a foam, it can lift grease and oil spots out of concrete in a jiffy.

Chico's investigation of manufacturing requirements suggests that small-scale manufacturing is quite feasible and that output could be adjusted over a wide range of volumes with little change in efficiency. Potential suppliers of raw materials have been contacted, and a long list of friends who are eager for part-time work ensures the availability of direct labor.

Maria has located a steel farm building for rent near the interstate highway in an area recently rezoned for commercial and industrial use. Initial cleanup, some insulation, additional lighting, gravel for the drive and loading area, and a small amount of additional office space are all that seem to be necessary to make the building suitable for their needs. She also has acquired a delivery van, which was used by a local florist before his retirement.

Elaina has worked out all of the details for advertising and other promotional activities that would be needed for the three forms of the product. She and Juan have determined the range of possible sales volumes for each form, assuming primary customers to be commercial laundries for the liquid, auto service centers for the solid, and service stations for the foam. Juan has determined optimal delivery routes and schedules to cover the midstate area and is now considering the possibility of adding delivery to two major metropolitan areas.

After much planning and several meetings with local financial institutions, the four have concluded that the product can be produced and marketed in only one of the three forms—liquid, solid, or foam—until successful financial performance of the venture is established. This success would require at least $30,000 of profit to be earned during the first year.

The four asked for your advice recently at a party. Rather than talk business at the party, you suggested that they send you the information they had gathered. A few days after the party, you received the following information from them:

| | Liquid | Solid | Foam |
|---|---|---|---|
| Selling price | $3.00 | $3.50 | $11.00 |
| Variable costs: | | | |
| Direct materials | $0.40 | $0.80 | $3.00 |
| Direct labor | 0.10 | 0.20 | 0.60 |
| Variable overhead | 0.15 | 0.30 | 0.90 |
| Variable selling and administrative | 0.35 | 0.20 | 0.50 |
| Total variable costs | $1.00 | $1.50 | $5.00 |
| Fixed costs: | | | |
| Factory overhead | $ 5,000 | $15,000 | $85,000 |
| Selling and administrative | 10,000 | 15,000 | 5,000 |

Sales volume information (all possible sales volumes between the estimated minimum and maximum are equally likely):

| | | | |
|---|---|---|---|
| Maximum sales volume | 20,000 bottles | 40,000 tubs | 25,000 cans |
| Minimum sales volume | 12,000 | 15,000 | 5,000 |
| Expected sales volume | 16,000 | 27,500 | 15,000 |

*Required:* (1) For each of the three forms of product, what is the
- (a) maximum possible profit?
- (b) minimum possible profit?
- (c) expected profit?
- (d) sales volume needed to earn $30,000?

(2) Which form of product seems favored relative to each of the calculations you made in (1)?

(3) Which form of the product would you recommend they introduce during the first year of operations? Why?

**11-44** You talk on the phone a lot to your friends back home. Each phone call is long distance, and you have been using a "10 cents a minute" phone card to pay for each call. You are considering signing up for a long-distance calling plan with a phone company. The company has two plans from which to choose. Plan 1 requires a person to pay $4.95 per month plus $0.07 per minute. Plan 2 requires a person to pay $8.95 per month plus $0.05 per minute. You have reviewed your calls in previous months and, on the average you talk to your friends long distance about 240 minutes per month.

*Required:* (1) What is the "break-even" point (in minutes) where it makes no difference which plan you select?
(2) Which of the two plans should you select? Why is it less expensive?

**11-45** Yesterday, you received the following letter for your advice column in the local paper:

**DR. DECISIVE**

Dear Dr. Decisive:

I read your column every day, and I think you can help me with this problem I am having with my boyfriend. This morning, as we were walking to the gym, we started having a nice, normal conversation about my aerobics class. Then, before I knew it, we had a major parting of the ways.

This all started when I mentioned that I didn't think it was fair that we had to pay a fee for each aerobics class we attended and that the $150 facilities use fee that each student pays at the beginning of the semester ought to cover it. He looked at me like I was an idiot and informed me that I was WRONG and must not have been paying attention in my accounting class. According to him, it is obvious that the aerobics fee is assessed to cover the aerobics instructor's salary. Well, it's not so obvious to me, and I need for you to tell him how wrong he is (he reads your column too). Until we get this cleared up, we can't go to the gym together. (How could I work out with such a pompous FOOL?). Just sign me . . .

"Nobody's Fool"

*Required:* Meet with your Dr. Decisive team and write a response to "Nobody's Fool."

# END NOTES

[a]John S. DeMott, "Small Factories' Big Lessons," *Nation's Business,* April 1995, 29, 30.
[b]Ibid.
[c]Ibid.
[d]Laura M. Litvan, "A Breath of Fresh Air," *Nation's Business,* March 1995, 53.
[e]Melinda Hemmelgarn, "Trip to factory reveals Girl Scout cookie facts." *Columbia Daily Tribune,* January 19, 2000, 2C.
[f]Ibid.
[g]Ibid.
[h]"Chocolate Bar Recalled as Allergy Precaution," *Columbia Daily Tribune,* April 22, 1995, 2A.
[i]"Something Fishy," *Fortune,* July 25, 1993, 14.

# DEVELOPING A BUSINESS PLAN FOR A MANUFACTURING COMPANY: BUDGETING

CHAPTER 12

"AT THE BEGINNING OF HIS UNDERTAKING, AND AT EVERY SUCCESSIVE STAGE, THE ALERT BUSINESS MAN STRIVES TO MODIFY HIS ARRANGEMENTS SO AS TO OBTAIN BETTER RESULTS WITH A GIVEN EXPENDITURE, OR EQUAL RESULTS WITH LESS EXPENDITURE."

—ALFRED MARSHALL

1. What are the similarities and differences between a large company's master budget and that of an entrepreneurial company?
2. What are the similarities and differences between a manufacturing company's master budget and that of a retail company?
3. How is a manufacturing company's operating cycle different from that of a retail company?
4. Is there a strategy a manufacturing company can use to complete its budget?
5. If a company's actual sales are different from its budgeted sales (or actual production is different from budgeted production) for the same time period, how can managers meaningfully evaluate how well the company met its cost goals?
6. How do budgets affect the business decisions that employees make?

Maybe you've had an experience similar to the following: "I went into the kitchen to make birthday cupcakes for my roommate to take to his fraternity meeting, only to find that I had forgotten to buy oil the last time I went grocery shopping. So, I went to the store and purchased some oil. After I got home, I started to gather together the ingredients and discovered that my roommate had used all the eggs the last time he volunteered to cook breakfast. Back to the store! By then I had already used up the hour I had budgeted for this project, but . . . he *is* my best friend, so I persevered. (Studying for my exam could wait.) The completed project was outstanding—two dozen *yummy* cupcakes. Unfortunately, the fraternity never got to taste them. When he was ready to go to his meeting, my roommate told me there would be 36 people at the meeting!!!! Back to the store again for three dozen cupcakes (they all had to look alike). I kept the ones I made for myself."

Imagine how much larger this problem would have been if this situation had occurred at **Sara Lee Corporation**, a company that manufactures multiple products, including desserts, and involves numerous people in the process! Large companies invest considerable time in the planning process to prevent problems such as this from occurring, and the master budget is one tool they use for planning.

## BUDGETING IN A MORE COMPLEX ENVIRONMENT

1 What are the similarities and differences between a large company's master budget and that of an entrepreneurial company?

A large company prepares budgets for the same reasons that a smaller company does. Besides describing a company's financial plans, budgets make other contributions to its planning, operating, and evaluating processes. They:

- Add discipline, or order, to the planning process
- Help managers identify and avoid potential operating problems
- Quantify plans
- Create a "benchmark" for evaluating the company's performance

However, a large company's budgets contain elements that a smaller company's budgets do not include. We next illustrate a master budget for Unlimited Decadence Corporation, a manufacturing company, and point out the similarities and differences between it and the budget of Sweet Temptations, the entrepreneurial retail company that we discussed in Chapter 4.

## THE BUDGET FRAMEWORK FOR PLANNING IN A MANUFACTURING COMPANY

2 What are the similarities and differences between a manufacturing company's master budget and that of a retail company?

As we discussed in Chapter 4, the form and the content of the individual schedules of a master budget differ from company to company for many reasons. However, even though they differ to some extent, the budget schedules of manufacturing companies and retail companies also contain many similarities because many of their activities are similar.

A master budget for a manufacturing company usually includes the following budget schedules:

1. Sales budget
2. Production budget
3. Direct materials purchases budget
4. Direct labor budget
5. Factory overhead budget

6. Selling expenses budget
7. General and administrative expenses budget
8. Capital expenditures budget
9. Cash budget (projected cash flow statement)
10. Projected income statement
11. Projected balance sheet

If you refer back to the budget schedules for a retail company that we discussed in Chapter 4, you will notice that a manufacturing company has more budget schedules than a retail company has. This should make sense when you remember that a manufacturing company *makes* the products that it sells rather than purchasing the products. The additional manufacturing activities must be added to the budget process. Exhibit 12-1 depicts Unlimited Decadence's master budget, composed of the eleven schedules listed above, and shows (with arrows) the important relationships among the schedules.

We will discuss the nature and purpose of these budget schedules and illustrate each of them, as we did in Chapter 4, so that you can see how Unlimited Decadence can describe its planned activities in a master budget. To simplify these illustrations, we assume in each of these budget schedules that Unlimited Decadence produces only one kind of candy—Darkly Decadent candy bars. However, companies that produce multiple products use the same procedures and logic in developing their budgets.

You should notice many similarities between the process of budgeting Unlimited Decadence's planned activities and the process that we used to describe the planned activities of Sweet Temptations. As you will see, the cyclical nature of a company's activities affects the budgeting process.

**EXHIBIT 12-1** **INTERRELATIONSHIPS AMONG BUDGET SCHEDULES IN THE MASTER BUDGET**

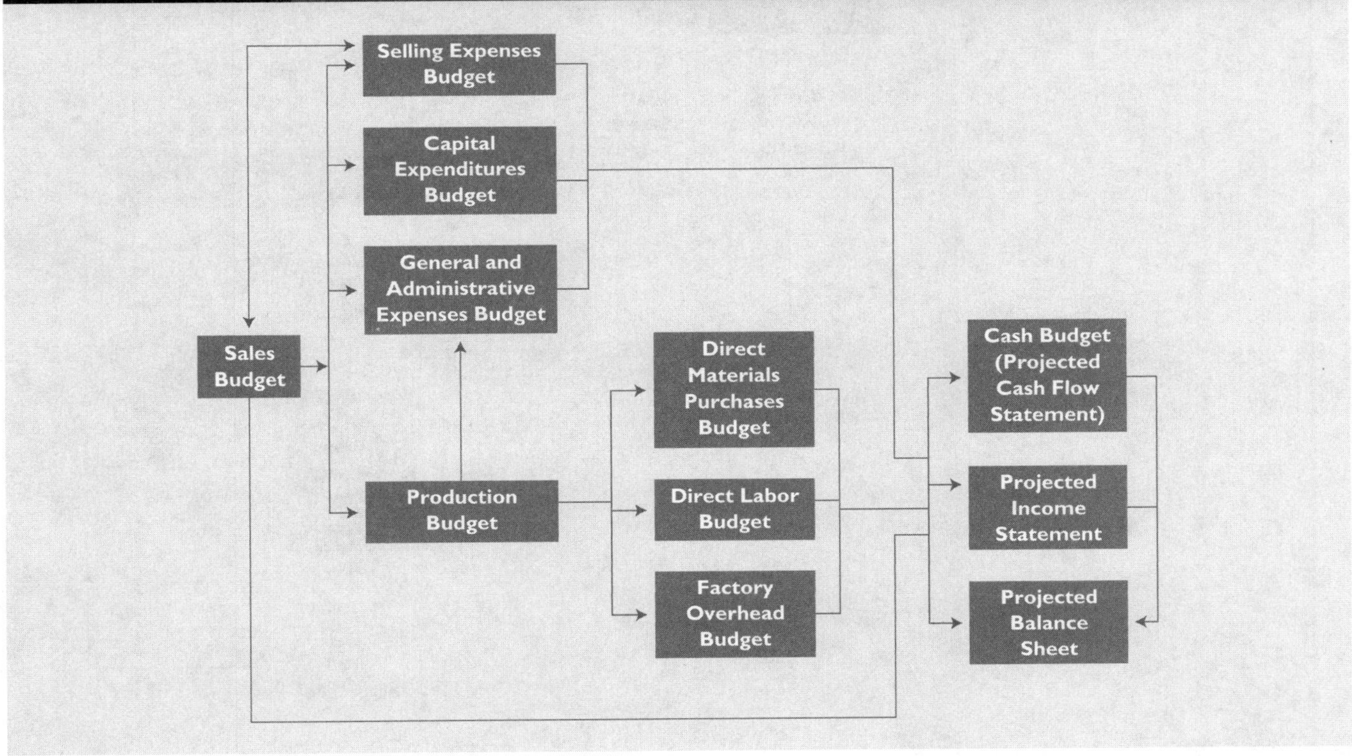

## The Operating Cycle of a Manufacturing Company

3 How is a manufacturing company's operating cycle different from that of a retail company?

Recall from Chapter 4 that the **operating cycle** of a company is the average time it takes the company to use cash to acquire goods and services, to convert these goods and services into products or services to sell, to sell these products and services to customers, and then to collect cash from customers for the sale. We can restate this definition specifically for a manufacturing company and say that the **operating cycle for a *manufacturing* company** is the average time it takes the company to use cash to acquire direct materials to use in manufacturing goods, to convert these direct materials into finished goods, to sell these goods to customers, and then to collect cash from customers for the sale. Unlimited Decadence's operating cycle is the time it takes to pay cash to purchase ingredients from its suppliers, to convert the ingredients into candy bars, to sell these candy bars to customers, and to collect cash from the customers. Exhibit 12-2 illustrates Unlimited Decadence's operating cycle. A company's master budget reflects and takes into account all the stages of its operating cycle. However, rather than beginning with expected cash payments, as the operating cycle does, a master budget begins with expected sales.

**EXHIBIT 12-2 UNLIMITED DECADENCE'S OPERATING CYCLE**

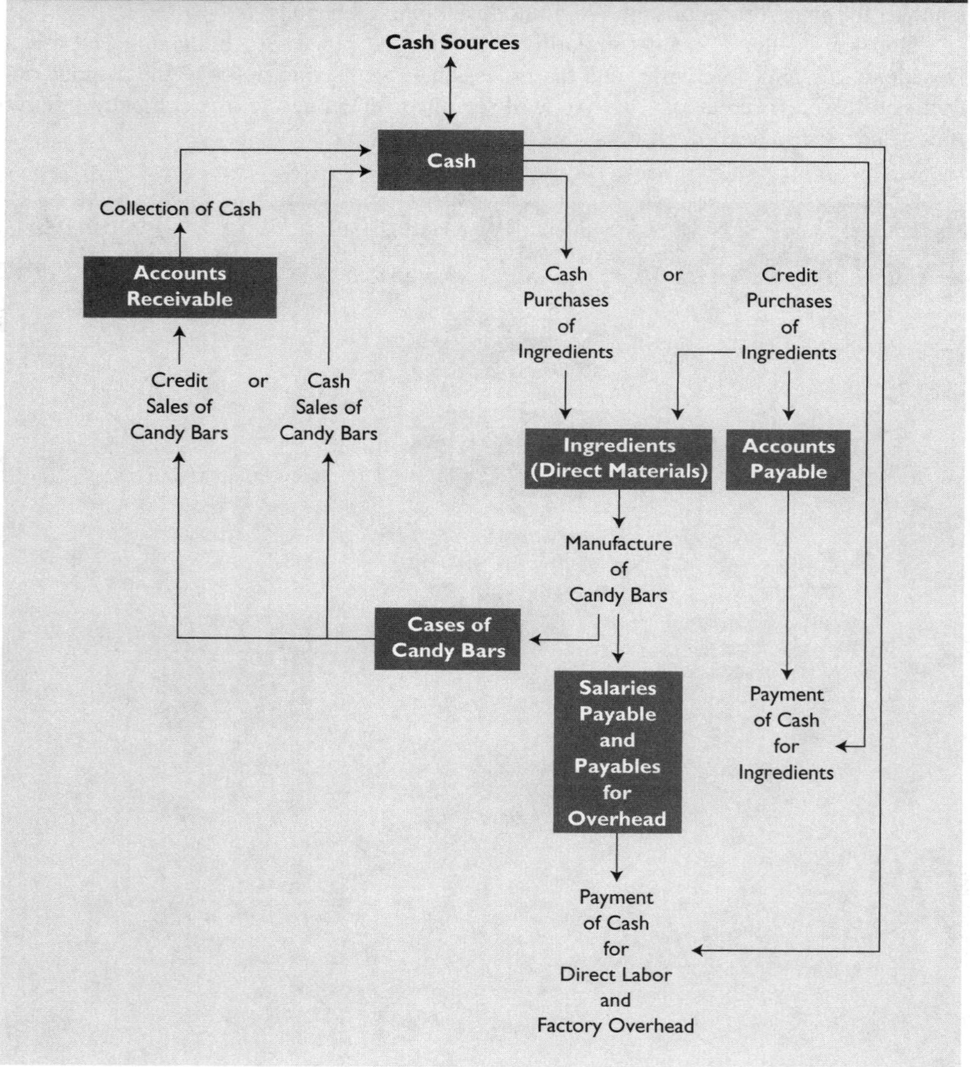

*Why do you think the budget begins with expected sales rather than expected cash payments? Given what you already know about budgeting, what do you think would be the effect of beginning the budget with cash payments instead?*

## Sales Budget: The Starting Point

4 Is there a strategy a manufacturing company can use to complete its budget?

As they do in a retail company, sales create the need for all the activities of a manufacturing company. Likewise, the sales budget directly or indirectly affects all of the other budget schedules. Remember from Chapter 4 that the **sales budget** shows the amount of inventory (in units) that the company expects to sell in each month of the budget period and the related revenues that the company expects to earn from each month's sales. Exhibit 12-3 shows Unlimited Decadence's sales budget for Darkly Decadent candy bars for the second quarter of the year 2009.[1] The sales figures are based on a market analysis conducted by Unlimited Decadence's marketing department and on the company's past sales figures. Notice that budgeted sales revenue is different from expected cash receipts in each month. This is because Unlimited Decadence gives its credit customers thirty days (n/30) to pay for their purchases,[2] so it expects to collect cash from its credit sales roughly one month after the sales occur.

*After looking at Unlimited Decadence's sales budget, do you think it has any cash customers? How do you know?*

## Production Budget

After estimating sales for the quarter, managers at Unlimited Decadence must decide how many cases of Darkly Decadent candy bars to produce and when to produce them. The production budget helps managers quantify these decisions. The **production budget** is a schedule showing how many units the company should produce during each budget period both to satisfy expected sales (from the sales budget) for that period and to end each

**EXHIBIT 12-3** **SALES BUDGET**

**UNLIMITED DECADENCE CORPORATION**
**Sales Budget**
**(in thousands)**
**Second Quarter 2009**

| | April | May | June | Quarter |
|---|---|---|---|---|
| Budgeted sales (cases) | 500 | 360 | 300 | 1,160 |
| Budgeted selling price per case | $ 16 | $ 16 | $ 16 | $ 16 |
| Budgeted sales revenue | $8,000 | $5,760 | $4,800 | $18,560 |
| Expected cash receipts | | | | |
| From March sales* | $5,840 | | | $ 5,840 |
| From April sales | | $8,000 | | $ 8,000 |
| From May sales | | | $5,760 | $ 5,760 |
| | $5,840 | $8,000 | $5,760 | $19,600 |

*Sales for March are 365 thousand cases

[1]To keep the budget schedules simple, in this chapter we assume that Unlimited Decadence sells only one type of candy bar—the Darkly Decadent candy bar. Therefore, we include only one sales budget and one production budget.

[2]We are assuming no cash discounts. If Unlimited Decadence gave its customers cash discounts, it would expect to collect cash sooner, but it also would expect to collect less cash because of the discount.

period with a desired finished goods inventory level. These production figures will form the basis for estimating the expenses that the company will incur in its manufacturing activity, and that the company will show on its projected income statement for the budget period. Managers also use the desired ending finished goods inventory for the budget period in estimating the inventory costs that appear on the projected balance sheet for the budget period.

In deciding what ending finished goods inventory levels to maintain, managers must balance several costs that are associated with inventories. Carrying inventories is expensive. For example, **Spangler Candy Co.**, the Bryan, Ohio candy cane manufacturer that we discussed in Chapter 11, begins in February to produce candy canes for the Christmas holidays.[a] Since it begins its production so early in the year, it must store the candy canes in a 215,000-square-foot warehouse. Besides the cost of the warehouse, Spangler has other costs associated with its inventory. These include the costs of keeping the company's money invested in inventory of candy canes, of handling inventory, and of paying insurance and taxes. Furthermore, by storing the inventory, Spangler risks theft, damage, or obsolescence of its product.

*Why do you think there is a cost associated with keeping the company's cash tied up in inventory? What is the cost?*

On the other hand, it also can be very expensive *not* to carry inventory. For example, costs can arise from having excessive production facilities just to meet peak production requirements, from working employees overtime to fill rush orders, or from losing sales because orders cannot be met. Every company must plan its inventory levels by keeping both the costs of carrying and the costs of not carrying inventory in mind, and by trying to maintain an optimal level of inventory on hand so that the combined total cost is the lowest possible amount.

Sometimes, after evaluating these costs, companies set desired ending finished goods inventory levels at a constant percentage of the following period's budgeted unit sales. This policy gives the company enough units of inventory to satisfy customer demand for a constant period of time beyond the end of the period, even if the company doesn't (or can't) produce any units. It also prevents the company from accumulating too much inventory. For example, Unlimited Decadence's policy is to have an ending finished goods inventory equal to 25 percent of the next month's anticipated sales of candy bars. Therefore, if sales occur as it expects, Unlimited Decadence will always have enough units at the end of the period to satisfy customer demand for about one week without producing any new cases of candy bars. If its actual ending inventory in any month is greater than 25 percent of the next month's expected sales, it will adjust the number of cases of candy bars it plans to manufacture in the next month. In Unlimited Decadence's situation, budgeted sales and budgeted production are linked together, as shown in the following diagram:

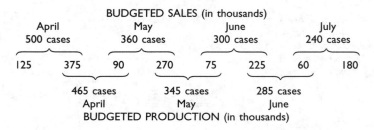

BUDGETED SALES (in thousands)

| April | | May | | June | | July | |
|---|---|---|---|---|---|---|---|
| 500 cases | | 360 cases | | 300 cases | | 240 cases | |
| 125 | 375 | 90 | 270 | 75 | 225 | 60 | 180 |
| | 465 cases | | 345 cases | | 285 cases | | |
| | April | | May | | June | | |

BUDGETED PRODUCTION (in thousands)

With this inventory policy, March's production would have been sufficient to cover three-fourths (75%) of March's sales and the first one-fourth (25%) of April's sales (125,000 cases). April's required production of 465,000 cases, then, must satisfy the last three-fourths of April's sales (375,000 cases) plus the first one-fourth of May's sales (90,000 cases) and so forth.

*What do you think should happen to next month's actual production if Unlimited Decadence sells more cases of candy bars this month than it budgeted? Why?*

Other companies, particularly those experiencing seasonal demand, might be better off having a policy of allowing finished goods inventories to gradually increase during low sales periods so that they can meet increased demand during high sales periods without having to undergo large changes in production levels.

*Think about a company's factory, equipment, employees, and inventories. How do you think large changes in production levels would affect each of these factors? How would such changes affect the company's costs?*

Exhibit 12-4 presents Unlimited Decadence's production budget for Darkly Decadent candy bars. Notice that we expressed this budget entirely in units (thousands of cases of candy bars). Also notice that Unlimited Decadence must have inventory available for each time period (month or quarter) equal to the sum of the budgeted sales of cases of candy bars for that time period and the desired ending inventory (in other words, enough to sell during the period and to still have the desired amount of inventory remaining after the sales). The total required cases must come from the period's beginning inventory and from any goods that Unlimited Decadence produces during the time period. Thus, for each period, the necessary production for that period is computed by subtracting the number of cases that Unlimited Decadence already has on hand at the beginning of the period (the beginning inventory) from the total number of cases required.

*By looking at this production budget, can you tell what Unlimited Decadence anticipates its July sales will be?*

Notice too the relationship between the monthly and the quarterly numbers. Just as occurs with a retail company, in a manufacturing company, the budgeted unit sales for the quarter equal the sum of the budgeted unit sales for all three months of the quarter. Unlimited Decadence's total sales for the second quarter of the year 2009 (1,160,000 cases) is the sum of its monthly sales for the quarter (500,000 + 360,000 + 300,000 cases). Similarly, the budgeted production for the quarter (1,095,000 cases) is the sum of the three monthly production requirements (465,000 + 345,000 + 285,000 cases). The desired

**EXHIBIT 12-4 PRODUCTION BUDGET**

**UNLIMITED DECADENCE CORPORATION**
**Production Budget**
**(in thousands of cases)**
**Second Quarter 2009**

| | April | May | June | Quarter |
|---|---|---|---|---|
| Budgeted sales (cases) | 500 | 360 | 300 | 1,160 |
| Add: Desired ending inventory of finished cases* | 90 | 75 | 60 | 60 |
| Total cases required | 590 | 435 | 360 | 1,220 |
| Less: Beginning inventory of finished cases | (125) | (90) | (75) | (125) |
| Budgeted production (cases) | 465 | 345 | 285 | 1,095 |

*One-fourth of next month's sales

ending and beginning inventories for the quarter, however, are simply equal to the desired ending inventory for the last month of the quarter (60,000 cases for June) and the beginning inventory for the first month of the quarter (125,000 cases for April), respectively. Unlimited Decadence's total requirement of cases of candy bars for the quarter is the quarter's budgeted unit sales (1,160,000 cases) plus its desired ending inventory (60,000 cases). Finally, note that each month's ending inventory is the following month's beginning inventory (April's desired ending inventory of 90,000 cases is the same as May's beginning inventory).

*Look at Unlimited Decadence's production budget again. If Unlimited Decadence had a policy of keeping ending finished goods inventory at a constant level, how do you think that would change each month's production from what Unlimited Decadence currently budgeted?*

## Direct Materials Purchases Budget

To manufacture goods, a company must have direct materials on hand. (Remember from Chapter 11 that direct materials physically become a part of a manufactured product.) Therefore, its managers must decide when to purchase direct materials, how many to purchase, and when to pay for these purchases. The direct materials purchases budget helps managers quantify these decisions. The **direct materials purchases budget** is a schedule that shows the number of direct material units that must be purchased in each budget period to meet production and ending direct materials inventory requirements. It also shows the costs related to those purchases and when the company expects to pay for them.

As you have probably observed, manufacturing companies often use many different direct materials in their products. They purchase these direct materials at widely differing prices. Unlimited Decadence, for example, uses sugar, milk products, cocoa beans, nuts, and emulsifiers in its products. Sugar, cocoa beans, and nuts are priced by the pound, emulsifiers by the carton, and milk products by the barrel. Because of differences like these, manufacturing companies often prepare a separate schedule for each direct material. However, despite these differences, the structures of the direct materials purchases schedules for all the direct materials are similar. Therefore, to avoid unnecessary repetition, we now illustrate Unlimited Decadence's direct materials purchases budget for only one of its direct materials—sugar.

### Direct Materials Purchases Requirement

The direct materials purchases budget initially shows the direct materials, in units (pounds, barrels, or cartons), that a company needs to have on hand during each budget period. This amount is the sum of the direct materials the company expects to use in production in each budget period and the desired ending inventory of direct materials. Suppose, for example, that Unlimited Decadence purchases sugar by the pound. The total sugar that Unlimited Decadence needs to have on hand in each month is the number of pounds of sugar it requires for the budgeted production of cases of chocolates that month plus the number of pounds of sugar it desires to have in its ending inventory. Exhibit 12-5 shows Unlimited Decadence's purchases budget for sugar. Notice that in April, Unlimited Decadence needs 1,860,000 pounds of sugar for the production of 465,000 cases of candy. Its desired ending inventory is 92,000 pounds of sugar, so the total sugar that it needs to have on hand in April is the sum of both, or 1,952,000 pounds of sugar. If it needs more than the amount of the month's beginning inventory of sugar (in April, 124,000 pounds), Unlimited Decadence must purchase enough sugar to make up the difference. We computed the number of pounds of sugar that Unlimited Decadence must purchase in April (1,828,000 pounds) by subtracting the number of pounds of sugar in the beginning inventory of sugar (124,000 pounds in April) from the total inventory of sugar required in that month (1,952,000 pounds).

Is this the type of sugar that Unlimited Decadence uses in its production of candy bars?

Unlimited Decadence determines the amount of sugar it needs for production in each budget period by multiplying its budgeted production by the standard number of pounds

## EXHIBIT 12-5 DIRECT MATERIALS PURCHASES BUDGET FOR SUGAR

**UNLIMITED DECADENCE CORPORATION**
**Direct Materials Purchases Budget, Darkly Decadent Candy Bar – Sugar**
**(in thousands)**
**Second Quarter 2009**

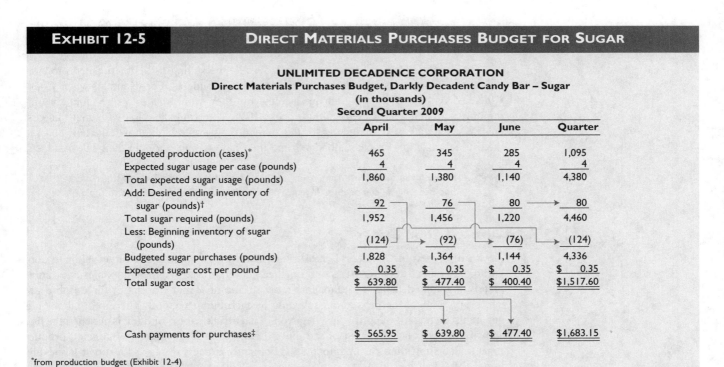

| | April | May | June | Quarter |
|---|---|---|---|---|
| Budgeted production (cases)* | 465 | 345 | 285 | 1,095 |
| Expected sugar usage per case (pounds) | 4 | 4 | 4 | 4 |
| Total expected sugar usage (pounds) | 1,860 | 1,380 | 1,140 | 4,380 |
| Add: Desired ending inventory of sugar (pounds)† | 92 | 76 | 80 | 80 |
| Total sugar required (pounds) | 1,952 | 1,456 | 1,220 | 4,460 |
| Less: Beginning inventory of sugar (pounds) | (124) | (92) | (76) | (124) |
| Budgeted sugar purchases (pounds) | 1,828 | 1,364 | 1,144 | 4,336 |
| Expected sugar cost per pound | $ 0.35 | $ 0.35 | $ 0.35 | $ 0.35 |
| Total sugar cost | $ 639.80 | $ 477.40 | $ 400.40 | $1,517.60 |
| Cash payments for purchases‡ | $ 565.95 | $ 639.80 | $ 477.40 | $1,683.15 |

*from production budget (Exhibit 12-4)
†1/15 of next month's expected sugar usage
‡Payments are made one month after credit purchases.

of sugar (4 pounds) needed to produce each case of candy. It bases the standard number of pounds of sugar needed per case on its engineering studies and production data from previous periods. The desired ending inventories of sugar used in this budget result from managers' decisions based on the same kinds of cost considerations (cost of carrying versus cost of not carrying inventories) that determine the desired finished goods inventory levels appearing in the production budget.

*What other similarities do you see between the direct materials purchases budget and the production budget?*

### Direct Materials Purchase Cost

Managers use anticipated direct materials purchase prices (which the company may obtain from its suppliers) to convert unit purchase requirements into direct materials purchase costs. Unlimited Decadence anticipates that it will pay $0.35 per pound of sugar. Multiplying the April budgeted sugar purchases of 1,828,000 pounds by $0.35 gives the direct materials purchases cost of $639,800. Managers then use the direct materials purchases cost to budget cash payments for direct materials purchases. The company's payment arrangement with its direct materials suppliers usually determines the timing of these payments. If Unlimited Decadence pays cash for sugar, for example, its cash payment each month for purchases of sugar equals the total sugar cost for that month. On the other hand, if Unlimited Decadence always pays for sugar on the thirtieth day after its purchases (with terms of n/30, as we assume in Exhibit 12-5),[3] the cash payment for sugar purchases each month approximately equals the total budgeted sugar cost for the previous month. For example, in May, the cash payment of $639,800 equals the total sugar cost for April.

[3]We assume that Unlimited Decadence's supplier offers no cash discounts. If there were cash discounts, Unlimited Decadence would make cash payments earlier, but these payments would be smaller because of the discounts.

*Look at the direct materials purchases budget again. Where did the beginning inventory and the ending inventory numbers for the quarter come from?*

Direct materials purchase costs can also affect the selling prices of finished products as well as future sales and direct materials purchases budgets. For example, when **Coca-Cola** and **Anheuser-Busch** companies found out they would have to pay more for aluminum cans, they raised their selling prices.[b] If the companies had known about this cost change when they were budgeting for the quarter, they would have shown the new costs in their direct materials purchases budgets and their new selling prices in their sales budgets.

*How do you think these companies' budgets would have been affected if their markets had been highly competitive? Why? What decisions would they have had to make?*

## Direct Labor Budget

As we discussed in Chapter 11, most manufacturing companies use direct labor to convert or assemble direct materials into finished goods, although some companies have completely automated factories. Managers must decide how many hours of direct labor are necessary to meet the production schedule in each budget period. The direct labor budget helps managers quantify this decision. The **direct labor budget** is a schedule that shows the hours and the cost of the direct labor required to meet the budgeted production. It also shows the cash payments the company expects to make for direct labor during each budget period.

To help you understand the concept of a direct labor budget, we illustrate a simple direct labor budget for Unlimited Decadence in Exhibit 12-6. The total hours of direct labor time required to meet each month's budgeted production of Darkly Decadent candy bars are computed by multiplying the month's budgeted production by the standard number of hours of direct labor needed to produce each unit of product. For example, to determine the amount of direct labor necessary for April's budgeted

**EXHIBIT 12-6 DIRECT LABOR BUDGET**

**UNLIMITED DECADENCE CORPORATION**
***Direct Labor Budget***
***(in thousands)***
***Second Quarter 2009***

| | April | May | June | Quarter |
|---|---|---|---|---|
| Budgeted production (cases)* | 465 | 345 | 285 | 1,095 |
| Direct labor time per case (hours per case) | 0.50 | 0.50 | 0.50 | 0.50 |
| Total direct labor hours required | 232.50 | 172.50 | 142.50 | 547.50 |
| Labor rate per hour | $ 12.00 | $ 12.00 | $ 12.00 | $ 12.00 |
| Budgeted labor cost | $2,790.00 | $2,070.00 | $1,710.00 | $6,570.00 |
| Add: Beginning wages payable balance† | 1,200.00 | 1,395.00 | 1,035.00 | 1,200.00 |
| Less: Ending wages payable balance† | (1,395.00) | (1,035.00) | (855.00) | (855.00) |
| Cash payments for direct labor | $2,595.00 | $2,430.00 | $1,890.00 | $6,915.00 |

*From production budget (Exhibit 12-4)
†Wages are paid two weeks after they are earned.

production (232,500 hours of labor), Unlimited Decadence's managers would multiply 465,000 cases (April's budgeted production) by 0.50 hours (the standard number of hours to produce a case of candy bars). Managers use these total direct labor hour requirements to help them anticipate the number of workers needed at various times of the year. Then they can make hiring and training plans and avoid costly overtime or production delays.

*When Techknits, Inc., the New York sweater manufacturer we mentioned in Chapter 11, computerized its looms, one person in the factory could run four looms instead of only one.[c] How do you think this change affected Techknits' direct labor budget?*

In Unlimited Decadence's direct labor budget, we assume that each case of Darkly Decadent candy bars requires one-half hour of direct labor time, and that the company pays all factory employees $12 per hour. These assumptions greatly simplify the illustration because manufacturing companies usually hire employees to perform a variety of skilled and unskilled direct labor operations at many different wage rates. Notice that we based the computation of total direct labor hours required on budgeted production (from the production budget in Exhibit 12-4) and that the total from the quarter is simply the sum of the amounts for the three months. Budgeted direct labor cost is computed by multiplying the total direct labor hour requirements by the wage rate per hour. For instance, Unlimited Decadence requires 232,500 total direct labor hours in April. Multiplying this by the labor rate of $12 per hour gives the budgeted direct labor cost for April ($2,790,000). The direct labor cost for a budget period may differ from the budgeted cash *payments* for direct labor for that same period. This happens whenever the period in which employees are paid differs from the budget period in which they worked. For example, Unlimited Decadence pays wages two weeks after its employees earn them. May's budgeted cash payment for direct labor consists of the last half of April's direct labor cost ($1,395,000) and the first half of May's direct labor cost ($1,035,000).

*In what month would Unlimited Decadence budget the cash payment for the other half of May's direct labor cost?*

Notice that the total cash payments for the quarter equal the sum of the cash payments for the three months in the quarter. Also notice that the beginning wages payable balance for the quarter is the same as the beginning wages payable balance for the *first month* of the quarter. The ending wages payable balance for the quarter is the same as the ending wages payable balance for the *last month* of the quarter.

*Look again at Unlimited Decadence's direct labor budget. Can you tell from the budget how much Unlimited Decadence budgeted for March's labor cost?*

## Factory Overhead Budget

All manufacturing companies incur overhead costs when they convert direct materials into finished goods. The **factory overhead budget** is a schedule showing estimates of all factory overhead costs and their related cash payments for each budget period. Managers base these factory overhead cost estimates on the production budget and on studies of the behavior of the various overhead costs, as we discussed in Chapter 11.

Exhibit 12-7 shows the factory overhead budget for Unlimited Decadence. Notice that we have separated fixed and variable overhead costs on this budget schedule. As you would expect, total variable costs fluctuate. Close examination reveals, in fact, that the budgeted variable cost totals for each month vary directly in proportion to changes in budgeted production levels. We show the variable cost per case of candy bars in parentheses in the variable costs section of the budget. (For instance, utilities costs are $0.05 per case.)

**EXHIBIT 12-7** **FACTORY OVERHEAD BUDGET**

**UNLIMITED DECADENCE CORPORATION**
*Factory Overhead Budget*
*(in thousands)*
*Second Quarter 2009*

| | April | May | June | Quarter |
|---|---|---|---|---|
| Budgeted production (cases)* | 465 | 345 | 285 | 1,095 |
| Variable overhead costs (rate): | | | | |
| Indirect labor ($.12 per case) | $ 55.80 | $ 41.40 | $ 34.20 | $ 131.40 |
| Indirect materials ($.08 per case) | 37.20 | 27.60 | 22.80 | 87.60 |
| Utilities ($.05 per case) | 23.25 | 17.25 | 14.25 | 54.75 |
| Other variable costs ($.07 per case) | 32.55 | 24.15 | 19.95 | 76.65 |
| Total variable costs ($.32 per case) | $148.80 | $110.40 | $ 91.20 | $ 350.40 |
| Fixed overhead costs: | | | | |
| Supervisory salaries | $114.00 | $114.00 | $114.00 | $ 342.00 |
| Depreciation of plant and equipment | 150.00 | 150.00 | 150.00 | 450.00 |
| Other fixed costs | 240.00 | 240.00 | 240.00 | 720.00 |
| Total fixed costs | $504.00 | $504.00 | $504.00 | $1,512.00 |
| Total factory overhead costs | $652.80 | $614.40 | $595.20 | $1,862.40 |
| Less: Depreciation of plant and equipment | (150.00) | (150.00) | (150.00) | (450.00) |
| Cash payments for factory overhead costs | $502.80 | $464.40 | $445.20 | $1,412.40 |

*From production budget (Exhibit 12-4)

However, fixed costs are the same in each month's budget. The fixed costs total $504,000 each month and consist of supervisory salaries, depreciation of plant and equipment, and other fixed costs.

Unlimited Decadence pays factory overhead costs (except for depreciation) in the period in which they are incurred. Recall from Chapter 5 that depreciation is an allocation of the cost (or, the difference between the original cost and the residual value) of plant and equipment to the periods of their use. There are cash flows associated with owning plant and equipment, but they are the payments associated with plant and equipment purchases (in the years that the company makes payments) and the cash receipts associated with selling or disposing of plant and equipment (in the years of disposal).[4] These cash flows do not correspond in amount in any period to the depreciation of the plant and equipment. Note that we have simply subtracted the depreciation expense ($150), which involves no corresponding cash flow, from the total factory overhead costs to determine the total monthly cash payments for factory overhead.

## Selling Expenses Budget

The selling expenses budget of a manufacturing company is developed in the same way as that of a retail company. A large company typically has more complicated budgets than does a small company, however. The selling expenses budget of a large company often shows sales-determined expenses separately from sales-determining expenses. **Sales-determined expenses** result from selling activities that are necessary to support the volume of budgeted sales. Managers estimate these expenses *after* they have developed the sales budget. For example, shipping expenses are sales-determined expenses. The estimated shipping expenses increase as projected sales increase. **Sales-determining expenses** result from selling activities that affect the sales volume. Managers must deliberately decide to

[4]A company includes these cash payments and receipts in its capital expenditures budget, which we will discuss in Chapter 20.

Where would Hershey's include the cost of this advertisement in its master budget?

implement the activities that generate sales-determining expenses. Sales-determining expenses *influence* the preparation of the sales budget. For example, Unlimited Decadence's advertising has an effect on the number of cases of candy bars that Unlimited Decadence sells. Therefore, advertising expenses are sales-determining expenses.

*Suppose Unlimited Decadence purchased network time for a commercial to be aired during the Super Bowl. What budget periods' sales do you think this advertising expense will influence? Why?*

Managers of a large company often spend a considerable amount of time and effort studying the factors that affect the sales volumes of its various products. Then they try to plan strategies to take advantage of those factors. In planning these strategies, they also consider general business and industry conditions, actions of competitors, and company policy.

Exhibit 12-8 shows Unlimited Decadence's selling expenses budget for the second quarter of the year 2009. Note that Unlimited Decadence has sales-determined shipping expenses of $0.30 per case *sold.* Notice also the similarity between this budget and that of Sweet Temptations (Exhibit 4-8).

## General and Administrative Expenses Budget

Like the selling expenses budget, the general and administrative expenses budget of a manufacturing company is developed in the same way as that of a retail company. However, a large company like Unlimited Decadence often groups and describes expenses by administrative activity or function. For example, expenses related to accounting, research and development, and legal activities might be shown separately. Such groupings are useful because they give managers an opportunity to review the commitment of resources to each function during the planning process. The groupings also provide a standard of comparison against which managers can evaluate the actual costs incurred in each activity or function. Exhibit 12-9 shows Unlimited Decadence's general and administrative expenses budget for the second quarter of the year 2009.

*How is this budget similar to that of Sweet Temptations (Exhibit 4-9)?*

Note that there are two "noncash" expenses (insurance and depreciation) that we did not include in the total cash payments for the second quarter of the year 2009. The reason we didn't include them is because Unlimited Decadence made (or will make) these cash payments in different time periods. It is common for a company to pay for some items before their costs are considered to be expenses. For example, a company may prepay insurance on its buildings and equipment. The $40,000 monthly insurance expense on Unlimited Decadence's general and administrative expenses budget reflects the expected "using up" of the insurance policy that it paid for earlier. Also, as we mentioned previously, it is uncommon for the cash payments associated with plant and equipment purchases to coincide with the depreciation of the plant and equipment.

**EXHIBIT 12-8 SELLING EXPENSES BUDGET**

**UNLIMITED DECADENCE CORPORATION**
***Selling Expenses Budget***
***(in thousands)***
***Second Quarter 2009***

| | April | May | June | Quarter |
|---|---|---|---|---|
| Budgeted sales (cases)* | 500 | 360 | 300 | 1,160 |
| Sales-determining expenses: | | | | |
| Advertising | $250 | $200 | $150 | $ 600 |
| Sales salaries | 225 | 225 | 225 | 675 |
| Other promotional efforts | 100 | — | — | 100 |
| Sales-determined expenses: | | | | |
| Shipping (variable at $.30 per case sold) | 150 | 108 | 90 | 348 |
| Total selling expenses | $725 | $533 | $465 | $1,723 |
| Cash payments for selling expenses† | $725 | $533 | $465 | $1,723 |

*From the sales budget (Exhibit 12-3)
†Cash payments will occur in the month of the expense.

**EXHIBIT 12-9** **GENERAL AND ADMINISTRATIVE EXPENSES BUDGET**

**UNLIMITED DECADENCE CORPORATION**
***General and Administrative Expenses Budget***
***(in thousands)***
***Second Quarter 2009***

| | April | May | June | Quarter |
|---|---|---|---|---|
| Accounting and clerical expenses | $201 | $201 | $ 201 | $ 603 |
| Administrative salaries | 134 | 134 | 134 | 402 |
| General expenses: | | | | |
| Insurance[*] | 40 | 40 | 40 | 120 |
| Property taxes[†] | 99 | 99 | 99 | 297 |
| Depreciation of office buildings and equipment | 83 | 83 | 83 | 249 |
| Total expenses | $557 | $557 | $ 557 | $1,671 |
| Schedule of cash payments: | | | | |
| Accounting and clerical expenses | $201 | $201 | $ 201 | $ 603 |
| Administrative salaries | 134 | 134 | 134 | 402 |
| Property taxes[†] | | | 1,188 | 1,188 |
| Total cash payments | $335 | $335 | $1,523 | $2,193 |

[*] The $40,000-per-month insurance expense is equal to the monthly reduction in the prepaid insurance account.
[†] Property taxes accrue each month and are paid in full in June each year.

## Capital Expenditures Budget

Adding to plant and equipment, replacing old machinery, remodeling or relocating office facilities, or developing a new product may involve large expenditures of cash. Such expenditures often result from a company's commitments to major programs or projects that may require several years to produce benefits for the company. For example, **Ford Motor Co.'s** automotive capital spending budget for 2006 was $7 billion, most of which was for new automotive development. Its new cars take five or six years to design.

Because of the cost and time requirements of major programs or projects, managers should not make capital expenditure commitments without a thorough and objective evaluation of the effect of the capital expenditures on the company's operations. Managers should also carefully plan the projects to be undertaken so that they will not interfere with the company's current operations. Such planning is aided by the capital expenditures budget. The **capital expenditures budget** is a set of schedules that shows the effects that each new project to be undertaken is expected to have on other master budget schedules. In this budget, managers use information gathered during project evaluations to show (1) the expected timing of project-related cash receipts and payments that affect the cash budget, (2) the costs of project-related assets to be acquired that affect the projected balance sheet, and (3) the project-related increases and decreases in factory overhead costs, selling expenses, general and administrative expenses, and perhaps sales that affect the budgets for those items as well as the projected income statement.

© CORBIS

How long do you think it took to design this vehicle?

An adequate illustration of a capital expenditures budget would unnecessarily complicate our discussion of the other budgets. However, the evaluation of proposals to invest company resources in long-term projects is important. Since Unlimited Decadence is planning no capital expenditures during the second quarter of the year 2009, we will postpone our discussion of the capital expenditures budget until Chapter 20 of Volume 2.

## Cash Budget (Projected Cash Flow Statement)

Remember from our Chapter 4 discussion that the cash budget helps managers anticipate the approach of cash shortages or excesses in time to avoid them. If managers expect temporary cash shortages to occur, they can provide potential lenders (such as banks) with the company's cash budget to show how the company will use borrowed cash and when the managers anticipate that the company will have enough cash to repay the loan. As soon as they know when to expect temporary cash excesses, managers can begin to identify temporary investments for this excess cash.

The cash budget may have three major sections: the operating activities section, the investing activities section, and the financing activities section.[5] The **operating activities section** [which is set up like the operating activities section (direct method) of the cash flow statement] summarizes the cash receipts and payments that managers expect to result from the company's planned operating activities. This section shows the net cash receipts (excess of operating receipts over operating payments) or the net cash payments (excess of payments over receipts) for each budget period. When the expected net cash receipts from operating activities is added to (or the net payments are deducted from) the period's beginning cash balance, the result is the expected ending cash balance from operating activities. For example, on Unlimited Decadence's cash budget (Exhibit 12-10), the May net cash receipts of $2,254,220 are added to May's beginning cash balance of $1,949,200 to get the anticipated ending cash balance from operating activities for May of $4,203,420. Notice that April's net cash *payment* of $72,250 is *subtracted* from April's beginning cash balance to get the expected ending cash balance from operating activities for April.

The **investing activities section** summarizes the cash transactions that managers expect to result from the company's investing activities. Normally, companies include here cash payments for the purchase of property, plant, and equipment as well as for the purchase of government securities and the stocks or bonds of other companies. They also include here cash receipts from the planned disposal of old property, plant, and equipment or from the expected sale of investments in stocks and bonds of other companies.

*Why do you think these cash receipts are included in the investing activities section?*

The net cash payments (receipts) from planned investment activities are subtracted from (added to) the anticipated ending cash balance from operating activities to arrive at the anticipated ending cash balance from operating and investing activities. If the anticipated ending cash balance from operating and investing activities is too low in any budget period, the company can arrange to borrow cash (a financing activity) or sell investments in time to avoid the cash shortage. If the balance is too high in any period, the company may plan to use the excess cash to repay loans taken in previous periods (another financing activity) or may invest its excess cash (as we discuss later).

The **financing activities section** shows the cash receipts and payments associated with planned financing activities, such as those we mentioned in the previous paragraph. This section includes cash receipts from borrowing money or from selling the company's own stock. It also includes cash payments to pay back loans or to repurchase the company's own stock.

*Why do you think these cash payments are included in the financing section?*

Adding the expected net financing receipts to (or deducting the net financing payments from) the anticipated cash balance from operating and investing activities gives the budgeted ending cash balance for the period. This ending cash balance is used as the cash balance for the projected balance sheet at the end of the period.

---

[5]Remember, a cash budget used for internal reporting (and sometimes used for external reporting) is similar to the cash flow statement for external reporting that we discussed in Chapter 8.

*What similarities and differences do you notice between a cash budget and the cash flow statement we discussed in Chapter 8?*

Exhibit 12-10 shows Unlimited Decadence's cash budget for the second quarter of the year 2009. Notice that except for the cash payment for income taxes, the operating activities section of the cash budget merely summarizes the receipts and payments computed in the company's previous budgets. The payment of income taxes must be based on the company's projected income statement. Notice in Exhibit 12-11 that we compute income tax

**EXHIBIT 12-10** **CASH BUDGET**

**UNLIMITED DECADENCE CORPORATION**
***Cash Budget***
***(in thousands)***
***Second Quarter 2009***

| | April | May | June | Quarter |
|---|---|---|---|---|
| Cash flows from operating activities: | | | | |
| Cash receipts from: | | | | |
| Sales[*] | $5,840.00 | $ 8,000.00 | $5,760.00 | $19,600.00 |
| Cash payments for: | | | | |
| Sugar purchases[†] | $ 565.95 | $ 639.80 | $ 477.40 | $ 1,683.15 |
| Other direct materials purchases[‡] | 1,188.50 | 1,343.58 | 1,002.54 | 3,534.62 |
| Direct labor[§] | 2,595.00 | 2,430.00 | 1,890.00 | 6,915.00 |
| Factory overhead[¶] | 502.80 | 464.40 | 445.20 | 1,412.40 |
| Selling expenses[**] | 725.00 | 533.00 | 465.00 | 1,723.00 |
| General and administrative expenses[††] | 335.00 | 335.00 | 1,523.00 | 2,193.00 |
| Income taxes[‡‡] | — | — | 473.48 | 473.48 |
| Total cash payments | $5,912.25 | $ 5,745.78 | $6,276.62 | $17,934.65 |
| Net cash receipts (payments) from operating activities | $ (72.25) | $ 2,254.22 | $ (516.62) | $ 1,665.35 |
| Add: Beginning cash balance | 1,021.45[§§] | 1,949.20 | 1,683.42 | 1,021.45 |
| Ending cash balance from operating activities | $ 949.20 | $ 4,203.42 | $1,166.80 | $ 2,686.80 |
| Cash flows from investing activities: | | | | |
| Cash payment for investment in capital stock | — | $(1,500.00) | — | $(1,500.00) |
| Net cash flow from investing activities | — | $(1,500.00) | — | $(1,500.00) |
| Ending cash balance from operating and investing activities | $ 949.20 | $ 2,703.42 | $1,166.80 | $ 1,186.80 |
| Cash flows from financing activities: | | | | |
| Cash receipts from bank loans | $1,000.00 | — | — | $ 1,000.00 |
| Cash payments for: | | | | |
| Repayment of loan | — | $(1,000.00) | — | (1,000.00) |
| Interest on loan[¶¶] | — | (20.00) | — | (20.00) |
| Net cash flow from financing activities | $1,000.00 | $(1,020.00) | — | $ (20.00) |
| Ending cash balance | $1,949.20 | $ 1,683.42 | $1,166.80 | $ 1,166.80 |

[*]From the sales budget (Exhibit 12-3)
[†]From the direct materials purchases budget (Exhibit 12-5)
[‡]From the other direct materials purchases budgets (not shown in this chapter)
[§]From the direct labor budget (Exhibit 12-6)
[¶]From the factory overhead budget (Exhibit 12-7)
[**]From the selling expenses budget (Exhibit 12-8)
[††]From the general and administrative expenses budget (Exhibit 12-9)
[‡‡]From the income statement (Exhibit 12-11)
[§§]From last quarter's balance sheet (Exhibit 12-12)
[¶¶]Although interest from borrowing is in the cash flows from financing activities section of the cash budget, it is shown in the cash flows from operating activities section of the cash flow statement.

expense to be $473,480. This is the same number we use for income tax *payments* in the cash budget for June because we are assuming that Unlimited Decadence pays income taxes at the end of each quarter for the income earned during the quarter.

Notice that Unlimited Decadence's cash budget shows a net cash payment of $72,250 from operating activities in April. This reduces the beginning cash balance of $1,021,450 to $949,200. Unlimited Decadence's management has adopted the policy of not allowing its cash balance to drop below $1 million at the end of any month, however. Hence, to have enough cash on hand, the company must acquire more cash. There are two major sources of additional cash: debt capital and equity capital.

### Debt Capital

**Debt capital** is money that a company borrows from creditors. This borrowed money, called the *principal,* must be paid back to the creditors. Furthermore, the company also must pay a specified amount of interest on the principal. This interest may take several forms:

1. A specific amount that the company pays at set intervals throughout the life of the loan
2. An amount computed on the unpaid balance and paid at the same time that the company makes partial payments on the loan
3. A set amount that the company pays all at once on the same date that it pays back the entire loan

Frequently a company signs a note payable for this debt, as we will discuss in Chapter 14.

### Equity Capital

**Equity capital** is money that a corporation brings in through the sale of the corporation's own stock (or, as we discussed in Chapter 4, through the contribution of cash to the company by the owner or owners, in the case of sole proprietorships and partnerships). A corporation can sell its own stock to current stockholders and/or others outside the corporation, who then become additional stockholders of the company. The corporation can use the money from the sale of this stock for many purposes. There is no obligation to pay it back. However, although corporations do not necessarily return the investments of owners, most pay dividends to stockholders as a return *on* their investments. Unlike debt capital, which requires a particular amount of interest to be paid at specific times, equity capital does not require the payment of dividends. We will discuss stocks and dividends more thoroughly in Chapter 24 of Volume 2.

### Obtaining Financing

In deciding whether to obtain financing through debt capital or equity capital, managers must consider several factors:

1. Whether they want the company to be obligated to a fixed cash payment (interest and principal)
2. How the interest rate on borrowed money compares with the company's anticipated dividend payments
3. Whether the current stockholders want to bring more stockholders into the company and, perhaps, share control of the company with them (meaning that the current stockholders would have relatively less "say" in the operations of the company and a smaller share of its income)

Because Unlimited Decadence's stockholders do not want to purchase more shares of Unlimited Decadence's stock or to share control of the company with new owners, Unlimited Decadence plans debt financing to cover this quarter's cash shortfalls. Unlimited

**"We need two hundred million bucks by Friday—any ideas?"**



Decadence has an arrangement with 2nd State Bank called a *line of credit,* which allows it to borrow up to $5 million, as needed, in even million-dollar increments. In other words, the amount of money borrowed by Unlimited Decadence at any time must be evenly divisible by $1 million. At no time can the total amount borrowed by Unlimited Decadence from 2nd State Bank exceed $5 million. Unlimited Decadence computes the loan's interest at the end of each month as 1% of the loan balance at the beginning of the month. Each time Unlimited Decadence borrows money, it takes out a loan (a note payable) at the beginning of the month in which it requires the money (in this case, the beginning of April). It pays back loans plus accumulated interest on the loans at the end of the first month in which it has enough cash, in excess of $1 million, to pay back the amount of the loan plus interest.

To meet its minimum cash balance policy, Unlimited Decadence must borrow $1 million at the beginning of April. Consistent with our earlier discussion, Unlimited Decadence shows this estimated April cash receipt from debt capital in the cash flows from financing activities section of its cash budget in Exhibit 12-10. This raises April's estimated ending cash balance (and May's beginning cash balance) to $1,949,200. When this beginning balance is added to the $2,254,220 estimated net cash receipts from May's operating activities, the projected ending cash balance from operating activities for May becomes $4,203,420.

### Repaying Debt and Interest

Once managers choose the type, amount, and timing of debt or equity financing, the cash budget provides information for planning either the repayment of the debt and the related interest or the payment of dividends. During periods of excess cash, managers will choose to pay back loans plus the interest that has accumulated on these loans. In the case of Unlimited Decadence's cash budget in Exhibit 12-10, since May's ending cash balance from operating activities of $4,203,420 is $3,203,420 greater than its required minimum ending cash balance of $1 million, Unlimited Decadence plans to repay its entire loan plus interest ($1,020,000) at the end of May. The $20,000 interest is two months' interest computed on the $1 million total loan balance carried through April and May. We will discuss short-term debt and long-term debt more thoroughly in Chapters 14 of this Volume and 22 of Volume 2 respectively.

### Investment of Excess Cash

After paying back its loan plus interest in May, Unlimited Decadence estimates that it will have $2,183,420 cash in excess of its desired minimum cash balance ($4,203,420 expected ending cash balance from operating activities − $1,020,000 planned repayment of bank loan plus interest − $1,000,000 minimum cash balance). In situations like this, where there is an expected excess of cash in a particular month, managers often will plan to "put this excess cash to work" earning interest or dividends for the company. So in May, Unlimited Decadence's managers tentatively plan to invest $1.5 million of the expected excess cash in low-risk capital stock. Notice in Exhibit 12-10 that Unlimited Decadence shows the $1,500,000 payment for the purchase of the stock in the cash flows from investing activities section of its cash budget.[6] Since its projected ending cash balance for June is above the desired minimum cash balance, Unlimited Decadence can plan to "hold" (not sell) its investment through June.

After summarizing its expected quarterly cash flows from operating activities, investing activities, and financing activities, Unlimited Decadence can estimate what its cash balance will be at the end of the second quarter. June's $1,166,800 expected ending cash balance will appear on Unlimited Decadence's projected balance sheet for June 30, 2009, as we show in Exhibit 12-12.

## Projected Income Statement

After generating all the previous budget schedules, managers develop a projected income statement to determine the company's profitability if it follows all its plans and if all the anticipated conditions occur. Exhibit 12-11 shows Unlimited Decadence's projected income statement for the second quarter of the year 2009. This statement is similar to Unlimited Decadence's *annual* income statement, which we discussed in Chapter 10, but with a few differences. Since Exhibit 12-11 shows a projected income statement, Unlimited Decadence computes its cost of goods sold directly on the statement. Because Unlimited Decadence is a manufacturing company, it computes its cost of finished goods available for sale ($14,684,700) by summing the beginning finished goods inventory ($1,500,000) from the end of the first quarter (March 31, 2009) balance sheet and the cost of goods manufactured this quarter ($4,752,300 direct materials used, $6,570,000 direct labor, and $1,862,400 factory overhead from the budget schedules). It then subtracts the ending finished goods inventory ($722,400) to determine its cost of goods sold ($13,962,300).

Since Unlimited Decadence is a corporation, it estimates its income tax expense by multiplying the expected income before income taxes ($1,183,700) by the anticipated 40% income tax rate. The amount of the income tax expense for the second quarter ($473,480) also appears in the cash budget for the second quarter (Exhibit 12-10). This is because we assume that Unlimited Decadence pays income taxes quarterly in the last month of the quarter in which income is earned. Unlimited Decadence's projected net income for the second quarter of 2009 is $710,220.

*Look at the cash budget again (Exhibit 12-10). Do you think the cash budget or the income statement should be developed first? Why?*

[6]Unlimited Decadence does not expect to receive a dividend this quarter. If it did expect to receive a dividend, it would include the estimated amount of the dividend as dividend revenue on its projected income statement, and as dividends received in the cash flows from operating activities section of the cash budget.

## Projected Balance Sheet

Finally, before implementing their plan of action, managers develop a projected balance sheet to show the resources that the company expects to have available to use and what it expects to owe creditors at the end of the quarter if it follows its plans and if anticipated conditions occur. Exhibit 12-12 shows Unlimited Decadence's *actual* balance sheet at the end of the first quarter of the year 2009 and its *projected* balance sheet for the end of the second quarter of 2009. The amounts on the projected balance sheet for Unlimited Decadence come from previous budget schedules and the previous quarter's actual balance sheet. After the second quarter of the year 2009, Unlimited Decadence expects to have $20,006,460 of total resources available to use and to owe creditors and employees a total of $2,096,240. The projected balance sheet completes the financial description of Unlimited Decadence's second-quarter plans.

**EXHIBIT 12-11 PROJECTED INCOME STATEMENT**

**UNLIMITED DECADENCE CORPORATION**
***Projected Income Statement***
***(in thousands)***
***Second Quarter 2009***

| | | | |
|---|---|---|---|
| Sales revenue | | | $18,560.00* |
| Cost of goods sold | | | |
| Beginning finished goods inventory (125 cases at $12/case) | | $ 1,500.00† | |
| Add: Cost of goods manufactured (1,095 cases): | | | |
| Direct materials used ($4.34 × 1,095) | $4,752.30‡ | | |
| Direct labor | 6,570.00§ | | |
| Factory overhead | 1,862.40¶ | | |
| Total cost of goods manufactured | | 13,184.70 | |
| Cost of finished goods available for sale | | $14,684.70 | |
| Less: Ending finished goods inventory | | (722.40)** | |
| Cost of goods sold | | | (13,962.30) |
| Gross profit | | | $ 4,597.70 |
| Operating expenses | | | |
| Selling expenses | | $ 1,723.00†† | |
| General and administrative expenses | | 1,671.00‡‡ | |
| Total operating expenses | | | (3,394.00) |
| Operating income | | | $ 1,203.70 |
| Other items | | | |
| Interest expense | | | (20.00)§§ |
| Income before taxes | | | $ 1,183.70 |
| Income tax expense | | | (473.48)¶¶ |
| Net income | | | $ 710.22 |

*From the sales budget (Exhibit 12-3)
†From last quarter's ending balance sheet
‡From the direct materials budgets (Exhibit 12-5) and other direct materials schedules not shown in this chapter
§From the direct labor budget (Exhibit 12-6)
¶From the factory overhead budget (Exhibit 12-7)
**[60 cases (from Exhibit 12-4) × $12.04]. Finished goods manufactured during the quarter are expected to cost $12.04 (rounded) per case.
††From the selling expenses budget (Exhibit 12-8)
‡‡From the general and administrative expenses budget (Exhibit 12-9)
§§Interest expense is $20 (1% × $1,000 × 2 months).
¶¶Income tax expense has been estimated based on a 40% income tax rate.

**EXHIBIT 12-12 ACTUAL AND PROJECTED BALANCE SHEETS**

**UNLIMITED DECADENCE CORPORATION**
***Balance Sheet***
***(in thousands)***
***March 31, 2009***

| | | |
|---|---|---|
| **Assets** | | |
| Current assets | | |
| Cash | $1,021.45 | |
| Accounts receivable | 5,840.00 | |
| Raw materials inventory | 134.54 | |
| Finished goods inventory | 1,500.00 | |
| Prepaid insurance | 840.00 | |
| Total current assets | | $ 9,335.99 |
| Property, plant, and equipment | | |
| Plant and equipment (net) | $6,408.00 | |
| Office buildings and equipment (net) | 5,301.46 | |
| Total property, plant, and equipment | | 11,709.46 |
| Total Assets | | $21,045.45 |
| **Liabilities** | | |
| Current liabilities | | |
| Accounts payable | $1,754.45 | |
| Wages payable | 1,200.00 | |
| Property taxes payable | 891.00 | |
| Total Liabilities | | $ 3,845.45 |
| **Stockholders' Equity** | | |
| Common stock, $3 par | $3,600.00 | |
| Additional paid-in capital | 4,540.00 | |
| Contributed capital | | $ 8,140.00 |
| Retained earnings | | 9,060.00 |
| Total Stockholders' Equity | | $17,200.00 |
| Total Liabilities and Stockholders' Equity | | $21,045.45 |

*continued*

## TECHNOLOGY AND BUDGETING

As you probably have observed, the budgeting process involves plenty of "number crunching." During our discussion of this process, you also should have observed how the numbers within and among budgets are interrelated. It is common for managers to review their budgets, notice a problem, and go "back to the drawing board" to refine the budget. But changing any aspect of the budget causes other numbers to change also (sort of a "domino effect"). Luckily, technological developments have made this process easier and much less time-consuming, and also have minimized errors. Many companies use spreadsheet programs, such as Excel, to simplify their budgeting processes. These programs take into account the interrelationships among the budget numbers. When managers change a number in a budget, spreadsheet programs automatically change the other numbers that are affected by the initial change.

Many other companies use their enterprise resource planning (ERP) systems as budgeting and planning tools. Remember from Chapter 10 that an ERP system involves integrated computer software that allows managers to "pick and choose" data from an integrated database that is relevant to particular activities or decisions. Since an ERP sys-

**EXHIBIT 12-12 ACTUAL AND PROJECTED BALANCE SHEETS—CONTINUED**

**UNLIMITED DECADENCE CORPORATION**
***Projected Balance Sheet***
***(in thousands)***
***June 30, 2009***

| | | |
|---|---|---|
| **Assets** | | |
| Current assets | | |
| Cash | $1,166.80* | |
| Marketable securities | 1,500.00† | |
| Accounts receivable | 4,800.00‡ | |
| Raw materials inventory | 86.80§ | |
| Finished goods inventory | 722.40¶ | |
| Prepaid insurance | 720.00** | |
| Total current assets | | $ 8,996.00 |
| Property, plant, and equipment | | |
| Plant and equipment (net) | $5,958.00†† | |
| Office buildings and equipment (net) | 5,052.46‡‡ | |
| Total property, plant, and equipment | | 11,010.46 |
| Total Assets | | $20,006.46 |
| **Liabilities** | | |
| Current liabilities | | |
| Accounts payable | $1,241.24§§ | |
| Wages payable | 855.00¶¶ | |
| Total Liabilities | | $ 2,096.24 |
| **Stockholders' Equity** | | |
| Common stock, $3 par | $3,600.00 | |
| Additional paid-in capital | 4,540.00 | |
| Contributed capital | | $ 8,140.00 |
| Retained earnings | | 9,770.22*** |
| Total Stockholders' Equity | | $17,910.22 |
| Total Liabilities and Stockholders' Equity | | $20,006.46 |

*From the cash budget (Exhibit 12-10)
†From the cash budget, investment in stock (Exhibit 12-10)
‡From the sales budget (Exhibit 12-3)
§From the raw materials purchases budget for sugar (Exhibit 12-5) and other direct materials budgets not shown in this chapter
¶From the projected income statement (Exhibit 12-11)
**$840 from beginning balance sheet minus $120 from the general and administrative expenses budget (Exhibit 12-9)
††$6,408 book value from beginning balance sheet minus $450 depreciation from factory overhead budget (Exhibit 12-7)
‡‡$5,301.46 book value from the beginning balance sheet minus $249 depreciation from the general and administrative expenses budget (Exhibit 12-9)
§§$400.40 from the direct materials purchases budget (Exhibit 12-5) and $840.84 other direct materials (budget not shown)
¶¶From the direct labor budget (Exhibit 12-6)
***$9,060 beginning retained earnings plus $710.22 net income minus $0 dividends

tem warehouses an integrated accounting system, the data necessary for budgeting and planning (and the resulting budget schedules) can be accessed by all budget participants during the budgeting process, allowing for greater coordination among the employees working on different parts of the master budget. **Owens Corning**, for example, recently implemented an ERP system from **SAP** that consolidated 200-plus different budgeting systems into fewer than ten. This resulted in the elimination of multiple data inputs and shortened the budget process.

Some companies are beginning to budget on the web. For instance, **Alfa Laval**, a Swedish manufacturer of industrial processing equipment, developed its own web budgeting application from scratch. The result is that the installation and maintenance of the system is fast and easy, and the web provides more employees access to the budgeting and planning process.

The use of technology in budgeting allows a company's managers to spend less time "crunching" numbers. This allows them to spend more time monitoring, analyzing, and reacting to developments in and around the company in a timely manner.

## RESPONSIBILITY CENTERS

A company uses the budgets we just discussed to provide a financial description of its plans. In addition, the information contained in these budgets can also be used to evaluate managers' performances. That is, after the budget period is over, the company can compare its *actual* revenues, costs, and profit with its *expected* revenues, costs, and profit from its various budgets to see how closely the company followed its plans.

A large company usually separates its operations into distinct responsibility centers for performance evaluation. A **responsibility center** is an identifiable portion or segment of a company's operations, the activities of which are the responsibility of a particular manager. Depending on the decision-making authority of that manager, a responsibility center may be evaluated as a cost center, a revenue center, a profit center, or an investment center.

A **cost center** is a responsibility center in which the manager who is responsible for its activities has decision-making authority over only the level of costs it incurs. The cost center manager has no influence over the amount of revenue ultimately received by the company or the level of investment in property, plant, and equipment used in operations. Because of this, a company evaluates a cost center manager by comparing the cost center's budgeted costs with its actual costs. For example, the foreman of a small machine shop in a large manufacturing company might be evaluated as a cost center manager. This approach is used because the foreman has no authority to influence the amount of revenue earned by (or investment made in) the machine shop, although the foreman's decisions affect the daily costs of the machine shop.

A **revenue center** (usually a sales department or branch) is a responsibility center in which the manager who has responsibility for its activities has decision-making authority over its revenues. The revenue center manager generally has no control over the costs incurred by the company or the level of investment in the property, plant, and equipment used in the revenue center's operations. For example, managers of the sales branch offices of a large manufacturing company make decisions about how to sell the product the company manufactures, but they have no control of the costs of manufacturing the product they sell or the investment in the equipment (e.g., salespersons' cars) used in the selling activities. A company evaluates the manager of a revenue center by comparing the center's actual revenues with its budgeted revenues.

A **profit center** is a responsibility center in which the manager has decision-making authority over both costs and revenues of a branch, division, or segment of a company. A company evaluates the manager of a profit center by comparing the center's budgeted profit with its actual profit. Decisions affecting revenues, such as which orders to accept and which prices to charge, affect profit. Decisions affecting costs also affect profit. Therefore profit is a convenient summary measure that a company can use to evaluate the performance of a manager who can control both costs and revenues by the decisions he or she makes.

An **investment center** is a responsibility center in which the manager has decision-making authority over costs, revenues, and the level of investment in property, plant, and equipment the center uses in its operations. A company sometimes can evaluate the manager of an investment center by judging the manager's decisions affecting the center's investment in plant and equipment separately from the manager's decisions affecting costs and revenues. More often, however, the manager's performance is evaluated using some comprehensive measure affected by all of the manager's decisions. A company commonly uses the ratio of profit earned by the center to the average investment in the center (which is sometimes called *return on average investment*) to evaluate the manager of an investment center.

Whichever type of responsibility center a company uses for a particular department or division, it must be certain that the manager has the *authority* to make decisions about the costs, revenues, or investments for which the manager is responsible. This concept is referred to as "having authority commensurate with responsibility." In the next section, we will discuss the use of flexible budgets and budget information in the evaluation of a cost center manager.

## FLEXIBLE BUDGETS

5 If a company's actual sales are different from its budgeted sales (or actual production is different from budgeted production) for the same time period, how can managers meaningfully evaluate how well the company met its cost goals?

One of the benefits of budgeting is that it provides a benchmark against which managers of a company can measure the results of actual activities to see how well the company met its goals. For a cost center, this comparison is typically quantified in a cost report. A cost report usually lists the budgeted costs, the actual costs incurred, and the differences between them. Such reports are most meaningful when the budgeted costs are developed to show the amounts expected to occur at the actual activity level attained. For example, it would be meaningful to compare the actual manufacturing costs incurred in producing 500,000 cases of candy bars during a period with the costs expected at a production level of 500,000 cases of candy bars. It would be less useful to compare them with the expenses expected at the production level of 465,000 cases of candy bars budgeted before the period began. A **flexible budget** is a cost or expense budget that shows expected costs or expenses at various activity levels.

For example, Exhibit 12-13 shows a flexible budget for Unlimited Decadence's manufacturing costs. Note in this exhibit how the variable manufacturing costs (direct materials, direct labor, and variable factory overhead) vary in proportion to production volume at the variable cost rates we previously assumed.

Recall that in the direct materials purchases budget (Exhibit 12-5) we assumed that each case of Darkly Decadent candy bars requires 4 pounds of sugar costing \$0.35 per pound. Thus each case requires \$1.40 of sugar. We also assumed that each case requires \$2.94 of other direct materials, for a total direct material cost of \$4.34 per case. Similarly, each case (Exhibit 12-6) requires \$6 of direct labor cost (1/2 hour at \$12 per hour). The factory overhead budget in Exhibit 12-7 shows the variable factory overhead cost rates per case of Darkly Decadent candy bars manufactured. Note that the fixed factory overhead costs do not vary with production volume, however. We illustrate the use of cost reports next using data from Unlimited Decadence's flexible manufacturing cost budget (Exhibit 12-13).

Suppose that the president of Unlimited Decadence wants to evaluate the performance of the manager of the company's manufacturing operations (a cost center) for the month of April 2009, which we now assume has just passed. The basis of the performance evaluation will be a comparison of actual and budgeted manufacturing costs for April. In this comparison, the president wants to include the cost of direct materials, direct labor, and factory overhead. The company actually produced 500,000 cases of candy instead of the 465,000 cases it had budgeted earlier. Assuming the actual costs shown in Exhibit 12-14, the president prepares the *erroneous* manufacturing cost report that we present in that exhibit.

As you might expect from looking at this cost report, the president was not pleased. Many of the actual costs exceeded the April budget, and the total actual costs appear to be greater than the total expected costs by \$298,800! However, the president would be mistaken in believing that the manager of the company's manufacturing operations has not kept the manufacturing costs under control.

The problem with the president's report is that it compares actual costs incurred in April, costs spent in producing 500,000 cases of candy bars, with April's original planning budget, which was based on the budgeted production of only 465,000 cases of candy bars. If he thinks about it for a minute, the president shouldn't be surprised at the higher actual costs. It makes sense that costs would be higher when the company produces more cases of candy bars. Since the original production budget (Exhibit 12-4) called for the production of 465,000 cases of candy bars in April, the direct materials cost, direct labor

**EXHIBIT 12-13 FLEXIBLE MANUFACTURING COST BUDGET**

**UNLIMITED DECADENCE CORPORATION**
***Flexible Cost Budget***
***(in thousands)***

| | Production Volume (Cases) | | | |
|---|---|---|---|---|
| | **200** | **300** | **400** | **500** |
| Direct materials ($4.34/case) | $ 868.00 | $1,302.00 | $1,736.00 | $2,170.00 |
| Direct labor ($6/case) | 1,200.00 | 1,800.00 | 2,400.00 | 3,000.00 |
| Factory overhead | | | | |
| Variable: | | | | |
| Indirect labor ($.12/case) | 24.00 | 36.00 | 48.00 | 60.00 |
| Indirect materials ($.08/case) | 16.00 | 24.00 | 32.00 | 40.00 |
| Utilities ($.05/case) | 10.00 | 15.00 | 20.00 | 25.00 |
| Other ($.07/case) | 14.00 | 21.00 | 28.00 | 35.00 |
| Fixed: | | | | |
| Supervisory salaries | 114.00 | 114.00 | 114.00 | 114.00 |
| Depreciation | 150.00 | 150.00 | 150.00 | 150.00 |
| Other | 240.00 | 240.00 | 240.00 | 240.00 |
| Total manufacturing costs | $2,636.00 | $3,702.00 | $4,768.00 | $5,834.00 |

cost, and factory overhead costs were estimated for that production level. The result is the misleading comparison in Exhibit 12-14.

We can correct the cost report, and make a meaningful cost comparison, by adjusting April's budget to show the costs expected to be incurred in producing 500,000 cases of candy bars. The flexible budget for manufacturing costs that we show in Exhibit 12-13 provides the budgeted cost information for the production level of *500,000* cases of candy bars. We used this budgeted information in the corrected manufacturing cost re-

**EXHIBIT 12-14 ERRONEOUS MANUFACTURING COST REPORT**

**UNLIMITED DECADENCE CORPORATION**
***Manufacturing Cost Report***
***(in thousands)***

| | **Original April Budget** | **Actual Costs** | **Favorable (Unfavorable) Difference** |
|---|---|---|---|
| Production (cases) | 465 cases | 500 cases | |
| Direct materials ($4.34/case) | $2,018.10 | $2,071.90 | $ (53.80) |
| Direct labor ($6/case) | 2,790.00 | 3,100.00 | (310.00) |
| Factory overhead | | | |
| Variable: | | | |
| Indirect labor ($.12/case) | 55.80 | 42.00 | 13.80 |
| Indirect materials ($.08/case) | 37.20 | 18.00 | 19.20 |
| Utilities ($.05/case) | 23.25 | 14.00 | 9.25 |
| Other ($.07/case) | 32.55 | 12.00 | 20.55 |
| Fixed: | | | |
| Supervisory salaries | 114.00 | 114.00 | — |
| Depreciation | 150.00 | 150.00 | — |
| Other | 240.00 | 237.80 | 2.20 |
| Total manufacturing costs | $5,460.90 | $5,759.70 | $(298.80) |

**EXHIBIT 12-15 CORRECTED MANUFACTURING COST REPORT**

**UNLIMITED DECADENCE CORPORATION**
***Manufacturing Cost Report***
***(in thousands)***

| | Adjusted April Budget | Actual Costs | Favorable (Unfavorable) Difference |
|---|---|---|---|
| Production (cases) | 500 cases | 500 cases | |
| Direct materials ($4.34/case) | $2,170.00 | $2,071.90 | $98.10 |
| Direct labor ($6/case) | 3,000.00 | 3,100.00 | (100.00) |
| Factory overhead | | | |
| Variable: | | | |
| Indirect labor ($.12/case) | 60.00 | 42.00 | 18.00 |
| Indirect materials ($.08/case) | 40.00 | 18.00 | 22.00 |
| Utilities ($.05/case) | 25.00 | 14.00 | 11.00 |
| Other ($.07/case) | 35.00 | 12.00 | 23.00 |
| Fixed: | | | |
| Supervisory salaries | 114.00 | 114.00 | — |
| Depreciation | 150.00 | 150.00 | — |
| Other | 240.00 | 237.80 | 2.20 |
| Total manufacturing costs | $5,834.00 | $5,759.70 | $74.30 |

port in Exhibit 12-15. When April's actual costs are subtracted from the correct budgeted costs, the president has a useful cost comparison for evaluating the manager's performance regarding April's manufacturing activity.

Notice that the restatement of Unlimited Decadence's manufacturing cost budget required the adjustment of only the variable manufacturing costs. The fixed costs are expected to be the same at either production level. Note also how the cost comparison presents a very different picture of performance. The revised manufacturing cost report shows total actual costs to be *lower* than total expected costs by $74,300, a *favorable* difference.

The idea of basing cost comparisons on flexible budgets adjusted to show expected costs at the actual activity level attained is an important one for evaluating costs. Using the flexible budget in this way makes the differences computed between budgeted and actual costs calculated in cost reports more meaningful. These differences can suggest possible areas of the company's operations that may need attention, such as an inexperienced worker who uses direct materials inefficiently or a machine that needs replacement. We will discuss the evaluation of differences between expected (standard) costs and actual costs in Chapter 17 of Volume 2.

*Look at the revised manufacturing cost report again (Exhibit 12-15). How might you explain the fact that actual direct labor costs were higher than the costs budgeted for the 500,000 cases produced?*

## BUSINESS ISSUES AND VALUES

**6** How do budgets affect the business decisions that employees make?

The master budget provides information that helps managers see the financial consequences of their planning decisions (if everything goes according to plan) before they implement those decisions. However, for everything to go according to plan, managers also must consider how their planning decisions influence the behavior of the people who will implement those plans.

Budgets can motivate employees to work toward the company's goals and can help them feel a sense of achievement when they achieve those goals. When the production supervisor at Unlimited Decadence completes production of Darkly Decadent candy bars on schedule and within budgeted costs, both she and her boss will be pleased.

On the other hand, budgets also can motivate employees to participate in activities that may be contrary to the company's goals, although these employees typically do not intend for these activities to undermine the company's goals. This may result in **suboptimization**, a condition in which the company earns less profit than it is capable of earning. For example, a problem can occur when a manager's performance evaluation (or compensation) is based on how well he or she keeps costs within the budget. The message the manager gets from the budget is that actual costs should not be more than budgeted (no matter what!). When this is the case, some managers will postpone necessary expenditures so their departments will "look better" when the actual performance of the department is compared with the budget. This practice of postponing necessary expenditures can hurt the company in the long run. For example, Hasty Transfer Company, with whom Unlimited Decadence contracts to ship candy to Sweet Temptations and other retail stores around the country, must periodically have its delivery trucks serviced. Failure to perform routine maintenance on these trucks could cause expensive repair problems in the future and could delay future shipments. If its customers use a different carrier in the meantime, Hasty may permanently lose their business. As you can see, a manager who skips maintenance on the trucks during the current budget period in order to stay within the budget may cause Hasty Transfer Company much bigger problems in the future.

Another, more colorful, example of behavior being motivated by the *perceived* message involves Custer's defeat at Little Bighorn, a defeat partially caused by his inaccurate assessment of the Indians' numbers.[d] U.S. Indian agents' profits were tied to the number of Indians on the reservations: the more Indians on the reservations, the greater were the agents' profits. Any agent who reported a decrease in the Indian population took a bite out of his own paycheck. Therefore, as you might expect, the agents were reluctant to report decreases in the numbers (even though thousands of Indians had fled the reservations). Custer assumed, from the reports of the agents, that the Indians were still residing on the reservations rather than joining forces with Sitting Bull, Crazy Horse, and Gall. Consequently, he grossly underestimated the strength of his enemies and, well, the rest is history.

*How do you think the Indian agents' compensation might have been restructured to cause a better outcome?*

When companies "roll over" their budgets from year to year (that is, last year's budgets become the starting point for this year's budgeting process), upper-level managers may be tempted to reduce this year's budget of a department that spent less money last year than it budgeted. Besides discouraging employees by reducing the resources they have to work with, the threat of a reduced budget usually causes employees to go on a last-minute "shopping spree," increasing end-of-budget-period expenditures in an effort to "hang on to" future resources (sometimes referred to as "use it or lose it").

*How do you think this type of last-minute spending might sabotage the company's goals?*

Unfortunately, sometimes managers' efforts backfire when they try to motivate employees through budgets. For example, sometimes managers set budget goals at a level that makes these goals too difficult to accomplish. When employees recognize that they cannot attain the goals that managers have set for them, they sometimes quit trying to attain those goals. Also, sometimes efforts to be fair can backfire. Departmental budgets may contain costs for activities that result in benefits for the department but over which the department manager has no control. For example, suppose Unlimited Decadence's marketing budget contains the same amount of air-conditioning costs that every other department's budget contains, even though the company has a central air-conditioning system that is used mostly to keep the kitchen-hot factory relatively cool. If Unlimited Decadence's president measures managers' performances against their budgets, a high electric bill for the company could reflect negatively on the marketing manager's performance, even though he had no control over the high air-conditioning costs. This situation could lower the manager's morale.

*Which would you prefer: your parents impose a budget on you for a week's vacation, or you participate with them in setting your vacation budget? Why?*

To help keep morale high, and to get better budget information, many companies use a participative budgeting process. **Participative budgeting** is budgeting in which department and division managers or teams participate with upper-level managers in the planning decisions that determine the goals and resource commitments for the activities of their departments, divisions, or teams. Upper-level company managers typically approach this process by providing mid- or lower-level managers or teams with a statement of company goals and with information about the availability of resources. A statement of company goals indicates to the budget participants the direction in which upper-level managers want the company to move. Department and division managers or teams use this information to set department, division, or team goals and to determine what resources would help them move toward the achievement of these goals. With participative budgeting, all departments, divisions, and teams, through their own goals and resources, do their part to help the company achieve the goals of upper-level managers. This situation—where department, division, or team goals support the company goals—is called **goal congruence**.

After determining goals, managers or team coordinators supply upper-level managers with information about the resource requirements necessary for each of their areas to meet these goals. Upper-level managers then review the goals and resource requirements for all areas of the company. Next, they either allocate the resources to the departments, divisions, or teams or ask them to refine and resubmit goals and resource requirements. Usually there is some "back and forth" between the areas and upper-level managers. This occurs because goals need to be refined and because often the total budget requests exceed the company's available resources.

Participative budgeting helps managers at all levels make planning decisions through this exchange of information. It helps managers arrive at decisions that complement each other and that aid the company in reaching the stated goals, and it ensures that different departments, divisions, teams, and levels of managers are aware of each other's plans and decisions.

In most large companies, budgeting is the responsibility of a budget committee, which is usually composed of representative managers of the functional areas of the company as well as other individuals affected by the budget. Having a budget committee can improve the effectiveness of the participative budgeting process by bringing these diverse individuals together to exchange information, to settle differences, to allocate resources based on the information they bring to the meeting, and to make other decisions. Having a budget committee can also improve the efficiency of the budgeting process by eliminating the time required by the "back and forth" process we just described.

Managers' participation on a budget committee takes on even more significance when a company operates in more than one country. Since countries' political, economic, and legal environments vary, communication and coordination among managers in different countries becomes more complicated. Think about how much communication and coordination must occur among the parts, assembly, and sales departments of a company. How can the parts department know how many parts to purchase or manufacture without knowing how many units will be assembled? And how can the assembly department know how many units to assemble without knowing projected sales? Now, picture **Ford Motor Co.**, with auto-parts plants in China, an assembly plant in Poland, and a sales office in Vietnam. In addition to handling language differences, the managers of these offices and factories must be prepared to change their plans and budgets when conditions change in these countries. For example, political unrest in Poland could cause delays in shipments of parts into the country or of automobiles out of the country.

*Which of Ford's budgets do you think would be affected by delays in shipments? How do you think the budgets would be affected?*

As you can see, a budget can "look great on paper" but not have the effects managers intended. The improper use of budgets can cause a company to lose the potential benefits of budgeting. Therefore, great care must be used in the budgeting process. A company can use participative budgeting and budget committees to improve goal congruence, coordination, and communication within the company. The planning and decision making that occur in the budget process require more than just consideration of the numbers. Managers must take into account how they will use the budgets and also how the budgets will affect the company's employees.

## SUMMARY

At the beginning of the chapter we asked you several questions. During the chapter, we asked you to STOP and answer some other questions to build your knowledge about specific issues. Be sure you answered these additional questions. Below are the questions from the beginning of the chapter, with a brief summary of the key points relating to the answers. Use your creative and critical thinking skills to expand on these key points to develop more complete answers to the questions and to determine what other questions you have that might lead you to learn more about the issues.

### 1 What are the similarities and differences between a large company's master budget and that of an entrepreneurial company?

A large company and an entrepreneurial (small) company budget for the same reasons. Both use sales budgets, purchases budgets, selling expenses budgets, general and administrative expenses budgets, cash budgets, projected income statements, and projected balance sheets. Generally, both large and small companies use similar structures for these budgets. However, a large company's selling expenses budget often shows sales-determined expenses separately from sales-determining expenses. Also, a large company's general and administrative expenses budget often shows expenses grouped by administrative activity or function. A large company often plans large programs or projects and quantifies them in a capital expenditures budget.

### 2 What are the similarities and differences between a manufacturing company's master budget and that of a retail company?

A manufacturing company has all of the budgets that a retail company has. However, a manufacturing company's purchases budget addresses the purchase of direct materials rather than the purchase of goods for resale. A manufacturing company develops additional budgets because it makes the products it sells. These additional budgets include the production budget, direct labor budget, and factory overhead budget.

### 3 How is a manufacturing company's operating cycle different from that of a retail company?

A retail company's operating cycle is the average time it takes the company to use cash to acquire goods for resale, to sell them to customers, and then to collect cash from the customers for the sale. A manufacturing company's operating cycle is the average time it takes the company to use cash to acquire direct materials to use in manufacturing goods, to convert these direct materials into finished goods, to sell these goods to customers, and then to collect cash from the customers for the sale. Although the operating cycles of these two types of companies are similar (the time involved from using cash to purchase finished products or direct materials through collecting cash from the customers for the sale of products), the difference between the two is the manufacturing company's conversion of the purchased materials into finished goods.

### 4 Is there a strategy a manufacturing company can use to complete its budget?

Yes, the strategy a manufacturing company can use to complete its budget is similar to that used by a retail company. The budgeting process for a manufacturing company begins with the sales budget because product sales affect all other company activities. By gathering various types of information, such as past sales data, knowledge about customer needs, industry trends, economic forecasts, and new technological developments, managers of a manufacturing company estimate the amount of inventory to be sold in each budget period. The managers plan cash collections from sales by examining the company's credit-granting policies.

After budgeting sales, managers of the manufacturing company determine the number of each of the company's products that it must manufacture in order to meet the planned sales and keep on hand a desired inventory of finished goods. Once the managers have forecasted production, they plan the amount and timing of direct materials purchases. To budget these purchases, the managers examine the costs associated with direct materials purchases and storage as well as the costs associated with not carrying enough inventory. They also consider forecasted production and the company's policy on direct materials inventory levels. After budgeting direct materials purchases, the managers plan the cash payments for these purchases by reviewing the payment agreements between the company and its suppliers.

Managers also estimate the amount of direct labor time and cost necessary to achieve the budgeted production level. They then plan the cash payments for the wages and salaries of the factory workers, basing these estimates on the agreed-upon wages for the workers and on the company's payroll schedule. The managers also use budgeted production to estimate the company's factory overhead costs. These costs may be based on agreements with indirect materials suppliers, agreed-upon wages and salaries, and past overhead costs. The managers then budget the company's selling and general and administrative expenses.

To budget all costs (expenses), the managers first must determine the behaviors of the costs (expenses). They budget fixed expenses by evaluating previous fixed expenses and then adjusting them (if necessary) according to the plans for the coming time period. They budget variable expenses by first observing what activity causes these expenses to vary, and then computing the total expenses by multiplying the cost per unit of activity by the activity level. The managers budget the cash payments for these expenses by reviewing the company's policy on the payment of expenses.

The managers then develop the cash budget, the projected income statement, and the projected balance sheet. The information for developing the cash budget comes from the other previously prepared budgets, as does the information for creating the projected income statement. The information for developing the balance sheet comes from previously developed schedules, the projected income statement, and the previous balance sheet.

### 5 If a company's actual sales are different from its budgeted sales (or actual production is different from budgeted production) for the same time period, how can managers meaningfully evaluate how well the company met its cost goals?

Managers use flexible budgets and cost reports to evaluate how well the company met its goals (as presented in the budget). Flexible budgets show expected costs at various activity levels, so if the actual activity level is different from the expected activity level, managers know what costs should have been at the actual activity level. Then, any differences between the costs budgeted and the actual costs for the actual activity level can suggest possible areas of the company's operations that may need attention.

### 6 How do budgets affect the business decisions that employees make?

Because a company uses budgets as one way to communicate to employees the company's goals and the activities needed to achieve them, managers must be sure that the budgets convey the proper messages. Employees behave in ways that they perceive will benefit them and that will, at the same time, achieve the goals of the company as communicated in the budget. But if the budget, or budget system, conveys the wrong message, employees are likely to act on the message they receive, which may not be in the best interest of the company. To maximize goal congruence through better communication, a company can use participative budgeting and a budget committee.

## Key Terms

**capital expenditures budget** *(p. 389)*
**cost center** *(p. 398)*
**debt capital** *(p. 392)*
**direct labor budget** *(p. 384)*
**direct materials purchases budget** *(p. 382)*
**equity capital** *(p. 392)*
**factory overhead budget** *(p. 385)*
**financing activities section** *(p. 390)*
**flexible budget** *(p. 399)*
**goal congruence** *(p. 403)*
**investing activities section** *(p. 390)*
**investment center** *(p. 398)*
**operating activities section** *(p. 390)*
**operating cycle** *(p. 378)*
**operating cycle for a *manufacturing* company** *(p. 378)*
**participative budget** *(p. 403)*
**production budget** *(p. 379)*
**profit center** *(p. 398)*
**responsibility center** *(p. 398)*
**revenue center** *(p. 398)*
**sales budget** *(p. 379)*
**sales-determined expenses** *(p. 386)*
**sales-determining expenses** *(p. 386)*
**suboptimization** *(p. 402)*

## Summary Surfing

Here is an opportunity to gather information on the Internet about real-world issues related to the topics in this chapter (for suggestions on how to navigate various organizations' Web sites to find the relevant information, see the related discussion in the Preface at the beginning of the book). Answer the following questions.

- Go to the **Entrepreneur.com** Web site. This site includes advice for setting up a business plan, including how to set prices. What are three different pricing methods? What is the biggest pricing mistake made by companies?

## Integrated Business and Accounting Situations

**Answer the Following Questions in Your Own Words.**

### Testing Your Knowledge

**12-1** Explain the contributions that budgets make to the planning, operating, and evaluating processes.

**12-2** What information does a sales budget convey?

**12-3** Is a sales budget for a manufacturing company different from a sales budget for a retail company? Why or why not?

**12-4** Describe why budgeted cash receipts in any given month might be different from budgeted sales revenue.

**12-5** What information does a production budget convey?

**12-6** What factors should managers consider when deciding what policy to establish about the size of the ending finished goods inventory in any budget period?

**12-7** Without referring back to the chapter, write an equation that can be used to compute budgeted production for any budget period.

**12-8** What information does a direct materials purchases budget convey?

**12-9** What similarities do you see between the logic of the production budget and that of the direct materials purchases budget?

**12-10** How does a company determine how many units of a particular direct material it needs for production in a budget period?

**12-11** What information does a direct labor budget convey?

**12-12** How does a company determine how many hours of direct labor are needed to meet each month's budgeted production?

**12-13** How is a direct materials purchases budget similar to a direct labor budget? How is it different?

**12-14** What information does a factory overhead budget convey?

**12-15** Describe why depreciation is subtracted from total overhead costs in determining cash payments for factory overhead costs.

**12-16** What are the similarities and differences between the selling expenses budget of a large company and that of a small company?

**12-17** How can you distinguish a sales-determined expense from a sales-determining expense?

**12-18** What are the similarities and differences between the general and administrative budget of a large company and that of a small company?

**12-19** What information does a capital expenditures budget convey?

**12-20** What information does a cash budget convey?

**12-21** What are the similarities and differences between a cash budget and a cash flow statement?

**12-22** How can managers predict when a company will need to borrow money, and how can they estimate how much money the company will need to borrow?

**12-23** What are the similarities and differences between debt capital and equity capital?

**12-24** What is a line of credit? Describe how it works.

**12-25** What information does a projected income statement convey?

**12-26** How are the cost of goods sold sections of the income statements of a retail company and a manufacturing company similar and different?

**12-27** What information is conveyed in the projected balance sheet?

**12-28** What is a responsibility center? Briefly describe the four types of responsibility center.

**12-29** Describe a flexible budget. How might a flexible budget help managers make decisions?

**12-30** Give three examples, in your own words, of how budgets can affect employee behavior.

**12-31** What is participative budgeting, and what are its advantages?

**12-32** What is a budget committee, and what are its advantages?

## Applying Your Knowledge

**12-33** The sales budget of Eau de Libre Corporation, a company that manufactures cologne ("One whiff makes you want to go to the library") for college students and sells the cologne mostly to students' parents, shows the following estimated sales:

| | |
|---|---|
| September | 70,000 bottles |
| October | 40,000 bottles |
| November | 50,000 bottles |
| December | 60,000 bottles |
| January | 55,000 bottles |

Each bottle sells for $10. All of Eau de Libre's sales are on account, and it expects to collect accounts receivable 15 days after making the sales. It gives no cash discounts. (Assume all months have 30 days.)

*Required:* Prepare a sales budget for the last three months of the year, including estimated cash receipts.

**12-34** Refer to 12-33. Eau de Libre's policy is to end each month with an inventory of finished goods on hand equal to 20% of the following month's estimated sales.

*Required:* Using the budgeted sales figures given in 12-33, prepare a production budget for the last three months of the year.

**12-35** Using the budgeted sales figures in 12-33, respond to the following, treating each independently.

*Required:* (1) Prepare a production budget for the last three months of the year, assuming that Eau de Libre wants to have 11,000 bottles in finished goods inventory at the end of each month.

(2) Prepare a production budget for the last three months of the year so that production is the same each month. Assume that Eau de Libre has a beginning finished goods inventory in October of 11,000 bottles and wants to have an ending finished goods inventory in December of 29,000 bottles.

**12-36** The production budget of the Birmingham Steal Corporation, a manufacturer of baseball uniforms, shows budgeted production (in uniforms) for December and the first four months of next year as follows:

| | **Uniforms** |
|---|---|
| December | 10,000 |
| January | 4,000 |
| February | 9,000 |
| March | 15,000 |
| April | 5,000 |

Each uniform requires 5 yards of heavy cotton costing $3 per yard. Birmingham Steal buys cotton on credit, paying in the month following the purchase. Its supplier offers no cash discounts.

*Required:* For each of the following two independent situations, prepare a direct materials purchases budget for the direct materials needed in the first three months of next year:

(1) Birmingham Steal's policy is to have direct materials in its raw materials inventory at the end of each month equal to 50% of the following month's usage requirement.

(2) Birmingham Steal's policy is to keep the direct materials in its raw materials inventory at the end of each month to a minimum, but without letting it fall below 5,000 yards. Assume that the December 1 raw materials inventory has 5,000 yards of direct materials and that the company's only supplier is willing to sell a maximum of 60,000 yards of cotton to the company per month.

**12-37** Refer to 12-36. Birmingham Steal Corporation uses 2 direct labor hours to produce one baseball uniform. The direct labor rate is $16 per hour. It pays three-fourths of each month's wages in the month earned. It pays the other one-fourth in the following month.

*Required:* Using the production information in 12-36, prepare a direct labor budget for the first three months of next year.

**12-38** Refer to 12-36. Birmingham Steal Corporation's variable factory overhead costs include utilities ($.20 per baseball uniform), supplies ($.05 per uniform), and other variable costs ($.12 per uniform). Fixed factory overhead costs include supervisory salaries ($20,000 per month), depreciation of plant and equipment ($5,500 per month), and other fixed costs ($12,000 per month). Birmingham Steal makes cash payments for factory overhead costs (except for depreciation) in the month these costs are incurred.

*Required:* Using the production information in 12-36, prepare a factory overhead budget for the first three months of next year.

**12-39** Brown's Feed Store ("We deliver to ewe") estimates its monthly selling expenses as follows:

| | |
|---|---|
| Advertising | $20,000 per month |
| Sales salaries | $18,000 per month |
| Sales calls on customers | $ 35.00 per lot |
| Commissions paid to sales personnel | $ 50.00 per lot |
| Delivery | $ 20.00 per lot |

Brown pays for selling expenses in the month after they are incurred. Using current plans, it estimates the following sales:

| | |
|---|---|
| March | 70 lots |
| April | 90 lots |
| May | 100 lots |
| June | 110 lots |

*Required:* Prepare a selling expenses budget for the second quarter for Brown's Feed Store.

**12-40** Olson Construction Company builds houses. It has completed two houses: the first priced at $95,000, and the second at $120,000. Olson pays the realtor 7% of the selling price when the house is sold. Two additional houses are under construction. Brunhilde Olson, the owner, estimates that in May, the company will pay $20,000 to workers, $42,000 for direct materials, and $60,000 to other companies for work she has subcontracted. The bank will make a minimum construction loan to Olson Construction of $50,000 at 12% per year on May 1 if the company needs it. Interest would be paid at the end of each month on that loan. If Olson doesn't borrow money on May 1, it will not be able to borrow cash until June 15. Brunhilde also wants to avoid having too much cash on hand. She has adopted a policy of investing "excess" cash in a 30-day certificate of deposit at the end of any month when the anticipated ending cash balance from operations exceeds $60,000, so that the ending cash balance is reduced to exactly $60,000. On April 30, Olson Construction Company has $25,000 cash on hand.

*Required:* (1) Prepare a cash budget for May, assuming that Olson Construction expects to sell only the $95,000 house.
(2) Prepare a cash budget for May, assuming that Olson Construction expects to sell both houses.

**12-41** Knob-Hill Corporation, a manufacturer of door knobs, budgeted its manufacturing costs for August at a production level of 10,000 door knobs. But it actually produced 12,500 door knobs because August sales were higher than it anticipated. Budgeted and actual costs are shown here:

| | Budgeted | Actual |
|---|---|---|
| Door knobs manufactured | 10,000 | 12,500 |
| Direct materials | $ 3,400 | $ 4,330 |
| Direct labor | 5,600 | 6,750 |
| Factory overhead | | |
| Variable: | | |
| Utilities | 360 | 443 |
| Supplies | 120 | 162 |
| Other | 400 | 370 |
| Fixed: | | |
| Supervisory salaries | 2,900 | 2,900 |
| Depreciation | 1,000 | 1,000 |
| Other | 600 | 660 |
| Total manufacturing costs | $14,380 | $16,615 |

*Required:* Prepare a manufacturing cost report comparing August's actual costs with a revised (flexible) budget based on the actual production level for August.

**12-42** Canine Cuisine Company, owned by Goode Doggie, produces dog food that it sells in 10-pound bags for $7.00 per bag. Other information about the company includes the following:

(a) Sales estimates for the first four months of the year are as follows: January—50,000 bags, February—40,000 bags, March—55,000 bags, and April—50,000 bags. The ending inventory of dog food each month is 20% of the next month's sales estimate (in bags). All sales are cash sales.
(b) Canine Cuisine makes the dog food from a mixture of direct materials costing $.10 per pound. Each month's ending inventory of direct materials (in pounds) is 50% of the next month's usage requirement. Payment for direct materials is made in the month of purchase, with no cash discounts taken.
(c) Each bag of dog food requires 0.10 hour of direct labor costing $10 per hour. Canine Cuisine pays three-fourths of each month's direct labor cost in the month incurred and one-fourth in the following month. The wages payable for direct labor at the beginning of January was $15,500 for the 62,000 bags of dog food produced in December.
(d) Canine Cuisine's variable factory overhead costs are $1.40 per bag produced, and fixed factory overhead is $60,000 per month (which includes $25,000 of depreciation). Factory overhead costs (except for depreciation) are paid in the month after they are incurred.
(e) Canine Cuisine pays both variable selling expenses of $1.00 per bag sold and fixed selling expenses of $10,000 per month in the same month incurred.
(f) General and administrative expenses totaling $65,000 per month (including $20,000 depreciation) are all fixed. Canine Cuisine pays them (except for depreciation) in the month after they are incurred.
(g) Canine Cuisine's cash balance on January 1 is $45,000.

*Required:* Prepare a production budget, a direct materials purchases budget, a direct labor budget, and a cash budget for each of the first two months of the year.

**12-43** Refer to 12-42. Assume that January's beginning finished goods inventory (10,000 bags) had a cost of $43,700, its budgeted production for January is 48,000 bags, and its budgeted ending finished goods inventory (8,000 bags) has a cost of $37,200.

*Required:* Prepare a projected income statement for the month of January for Canine Cuisine Company (assuming Canine is a sole proprietorship).

**12-44** Refer to 12-42 and 12-43. At the beginning of January, Canine Cuisine Company's raw materials inventory was $24,000, its property, plant, and equipment (net) was $265,000, and its Goode Doggie capital was $195,400. It had no goods-in-process inventory or long-term liabilities at the beginning or end of January.

*Required:* Prepare a projected classified balance sheet at the end of January for Canine Cuisine Company. List total current liabilities as one amount.

**12-45** Mammoth Manufacturing Company set its production budget at 180,000 units per month during the second quarter of the year (assuming 45,000 units per week and four weeks per month). It developed all manufacturing cost budgets from this production budget. The following factory overhead budget for April applies to May and June as well.

**MAMMOTH MANUFACTURING COMPANY**
***Factory Overhead Budget***
***April***

| | |
|---|---|
| Budgeted production | 180,000 units |
| Variable overhead costs: | |
| Utilities | $ 10,800[a] |
| Supplies | 9,000[b] |
| Maintenance | 5,400[b] |
| Materials handling | 11,700[b] |
| Other variable costs | 14,400[b] |
| Total variable overhead | $ 51,300 |
| Fixed overhead costs: | |
| Supervisory salaries | $ 26,000[b] |
| Depreciation of plant and equipment | 35,000 |
| Insurance and property taxes on plant and equipment | 14,000[c] |

| | |
|---|---|
| Other fixed costs | 25,000[b] |
| Total fixed overhead | $100,000 |
| Total factory overhead | $151,300 |

[a]Paid in the following month
[b]Paid in same month
[c]Insurance was prepaid; taxes are paid in December.

Utility costs incurred in March were $10,200. The factory may have to close during the last week in May because of some difficulty the company is having with the renegotiation of a labor contract. If this happens, production in May will fall to 135,000 units. This lost production will need to be made up in June for the company to avoid losing sales. Mammoth is concerned about the effects that closing the factory the first week in May will have on its cash budget .

*Required:* On one schedule, prepare monthly factory overhead budgets (adjusting them where necessary for the effect of the one-week closing of the factory) for April, May, and June. Include the estimated monthly cash payments for factory overhead costs.

## Making Evaluations

**12-46** Exhibit 12-2 shows a diagram of a manufacturing company's operating cycle.

*Required:* Make a diagram of your own, and indicate on it where you think each budget fits. Briefly describe why you placed each budget where you did.

**12-47** The quarter column in a budget sometimes sums the amounts in the other columns and sometimes doesn't sum them.

*Required:* Carefully describe how you can decide, when developing a budget, whether to add monthly data together to get a quarterly amount or whether to determine that quarterly amount some other way. Give an example of when you would use each method. In your example of using some other way to determine the quarterly amount, describe what that other way would be.

**12-48** Suppose you and a team of managers of a company are trying to decide whether the company should obtain financing through debt capital or equity capital.

*Required:* What questions must you answer? How would the answers to these questions affect your decision?

**12-49** Suppose you are the controller of the multinational Crescent Hardware and Software Company, which manufactures crescent wrenches and crescent rolls (and is based in the Crescent City—New Orleans). Your boss, Rosie Hammerschmidt, is interested in forming a budget committee for the company and has asked you to suggest its membership.

*Required:* Write Ms. Hammerschmidt a memo describing whom you would include on this committee and the rationale for each of your choices.

**12-50** The Best Defense Corporation has just begun manufacturing burglar alarm systems called *Offense.* The sales estimate for April, the company's first month of operations, is 200 systems. Sales are expected to increase to 300 systems in May and 400 systems in June, and then to stay at 500 systems each month for the rest of the year. Best is planning to sell these systems for $320 each and to extend credit to its customers up to 60 days. Best gives no cash discounts. It expects to collect 10% of its accounts receivable in the month of sales, 30% in the month following sales, and 58% in the second month following sales. It estimates that 2% of its sales will not be collectible.

*Required:* (1) Prepare a sales budget for the first six months of Best's operations, including expected cash receipts from sales for each month.
(2) Do you agree with Best's credit policy? If so, what do you like about it? If not, what concerns do you have about the policy? In either case, what do you recommend to improve Best's credit policy?
(3) How do you think the 2% of uncollectible sales should affect the accounting equation? Why?

**12-51** Stick With Us Company will begin operations next January to produce glue. Estimates of sales quantities and direct materials and direct labor costs are as follows:

| Tubes to be Sold | | Direct Materials and Direct Labor Costs per Tube | |
|---|---|---|---|
| January | 30,000 | Direct materials | |
| February | 50,000 | (4 lbs @ $1.50 per lb.) | $6.00 |
| March | 40,000 | Direct labor | |
| April | 20,000 | (1/4 hr.@$9.00 per hr.) | 2.25 |
| | | | $8.25 |

The following information is also available:

(a) Monthly production should be scheduled so that the ending inventory of finished tubes of glue is 50% of the next month's expected sales of tubes.

(b) Direct materials inventory (in pounds) at the end of each month should be 25% of the next month's usage requirement. Direct materials will be paid for in the month following their purchase, with no cash discounts. Assume Stick has no direct materials inventory on January 1.

(c) Stick pays wages in the month the labor cost is incurred.

*Required:* (1) Prepare a production budget for January, February, and March.
(2) Prepare a direct materials purchases budget for January and February.
(3) Prepare a direct labor budget for January and February.
(4) Do you think it is reasonable for this company to set desired finished goods inventory levels as a constant percentage of the next month's expected sales, and desired direct materials inventory as a constant percentage of the next month's usage requirement? What do you think are the advantages and disadvantages of this policy?

**12-52** In the chapter, we mentioned that **Coca-Cola** raised its selling prices after it had to pay more for aluminum cans. Suppose you were employed by Coca-Cola at that time and were involved in this decision.

*Required:* What other alternatives might you have considered besides raising prices? How would these alternatives have affected Coca-Cola's budgets?

**12-53** Suppose that you are the head of production at Tiny Tyke Toy Company and that the accounting department has developed the following cost report for your department for the month of October.

**TINY TYKE TOY COMPANY**
***Manufacturing Cost Report***
***October***

| | Original October Budget | Actual Costs | Favorable (Unfavorable) Difference |
|---|---|---|---|
| Production (units) | 10,000 units | 11,000 units | |
| Direct materials | $ 3,000 | $ 3,200 | $ (200) |
| Direct labor | 12,500 | 13,600 | (1,100) |
| Factory overhead | | | |
| Variable: | | | |
| Utilities | 2,000 | 2,160 | (160) |
| Supplies | 500 | 540 | (40) |
| Other | 750 | 830 | (80) |
| Fixed: | | | |
| Supervisory salaries | 4,000 | 4,000 | — |
| Depreciation | 2,500 | 2,500 | — |
| Other | 5,500 | 5,550 | (50) |
| Total manufacturing costs | $30,750 | $32,380 | $(1,630) |

Your boss, who also has a copy of this report, has asked you to write her a memo explaining the "cost overruns" and describing a plan to keep costs more in line with the budget.

*Required:* Write a memo responding to your boss's request.

**12-54** Yesterday, you received the following letter in the mail for your advice column in the local paper:

**DR. DECISIVE**

Dr. Decisive:

What is going on in this country? Doesn't anybody have any scruples anymore? Even my boyfriend is sliding. See if you agree with me.

My boyfriend's roommate, let's call him "Ethics," was just hired to be the new manager of the advertising department for a large furniture manufacturer. In his first few days at the company, "Ethics" learned, through the overactive company grapevine, that the company values a manager's ability to keep his or her department's costs within the limits of the budgeted costs. "Ethics" has always been concerned about his image and wants to "come on like gangbusters." Get this: he has decided to overestimate next year's budgeted costs for his department just to make himself look better on his end-of-year performance evaluation. My boyfriend says that this is normal behavior and that the company expects its managers to do this.

We just studied budgeting in my accounting class, and from what I learned, the decision made by "Ethics" will have effects both inside and outside the company. At a minimum, I can see it affecting a bank's loan decision, the way resources are allocated among the departments of the company, the activities of the employees in his department, and the success of the company as a whole. I'm sure that you agree with me that "jerk," I mean "Ethics," is not making a benign decision. Both my boyfriend and what's-his-name think I am overreacting. Will you please explain to them (in as much detail as you can) why I am right and that I am reacting in a mature, rational manner? Thanks (I read your column every day). Please sign me

"Watchdog"

*Required:* Meet with your Dr. Decisive team and write a response to "Watchdog."

## END NOTES

[a]John S. DeMott, "Small Factories' Big Lessons," *Nation's Business,* April 1995, 29, 30.

[b]Erle Norton, "High Raw-Material Costs Lift Price Tags," *Wall Street Journal,* April 27, 1995, A2.

[c]John S. DeMott, "Small Factories' Big Lessons," *Nation's Business,* April 1995, 29, 30.

[d]Evan S. Connell, *Son of the Morning Star* (San Francisco: North Point Press, 1984).

# PART 5

# MANAGING, REPORTING, AND EVALUATING CORPORATE LIQUIDITY

This section consists of two chapters which discuss issues involving a corporation's liquidity. After reading these chapters, you will be able to:

- *understand the importance of managing and reporting on a corporation's liquidity*
- *explain the management policies and control procedures for accounts receivable and cash receipts*
- *explain the management policies and control procedures for accounts payable and cash payments*
- *account for international sales and purchases*
- *report on a corporation's accrued liabilities and loss contingencies*
- *use intracompany and intercompany analysis to evaluate a corporation's liquidity*

CHAPTER

13

# REVENUES AND CASH COLLECTIONS

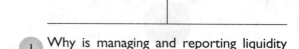

"FIRMS HAVE NO DESIRE TO GO BANKRUPT, SO IT IS NO SURPRISE THAT ONE OF THE CRUCIAL GOALS OF FINANCIAL MANAGEMENT IS ENSURING FINANCIAL VIABILITY. THIS GOAL IS OFTEN MEASURED IN LIQUIDITY . . ."

—STEVEN A. FINKLER

1. Why is managing and reporting liquidity important?
2. Why might a company offer credit sales, and what management policies should exist for accounts receivable?
3. How does a company report credit sales and net sales?
4. How does a company determine the amount of its bad debts expense, and how does it report the related amounts on its financial statements?
5. What is an exchange rate, and how does an exchange gain (loss) arise from a credit sale made to a company in another country?
6. How does a company account for cash collected prior to sales?
7. What are the important characteristics of a note receivable, and how is interest computed?
8. What are cash equivalents and what items does a company include in its cash and cash equivalents?

On **Hershey Foods**' (maker of "Kisses") December 31, 2005 balance sheet, the company reported that it had $626 million of cash and cash equivalents and receivables—14.6 percent of its total assets. On February 28, 2006, **Rocky Mountain Chocolate Factory's** balance sheet total for the same categories was slightly less than $6.8 million. Given that its total assets were about $19.1 million, 35.6 percent of Rocky Mountain's assets were these current assets. These dollar amounts of current assets shown on Hershey Foods' and Rocky Mountain's balance sheets resulted from prior management decisions as well as from the accounting methods used to keep track of the various categories of balance sheet accounts.

There are various ways to understand the meaning of the information reported by these companies. For example, if one piece of Hershey's candy sold for an average of five cents, its cash and cash equivalents and receivables account balances held the dollar equivalent of over 12.5 billion pieces! Hershey Foods' $626 million total for the three categories of current assets is 92 times greater than Rocky Mountain Chocolate Factory's $6.8 million. Should you conclude that Hershey has operations that are 92 times larger than those of Rocky Mountain? Another way to think about these amounts is to think about the business operations that create them. For example, accounts receivable result from making credit sales. In their respective income statements, Hershey Foods reported revenue of $4.8 billion and accounts receivable of $559 million. Rocky Mountain Chocolate Factory reported revenue of $21.1 million and accounts receivable of $3.3 million. So Hershey Foods' revenue was 8.2 times its accounts receivable, while Rocky Mountain Chocolate Factory's was 6.6 times.

*Can you conclude whether Hershey Foods or Rocky Mountain Chocolate Factory is better at managing its accounts receivable? What factors besides these amounts on the balance sheets and income statements of the two companies should you consider?*

Why do these and other companies hold these current assets? Large companies hold short-term assets for the same reasons as do small companies like Sweet Temptations: because the companies pay off short-term obligations as they come due, sell on credit to customers, and prepay for some items. (Companies also may hold short-term assets to sell to their customers or in anticipation of purchasing long-term assets, retiring long-term debt, or distributing cash dividends. We will discuss these issues in later chapters.) The amount that a company reports for each of these short-term assets varies within and across

© PHOTOPIA

If you had an inventory of Hershey's Kisses at home or in your dorm room or apartment, how quickly do you think you would "sell" them to your friends?

industries. However, one issue does not vary: effectively managing and reporting on liquidity is an important part of the accounting and finance function of every company.

In Chapters 13 and 14 we discuss liquidity. Think about these two chapters together. In Chapter 13, we first provide a framework for examining liquidity management and reporting issues. This framework provides a basis for discussing specific liquidity management topics. Second, we discuss management and reporting issues for accounts receivable and notes receivable as well as for a liability—unearned revenue—because they all relate to the selling of goods and services and the collection of cash from customers. We also discuss how a company accounts for credit sales to customers in other countries. We will discuss inventories and short-term investments (marketable securities) in later chapters. We also evaluate management and reporting issues for a company's cash balance in Chapter 13. In Chapter 14, we discuss management and reporting issues for accounts payable, additional types of current liabilities, prepaid items, and contingent liabilities. We also discuss how a company accounts for credit purchases from companies in other countries. We conclude the chapter with a discussion on evaluating a company's liquidity position. This evaluation section draws from information you will learn in both chapters.

As you will see, many aspects of liquidity management and reporting are similar for entrepreneurial businesses and large companies. We will concentrate on building on what you have learned in earlier chapters about these assets and liabilities. Although our focus is on large businesses that are usually organized as corporations, we will continue to use the general term *company* unless the discussion relates only to a corporation, such as when we discuss income taxes.

## THE IMPORTANCE OF MANAGING AND REPORTING ON LIQUIDITY

1 Why is managing and reporting liquidity important?

Recall from Chapter 7 that **liquidity** refers to how quickly a company can convert its assets into cash to pay its bills. Cash, then, is the most liquid asset. Cash equivalents,[1] accounts receivable, and notes receivable are considered the next most liquid because they may be turned into cash in the near term. Managers and external users are interested in the liquidity of a company's assets because it affects the company's ability to pay its short-term liabilities. They assess a company's *liquidity position* by comparing the composition and amounts of its short-term assets and short-term liabilities. Also recall from Chapter 7 that managers and external users may use the quick ratio to assess liquidity. We will revisit this ratio in Chapter 14 (and discuss the current ratio in Chapter 19). **Liquidity management** refers to a company's policies and activities that control its liquidity position. In other words, it refers to how a company manages cash, receivables, and current liabilities.

Why do managers and external users need to understand liquidity? From any user's perspective, it is important to understand the types of economic resources or economic obligations that each balance sheet item represents. If an external user does not know what "cash equivalents" or "accrued expenses" are, how can he or she include them in a business decision? From a manager's perspective, it is important to understand how liquidity can be managed to improve company performance. If a manager is not aware that faster collection of receivables and slower payment of payables (without alienating the other party in each case) will increase the amount of cash that may be invested in some type of interest-earning account, how can these techniques be used to improve profits? So both external users and managers need to understand how a company's policies and activities affect its liquidity position.

In our discussion of the evaluation and management of a company's liquidity, we use an integrated approach. In other words, you need to understand what is important about each type of current asset and current liability *and* how these account balances are related to each other. We use this integrated approach for three reasons. First, managers do not make liquidity decisions for one type of cash-related activity without considering the effect on related activities. For example, managers realize that making it easier for cus-

[1]Cash equivalents are very short-term investments that are easily converted into cash. We will discuss them later in the chapter.

tomers to obtain credit probably makes it more difficult for the company to collect cash from credit sales. Second, external users do not evaluate a company's liquidity only by examining each current asset or liability separately. For instance, they realize that a large cash balance does not always mean that a company's liquidity position is good; for example, the company may owe a relatively large amount of short-term debt. Also, the return earned on the cash is probably low. Finally, to assess liquidity, managers and external users use financial statement ratios composed of several items.

*Don't let our use of an "integrated approach" worry you. To understand how to use many things, you must understand each part and how the parts fit together. Can you drive a car safely without knowing the difference between the gas pedal and the brake pedal? We are simply applying this same logic to liquidity. Can you think of other examples in which an integrated approach to understanding is needed?*

## What You Need to Know to Evaluate an Account Balance

Exhibit 13-1 shows the current assets and current liabilities for Unlimited Decadence at December 31, 2008. Each asset and liability amount includes the results of all the transactions and events related to that specific account to date. To evaluate an account balance, you need to understand that company policies and activities (1) affect how these transactions and events happen (and therefore affect the account balances) and (2) occur within the larger business and economic environment.

For example, what do you need to know to evaluate an accounts receivable balance? We devote a section of this chapter to receivables, but we briefly answer this question now. The answer illustrates our approach to helping you learn about every account balance, not just accounts receivable. A year-end accounts receivable balance is calculated as follows, and the amounts appear on each of the financial statements as indicated:

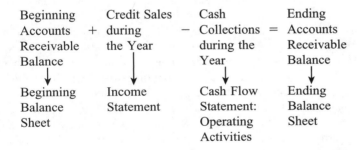

| | | | | | | |
|---|---|---|---|---|---|---|
| Beginning Accounts Receivable Balance | + | Credit Sales during the Year | − | Cash Collections during the Year | = | Ending Accounts Receivable Balance |
| ↓ | | ↓ | | ↓ | | ↓ |
| Beginning Balance Sheet | | Income Statement | | Cash Flow Statement: Operating Activities | | Ending Balance Sheet |

**EXHIBIT 13-1 UNLIMITED DECADENCE: BALANCES FOR CURRENT ASSET AND CURRENT LIABILITY ACCOUNTS, DECEMBER 31, 2008**

| (in thousands) | |
|---|---|
| Current assets | |
| Cash and cash equivalents | $1,020 |
| Accounts receivable (net) | 5,855 |
| Short-term notes receivable | 100 |
| Inventories | 1,610 |
| Total current assets | $8,585 |
| Current liabilities | |
| Accounts payable | $1,450 |
| Accrued liabilities | 500 |
| Taxes payable | 2,000 |
| Short-term notes payable | 150 |
| Total current liabilities | $4,100 |

Since the ending accounts receivable balance is the net result of these three components, to evaluate a company's accounts receivable you must understand how it reports these components in each of the financial statements and how the components relate to each other. First, increases in accounts receivable result from credit sales. Thus, you need to understand how a company processes its credit sales. Equally important, you need to realize that credit policies (guidelines about which customers are given credit and about the terms of the credit) also affect accounts receivable. Second, decreases in accounts receivable result from cash collections. So, you need to understand how a company processes its cash receipts. You also need to recognize that policies about methods of cash collection and cash discounts affect accounts receivable. Finally, recall from Chapter 9 that companies show accounts receivable in the balance sheet at their net realizable value (Accounts Receivable [net] = Total Accounts Receivable − Estimated Amount of Uncollectible Accounts). Thus, GAAP reporting requirements and management practices affect the amount of a company's estimate of its uncollectible accounts (not included in the equation we showed earlier).

This method of analysis holds true for every account balance. Company activities and policies as well as the business and economic environment affect the transactions and events that result in a year-end account balance. To be able to evaluate the financial performance of a company, you need to understand how these factors affect each financial statement item.

### Our Approach to Studying Liquidity

The highlighted areas in Exhibit 13-2 show which balance sheet items we discuss in this chapter and in Chapter 14. This should help you visualize how managers and external users approach their study of liquidity. Liquidity management can be broken down into five areas, as follows: (1) **accounts receivable management**, which involves setting and following policies for granting credit and processing credit sales; (2) **cash receipts management**, which involves setting and following policies for collecting cash from credit or cash sales (or in advance of sales), processing cash collections, and depositing cash collections into the company's bank account; (3) **accounts payable management**, which involves setting and following policies for authorizing and making purchases and for processing credit purchases; (4) **cash payments management**, which involves setting and following policies for paying for cash or credit purchases and processing cash payments; and (5) **cash balance management**, which involves setting and following policies for maintaining an optimal amount of cash. A company may invest excess cash in cash equivalents or short-term marketable securities (which we will discuss in Chapter 23) to earn investment income.

Exhibit 13-3 illustrates the scope of liquidity management over each of these five areas. In this exhibit, we show the financial statement items affected by liquidity management and provide *one* example of a policy and an activity for each area.

*Take some time to study Exhibit 13-3. How does it relate to our descriptions of each area? Notice what is written on the right side of the exhibit. Can you explain each of these items?*

## Managing Accounts Receivable

Accounts receivable are the amounts owed to a company for its credit sales. Many companies sell goods on credit as a routine part of business and expect to collect these amounts in cash within a relatively short period of time. For example, Hershey Foods had sales of $4.8 billion in 2005, and its average accounts receivable were $484 million. In the candy manufacturing industry, the number of days it takes to collect these receivables averages about 40 days. Unlimited Decadence has accounts receivable (net) of $5,855,000 at December 31, 2008.

**EXHIBIT 13-2 ANALYSIS OF A COMPANY'S BALANCE SHEET: LIQUIDITY**

*Assets*

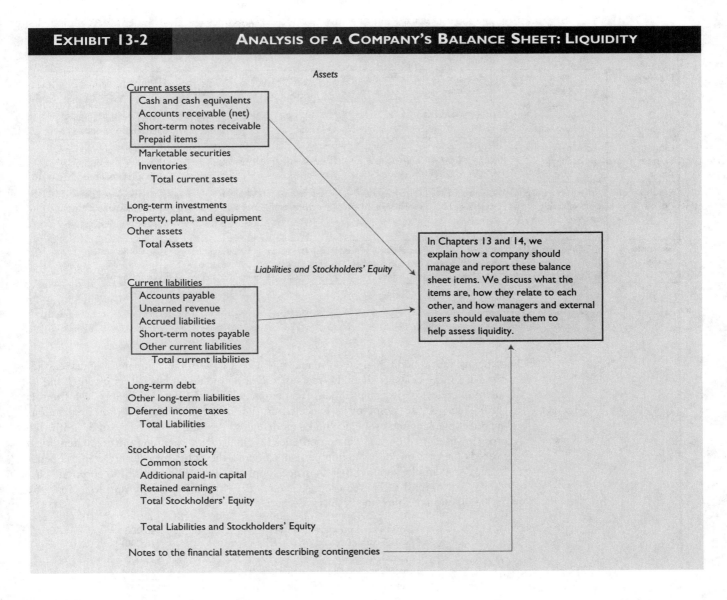

Current assets
- Cash and cash equivalents
- Accounts receivable (net)
- Short-term notes receivable
- Prepaid items
- Marketable securities
- Inventories
- Total current assets

Long-term investments
Property, plant, and equipment
Other assets
Total Assets

*Liabilities and Stockholders' Equity*

Current liabilities
- Accounts payable
- Unearned revenue
- Accrued liabilities
- Short-term notes payable
- Other current liabilities
- Total current liabilities

Long-term debt
Other long-term liabilities
Deferred income taxes
Total Liabilities

Stockholders' equity
- Common stock
- Additional paid-in capital
- Retained earnings
- Total Stockholders' Equity

Total Liabilities and Stockholders' Equity

Notes to the financial statements describing contingencies

In Chapters 13 and 14, we explain how a company should manage and report these balance sheet items. We discuss what the items are, how they relate to each other, and how managers and external users should evaluate them to help assess liquidity.

## The Reasons for Offering Credit Sales

**2** **Why might a company offer credit sales, and what management policies should exist for accounts receivable?**

Why does a company grant credit? As we discussed in Chapter 9, (1) it may be more convenient to sell on credit than for cash; (2) offering credit may encourage a customer to buy an item that the customer might not otherwise purchase; and (3) allowing customers to pay *after* receiving the goods signals product quality and a commitment to customers.

*Have you noticed that companies sometime sell goods on a "cash and carry" basis? What does this mean? What should companies and customers think about before using the "cash and carry" basis?*

A company has two major concerns with credit sales.[2] First, credit sales require managers to be involved in receivables and cash-collection management; therefore, the

[2]In this section we are *not* discussing bank credit card (VISA, Mastercard) sales. A company treats these sales as cash sales, except that it must pay a percentage of the amount of the sale (generally between 1% and 5%) to the credit card company. So, credit cards are an example of "outsourcing" the credit evaluation and collection functions, thereby transferring the costs and risks to the credit card company.

## EXHIBIT 13-3 THE SCOPE OF LIQUIDITY MANAGEMENT

| | | | | | | |
|---|---|---|---|---|---|---|
| **Financial Statement Items** | Sales Revenue and Accounts Receivable | Accounts Receivable and Cash | Cash and Cash Equivalents | Cash and Accounts Payable | Accounts Payable and Expenses or Assets | Activities are recorded in the accounting system, and the account balances are reported in the financial statements. |
| **Liquidity Management Area** | Accounts receivable management | Cash receipts management | Cash balance management | Cash payments management | Accounts payable management | Company activities are managed accordng to company policies. |
| **Example of Policy** | Sales personnel must receive credit approval before making sale. | Cash receipts are deposited daily. | Cash balance is monitored daily to ensure proper balance. | Cash payments are made only for approved purchases. | All purchases must be approved by company employee. | Company policies influence activities. |
| **Example of Activity** | Credit sales are made to customer with approved credit. | Cash is collected from credit sale. | Excess cash is used to purchase cash equivalents.* | Cash is paid to suppliers for credit purchases. | Items are purchased on credit from supplier. | Activities are influenced by company policies. |

*If the excess cash will not be needed in the near term, the company may invest in short-term marketable securities (which we will discuss in Chapter 23 of Volume 2).

company incurs additional credit management costs. Also, the company might incur additional selling costs, such as the costs of soliciting the credit customers. Second, the issue of uncollectible accounts arises. If a company cannot effectively collect cash from its credit sales, it loses some of its expected profits from credit sales. So if a company has uncollectible accounts, should it make credit sales? As long as the increase in profit (the gross profit earned from the increased sales less the cost of operating the credit activities) exceeds the cost of not collecting certain accounts, the policy of offering credit is beneficial. For example, suppose that an office supply retailer decides to sell to corporate customers and so must offer credit terms. The retailer expects its annual sales to increase by $100,000 and the following results to occur:

| | |
|---|---|
| Gross profit on increased sales | $40,000 |
| Less: Costs of operating the credit activities | (15,000) |
| Increase in profit | $25,000 |
| Less: Uncollectible additional credit sales | (5,000) |
| Net increase in profit | $20,000 |

In this example, even though the company incurred a cost from not collecting certain accounts, the decision to offer credit terms on sales to corporate customers would increase the company's profit. We will discuss accounting for the uncollectible accounts receivable later in this chapter.

*How would you, as a manager, use break-even analysis to decide whether to offer credit?*

In practically every large company, the benefits from offering credit sales outweigh the associated costs. Any company that has transactions with other companies will have accounts receivable; these companies may have *only* credit sales and never make cash sales. Companies that deal only with customers who pay cash or use bank credit cards will *not* have accounts receivable.

*Can you name a company that makes all its sales on credit? that makes all its sales for cash?*

### Accounts Receivable Subsidiary File

As a company increases in size, it needs more accounts to record specific types of accounting information. A larger company, for example, is likely to own more assets and different types of assets (e.g., buildings and equipment). In addition, it will have more customer accounts from sales on credit.

To keep up-to-date records of transactions with individual credit customers, a larger company sets up an accounts receivable subsidiary file. An **accounts receivable subsidiary file** contains the individual accounts of all the customers that purchase from the company on credit.[3] Whenever a company makes a credit sale to a customer, it records an increase in the customer's account in this subsidiary file. When a customer pays its account, the company records a decrease in the customer's account in this file. Thus, at all times the company knows the balance in each customer's account. As we will discuss later, this information is very helpful in deciding whether to extend additional credit to a customer and in determining which customers need to be reminded to pay their bills.

When a company uses an accounts receivable subsidiary file, it still keeps a single Accounts Receivable account in its columnar accounting system (to maintain the equality of the accounting equation). The Accounts Receivable account is referred to as a **control account**. The balance of the Accounts Receivable control account must always equal the total of the individual customer accounts in the accounts receivable subsidiary file on each balance sheet date. This means that each time a company records a transaction (e.g., credit sale, collection) in a customer's account in the subsidiary file, it must also record the transaction in the Accounts Receivable control account. A company's enterprise resource planning (ERP) system can easily be designed to do this. In order to maintain internal control over its accounts receivable, a company checks that the total of the balances of all the customers' accounts in its accounts receivable subsidiary file is equal to the balance of its Accounts Receivable control account.

## ACCOUNTS RECEIVABLE

In the first part of the book (particularly Chapters 5–9) we discussed credit sales and accounts receivable in an entrepreneurial environment. Some of that discussion also applies to our analysis of large companies. Here are the basic management policies that apply to accounts receivable in large companies.

1. *Granting credit.* A company should have control policies to govern which customers are granted credit and how much credit it allows.
2. *Recording credit sales, returns, and allowances.* A company generally records credit sales in the accounting system when it transfers the goods to the customer. It also records any sales returns or allowances in the accounting system as they occur.
3. *Monitoring accounts receivable balances.* A company should have control policies to monitor the accounts receivable balances of its customers. It should send periodic (monthly) statements to its customers. It should deny additional credit to customers with overdue balances. It should monitor its bad debts. If the total accounts receivable balance becomes relatively large, it should investigate the reasons for the growth. If cash collections have slowed, it should examine its credit policies.
4. *Reporting accounts receivable according to GAAP.* GAAP requires that every company report accounts receivable at the net realizable value on its balance sheet.

Items 1, 2, and 3 relate mainly to accounts receivable management. Item 4 refers to how a company reports accounts receivable on its balance sheet. In the following sections

[3]If a company requires customers to sign a promissory note, it may also have a subsidiary file for notes receivable.

we will build on these items to discuss the managing and reporting of accounts receivable in a large-company environment.

## Granting Credit

How does a company decide which customers to extend credit to and how much credit to allow? In Chapter 9 we explained that smaller companies ask potential credit customers to complete formal credit applications for evaluation and approval decisions. This process also is common for large companies. In addition, large companies use three other policies to reduce the risks associated with selling goods on credit.

First, companies often establish personnel policies that prohibit sales personnel from having the authority to approve credit sales. A salesperson who also has the ability to approve credit has an incentive to grant more credit than customers deserve, in order to increase the salesperson's dollar amount of sales. This is especially true if the company pays commissions to sales personnel.

At Unlimited Decadence, a credit department processes all credit applications. The credit manager reports to the Vice-President of Finance. On the other hand, the sales personnel report to the Vice-President of Sales. This organizational structure separates credit approval and sales responsibilities.

*Do you think a company's credit department and its sales department might disgree about who should be granted credit? Why or why not? How can these disagreements be resolved?*

Second, before agreeing to sell goods on credit, companies sometimes require customers to submit letters of credit from their banks. A **letter of credit**, written by a customer's bank, ensures payment to the selling company when that company presents the bank with documents that show it met the conditions of the sale. In essence, the bank that issues the letter of credit guarantees that payment will be made to the seller when the transaction between the seller and the buyer is complete. If a company's sale involves a letter of credit, the risk of granting credit is reduced because the process now involves the creditworthiness of the buyer's bank.

U.S. companies commonly require letters of credit from customers when they make international sales. The letters are important because managers usually have less knowledge about business in foreign countries or about a specific foreign customer. There also may be increased risk from war, civil strife, different business practices, or an inability to convert local currencies to U.S. dollars.

Third, companies that sell goods on credit to international customers sometimes purchase export insurance as a way to reduce credit risk. **Export insurance** eliminates a company's risk of not receiving payment for the goods it sold internationally; if it does not receive payment, the insurance company must pay. Regardless of the credit policies used by a company, it should approve credit before each credit sales transaction. By doing this, a company improves the collectibility of every receivable.

## Recording Credit Sales, Returns, Allowances, and Discounts in the Accounting System

3 How does a company report credit sales and net sales?

According to GAAP, when collection from a sale is likely, a company records a revenue transaction in the accounting period in which it earns the revenue—usually when the selling company transfers the goods to the customer or performs the service. So, Unlimited Decadence earns revenue when it ships chocolates to its customers because its policies ensure that it has a high probability of collecting the receivable. Once the accounting department matches the approved sales order, shipping document, and sales invoice, it has evidence that the sale occurred, and it can record the sales transaction. For example, assume that on April 15, 2008, Bayside Candies Company ordered 300 boxes of chocolates on credit from Unlimited Decadence for $1,350 ($4.50 per box). Further, Bayside requests that 100 of the boxes have specialized Mother's Day wrapping. On April 17, Unlimited Decadence ships the 300 boxes of chocolates and records the credit sale as follows[4]:

| **Assets** | = | **Liabilities** | + | **Stockholders' Equity** | | |
|---|---|---|---|---|---|---|
| | | | | ***Net Income*** | | |
| | | | | **Revenues** | – | **Expenses** |
| Accounts Receivable (Bayside Candies) | | | | Sales Revenue | | |
| +$1,350 | | | | +$1,350 | | |

**FINANCIAL STATEMENT EFFECTS**

Increases current assets and total assets on ***balance sheet***. Increases revenues, which increases net income on ***income statement*** (and therefore increases stockholders' equity on ***balance sheet***).

Both Accounts Receivable[5] and Sales Revenue increase by $1,350 as a result of the sale.

It is not always clear when credit sales have taken place and what dollar amount of sales a company should show on an income statement. For example, a manufacturing company whose customers (e.g., retail stores) will resell the goods to consumers often provides the customer an opportunity to return goods that it doesn't sell. This is especially true if the product is defective or is newly developed and the retailer is not sure how many retail customers will purchase it. Similarly, some companies guarantee to have the lowest-priced products. If a customer finds a lower price on the same product elsewhere, these companies refund the difference and perhaps return an additional amount.

*Would you recommend that a company not record revenue until such options have expired? For example, should the publisher of this book not record revenue until your right to return it to the bookstore has expired?*

How should these types of sales policies affect a company's accounting procedures for reporting sales on the income statement and accounts receivable on the balance sheet? Recall from Chapter 6 that companies show sales revenues on the income statement at a *net* amount. **Sales revenue (net)**, or **net sales** for an accounting period equal the total sales minus sales returns and allowances and sales discounts for that period. A **sales return** occurs when a customer returns goods that the company previously recorded as a sale and the customer receives a refund in exchange for the goods. A **sales allowance** occurs when a company refunds a portion of the sales price after the original sale occurred. A **sales discount** (also called a *cash discount*) is a reduction in the invoice price because the customer pays within the discount period.

A company may use the accounting information in its ERP system to keep track of sales returns and allowances. Managers monitor the volume of returns and allowances for three basic reasons. First, a relatively high level of sales returns may indicate that sales personnel are persuading customers to make unwanted purchases. If sales personnel are not at least partly responsible for the costs associated with sales returns, they may use a lenient sales return policy, to their personal (not the company's) advantage. Perhaps you have been in a situation where the salesperson says, "Go ahead, buy it now while we have it on sale. You can always bring it back later if you change your mind." (Some companies, however, use liberal return policies as a deliberate way to generate more sales. They *encourage* sales personnel to stress the return policy when trying to make a sale because they assume that few customers will return the item.) Second, a relatively high level of

[4]Since Unlimited Decadence uses a perpetual inventory system, it also would record an increase in Cost of Goods Sold and a decrease in Inventory for the *cost* of the inventory sold. For the sake of simplicity, we do not show the entry here or in other sales transactions later in the chapter. We discussed the perpetual inventory system in Chapter 5 and will expand on it in Chapter 19 of Volume 2.

[5]Note that Unlimited Decadence uses an accounts receivable subsidiary file. Therefore, it records the transaction both in the Accounts Receivable control account and in the account of the individual customer, Bayside Candies. We show this here and later in the chapter (and in Chapter 14) by listing the customer's name in parentheses in the account title.

sales returns may indicate problems with product quality or product demand. Therefore, many companies require sales personnel to find out why goods are being returned. Finally, a relatively high level of sales allowances may result from shipping or warehouse problems. A sales allowance often is given to customers if goods are slightly damaged or do not match the description of the goods that were ordered (e.g., if Unlimited Decadence shipped the wrong flavor of candy).

To continue the example of the sale to Bayside Candies when the boxes arrive at Bayside on April 19, its receiving department personnel inspect the order and find that none of the boxes have the special Mother's Day wrapping. On being notified of the mistake on April 20, Unlimited Decadence offers to reduce the sales price for the entire shipment by $1 per box ($300). Bayside agrees, and on April 24, 2008, Unlimited Decadence records the sales allowance as follows:

**FINANCIAL STATEMENT EFFECTS**

Decreases current assets and total assets on ***balance sheet***. Decreases *net* revenues, which decreases net income on ***income statement*** (and therefore decreases stockholders' equity on ***balance sheet***).

| **Assets** | = | **Liabilities** | + | **Stockholders' Equity** | | |
|---|---|---|---|---|---|---|
| | | | | ***Net Income*** | | |
| | | | | **Revenues** | − | **Expenses** |
| Accounts Receivable (Bayside Candies) | | | | Sales Revenue | | |
| Bal $1,350 | | | | | | |
| −300 | | | | −$300 | | |
| Bal $1,050 | | | | | | |

*Why would both companies agree to the sales allowance rather than deciding that Bayside should return the boxes?*

Unlimited Decadence decreases Accounts Receivable by $300 because Bayside now owes it only $1,050, not the original $1,350. The company decreases the Sales Revenue account by $300 for the sales allowance. The negative amounts are "coded" (e.g., SA for sales allowance). When Unlimited Decadence's managers want to know the types and amounts of sales returns and allowances, they use the company's ERP system (as we discussed in Chapter 10) to electronically "sort" the entries in the Sales Revenue account column to identify these items.

Suppose instead that Bayside returned the 100 boxes that did not have the special wrapping. Unlimited Decadence would record the sales return of $450 ($4.50 per box) in the same way that we just showed for the sales allowance (except recording $450 rather than $300). However, since Unlimited Decadence receives the boxes back, and since it uses the perpetual inventory system, it also must record an increase in Inventory and a decrease in Cost of Goods Sold. In other words, it reverses the sale *and* the cost of the sale. If we assume that each box cost $2.50, Unlimited Decadence would record the return as follows:

**FINANCIAL STATEMENT EFFECTS**

Decreases current assets and total assets on ***balance sheet***. Decreases *net* revenues and cost of goods sold, which decreases net income on ***income statement*** (and therefore decreases stockholders' equity on ***balance sheet***).

| **Assets** | | = | **Liabilities** | + | **Stockholders' Equity** | | |
|---|---|---|---|---|---|---|---|
| | | | | | ***Net Income*** | | |
| | | | | | **Revenues** | − | **Expenses** |
| Accounts Receivable (Bayside Candies) | Inventory | | | | Sales Revenue | | Cost of Goods Sold |
| −$450 | +$250 | | | | −$450 | − | −$250 |

A company also uses its accounting system to keep track of its sales discounts. In Chapter 6, we explained how a company may offer a sales (cash) discount to credit customers to encourage them to pay their accounts receivable within a relatively short period of time, usually 10 to 15 days. Recall that a sales discount is a percentage reduction of the invoice price; the selling company grants this discount in return for the customer's early payment. The sales discount arrangement is shown on the invoice in a standard format such as "2/10, n/30." This means that the selling company grants a 2% discount if the customer pays within 10 days. Otherwise the entire dollar amount of the invoice (referred to as the *gross amount*) is due within 30 days.

We show how a company handles sales discounts by focusing on one transaction. (In Chapter 14 we will discuss why managers usually should take advantage of the discount.) Assume that Unlimited Decadence offers discount terms of 2/10, n/30 to all its customers and that Pinecrest Candies purchases 400 boxes of chocolates on April 5, 2008 for $4.50 per box. Unlimited Decadence sends a sales invoice to Pinecrest for $1,800 (400 × $4.50). The invoice states that Unlimited Decadence will give a 2% discount to Pinecrest if it receives payment within 10 days.

On April 5, 2008, Unlimited Decadence records this sale by increasing accounts receivable and sales revenue by $1,800. Now, assume that on April 12, 2008, Unlimited Decadence receives a check from Pinecrest in payment of the account receivable. Because Pinecrest pays within 10 days of the sale, it takes the 2% discount. Pinecrest's check is for $1,764, which reflects the 2% cash discount of $36 ($1,800 × 0.02). Unlimited Decadence records the April 12 cash receipt as follows:

| **Assets** | | = | **Liabilities** | + | **Stockholders' Equity** | | |
|---|---|---|---|---|---|---|---|
| | | | | | ***Net Income*** | | |
| | | | | | **Revenues** | − | **Expenses** |
| Cash | Accounts Receivable (Pinecrest Candies) | | | | Sales Revenue | | |
| | Bal $1,800 | | | | | | |
| +$1,764 | −1,800 | | | | −$36 | | |
| | Bal $ 0 | | | | | | |

**FINANCIAL STATEMENT EFFECTS**

Decreases current assets and total assets on ***balance sheet***. Decreases *net* revenues, which decreases net income on ***income statement*** (and therefore decreases stockholders' equity on ***balance sheet***). Increases cash flows from operating activities on ***cash flow statement***.

The company decreases the Sales Revenue account by $36 for the sales discount. The negative amounts are "coded" (e.g., SD for sales discount) so that when Unlimited Decadence's managers want to know the types and amounts of sales discounts, they use the company's ERP system to electronically "sort" the entries in the Sales Revenue account column to identify these items.

*Why do you think that Unlimited Decadence decreases Accounts Receivable by $1,800 instead of $1,764?*

## Business Issues and Values in Recording Credit Sales

How does recording credit sales affect the ability of external users to rely on the income reported on an income statement? Unfortunately, sometimes managers become too aggressive in their decisions about when to report revenue, and how much to report. Managers may do this in order to make themselves look good, or to meet the revenue and profit expectations of Wall Street. A recent Securities and Exchange Commission study indicated that the issues of when to report revenue, and how much to report, cause over half the financial reporting errors and frauds in financial statements. These problems arise for many reasons including reporting revenue before it is earned, when its collectibility is very uncertain, or when it is contingent on some future event.

For example, in 2006 **Nortel Networks** announced the *third* restatement of its 2003 and 2004 financial statements. This latest restatement reduced its reported revenue in 2003 and 2004 by $261 million and $312 million, respectively. This means that Nortel previously reported revenue of $573 that it had not yet earned. As a result of this restatement, among other changes, its net income was reduced by $125 million and $131 million in those two years. Also in 2006, **The Warnaco Group** (maker of Calvin Klein jeans, Speedo swimsuits, and other apparel) said it would restate its results for 2005 and the first quarter of 2006 due to errors in accounting for sales returns and allowances that overstated its net revenues. The restatement is expected to reduce Warnaco's earnings per share by 5 to 7 cents per share.

Investors and creditors need to be aware that companies differ in how they interpret GAAP for similar sales transactions. As business deals become more complicated, defining when sales revenue is earned (and collectible) becomes more difficult.

## Monitoring Accounts Receivable Balances

Although companies require customers to show that they have the *ability* to pay for credit sales, this does not mean that customers always pay. As we discussed in Chapter 9, when making credit sales, the company does not know *which* customers will not pay. (Again, if it knew at the time of sale that a particular customer would not pay, it would not make the sale.)

Large companies, like small ones, monitor customers' accounts receivable balances to help decrease the number of accounts that will be uncollectible. An accounts receivable subsidiary file is very useful for this purpose because it enables a company to more easily analyze each customer's account. A company sends notices to customers with overdue amounts. If a customer does not pay within a reasonable period of time, the credit manager should contact the customer to discuss the problem and try to work out a payment schedule. If that doesn't work, a company may take legal action against the customer by filing a lawsuit to force payment or may turn the account over to a collection agency.

Whether making credit sales to attract customers or to increase their convenience, a company records the costs associated with making these sales as an expense and separates them into two types: (1) the administrative expenses associated with making credit sales, including the costs of processing customers' credit applications, sending out monthly statements, and contacting overdue accounts; and (2) the *bad debts expense* caused by customers never paying off their accounts receivable balances.

**Bad debts expense** is the expense that represents the estimated cost, for the accounting period, of the eventual noncollection of accounts receivable. A company records the expense (and a reduction in the net accounts receivable, as we will discuss later) in the accounting system through an end-of-period adjustment. Recording bad debts expense in the accounting records is not as straightforward as recording other costs. Customers do not telephone the company to announce: "We are going to keep the goods you just sold us, but we are never going to pay for them. Please consider us a bad debt." Rather, a company *estimates* and reports the bad debts expense in the period of the credit sale and *not* in the period when the company discovers that a customer cannot pay. This is an example of the matching principle we discussed in Chapter 9.

*Once a company has estimated the amount of accounts receivable that will be uncollectible, do you think it can just erase the total amount for accounts receivable that is in the accounting records and replace it with the net accounts receivable amount? Why or why not? How should it make this change in the accounting records?*

For example, assume that at December 31, 2008, Unlimited Decadence has accounts receivable of $6 million and estimates that its bad debts expense for 2008 is $134,000 (later we will discuss how it computed this amount). It records this amount as follows:

**FINANCIAL STATEMENT EFFECTS**

Decreases *net* accounts receivable, current assets, and total assets on ***balance sheet***. Increases expenses, which decreases net income on ***income statement*** (and therefore decreases stockholders' equity on ***balance sheet***).

| **Assets** | | | = | **Liabilities** | + | **Stockholders' Equity** | | |
|---|---|---|---|---|---|---|---|---|
| | | | | | | ***Net Income*** | | |
| Accounts Receivable | | Allowance for Bad Debts | | | | **Revenues** | − | **Expenses** Bad Debts Expense |
| Bal $6,000,000 | − | Bal $ 11,000 | | | | | | |
| | − | +134,000 | | | | | − | +$134,000 |
| Bal $6,000,000 | − | Bal $145,000 | | | | | | |

*$134,000 probably seems like a large amount to you. How would you decide if it is a large amount for Unlimited Decadence?*

Note that Unlimited Decadence did not reduce the Accounts Receivable account directly in this entry because it does not yet know which credit customers will not pay. Instead it *increases* an Allowance for Bad Debts account (sometimes called Allowance for Doubtful Accounts or Allowance for Uncollectible Accounts). On the balance sheet, the company subtracts the balance of the Allowance for Bad Debts account from the balance in the Accounts Receivable account to report the net realizable value of the accounts receivable (the amount of cash the company expects to collect). That is why we show a minus sign (−) in the column before the allowance account balance. Allowance for Bad Debts is a contra-account. A **contra-account** is an account that has the effect of reducing the balance in another account. The company includes the bad debts expense (sometimes called *Provision for Credit Losses*) on the income statement as a part of its operating expenses.

*Can you think of other possible contra accounts?*

## Write-off of an Uncollectible Account

Eventually a manager will judge that certain customer accounts are uncollectible. This may occur because a customer filed for bankruptcy, left no forwarding address and cannot be found, or went out of business. At this time the company "writes off" (eliminates) the customer's account receivable, and an equal amount of the allowance for bad debts, because it knows it will not collect an amount previously included in its estimate of uncollectible accounts. It still expects to collect the *same* amount of its total accounts receivable as it did before the write-off. Therefore the write-off does *not* affect the total assets or expenses of the company. Remember that the company recorded both the expense and the reduction in the asset in the period of the credit sale by using an end-of-period adjustment.

A manager authorizing a write-off is, in essence, saying, "Now I know for whom I was creating that allowance." Therefore, the write-off does *not* affect the company's balance sheet or its income statement—the effects on those two statements were recorded when the company made the bad debt estimate. The company records the write-off by reducing the accounts receivable balance and the allowance account by the same amount. For example, assume the Chocolate Candies Cafe owes Unlimited Decadence $8,000 from a sale two years ago. Unlimited Decadence no longer believes that the amount is collectible and writes off this receivable early in 2009 as follows:

| **Assets** | | | | | = | **Liabilities** | + | **Stockholders' Equity** |
|---|---|---|---|---|---|---|---|---|
| | Accounts Receivable | | | Allowance for Bad Debts | | | | |
| Bal | $6,000,000 | − | Bal | $145,000 | | | | |
| | −8,000 | − | | −8,000 | | | | |
| Bal | $5,992,000 | − | Bal | $137,000 | | | | |

**FINANCIAL STATEMENT EFFECTS**

No effect on *net* accounts receivable, current assets, and total assets on ***balance sheet***.

Unlimited Decadence decreases both its Allowance for Bad Debts and its Accounts Receivable by $8,000. Also, for control purposes, Unlimited Decadence will make a note of this write-off in Chocolate Candies Cafe's credit file in its ERP system. Note that this write-off has no effect on Unlimited Decadence's net accounts receivable:

| | **Before the Write-off** | **After the Write-off** |
|---|---|---|
| Accounts receivable (assumed) | $6,000,000 | $5,992,000 |
| Less: Allowance for bad debts | (145,000) | (137,000) |
| Net accounts receivable | $5,855,000 | $5,855,000 |

*Do you think managers would prefer to write off a receivable at the end of the year or wait until the next year? Explain your answer.*

If the company's estimates are accurate and it writes off its uncollectible accounts before the end of the year, then the balance of its Allowance for Bad Debts account before the year-end adjustment will be zero. However, since estimates are "best guesses" and a company is unlikely to write off its accounts so quickly, a company's Allowance for Bad Debts account will frequently have a year-end balance. For example, suppose that Unlimited Decadence has a receivable from another company that declares bankruptcy. It might take more than a year for the courts to rule on how much Unlimited Decadence will receive and, therefore, how much it will write off.

In summary, a company computes the year-end balance of its Allowance for Bad Debts as follows:

| | | | | | | |
|---|---|---|---|---|---|---|
| Beginning Allowance Balance | + | Bad Debts Expense for the Year | − | Write-offs for the Year | = | Ending Allowance Balance |

A company computes the year-end balance of its Accounts Receivable as follows:

| | | | | | | | | |
|---|---|---|---|---|---|---|---|---|
| Beginning Accounts Receivable Balance | + | Credit Sales during the Year | − | Cash Collections of Accounts Receivable during the Year | − | Write-offs of Accounts Receivable for the Year | = | Ending Accounts Receivable Balance |

Note that this equation differs from the equation given in our discussion at the beginning of the chapter because we now include write-offs.

*Do you think that reporting bad debt expense in the period of the sale results in better income measurement and asset valuation than reporting the expense when the receivable is written off? Explain your answer.*

## Technology and Receivables Management

*How have computers changed your everyday life? Think about how technology affects your job or the job of a friend. How do you think technology affects large companies and their receivables management?*

Do all companies manage liquidity using the same methods? No: as we discussed in Chapter 10 for enterprise resource planning (ERP) systems, an increasing number of large companies are reengineering all or parts of their accounting and finance functions, especially liquidity-management activities. **Reengineering** is the process of analyzing and redesigning an activity to make it more effective and efficient. In most cases, it involves taking advantage of new technologies.

In receivables management, reengineering has changed the way many large companies grant credit, record credit sales, and monitor receivables. For example, some companies now approve credit applications by using a special type of computer program, called a *neural network.* Credit applications are entered electronically and the program "thinks" like a credit analyst and decides whether or not to approve credit. Thanks to such technology, applications are processed more quickly and conveniently, allowing customers earlier access to credit, and saving the company personnel costs and reducing its bad debts.

*Do you think this technology means that a customer is less likely to shop around for a better deal?*

Many large companies now process and record credit sales with trusted customers (called *trading partners*) using Electronic Data Interchange (EDI) in e-business (as we discussed in Chapter 10). With EDI, the computers of the two companies are linked. When a customer wants to make a purchase, it views the seller's products and price lists from its own computer and submits orders directly into the seller's computerized sales-processing system. The system automatically prepares shipping documents and sales invoices, and distributes them electronically to the company's shipping department and to the customer's accounts payables management system. The computer programs have built-in controls to monitor the size and frequency of customers' orders. They print out a list of "unusual-looking" transactions daily, to be reviewed by managers to ensure that each transaction was authorized properly.

Technology also assists with monitoring a company's receivables. Computer programs can electronically check the ages of customers' balances and automatically send "past due" notices to customers. The programs can also change the information in the notices as the accounts become more overdue (and include appropriate advertising for each specific customer).

## Reporting Accounts Receivable

4 How does a company determine the amount of its bad debts expense, and how does it report the related amounts on its financial statements?

Although we explained in Chapter 9 and in the previous section that companies show accounts receivable on the balance sheet at net realizable value, we did not explain *how* they calculate the amounts of the bad debts expense and the allowance for bad debts. When a company prepares financial statements, it uses one of two methods to calculate these amounts: (1) the aging method or (2) the percentage of sales method. The basic difference between the two is that the aging method calculates the estimate of the *balance* in the Allowance for Bad Debts account to use in determining the net realizable value for Accounts Receivable. Under this method, the bad debts expense is the amount needed to obtain the *required allowance balance.* On the other hand, the percentage of sales method calculates the *amount of bad debts expense* to include on the income statement of the current period. It ignores any balance in the Allowance for Bad Debts. We will explain the aging method and then briefly discuss the percentage of sales method.

### Aging Method of Estimating Bad Debts

A company using the **aging method** estimates the amount of bad debts based on the age of the individual amounts included in the ending balance of its Accounts Receivable (how long these amounts have been owed to the company). It does this because the older the receivable, the less likely the company is to collect it. Therefore, the aging method is generally considered to be better for estimating, at the end of the period, the net accounts receivable that will be collectible. Because of this accounts receivable focus, the aging method is called a "balance sheet approach" to estimating bad debts. Note that this method does *not* directly consider the dollar amount of credit sales that occurred during the accounting period.

*Do you agree that the accounts receivable ending balance may include uncollected credit sales from previous periods and not include most credit sales from this period? Why or why not?*

A company uses four steps in the aging method. First, it categorizes the accounts receivable for its individual customers (from its accounts receivable subsidiary file) into age groups based on the length of time they have been outstanding. For example, Unlimited Decadence divides its accounts receivable into groups of balances that are (1) not yet past due, (2) 1–30 days past due, (3) 31–60 days past due, (4) 61–120 days past due, and (5) more than 120 days past due. It divides the customers' balances into groups because older accounts are more likely to be uncollectible.

Second, the company multiplies the total dollar amount for each age group by the percentage of that group's amount that it estimates to be uncollectible. It bases each group's uncollectible percentage on its past experience in collecting receivables. For example, for its December 31, 2008, balance sheet, Unlimited Decadence uses its ERP system to analyze its past performance in collecting receivables (or uses industry estimates), develops an estimated percentage that is uncollectible for each age group, and calculates the dollar amount uncollectible for each age group as follows:

| Age Group | Amount | | Estimated Percentage Uncollectible | | Estimated Uncollectible Amount |
|---|---|---|---|---|---|
| Not yet past due | $3,000,000 | × | 0.1% | = | $ 3,000 |
| 1–30 days past due | 1,500,000 | × | 1 | = | 15,000 |
| 31–60 days past due | 900,000 | × | 3 | = | 27,000 |
| 61–120 days past due | 400,000 | × | 10 | = | 40,000 |
| 121+ days past due | 200,000 | × | 30 | = | 60,000 |
| Total | $6,000,000 | | | | $145,000 |

Third, the company sums the estimated uncollectible amounts to calculate the required ending balance in the Allowance for Bad Debts. As shown in the preceding schedule, the total for Unlimited Decadence on December 31, 2008 is $145,000.

Fourth, the company makes a year-end adjustment to *bring the balance in the Allowance account up to the calculated balance.* The amount of the adjustment depends on the existing balance in the Allowance account before the adjustment. We assume that before its 2008 year-end adjustment, Unlimited Decadence has a beginning balance of $11,000 in its Allowance account. The balance in Bad Debts Expense before the adjustment is $0 because we assume that the year-end adjustment is the only time during the year that a company records bad debts. (A company could, however, record bad debts expense during the year, say quarterly.) The amount of the end-of-period adjustment is the amount needed to increase the existing balance of Allowance for Bad Debts up to the estimated amount calculated by the aging analysis. Unlimited Decadence calculates the amount as follows:

$$\text{Required end-of-period adjustment} = \$145{,}000 \text{ required balance} - \$11{,}000 \text{ existing balance} = \underline{\underline{\$134{,}000}}$$

At the end of 2008, Unlimited Decadence records $134,000 as Bad Debts Expense and increases its Allowance for Bad Debts by $134,000 as follows:

**FINANCIAL STATEMENT EFFECTS**

Decreases *net* accounts receivable, current assets, and total assets on ***balance sheet.*** Increases expenses, which decreases net income on ***income statement*** (and therefore decreases stockholders' equity on ***balance sheet***).

| **Assets** | | | = | **Liabilities** + | **Stockholders' Equity** — **Net Income** — **Revenues** − **Expenses** |
|---|---|---|---|---|---|
| Accounts Receivable | − | Allowance for Bad Debts | | | Bad Debts Expense |
| Bal $6,000,000 | − | Bal $ 11,000 | [12/31/08 balances before adjustment] | − | $ 0 |
| | − | +134,000 | [12/31/08 adjustment] | − | +134,000 |
| Bal $6,000,000 | − | Bal $145,000 | [12/31/08 balances after adjustment] | − | $134,000 |

The Allowance account increases from $11,000 to the required (calculated) balance of $145,000. Unlimited Decadence subtracts this balance from the $6,000,000 ending Accounts Receivable balance to determine the net realizable value of $5,855,000, which it reports on its December 31, 2008 year-end balance sheet. It includes the bad debts expense of $134,000 on its 2008 income statement. Exhibit 13-4

**EXHIBIT 13-4 DESCRIPTION OF ACCOUNTS RECEIVABLE ON A BALANCE SHEET**

**UNLIMITED DECADENCE**
**Balances for Current Asset Accounts**
**December 31, 2008**
***(in thousands)***

| | |
|---|---|
| Current assets | |
| Cash and cash equivalents | $1,020 |
| Accounts receivable (net) | 5,855 |
| Short-term notes receivable | 100 |
| Inventories | 1,610 |
| Total current assets | $8,585 |

**Accounts receivable** (gross) is the total amount owed to a company by customers for credit sales.

**Allowance for bad debts** is the amount the company expects not to be paid.

**Accounts receivable** *(net)* is the amount the company expects to collect.

GAAP requires that a company report its accounts receivable on its balance sheet at the *net realizable value* (i.e., the amount of cash the company expects to collect from customers).

The net amount shown for Unlimited Decadence's accounts receivable represents the total amounts owed to Unlimited Decadence from customers at December 31, 2008, *less* an allowance for accounts receivable estimated to be uncollectible. The calculation is (in thousands of dollars):

| Total accounts receivable owed to Unlimited Decadence | − | Allowance for bad debts | = | Accounts receivable (net) |
|---|---|---|---|---|
| $6,000 | − | $145 | = | $5,855 |

summarizes the reporting of accounts receivable, using the amounts calculated above under the aging method.

In addition to using an aging analysis to determine the bad debts expense at year-end, many companies do an aging analysis on a quarterly, monthly, or more frequent basis. By watching which customers' accounts are moving to an older age group, the company can closely monitor which customers may not pay their accounts.

### Percentage of Sales Method of Estimating Bad Debts

A company using the **percentage of sales method** estimates its bad debts expense by multiplying the net credit sales of the period by the percentage of these sales it estimates to be uncollectible. The company may use its ERP system to base the percentage on its history of writing off bad debts (or on industry statistics). Because the estimate is based on the dollar amount of credit sales reported on the income statement, the percentage of sales method is called an "income statement approach" to calculating bad debts expense.

For instance, assume that Unlimited Decadence had $72 million in credit sales during 2008. Further, based on prior experience, assume it estimates that 0.2% of its credit sales will be uncollectible. If Unlimited Decadence uses the percentage of sales method, it records bad debts expense for 2008 at $144,000 ($72 million × 0.002). If we again assume that Unlimited Decadence has a beginning balance of $11,000 in its Allowance account, the balance in its Allowance for Bad Debts at the end of 2008 would be $155,000.

*Why do you think that Unlimited Decadence uses higher percentages in the aging schedule than it uses in the percentage of sales method? Since the percentage of sales and aging methods produce different amounts, is one right and the other wrong?*

Notice that when a company uses the percentage of sales method, the year-end adjustment is designed so that the *calculated* amount of bad debts expense (in this case, $144,000) is the amount of the *bad debts expense* that the company reports. The year-end balance in Allowance for Bad Debts is the sum of the balance before the adjustment plus the calculated amount of bad debts expense. This method does not consider the age of the receivables, or an evaluation of the collectibility of individual receivables.

*What do you think managers (of companies that use the percentage of sales method) will do if they notice that the balance of the Allowance for Bad Debts is getting larger and larger at the end of every year? Why would this happen?*

## Technology and Management of Accounts Receivable

Many large companies are reengineering their management of accounts receivable to reduce the costs of handling collections of receivables and to speed up the depositing of cash receipts into their bank accounts. They often use two strategies: (1) lockbox systems and (2) electronic cash-collection procedures.

A **lockbox system** is a cash-collection method in which customers mail their payments to the company's post office box, which is monitored by its bank. Bank employees—not company employees—compare payment notices with customers' checks, total the day's receipts, and deposit the checks. Then they send the payment notices to the company so that it can record the transactions in its accounting system. Companies that have multistate operations use several lockboxes. By using a lockbox system, a company reduces the number of employees it needs to manage receivables, and it deposits its cash receipts very quickly. **Wells Fargo Bank**, for instance, advertises that it processes company lockbox receipts six days a week, works three shifts of employees per day, reports to the company up to four times a day, and picks up mail eight or nine times every working day.

Increasingly, companies are adopting electronic cash-collection procedures. With **electronic cash-collection procedures,** customers make payments by a direct transfer of funds from their bank accounts to the company's bank account. Electronic cash collections are commonly used by a company's EDI (Electronic Data Interchange) partners. The advantages of electronic cash-collection procedures are that there are no mailed-in receipts to open, no checks to process, and no payment notices to match. However, the company, its customers, and the banks for both parties must agree to the electronic collection procedures. Wells Fargo Bank also advertises that it performs electronic transfer services for its banking customers.

## Business Issues and Values in Recording Bad Debts

In its 2005 annual report, **U.S. Bancorp** reported that its bad debts expense was $666 million, $669 million, and $1,254 million in 2005, 2004, and 2003, respectively. The bank wrote-off loans of $949 million, $1,074 million, and $1,494 million in each of these years.

*Explain why the changes might have occurred in U.S. Bancorp's bad debts. Why might the shareholders of U.S. Bancorp be interested in the changes in the amounts?*

# COMPUTING THE AMOUNT OF SALES MADE TO COMPANIES IN OTHER COUNTRIES

**5** What is an exchange rate, and how does an exchange gain (loss) arise from a credit sale made to a company in another country?

As U.S. companies expand their operations, they frequently become involved in transactions with customers and suppliers in other countries. For example, a U.S. company may decide to expand its revenue opportunities by selling its products in foreign countries. Or, a U.S. company may decide that it can purchase inventory at a lower cost or acquire machinery that is more efficient from a company based in a foreign country. In each of these situations, the U.S. company must record the transaction in U.S. dollars, although the price may be stated in terms of a foreign currency. Since these types of transactions are becoming more common, even among small companies, you should have a basic understanding of these international issues. In this chapter we discuss the recording of international sales. In Chapter 14, we will discuss the recording of international purchases. But first we discuss exchange rates.

An **exchange rate** measures the value of one currency in terms of another currency. Unfortunately, some exchange rates are commonly expressed in U.S. dollars whereas others are expressed in terms of the number of foreign units that are equal to the U.S. dollar. For example, recently the British pound was quoted at a rate of $1.88. This rate means that it takes $1.88 to buy one British pound; that is, the pound is a larger unit than the U.S. dollar. In contrast, the Swiss franc was recently quoted at a rate of 1.23 francs to the U.S. dollar. This rate means that it takes 1.23 francs to buy $1; that is, the franc is a smaller unit than the dollar. To avoid confusion, in this book we always quote exchange rates in terms of the number of U.S. dollars that is equivalent to one unit of the foreign currency. Therefore, for the British pound and the Swiss franc, we use exchange rates of $1.88 for the pound and $0.81 (1 ÷ 1.23) for the franc. The general rule is that a foreign currency is converted into U.S. dollars as follows:

$$\text{Amount in U.S. Dollars} = \text{Foreign Currency Amount} \times \underset{\text{(stated in dollars)}}{\text{Exchange Rate}}$$

We illustrate some recent exchange rates in Exhibit 13-5.

*Pick the currency of a country you have visited or would like to visit and look up its exchange rate. Is its currency larger or smaller than the U.S. dollar?*

© PHOTODISC/GETTY IMAGES

When a company and its customer are in different countries that use different currencies, how do you think they arrive at an agreed-upon selling price?

**EXHIBIT 13-5** **EXCHANGE RATES**

| Currency (Country) | Price in U.S. Dollars |
|---|---|
| Pound (Britain) | $1.8847 |
| Dollar (Canada) | 0.8910 |
| Euro | 1.2829 |
| Shekel (Israel) | 0.2292 |
| Yen (Japan) | 0.0086 |
| Peso (Mexico) | 0.0926 |
| Riyal (Saudi Arabia) | 0.2666 |
| Won (South Korea) | 0.0010 |
| Franc (Switzerland) | 0.8113 |

*Source: The Wall Street Journal,* August 18, 2006.

Since an exchange rate represents the price of one currency in terms of another, rates change continuously as supply and demand for currencies change. These changes are often described by terms such as strong (rising) and weak (falling). To understand these changes, consider the exchange rate for the pound in Exhibit 13-5: $1.6193. If the dollar weakens against the pound, the price (exchange rate) of the pound rises when stated in terms of the dollar. For example, a change in the rate to $1.65 would be a weakening of the dollar because it now takes more dollars to buy one pound. Saying that the dollar is weakening is the same as saying that the pound is strengthening.

*Wait a few days and look up the exchange rate you used in the previous STOP. Has the currency strengthened or weakened?*

As we explained earlier, many U.S. companies conduct transactions with customers in foreign countries. Sometimes the companies agree on a price stated in U.S. dollars. For example, most sales of crude oil are stated in terms of the U.S. dollar. In these situations, there is no accounting issue; the transaction is recorded as we discussed earlier in this chapter. For example, if a U.S. oil company sells 10,000 barrels of crude oil to Mexico, the price would be quoted in dollars and not in the equivalent amount of pesos. If the price was $25 per barrel, the company would record a sale and the related cash receipt of $250,000 ($25 × 10,000).

In many situations, however, the companies agree on a price stated in terms of the foreign currency. In these cases, the U.S. company must record the transaction in U.S. dollars. Therefore, the company must convert the foreign currency amount into dollars at the exchange rate on the day of the transaction. Also, transactions between companies in different countries usually involve credit terms, if only to allow time for the processing of the orders, shipments, and payments across international borders. In addition, currency exchange rates change continuously. As a result, the exchange rate is likely to change between the date the U.S. company records a credit sale and the date it receives the payment. On the date of the cash receipt, then, the company records an exchange gain or loss to account for the difference between the selling price and the amount of the cash receipt. An **exchange gain or loss** is caused by a change in the exchange rate between the date that a company records a credit sale and the date the company collects the cash. More specifically, exchange gains and losses occur for credit sales as follows:

1. An exchange *gain* occurs when the exchange rate *increases* between the date a company records a *receivable* and the date the company *collects* the cash.
2. An exchange *loss* occurs when the exchange rate *declines* between the date a company records a *receivable* and the date the company *collects* the cash.

To understand an exchange loss that occurs when the exchange rate declines between the date a credit sale is recorded and the date the cash is collected, suppose that Unlimited Decadence sells candy to the Herrmann Company, a German company, on credit and agrees to a price of 300,000 Euros rather than a price in dollars. On the date of the sale, the exchange rate is $1.28 (1 Euro = $1.28), and therefore Unlimited Decadence records the sale of $384,000 (300,000 Euros × $1.28) as follows:

| Assets | = | Liabilities | + | Stockholders' Equity | | |
|---|---|---|---|---|---|---|
| | | | | Net Income | | |
| | | | | Revenues | − | Expenses |
| Accounts Receivable (Herrmann Company) | | | | Sales Revenue | | |
| +$384,000 | | | | +$384,000 | | |

**FINANCIAL STATEMENT EFFECTS**

Increases current assets and total assets on ***balance sheet***. Increases revenues, which increases net income on ***income statement*** (and therefore increases stockholders' equity on ***balance sheet***).

Herrmann Company has an obligation to pay 300,000 Euros regardless of the exchange rate on the date of payment. If the exchange rate is $1.26 when Herrmann pays the amount owed, Unlimited Decadence can convert those Euros into only $378,000 (300,000 Euros × $1.26). As a result, it has an exchange *loss* of $6,000 ($378,000 − $384,000), which it records at the time of the cash collection as follows:

| Assets | | = | Liabilities | + | Stockholders' Equity | | |
|---|---|---|---|---|---|---|---|
| | | | | | Net Income | | |
| | | | | | Revenues (Gains) | − | Expenses (Losses) |
| Cash | Accounts Receivable (Herrmann Company) | | | | | | Exchange Loss |
| +$378,000 | −$384,000 | | | | | − | +$6,000 |

**FINANCIAL STATEMENT EFFECTS**

Decreases current assets and total assets on ***balance sheet***. Increases losses (in "other items"), which decreases net income on ***income statement*** (and therefore decreases stockholders' equity on ***balance sheet***). Increases cash flows from operating activities on ***cash flow statement***.

Unlimited Decadence also can compute the exchange loss by multiplying the amount of the receivable by the change in the exchange rate [300,000 Euros × ($1.28 − $1.26) = $6,000]. Remember that Herrmann Company still pays 300,000 Euros; it is Unlimited Decadence that has the exchange loss.

Note that the U.S. company (Unlimited Decadence) experienced an exchange loss because it agreed to a transaction expressed in terms of a foreign currency. In such a situation, the U.S. company accepts the risks associated with changes in the exchange rate. If a U.S. company agrees to a transaction in U.S. dollars, the foreign company accepts, and the U.S. company avoids, the risks associated with changes in the exchange rate.

A potential disadvantage of selling to companies in other countries is that it may take longer to collect from them. For example, a recent Dun & Bradstreet study indicated that U.S. companies pay their bills, on average, in 30 to 60 days, whereas in Germany the average time is 30 to 90 days.

## UNEARNED REVENUE

**6** How does a company account for cash collected prior to sales?

A company usually collects cash from a customer at the time of the sale or *after* the sale, as we discussed earlier in the chapter. In some industries, however, it is common for the selling company to collect cash from customers *before* it delivers the goods or provides the services that the customers purchased. For example, magazine publishers require customers to pay for subscriptions before many of the issues being purchased are even written, much less delivered to the customer.

*Have you paid for goods or services in advance? What did you purchase? What are some other examples of goods or services that people pay for before they actually receive what they purchased?*

When a company collects cash before it delivers the goods or services, it records a current liability often called **unearned revenue**. You may think that this is a confusing label because the term "revenue" means that the company has done what it has to do to earn revenue. However, "unearned" indicates that the earning process is not complete. Some companies use a less confusing title such as "products (or services) to be provided."

*Do you agree with the following statement? "Accounts receivable are the amounts owed to a company for credit sales already recorded, whereas unearned revenues are the amounts received by a company for sales it will record in the future." Why or why not?*

A company records this liability (unearned revenue) because it accepts an obligation to provide goods or services in the future as a result of collecting cash now. Remember that a company does not record revenue until it provides the goods or services. A magazine publishing company, then, earns subscription revenue one issue at a time as it delivers magazines to customers who already paid for that issue. Every time the company delivers an issue of the magazine, it reduces that portion of the unearned revenue and increases revenue.

For example, suppose that Bookworm Publishing Corporation publishes *Enlightened Lite,* a new-age magazine that comes out monthly. The magazine publishes poetry, humorous short stories, recipes, and critiques of self-help books. Bookworm's fiscal year ends on December 31. On November 19, the company received a check for $3,600 from Aroma Health Stores for 100 annual subscriptions (12 monthly issues each, starting in December) of *Enlightened Lite.* Aroma owns 100 retail health-aid stores and wants each store manager to read the magazine. Bookworm Publishing records the cash receipt as follows:

**FINANCIAL STATEMENT EFFECTS**

Increases current assets and total assets on ***balance sheet***. Increases current liabilities and total liabilities on ***balance sheet***. Increases cash flows from operating activities on ***cash flow statement***.

| **Assets** | = | **Liabilities** | + | **Stockholders' Equity** |
|---|---|---|---|---|
| Cash | | Unearned Subscription Revenue | | |
| +$3,600 | | +$3,600 | | |

Bookworm increases Cash by the $3,600 it received. Because it collected the cash before it delivers any issues of the magazine to Aroma Health Stores, it increases Unearned Subscription Revenue, a current liability account, for the entire amount of the cash receipt.

*If Bookworm received payment for two-year subscriptions, do you think it would classify the entire amount as a current liability? Why or why not?*

On December 1, Bookworm sends out 100 copies of its December issue of *Enlightened Lite* to Aroma Health Stores and records the event as follows:

**FINANCIAL STATEMENT EFFECTS**

Decreases current liabilities and total liabilities on ***balance sheet***. Increases revenues, which increases net income on ***income statement*** (and therefore increases stockholders' equity on ***balance sheet***).

| **Assets** | = | **Liabilities** | + | **Stockholders' Equity** | | |
|---|---|---|---|---|---|---|
| | | | | ***Net Income*** | | |
| | | | | **Revenues** | − | **Expenses** |
| | | Unearned Subscription Revenue | | Subscription Revenue | | |
| | | −$300 | | +$300 | | |

By sending out one issue of its magazine, Bookworm Publishing earns $300 (1/12 of the $3,600 received from Aroma). Therefore it reduces its liability to Aroma by this same amount. Every month when Bookworm mails out an issue of *Enlightened Lite* to Aroma Health Stores, it records a decrease in its liability and an increase in its revenue.

Exhibit 13-6 summarizes how Bookworm Publishing calculates the Unearned Subscription Revenue balance for Aroma Health Stores on December 31. Bookworm reports the total balance for all its customers in its Unearned Subscription Revenue account in the current liabilities section of its December 31, 2008 balance sheet.

**EXHIBIT 13-6** **BOOKWORM PUBLISHING'S YEAR-END SUBSCRIPTION REVENUE FOR ONE CUSTOMER: AROMA HEALTH STORES**

Unearned Subscription Revenue

| | |
|---|---|
| 11/19 | + $3,600 |
| 12/1 | − 300 |
| 12/31 | $3,300 |

Bookworm sells 100 annual subscriptions to Aroma Health Stores. Because it has sent none of the magazines to Aroma, Bookworm records a liability for the total amount of cash received (100 subscriptions at $36 per subscription = $3,600).

Bookworm Publishing mails its December issue to all customers. By sending 100 copies of its magazine to Aroma Health Stores, it has now earned 1/12 of this unearned revenue. It reduces the account by $300 because $3,600 ÷ 12 = $300.

Bookworm Publishing's liability to Aroma Health Stores at 12/31 is $3,300, which represents the value of 100 copies of each of the 11 issues that Bookworm will deliver next year. To determine the amount to be reported as a current liability on its 12/31 balance sheet, it adds this amount to the balances of the Unearned Subscription Revenue for all other customers.

*Why might Bookworm ship its January issue in late December?*

Airline companies have significant unearned revenues because they require customers to pay before flying. For example, on its December 31, 2005 balance sheet, **Southwest Airlines** reports an "air traffic liability" of $649 million, which is equal to approximately 17 percent of its current liabilities.

*Explain how this information affects your evaluation of Delta's liquidity.*

In summary, a company calculates its year-end unearned revenue balance, as shown below, and includes the amounts on each of the financial statements as indicated:

| | | | | | | |
|---|---|---|---|---|---|---|
| Beginning Unearned Revenue Balance | + | Cash Collected during the Year for Goods Not Yet Delivered or Services Not Yet Provided | − | Amounts Earned during the Year | = | Ending Unearned Revenue Balance |
| ↓ | | ↓ | | ↓ | | ↓ |
| Beginning Balance Sheet: Current Liabilities | | Cash Flow Statement: Operating Activities | | Income Statement | | Ending Balance Sheet: Current Liabilities |

## NOTES RECEIVABLE

7 What are the important characteristics of a note receivable, and how is interest computed?

Many companies also sell goods to customers under more formal, extended credit arrangements. In this situation, the selling company usually requires the customer to sign a promissory note. A **note** is a written legal document in which the maker of the note (in our case, the customer) makes an unconditional promise to pay another party (in our case, the selling company) a certain amount of money on an agreed future date. Because the selling company expects to receive the cash that its customer promised, the amount the customer owes is called a **note receivable**.

For these sales, a company manages the activities of granting credit, recording credit sales, and monitoring notes receivable balances using methods similar to those used in managing accounts receivable. For credit sales that involve promissory notes, managers and external users must still be concerned with the criteria used to judge whether a sale has actually occurred, as we discussed earlier. The same questions about transfer of goods and services to the customer and the likelihood of sales returns must be answered. So, why use a promissory note instead of an account receivable? A company may require a customer to sign a promissory note if the amount of the credit sale is relatively large, the length of time between the sale and the eventual cash collection is relatively long (and so interest is paid), or the creditworthiness of the customer is questionable. Because a promissory note is a written, legal document, many companies want the added security that is provided by a note.

*If you loaned a friend $5, would you want a note in exchange? What if you loaned $5,000?*

Exhibit 13-7 provides an example of a promissory note. In our example, Burgen Candies makes a major purchase and agrees to pay Unlimited Decadence $10,000 plus interest (computed based on an annual interest rate of 12%) on February 1, 2009. Because Burgen Candies is a new company and it wants to delay payment until it is more established, Unlimited Decadence requires it to sign a note. The **principal** or **face value** of the note is the amount stated on the note—in our case, $10,000. The **maturity date** (February 1, 2009) is the specific day when the company that made and signed the note (called the **maker**) promises to pay the principal and interest amounts to the note holder (called the **payee**). Three factors determine the amount of interest owed to the payee: (1) the face value (principal) of the note, (2) the interest rate stated on the note, and (3) the length of time between the date the note is issued and the maturity date. The general rule for computing interest is as follows:

$$\text{Interest} = \text{Principal of the Note} \times \text{Annual Rate of Interest} \times \text{Period of Time the Note Is Outstanding in Years or Fraction of a Year}$$

This equation is often referred to as I = PRT. The **maturity value of the note** is the total of the principal plus the interest due on the maturity date and is the amount the maker must pay the payee on that date.

## EXHIBIT 13-7 PROMISSORY NOTE FROM BURGEN CANDIES TO UNLIMITED DECADENCE

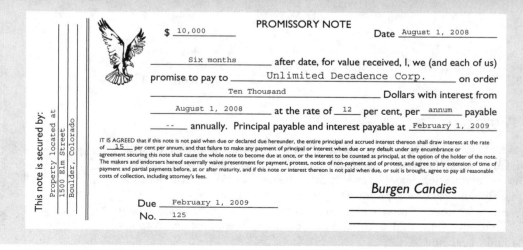

This note is secured by:
Property located at
1500 Elm Street
Boulder, Colorado

PROMISSORY NOTE

$ 10,000 Date August 1, 2008

Six months after date, for value received, I, we (and each of us) promise to pay to Unlimited Decadence Corp. on order Ten Thousand Dollars with interest from August 1, 2008 at the rate of 12 per cent, per annum payable -- annually. Principal payable and interest payable at February 1, 2009

IT IS AGREED that if this note is not paid when due or declared due hereunder, the entire principal and accrued interest thereon shall draw interest at the rate of 15 per cent per annum, and that failure to make any payment of principal or interest when due or any default under any encumbrance or agreement securing this note shall cause the whole note to become due at once, or the interest to be counted as principal, at the option of the holder of the note. The makers and endorsers hereof severrally waive presentment for payment, protest, notice of non-payment and of protest, and agree to any extension of time of payment and partial payments before, at or after maturity, and if this note or interest thereon is not paid when due, or suit is brought, agree to pay all reasonable costs of collection, including attorney's fees.

Due February 1, 2009

No. 125

Burgen Candies

*Did you get all of those terms straight? Use our Burgen Candies example to see how well you understand this section so far. Based on our example, answer the following questions:*

1. *Who is the maker of the note?*
2. *Who is the payee of the note?*
3. *When was the note signed?*
4. *What is the face value of the note?*
5. *When is the maturity date of the note?*
6. *What is the annual interest rate on the note?*
7. *How long is the time between the date the note is issued and the maturity date?*
8. *How much is the interest due on the maturity date?*
9. *How much is the maturity value of the note?*

*How did you do?[6] Make sure you have this information correct because we will use it as we continue our notes receivable example.*

## Recording Receipt of a Note Receivable

Unlimited Decadence records the $10,000 sale when it receives the note from Burgen Candies on August 1, 2008 (the date on the note), as follows:

| **Assets** | = | **Liabilities** | + | **Stockholders' Equity** | | |
|---|---|---|---|---|---|---|
| | | | | ***Net Income*** | | |
| | | | | **Revenues** | – | **Expenses** |
| Notes Receivable | | | | Sales Revenue | | |
| +$10,000 | | | | +$10,000 | | |

**FINANCIAL STATEMENT EFFECTS**

Increases current assets and total assets on ***balance sheet***. Increases revenues, which increases net income on ***income statement*** (and therefore increases stockholders' equity on ***balance sheet***).

Both Notes Receivable and Sales Revenue increase by $10,000 as a result of the sale.

*Can you explain why a company's interest revenue may be different from the interest it received in any accounting period?*

## Recording Accrued Interest

From the day a customer signs a promissory note until the maturity date of the note, the selling company earns the interest associated with the note. It *earns* interest continuously during this time period even though it may not *collect* the interest until the maturity date. By saying that interest is earned continuously, we mean that, for example, after one day of holding a note, a company has earned one day's worth of interest. This holds true for one week, one month, and so on, regardless of when the company receives the interest.

Exhibit 13-8 shows how much interest Unlimited Decadence earns while it holds Burgen Candies' $10,000 promissory note. As we show in the exhibit, we calculate one month's interest as follows:

$$\text{Interest} = \text{Principal of the Note} \times \text{Annual Rate of Interest} \times \text{Period of Time the Note Is Outstanding in Years or Fraction of a Year}$$

$$= \$10{,}000 \times 0.12 \times 1/12$$

$$= \underline{\underline{\$100}}$$

Unlimited Decadence earns $600 ($10,000 × 0.12 × 6/12) interest over the six-month life of the note. Another way to think of the total amount of interest is to multiply the interest earned per month by the number of months. Unlimited Decadence earns $100 in interest per month for six months for a total of $600.

[6] Here are the answers: (1) Burgen Candies (2) Unlimited Decadence Corporation (3) August 1, 2008 (4) $10,000 (5) February 1, 2009 (6) 12% (7) One-half of a year (six months) (8) $10,000 × 0.12 × 1/2 = $600 (9) $10,000 + $600 = $10,600.

## EXHIBIT 13-8 EXPLANATION OF INTEREST EARNED BY UNLIMITED DECADENCE ON PROMISSORY NOTE FROM BURGEN CANDIES

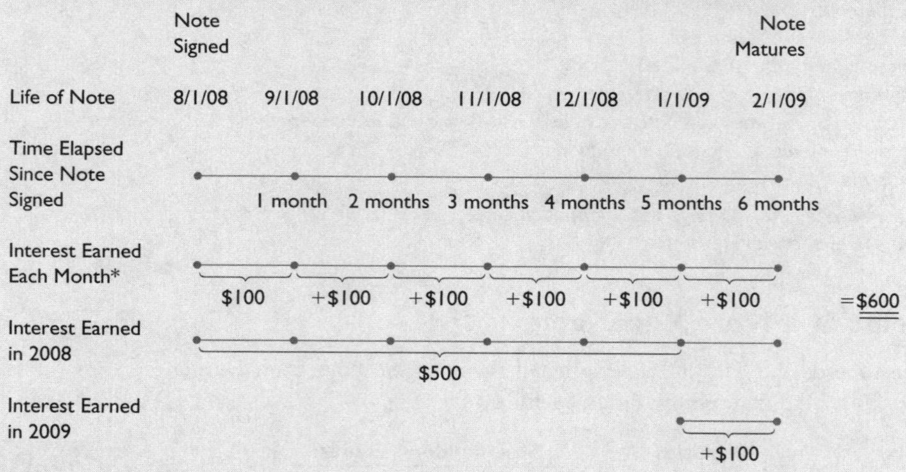

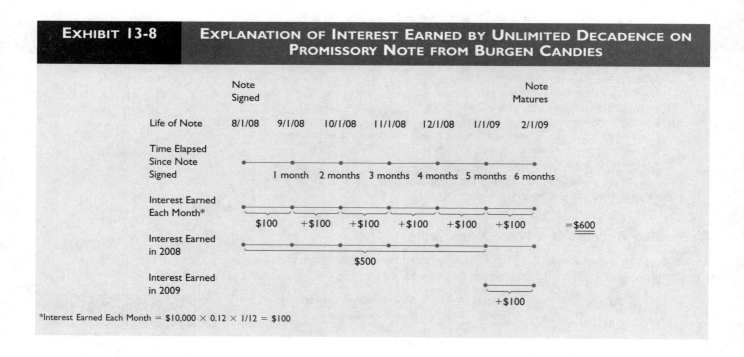

*Interest Earned Each Month = $10,000 × 0.12 × 1/12 = $100

We focus on the concept of earning interest over time because a company must report, on its financial statements for a period, the interest that it has earned during the period (even if it has not yet collected the interest). Unlimited Decadence is to receive the $10,000 face value of Burgen Candies' note and the $600 in interest on February 1, 2009, but its fiscal year ends on December 31, 2008. Although Unlimited Decadence has not received any cash from Burgen Candies its financial statements for 2008 must include the amount of interest the company has earned through December 31, 2008.

You can see in Exhibit 13-8 that at December 31, 2008, five months have passed since Unlimited Decadence received the $10,000 note. Thus, Unlimited Decadence's accounting records should show that it earned $500 ($10,000 × 0.12 × 5/12) of interest during 2008 from holding Burgen Candies' note. Also, the records should show that Unlimited Decadence has a legal right to collect the interest at a later date. So Unlimited Decadence makes an end-of-period adjustment to record the $500 as follows:

**FINANCIAL STATEMENT EFFECTS**

Increases current assets and total assets on ***balance sheet.*** Increases revenues (in "other items"), which increases net income on ***income statement*** (and therefore increases stockholders' equity on ***balance sheet***).

| **Assets** | = | **Liabilities** | + | **Stockholders' Equity** | | |
|---|---|---|---|---|---|---|
| | | | | ***Net Income*** | | |
| | | | | **Revenues** | − | **Expenses** |
| Interest Receivable | | | | Interest Revenue | | |
| +$500 | | | | +$500 | | |

Both Interest Receivable and Interest Revenue increase by $500 as a result of the adjustment. Every time a company prepares financial statements, it must determine whether or not it has earned any interest that it has not yet recorded in its accounting system. If so, it makes an end-of-period adjustment to record the interest receivable and the interest revenue.

## Recording the Cash Receipt

Assume that on February 1, 2009, Burgen Candies pays Unlimited Decadence the $10,600 maturity value of the note. Unlimited Decadence records this transaction as follows:

| Assets | | | = Liabs. | + Stockholders' Equity: Net Income (Revenues − Expenses) |
|---|---|---|---|---|
| Cash | Notes Receivable | Interest Receivable | | Revenues: Interest Revenue |
| | Bal $10,000 | Bal $500 | | |
| +$10,600 | −10,000 | −500 | | +$100 |
| | Bal $ 0 | Bal $ 0 | | |

**FINANCIAL STATEMENT EFFECTS**

Increases current assets and total assets on ***balance sheet.*** Increases revenues (in "other items"), which increases net income on ***income statement*** (and therefore increases stockholders' equity on ***balance sheet***). Increases cash flows from operating activities on ***cash flow statement.***

Notice how this transaction affects Unlimited Decadence's financial statements. Cash increases by the $10,600 received from Burgen Candies. Interest revenue increases by the $100 ($10,000 × 0.12 × 1/12) interest earned from holding the note during January, as we show in Exhibit 13-8. Unlimited Decadence decreases the Notes Receivable account and the Interest Receivable account related to Burgen Candies' note by $10,000 and $500, respectively, because the customer no longer owes the principal or the interest recorded in December. The collection of the $600 interest and the $10,000 principal are both included in the cash flows from operating activities because the note receivable resulted from a sale by Unlimited Decadence. If the note receivable had resulted from a loan by Unlimited Decadence, the collection of the $10,000 principal would be classified as an investing activity in the cash flow statement.

## REPORTING CASH AND CASH EQUIVALENTS

8 What are cash equivalents and what items does a company include in its cash and cash equivalents?

On any given day, a company wants to have enough cash in its bank account to cover all the payments that will clear its account on that day, but not so much cash that it forgoes earning interest by not investing any excess cash. Large companies routinely take advantage of the money market (i.e., the market for buying and selling very short-term interest-bearing investments) by using excess cash to purchase cash equivalents. Many companies report cash and cash equivalents on their balance sheets. **Cash equivalents** are investments that are short-term, earn interest, are highly liquid, and involve very little risk. Examples of cash equivalents are short-term government notes and commercial paper (loans)

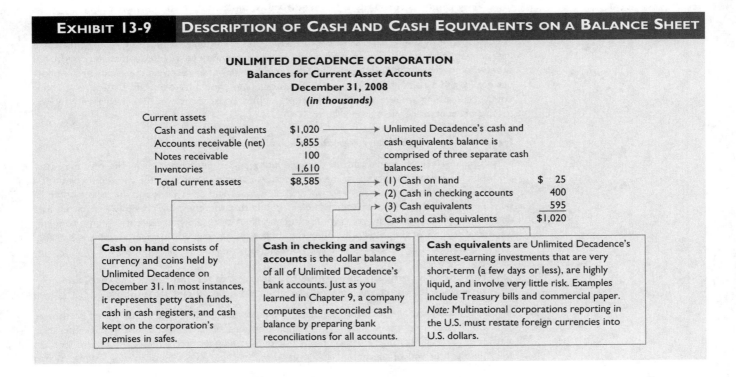

### EXHIBIT 13-9 DESCRIPTION OF CASH AND CASH EQUIVALENTS ON A BALANCE SHEET

**UNLIMITED DECADENCE CORPORATION**
**Balances for Current Asset Accounts**
**December 31, 2008**
***(in thousands)***

| Current assets | |
|---|---|
| Cash and cash equivalents | $1,020 |
| Accounts receivable (net) | 5,855 |
| Notes receivable | 100 |
| Inventories | 1,610 |
| Total current assets | $8,585 |

Unlimited Decadence's cash and cash equivalents balance is comprised of three separate cash balances:

| | |
|---|---|
| (1) Cash on hand | $ 25 |
| (2) Cash in checking accounts | 400 |
| (3) Cash equivalents | 595 |
| Cash and cash equivalents | $1,020 |

**Cash on hand** consists of currency and coins held by Unlimited Decadence on December 31. In most instances, it represents petty cash funds, cash in cash registers, and cash kept on the corporation's premises in safes.

**Cash in checking and savings accounts** is the dollar balance of all of Unlimited Decadence's bank accounts. Just as you learned in Chapter 9, a company computes the reconciled cash balance by preparing bank reconciliations for all accounts.

**Cash equivalents** are Unlimited Decadence's interest-earning investments that are very short-term (a few days or less), are highly liquid, and involve very little risk. Examples include Treasury bills and commercial paper. *Note:* Multinational corporations reporting in the U.S. must restate foreign currencies into U.S. dollars.

issued by corporations. Cash balance managers of large companies manage large sums of cash so precisely that they can purchase cash equivalents for just one day. The cash equivalents are so liquid that companies can exchange them for cash almost instantly (and earn interest on these investments) and adjust checking account balances very quickly. Communication technology provides a global marketplace for buying and selling cash equivalents.

In addition to checking accounts and cash equivalents, large companies may have petty cash funds, as we discussed in Chapter 9. A company includes the balance of the petty cash account, the reconciled cash balance of the checking account(s), and the cash equivalents as a current asset, Cash and Cash Equivalents, on its balance sheet. Recall that because of the liquidity of this asset, a company lists the total of Cash and Cash Equivalents as the first item of current assets. In Exhibit 13-9, we explain Unlimited Decadence's December 31, 2008 cash balance of $1,020.

## SUMMARY

At the beginning of the chapter we asked you several questions. During the chapter, we asked you to STOP and answer some additional questions to build your knowledge about specific issues. Be sure you answered these additional questions. Below are the questions from the beginning of the chapter, with a brief summary of the key points relating to the answers. Use your creative and critical thinking skills to expand on these key points to develop more complete answers to the questions and to determine what other questions you have that might lead you to learn more about the issues.

### 1 Why is managing and reporting liquidity important?

Managers and external users are interested in the liquidity of a company's assets because it affects the company's ability to pay its short-term liabilities. They assess a company's liquidity position by comparing the composition and amounts of its short-term assets and its short-term liabilities. From an external user's perspective, it is important to understand the types of economic resources or economic obligations that each balance sheet item represents. From a manager's perspective, it is important to understand how liquidity can be managed to improve company performance.

### 2 Why might a company offer credit sales, and what management policies should exist for accounts receivable?

A company might offer credit sales because selling on credit may be more convenient than selling for cash, because offering credit may encourage customers to buy items that they might not otherwise purchase, and because allowing customers to pay after receiving the goods signals product quality and a commitment to customers. A company should have policies that cover granting credit, recognizing when a credit sale occurs, monitoring accounts receivable balances, and reporting accounts receivable according to GAAP.

### 3 How does a company report credit sales and net sales?

A company reports credit sales in the accounting period in which it earns the revenue—usually when it transfers the goods to the customer. A company's net sales for an accounting period equals its total sales minus sales returns and allowances and sales discounts for that period. A sales return occurs when a customer returns goods that the company previously recorded as a sale and receives a refund in exchange for the goods. A sales allowance occurs when a company refunds a portion of the sales price after the original sale occurred. A sales discount is a reduction in the amount collected because the customer pays within the discount period.

### 4 How does a company determine the amount of its bad debts expense, and how does it report the related amounts on its financial statements?

A company using the aging method estimates the amount of bad debts expense based on the age of the individual accounts included in the ending balance of its Accounts Receivable. The aging method is generally considered to be better for determining the net accounts receivable that are collectible at the end of the period and is called a "balance sheet approach" for estimating bad debts. A company using the percentage of sales method estimates its bad debts expense by multiplying its net credit sales of the period by the percentage of these sales that it estimates to be uncollectible. The percentage of sales method is called an "income statement approach." Both Allowance for Bad Debts and Bad Debts Expense increase as a result of recording the estimate. A company includes the amount of its Bad Debts Expense on the income statement as a part of its operating expenses. It subtracts the Allowance for Bad Debts balance from the Accounts Receivable balance, so that the net Accounts Receivable reported on its balance sheet is the net realizable value (the amount of cash it expects to collect).

### 5 What is an exchange rate, and how does an exchange gain (loss) arise from a credit sale made to a company in another country?

An exchange rate measures the value of one currency in terms of another currency. In this book we always quote exchange rates in terms of the number of U.S. dollars that is equivalent to one unit of the foreign currency. An exchange gain or loss is caused by a change in the exchange rate between the date a company records a credit sales transaction and the date the company collects the cash. More specifically, for credit sales, an exchange gain occurs when the exchange rate increases between the date a company records a receivable and the date the company collects the cash, and an exchange loss occurs when the exchange rate declines between the date a company records a receivable and the date the company collects the cash.

### 6 How does a company account for cash collected prior to sales?

When a company collects cash from customers before it delivers the goods or provides the services that they purchased, it records a current liability, often called Unearned Revenue. A company records this liability (Unearned Revenue) because it accepts an obligation to provide goods or services in the future as a result of receiving cash now. The company records revenue and reduces Unearned Revenue when it provides the goods or services.

### 7 What are the important characteristics of a note receivable, and how is interest computed?

The principal or face value of the note is the amount that is stated on the note. The maturity date is the date when the company that made and signed the note (called the *maker*) promises to pay the principal and interest amounts to the note holder (called the *payee*). Three factors determine the amount of interest owed to the payee: (1) the face value (principal) of the note; (2) the interest rate stated on the note; and (3) the length of time between the date the note is issued and the maturity date. The equation for computing interest is as follows:

$$\text{Interest} = \text{Principal of the Note} \times \text{Annual Rate of Interest} \times \text{Period of Time the Note Is Outstanding in Years or Fraction of a Year}$$

The maturity value of the note is the total of the principal plus the interest due on the maturity date.

### 8 What are cash equivalents and what items does a company include in its cash and cash equivalents?

A company invests excess cash in cash equivalents, which are investments that are short-term, earn interest, are highly liquid, and involve very little risk. A company includes the balance of the petty cash account, the reconciled cash balance of the checking account(s), and the cash equivalents as a current asset, Cash and Cash Equivalents, on its balance sheet.

## KEY TERMS

**accounts payable management** *(p. 420)*
**accounts receivable management** *(p. 420)*
**accounts receivable subsidiary file** *(p. 423)*
**aging method** *(p. 431)*
**bad debts expense** *(p. 428)*
**cash balance management** *(p. 420)*
**cash equivalents** *(p. 443)*

**cash payments management** *(p. 420)*
**cash receipts management** *(p. 420)*
**control account** *(p. 423)*
**contra-account** *(p. 429)*
**electronic cash-collection procedures** *(p. 434)*
**exchange gain or loss** *(p. 436)*
**exchange rate** *(p. 435)*
**export insurance** *(p. 424)*
**letter of credit** *(p. 424)*
**liquidity** *(p. 418)*
**liquidity management** *(p. 418)*
**lockbox system** *(p. 434)*
**maker** *(p. 440)*
**maturity date** *(p. 440)*
**maturity value of the note** *(p. 440)*
**net sales** *(p. 425)*
**note** *(p. 439)*
**note receivable** *(p. 439)*
**payee** *(p. 440)*
**percentage of sales method** *(p. 433)*
**principal (face value)** *(p. 440)*
**reengineering** *(p. 430)*
**sales allowance** *(p. 425)*
**sales discount** *(p. 425)*
**sales return** *(p. 425)*
**sales revenue (net)** *(p. 425)*
**unearned revenue** *(p. 437)*

## SUMMARY SURFING

Here is an opportunity to gather information on the Internet about real-world issues related to the topics in this chapter (for suggestions on how to navigate various companies' Web sites to find their financial statements and other information, see the related discussion in the Preface at the beginning of the book). Answer the following questions.

- Go to the **Southwest Airlines** Web site. Find the amount of the "air traffic liability" on its most recent balance sheet. How does this amount compare with the 2005 amount discussed in the chapter, and what does it tell you about the airline's performance?
- Go to the **Yahoo! Finance** Web site. Click on Investing; then click on *Currency Exchange Rates*. Has the dollar strengthened or weakened since August 18, 2006 against each of the currencies listed both on your screen and in Exhibit 13-5?

## INTEGRATED BUSINESS AND ACCOUNTING SITUATIONS

**Answer the Following Questions in Your Own Words.**

### Testing Your Knowledge

**13-1** What is liquidity management, and why do users need to understand liquidity?

**13-2** What does a user need to know to evaluate an account balance?

**13-3** Identify the five areas of liquidity management.

**13-4** Why do companies make credit sales to customers?

**13-5** What is an accounts receivable subsidiary file, and how does it relate to the Accounts Receivable control account?

**13-6** What are the basic management policies over accounts receivable for large companies?

**13-7** Identify three additional controls used by large companies in granting credit.

**13-8** Explain the difference between a sales return, a sales allowance, and a sales discount.

**13-9** What is bad debts expense, and when is it measured and reported?

**13-10** How does the reporting of bad debts affect a company's financial statements?

**13-11** How does a company record the write-off of an uncollectible account, and how does the write-off affect the net accounts receivable?

**13-12** Briefly explain how large companies are reengineering their liquidity management activities.

**13-13** What are the two methods of calculating the bad debts expense and the allowance for bad debts?

**13-14** Briefly explain how a company estimates bad debts expense using the aging method.

**13-15** Briefly explain how a company estimates bad debts expense using the percentage of sales method.

**13-16** Explain the meaning of (a) an exchange rate and (b) an exchange gain and an exchange loss in regard to credit sales.

**13-17** What is unearned revenue? Give an example (other than those in the chapter).

**13-18** Why might a company require a customer to sign a note receivable for a credit sale?

**13-19** Briefly explain how to record the receipt of a note receivable, the related accrued interest, and the payment of the note by the customer.

**13-20** Define the term *cash equivalents,* and explain why a company would have them.

**13-21** Identify what is included in Cash and Cash Equivalents reported on a company's balance sheet.

## Applying Your Knowledge

**13-22** Garcia Company has always required its customers to pay cash for purchases. It is considering making credit sales and has come to you for advice on this issue. You determine that Garcia has made sales of $800,000 each year for the past several years, on which it has earned a gross profit of 40%. Basing your calculations on industry information, you estimate that Garcia's sales will increase by 15% if it makes credit sales. However, bad debts are likely to be about 2% of credit sales, and additional variable selling expenses will be about 5% of credit sales. In addition, the cost of operating the credit department is estimated to be $20,000.

*Required:* (1) Prepare a schedule to determine whether Garcia's profit will increase if it makes credit sales.
(2) What other issues regarding profitability should Garcia consider before deciding whether to make credit sales?

**13-23** Miatarus Company had gross sales for the current year of $920,000. Sales returns were $25,000, and sales allowances were $10,000. Of these net sales, 60% were credit sales with terms of 2/10, n/30. Customers took the sales (cash) discount on 90% of their net credit purchases.

*Required:* (1) Compute the company's net sales for the current year.
(2) Why is it important for users to know a company's gross sales and net sales?

**13-24** On April 6, Softwinds Fans Corporation sold inventory costing $3,000 to Tail Company at a selling price of $5,820. On April 8, Tail returned inventory with a selling price of $760 (cost of $400) purchased on April 6 because the inventory did not match what was ordered. Softwinds uses a perpetual inventory system.

*Required:* (1) Assuming that the inventory was sold for cash, record the preceding transactions.
(2) Assuming instead that the inventory was sold on credit, record the preceding transactions.

**13-25** On October 4, Shearson Woodworks sold $15,000 of merchandise on credit to Lin Furniture Mart, with terms of 3/10, n/30. Shearson uses the perpetual inventory system; the cost of the inventory sold was $9,000.

*Required:* (1) Assume that Lin pays for the purchase on October 12. Record the sale and collection.
(2) Assume that Lin pays for the purchase on October 30. Record the sale and collection.

**13-26** Your friend Jacob Thomon applied for a summer internship with McClellan Industries. McClellan set up its internship program for college freshmen two years ago. The program is designed to provide outstanding students who are in their early years of college with some hands-on business experience. McClellan hopes that the students' experiences will encourage them to pursue some type of business major in college.

After submitting his application, Jacob received a letter from McClellan Industries. The letter stated that this summer's remaining internship opening is in its accounting department. It specifically mentioned that the intern will spend the summer helping reengineer the company's accounts receivable controls and policies. Jacob knows that you are taking this accounting course. He comes over to your place for some advice. He asks several questions:

(1) "What the heck is reengineering?"
(2) "What is the letter from McClellan talking about when it says 'accounts receivable controls and policies'? What are some of these controls and policies?"
(3) "How can accounts receivable controls and policies be reengineered?"

*Required:* Prepare a written response to each of Jacob's questions.

**13-27** At the end of 2008, before the bad debts end-of-period adjustment, Satterly Corporation had an accounts receivable balance of $129,000 and an allowance for bad debts balance of $400. Using an aging analysis, Satterly estimated that its allowance account should have a balance of $9,000 at the end of 2008. On January 2, 2009, Satterly determined that a $1,500 account receivable was not collectible, so it wrote off the customer's account.

*Required:* (1) Record the bad debts adjustment at the end of 2008.
(2) Show how the net accounts receivable would be reported on Satterly's December 31, 2008 balance sheet.
(3) Record the write-off of the account receivable on January 2, 2009.
(4) Assuming no accounts receivable were collected in early January, show the net accounts receivable at the end of the day on January 2, 2009.
(5) Explain the difference between your answers to (2) and (4).

**13-28** On December 31, Taylor Corporation has an accounts receivable balance of $180,000 and an Allowance for Bad Debts balance of $500. In analyzing its individual accounts receivable, Taylor determines that accounts receivable of $100,000 are not yet past due, $50,000 are between 1 and 60 days past due, $20,000 are between 61 and 120 days past due, and $10,000 are over 120 days past due. Based on past experience, Taylor estimates that it will not collect ½ percent of accounts not yet due, 1 percent of accounts between 1 and 60 days past due, 3 percent of accounts between 61 and 120 days past due, and 10 percent of accounts over 120 days past due.

*Required:* (1) Prepare an aging analysis to determine the amount of Taylor Corporation's estimated uncollectible accounts at the end of the year.
(2) Prepare the year-end bad debts adjustment.
(3) Show how Taylor would report its net accounts receivable on its December 31 balance sheet.

**13-29** Andrews Corporation uses the aging method for its uncollectible accounts. At the end of the year, its accounts receivable were categorized as follows:

| Age Group | Amount | Estimated Percentage Uncollectible |
|---|---|---|
| Not yet past due | $ 80,000 | ½% |
| 1–30 days past due | 45,000 | 1 |
| 31–60 days past due | 20,000 | 2 |
| 61–90 days past due | 12,000 | 4 |
| >90 days past due | 8,000 | 7 |
| | $165,000 | |

Before Andrews recorded the bad debts expense end-of-period adjustment, the balance in Allowance for Bad Debts was $400.

*Required:* (1) Calculate the amount of Andrews' estimated uncollectible accounts at the end of the year.
(2) Prepare the bad debts end-of-period adjustment.
(3) Show how the net accounts receivable would be reported in Andrews' balance sheet at the end of the year.
(4) Discuss the effect on Andrews' year-end financial statements if the end-of-period adjustment had not been made in (2). Ignore income taxes.

**13-30** The Redford Optical Supplies Corporation uses the percentage of sales method for estimating its bad debts expense. In 2008 the corporation sold on credit $350,000 of glasses and lenses and had sales returns and allowances from credit sales of $20,000. In past years, approximately 1 percent of net credit sales have been uncollectible. At the end of Redford's fiscal year, before the bad debts expense end-of-period adjustment is made, the accounts receivable balance was $75,000 and the allowance for bad debts balance was $500.

*Required:* (1) Compute the dollar amount of bad debts expense that Redford should include on its 2008 income statement.
(2) Prepare the bad debts end-of-period adjustment.
(3) Show how the net accounts receivable would be reported on Redford's balance sheet at the end of 2008.
(4) Discuss the effect on Redford's 2008 financial statements if the end-of-period adjustment had not been made in (2). Ignore income taxes.

**13-31** Use the same facts for Redford Optical Supplies Corporation in 13-30, but assume Redford uses the aging method for calculating bad debts expense and the allowance for bad debts. In using the aging method, Redford has found that 2 percent of accounts receivable that are not yet past due at the end of any particular year are never collected and 5 percent of accounts receivable that are overdue at year-end are never collected. Of the accounts receivable balance at the end of 2008, 40% are not yet past due.

*Required:* (1) Compute the dollar amount of bad debts expense that Redford should include on its 2008 income statement.
(2) Show how the net accounts receivable would be reported on Redford's balance sheet at the end of 2008.

**13-32** On June 20, 2008, Livingstone Company, a U.S. company, sold merchandise on credit to Schloss Company, a Swiss company, for 25,000 francs. The Livingstone Company received payment for the merchandise on July 10, 2008. The exchange rates on June 20 and July 10 were $0.70 and $0.67, respectively.

*Required:* (1) Record the sale and collection.
(2) Prepare the July 10 entry for Livingstone to record the collection if, instead, the exchange rate was $0.72 on this date.

**13-33** On November 1, 2008, Lindner Corporation received $7,200 from Slater Insurance Agency in advance for six months of rent on office space.

*Required:* (1) Record the receipt of the rent by Lindner.
(2) Record Lindner's end-of-period adjustment.

**13-34** Boston Publishing Company publishes a hobby magazine titled *Crocheting Today* every month. The company sells annual subscriptions for $48. On March 1, 2008, the company received payment for 1,000 subscriptions for this monthly magazine. On March 1, 2009, the company received payment for 600 annual renewals and 800 new subscriptions for this magazine. On July 2, 2009, the company received payment for another 300 subscriptions to the magazine.

*Required:* (1) Compute the amount of cash the company received from these subscriptions during (a) 2008 and (b) 2009.
(2) Compute the amount of revenue the company recorded from these subscriptions in (a) 2008 and (b) 2009.

(3) Explain why the cash the company received from these subscriptions during 2008 and 2009 was not recorded as revenue at the time the cash was received.

(4) Compute the amount of the liability the company owed to these subscribers at the end of (a) 2008 and (b) 2009. Explain why these amounts were current liabilities for the company.

**13-35** The Nicholson Paving Corporation had the following short-term notes receivable outstanding during 2008:

| Amount | Date Issued | Date Due | Interest Rate |
|---|---|---|---|
| $ 6,000 | January 1, 2008 | March 1, 2008 | 8% |
| 8,000 | May 1, 2008 | November 1, 2008 | 12% |
| 10,000 | October 2, 2008 | April 2, 2009 | 9% |

Nicholson collects all the interest on each note on the maturity date.

*Required:* (1) Compute the interest revenue earned by The Nicholson Paving Corporation during 2008. For simplicity, compute interest based on the number of months that each note was outstanding.

(2) Prepare the adjustment (if any) that Nicholson needs to make at the end of 2008.

**13-36** Summertime Equipment Corporation's fiscal year ends on December 31. It has the following short-term notes receivable outstanding during 2008:

| Amount | Date Issued | Life of Note | Interest Rate |
|---|---|---|---|
| $3,000 | February 1 | 3 months | 8% |
| 5,000 | September 1 | 6 months | 10% |
| 2,000 | December 1 | 9 months | 12% |

Summertime collects all the interest on each note on the maturity date.

*Required:* (1) Compute the interest revenue (to the nearest month) that Summertime will report for these notes on its 2008 income statement.

(2) Compute the amount of interest receivable that Summertime will report for these notes on its 2008 ending balance sheet.

(3) Compute the interest revenue that Summertime will report for these notes on its 2009 income statement.

**13-37** On April 1, 2008, O'Neill Farm Equipment Company sold a tractor to Klemme Farms for $60,000 and agreed to delay collection of the selling price until six months later (after the harvest). Klemme Farms issued a note that was dated April 1, 2008, and that had an interest rate of 10%. The tractor cost O'Neill $45,000, and it uses a perpetual inventory system. The note was paid on schedule.

*Required:* (1) (a) Who is the maker of the note?

(b) Who is the payee of the note?

(c) When was the note signed?

(d) What is the face value of the note?

(e) When is the maturity date of the note?

(f) What is the annual interest rate on the note?

(g) How long is the time between the date the note is issued and the maturity date?

(h) How much is the interest due on the maturity date?

(i) How much is the maturity value of the note?

(2) Show how the April 1 transaction was recorded by O'Neill.

(3) Show how the collection of the note receivable was recorded by O'Neill.

**13-38** Farrell Corporation is preparing its ending 2008 balance sheet. In its accounting records, it has a reconciled cash balance of $47,200, petty cash of $2,700, cash equivalents of $10,300, and marketable securities of $14,000.

*Required:* Compute the amount that Farrell should report as Cash and Cash Equivalents on the balance sheet.

## Making Evaluations

**13-39** A friend of yours who owns a retail store is considering expanding her business by selling on credit to other small businesses. Knowing that you are in an accounting class, she asks for your advice.

*Required:* Write your friend a short report explaining the advantages and disadvantages of offering credit sales. Then write a "memo for the file" outlining how you would use your knowledge of break-even analysis to analyze the decision after you estimated the necessary information.

**13-40** The Midler Boutique has significantly expanded its sales in recent years by offering a liberal credit policy. As a result, bad debt losses have also increased. The owner has prepared the following summarized income statements:

| | 2005 | 2006 | 2007 | 2008 |
|---|---|---|---|---|
| Sales on credit | $32,000 | $50,000 | $70,000 | $90,000 |
| Cost of goods sold | (12,000) | (19,000) | (26,000) | (33,000) |
| Bad debt expense | (1,302) | (2,250) | (3,260) | (4,320) |
| Other expenses | (10,000) | (12,000) | (14,000) | (16,000) |
| Net Income | $ 8,698 | $16,750 | $26,740 | $36,680 |
| Accounts written off | $ 200 | $ 1,000 | $ 1,600 | $ 2,000 |

The company uses the percentage of sales method to calculate its bad debts expense. The accounts written off each year relate to credit sales made in the previous year.

*Required:* Prepare for Ms. Midler a report that explains the trend in bad debts as compared with other items on the income statement. Does it appear that the liberal credit policy is successful? What do you think the bad debts expense for 2009 should be if credit sales were $120,000 that year?

**13-41** Three years ago, Trevor and Jill Davey formed a company called The Bicycle Boutique. Sales have slowly increased each year, and the reputation of the company in the community has steadily improved. However, because of limited resources, the company has made only cash sales. With the increase in the prices for modern sophisticated bikes, the Daveys have decided that it would be desirable to offer credit card sales and to sell on credit.

Sales for the last three years have been $100,000, $140,000, and $190,000, respectively. The gross profit has consistently been 40% of sales. The Daveys believe that sales would increase by 50% next year if the "cash only" sales policy is not changed but would double under the new policy. They expect only 30% of the sales to be cash sales, with the remaining sales to be equally split between credit card sales and credit sales. The credit card receipts will be deposited immediately in a local bank. The fee on credit card sales will be 4%. It is expected that credit sales will be made evenly throughout the year, will be collected on average after two months, and that 2% will not be collectible.

To implement the new policy regarding credit sales, the company has applied for a bank loan of $150,000, to be paid back in one year. The bank will charge interest of 12% and has asked for certain financial information.

*Required:* (1) Prepare a schedule that shows the cash receipts expected for the next year under the old policy and under the new policy.
(2) Should the company prefer credit card sales or credit sales?
(3) Should the company implement the new policy?

**13-42** Your friend has operated a business for two years and has made many sales on credit. His accountant has told him that he must estimate the amounts that will be uncollectible in the future to include in this year's financial statements. Your friend is upset because he does not want "guesses" appearing in the financial statements and because he knows that accounting information should be reliable and accurate. Since he knows that you are currently studying accounting, he buys you dinner and before picking up the check asks you for your opinion.

*Required:* How would you answer your friend? Explain why the accountant is suggesting that an estimate of uncollectible accounts be included in this year's financial statements and why your friend's concerns are not critical.

**13-43** According to their annual reports, **Harrahs Entertainment** and **MGM Mirage**, operators of casinos in Las Vegas and other locations, reported the following information:

**HARRAH'S ENTERTAINMENT**

| Year ended December 31 (in millions) | 2005 | 2004 | 2003 |
|---|---|---|---|
| Revenues | $8,462.3 | $5,411.1 | $4,656.4 |
| Less: Complimentary allowances | (1,351.3) | (862.8) | (707.5) |
| | $7,111.0 | $4,548.3 | $3,948.9 |

Revenue Recognition. Casino revenues consist of net gaming wins. Food and beverage and rooms revenues include the aggregate amounts generated by those departments at all consolidated casinos and casino hotels.

Casino promotional allowances consist principally of the retail value of complimentary food and beverages, accommodations, admissions and entertainment provided to casino patrons. Also included is the value of coupons redeemed for cash at our properties. The estimated costs of providing such complimentary services, which we classify as casino expenses for continuing operations through interdepartmental allocations, were as follows:

| | 2005 | 2004 | 2003 |
|---|---|---|---|
| Food and beverage | $ 396.3 | $ 240.8 | $ 204.8 |
| Rooms | 123.4 | 82.9 | 77.4 |
| Other | 71.0 | 50.2 | 25.7 |
| | $ 590.7 | $ 373.9 | $ 307.9 |

**MGM MIRAGE**

| Year ended December 31 (in thousands) | 2005 | 2004 | 2003 |
|---|---|---|---|
| Revenues | $7,084,169 | $4,672,488 | $4,275,766 |
| Less: Promotional allowances | (602,202) | (434,384) | (413,023) |
| | $6,481,967 | $4,238,104 | $3,862,743 |

Revenue Recognition and Promotional Allowances: Casino revenue is the aggregate net difference between gaming wins and losses. The retail value of accommodations, food and beverage, and other services furnished to guests without charge is included in gross revenue and then deducted as promotional allowances. The estimated cost of providing such promotional allowances is primarily included in casino expenses as follows:

| Year ended December 31 | 2005 | 2004 | 2003 |
|---|---|---|---|
| Rooms | $ 82,009 | $ 63,652 | $ 64,103 |
| Food and beverage | 255,201 | 191,695 | 178,399 |
| Other | 35,242 | 25,213 | 21,560 |
| | $372,452 | $280,560 | $264,062 |

*Required:* (1) Do the two companies use the same accounting policies? Explain whether you agree with the policy or policies. Explain which disclosure you prefer.
(2) Are there significant differences between the two companies for the amount of the complimentary (promotional) allowances they give?
(3) Are there significant differences between the two companies for the cost of the complimentary (promotional) allowances they give?

**13-44** **Eastman Kodak Company** reported the following in its 2005 annual report relating to accounts receivable (amounts in millions of dollars):

| Dec. 31 | 2005 | 2004 |
|---|---|---|
| Receivables | | |
| Trade receivables | $2,447 | $2,137 |
| Miscellaneous receivables | 313 | 407 |
| Total (net of allowances of $162 and $127) | $2,760 | $2,544 |

Of the total trade receivable amounts of $2,447 million and $2,137 million as of December 31, 2005 and 2004, respectively, approximately $374 million and $492 million, respectively, are expected to be settled through customer deductions in lieu of cash payments. Such deductions represent rebates owed to the customer and are included in accounts payable and other current liabilities in the accompanying Consolidated Statement of Financial Position at each respective balance sheet date.

*Required:* (1) How could you determine if the December 31, 2005 allowance for bad debts is reasonable? (*Hint:* No calculations are required.)

(2) Eastman Kodak's sales in 2005 were $14,268. Assume that all sales were made on credit, the bad debts expense for 2005 was $120, and the bad debts relate only to trade receivables. Compute the amount of bad debts written off in 2005 and the cash collected from sales in 2005.

(3) Why did Eastman Kodak disclose that some of its trade receivables would be settled through customer deductions?

(4) Eastman Kodak's sales in 2004 were $13,517 and assume that its bad debts expense was $112. Evaluate how the company's management of its accounts receivable changed in 2005 compared to 2004.

**13-45** __Kohl's Corporation__ included the following information in its 10-K report:

The company's accounts receivable at January 28, 2006 increased $262.4 million, or 18.9%, over the January 29, 2005 balance. The increase is primarily due to a 18.6% increase in proprietary credit card sales and a decrease in payment rates. Net write-offs increased to 1.0% of Kohl's charge sales in fiscal 2005 from 0.9% in fiscal 2004. The Company's incremental bad debt expense related to the revised bankruptcy legislation, effective October 17, 2005, was $3.2 million. The Company believes write-offs of delinquent accounts were accelerated due to the bankruptcy legislation. As a result, the allowance for doubtful accounts was reduced to 1.6% of gross accounts receivable in fiscal 2005 from 1.7% in fiscal 2004. The Company's credit card program supports earnings growth by driving sales through promotional events and through the growth in the proprietary credit card financial performance. The following table summarizes information related to Kohl's proprietary credit card receivables:

| | January 28, 2006 | January 29, 2005 | January 31, 2004 |
|---|---|---|---|
| | | ($ In Thousands) | |
| Gross accounts receivable | $1,678,400 | $1,414,289 | $1,172,678 |
| Allowance for doubtful accounts | $ 26,335 | $ 24,657 | $ 22,521 |
| Allowance as a % of gross accounts receivable | 1.6% | 1.7% | 1.9% |
| Accounts receivable turnover (rolling 4 quarters)* | 3.8x | 3.8x | 3.6x |
| Proprietary credit card share | 40.6% | 39.2% | 36.0% |
| Accounts over 60 days past due | 2.4% | 2.5% | 2.7% |

* Credit card sales divided by average quarterly gross accounts receivable

*Required:* Assume you are a financial analyst. Write a report that explains Kohl's disclosures for your clients who you know are not financially sophisticated.

**13-46** Your friend works part-time at a local company. He is concerned about some of the practices he has observed and asks for your advice. "I was surprised to see the sales manager agree to open a new credit account over the phone. When I asked him about that, he said: 'We have been trying to get that account for years. I couldn't keep them waiting.' Then when I was working in the warehouse, the employees would sometimes accept returns from customers' trucks. They just wrote a note on the customer's invoice. Then I was talking to the bookkeeper about uncollectible accounts, and she said: 'Handling a bad debt is easy. I just press the delete button on my computer.' She also told me she hates the new year because that is when the company president makes her write off all the uncollectible accounts. He never wants to do them at the end of the year because he says they will affect that year's performance. She also said that it upsets her to think of all the previous year's sales that are now not going to be paid for."

*Required:* Write a short report outlining the advantages and disadvantages of the activities your friend observed. For each situation, explain what policy you would recommend.

**13-47** In its December 31, 2005 balance sheet, **UAL** (the parent company of United Airlines) reported the following amounts (in millions), respectively:

| | 2005 | 2004 |
|---|---|---|
| Current assets | $4,259 | $3,914 |
| Cash and cash equivalents | 1,761 | 1,223 |
| Short-term investments | 77 | 78 |
| Receivables | 839 | 951 |
| Current liabilities | 5,234 | 6,461 |
| Advance ticket sales | 1,575 | 1,361 |

*Required:* Using ratio analysis, explain whether or not United Airlines' liquidity position has improved from December 31, 2004 to December 31, 2005. Explain which single measure of the company's liquidity you would prefer to use.

**13-48** **Fifth Third Bancorp** reported the following in its 2005 annual report relating to loans (and leases) and loan losses (amounts in millions of dollars):

| Dec. 31 | 2005 | 2004 |
|---|---|---|
| Total portfolio loans | $ 69,925 | $ 59,808 |
| Allowance for loan losses | (744) | (713) |
| Total portfolio loans, net | $ 69,181 | $ 59,095 |

Transactions in the allowance for loan (and lease) losses for the years ended December 31:

| | 2005 | 2004 |
|---|---|---|
| Balance at January 1 | $ 713 | $ 697 |
| Losses charged off | (373) | (321) |
| Recoveries of losses previously charged off | 74 | 69 |
| Net charge-offs | (299) | (252) |
| Provision for loan and lease losses | 330 | 268 |
| Balance at December 31 | $ 744 | $ 713 |

*Required:* (1) Explain why accounting principles require that estimates of bad debts must be made.

(2) Explain the information for the bank's allowance for credit losses for 2005.

(3) Compute the net new loans provided by the bank during 2005.

(4) Evaluate how the bank's management of its bad debts changed in 2005 compared to 2004.

**13-49** Yesterday, you received the letter shown on the following page for your advice column in the local paper:

## Dr. Decisive

Dear Dr. Decisive:

My brother and I are having a fight over bad debts. I think he owes me $10, and he disagrees. But seriously, he is an engineer, and you know how they like all their numbers to be precise. The other day I showed him a newspaper report in which a bank president was saying that the bank had some bad real estate loans and so would have a large bad debt expense this year and for the next couple of years. My brother said that the bank president's statement was crazy and that the bank should wait until the loans were written off before recording them as an expense. I was trying to tell him that the bank should record them all as expenses now. But whoever is right, we both disagree with the bank president.

Call me "Confused Again."

*Required:* Meet with your Dr. Decisive team and write a response to "Confused Again."

CHAPTER

14

# EXPENSES AND CASH PAYMENTS

"READY MONEY IS ALADDIN'S LAMP."

—GEORGE GORDON NOEL BYRON

1. Why does a large company make purchases on credit, and how should it manage and record accounts payable?
2. How does an exchange gain (loss) arise from a credit purchase made from a company in another country?
3. What are accrued liabilities, and what types does a company often have?
4. What types of taxes do an employee and a company incur, and how does the company record them?
5. How is accounting for a short-term note payable similar to accounting for a short-term note receivable?
6. What are prepaid items, and how does a company account for them?
7. What are loss contingencies, and how does a company report or disclose them?
8. What can external users learn from analyzing a company's liquidity?

**Hershey Foods**' (maker of "Hugs") December 31, 2005 balance sheet listed $1,518 million of current liabilities—35.3 percent of its total assets. On February 28, 2006, **Rocky Mountain Chocolate Factory's** balance sheet total for the same categories was slightly more than $2.9 million. Given that its total assets were about $19.1 million, Rocky Mountain's current liabilities were equal to 15.2 percent of its total assets. These dollar amounts of current liabilities shown on Hershey Foods' and Rocky Mountain's balance sheets resulted from prior management decisions as well as from the accounting methods used to keep track of the various categories.

There are various ways to understand the meaning of the information reported by these companies. For example, if one piece of Hershey's candy cost an average of three cents to manufacture, these current liability account balances held the dollar equivalent of over 50 billion pieces! Hershey Foods' $1,518 million in current liabilities is over 523 times greater than Rocky Mountain Chocolate Factory's $2.9 million. Should you conclude that Hershey has operations that are 523 times larger than those of Rocky Mountain? Another way to think about these amounts is to think about the business operations that create them. For example, accounts payable result from making credit purchases. In their respective income statements, Hershey Foods reported cost of goods sold of almost $2.9 billion and accounts payable of $168 million, while Rocky Mountain Chocolate Factory reported cost of goods sold of $14.0 million and accounts payable of $507.5 thousand. So Hershey Foods' cost of goods sold was 17.3 times its accounts payable, while Rocky Mountain Chocolate Factory's was 27.6 times.

*Can you conclude whether Hershey Foods or Rocky Mountain Chocolate Factory is better at managing its accounts payable? What factors besides these amounts on the balance sheets and income statements of the two companies should you consider?*

As we discussed in Chapter 13, managers and external users assess a company's liquidity position by comparing the composition and amounts of the company's current assets *and* its current liabilities. If you have information only about a company's current assets, you cannot properly assess liquidity.

In this chapter, we continue our discussion of the balance sheet items that affect a company's liquidity position. In Chapter 13 we provided an analysis of the management and reporting of three current assets—cash, accounts receivable, and notes receivable—

© PHOTOPIA

If you had an inventory of Hershey's Hugs at home or in your dorm room or apartment, how many times a year do you think you would have to purchase replacements?

and a current liability, unearned revenue. All these items relate to the reporting of revenue. In this chapter we describe and analyze how a company manages and reports its current liabilities and one current asset, all of which relate to the reporting of expenses.

We organize the chapter as follows. First, we discuss the management and reporting of accounts payable. We explain how companies manage purchases on credit and accounts payable, including purchases discounts, and how they report accounts payable in the balance sheet. Second, we discuss additional types of current liabilities. These other liabilities are an important aspect of a company's liquidity. For example, although Hershey Foods reported in its December 31, 2005 balance sheet that it owed $1,518 million in current liabilities, 89 percent of these liabilities were *not* accounts payable. Third, we discuss prepaid items, an asset that relates to payments of expenses. Finally, we discuss how to evaluate a company's liquidity position using information from Chapter 13 and this chapter.

## MANAGING AND RECORDING ACCOUNTS PAYABLE

1 Why does a large company make purchases on credit, and how should it manage and record accounts payable?

Recall from Chapter 9 that accounts payable are the amounts owed by a company to its suppliers for previous credit purchases of inventory and supplies. A large company makes purchases on credit for many of the same reasons that a small company does: (1) purchasing on credit is often more convenient than purchasing with cash, (2) purchasing on credit delays paying for purchases and, by doing so, results in a short-term "loan" from the supplier, and (3) purchasing on credit gives the company an opportunity to assess the quality of the item before making the cash payment. At December 31, 2008, Unlimited Decadence owes $1,450,000 in accounts payable, as we showed in Exhibit 13-1.

Accounts payable management involves establishing procedures, policies, and activities that govern credit purchases. One procedure that a large company will use to help manage its accounts payable is to create an accounts payable subsidiary file. An **accounts payable subsidiary file,** which contains the individual accounts of all the suppliers that sell to the company on credit, works the same way as an accounts receivable subsidiary file (discussed in Chapter 13). Whenever the company purchases on credit or pays a supplier, it records the transaction in the individual supplier's account in the subsidiary file. In this way, the company keeps up-to-date records of its transactions with its suppliers. As we will discuss later, this is important so that the company can monitor its purchases discounts, returns, and allowances. The company also keeps an Accounts Payable **control account** to control the individual supplier accounts in the subsidiary file and to help the company monitor its existing total Accounts Payable balance. The balance of the Accounts Payable control account must always be equal to the total of the accounts payable subsidiary file on each balance sheet date. Thus, when a company records an accounts payable transaction in the individual subsidiary file account, it must also record the transaction in the control account. Before the company issues its financial statements, it prepares a schedule of the individual supplier account balances to prove the equality of the Accounts Payable control account and the subsidiary file.

In general, companies should establish the following policies over credit purchases:

1. *A company should separate purchasing duties from record-keeping duties and/or from control of the asset.* Separating these duties helps prevent one employee from making a purchase through the company and stealing the purchased goods for personal use. For example, say that one employee is in charge of processing the accounting records for a company's computer purchases *and* also has the authority to order its equipment. In this situation, the employee could order a laptop computer to be delivered to his or her office, process the purchase for the company to make the payment, take the computer home, and then later remove the computer from the company's accounting records.
2. *A company should restrict the ability of employees to obligate the company to pay for credit purchases.* A company should set up a purchasing department to control

the purchasing process. This department should investigate potential suppliers and identify the best prices and payment terms for goods that meet the company's quality standards. Restricting purchases to employees in the purchasing department should prevent other employees from making unnecessary or costly credit purchases.

3. *A company should authorize cash payments only for goods that have been received and properly documented.* Because a company should separate the duties related to purchasing, record keeping, and control of assets, it needs some type of documentation to ensure that it doesn't make cash payments for goods that it didn't order or didn't receive. A company should authorize cash payments only if the purchase order and the receiving report match the supplier's invoice—that is, only if the supplier's invoice reflects what the company received from the supplier and what the company ordered. If the receiving report indicates a problem with purchased goods and the company keeps the goods anyway (e.g., the goods have minor damage), the accounts payable department should ask the supplier for a reduction in the sales price (known as a *purchases allowance*).
4. *A company should require the submission of accounts payable documents to the cash payments department in a timely manner to take advantage of purchases discounts.* Recall from Chapter 13 that a selling company often offers sales discounts to customers if they pay by a certain date. The company buying the goods refers to this as a *purchases discount.* Accounts payable department employees should analyze the potential savings from taking purchases discounts and, when beneficial, notify cash payments personnel that they should make a timely payment.

Here's an example. Suppose that on July 3, 2008, Unlimited Decadence is running low on cocoa. The employee who monitors cocoa for the company contacts the purchasing department and requests that more cocoa be purchased. The purchasing department checks the purchases budget to see if this seems like a reasonable and expected request. If so, an employee in the purchasing department checks current prices for cocoa and completes a purchase order, which is approved by a supervisor. The **purchase order** documents the details of a purchase (e.g., item number, quantity, price) and provides a written record of the purchase approval. The purchasing department sends a copy of the approved purchase order to Unlimited Decadence's cocoa supplier, Cool Cocoa Inc. So, Unlimited Decadence has now completed its order for, say, $35,000 of cocoa.

Cool Cocoa ships the cocoa to Unlimited Decadence and mails it an invoice. When the cocoa arrives at Unlimited Decadence's receiving dock on July 24, 2008, the employees check the goods against a copy of the purchase order to see that the correct goods arrived. If the goods match the purchase order, the employees accept delivery of the goods and complete a form called a *receiving report*. The **receiving report** documents the type, quantity, and condition of goods received by the company.

Employees in the accounting department match the July 3, 2008 purchase order with the corresponding receiving report and the invoice from the supplier. If all the information on each document is consistent, since Unlimited Decadence uses a perpetual inventory system and an accounts payable subsidiary ledger, it records the transaction as follows:

| **Assets** | = | **Liabilities** | + | **Stockholders' Equity** |
|---|---|---|---|---|
| Raw Materials Inventory | | Accounts Payable (Cool Cocoa Inc.) | | |
| +$35,000 | | +$35,000 | | |

**FINANCIAL STATEMENT EFFECTS**

Increases current assets and total assets on ***balance sheet.*** Increases current liabilities and total liabilities on ***balance sheet.***

## Purchases Discounts

A **purchases discount** (also called a *cash discount*) is a reduction in the invoice price because the purchaser pays within the discount period. In Chapters 6 and 13, we explained how a company may offer a sales (cash) discount to credit customers to encourage them to pay their accounts receivable within a relatively short period of time, usually

10 to 15 days. Recall that a sales discount is a percentage reduction of the invoice price that the selling company grants in return for the customer's early payment. The sales discount is shown on the invoice in a standard format such as "2/10, n/30." This means that the selling company grants a 2% discount if the customer pays within 10 days. Otherwise, the entire dollar amount of the invoice (referred to as the *gross amount*) is due within 30 days.

*Explain whether, as a manager, you would be more interested to know the amount of the purchases discounts taken or the amount of the available discounts that the company did not take.*

Now we discuss how a company handles purchases discounts. Again we focus on the transaction in which Unlimited Decadence purchases cocoa at a cost of $35,000. Assume that Cool Cocoa offers discount terms of 2/10, n/30. On July 24, 2008, Unlimited Decadence receives the cocoa. It has two alternate methods to use to record the purchase—the gross method and the net method.

### Recording Purchases Using the Gross Method

If Unlimited Decadence uses the gross method, it records the purchase of the cocoa on July 24, 2008, at the total invoice price of $35,000, as we illustrated earlier. The purchasing department employees forward the purchase documents to the cash payments department so that the company can make the payment within the discount period.

Assume that on July 31, 2008, Unlimited Decadence pays for the cocoa by mailing a check. Because it pays within 10 days of the purchase, it takes the 2% discount. Its check is for $34,300, the $35,000 invoice price less the $700 (2% × $35,000) discount. Unlimited Decadence records the cash payment as follows:

**FINANCIAL STATEMENT EFFECTS**

Decreases current assets and total assets on ***balance sheet.*** Decreases current liabilities and total liabilities on ***balance sheet.*** Decreases cash flows from operating activities on ***cash flow statement.***

| Assets | | = | Liabilities | + | Stockholders' Equity |
|---|---|---|---|---|---|
| Cash | Raw Materials Inventory | | Accounts Payable (Cool Cocoa Inc.) | | |
| | Bal $35,000 | | Bal $35,000 | | |
| −$34,300 | −700 | | −35,000 | | |
| | Bal $34,300 | | Bal $ 0 | | |

Cash decreases by $34,300, the amount of the check, whereas Accounts Payable decreases by $35,000, the original amount of the purchase. Even though Unlimited Decadence paid only $34,300, it reduces Accounts Payable by $35,000 because it has satisfied its entire obligation to Cool Cocoa. Unlimited Decadence records the $700 purchases discount as a decrease in the Raw Materials Inventory account because inventory should be recorded at the acquisition cost—in this case, $34,300. It reports any balance in the Accounts Payable account at the end of the accounting period as a current liability on the year-end balance sheet.

Alternatively, if Unlimited Decadence does *not* pay within the 10-day discount period, when it does pay it simply reduces both Cash and Accounts Payable by $35,000.

*Do you think a company could treat the amount of purchases discounts it takes as an increase in income? Why or why not?*

### Recording Purchases Using the Net Method

If Unlimited Decadence uses the net method, it records the purchase of the cocoa at the total invoice price less the discount (that is, the net price), or $34,300, as follows:

**FINANCIAL STATEMENT EFFECTS**

Increases current assets and total assets on ***balance sheet.*** Increases current liabilities and total liabilities on ***balance sheet.***

| Assets | = | Liabilities | + | Stockholders' Equity |
|---|---|---|---|---|
| Raw Materials Inventory | | Accounts Payable (Cool Cocoa Inc.) | | |
| +$34,300 | | +$34,300 | | |

Now on July 31, 2008, when Unlimited Decadence pays for the cocoa by mailing a check, it takes the 2% discount and only pays $34,300, which it records as follows:

| **Assets** | = | **Liabilities** | + | **Stockholders' Equity** |
|---|---|---|---|---|
| Cash | | Accounts Payable (Cool Cocoa Inc.) | | |
| | | Bal $34,300 | | |
| −$34,300 | | − 34,300 | | |
| | | Bal $ 0 | | |

**FINANCIAL STATEMENT EFFECTS**

Decreases current assets and total assets on ***balance sheet***. Decreases current liabilities and total liabilities on ***balance sheet***. Decreases cash flows from operating activities on ***cash flow statement***.

Alternatively, if Unlimited Decadence does not pay within the 10-day discount period, it must pay $35,000, which it records as follows:

| **Assets** | = | **Liabilities** | + | **Stockholders' Equity** | | |
|---|---|---|---|---|---|---|
| | | | | ***Net Income*** | | |
| | | | | **Revenues** | − | **Expenses** |
| Cash | | Accounts Payable (Cool Cocoa Inc.) | | | | Purchases Discounts Lost |
| | | Bal $34,300 | | | | |
| −$35,000 | | −34,300 | | | − | +$700 |
| | | Bal $ 0 | | | | |

**FINANCIAL STATEMENT EFFECTS**

Decreases current assets and total assets on ***balance sheet***. Decreases current liabilities and total liabilities on ***balance sheet***. Increases expenses (in "other items"), which decreases net income on ***income statement*** (and therefore decreases stockholders' equity on ***balance sheet***). Decreases cash flows from operating activities on ***cash flow statement***.

Cash decreases by $35,000, the amount of the check, whereas Accounts Payable decreases by $34,300, the original amount at which Unlimited Decadence recorded the purchase. Unlimited Decadence records the $700 difference as Purchases Discounts Lost, which is an expense account similar to interest expense.

### Management Issues

Although most companies use the gross method, the net method has advantages for the managers of a company. Managers typically take advantage of purchases discounts. Think about how much it costs not to! Consider the Unlimited Decadence example. If the company takes advantage of the discount, it pays 2% less by paying 20 days earlier (the 30 days allowed for payment minus the 10-day discount period). This is an approximate annual interest cost of 36% [2% × (360 ÷ 20)]! Unlimited Decadence would save even if it had to borrow money from a bank to pay for the purchases within the discount period.

*What do you think would be the interest cost if the company didn't pay for 60 days? What other consequences might follow from this decision?*

Given the high cost of *not* taking a discount, managers should be interested in knowing if any discounts have not been taken. The net method indicates this fact directly because the Purchases Discounts Lost account keeps track of any discounts *not taken.* In contrast, the gross method keeps track only of the discounts that *were taken* (by reducing the Inventory account). It does not show the discounts that were available but were *not* taken.

## Purchases Returns and Allowances

Recall from Chapter 13 that a company may report a sales return or allowance that it gives a customer for, say, damaged goods. The customer (the purchaser) has a purchases return or allowance. A **purchases return** occurs when a company *returns* goods that it previously recorded as a purchase and receives a refund in exchange for the goods. A **purchases allowance** occurs when a company *keeps* the goods that it previously recorded as a purchase and later receives a refund of a portion of the purchase price.

A company may use the accounting information in its ERP system to keep track of purchases returns and allowances. Managers monitor the volume of returns and allowances for three basic reasons. First, a relatively high level of purchases returns may indicate that the purchasing department personnel are being persuaded to make unwanted purchases. As we discussed in Chapter 13, some companies want their sales personnel to encourage a purchase by reminding the customers how easy it is to return the item. Second, a relatively high level of purchases returns may indicate problems with the suppliers' product quality. Therefore, companies should require purchasing department personnel to find out why goods are being returned. Finally, a relatively high level of purchases allowances may result from suppliers' shipping or warehouse problems. A purchases allowance is often obtained if goods are slightly damaged or do not match the description of the goods that were ordered.

For example, assume that on September 7, 2008, Unlimited Decadence ordered 10,000 pounds of sugar on credit from Sugar Supply Company for $0.35 per pound, for a total cost of $3,500. On September 18, Unlimited Decadence receives the sugar and records the purchase (using the gross method) in its Raw Materials Inventory and Accounts Payable accounts. Its receiving department personnel inspect the order and find that the sugar is of the wrong quality. After being notified of the mistake on September 20, Sugar Supply Company offers to reduce the sales price for the entire shipment by $0.05 per pound ($500). Unlimited Decadence agrees because it can use the sugar in a different candy bar without affecting the quality, and it records the purchases allowance as follows:

**FINANCIAL STATEMENT EFFECTS**

Decreases current assets and total assets on ***balance sheet***. Decreases current liabilities and total liabilities on ***balance sheet***.

| **Assets** | = | **Liabilities** | + | **Stockholders' Equity** |
|---|---|---|---|---|
| Raw Materials Inventory | | Accounts Payable (Sugar Supply Co.) | | |
| Bal $3,500 | | Bal $3,500 | | |
| −500 | | −500 | | |
| Bal $3,000 | | Bal $3,000 | | |

*Why would both companies agree to the purchases allowance rather than agreeing that Unlimited Decadence will return the sugar?*

Unlimited Decadence decreases Accounts Payable by $500 because it now owes only $3,000, not the original $3,500. The company decreases the Raw Materials Inventory account by $500 for the purchases allowance. The company would also record a purchases return in the same way. The company reports the balance of the Raw Materials Inventory account on its balance sheet; note that this account balance includes the amounts of purchases less the purchases returns and allowances. For internal control purposes, Unlimited Decadence's managers want to know whether the types and amounts of purchases returns and allowances were due to errors by its purchasing department, or delivery of poor quality goods (or errors) by its suppliers. An ERP system can help a company's managers identify a list of these items by electronically sorting the information in the Raw Materials Inventory account.

*Why do you think a company reports accounts receivable as a net amount, but accounts payable as a gross amount?*

## Purchase Transactions in a Foreign Currency

2 How does an exchange gain (loss) arise from a credit purchase made from a company in another country?

As we explained in Chapter 13, many U.S. companies conduct transactions with customers in foreign countries. Here we discuss transactions involving the purchase of inventory when the company and its supplier agree on a price stated in terms of the foreign currency. In these cases, the U.S. company must record the purchase in U.S. dollars. Therefore, the company must convert the foreign currency amount into dollars at the exchange rate on the day of the transaction. As we discussed in Chapter 13, transactions between companies in different countries usually involve credit terms, if only to allow time for the processing of the orders, shipments, and payments across international borders. In addition, currency exchange rates change continuously. As a result, the exchange rate is likely to have changed between the date the U.S. company records a credit purchase and the date it makes the payment for that purchase. On the date of payment, then, the company must record an exchange gain or loss to account for the difference between the purchase price and the amount of the cash payment. An **exchange gain or loss** is caused by a change in the exchange rate between the date that a company records a credit purchase and the date that the company pays the cash. More specifically, exchange gains and losses occur for credit purchases as follows:

1. An exchange *gain* occurs when the exchange rate *declines* between the date a company records a *payable* and the date the company *pays* the cash.
2. An exchange *loss* occurs when the exchange rate *increases* between the date a company records a *payable* and the date the company *pays* the cash.

To understand an exchange gain that occurs when the exchange rate declines between the date a credit purchase is recorded and the date the cash is paid, suppose that Unlimited Decadence purchases sugar from a Brazilian company and agrees to a price of 600,000 reals rather than a price in dollars. On the date of the purchase, the exchange rate is \$0.46 (one real = \$0.46); therefore, Unlimited Decadence records the purchase of the inventory at \$276,000 (600,000 reals × \$0.46) as follows:

| **Assets** | = | **Liabilities** | + | **Stockholders' Equity** |
|---|---|---|---|---|
| Raw Materials Inventory | | Accounts Payable (Brazilian Company) | | |
| +\$276,000 | | +\$276,000 | | |

FINANCIAL STATEMENT EFFECTS

Increases current assets and total assets on ***balance sheet***. Increases current liabilities and total liabilities on ***balance sheet***.

The Brazilian company has a right to receive 600,000 reals, and Unlimited Decadence is obligated to pay sufficient dollars that will convert to 600,000 reals on the date that the payment is made. Now assume that the exchange rate on the date of payment is \$0.44 (one real = \$0.44). In this case, since only \$0.44 now buys one real, Unlimited Decadence will have to pay fewer dollars to buy 600,000 reals. That is, the real has become less expensive. More specifically, Unlimited Decadence has to pay only \$264,000 (600,000 reals × \$0.44). Therefore, it has incurred an exchange *gain* of \$12,000 (\$276,000 − \$264,000), which it records at the time of the cash payment as follows:

| **Assets** | = | **Liabilities** | + | **Stockholders' Equity** | | |
|---|---|---|---|---|---|---|
| | | | | ***Net Income*** | | |
| | | | | **Revenues (Gains)** | − | **Expenses (Losses)** |
| Cash | | Accounts Payable (Cool Cocoa Inc.) | | Exchange Gain | | |
| −\$264,000 | | −\$276,000 | | +\$12,000 | | |

FINANCIAL STATEMENT EFFECTS

Decreases current assets and total assets on ***balance sheet***. Decreases current liabilities and total liabilities on ***balance sheet***. Increases gains (in "other items"), which increases net income on ***income statement*** (and therefore increases stockholders' equity on ***balance sheet***). Decreases cash flows from operating activities on ***cash flow statement***.

The exchange gain occurs because Unlimited Decadence has to pay only \$264,000 to settle the debt it originally recorded at \$276,000. It can also compute the gain by multiplying the amount owed by the change in the exchange rate [600,000 reals × (\$0.46 − \$0.44) = \$12,000]. Remember that the Brazilian company still receives 600,000 reals; it is Unlimited Decadence that has the exchange gain.

Note that the U.S. company (Unlimited Decadence) experienced the exchange gain because it agreed to a transaction expressed in terms of a foreign currency. In such situations, the U.S. company accepts the risks associated with exchange rate changes. When the transaction is expressed in U.S. dollars, the foreign company accepts, and the U.S. company avoids, the risks associated with exchange rate changes.

## Technology and Accounts Payable Management

As for the other areas of liquidity management, a rethinking of accounts payable management and the emergence of new technologies are changing accounts payable policies and activities for many large companies. Companies often use three innovations.

First, many large companies, as part of their ERP systems, are reengineering the purchase requisition and ordering process for small-dollar purchases. Streamlining this process can save large companies millions of dollars. Using a traditional purchasing system, processing one purchase order costs between $50 and $300 regardless of the cost of the goods being ordered, so the cost of processing the paperwork often exceeds the value of the items being purchased! Realizing this, many companies are replacing their old process with a procurement card system.

Similar to a credit card, a **procurement card** permits employees responsible for keeping supplies in stock to purchase directly from suppliers. The card records each transaction electronically with the company's bank. The company's accounting system processes only the aggregate total of all of these purchase transactions instead of processing each individual transaction. Electronic controls prevent misuse of the card by restricting which suppliers can access the card and limiting the dollar amount of purchases charged each month. Procurement cards eliminate the need for purchase requisitions, reduce the handling of invoices, speed up the delivery of supplies, and lower costs.

Second, many companies use EDI technology (as we discussed in Chapter 13) in their accounts payable management, mainly for large-dollar inventory purchases from their e-business trading partners. Under EDI, when a company purchases raw materials, its purchasing department personnel access its trading partner's current inventory price lists and then, using these prices, place the purchase order electronically. Computer controls restrict (1) who can place orders, (2) which trading partners the purchasing department personnel can use for specific types of purchases, and (3) the size and frequency of orders.

With EDI, electronic invoices received from trading partners automatically update the company's accounts payable system. The computer checks the information on the invoice (price, description of goods, quantity, etc.) against the electronic purchase order, confirms receipt of the proper goods by checking computerized inventory-receiving reports, and approves the transaction for entry into the accounting records.

Third, some companies are outsourcing accounts payable in much the same way that they outsource cash payments. Outsourcing accounts payable may reduce the fixed personnel costs associated with managing accounts payable internally, give the company immediate access to new and efficient technologies, and improve its controls over accounts payable.

## Additional Current Liabilities

Accounts payable is not the only current liability shown on a company's balance sheet. Remember that accounts payable represent only amounts owed to suppliers for credit purchases of supplies and inventory. Companies also engage in many other activities that lead to reporting current liabilities. For instance, when a company's employees work for a day, the company incurs an obligation to pay them. There are many specific current liabilities that a company might report on its balance sheet. We discuss three of the most common types: (1) accrued liabilities, (2) taxes, and (3) short-term notes payable.

## Accrued Liabilities

3 What are accrued liabilities, and what types does a company often have?

On its December 31, 2005 balance sheet, Hershey Foods reported nearly $508 million of accrued liabilities, which was over 33% of its total of $1,518 million in current liabilities. For managers and external users to assess a company's liquidity, they must understand what accrued liabilities are and why companies report them.

**Accrued liabilities** are short-term obligations (other than accounts payable) that a company owes at the end of an accounting period and that result from the company's operating activities during the period. A company's utility bill that covers the last month in an accounting period (and that it will pay in the next accounting period) is an example of an accrued liability. In most instances, a company records its accrued liabilities by making end-of-period adjustments to its accounts. It makes these adjustments so that it records all the expenses for the accounting period and the related amounts it owes at the end of the period and correctly reports them in the period's financial statements.

*Assume that it is March 31, 2008, and Unlimited Decadence is about to prepare its financial statements for the first quarter of 2008. Its Utilities Expense account includes the following amounts:*

| Utilities Expense |
|---|
| +$16,800 |
| + 14,800 |

*Do you think Unlimited Decadence's accounting system shows all of its utilities expense for the first quarter of 2008? Why or why not? What does Unlimited Decadence need to do, if anything, to ensure that it includes the proper amount of utilities expense in its income statement?*

We discuss two specific types of accrued liabilities: (1) salaries (wages) and (2) warranties.

## Accrued Salaries

Many manufacturing companies, such as candy manufacturers, pay employees weekly or biweekly (e.g., every other Friday). During an accounting period, a company records salaries as an expense on the day that it pays the employees. At the end of an accounting period, however, its employees may have worked several days since their last payday. The amount of salaries that a company owes its employees on the balance sheet date is called **accrued salaries**, **salaries payable**, or **wages payable**.

For example, assume that Unlimited Decadence is preparing its financial statements for the year ending December 31, 2008. Further, assume that it pays its employees $1 million of salaries each week (five-day week), with every Monday being payday. Exhibit 14-1 shows Unlimited Decadence's pay schedule for the week that includes December 31, 2008. Notice that December 31, 2008 is on a Wednesday. This means that on December 31, 2008, Unlimited Decadence owes its employees for the work they performed on Tuesday and Wednesday of this week (since the last payday). As we show in Exhibit 14-1, the salaries for these two days total $400,000. To ensure that its financial statements correctly include these salaries, Unlimited Decadence makes the entry shown in Exhibit 14-1.

Both Salaries Expense and Salaries Payable increase by the amount of the salaries owed, $400,000. Unlimited Decadence includes the $400,000 salaries expense for the last two working days of the year in the total salaries expense that it reports as an operating expense on its income statement for 2008. It reports the $400,000 salaries payable as part of its accrued liabilities in the current liabilities section of its December 31, 2008 balance sheet.[1] As you can see in Exhibit 14-1, on the next payday (January 5, 2009), Unlimited Decadence pays $1 million but has an expense of only $600,000 for 2009 because its employees worked only three days in January (we assume that salary costs are not affected by holidays).

## Warranty Liabilities

When a company offers a warranty on a product it sells, it agrees to repair or replace it for a specified period of time if it is defective. Do you check what type of warranty comes with the products you purchase? Depending on the type of product, you may see all sorts of warranties: "30 days parts and labor," "3 years bumper-to-bumper," "complete

[1]In this discussion and our previous discussions on salaries, we ignore payroll taxes. We will discuss them in a later section on taxes.

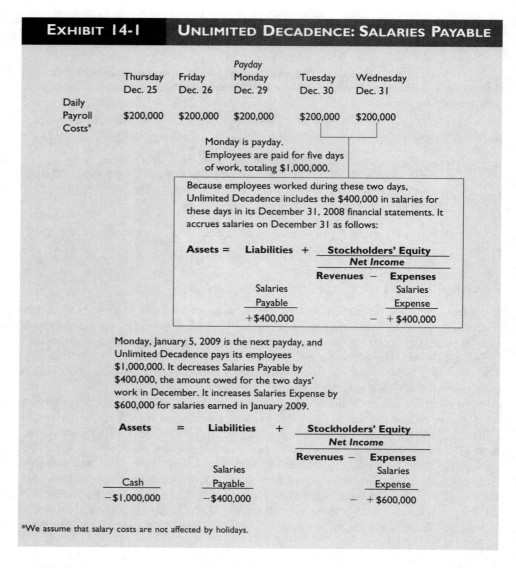

## EXHIBIT 14-1 UNLIMITED DECADENCE: SALARIES PAYABLE

| | Thursday Dec. 25 | Friday Dec. 26 | *Payday* Monday Dec. 29 | Tuesday Dec. 30 | Wednesday Dec. 31 |
|---|---|---|---|---|---|
| Daily Payroll Costs* | $200,000 | $200,000 | $200,000 | $200,000 | $200,000 |

Monday is payday.
Employees are paid for five days of work, totaling $1,000,000.

Because employees worked during these two days, Unlimited Decadence includes the $400,000 in salaries for these days in its December 31, 2008 financial statements. It accrues salaries on December 31 as follows:

| Assets = | Liabilities + | Stockholders' Equity | |
|---|---|---|---|
| | | ***Net Income*** | |
| | | **Revenues** – | **Expenses** |
| | Salaries Payable | | Salaries Expense |
| | +$400,000 | – | +$400,000 |

Monday, January 5, 2009 is the next payday, and Unlimited Decadence pays its employees $1,000,000. It decreases Salaries Payable by $400,000, the amount owed for the two days' work in December. It increases Salaries Expense by $600,000 for salaries earned in January 2009.

| Assets = | Liabilities + | Stockholders' Equity | |
|---|---|---|---|
| | | ***Net Income*** | |
| | | **Revenues** – | **Expenses** |
| Cash | Salaries Payable | | Salaries Expense |
| –$1,000,000 | –$400,000 | – | +$600,000 |

*We assume that salary costs are not affected by holidays.

satisfaction or your money back." Here's what is written on the side of a package of M&M's Chocolate Candies:

> "M&M's"® Chocolate Candies are made of the finest ingredients. This product should reach you in excellent condition. Satisfaction guaranteed or we will replace it. We value your questions or comments.
> Call **1-800-627-7852**
> M-F, 8:30 AM to 5 PM EST.
> Please save the unused product and the wrapper.

*Explain whether you think that a company increases the selling price of a product because it offers a warranty.*

The costs that a company incurs to fulfill its warranty promises are an expense associated with selling the goods. Under GAAP, a company matches the cost of providing warranties as an expense against the revenues it earned from the sale of the products *in the period of the sale*. For example, suppose you buy a Ford on May 20, 2008, and the warranty is for five years or 60,000 miles. On June 17, 2008, you have a problem, which the dealer fixes at a cost of $100. The dealer bills Ford Motor Company for the $100, and Ford records the following when it pays the dealer:

| Assets | = | Liabilities | + | Stockholders' Equity: Net Income: Revenues | − | Stockholders' Equity: Net Income: Expenses |
|---|---|---|---|---|---|---|
| Cash | | | | | | Warranty Expense |
| −$100 | | | | | − | +$100 |

> **FINANCIAL STATEMENT EFFECTS**
>
> Decreases current assets and total assets on ***balance sheet***. Increases expenses, which decreases net income on ***income statement*** (and therefore decreases stockholders' equity on ***balance sheet***). Decreases cash flows from operating activities on ***cash flow statement***.

Because warranties tend to last for several months or years, customers who purchase a company's goods in one accounting period may in a later accounting period require the company to honor its warranty on those goods. For example, when you bought your Ford, you received a five-year, 60,000-mile warranty from **Ford Motor Company**. So when Ford prepares its financial statements for the period ending December 31, 2008, it calculates and records the estimated cost of meeting the remaining warranties on current-period sales. Suppose that on December 31, 2008, Ford estimates that the warranty on the car it sold you in 2008 will cost another $900 before expiring. It records this warranty cost as follows:

| Assets | = | Liabilities | + | Stockholders' Equity: Net Income: Revenues | − | Stockholders' Equity: Net Income: Expenses |
|---|---|---|---|---|---|---|
| | | Accrued Warranty Liability | | | | Warranty Expense |
| | | | | | − | Bal $ 100 |
| | | +$900 | | | − | +900 |
| | | | | | − | Bal $1,000 |

> **FINANCIAL STATEMENT EFFECTS**
>
> Increases current liabilities and total liabilities on ***balance sheet***. Increases expenses, which decreases net income on ***income statement*** (and therefore decreases stockholders' equity on ***balance sheet***).

By recording this estimate, Ford increases its Warranty Expense by $900, to $1,000, for your car. As a result of this accrual, its Warranty Expense account for 2008 now includes all of the warranty costs associated with the sale made in 2008. Ford records and reports the total warranty expense for *all* its sales for the year as an operating expense on its 2008 income statement. Also, as a result of this accrual, its Accrued Warranty Liability increases by $900, the estimated cost of the remaining warranties. Ford records and reports the total accrued warranty liability for *all* its sales in the liability section of its December 31, 2008 balance sheet. During the next five years, whenever you claim the warranty associated with the 2008 sale, Ford will reduce the accrued warranty liability and will reduce cash or inventory.

*Since your warranty has a life of five years, explain whether Ford should report all of the warranty liability as a current liability or part of the warranty liability as a current liability and part as a noncurrent liability.*

Warranty costs can substantially affect a company's profitability. For example, a recent article in *Business Week* quoted a Deutsche Bank study that estimated Ford's average warranty costs per vehicle to be $650 for a total of $2.6 billion per year, compared to General Motors' $550, and only $400 for Toyota. Although the warranty expense reduces net income, providing a warranty to customers should increase sales. However, increasing or excessive warranty costs usually signal problems with the quality of the goods that a company manufactures and sells. Managers and external users monitor a company's warranty costs to determine if a company has quality-control problems.

*Explain other issues managers should consider as they evaluate warranty cost. Explain whether you would or would not purchase an extended warranty on your new car.*

# TAXES

4 What types of taxes do an employee and a company incur, and how does the company record them?

A **tax** is an amount of money that a government requires a taxable entity (e.g., an individual or a company) to pay. For example, in the United States, if you earn a certain minimum amount of personal income, the federal government requires you to pay income taxes. Companies incur many different kinds of taxes, including federal and state payroll taxes ("social security" and "unemployment" taxes), federal and state income taxes, state and local sales taxes (if they sell to retail customers), and state and local property taxes.

*At December 31 of any year, do you have a personal income tax liability or asset? Why?*

Managers and external users should understand that taxes are a significant cost of doing business. For instance, in 2005 Hershey Foods earned $773 million in income before income taxes. In that same year, it reported income tax expense of $280 million. Keep in mind that the $280 million does not include the amounts for other types of taxes that Hershey incurred during 2005.

Taxes that a company owes but has not paid at the balance sheet date are referred to as **accrued taxes**, or **taxes payable**. We explain three types of taxes: payroll, income, and sales taxes.

## Payroll Taxes

If you talk about payroll taxes with a company's managers or its employees, you may hear two different perspectives. You may hear an employee say, "There is a big difference between the amount of income I earn (the **gross pay**) and the amount of my take-home pay (the **net pay**). Taxes take a big chunk out of my paycheck." The amount of an employee's net pay is usually quite a bit smaller than the gross pay because the employer is required by law to withhold certain taxes from the employee's earnings and send those taxes to the government.

On the other hand, you may hear a manager say, "The wages we pay our employees are only part of our total payroll costs. The cost of payroll taxes adds tremendously to our labor costs." This manager is referring to the fact that, in the United States, federal and state governments require employers to pay certain taxes on their employees' earnings.

A company's accounting system must keep track of the payroll taxes incurred by both the employees and the company. In the next three sections, we describe three types of payroll taxes and show how Unlimited Decadence calculates the net pay of one employee for a single pay period.

### Federal and State Income Taxes on Employees

Calculating federal and state income taxes for individual taxpayers in the United States is complex, and paying personal income taxes is the employee's, not the employer's, responsibility. However, employers, such as Unlimited Decadence, are required to withhold federal and state income taxes from their employees' pay and periodically to send the money withheld to the appropriate tax authorities. Governments set up this "pay-as-you-go" withholding of income taxes to increase the likelihood of collecting the taxes that are due.

A company, with the aid of its employees and government forms, calculates the dollar amount of taxes to withhold from each employee's paycheck for each pay period throughout the year. This amount varies considerably among employees depending on a variety of tax-related factors, including how much income they earn, their tax status (married or single), and the number of dependents they claim. If an individual employee's pay varies between pay periods, the company calculates this withholding amount each time it pays the employee. Every pay period, the company deducts the appropriate amount of tax from each employee's gross pay.

For example, assume that Charlie Hill earns $15 per hour working for Unlimited Decadence as a machine operator. Further assume that he works 40 hours per week. Mr.

Hill's gross pay for the pay-week (remember that Unlimited Decadence's payday is Monday) ending February 25, 2008, is \$600 (\$15 $\times$ 40 hours). However, Mr. Hill does not receive a paycheck for this gross amount. Unlimited Decadence uses federal and state income tax tables to determine how much federal and state income tax to withhold from Mr. Hill's pay. In this example, we assume that Mr. Hill's federal and state income tax withholdings total \$95.

### Federal Social Security and Medicare Taxes

Unlimited Decadence also must withhold federal social security and Medicare taxes from Mr. Hill's gross pay. Under the Federal Insurance Contributions Act (FICA), the U.S. government collects social security taxes from employees *and* employers. The amounts generated from FICA taxes provide the cash used to pay current benefits to qualified participants in the government's social security and Medicare system. In other words, the government does *not* save the dollars you pay into the system while you are in the workforce to support your financial needs during your retirement years. These dollars go to support those who are currently retired and eligible for benefits.

*When you retire in, say, 2059, who do you think will pay your social security benefits?*

For both the employer and the employee, FICA taxes are composed of two parts: (1) social security taxes and (2) Medicare taxes. Congress periodically increases the FICA rates. At the time we wrote this book, the social security tax rate was 6.20% of wages and salaries up to \$98,700—neither you nor the company you worked for would pay social security tax on any wages or salaries you earned in excess of \$98,700 per year. The Medicare tax rate was 1.45%, with no upper limit on the amount of salary taxed.

*Do you think Mr. Hill will have social security and Medicare taxes deducted from his gross pay every week during 2008? Why or why not?*

Using the rates in effect when we wrote this book, Unlimited Decadence calculates social security and Medicare payroll tax deductions for Mr. Hill as follows:

| | |
|---|---|
| Mr. Hill's Social Security Taxes Withheld from His Weekly Pay | = Gross Pay $\times$ 6.20% |
| | = \$600 $\times$ 0.062 |
| | = \$37.20 |
| Mr. Hill's Medicare Taxes Withheld from His Weekly Pay | = Gross Pay $\times$ 1.45% |
| | = \$600 $\times$ 0.0145 |
| | = \$8.70 |
| Mr. Hill's Total FICA Taxes Withheld from His Weekly Pay | = Social Security Taxes + Medicare Taxes |
| | = \$37.20 + \$8.70 |
| | = \$45.90 |

Based on these calculations, Unlimited Decadence withholds \$45.90 in FICA taxes from Mr. Hill's gross pay. Assuming Mr. Hill has no other employee deductions,[2] his net pay for the week is \$459.10 (\$600 − \$95 − \$45.90).

Remember that *both* the employee *and* the employer pay FICA taxes. Thus, after withholding \$45.90 from Mr. Hill's pay, Unlimited Decadence must pay \$91.80 (\$45.90 for the employee portion of the tax withheld from the employee's paycheck plus \$45.90 for the employer portion of the tax) of FICA taxes to the government.

[2]Employees often pay for programs such as medical insurance, union dues, and charitable contributions (e.g., the United Way) through payroll deductions. The employer must keep track of the appropriate deductions from each employee's pay and send the correct amounts to the various agencies.

### Federal and State Unemployment Taxes

Under the Federal Unemployment Tax Act (FUTA), federal and state governments collect unemployment taxes from companies to support unemployment insurance payments to workers who lose their jobs. These FUTA taxes are paid only by employers (*not* employees). At the present time, FUTA taxes are assessed at a maximum rate of 6.2% on the first $7,000 paid to each employee in each year. Of the 6.2%, 5.4% is paid to the state if it levies an approved unemployment tax. However, most states allow a company with a good employment record to receive a good "merit rating" and receive a reduction in the tax rate.

To determine whether Unlimited Decadence is required to pay FUTA taxes on Mr. Hill's February 25, 2008 gross pay, it must calculate the amount of wages earned this year by Mr. Hill. The pay-week ending February 25, 2008 is the eighth week of the year. Including his February 25 paycheck, Mr. Hill has received $4,800 so far this year ($600 per week × 8 weeks). Because Mr. Hill has not yet received $7,000 during 2008, Unlimited Decadence is required to pay FUTA taxes on Mr. Hill's gross pay. Using the 6.2% rate, Unlimited Decadence must pay $37.20 ($600 × 6.2%) in FUTA taxes to the U.S. government because of Mr. Hill's work during the pay-week ending February 25, 2008. However, it pays no FUTA taxes on any income it pays an employee above $7,000 during the year.

### Recording Payroll and Payroll Taxes

Computerized payroll systems are designed to calculate an employee's gross pay and net pay. The payroll software is constantly updated for changes in pay rates, payroll taxes, or other employee deductions to ensure that a company accounts for its payroll properly. Even though computers make the payroll calculations, it is important that managers, investors, and creditors understand how payroll taxes affect a company's expenses. For example, if you don't understand payroll tax laws, it is easy to underestimate the total cost associated with hiring new employees.

Exhibit 14-2 shows the impact of the payroll tax items on Charlie Hill's net pay. Mr. Hill's gross pay of $600 is reduced by $95 in federal and state income tax withholding

**EXHIBIT 14-2 PAYROLL AND EMPLOYEE PAYROLL TAXES: UNLIMITED DECADENCE**

Employee payroll taxes that affect Mr. Hill's net pay for the pay-week ending February 25, 2008, are as follows:

| | |
|---|---|
| $600.00 | Gross pay (40 hours × $15) |
| (95.00) | Federal and state income tax withheld |
| (45.90) | FICA taxes withheld (social security taxes of $37.20 and medicare taxes of $8.70) |
| $459.10 | |

On February 25, 2008, Unlimited Decadence records Mr. Hill's salary as follows:

| Assets | = | Liabilities | | + | Stockholders' Equity | | |
|---|---|---|---|---|---|---|---|
| | | | | | Net Income | | |
| | | | | | Revenues | − | Expenses |
| Cash | | Federal and State Income Taxes Payable | FICA Taxes Payable | | | | Salaries Expense |
| −$459.10 | | +$95.00 | +$45.90 | | | − | +$600 |

Salaries Expense increases by the $600 gross amount of Mr. Hill's pay—Unlimited Decadence's cost of his salary for the week. Two liability accounts increase by $95 and $45.90 because Unlimited Decadence collects these taxes for the government and owes these amounts. Cash decreases by the $459.10 amount of Mr. Hill's net pay. If Unlimited Decadence owes payroll tax liabilities at year-end, it reports them in the current liability section of its balance sheet.

**FINANCIAL STATEMENT EFFECTS**

Decreases current assets and total assets on ***balance sheet***. Increases current liabilities and total liabilities on ***balance sheet***. Increases expenses, which decreases net income on ***income statement*** (and therefore decreases stockholders' equity on ***balance sheet***). Decreases cash flows from operating activities on ***cash flow statement***.

and $45.90 in social security and Medicare taxes, resulting in net pay of $459.10. We also show how Unlimited Decadence records Mr. Hill's weekly pay in its accounting system. Note that it bases the amount of salary expense on Mr. Hill's gross pay. The gross pay is part of the cost to Unlimited Decadence for his employment. The amount of taxes withheld from Mr. Hill's pay are liabilities of Unlimited Decadence until it pays them to the governmental agencies. If it owes these taxes at the balance sheet date, Unlimited Decadence reports the amounts as current liabilities on its ending balance sheet. Then when Unlimited Decadence pays the government for these taxes, it reduces the related liabilities.

Exhibit 14-3 shows how Unlimited Decadence records the employer-related payroll taxes it incurred as a result of employing Mr. Hill for the week. Recall that Unlimited Decadence incurred $45.90 in FICA taxes and $37.20 in FUTA taxes because of Mr. Hill's employment. As a result of Mr. Hill's employment for the pay-week ending February 25, 2008, Unlimited Decadence records an increase of $83.10 ($45.90 + $37.20) in its Payroll Taxes Expense and an increase in each tax liability. If Unlimited Decadence owes these taxes at the balance sheet date, it reports these amounts as current liabilities on its ending balance sheet. When Unlimited Decadence pays the government for these taxes, it reduces the related liabilities.

Remember that we based our example on only one employee, Mr. Hill. Unlimited Decadence's total expense for employees' salaries for the pay-week ending February 25, 2008, and for every week, is the sum of these expenses for all employees. Also, if Unlimited Decadence accrues salaries (or wages) at the end of an accounting period as we showed earlier, it accrues payroll taxes at the same time.

## Income Taxes

In Chapter 10 we explained that one major difference between a corporation and a partnership or sole proprietorship is that a corporation is subject to federal and state income taxes. Therefore, a corporation must include the effects of its own income taxes on its financial statements. It includes income tax expense on its income statement because income taxes are a cost of doing business. Similarly, if it owes federal and/or state income

### EXHIBIT 14-3 EMPLOYER PAYROLL TAXES: UNLIMITED DECADENCE

Employer payroll taxes for Unlimited Decadence caused by Mr. Hill's employment for the pay-week ending February 25, 2008, are as follows:

| | |
|---|---|
| $45.90 | Employer's FICA taxes owed on Mr. Hill's gross pay (social security taxes of $37.20 and medicare taxes of $8.70) |
| 37.20 | FUTA taxes owed on Mr. Hill's gross pay |
| $83.10 | |

On February 25, 2008, Unlimited Decadence records the payroll taxes associated with Mr. Hill's salary as follows:

| Assets | = | Liabilities | | + | Stockholders' Equity | | |
|---|---|---|---|---|---|---|---|
| | | | | | Net Income | | |
| | | | | | Revenues | − | Expenses |
| | | FUTA Taxes Payable | FICA Taxes Payable | | | | Payroll Tax Expense |
| | | +$37.20 | +$45.90 | | | − | +$83.10 |

Two liability accounts increase by $37.20 and $45.90. Payroll Tax Expense increases by the $83.10 cost of employing Mr. Hill. If Unlimited Decadence owes payroll tax liabilities at year-end, it reports them in the current liability section of its balance sheet.

**FINANCIAL STATEMENT EFFECTS**

Increases current liabilities and total liabilities on ***balance sheet.*** Increases expenses, which decreases net income on ***income statement*** (and therefore decreases stockholders' equity on ***balance sheet***).

taxes at the end of an accounting period, it reports these amounts as current liabilities on its ending balance sheet.

As we explained in Chapter 10, a corporation computes the income tax expense related to its "income before income taxes" each time it prepares an income statement; it computes this expense by multiplying its pretax income by the applicable tax rate. Since a corporation usually pays its income taxes after the end of the accounting period, it must accrue an expense and a liability through an end-of-period adjustment.[3]

For example, assume that Unlimited Decadence's income before income taxes for 2008 is $4.9 million (as we showed in Exhibit 10-6) and that it is subject to an income tax rate of 40%. Its income tax expense for 2008 is $1.96 million ($4.9 million × 0.40), and it records this amount as follows:

**FINANCIAL STATEMENT EFFECTS**

Increases current liabilities and total liabilities on ***balance sheet***. Increases expenses, which decreases net income on ***income statement*** (and therefore decreases stockholders' equity on ***balance sheet***).

| **Assets** | = | **Liabilities** | + | **Stockholders' Equity** | | |
|---|---|---|---|---|---|---|
| | | | | ***Net Income*** | | |
| | | | | **Revenues** | − | **Expenses** |
| | | Income Taxes Payable | | | | Income Tax Expense |
| | | +$1,960,000 | | | − | +$1,960,000 |

Both Income Tax Expense and Income Taxes Payable increase by $1.96 million, the amount of the taxes. Unlimited Decadence reports the Income Tax Expense amount on its 2008 income statement and reports the Income Taxes Payable amount with its other taxes payable in the current liabilities section of its December 31, 2008 balance sheet.

## Sales Taxes

So far in this book, whenever we discussed sales, for simplicity we ignored sales taxes. However, most states and local communities in the United States require customers to pay a sales tax on many types of products purchased. A company is required to collect state and local sales taxes from its retail customers at the time they purchase its products. (States usually require sales tax to be paid only on sales to the final retail purchaser and not on

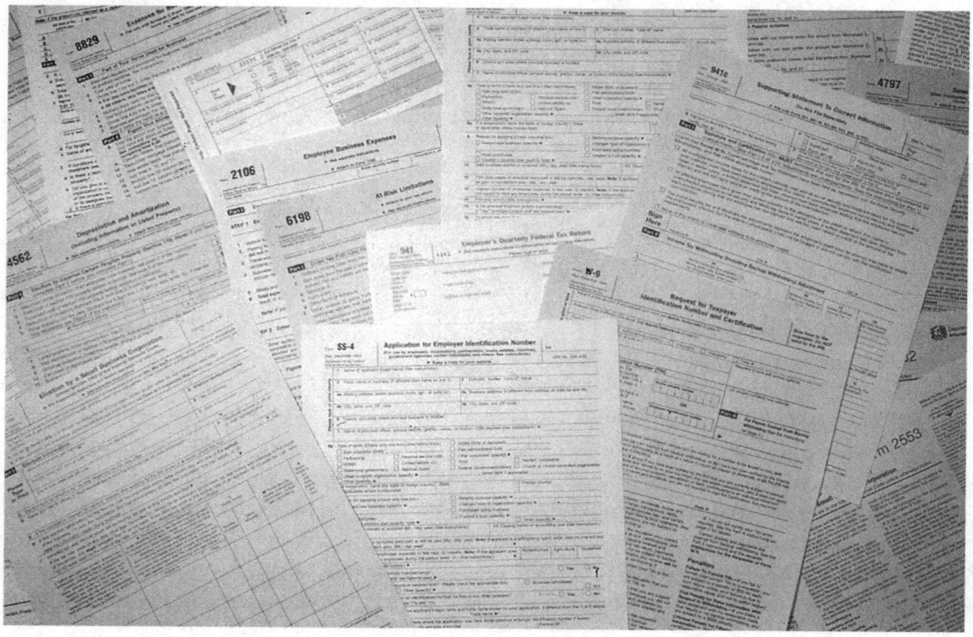


© PHOTOPIA

Some corporations claim that computing their income taxes is complicated. Do you agree?

[3]Like individuals, corporations are required to make tax payments throughout the year. For simplicity, we ignore this issue.

sales from a manufacturing company to a retail company.) Almost every time you purchase a product, you hear the salesperson say, "And with sales tax, your total comes to . . ."

At the time of sale, a company is acting as a collection agency for the state and/or local government. Therefore the sales tax it collects and then pays is neither a revenue nor an expense. The collection of the tax from the customer, however, does create a liability for the company because it receives cash that it owes to the state. It eliminates the liability when it pays the state. For example, if Unlimited Decadence makes a $10,000 credit sale that is subject to a 5% sales tax, it records the transaction as follows:

| Assets | = | Liabilities | + | Stockholders' Equity | | |
|---|---|---|---|---|---|---|
| | | | | ***Net Income*** | | |
| | | | | **Revenues** | − | **Expenses** |
| Accounts Receivable | | Sales Tax Payable | | Sales Revenue | | |
| +$10,500 | | +$500 | | +$10,000 | | |

**FINANCIAL STATEMENT EFFECTS**

Increases current assets and total assets on ***balance sheet***. Increases current liabilities and total liabilities on ***balance sheet***. Increases revenues, which increases net income on ***income statement*** (and therefore increases stockholders' equity on ***balance sheet***).

Accounts Receivable increases by $10,500, which is the amount of the sale ($10,000) plus the amount of the 5% tax ($10,000 × 5% = $500). Sales Revenue increases by $10,000, the amount of the sale. Because Unlimited Decadence must pay the amount of the sales tax to the state and local government at a later date, Sales Taxes Payable increases by $500. When Unlimited Decadence pays the sales tax to the state, it reduces the Sales Taxes Payable. If it has not paid these taxes by the balance sheet date, Unlimited Decadence reports them as a current liability on its ending balance sheet.

### Other Taxes

Companies in the United States are also subject to many other types of taxes. At the state level, companies are required to pay franchise taxes. A franchise tax is simply a tax that the state levies on all companies for "doing business" in the state. For example, in recent years California has collected around $22 billion annually in company franchise taxes. It bases the amount of the franchise tax on the company's income in the preceding year.

Almost all companies are required to pay property taxes. These are often called *ad valorem* taxes. Municipalities, school districts, counties, states, and other governmental entities that have taxing authority may levy property taxes on a company's land, buildings, or real estate. For example, the state of Missouri levies taxes on the value of a company's real estate. Local governments generally tax a company on the value of its land and buildings.

A company records the costs of its franchise taxes, property taxes, and other types of taxes as expenses in the accounting period in which it incurs them. If it has not paid these taxes by the end of an accounting period, it reports them in the current liability section of its ending balance sheet.

## SHORT-TERM NOTES PAYABLE

5 How is accounting for a short-term note payable similar to accounting for a short-term note receivable?

As we discussed in Chapter 13, some companies also sell goods to customers in return for a promissory note. When a company is the maker of the promissory note, it records a short-term note payable. A company may purchase goods using a promissory note for one of several reasons: (1) because the dollar amount of the purchase is relatively large compared with most of the selling company's credit sales, (2) because the purchasing company does not want to pay for the goods within the normal time frame offered by the selling company's credit department, or (3) because the purchasing company's credit worthiness is questionable.

Accounting for short-term notes payable is a "mirror image" of accounting for short-term notes receivable. Whereas a company earns interest revenue during the time it holds a note receivable, a company incurs interest expense during the time it owes a note payable. The amount of interest expense that a company incurs depends on the face value of the note, the note's interest rate, and the note's life. At the end of the accounting period, the company computes any accrued interest in the same way that we discussed for notes receivable. For notes payable, however, a company records the amount of interest as Interest Expense and Interest Payable. In addition to reporting the face value of short-term notes payable as a current liability on its balance sheet, a company includes the amount of interest payable in its total for accrued liabilities. The company reports the related interest expense in the "other items" section of its income statement. The interest paid and the principal paid are both included in the cash flow from operating activities section of the cash flow statement because the note payable resulted from a purchase of goods. If the note payable had resulted from borrowing money, the principal payment would be classified as a financing activity in the cash flow statement.

*Do you think that a balance sheet would be more useful if the assets and liabilities related to revenues were separated from the assets and liabilities related to expenses? Why or why not?*

## PREPAID ITEMS

6 What are prepaid items, and how does a company account for them?

A company often pays for goods or services *after* it has acquired or used them, as we discussed earlier in the chapter. In some industries, however, it is common for the buying company to pay cash *before* the selling company delivers the goods or provides the services that the buying company purchased. For example, landlords require tenants to pay rent before being allowed to use the property, and insurance companies require policyholders to pay premiums before their policy is in effect.

*Why do you think that in some industries, purchasers are required to pay in advance, whereas in others they pay in arrears?*

When a company pays for goods or services before using them, it doesn't record the expense at this time. Instead it records a current asset often called a **prepaid item**. Sometimes companies call this asset a *prepaid expense,* but many people think it is confusing to have the term "expense" in the name of an asset. Also, don't forget that many other assets are eventually going to be recorded as expenses and could also be labeled prepaid expenses.

*Would you call a building a prepaid expense? Why or why not?*

A purchasing company records a prepaid item as an asset because it has paid for a good or service that it will use in the future. It records an expense for the portion of the asset it uses, and it reduces the prepaid item as an end-of-period adjustment. The company includes the expense as an operating expense on its income statement and the remaining amount of the prepaid item as a current asset on its ending balance sheet. For example, a company paying $12,000 on October 1 for a one-year insurance policy records an asset, called *prepaid insurance.* At the end of the year, it records insurance expense for the amount used up, $3,000 [($12,000 ÷ 12) × 3 months], and reduces the prepaid insurance by the same amount. On the ending balance sheet, it reports the prepaid insurance at $9,000 ($12,000 − $3,000).

*Do you agree with the following statement? "Payables are the amounts owed because the company will record an expense in the future, whereas prepaids are the amounts that have already been recorded as an expense." Why or why not?*

## LOSS CONTINGENCIES

7 What are loss contingencies, and how does a company report or disclose them?

If you are deciding whether to invest in a company, would you want to know if the company promised to pay off another company's debt if it went unpaid? Would you want to know that the company is a defendant in a major lawsuit and may have to pay a large amount in damages if it loses? We are sure that your answer to both these questions is "yes." If this company has to pay off another company's debts or loses a major lawsuit, the financial situation of the company may drastically change. Its risk would be higher, and its financial flexibility and liquidity would be lower. In an investment decision about this company, you would probably like to have two additional pieces of information about each of these situations so you can make a more informed investment decision. First, you would want to know how likely it is that the company will actually have to pay. Second, you would want some estimate of what the dollar amount of the payment may be.

Situations such as the two described above are referred to as *contingencies*. A **contingency** is an existing condition that will lead to a gain or loss if a future event occurs (or fails to occur). A gain is like a revenue because it increases income and stockholders' equity, and a loss is like an expense because it reduces income and stockholders' equity. For example, the company faces a monetary loss *if* it loses the lawsuit. GAAP has more detailed rules for *loss* contingencies and the related liability (or reduction of an asset) because these affect investors and creditors negatively.

*Of the topics we have discussed in Chapters 13 and 14, can you think of any that are examples of loss (expense) contingencies?*

GAAP requires a company to either report or disclose certain information about loss contingencies in its financial statements depending on two conditions: (1) the likelihood that the future event will occur and (2) the ability to estimate the dollar amount associated with the contingency. The likelihood that the future event will occur falls into three levels, according to GAAP:

1. *Probable:* the chance that the future event will occur is likely
2. *Reasonably possible:* the chance that the future event will occur is more than remote but less than probable
3. *Remote:* the chance that the future event will occur is slight

Note that these levels are *not* defined in terms of a percentage probability. Their application requires good judgment by the company's managers, accountants, and lawyers.

The method that a company is required to use to report or disclose loss contingencies depends on the degree of certainty and measurability associated with the future event.

1. *Report in the financial statements:* a company reports an estimated loss from a loss contingency in its financial statements as a reduction in income (either as an expense or as a loss) and a liability (or reduction of an asset) if *both* of the following conditions are met:
   (a) it is *probable* that the future event related to the loss contingency will occur, and
   (b) the amount of the loss can be *reasonably estimated.*
2. *Disclose in the notes to the financial statements:* a company discloses an estimated loss from a loss contingency in the notes to its financial statements if it is *reasonably possible* that the future event related to the loss contingency will occur. A company also discloses a loss that is probable, but cannot be reasonably estimated.

*How do you think a company would report or disclose a loss contingency that is probable but not measurable? measurable but not probable?*

If the likelihood of the future event related to a loss contingency is remote, GAAP does not require that a company report an estimated loss in its financial statements or disclose the estimated loss in the notes (unless it is a guarantee of another company's debt).

Since a contingency requires an estimate, a company will rarely consider a single amount. Instead it will evaluate alternate amounts. When a single amount is the best estimate, the company uses that amount. Otherwise the company uses the minimum amount of the range of its estimates.

*Do you think that companies have contingent assets? If so, what is an example? If not, why not?*

**Bristol-Myers Squibb**, a pharmaceutical company, reports in its income statements for 2005, 2004, and 2003 that it had litigation expenses of $269 million, $420 million, and $199 million, respectively. It reports in its balance sheet, litigation liabilities of $493 million and $186 million at December 31, 2005 and 2004, respectively. In its notes, the company explains that it records accruals (liabilities) for contingencies such as lawsuits, claims, proceedings, and investigations that are pending against the company when "it is probable that a liability will be incurred and the amount of the loss can be reasonably estimated. These matters involve antitrust, securities, patent infringement, pricing, sales and marketing practices, environmental, health and safety matters, product liability and insurance coverage." The company also says that "management continues to believe . . . that during the next few years, the aggregate impact, . . . of these and other legal matters affecting the company is reasonably likely to be material to the company's results of operations and cash flows, and may be material to its financial condition and liquidity." The company then uses nine pages to provide further explanations of three categories of contingencies.

The first category, Intellectual Property, is for patent infringement lawsuits related to its best selling drug, Plavix. The second category, Other Intellectual Property Litigation, involves lawsuits and other legal matters related to five different drugs. The third category, Securities Litigation, is divided into eight separate subcategories describing lawsuits regarding alleged violations of federal securities laws and regulations. These notes disclose millions of dollars of current litigation, but millions more may result from future litigation issues (no wonder drugs are so expensive!). So the user of financial statements must be very careful when using the financial statements of companies that have significant litigation issues.

## EVALUATION OF A COMPANY'S MANAGEMENT OF ITS LIQUIDITY POSITION

8 What can external users learn from analyzing a company's liquidity?

In Chapters 13 and 14 we have discussed how a company manages and reports the current assets (except inventory and marketable securities) and liabilities that affect its liquidity position. It is important for you to understand these assets and liabilities and how they relate to each other as we discuss the evaluation of a company's liquidity.

External users evaluate a company's liquidity position for two main reasons. First, they evaluate the company's liquidity to help assess its ability to meet short-term obligations. External users realize that if a company cannot pay its obligations as they come due, it risks going out of business. A company that fails to pay its short-term obligations will have difficulty purchasing on credit or borrowing money. Second, external users evaluate a company's liquidity to help assess its financial flexibility. A company in a good liquidity position can take better advantage of business opportunities such as aggressively marketing its products or investing for growth.

External users must understand two basic aspects of accounting to be able to evaluate a company's liquidity position. First, they need to know the assets and liabilities that affect liquidity. You learned about this aspect in these two chapters. Second, investors and creditors must understand how to perform financial statement analysis. In Chapter 10 we described several types of financial statement analyses. Here, we will apply what you learned in these chapters.

Recall from Chapter 10 that investors and creditors use ratio analysis, horizontal analysis, and vertical analysis to evaluate liquidity. They may perform these types of analyses only on the company being evaluated (intracompany analysis), and/or they may compare the company's liquidity position with industry averages and with the liquidity positions of similar companies (intercompany analysis). We separate our discussion of evaluating company liquidity into two sections: intracompany analysis and intercompany analysis.

## Intracompany Analysis of Liquidity

Assume that you are a stockholder in **Rocky Mountain Chocolate Factory**. On May 27, 2006, you received Rocky Mountain's 2006 annual report, and you turned to the February 28, 2006 and February 28, 2005 comparative balance sheets to determine how well the company has managed its liquidity position. We show amounts included as current assets and current liabilities on these balance sheets in Exhibit 14-4. Note that the company uses a *fiscal year* that is different from the calendar year.

*Why do you think the company has a balance sheet dated at the end of February?*

How would you start your analysis? You should probably perform three steps. First, you should examine the balance of each account that affects liquidity for both years. Think about the liquidity management policies and activities that affect each balance. For instance, ask yourself: "Are the balances on February 28, 2006 similar to those on February 28, 2005? Did any balances change dramatically? If so, what could have caused the change?" By familiarizing yourself with the balances, you can anticipate the findings that percentage analysis or ratio analysis may produce.

For example, we can see in Exhibit 14-4 that Rocky Mountain's accounts receivable (net) balance on February 28, 2006 ($3,296,690) is larger than it was on February 28, 2005 ($2,943,835). There are several possible explanations for this increase. Some explanations are positive, whereas others indicate potential problems. If accounts receivable increased because of an overall increase in credit sales to good customers, the increase is good news. If the increase in accounts receivable is not accompanied by an increase in sales from the fiscal year ending February 28, 2005, to the fiscal year ending February 28, 2006, this increase may signal a slowdown in cash collections. You can get a better picture of the changes that occurred in these balances by using horizontal analysis to

**EXHIBIT 14-4 ROCKY MOUNTAIN CHOCOLATE FACTORY, INC.: CURRENT ASSET AND CURRENT LIABILITY AMOUNTS AS A PERCENTAGE OF TOTAL ASSETS**

| | February 28, 2006 | % | February 28, 2005 | % |
|---|---|---|---|---|
| CURRENT ASSETS | | | | |
| Cash and cash equivalents | $ 3,489,750 | 18.3 | $ 4,438,876 | 23.1 |
| Accounts receivable, less allowance for doubtful accounts of $46,920 and $80,641 | 3,296,690 | 17.3 | 2,943,835 | 15.3 |
| Notes receivable | 116,997 | 0.6 | 451,845 | 2.3 |
| Refundable income taxes | — | — | 364,630 | 1.9 |
| Inventories, less reserve for slow moving inventory of $61,032 and $127,345 | 2,938,234 | 15.4 | 2,518,212 | 13.1 |
| Deferred income taxes | 117,715 | 0.6 | 156,623 | 0.8 |
| Other | 481,091 | 2.5 | 250,886 | 1.3 |
| Total current assets | $10,440,477 | 54.8 | $11,124,907 | 57.8 |
| CURRENT LIABILITIES | | | | |
| Current maturities of long-term debt | $ — | — | $ 126,000 | 0.6 |
| Accounts payable | 1,145,410 | 6.0 | 1,088,476 | 5.7 |
| Accrued salaries and wages | 507,480 | 2.7 | 1,160,937 | 6.0 |
| Other accrued expenses | 750,733 | 3.9 | 324,215 | 1.7 |
| Dividend payable | 504,150 | 2.6 | 417,090 | 2.2 |
| Total current liabilities | $ 2,907,773 | 15.3 | $ 3,116,718 | 16.2 |

*Note:* Total assets at February 28, 2006 are $19,057,480 and at February 28, 2005 are $19,247,974.

calculate the percentage change in the balances from 2005 to 2006. Accounts receivable, for instance, increased by 12% ($3,296,690 ÷ $2,943,835 = 1.12, rounded) from 2005 to 2006. Rocky Mountain's sales increased by 15.3% (amounts not shown in Exhibit 14-4), so its accounts receivable has decreased in relation to its sales. This is a positive sign in regard to its liquidity. You can also compare the percentage increase in accounts receivable with percentage changes in other liquidity-related accounts. But note that receivables may not all have the same liquidity. For example, a company may expect to collect accounts receivable sooner than notes receivable. Note also that Rocky Mountain's allowance for doubtful accounts (allowance for bad debts) decreased in 2006. The company may be managing its receivables better and may be more optimistic about collecting them, thereby sending another positive signal about its liquidity.

*If a company's accounts receivable increased by 12%, would you expect a similar increase in its accounts payable? Why or why not?*

Second, you should examine how Rocky Mountain's liquidity position has changed from February 28, 2005, to February 28, 2006, by converting the dollar balances for each current asset and current liability to percentages of the company's total assets. This is done by dividing the balance of each current asset and current liability by the amount of total assets. This vertical analysis is important because although the current-year account balances may be significantly different from the account balances of the past year, the whole company may have grown (or shrunk) by the same proportion. Rocky Mountain's total assets at February 28, 2006, and February 28, 2005, are $19,057,480 and $19,247,974, respectively. In Exhibit 14-4, for each year we calculated each of Rocky Mountain's current asset and current liability balances as a percentage of that year's total assets. For example, the increase in Rocky Mountain's other accrued expenses balance from $324,215 to $750,733 may seem more significant when we realize that the relation to total assets has increased from 1.7% to 3.9%.

*What other insights do you gain by examining Exhibit 14-4? What questions about Rocky Mountain's liquidity position occur to you when you examine this exhibit?*

Third, you should calculate liquidity ratios for February 28, 2006, and February 28, 2005. Two of the most commonly used ratios are the quick ratio and the accounts receivable turnover ratio.[4] We introduced these ratios in earlier chapters. The quick ratio is calculated as follows:

$$\text{Quick Ratio} = \frac{\begin{array}{c}\text{Cash and Cash Equivalents} + \text{Short-Term Investments}\\ + \text{Accounts Receivable} + \text{Notes Receivable (short-term)}\end{array}}{\text{Current Liabilities}}$$

The quick ratio compares the company's dollar amount of those current assets that can be most easily converted into cash with the dollar amount of the company's current liabilities. The larger the ratio, the better position the company is in to meet its short-term obligations. The quick ratio of Rocky Mountain on February 28, 2006, is 2.37 and on February 28, 2005, is 2.51. Since the 2006 ratio is slightly lower than the 2005 ratio, this trend indicates a decrease in Rocky Mountain's liquidity position.

*When computing the quick ratio, would you include unearned revenue in the denominator? Why or why not?*

The accounts receivable turnover ratio is calculated as follows:

$$\text{Accounts Receivable Turnover} = \frac{\text{Net Sales}}{\text{Average Net Accounts Receivable}}$$

[4]We will discuss the current ratio and the inventory turnover ratio for large companies in Chapter 19 of Volume 2.

Dividing net sales[5] by average net accounts receivable shows how many times the average accounts receivable are *turned over,* or collected, during each accounting period. Notice that we use the *average* net accounts receivable, as opposed to the balance at the beginning or the end of the accounting period, as the denominator in this ratio. The average net accounts receivable is calculated as follows:

$$\text{Average Net Accounts Receivable} = \frac{\begin{matrix}\text{Beginning Net} & & \text{Ending Net} \\ \text{Accounts Receivable} & + & \text{Accounts Receivable}\end{matrix}}{2}$$

A company uses this average amount because it is usually a better measure of the dollar amount of accounts receivable that the company managed during the accounting period than is the accounts receivable balance at the beginning or the end of the year. The accounts receivable turnover ratio is a measure of the efficiency with which a company collects its receivables. As a general rule, the higher the turnover, the better it is for the company because the company has fewer resources tied up in accounts receivable, collects these resources at a faster pace, and usually has fewer uncollectible accounts. Too high a turnover rate, however, might indicate that the company is too aggressive in its collection policies and is alienating its customers. A company often divides its accounts receivable turnover into the number of days in the business year; this shows the average number of days required for the company to collect its accounts receivable. External users compare a company's average collection period with the number of days the company gives its customers to pay for credit purchases (i.e., credit terms). This comparison provides investors and creditors with an indication of how effectively the company manages its accounts receivable and cash receipts.

Using information from Rocky Mountain's annual report, we calculated the company's accounts receivable turnover ratio and its average collection period (assuming a 365-day business year) for fiscal 2006 and fiscal 2005, as we show in Exhibit 14-5. As you can see, Rocky Mountain's collection period has increased from 50 days in fiscal 2005 to 51 days in fiscal 2006. Thus, Rocky Mountain is collecting its accounts receivable a little less effectively.

Another ratio that some users find helpful is the accounts payable turnover ratio, which is calculated as follows:

$$\text{Accounts Payable Turnover} = \frac{\text{Cost of Goods Sold}}{\text{Average Accounts Payable}}$$

This ratio measures the number of times that accounts payable turn over during the year. Using information from Rocky Mountain's annual report, we calculated the company's accounts payable turnover ratio for fiscal 2006 and fiscal 2005 and its average payment period, as we show in Exhibit 14-5. As you can see, Rocky Mountain's accounts payable payment period has decreased from 32 days in fiscal 2005 to 29 days in fiscal 2006. Thus, Rocky Mountain is paying its accounts payable more quickly in 2006 than 2005. A company with too low an accounts payable turnover may not be paying creditors on a timely basis and may be in financial difficulty. Alternatively, a company with too high a turnover may be paying too quickly and losing the "free" credit provided by accounts payable. A user may prefer to compute the accounts payable turnover ratio using purchases as the numerator because purchases are more closely related to accounts payable than is cost of goods sold. Since companies typically don't report purchases, the external user needs to compute the amount by adding the ending inventory to the cost of goods sold and subtracting the beginning inventory.

[5]As we discussed in Chapter 7, if a company's net *credit* sales are known, you should use this amount in the calculation.

## EXHIBIT 14-5 ROCKY MOUNTAIN CHOCOLATE FACTORY, INC.: ACCOUNTS RECEIVABLE AND ACCOUNTS PAYABLE RATIOS

*Fiscal Year Ending February 28, 2006*

$$\text{Accounts Receivable Turnover} = \frac{\$22{,}343{,}209}{(\$2{,}943{,}835 + \$3{,}296{,}690) \div 2} = 7.2$$

$$\text{Number of Days in Collection Period} = \frac{365 \text{ days}}{7.2} = 51 \text{ days}$$

$$\text{Accounts Payable Turnover} = \frac{\$13{,}956{,}550}{(\$1{,}088{,}476 + \$1{,}145{,}410) \div 2} = 12.5$$

$$\text{Number of Days in Payment Period} = \frac{365 \text{ days}}{12.5} = 29 \text{ days}$$

*Fiscal Year Ending February 28, 2005*

$$\text{Accounts Receivable Turnover} = \frac{\$19{,}380{,}861}{(\$2{,}388{,}848 + \$2{,}943{,}835) \div 2} = 7.3$$

$$\text{Number of Days in Collection Period} = \frac{365 \text{ days}}{7.3} = 50 \text{ days}$$

$$\text{Accounts Payable Turnover} = \frac{\$11{,}741{,}205}{(\$952{,}542 + \$1{,}088{,}476) \div 2} = 11.5$$

$$\text{Number of Days in Payment Period} = \frac{365 \text{ days}}{11.5} = 32 \text{ days}$$

*Note:* Listed below are the dollar numbers we used to calculate the accounts receivable ratios for Rocky Mountain. Make sure you understand how each ratio was calculated.

| *Net sales* | *Cost of sales* |
|---|---|
| 2006: $22,343,209 | 2006: $13,956,550 |
| 2005: $19,380,861 | 2005: $11,741,205 |

| *Net accounts receivable* | *Accounts payable* |
|---|---|
| 2/28/2006: $3,296,690 | 2/28/2006: $1,145,410 |
| 2/28/2005: $2,943,835 | 2/28/2005: $1,088,476 |
| 2/29/2004: $2,388,848 | 2/29/2004: $ 952,542 |

*Can you use the information in Exhibit 14-4 to discover other useful information?*

## Intercompany Analysis of Liquidity

When you complete an *intra*company analysis of a company's liquidity position, you learn how the company's position has changed since previous years. However, to gauge how well the company has managed its liquidity, you also should use *inter*company analysis to compare the company's liquidity position with the liquidity position of similar companies or with industry averages. Investors and creditors can find industry-level financial data from information services companies such as **Dun & Bradstreet**, **Moody's**, and **Standard & Poor's**.

By comparing Rocky Mountain's February 28, 2006, and February 28, 2005, quick ratios and its fiscal 2006 and 2005 accounts receivable turnover ratios, the numbers of days in its collection period, accounts payable turnover ratios, and the number of days in its payment period we can analyze Rocky Mountain's liquidity position. But are the ra-

**EXHIBIT 14-6** **COMPARISON OF INDUSTRY AVERAGES FOR LIQUIDITY: ROCKY MOUNTAIN CHOCOLATE FACTORY AND OTHER CANDY MANUFACTURERS**

| | Rocky Mountain 2006 | Industry Averages |
|---|---|---|
| Quick Ratio | 2.37 | 1.7 |
| Accounts Receivable Turnover Ratio | 7.2 | 12.2 |
| Number of Days in Collection Period | 51 | 30 |
| Accounts Payable Turnover Ratio | 12.5 | 15.2 |
| Number of Days in Payment Period | 29 | 24 |

tios and amounts good or bad? Do the fiscal 2006 accounts receivable turnover ratio of 7.2 and the collection period of 51 days indicate that the company's accounts receivable are being managed effectively? In Exhibit 14-6, we list the industry averages for candy manufacturers.

By studying Exhibit 14-6, you can see that Rocky Mountain has a better-than-average quick ratio. This means Rocky Mountain has slightly more cash, short-term investments, and accounts and notes receivable compared with its total dollar amount of current liabilities. Its accounts receivable turnover (and the collection period) are much worse than the industry averages. Furthermore, its accounts payable turnover is much slower than the industry average. So, Rocky Mountain's liquidity position is generally worse than the industry average. Therefore, investors and creditors may have some concerns about Rocky Mountain's current overall liquidity position, and may need to monitor the company's ongoing overall liquidity position.

*If some companies in the industry make significant cash sales, how would your interpretation of their quick ratios and their accounts receivable turnover ratios be affected?*

## BUSINESS ISSUES AND VALUES

In this chapter and Chapter 13 we explained how companies record and report several types of current assets and current liabilities using GAAP. We also explained how managers, investors, and creditors use financial statements to assess a company's liquidity position. Because investors and creditors make business decisions that are based on their assessment of a company's financial statements, a manager may be tempted to make the company appear more liquid, or more financially flexible, than it really is.

In Chapter 13, we discussed how a company may record credit sales very aggressively, stretching its interpretation of GAAP. By recording credit sales before the revenue is earned, a company may *overstate* its accounts receivable and net income for the accounting period. Alternatively, a company might understate its expected future sales returns, which would overstate sales (net) and net income. Also, because the dollar amount in accounts receivable is higher than it should be, the quick ratio may be overstated.

When it comes to reporting current liabilities, a manager may be tempted to *understate* the company's liabilities. For example, a company may intentionally underestimate warranty liabilities by using a lower estimate of warranty claims outstanding at year-end. Similarly, a company may indicate that a loss contingency is only remotely possible even though it knows that the probability is much higher.

If a company's current liabilities are understated, its quick ratio is higher than it should be. Thus, the company's liquidity position looks better, making the company seem to have more financial flexibility. By relying on these inflated ratios, external users may make wrong business decisions—make a loan to a company that is more risky than they believed it was or pay more than they should for shares of a company's common stock. If managers intentionally misstate financial statements, they have broken the law. They have committed what is called "management fraud" and can be arrested and prosecuted for their actions.

*Do you think a manager should be pessimistic about warranty costs or contingent liabilities to make sure that the company's liquidity position is not overstated? Why or why not? What should the manager do?*

## SUMMARY

At the beginning of the chapter we asked you several questions. During the chapter, we asked you to STOP and answer some additional questions to build your knowledge about specific issues. Be sure you answered these additional questions. Below are the questions from the beginning of the chapter, with a brief summary of the key points relating to the answers. Use your creative and critical thinking skills to expand on these key points to develop more complete answers to the questions and to determine what other questions you have that might lead you to learn more about the issues.

### 1 Why does a large company make purchases on credit, and how should it manage and record accounts payable?

A large company makes purchases on credit for many of the same reasons that a small company does: (1) purchasing on credit is often more convenient than purchasing with cash, (2) purchasing on credit delays paying for purchases and, by doing so, results in a short-term "loan" from the supplier, and (3) purchasing on credit gives the company an opportunity to assess the quality of the item before making the cash payment. In general, a company should establish the following policies for credit purchases: (1) separate purchasing duties from record-keeping duties and/or control of the asset, (2) restrict the ability of employees to obligate the company to pay for credit purchases, (3) authorize cash payments only for goods that have been received and properly documented, and (4) require submission of accounts payable documents to the cash payments department in a timely manner to take advantage of purchases discounts. When the company purchases inventory and uses the gross method, it increases inventory and accounts payable for the total amount of the purchase. When it pays for the purchases and takes a discount, it decreases cash for the net amount, inventory for the amount of the discount, and accounts payable by the gross amount of the purchase. Alternatively, if the company does not pay within the discount period, it simply reduces cash and accounts payable. If a company uses the net method, it records the inventory at the total invoice price less the discount (that is, at the net price). When it pays the invoice, it reduces cash and accounts payable by the net amount. Alternatively, if it does not pay within the discount period, it decreases cash by the gross amount, decreases accounts payable by the net amount, and records the difference as purchases discounts lost, which is an expense account similar to interest expense.

### 2 How does an exchange gain (loss) arise from a credit purchase made from a company in another country?

An exchange gain or loss is caused by a change in the exchange rate between the date that a company records a credit purchase transaction and the date that the company pays the cash. More specifically, an exchange gain occurs when the exchange rate declines between the date a company records a payable and the date the company pays the cash, and an exchange loss occurs when the exchange rate increases between the date a company records a payable and the date the company pays the cash.

### 3 What are accrued liabilities, and what types does a company often have?

Accrued liabilities are short-term obligations (other than accounts payable) that a company owes at the end of an accounting period and that result from the company's operating activities during the period. Examples include a company's utility bill for the last month in an accounting period (which it will pay in the next accounting period), salaries (wages) that have been earned by employees but have not yet been paid, and warranties that apply to products sold during the period and that will be honored in future year(s).

### 4 What types of taxes do an employee and a company incur, and how does the company record them?

If an employee earns a certain minimum amount of personal income, the federal government requires the employee to pay income taxes, as well as social security and Medicare taxes. A company incurs federal and state payroll taxes (social security and unemployment taxes), federal and state income taxes, state and local sales taxes (if it sells to retail customers), and state and local property taxes. For the employee, the company records gross pay as an expense, deducts taxes owed by the employee, and pays the employee the net pay. It sends the employee's taxes withheld to the appropriate governments. The company also records its payroll expenses and later sends the amounts to the appropriate governments.

### 5 How is accounting for a short-term note payable similar to accounting for a short-term note receivable?

Accounting for a short-term note payable is a "mirror image" of accounting for a short-term note receivable. Whereas a company earns interest revenue during the time it holds a note receivable, a company incurs interest expense during the time it owes a note payable. The amount of interest expense that a company incurs depends on the face value of the note, its interest rate, and its life. At the end of the accounting period, the company computes any accrued interest in the same way it does for a note receivable. For notes payable, however, a company records the amount of interest as interest expense and interest payable. In addition to reporting the face value of a short-term note payable as a current liability on its balance sheet, a company includes the amount of interest payable in its total for accrued liabilities. The company reports the related interest expense in the "other items" section of its income statement. The interest paid and the principal paid are both included in the cash flows from operating activities section of the cash flow statement if the note payable resulted from the purchase of goods.

### 6 What are prepaid items, and how does a company account for them?

Prepaid items arise when a purchasing company pays cash before the selling company delivers the goods or provides the services that were purchased. For example, landlords require tenants to pay rent before being allowed to use the property, and insurance companies require policyholders to pay premiums before their policy is in effect. A purchasing company records a prepaid item as an asset because it has paid for a good or service that it will use in the future. It records an expense for the portion of the asset it uses and reduces the prepaid item as an end-of-period adjustment. The company includes the expense as an operating expense on its income statement and the remaining amount of the prepaid item as a current asset on its ending balance sheet.

### 7 What are loss contingencies, and how does a company report or disclose them?

A contingency is an existing condition that will lead to a gain or loss if a future event occurs (or fails to occur). GAAP requires a company to either report or disclose certain information about loss contingencies in its financial statements depending on two conditions: (1) the likelihood that the future event will occur, and (2) the ability to estimate the dollar amount associated with the contingency. The likelihood that the future event will occur falls into three levels, according to GAAP: (1) probable, (2) reasonably possible, and (3) remote. The method that a company is required to use to report or disclose loss contingencies depends on the degree of certainty that is associated with the future event: (1) if it is probable that the future event related to the loss contingency will occur and the amount of the loss can be reasonably estimated, a company reports an estimated loss from a loss contingency on its financial statements as a reduction in income (either as an expense or a loss) and as a liability (or reduction of an asset); (2) if it is reasonably possible that the future event related to the loss contingency will occur, a company discloses an estimated loss from a loss contingency in the notes to its financial statements. If the likelihood of the future event related to a loss contingency is remote, GAAP does not require that a company report an estimated loss in the financial statements or disclose the loss in the notes (unless it is a guarantee of another company's debt).

### 8 What can external users learn from analyzing a company's liquidity?

External users evaluate a company's liquidity position for two main reasons. First, they evaluate the company's liquidity to help assess its ability to meet short-term obligations. External users realize that if a company cannot pay its obligations as they come due, it risks going out of business. A company that fails to pay its short-term obligations will have difficulty purchasing on credit or borrowing money. Second, external users evaluate a company's liquidity to help assess its financial flexibility. A company in a good liquidity position can take better advantage of business opportunities such as aggressively marketing its products or investing for growth. External users must understand two basic aspects of accounting to be able to evaluate a company's liquidity position. First, they need to know the assets and liabilities that affect liquidity. Second, they must understand how to perform financial statement analysis using ratio analysis, horizontal analysis, and vertical analysis. They may perform these types of analyses only on the company being evaluated (intracompany analysis), and/or they may compare the company's liquidity position with industry averages and with the liquidity positions of similar companies (intercompany analysis).

## Key Terms

**accounts payable subsidiary file** *(p. 458)*
**accrued liabilities** *(p. 464)*
**accrued salaries** *(p. 465)*
**accrued taxes** *(p. 468)*
**contingency** *(p. 475)*
**control account** *(p. 458)*
**exchange gain or loss** *(p. 463)*
**gross pay** *(p. 468)*
**net pay** *(p. 468)*
**prepaid item** *(p. 474)*
**procurement card** *(p. 464)*
**purchase order** *(p. 459)*
**purchases allowance** *(p. 461)*
**purchases discount** *(p. 459)*
**purchases return** *(p. 461)*
**receiving report** *(p. 459)*
**salaries payable** *(p. 465)*
**tax** *(p. 468)*
**taxes payable** *(p. 468)*
**wages payable** *(p. 465)*

## Summary Surfing

Here is an opportunity to gather information on the Internet about real-world issues related to the topics in this chapter (for suggestions on how to navigate various companies' Web sites to find their financial statements and other information, see the related discussion in the Preface at the beginning of the book). Answer the following questions.

- Go to the **Yahoo! Finance** Web site. Click on Investing; then click on *Currency Exchange Rates*. Has the dollar strengthened or weakened against the Brazilian real since Unlimited Decadence's purchase discussed in the chapter? If the company purchased sugar when the exchange rate was $0.50 and paid at the current exchange rate, would the company have an exchange gain or loss?
- Go to the **Hershey Company** Web site. Find the company's 10-K filed for the most recent year. Explain how the company's liquidity has changed in the last year.

# INTEGRATED BUSINESS AND ACCOUNTING SITUATIONS

**Answer the Following Questions in Your Own Words.**

## Testing Your Knowledge

**14-1** Why does a large company make purchases on credit?

**14-2** What is an accounts payable subsidiary file, and how does it relate to the Accounts Payable control account?

**14-3** What are the basic management policies over credit purchases for large companies?

**14-4** What is the difference between a purchase order and a receiving report?

**14-5** Briefly explain how a company records and reports a purchases discount taken under (a) the gross method and (b) the net method.

**14-6** Explain the difference between a purchases return and a purchases allowance.

**14-7** Explain the difference between an exchange gain and an exchange loss in regard to credit purchases.

**14-8** Briefly explain what innovations a company might use for its accounts payable management.

**14-9** What are accrued liabilities, and what effect do they have on a company's financial statements?

**14-10** What are accrued salaries? How is the dollar amount of salaries payable calculated at the end of an accounting period?

**14-11** What is a product warranty? What does the dollar amount of accrued warranty liability reported on a company's ending balance sheet represent?

**14-12** Identify three types of payroll taxes, and explain whether employees, employers, or both are responsible for each type of tax.

**14-13** Why might a company be required to issue a short-term note payable when it purchases inventory? How does the company report this note on its ending balance sheet?

**14-14** What is a prepaid item, and how is it adjusted at the end of an accounting period?

**14-15** What is a loss contingency, and what are the two conditions that must be considered in determining how to account for it?

**14-16** When does a company report a loss contingency in its financial statements?

**14-17** When does a company disclose a loss contingency in the notes to its financial statements?

**14-18** Why do external users evaluate a company's liquidity position?

**14-19** Briefly discuss how you would use intracompany analysis to evaluate a company's liquidity management.

**14-20** How is a company's quick ratio calculated, and what does it show?

**14-21** How is a company's accounts receivable turnover ratio calculated, and what does it measure?

**14-22** How is a company's accounts payable turnover ratio calculated, and what does it measure?

**14-23** Briefly discuss how you would use intercompany analysis to evaluate a company's liquidity management.

## Applying Your Knowledge

**14-24** On May 3 Morgan Furnace Company, which uses a perpetual inventory system, purchased $16,000 of furnaces from Tam Mfg. on credit with terms 3/10, n/30.

*Required:* (1) Using the gross method, record Morgan's purchase and payment assuming (a) Morgan paid for the purchase on May 12, and instead (b) Morgan paid for the purchase on May 30.
(2) Using the net method, record Morgan's purchase and payment assuming (a) Morgan paid for the purchase on May 12, and instead (b) Morgan paid for the purchase on May 30.

**14-25** On September 21 the purchasing department of Sherman Hardware Corporation purchased raw materials costing $15,000 on credit from Adams Supply Company. Adams offered Sherman purchases discount terms of 2/15, n/30. Sherman uses a perpetual inventory system and the gross method of recording purchases discounts.

*Required:* (1) Show how Sherman records the credit purchase and its cash payment in its accounting system (a) if Sherman's accounting department waits 30 days from the date of the purchase before it pays Adams for this purchase, and instead (b) if Sherman's accounting department pays for the purchase within 15 days from the date of the purchase.
(2) If Sherman sells this inventory for $24,000, what is the gross profit from the sale under (a) and (b)? Explain the difference between these two amounts.
(3) What would your answers to (2) be if Sherman had been using the net method of recording purchases discounts? What is the reason for any difference between your answers to (2) and (3)?
(4) What is the approximate interest cost (percentage) assuming a 360-day year if Sherman chooses not to pay for its purchases within the purchases discount period?

**14-26** On July 1, Nikko Company purchased merchandise costing $14,000 on credit from Ham Company under terms n/30. When it received the merchandise, an inspection revealed that some was of inferior quality. Instead of returning the merchandise to Ham, Nikko was granted an allowance of $1,700, and it planned to sell the merchandise at its annual "sidewalk sale." Nikko uses the gross method to record its purchases.

*Required:* (1) Show how Nikko Company would record the purchase, allowance, and payment.
(2) What source documents would be used to record each transaction?
(3) What is the net amount of the inventory after these transactions have been recorded?

**14-27** On January 15, Seagle Company, a U.S. company, acquired machinery on credit from Cleese Company, a British company, for 12,000 pounds. The Seagle Company paid for the machine on January 30. The exchange rates on January 15 and January 30 were $1.60 and $1.55, respectively.

*Required:* (1) Record the purchase and the payment.
(2) Record the payment on January 30 if, instead, the exchange rate was $1.67 on this date.

**14-28** The Clinkscales Brass Fittings Company has 100 employees, each of whom earns $440 per week for a five-day work week (Monday through Friday). The employees are paid every Thursday at the end of the day. September 30, the end of the company's fiscal year, falls on Monday.

*Required:* (1) Record the end-of-period adjustment for salaries on September 30.
(2) Record the entry for the payment of salaries on October 3.

(3) Explain the effect on Clinkscales' financial statements for the fiscal year if it had not made the end-of-period adjustment in (1). Ignore income taxes.

**14-29** On October 2, 2008, Scotch Company purchased two acres of land from Irist Company at a cost of $20,000. The Scotch Company signed (issued) a one-year, 10% note requiring it to repay the $20,000 principal plus $2,000 interest on October 1, 2009 to Irist Company. Irist Company had originally purchased the land for $20,000.

*Required:* (1) Record the purchase of the land and the December 31 end-of-period adjustment for Scotch Company.
(2) Record the sale of the land and the December 31 end-of-period adjustment for Irist Company.

**14-30** The following list of accounts and account balances was taken from the accounting records of Mane Lettering Company:

| Account Title | Account Balance Before Adjustment | Account Balance After Adjustment |
|---|---|---|
| Prepaid Insurance | $2,400 | $1,800 |
| Salaries Payable | 0 | 7,300 |
| Unearned Rent Revenue | 9,800 | 5,600 |

*Required:* For each account enter the beginning balance, prepare the end-of-period adjustment that caused the change in the account balance, and enter the ending balance.

**14-31** On December 31 of the current year, Rulem Company provides you with the following information:
(a) Accrued interest on a note payable amounts to $1,700 at year-end.
(b) Prepaid insurance that expired during the year totals $5,000 at year-end.
(c) Unearned rent revenue that was earned during the year totals $7,200 at year-end.

*Required:* (1) Record the end-of-period adjustment of Rulem for each of the preceding items.
(2) Explain the effect on Rulem's current financial statements if each of the end-of-period adjustments had not been made. Ignore income taxes.

**14-32** During 2008, Ryan Appliance Wholesalers sold electric toasters with one-year warranties. By the end of the year, the company had repaired 300 toasters at an average cost (paid in cash) of $8 each. On December 31, 2008, the company estimated that, in 2009, it would repair, at an average cost of $8 per toaster, 500 toasters sold in 2008.

*Required:* (1) Record the repair of the toasters during 2008.
(2) Record the end-of-period adjustment for 2008.
(3) Show how the warranty expense and liability would be reported on the company's 2008 financial statements.

**14-33** Lisa Renet manages Seasons Catering Company. Her annual salary is $120,000, which is earned evenly over the year. Each month, Renet has $2,400 in federal and state income taxes withheld. For simplicity, assume the FICA tax rate is 8% up to a maximum salary of $100,000. Assume that FUTA taxes are 6.2% on the first $7,000 of an employee's gross pay. Renet pays $100 per month for medical insurance; the company withholds this amount from her paycheck and also contributes an equal amount.

*Required:* (1) For the month of January, calculate (a) Renet's net pay and (b) Seasons Catering Company's salary expense and payroll tax expense associated with Renet's employment.
(2) For the month of December, calculate (a) Renet's net pay and (b) Seasons Catering Company's salary expense and payroll tax expense associated with Renet's employment.
(3) Are the amounts you calculated in (2) the same as the amounts you calculated in (1)? Why or why not?

**14-34** For the employees of McKinley Plastics Company, the gross pay and the federal income tax withheld in the first week of February 2008 were as follows:

| Employee | Gross Pay | Income Tax Withheld |
|---|---|---|
| Carver, James | $1,200 | $168 |
| Webb, Steve | 1,400 | 216 |
| Bailey, Doreen | 2,000 | 308 |

For simplicity, assume FICA taxes are withheld at an 8% rate. FUTA taxes are 6.2%. Each employee has a $5 union fee deducted from each paycheck.

*Required:* (1) Compute the net amount paid to each employee.
(2) Compute the total salaries expense and payroll tax expense incurred by McKinley for the first week of February.
(3) Record (a) the salaries expense and (b) the payroll tax expense of McKinley for the first week of February, assuming the FICA taxes, FUTA taxes, and union dues will be remitted by McKinley in March.

**14-35** During 2008, Caran Cutlery Company made cash sales of $90,000, on which a 5% sales tax was imposed. The sales tax was collected from the customer at the time of each sale. By the end of the year, 75% of the sales tax collected had been remitted to the state.

*Required:* (1) Show how Caran Cutlery should record the preceding events for 2008.
(2) Show how Caran Cutlery would report the sales tax liability at the end of 2008.

**14-36** On December 31, 2008, Adams Advertising Company was preparing its 2008 financial statements and estimated that its property taxes for the period from July 1, 2008 to June 30, 2009 would be $100,000. On February 10, 2009, Adams received and paid its property tax bill for $100,000.

*Required:* (1) Show how Adams should record the preceding events on (a) December 31, 2008, and (b) February 10, 2009.
(2) What would be the effect on the 2008 financial statements if Adams had not recorded its property taxes on December 31, 2008? Ignore income taxes.

**14-37** On August 1, 2008, Taft Trailer Company purchased inventory for $120,000 and issued a 10%, six-month note due February 1, 2009 to the seller. The company uses a perpetual inventory system and pays all interest on the maturity date.

*Required:* (1) Record (a) the purchase of the inventory, (b) the accrual of interest at year-end, and (c) the repayment of the note.
(2) Show how Taft Trailer Company would report the liabilities at the end of 2008.

**14-38** On October 30, 2008, Sheller Manufacturing Company (whose fiscal period is a calendar year) paid six months' rent in advance on its factory, at $10,000 a month.

*Required:* (1) Record the payment of the rent and any other entry you think is appropriate in 2008.
(2) Show how the rent accounts would be reported on Sheller's 2008 financial statements.
(3) If Sheller had recorded the entire $60,000 as rent expense on October 31, 2008, what adjustment at the end of 2008 would you recommend to correct its accounting records? Why?

**14-39** Wanchez Company is a defendant in a lawsuit resulting from injuries sustained by a customer. During 2008, the customer filed suit against the company for $700,000; the company's lawyers feel that the customer is at least partially at fault. The suit is expected to be "settled" in 2009.

*Required:* For each of the following alternatives, show how the company would report or disclose the preceding information in its 2008 annual report.

(1) The company's lawyers think that the lawsuit will probably be settled for between $50,000 and $100,000, with $80,000 being the most likely amount.
(2) The company's lawyers think that it is reasonably possible the customer will win the lawsuit. If so, the amount of the settlement will likely be somewhere between $50,000 and $100,000.

**14-40** At the beginning of 2008, Fresco Manufacturing Company had accounts receivable (net) of $36,000. During 2008, Fresco made net sales of $420,000 under terms of 1/10, n/30, while operating on a 300-day business year. At the end of 2008, the company had current liabilities of $60,000, as well as the following current assets:

| | |
|---|---|
| Cash and cash equivalents | $12,000 |
| Accounts receivable (net) | 40,000 |
| Notes receivable | 12,000 |
| Inventories | 83,000 |
| Marketable securities | 6,000 |
| Prepaid items | 4,000 |

*Required:* (1) Compute Fresco's quick ratio at the end of 2008. How does this compare with the industry average of 1.05?
(2) Compute Fresco's accounts receivable turnover ratio and the number of days in its collection period. What do you think of its collection efforts?

## Making Evaluations

**14-41** If you have (or used to have) a job, think about the controls you have seen regarding purchases and cash payments.

*Required:* Explain the controls you observed. Are there any areas in which you would recommend improvements?

**14-42** Your friend works at a local company part-time helping with the accounts payable. He has observed that the company uses the gross method of accounting for purchases discounts and wonders what the differences are between this method and the net method.

*Required:* Write a short report explaining the difference between the gross and the net methods, and include your recommendation about which method the company should use.

**14-43** Use your paycheck stub from a job where you work (or have worked).

*Required:* Determine the amount of your gross pay and net pay. Analyze how your pay affects the company's financial statements. Can you identify the payroll costs the company incurred by employing you?

**14-44** The Zanzibar Company has a significant increase in business around Christmas. In past years it has hired 10 extra employees for December, with each employee working 200 hours. As a result of using seasonal employees, the company pays the full 5.4% of the 6.2% FUTA tax to the state on these salaries as well as on the salaries of its 20 year-round employees. The company is confident that if it did not have this seasonal employment problem, it could achieve a merit rating and could pay only 4.6% to the state for the FUTA tax. The company estimates that hiring each employee costs $50 in interviewing and processing costs. As an alternative for 2008, Zanzibar Company is considering using employees provided by Temphelp, a company that specializes in providing temporary employees. Zanzibar would have to pay Temphelp $9 per hour per employee, but Temphelp would pay all social security and federal and state unemployment taxes.

*Required:* Using the rates provided in this chapter, what is the company wage rate at which it would make no difference to Zanzibar Company if it hired its own employees or used Temphelp?

**14-45** The Slamming Sam Golf Club Company decided to expand its manufacturing operations as a result of receiving a new order for golf clubs from a distributor. On July 1, 2008, the company acquired a new machine for manufacturing the clubs, from a supplier at a cost of $500,000. The supplier offers to accept either immediate payment or a nine-month note with interest of 10%. The company expects to produce 5,000 clubs during the remaining six months of the year and incur materials costs of $30 for each club evenly over the period. Since Slamming Sam will not sell the clubs to the public until the spring of 2009, the materials supplier offers terms of immediate payment less a 5% discount if paid within ten days, or full payment within two months, or delayed payment until 2008 with interest charged at 12% after two months until full payment is received.

*Required:* Compute the amount of the liabilities that the company will have on December 31, 2008, under each of the alternative situations. (Assume a 360-day year.)

**14-46** According to Fortune magazine, the following amounts were used to compute the "net profits" of the movie *Indecent Proposal:*

| | |
|---|---|
| Gross receipts | $162,235,826 |
| Less: Distribution fees | 56,338,707 |
| Gross after distribution fees | $105,897,119 |
| Less: Accounts receivable (net of distribution fees) | 5,163,725 |
| Balance | $100,733,394 |
| Less: Distribution expenses | 55,062,679 |
| Balance | $ 45,670,715 |
| Less: Interest on negative cost | 8,002,432 |
| Negative cost | 73,418,212 |
| Net profits | $ (35,749,929) |

Many of the second-tier stars, writers, and producers receive bonuses based on net profits.

*Required:* Explain what you think each of the items represents. Explain whether the calculation of the net profits seems reasonable to you.

**14-47** General Electric disclosed the following information in its 2005 annual report:

**Product warranties**

We provide for estimated product warranty expenses when we sell the related products. Because warranty estimates are forecasts that tare based on the best available information—mostly historical claims experience—claims costs may differ from amounts provided. An analysis of changes in the liability for product warranties follows.

| (In millions) | 2005 | 2004 | 2003 |
|---|---|---|---|
| Balance at January 1 | $1,326 | $1,437 | $1,304 |
| Current year provisions | 448 | 720 | 751 |
| Expenditures | (699) | (838) | (749) |
| Other changes | — | 7 | 131 |
| Balance at December 31 | $1,075 | $1,326 | $1,437 |

The company's total revenues were $149,702 in 2005 and $134,481 in 2004. Its sales of goods was $59,837 in 2005 and $55,005 in 2004 and its cost of goods sold was $46,169 in 2005 and $42,645 in 2004.

*Required:* (1) Why does General Electric estimate its warranty expense?
(2) Explain the information for GE's product warranty liabilities for 2005.
(3) Evaluate how GE's management of its warranty expense changed in 2005 compared to 2004.

**14-48** Molson Coors reported the following in its income statement (in thousands):

| Year Ended | Dec. 25, 2005 | Dec. 26, 2004 | Dec. 28, 2003 |
|---|---|---|---|
| Sales | $7,417,702 | $5,819,727 | $5,387,220 |
| Beer excise taxes | (1,910,796) | (1,513,911) | (1,387,107) |
| Net sales | $5,506,906 | $4,305,816 | $4,000,113 |

*Required:* (1) Why do you think that Molson Coors uses a different date for each year-end?
(2) In the chapter, we explained that sales taxes are not included as part of revenue. Explain why you think that Molson Coors uses its form of disclosure for beer excise taxes.

**14-49** In its 2005 annual report, **The Stanley Works** disclosed the following:

The Company's policy is to accrue environmental investigatory and remediation costs for identified sites when it is probable that a liability has been incurred and the amount of loss can be reasonably estimated. The amount of liability recorded is based on an evaluation of currently available facts with respect to each individual size and includes such factors as existing technology, presently enacted laws and regulations, and prior experience in remediation of contaminated sites. The liabilities recorded do not take into account any claims for recoveries from insurance or third parties. As assessments and remediation progress at individual sites, the amounts recorded are reviewed periodically and adjusted to reflect additional technical and legal information that becomes available. As of December 31, 2005 and January 1, 2005, the Company had reserves of $21.3 million and $13.6 million, respectively, for remediation activities associated with Company-owned properties as well as for Superfund sites, for losses that are probable and estimable. Of the 2005 amount, $3.4 million is classified as current and $17.9 million as long-term. The range of environmental remediation costs that is reasonably possible is $19.4 million to $37.0 million which is subject to change in the near term. The Company may be liable for environmental remediation of sites it no longer owns. Liabilities have been recorded on those sites in accordance with policy.

*Required:* (1) Why did the company accrue these amounts?
(2) Why did the amount increase during 2005?
(3) Why does the company also give a range of estimates?

**14-50** **Crown Holdings** reported the following information related to its asbestos litigation in its 2005 annual report (dollar amounts in millions):

During 2005, 2004, and 2003, respectively, Crown Holdings (i) received 9,000, 13,000 and 36,000 new claims, (ii) settled or dismissed 4,000, 14,000 and 20,000 claims and (iii) had 79,000, 74,000 and 75,000 claims outstanding at the end of the respective years.

During 2005, 2004, and 2003, respectively, the Company (i) recorded pre-tax charges of $10, $35 and $44 to increase its accrual, (ii) made asbestos-related payments of $29, $41 and $68 and (iii) had outstanding accruals of $214, $233 and $239 at the end of the year.

*Required:* (1) Explain the information for Crown Holdings asbestos-related claims.
(2) Explain how Crown Holdings' performance has changed in the past three years.

**14-51** Excerpts from the 2005 annual report for **Colgate-Palmolive** are shown below:

**Consolidated Balance Sheets**

| As of December 31 | 2005 | 2004 |
|---|---|---|
| **Assets** | | |
| Current Assets | | |
| Cash and cash equivalents | $ 340.7 | $ 319.6 |
| Receivables (less allowances of $41.7 and $47.2, respectively) | 1,309.4 | 1,319.9 |
| Inventories | 855.8 | 845.5 |
| Other current assets | 251.2 | 254.9 |
| Total current assets | $ 2,757.1 | $2,739.9 |
| Property, plant and equipment, net | 2,544.1 | 2,647.7 |
| Goodwill | 1,845.7 | 1,891.7 |
| Other intangible assets, net | 783.2 | 832.4 |
| Other assets | 577.0 | 561.2 |
| Total assets | $ 8,507.1 | $8,672.9 |
| **Liabilities and Shareholders' Equity** | | |
| Current Liabilities | | |
| Notes and loans payable | $ 171.5 | $ 134.3 |
| Current portion of long-term debt | 356.7 | 451.3 |
| Accounts payable | 876.1 | 864.4 |
| Accrued income taxes | 215.5 | 153.1 |
| Other accruals | 1,123.2 | 1,127.6 |
| Total current liabilities | $ 2,743.0 | $2,730.7 |

**Consolidated Statements of Income**

| For the years ended December 31 | 2005 | 2004 | 2003 |
|---|---|---|---|
| Net sales | $11,396.9 | $10,584.2 | $9,903.4 |
| Cost of sales | 5,191.9 | 4,747.2 | 4,456.1 |
| Gross profit | $ 6,205.0 | $ 5,837.0 | $5,447.3 |
| Selling, general and administrative expenses | 3,920.8 | 3,624.6 | 3,296.3 |
| Other (income) expense, net | 69.2 | 90.3 | (15.0) |
| Operating profit | $ 2,215.0 | $ 2,122.1 | $2,166.0 |

*Required:* (1) Compute the quick ratio on December 31, 2005, and 2004, as well as the accounts receivable turnover ratio, and the accounts payable turnover ratio for fiscal years 2005 and 2004. The accounts receivable and accounts payable at December 31, 2003 were $1,222.4 and $753.6, respectively. Write a short report evaluating the performance of Colgate-Palmolive.

(2) In Management's Discussion and Analysis, the company discloses that sales volume in the Oral, Personal, and Household Care segment grew 8% in 2005 to $9,876.7 million from $9,151.1 in 2004. Compute the average amount by which the company's sales prices changed from 2004 to 2005.

(3) In Management's Discussion and Analysis, the company disclosed that worldwide net sales increased 7.5% on volume gains of 5.5%. Explain why the increases are different.

**14-52** Yesterday, you received the following letter for your advice column in the local paper:

## DR. DECISIVE

Dear Dr. Decisive:

Following a trip with my girlfriend and my family, I recently [see Chapter 5] wrote to ask you whether frequent flyer miles are an asset or an expense for a company that has accumulated them. Soon thereafter, we started arguing about whether the airline has a liability for frequent flyer miles "earned" by its customers. I say no. For example, I earned 12,000 miles on my trip to Hawaii, but I have to have 25,000 miles to get a free ticket. And I doubt I will travel much in the next few years because my parents won't take me on another trip. My girlfriend says there is a liability because many business executives fly all the time and get lots of miles that they use. But I respond that they often don't have time to use the miles. Then my smart-aleck little brother, who thinks he knows everything, agreed with my girlfriend but asked how the airline would know how much to record as the value of the liability. Help me before my girlfriend dumps me for my little brother.

Please sign me: "Wrestling Fan (Part 2)."

*Required:* Meet with your Dr. Decisive team and write a response to "Wrestling Fan (Part 2)."

# GLOSSARY

Parentheses indicate page references.

## A

**Accounting and auditing knowledge** A category of the business person's knowledge base that includes the ability to construct accounting data, as well as the ability to use this data to make decisions, to exercise judgments, to evaluate risks, and to solve problems (39)

**Accounting equation** Assets = Liabilities + Owner's Equity (131, 200)

**Accounting period** Time span for which a company reports its revenues and expenses (140)

**Accounting system** Process used to identify, measure, record, and retain information about a company's activities so that the company can prepare its financial statements (130)

**Accounts** Documents used to record and retain the monetary information from a company's transactions (135)

**Accounts payable** Amounts owed to suppliers for credit purchases (131, 289)

**Accounts payable management** Setting and following policies for authorizing and making purchases and for processing credit purchases (420)

**Accounts payable subsidiary file** Contains the individual accounts of all the suppliers that sell to the company on credit (458)

**Accounts receivable** Amounts owed by customers to the company (131, 282)

**Accounts receivable management** Setting and following policies for granting credit and processing credit sales (420)

**Accounts receivable subsidiary file** Contains the individual accounts of all the customers that purchase from the company on credit (423)

**Accounts receivable turnover** Net credit sales divided by average accounts receivable (215)

**Accrual accounting** Recording revenues and related expense transactions in the same accounting period that goods or services are provided, regardless of when cash is received or paid (141, 241)

**Accrued liabilities** Short-term obligations (other than accounts payable) that a company owes at the end of an accounting period and that result from the company's operating activities during the period (464)

**Accrued salaries** The amount of salaries that a company owes its employees on the balance sheet date (465)

**Accrued taxes** Taxes that a company owes but has not paid at the balance sheet date (468)

**Accumulated depreciation** Total amount of depreciation expense recorded over the life of an asset to date (203)

**Additional paid-in capital** Difference between the selling price and the par value in each stock transaction (316)

**Adjusting entries** Journal entries that a company makes at the end of its accounting period to bring the company's revenue and expense account balances up-to-date and to show the correct ending balances in its asset and liability accounts (179)

**Agent** Person who has the authority to act for another (305)

**Aging method** Estimates the amount of bad debts based on the age of the individual amounts included in the ending balance of accounts receivable (431)

**Annual report** Document that includes a company's income statement, balance sheet, and cash flow statement, along with other related financial accounting information (19, 319)

**Articles of incorporation** State-approved documents required to obtain permission to act as a corporation (308)

**Assets** A company's economic resources that it expects will provide future benefits to the company (17, 130, 202)

**Attribute listing** Listing the characteristics of an object or idea to gain insights into its possible usefulness (42)

**Audit committee** A part of a company's board of directors that is responsible for overseeing the financial reporting process of the company and the involvement of both the company's managers and its auditor in that process (321)

**Audit report** Report issued by an auditor stating that an audit was performed for a company which expresses an opinion as to how well the company's financial statements comply with GAAP (321)

**Auditing** Examination of a company's accounting records and financial statements by an independent certified public accountant (320)

**Average cost flow assumption** Allocates the average cost per unit for the period to both the ending inventory and the cost of goods sold

## B

**Bad debts expense** Expense that represents the estimated cost, for the accounting period, of the eventual noncollection of accounts receivable (428)

**Balance** The amount in an account column at the beginning of the period plus the increases and minus the decreases recorded in the column during the period. (136)

**Balance sheet** Accounting report that summarizes a company's financial position (assets, liabilities, and owner's equity) on a given date (17, 200)

**Bank reconciliation** Schedule used to analyze the difference between the ending cash balance in a company's accounting records and the ending cash balance reported by the bank on the company's bank statement (275)

**Bank statement** Statement which summarizes a company's banking activities during the month (274)

**Book value** Asset's original cost minus the related accumulated depreciation (203)

**Brainstorming** Process where members of a group try to generate as many solutions as possible to a particular problem (41)

**Break-even point** Unit sales volume at which a company earns zero profit (73)

**Budget** Report that gives a financial description of one part of a company's planned activity (93)

**Budgeting** Process of quantifying manager's plans and showing the impact of these plans on a company's operating activities (14, 93)

**Business plan** Describes a company's goals and its plans for achieving those goals (61)

## C

**Capital** Funds a company uses to operate or expand its operations (6, 65)

**Capital expenditures budget** Set of schedules that shows the effects that each new project to be undertaken is expected to have on the other master budget schedules (389)

**Capital stock** Units of ownership in a corporation that are given to owners in exchange for capital (315)

**Carrying costs** Costs per unit of keeping an inventory item on hand

**Cash** Money on hand, deposits in checking and savings accounts, and checks and credit card invoices that a company has received from its customers but not yet deposited (272)

**Cash balance management** Setting and following policies for maintaining an optimal amount of cash (420)

**Cash budget** Budget showing a company's expected cash receipts and payments and how they affect the company's cash balance (107)

**Cash discount** Percentage reduction of the invoice price if the customer pays the invoice within a specified period (173)

**Cash equivalents** Investments that are short-term, are highly liquid, and involve very little risk (443)

**Cash flow return** Company's cash flows divided by the dollar amount of its assets or owner's equity (246)

**Cash flow statement** Accounting report that summarizes a company's cash receipts, cash payments, and net change in cash for a specific time period (19, 232)

**Cash payments management** Setting and following policies for paying for cash or credit purchases and processing cash payments (420)

**Cash receipts management** Setting and following policies for collecting cash from credit or cash sales (420)

**Certified public accountant** Public accountant who has met the requirements of the state and who holds a license to practice accounting

**Classified balance sheet** Balance sheet which shows subtotals for assets, liabilities, and owner's equity in related groupings (202)

**Closely-held corporation** Corporation owned by a small number of investors (308)

**Closing entries** Entries made by a company at the end of an accounting period to create a zero balance in each revenue, expense, and withdrawals T-account, and to update the owner's equity by transferring the balances in the revenue, expense, and withdrawals T-accounts to the T-account for owner's capital (185)

**Common stock** Ownership unit of a corporation (315)

**Comparative financial statements** Financial statements from previous years included in a company's annual report to help external users in their analyses (319)

**Conceptual framework** Set of concepts that provides a logical structure for financial accounting and reporting (312)

**Contingency** Existing condition that will lead to a gain or loss if a future event occurs (475)

**Contra account** Account that has the effect of reducing the balance in another account (429)

**Contributed capital** Total investments made by stockholders in the corporation (315)

**Contribution margin per unit** Difference between the sales revenue per unit and the variable costs per unit (75)

**Control account** General ledger account that takes the place of the individual accounts in the subsidiary ledger (423, 458)

**Controller** High-level management accountant who coordinates a company's internal (management) accounting activities and the preparation of its financial reports

**Corporation** Company organized as a separate legal entity, or body (separate from its owners), according to the laws of a particular state (7, 306)

**Cost accounting (Cost analysis)** Process of determining and evaluating the costs of specific products or activities of a company (14)

**Cost center** Responsibility center in which the manager who is responsible for its activities can control only the level of costs it incurs (398)

**Cost of ending inventory** Dollar amount of merchandise on hand, based on a physical count, at the end of the accounting period (178)

**Cost of goods sold** Major expense of a retail company consisting of the cost of the goods (merchandise) that it sells during the accounting period (175)

**Cost report** Report showing a comparison between a company's budgeted and actual expenses for an accounting period (111)

**Cost-volume-profit (C-V-P) analysis** Shows how profit is affected by changes in sales volume, selling prices of products, and the various costs of a company (68)

**Creative thinking** Process of actively generating new ideas to discover solutions to a problem (40)

**Credit memo** Business document that lists the information for a sales return or allowance (174)

**Creditors** External parties to whom a company owes debts (131)

**Creditors' equity** Claims by creditors against the assets of a company (131)

**Critical thinking** Process that evaluates the ideas generated by creative thinking (42)

**Current assets** Cash and other assets that a company expects to convert into cash, sell, or use up within one year (202)

**Current liabilities** Obligations that a company expects to pay within one year by using current assets (204)

**Current ratio** Current assets divided by current liabilities (207)

# D

**Data warehouse** The software in an ERP system that stores many types of data (e.g., units, quantities, times, prices, names, pay rates, addresses) that can be retrieved by using data mining. (311)

**Debt capital** Money that a company borrows from creditors (392)

**Debt ratio** Total liabilities divided by total assets (209)

**Deductive logic** Reasoning that moves from general to specific (45)

**Deposit in transit** A cash receipt that a company has added to its Cash account but that the bank has not deducted from the cash balance reported on the bank statement because the check has not yet "cleared" the bank (275)

**Depreciation expense** Part of the cost of property, plant, and equipment (physical asset) that a company allocates as an expense to each accounting period in which the company uses the asset (151)

**Direct labor** Labor of the employees who work with direct materials to convert or assemble them into a finished product (344)

**Direct labor budget** Schedule that shows the hours and the cost of the direct labor required to meet the budgeted production (384)

**Direct materials** Raw materials that physically become part of a manufactured product (344)

**Direct materials purchases budget** Schedule that shows the number of direct material units that must be purchased in each budget period to meet production and ending direct materials inventory requirements (382)

**Direct method** Subtracting the operating cash outflows from the operating cash inflows to determine the net cash provided by (or used in) operating activities on the cash flow statement (236)

**Distribution** Making products available to customers through physical distribution systems (310)

**Double taxation** Occurs when a corporation is taxed on its taxable income and then its stockholders are taxed on the dividends they receive from the corporation (307)

**Drawing analogies** Making connections among facts, ideas, or experiences that are normally considered separately (41)

**Dual effect of transactions** A company must make at least two changes in its assets, liabilities, or owner's equity when it records each transaction (132)

# E

**Earning process** Purchasing (or producing) inventory, selling the inventory (or services), delivering the inventory (or services), and collecting and paying cash (140)

**Earnings per share (EPS)** Amount of net income earned for each share of common stock (319)

**E-business** Transactions conducted electronically (312)

**E-commerce** A method of conducting business where companies and consumers buy and sell goods and services over the Internet (37)

**Electronic cash-collection procedures** An accounts receivable management strategy in which a company's customers make payments by a direct transfer of funds from their bank accounts to the company's bank accounts (434)

**End-of-period adjustments** Increases or decreases to account balances at the end of the period to reflect the costs of providing goods or services that are not supported by source documents (149)

**Enterprise resource planning (ERP) system** Information system involving computer software that records and stores many different types of data in a data warehouse (310)

**Entity** Separation of accounting records of a company from the records of the company's owner or owners (127)

**Entrepreneur** Individual who is willing to risk the uncertainty of starting a company in exchange for the reward of earning a profit (and the personal reward of seeing the company succeed) (6)

**Equity** Claims by creditors and owner(s) against the assets of a company (131)

**Equity capital** Money that a corporation brings in through the sale of the corporation's own stock (392)

**Evaluating** Management activity that measures a company's actual operations and progress against standards or benchmarks (12)

**Exchange gain or loss** Caused by a change in the exchange rate between the date that a company records a credit sale (purchase) and the date that the company collects (pays) the cash (436, 463)

**Exchange rate** Measures the value of one currency in terms of another currency (435)

**Expenses** Costs a company incurs to provide goods or services to its customers during an accounting period (17, 139)

**Export insurance** An insurance policy that companies purchase to reduce the risks associated with selling goods on credit to international customers (424)

**External users** Individuals outside of a company who use the company's information for decision making (10)

# F

**Factory overhead** All items, other than direct materials and direct labor, that are necessary for the manufacture of a product (346)

**Factory overhead budget** Schedule showing estimates of all factory overhead costs and their related cash payments for each budget period (385)

**Finance** Plans a company's capital requirements for both the short and the long term (310)

**Financial accounting** Identification, measurement, recording, accumulation, and communication of economic information about a company for external users to use in their various decisions (15)

**Financial flexibility** Company's ability to adapt to change (181, 208)

**Financial Highlights** Financial summaries (5-, 10-, or 15-year) of key data from a company's financial statements in its annual reports (321)

**Financial statements** Accounting reports used to summarize and communicate financial information about a company (17)

**Financial Summaries** Financial highlights (5-, 10-, or 15-year) of key data from a company's financial statements in its annual reports (321)

**Financing activities** Obtaining capital from the owner and providing the owner with a return on investment, as well as obtaining capital from creditors and repaying the amounts borrowed (235)

**Financing activities section** Section of a company's cash flow statement (or cash budget) that shows the cash receipts and payments from its actual (or planned) financing activities (108, 390)

**Finished goods inventory** Finished products that are ready to be sold (343)

**Fixed costs** Costs that are constant in total and that are not affected by changes in volume (69)

**Fixed overhead volume variance** Difference between the amount of applied fixed overhead and the amount of budgeted fixed overhead

**Flexibility** Spectrum of ideas generated (40)

**Flexible budget** Cost or expense budget that shows expected costs or expenses at various activity levels (399)

**Fluency** Measure of the number of ideas generated or solutions proposed by the problem solver (40)

# G

**Gains** Increases in a corporation's income (and therefore its stockholders' equity) that result from transactions unrelated to providing goods and services (318)

**General accounting** Duty of a management accountant to design and operate a company's integrated accounting system

**General and administrative expenses** Operating expenses related to the general management of a company (179)

**General and administrative expenses budget** Budget showing the expenses and related cash payments associated with expected activities other than selling (105)

**General knowledge** A category of the business person's knowledge base that encompasses knowledge about history and cultures; an ability to interact with people who have dissimilar ideas; a sense of the contrasting economic, political, and social forces in the world and of the magnitude of world issues and ideas; and experience in making value judgments (39)

**Generally accepted accounting principles (GAAP)** Currently accepted principles, procedures, and practices that are used for financial accounting in the United States (16)

**Goal congruence** Situation where department, division, or team goals support the company's goals (403)

**Goods-in-process inventory** Products that a company has started manufacturing but that are not yet complete (343)

**Gross pay** The amount of an employee's earnings before payroll taxes are deducted (468)

**Gross profit** Net sales minus cost of goods sold (178)

**Gross profit percentage** Gross profit divided by net sales (182)

# H

**High-low method** Method that allows a decision-maker to quickly estimate the fixed and variable components of a mixed cost (353)

**Historical cost concept** Concept that a company records its transactions based on the dollars exchanged at the time the transaction occurred (129)

**Horizontal analysis** Shows the changes in a company's operating results over time in percentages as well as in dollar amounts (325)

**Human resources** Managing the company's employee-related activities, such as recruiting, hiring, training, and compensating employees, as well as providing a safe workplace (310)

# I

**Income from continuing operations** Reports a corporation's revenues and expenses that resulted from its ongoing operations (318)

**Income statement** Accounting report that summarizes the results of a company's operating activities for a specific time period (17)

**Income tax expense** Income taxes that a corporation must pay on its earnings (318)

**Incorporation** Process of filing the required documents and obtaining permission from a state to operate as a corporation (308)

**Independent** In the process of evaluating ideas, relying on one's own conclusions rather than relying on the conclusions of others (42)

**Indirect labor** Labor that is not traceable to individual products (346)

**Indirect materials** Raw materials that are not traceable to individual products (346)

**Indirect method** Adjusting net income to compute net cash provided by operating activities on the cash flow statement (236)

**Inductive logic** Reasoning that moves from the specific to the general (45)

**Initial public offering (IPO)** Corporation's first sale of its common stock to the public, after which the stock begins to trade in a secondary market (309)

**Integrated accounting system** Means by which accounting information about a company's activities is identified, measured, recorded, and retained so it can be communicated in an accounting report (10)

**Intercompany analysis** Comparing a company's performance with that of competing companies, industry averages, or averages in related industries (324)

**Interim financial statements** Financial statements prepared for a period of less than one year (323)

**Internal control** Procedures needed to safeguard a company's economic resources and to promote the efficient and effective operation of its accounting system

**Internal control structure** Set of policies and procedures that directs how employees should perform a company's activities (272)

**Internal users** Managers within a company who use information about the company for decision-making (10)

**Intracompany analysis** Comparing a company's current operations and financial position with its past results or with its expected results (324)

**Inventory** Merchandise a retail company is holding for resale (175, 285)

**Inventory turnover** Cost of goods sold divided by average inventory (214)

**Investing activities section** Section of a company's cash flow statement (or cash budget) that shows the cash receipts and payments from its actual (or planned) investing activities (108, 390)

**Investment center** Responsibility center in which the manager has decision-making authority over costs, revenues, and the level of investment in property, plant, and equipment the center uses in its operations (398)

**Investments portfolio** All of a company's investments in securities of other companies

# J

**Joint ownership** Characteristic of a partnership that all partners jointly own all the assets of the partnership (305)

# L

**Legal capital** Amount of stockholder's equity of a corporation that it cannot distribute to stockholders (315)

**Letter of credit** Letter written by a customer's bank ensuring that payment to the selling company will occur when that company presents the bank with documents that show that it has met the conditions of the sale (424)

**Letter to Shareholders** A section of a company's annual report in which the company's managers report on how well (or poorly) the corporation performed over the past year, specifically in regard to its liquidity, capital, and results of operation (322)

**Liabilities** A company's economic obligations (debts) owed to its creditors (17, 131, 204)

**Limited life** Occurs when a company's life is linked directly to the operating intentions of its owner (304, 305)

**Line of credit** Amount of money a company is allowed to borrow with a prearranged, agreed-upon interest rate and a specific payback schedule (66)

**Liquidity** Measure of how quickly an asset can be converted into cash or a liability can be paid (206, 418)

**Liquidity management** A company's policies and activities that control its liquidity position (418)

**Lockbox system** Cash-collection method in which customers mail their payments to the company's post office box, which is monitored by the bank (434)

**Long-term capital** Capital which will be repaid to creditors or returned to investors after more than one year (67)

**Long-term investments** Items such as notes receivable, government bonds, bonds and capital stock of corporations, and other securities which a company intends to hold for more than one year (203)

**Losses** Decreases in a corporation's income (and therefore its stockholders' equity) that result from transactions unrelated to providing goods and services (318)

# M

**Maker** Company that made and signed a note (440)

**Management accounting** Identification, measurement, recording, accumulation, and communi-cation of economic information about a company for internal users in management decision making (13)

**Management by exception** Management principle where an entrepreneur (or manager) focuses on improving the activities that show significant differences between budgeted and actual results (94)

**Management Discussion and Analysis (MD&A)** Portion of the annual report where managers comment on how well (or poorly) the corporation performed over the past year, specifically in regard to its liquidity, capital, and results of operations (321)

**Manufacturing company** Company that makes its products and then sells these products to its customers (5)

**Margin of safety** Amount that sales (in units) can decrease without a loss; the difference between the estimated sales volume and the break-even sales volume (363)

**Marketing** Identifies consumer needs, analyzes consumer behavior, evaluates customer satisfaction, and promotes a company's products (310)

**Master budget** Set of interrelated reports showing the relationships among a company's goals to be met, activities to be performed, resources to be used, and expected financial results (96)

**Matching principle** To determine its net income for an accounting period, a company computes and deducts the total expenses from the total revenues earned during the period (141)

**Material** Occurs when a monetary amount is large enough to make a difference in a user's decision (313)

**Maturity date** Specific day when a company that issued a bond (or note) promises to pay the principal (and interest) amounts to the bond (or note) holder (440)

**Maturity value of the note** The amount (principal plus interest) the maker of a note must pay the payee on the maturity date (440)

**Merchandising company** Company that purchases goods (sometimes referred to as merchandise or products) for resale to its customers (4)

**Mixed costs** Costs which have elements of both variable and fixed costs (351)

**Monetary unit concept** Concept that transactions are to be recorded in terms of money (128)

# N

**Net assets** Assets minus liabilities (132)

**Net income** Excess of a company's revenues over its expenses from providing goods or services to its customers during a specific time period (17, 139)

**Net loss** Excess of a company's expenses over its revenues from providing goods or services to its customers during a specific time period (17)

**Net pay** The amount of earnings after payroll taxes have been deducted (468)

**Net purchases** Amount of merchandise purchases adjusted for purchase returns, allowances, and discounts (178)

**Net sales** Total sales minus the sales discounts and sales returns and allowances for an accounting period (425)

**Noncurrent liabilities** Obligations that a company does not expect to pay within one year (204)

**Normal activity** Average of a company's expected future annual production volumes

**Note** Written legal document in which the maker of the note makes an unconditional promise to pay another party a certain amount of money on an agreed future date (439)

**Note payable** A legal document promising to pay a given amount on a given future date

**Note receivable** A note for which a selling company expects to receive cash from its customer on a specified future date (439)

**Notes to the financial statements** Inform external users of a company's annual report about its accounting policies and of important financial information that is not reported in the company's financial statements (320)

**NSF (not sufficient funds) check** A customers check that has "bounced" (the company's bank is unable to collect because the customer's bank account has insufficient funds to cover the check) (275)

**Number of days in the collection period** Number of days in a company's business year divided by its accounts receivable turnover (216)

**Number of days in the selling period** Number of days in a company's business year divided by its inventory turnover (215)

# O

**Objectivity** Quality of being unbiased in critical thinking (42)

**Operating** Management activity that enables a company to conduct its business according to its plan (11)

**Operating activities** Include the primary activities of buying, selling, and delivering goods for sale, as well as providing services (235)

**Operating activities section** Section of a company's cash flow statement (or cash budget) that summarizes the cash receipts and payments from its actual (or planned) operating activities (108, 390)

**Operating capability** Company's ability to continue a given level of operations (181, 214)

**Operating cycle** Average time it takes a company to use cash to buy or produce goods (or services) for sale, to sell these goods (or services) to customers, and to collect cash from its customers (241, 378)

**Operating cycle for a manufacturing company** The average time it takes a manufacturing company to use cash to acquire direct materials to use in manufacturing goods, to convert these direct materials into finished goods, to sell these goods to customers, and then to collect cash from customers for the sale (378)

**Operating expenses** Expenses (other than cost of goods sold) that a company incurs in its day-to-day operations (178)

**Operating income** All the revenues earned less the expenses incurred in the primary operating activities of a company (170, 180, 318)

**Ordering costs** Costs of placing and receiving each inventory order

**Organizational and business knowledge** A category of the business person's knowledge base that includes an understanding of the effects of economic, social, cultural, and psychological forces on companies; an understanding of how companies work; and understanding of methods and strategies for managing change; and an understanding of how technology helps organizations (39)

**Other items** Revenues and expenses that are not directly related to the primary operations of a company (170, 180, 318)

**Outsourcing** Occurs when a company turns over the management of a function to an outside specialist

**Outstanding check** A check that a company has written and deducted from its Cash account but that the bank has not deducted from the cash balance reported on the bank statement because the check has not yet "cleared" the bank (275)

**Overhead budget variance** Difference between the total overhead budgeted and the total overhead incurred

**Owner's equity** Owner's current investment in the assets of a company (18, 131, 205)

# P

**Par value** Monetary amount per share that must be kept in a corporation as legal capital (315)

**Participative budget** Budgeting in which department and division managers or teams participate with upper-level managers in the planning decisions to determine the goals and resource commitments for the activities of their departments, divisions, or teams (403)

**Partners' equity** The partners' current investment in the assets of the company (131)

**Partnership** Company owned by two or more individuals who each invest capital, time, and/or talent into the company and share in its profits and losses (7, 305)

**Partnership agreement** Contract signed by partners of a partnership before the company begins operations (7, 305)

**Payee** Holder of a note receivable (440)

**Percentage analysis** Financial analysis in which financial statement information is converted from dollars to percentages (325)

**Percentage of sales method** Estimates bad debts expense by multiplying the net credit sales of the period by the percentage of these sales that is estimated to be uncollectible (433)

**Periodic inventory system** System that does not keep a continuous record of the inventory on hand and sold, but determines the inventory at the end of each accounting period by physically counting it (176)

**Permanent accounts** Accounts used for the life of a company to record the effects of its transactions on its balance sheet (assets, liabilities, and owner's capital accounts) (169)

**Perpetual inventory system** System that keeps a continuous record of the cost of inventory on hand and the cost of inventory sold (175)

**Petty cash fund** Specified amount of money that is under the control of one employee and that is used for making small cash payments for a company (280)

**Piggybacking** Process of generating ideas from other ideas (41)

**Planning** Management activity that establishes a company's goals and the means of achieving these goals (11)

**Practical capacity** Volume of activity at which the company's manufacturing facilities are capable of operating per year under practical conditions, allowing for usual levels of efficiency

**Preferred stock** Type of capital stock issued for which stockholders receive certain additional rights in exchange for giving up some of the usual stockholders' rights (315)

**Prepaid insurance** Cost paid for the right to insurance protection (131)

**Prepaid item** Current asset (economic resource) that a company records when it pays for goods or services before using them (474)

**Price standard** Cost that a company should incur to acquire one unit of input for its manufacturing process (350)

**Price standard for factory overhead** Standard predetermined overhead rate

**Principal** Stated value on a note that must be paid on the maturity date (440)

**Procurement card** Similar to a credit card, permits employees responsible for keeping supplies in stock to purchase directly from suppliers (464)

**Product sales mix** Relative proportion of units of the different products that a company sells (357)

**Production** Manufacturing activity that uses people and equipment to convert materials, components, and parts into products that the company will sell to customers (310)

**Production budget** Schedule showing how many units a company should produce during each budget period both to satisfy expected sales for that period and to end each period with a desired finished goods inventory level (379)

**Profit** Difference between the total revenues of a company and the total costs (expenses) of the company during a specific time period (17)

**Profit center** Responsibility center in which the manager has decision-making authority over both costs and revenues (398)

**Profit margin** Net income divided by net sales (182)

**Projected balance sheet** Statement summarizing a company's expected financial position (assets, liabilities, and owner's equity) at the end of a budget period (111)

**Projected income statement** Statement summarizing a company's expected revenues and expenses for the budget period (109)

**Property and equipment** All of the physical (tangible), long-term assets a company uses in its operations (203)

**Prospectus** Corporation's financial reports and other information which must be provided to potential investors when the corporation offers stock for public sale (323)

**Publicly available information** Any information released to the public; it may come directly from a corporation or from secondary sources (319)

**Publicly held corporation** Sells its stock to the general public (309)

**Purchase order** Document authorizing a supplier to ship the items listed on the document at a specific price (285, 459)

**Purchases allowance** Occurs when a company keeps damaged goods that it previously recorded as a purchase, and later receives a refund of a portion of the purchase price (461)

**Purchases budget** Budget showing the purchases (in units) required in each month to make the expected sales in that month (from the sales budget) and to keep inventory at desired levels (102)

**Purchases discount** Reduction in the invoice price because the purchaser pays within the discount period (459)

**Purchases return** Occurs when a company returns goods that it previously recorded as a purchase and receives a refund in exchange for the goods (461)

# Q

**Quantity discount (Trade discount)** Reduction in the sales price of a good or service because of the number of items purchased or because of a sales promotion (173)

**Quantity standard** Amount of an input that a company should use to produce a unit of product in its manufacturing process (349)

**Quantity standard for factory overhead** Volume of production activity (direct labor hours, machine hours, or other measure of activity) that should be used to produce one unit of product

**Quick ratio** Quick assets divided by current liabilities (208)

# R

**Ratio analysis** Computations made in financial analysis in which an item on a company's financial statements is divided by another related item (182, 325)

**Raw materials** Materials, ingredients, and parts that make up a company's manufactured products (340)

**Raw materials inventory** Raw materials a company uses either directly or indirectly in manufacturing its products (343)

**Receiving report** Documents the type, quantity, and condition of goods received by a company (459)

**Records revenues** A company does this during the accounting period in which the revenues are earned and are collectible (or collected) (140)

**Reengineering** Process of analyzing and redesigning an activity to make it more effective and efficient (430)

**Relevant** Having the capacity to influence a user's decision (313)

**Relevant range** Range of volumes over which cost estimates are needed for a particular use and over which observed cost behaviors are expected to remain stable (355)

**Reliable** Having the capability of being verified (313)

**Residual equity** Term that is used to refer to owner's equity because creditors have first legal claim to a company's assets (131)

**Residual value** Estimated cash to be received from the sale or disposal of an asset at the end of its estimated service life

**Responsibility center** Identifiable portion or segment of a company's operations, the activities of which are the responsibility of a particular manager (398)

**Retail company's operating cycle** The average time it takes a retail company to use cash to buy goods for sale (called inventory), to sell these goods to customers, and to collect cash from its customers (94)

**Retained earnings** A corporation's total lifetime net income that has been reinvested in the corporation and not distributed to stockholders as dividends (315, 317)

**Return** Money received from investment and credit decisions (61)

**Return on owner's equity** Net income divided by average owner's equity (213)

**Return on total assets** Net income and interest expense are added together and then divided by average total assets (212)

**Revenue center** A responsibility center in which the manager who is responsible for its activities has decision-making authority over its revenues (398)

**Revenues** Prices charged to a company's customers for the goods or services the company provides to them (17, 139)

**Risk** Amount of uncertainty that exists about the future operations of a company (61, 181)

# S

**Salaries payable** The amount of salaries that a company owes its employees on the balance sheet date (465)

**Sales allowance** When a customer agrees to keep damaged merchandise and the company refunds a portion of the original sales price (174, 425)

**Sales budget** Budget showing the number of units of inventory that a company expects to sell each month, the related monthly sales revenue, and in which months the company expects to collect cash from these sales (98, 379)

**Sales discount** Percentage reduction of the invoice price if the customer pays the invoice within a specified period (173, 425)

**Sales order** Source document (either on paper or in a computer file) that includes specific information about a sale

**Sales return** When a customer returns previously purchased merchandise and receives a refund (174, 425)

**Sales revenue (net)** Total sales minus sales returns and allowances and sales discounts for an accounting period (425)

**Sales-determined expenses** Result from selling activities that are necessary to support the volume of budgeted sales (386)

**Sales-determining expenses** Result from selling activities that affect the sales volume (386)

**Scatter diagram** Pattern of points on a graph that allow the approximation of a straight line (352)

**Secondary equity market** Where investors buy the stock of corporations from other investors rather than from the corporations (309)

**Segment** Separate major line of business whose assets, results of operations, and activities can clearly be separated from the rest of the corporation

**Selling expenses** Operating expenses related to the sales activities of a company (179)

**Selling expenses budget** Budget showing the expenses and related cash payments associated with planned selling activities (104)

**Service company** Company that performs services or activities that benefit individuals or business customers (4)

**Service company's operating cycle** The average time it takes a service company to use cash to acquire supplies and services, to sell the services to customers, and to collect cash from its customers (95)

**Service life** Life over which a company expects an asset to be useful

**Short-term capital** Capital which will be repaid within a year or less (66)

**Sole proprietorship** Company owned by one individual who is the sole investor of capital into the company (7, 304)

**Solvency** Company's long-term ability to pay its debts as they come due (17)

**Solvent** When a company is capable of paying off its debts (6)

**Source document** Business record used as evidence that a transaction has occurred (128)

**Specific identification method** Allocates costs to cost of goods sold and to ending inventory by assigning to each unit sold and to each unit in ending inventory the cost to a company of purchasing that particular unit (287)

**Standard costs** Costs that a company should incur in performing an activity or producing a product under a given set of planned operating conditions (348)

**Standard cost system** Assigns standard costs rather than actual costs to each inventory account

**Statement of changes in owner's equity** Statement that summarizes the transactions that affected owner's equity during the accounting period (18, 184)

**Stockholders (Shareholders)** Owners of a corporation who hold shares of the corporation's capital stock (306)

**Stockholders' equity** Owners' equity of a corporation, consisting of contributed capital and retained earnings (18, 131, 315)

**Suboptimization** A condition in which a company earns less profit than it is capable of earning (402)

# T

**Tax** Amount of money that a government requires a taxable entity to pay (468)

**Taxes payable** Taxes that a company owes but has not paid at the balance sheet date (468)

**Temporary accounts** Accounts used for one accounting period to record the effects of a company's transactions on its net income (revenues and expenses) (169)

**10-K report** Report filed with the SEC including a corporation's annual report and other information such as officers' names, salaries, and stock ownership (323)

**Total contribution margin** Difference between the total sales revenue and the total variable costs (75)

**Total cost** Sum of the fixed costs and variable costs at a given volume (72)

**Total equity** Total of the liabilities and owner's equity (131)

**Total overhead variance** Difference between total factory overhead cost applied and total factory overhead cost incurred in a standard cost system

**Trading securities** Investments in securities that a company holds for a very short time to earn profits from short-term differences in the selling prices of the securities

**Transaction** Exchange of property or service by a company with another entity (128)

# U

**Unearned revenue** Obligation of a company to provide goods or services in the future, resulting from an advance receipt of cash (437)

**Unlimited liability** Owners of a sole proprietorship or partnership must assume personal responsibility for the debts incurred by their company (304)

# V

**Valid** Showing a realistic picture of what is meant to be represented by the information (314)

**Variable cost** Cost that is constant per unit and that changes in total in direct proportion to changes in volume (70)

**Variable manufacturing cost** Constant for each unit produced but varies in total in direct proportion to the volume produced (350)

**Variance** Difference between a standard cost and an actual cost (349)

**Vertical analysis** Shows each item in a financial statement of a given period or date both as a percentage of another item on the statement and as a dollar amount (325)

**Volume** Activity level in a company (68)

# W

**Wages and salaries payable** Amounts owed to employees for work they have done (131, 465)

**Withdrawals** Payments from the company to the owner (144)

**Working capital** A company's current assets minus its current liabilities (206, 269)

# INDEX

**Bold** indicates key terms.

# D



# E



# F

# Q



# R



# S

## T



## U



## V



## W



## Y